THE OXFORD ILLUSTRATED HISTORY OF
GREECE AND THE
HELLENISTIC WORLD

The fifteen scholars who have contributed to *The Oxford Illustrated History of Greece and the Hellenistic World* are all distinguished authorities in their field. They are:

GEORGE FORREST, New College, Oxford, *Greece: The History of the Archaic Period*

OLIVER TAPLIN, Magdalen College, Oxford, *Homer*

JASPER GRIFFIN, Balliol College, Oxford, *Greek Myth and Hesiod*

EWEN BOWIE, Corpus Christi College, Oxford, *Lyric and Elegiac Poetry*

MARTIN WEST, Royal Holloway and Bedford New College, London, *Early Greek Philosophy*

SIMON HORNBLOWER, Oriel College, Oxford, *Greece: The History of the Classical Period*

PETER LEVI, St Catherine's College, Oxford, *Greek Drama*

OSWYN MURRAY, Balliol College, Oxford, *Greek Historians* and *Life and Society in Classical Greece*

JULIA ANNAS, University of Arizona, *Classical Greek Philosophy*

ROBERT PARKER, Oriel College, Oxford, *Greek Religion*

JOHN BOARDMAN, Lincoln College, Oxford, *Greek Art and Architecture*

SIMON PRICE, Lady Margaret Hall, Oxford, *Greece: The History of the Hellenistic Period*

ROBERT LANE FOX, New College, Oxford, *Hellenistic Culture and Literature*

JONATHAN BARNES, Balliol College, Oxford, *Hellenistic Philosophy and Science*

ROGER LING, University of Manchester, *Hellenistic and Graeco-Roman Art*

THE OXFORD
ILLUSTRATED HISTORY OF
GREECE AND THE HELLENISTIC WORLD

Edited by
JOHN BOARDMAN
JASPER GRIFFIN
OSWYN MURRAY

OXFORD
UNIVERSITY PRESS

OXFORD

UNIVERSITY PRESS

Great Clarendon Street, Oxford ox2 6DP

Oxford University Press is a department of the University of Oxford.
It furthers the University's objective of excellence in research, scholarship,
and education by publishing worldwide in

Oxford New York

Athens Auckland Bangkok Bogotá Buenos Aires Calcutta
Cape Town Chennai Dar es Salaam Delhi Florence Hong Kong Istanbul
Karachi Kuala Lumpur Madrid Melbourne Mexico City Mumbai
Nairobi Paris São Paulo Shanghai Singapore Taipei Tokyo Toronto Warsaw

with associated companies in Berlin Ibadan

Oxford is a registered trade mark of Oxford University Press
in the UK and in certain other countries

First published 1986 by Oxford University Press
First issued in two volumes as an Oxford University Press paperback
and as a simultaneous hardback 1988
Reissued in paperback 2001

Library of Congress Cataloging in Publication Data
The Oxford history of the classical world/edited by John Boardman,
Jasper Griffin, Oswyn Murray.
Originally published as 1 v.: 1986.
Includes bibliographies and index.
Contents: [1] Greece and the Hellenistic world.
1. Civilization, Classical.   I. Boardman, John, 1927–
II. Griffin, Jasper.   III. Murray, Oswyn.
938—dc19 [DE59.094   1988]   87-34814
ISBN 0-19-285438-0 (paperback)

1 3 5 7 9 10 8 6 4 2

Printed in Italy

CONTENTS

LIST OF COLOUR PLATES

LIST OF MAPS

ACKNOWLEDGEMENTS

THE editors wish to express their thanks to the many institutions and individuals named in the List of Illustrations for provision of photographs and drawings, and permission to use them; and to Philippa Lewis who did the picture research. The pictures and captions for Chapters 1–12 were chosen by John Boardman; a special debt of gratitude is owed to Roger Ling who chose the pictures and wrote the captions for Chapters 13–16 in this volume. Oswyn Murray compiled the Chronological Charts. The Index was compiled by Peter Tickler. Many members of the Press have devoted their skills to the creation of this volume, but our principal debt must be to the authors for their patient co-operation.

NOTE

The Oxford History of the Classical World was originally published as one volume. For this Oxford Paperback edition, it appears as two books: *Greece and the Hellenistic World* and *The Roman World*. Where a cross-reference refers to *The Roman World* this is given as (for example): Vol. 2, p. 100.

Introduction

❧❧

JASPER GRIFFIN

T HE history of Greece and Rome can be looked at in two different ways. It can be seen as forming a single whole, all the way from the emergence of the Greek city-state (the *polis*) in the eighth century BC to the enormous expansion and eventual disintegration of the Roman Empire, a society which rested on Roman military and political power but whose culture, literature, and arts were truly Graeco-Roman. It can also be seen as two separate stories: first, the rise of the Greek *polis* from poverty and obscurity to the self-confident splendours of the 'classical' period in the fifth century BC, its extension over great areas of Asia by the conquests of Alexander, and its eventual subjugation by the Roman legions. Then there is the second story: the small city of Rome fighting its way to supremacy, first in Italy, and then in the whole of the Mediterranean basin; losing its republican constitution and becoming an Empire; conquering and exploiting the cities and kingdoms of Greece, and ruling the world until the 'barbarians' gradually became too strong and transformed the empire into a number of states which rested on quite different practices and beliefs. Each of these two perspectives contains some important truth.

The truly creative period of antiquity is quite a short part of that very long tale. The decisive advance was made in the archaic and classical periods of Greece, from the late eighth to the early fourth century BC. In that short period, in a small area of the eastern Mediterranean, societies emerged which are uniquely important to us. It was there that democracy was invented and argued about, achieved and attacked. Romans disapproved of democracy, and after the conquest of Greece by the Macedonian kings, and then by the Roman Republic, democracy was suppressed in favour of the domination of the upper class. Other basic questions were discussed, in works of literature which have survived the centuries. Is slavery wrong ('against nature')? What is the ultimate source of law, human or divine? Should the family be abolished in favour of the state? (Plato abolished it in theory, and the Spartans went a long way towards abolishing it in fact.) Is civil disobedience sometimes right? (Sophocles' *Antigone* is a classic discussion.) What is the right relation of the sexes? (Plato envisaged, and Aristophanes burlesqued, the idea of women holding political. power.) How can the rule of law be established over blood-feud and family loyalties? What justifies a state in ruling other states, or is there no such thing as justification, but only the ruthless logic of power? (This greatly exercised Thucydides.) What is the ideal size for a community? What is the role of heredity and what of education in the formation of character? It is notable that the decline in creative thought in Greece went along with the loss of political independence.

It is in this period, too, that the characteristic literary and artistic forms were devised. First came the epic, the narration of heroic deeds in elevated verse: Homer is the ultimate model of Virgil, Dante, Tasso, and Milton. Then lyric poetry, tragedy, and comedy, the forms practised by Shakespeare; then prose takes its place beside poetry, with history, philosophy, oratory, and (in Xenophon's *Cyropaedia*) the ancestor of the novel. As these forms were to dominate the high literature of subsequent Europe, so too the visual arts were to be deeply impressed by the bronze and marble statues, the pillars and porticoes of the buildings, the scientific layout of cities. Hippodamus of Miletus was basing cities on a rectangular grid pattern in the middle of the fifth century BC. Every modern bank and every parliament building which offers the world a pillared portico at its entrance is testifying to the lasting influence of the architecture of Greece, as domes and triumphal arches testify to that of Rome. And European literature and art alike show the haunting power of Greek mythology, from the art of Michelangelo and Rubens to the poetry of Milton and Keats. Helen of Troy, Oedipus, Narcissus, the Minotaur at the heart of the labyrinth: these and others are archetypal figures still.

The philosophical legacy, too, is vast. Plato and Aristotle have been the most influential philosophers in Western history both on academic and on Christian thinkers: one might mention the influence of Plato on St Augustine, and that of Aristotle on St Thomas Aquinas. 'In the beginning was the Word' is intelligible only in the light of Greek theories of the Logos. The idea of a university goes back to Plato's school at Athens, which lasted for nearly a thousand years. From Greece it passed to Europe by way of the Arabs, like the text of Aristotle; universities spread north from Salerno, where contact with the Muslim East had planted the seed. Textual criticism began with the study of corrupt texts of classical authors. Such words as 'museum', 'inspiration', 'poet laureate', reveal their ancient connections: a temple of the Muses, the 'breathing into' a poet of his inexplicably splendid verse by some supernatural force, the crowning of a successful poet with laurel. The modern cult of athletics and the revival of the Olympic games are of course strongly Greek.

The period covered in this book begins with the emergence of a recognizably Greek culture in a number of small communities around the Aegean, dwarfed by the ancient cultures of Egypt and Mesopotamia. It has a high point in the defeat by the Greek cities of the enormous armies of the Persian king. It ends with that culture, mature and self-confident, in command of great kingdoms: with Macedonians ruling on the Euphrates and the Nile, and Greek cities flourishing in

A RIVER VALLEY IN ARCADIA, east of Olympia. Rivers in such a landscape are treacherous in flood, though commonly dry in midsummer, and have carried away much cultivable soil even since antiquity when the land may have been better wooded.

Sicily, Italy, and Cyrenaica, at Marseilles, Alexandria, and Naples. It is an extraordinary expansion in scale, and wherever the Greeks went they took with them their texts of Homer, their educational system, their styles of building and art. Some cities achieved democracy, others were dominated by aristocracies; almost all were at times ruled by 'tyrants', self-made dictators; some cities managed to dominate others, while some formed themselves into equal leagues. There is great variety, along with the underlying unity which left a Greek in no doubt who was Greek ('Hellene', as the people whom we call Greek still call themselves), and who was a 'barbarian'—originally, a person of unintelligible speech, who just said 'Bar bar'.

Who were the Greeks? Their ancestors, like those of the Romans, belonged to the great Indo-European family of peoples, which spread in the course of many centuries from an original home somewhere near the Caucasus into India, Iran, and Europe. They began to enter Greece from the north about 1900 BC. From the great steppes they entered a world in which the sea was of primary importance for communications; the land of Greece is mountainous, broken up into a multitude of separate small plains, river valleys, and islands. The fierce particularity of classical Greece, in which every city as a matter of course had its own coinage and even its own calendar, with jealous hostility and intermittent war the rule between neighbouring cities, is clearly connected with the terrain. The climate of Greece is temperate, although the Aegean Sea is notorious for sudden storms, and a man needed little—by the standards of the wet and chilly North—for reasonable comfort. Open-air gatherings and a life largely lived out of doors came naturally in such surroundings. However spectacular the public buildings on the Acropolis, the life-style of a classical Athenian was very modest. The Greeks themselves said that poverty was their great instructor in hardihood and self-reliance, unlike the soft and wealthy peoples of the East.

Mycenaean Greece was culturally dependent on the sophisticated arts of the Minoans, the non-Indo-European people flourishing on Crete and some of the Aegean islands. It was in contact also with other ancient cultures of the Near East: Hittites, Egyptians, Syrians. The sea made it natural for Greeks to turn to neighbouring maritime peoples rather than to the hill-dwellers who lived on the European mainland. Egypt and Asia Minor were more interesting than Macedonia or Illyria. From those already ancient cultures the early Greeks learned many things: the names of exotic gods and goddesses such as Hera and Athena, who became fully naturalized, part of the classic pantheon; luxury arts; music and poetry. When all the other arts were temporarily lost in the dark age which followed the fall of the Mycenaean citadels about 1150 BC, poetry and song survived, and kept alive the memory of an age of great kings and heroes, of Mycenae not an abandoned ruin but rich in gold, the seat of Agamemnon, king of men. The Bronze Age Mycenaean culture was the setting of the myths, whose importance for classical Greece cannot be exaggerated. In the dark age which followed its 'fall, the complex inheritance from the earlier centuries was digested and organized. At its end the pantheon is

THE LION GATE AT MYCENAE. This monumental gateway to the citadel at Mycenae was built in the mid thirteenth century BC and was never lost to view. It, and the massive walls, thought by classical Greeks to have been built by giants, were a reminder to them of the achievements of their Age of Heroes, the period about which Homer sang. It is shown in this old photograph as it may have appeared to the Greeks themselves.

virtually complete, and religion has taken its lasting form; contact with the East is restored; and the *polis*, the independent city-state, is settling into its classic shape.

It is a revealing piece of evidence for the importance of the surrounding cultures that in Greek most names of musical instruments, and even those of many poetical forms, such as elegy, hymn, and iambus, are loan-words from languages which were not Indo-European. Poetry and literature always remained the supreme arts in Greece, both in social prestige and in impact; and their forms, like their mythical content, went ultimately back to a time when the ancestors of the Greeks found themselves arriving in a world of settled dwellings, palaces, frescoes, and music. That early contact must be a great part of the explanation for the Greek achievement. Their distant kinsmen who invaded the Indus valley found there cities and temples, which gave a flying start to Aryan culture in India; the first Greeks, similarly, were helped by contact with sophisticated societies to develop along lines very different from the Germans and the Celts, wandering in the northern forests, who remained for centuries in something far more like the original tribal society.

The Greeks themselves were aware of their debt to Phoenicia for the origin of

A VIEW EAST ACROSS THE EUROTAS VALLEY, near Sparta, from the Byzantine hill-town of Mistra. This is one of the broader, fertile valleys of south Greece, some 5 km across and with easy access to the sea at the south: an easier landscape than most in the Peloponnese but dominated by the massif of Mount Taygetus on the east.

their alphabet, to Egypt for their early style of sculpture, to Babylon for mathematics. In Greece all these things developed in a particular and characteristic way, sculpture, for instance, achieving a realism and also a range quite different from Egyptian art, while in mathematics a keen and novel interest arose in questions of proof and the basing of the whole system on axiomatic foundations. The alphabet was perfected into a script which, in its Roman form, has satisfied the western world ever since. Above all, the human scale, both in art and in society, characterized Greece. The independent city-state, in which alone a man could develop to the full as a citizen, is the central Greek achievement. It was possible because the great kingdoms of the East, which were close enough to give instruction and inspiration, were not close enough to subjugate Greece: when the Persian king Xerxes finally tried, it was too late.

Greek culture was competitive. Each successive historian and philosopher made a point of showing how he improved on his predecessor, and the dialogues of Plato are full of rival experts and thinkers competing for victory in argument. The great Panhellenic occasions, at Olympia and Delphi, centred on athletic competitions; when tragedies or comedies were put on in Athens, it seemed natural that they should be ranged in order by a panel of judges. Each city aimed to outdo its neighbours in splendour.

Greek culture was also marked in all its aspects by an extraordinarily strong feeling for form. That was what gave Greek art and literature their immense impact on the other societies with whom they came into contact. The formal perfection of Greek architecture and town planning, the self-conscious precision of the statues, the strict and exacting requirements which were felt to be appropriate to each genre of literature: all these trained in the audience a demanding and knowledgeable taste. Those who acquired that taste—Etruscans, Lydians, Lycians, the indigenous peoples of Sicily and Syria—found their own native productions by contrast embarrassingly crude and provincial. Only works in the Greek style would do, and literature in the Greek language. The other languages failed to produce literature, and (with the exception of Hebrew) were marked for disappearance. Only in Rome was the heroic decision taken to avoid the easy option of writing in Greek, and to embark on the enormous task of creating in Latin a literature which could be judged by the most exacting Greek standards.

This aesthetic precision must also explain in large part the failure of the Greeks to achieve more technical progress. Even such simple devices as the windmill and the screw were invented late and exploited little by a people ingenious enough to devise machines powered by steam. The existence of slavery does not account for this: slaves were a small part of the work-force in Greece. There was a general preference for aesthetic perfection rather than innovation—a thought-provoking contrast with our own age. We could take as symbolic the riders on the Parthenon frieze, controlling their mounts without stirrups: their beauty is marvellous, and the absence of gear increases it, but the early mediaeval invention of the stirrup would transform the power of cavalry.

The world of early Greece is distant from ours, far removed in space, time, and scale. Other societies have existed, in many ways equally interesting: the early civilization of China, for instance, and of India and Peru. But Greece is linked with us in ways in which those other societies, by the accident of history, are not. John Stuart Mill said that the defeat of King Xerxes at the battle of Salamis was, even as a fact in English history, more important than the Norman Conquest. It made possible the development of an independent society in Greece with its characteristic art and thought, which, through its cultural ascendancy over Rome, was to become the ancestor of the thought and art of Europe. Roman power and organization conquered Greece and oppressed it, but they also carried, wherever the invincible legions went, the culture of that extraordinary people. In the words of the Roman poet Horace, 'Greece though conquered took her fierce conqueror captive, and brought in the arts to the uncivilized Latin peoples'. Ever since then, Greece and Rome have never been lost to sight. Europe has always been aware that another high culture preceded its own, and that awareness has given a distinctively long perspective to European thought.

For many centuries the culture of Greece and Rome was *the* culture of Europe, 'classical' in the sense of being the standard by which everything else was judged. Schools and universities devoted themselves to the study of antiquity with a single-mindedness which must seem to us eccentric or perverse. We can hardly now make

THE APPROACH TO DELPHI FROM THE EAST, through the foothills of Mount Parnassus. Land communications in Greece were not easy, and often circuitous: one reason for preferring coastwise traffic by water where possible. These lower slopes may have been better wooded in antiquity, but limited farming has always been possible between the rocky outcrops, and there are good upland pastures.

sense of the idea of a past society serving in that way as a standard of judgement. But still, because of our unbroken connection with the poetry and science of Greece, to study it is to learn about ourselves, too. For the last advantage which the classical world has over all others is that it alone is both related and also strange to us: related, because we recognize the stories and the speculations as akin to ours (the moral dilemma of Antigone, the atomic theory, the idea that fossils of sea-creatures found on hills show that they were once under water); strange, because these people did things in many ways so differently from us. They worshipped many gods, they owned slaves, they had different ideas about sex. To see that such things can be true of people whom in some ways we find intelligible and recognizable can help to deliver us from the tyranny of the present, from the assumption that our own habits of action and thought are really inescapable, and from the idea that there are no alternatives. That is the liberating power of the past.

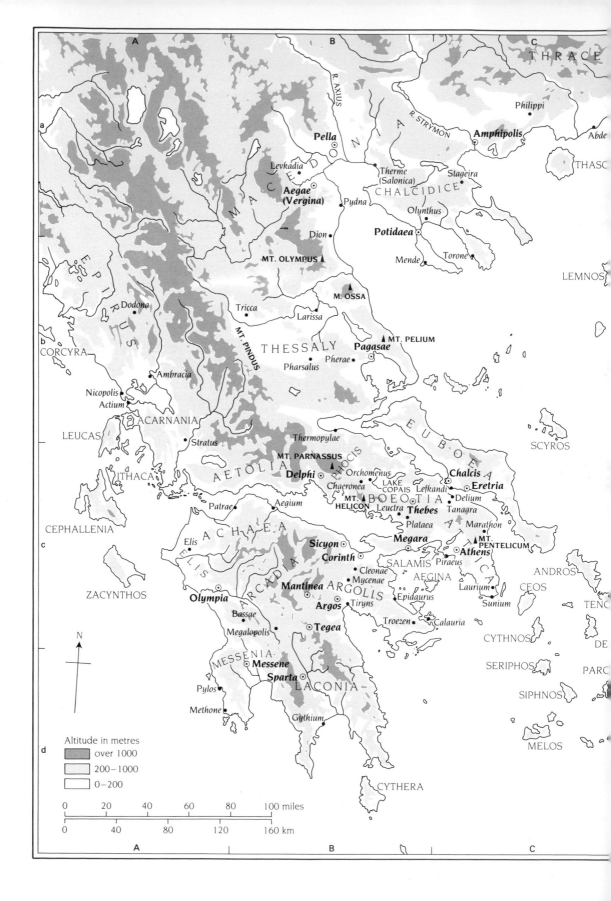

THRACE

Philippi

Abde

R. AXIUS

R. STRYMON

Amphipolis

THASC

Pella

M
A
C
E
D
O
N
I
A

Levkadia

Therme
(Salonica)

Stageira

CHALCIDICE

**Aegae
(Vergina)**

Pydna

Olynthus

LEMNOS

Dion

Potidaea

Mende

Torone

MT. OLYMPUS ▲

E
P
I
R
U
S

Dodona

Tricca

M. OSSA ▲

▲ MT. PELIUM

b

CORCYRA

Larissa

THESSALY

Pagasae

MT. PINDUS

Ambracia

Pherae

Nicopolis

Pharsalus

Actium

E
U
B
O
E
A

ACARNANIA

LEUCAS

Stratus

Thermopylae

SCYROS

MT. PARNASSUS ▲

ITHACA

A E T O L I A

PHOCIS

Delphi ⊙

Chalcis

Orchomenus

Lefkandi

⊙ **Eretria**

Chaeronea

LAKE
COPAIS

Delium

Patrae

Aegium

MT.
HELICON

B O E O T I A

Leuctra

Tanagra

A C H A E A

Thebes

Plataea

Marathon

CEPHALLENIA

Elis

Sicyon ⊙

Megara

MT.
PENTELICUM ▲

E
L
I
S

Corinth ⊙

Cleonae

SALAMIS

⊙ **Athens**

Piraeus

ZACYNTHOS

A
R
C
A
D
I
A

Mycenae

AEGINA

ANDROS

Mantinea ⊙

ARGOLIS

CEOS

TENC

Olympia ⊙

Bassae

Argos ●

Tiryns

Epidaurus

Laurium

Megalopolis

Tegea ⊙

Troezen

Calauria

Sunium

CYTHNOS

DE

MESSENIA

SERIPHOS

PARC

Messene ⊙

SIPHNOS

Pylos

Sparta ⊙

LACONIA

MELOS

Methone

Gythium

N

Altitude in metres

over 1000

200–1000

0–200

CYTHERA

| 0 | 20 | 40 | 60 | 80 | 100 miles |
| 0 | 40 | 80 | 120 | 160 km |

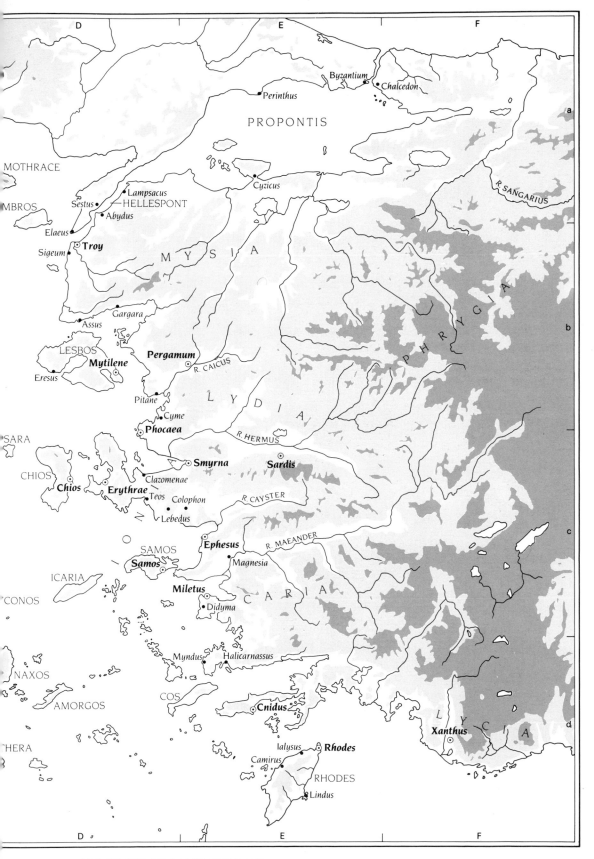

D   E   F

Byzantium
Chalcedon
•*Perinthus*

PROPONTIS

R. SANGARIUS

a

MOTHRACE

MBROS   •*Lampsacus*   •*Cyzicus*
Sestus•—HELLESPONT
•*Abydus*

Elaeus•
Sigeum ◉**Troy**   M Y S I A

P H R Y G I A

b

•*Assus*   *Gargara*•

LESBOS   **Pergamum**•
Mytilene•   *R. CAICUS*
•*Eresus*

L Y D I A

•*Pitane*
•*Cyme*
Phocaea•   *R. HERMUS*

SARA

CHIOS   ◉**Smyrna**   ◉**Sardis**
Chios◉ *Clazomenae*
Erythrae• •*Teos*
Z •*Colophon*
•*Lebedus*   *R. CAYSTER*

c

ICARIA   SAMOS
Samos◉ ◉**Ephesus**   *R. MAEANDER*
•*Magnesia*

CONOS

Miletus◉   C A R I A
•*Didyma*

NAXOS

•*Myndus* •*Halicarnassus*

AMORGOS   COS

L Y C I A

d

THERA   ◉**Cnidus**
Xanthus◉
•*Ialysus* •**Rhodes**
•*Camirus*
RHODES
•*Lindus*

D   E   F

MAP I. GREECE AND THE AEGEAN WORLD

I

Greece: The History of the Archaic Period

⚜

GEORGE FORREST

The Emergence of the Polis

FOR most historians the characteristic and peculiar element in Greek political life has been the *polis*, the city-state, an institution of which any precise definition obscures the variety in size or shape or social and political organization. Very roughly, it was a community of citizens (adult males), citizens without political rights (women and children), and non-citizens (resident foreigners and slaves), a defined body, occupying a defined area, living under a defined or definable constitution, independent of outside authority to an extent that allowed enough of its members to feel that they were independent. The land at large may have been virtually empty of residents or occupied by farmhouses or villages or even small towns, but there had to be one focal point, religious, political, administrative, around which usually grew up (Sparta was a notable exception) a city, the *polis* proper, usually fortified, always offering a market (an *agora*), a place of assembly (often the *agora* itself), a seat of justice and of government, executive and deliberative, in the early period monarchic or aristocratic in type, later usually oligarchic or democratic.

The physical base was almost essential, but even more so was the sense of community. 'We Athenians have a city so long as we have our ships', Themistocles was to say at Salamis (below, p. 39). So too the notion of independence. Some part of it could be shed involuntarily, by acceptance of tribute-paying to a stronger power, or voluntarily, by joining an alliance or even a federation (the Thessalian or Boeotian, for instance), but a sense of 'autonomy' had to be there. This institution at its best, the ancient theorists argued, should be neither too large nor too small, neither too self-sufficient nor too dependent, neither too oligarchic nor too democratic. Certainly, for the archaic and classical periods, most historians have been right to regard the *polis* as the characteristic form of political organization; certainly, too, many *poleis* approached somewhere near the happy norm. But recent enquiries have drawn attention to two other factors which in earlier years will somehow have influenced the origins of the city and may have continued for some time to colour its development.

The first of these is the repopulation of large tracts of the Greek countryside after the collapse of Mycenaean society. The immediate consequence of this collapse was a long period of chaotic tribal wandering which by about 1000 BC had set the pattern for the future: Dorians, newcomers from the north, in most of the Peloponnese, Crete, south-west Asia Minor and its offshore islands; Ionians in Attica, Euboea, most of the Aegean islands, and on the central coast of Asia Minor; in the north, in Lesbos, and north-west Asia Minor a mixture which we may roughly call Aeolian. But at the start most of the settlements were small nuclei with much land around them left to occupy.

The second factor is the appearance of associations of communities, clearly linked with, but not necessarily in all respects coterminous with, this repopulation. Greek tradition hands on several examples of such associations, some mere hazy recollections, some surviving as more or less empty religious institutions, some few surfacing occasionally in later political life. The six Dorian cities of south-west Asia Minor; the twelve Ionian states to the north, capable once of concerted action in the 'Meliac' war, too far away in time to be properly recalled; the amphictyony (a league of neighbours) of Anthela at Thermopylae which owed survival and prosperity to its association with the sanctuary of Apollo at Delphi. Except in the last case, however, vagueness of information has tended to divert attention to more solid things, to Athens, Sparta, Corinth, to real city-states.

But excavations of the last decade or so awaken interest and prompt a new perception. There existed archaeologically in central Greece an area of common culture: southern Thessaly, Boeotia, Euboea, and the islands around its eastern coast, an area which has been given new focus by the discovery of a major settlement at Lefkandi on the west coast of Euboea, half-way between what have hitherto been regarded as the island's two main cities, Chalcis and Eretria. Stunningly prosperous (by contemporary standards) throughout the Dark Age, say 1100 to 750, it appears to have reached a height of wealth in the late ninth century, but more than a century earlier it could offer the tomb of a hero, buried with his consort and with his horses, of unparalleled grandeur and wealth. On available archaeological evidence Lefkandi was the core of the wider community. Was it also the religious core? It is tempting to say that it was not, to think rather of Thermopylae some 60 miles to the north across the narrow water, the site of the amphictyony which, it was said, originally included precisely those same peoples, Thessalians, Boeotians, the smaller tribes between them and the Ionians, no doubt the Ionians of Euboea. Did it, or Thermopylae, provide any kind of political core? Who knows? But stories or hints of early collaboration, commercial and military, between various parts of the area, read against the firm archaeological background and with the likelihood of some religious association, argue for some much greater degree of cohesion than has previously been countenanced.

LEFKANDI. The site lies on the shore of the Straits of Euboea, between Chalcis and Eretria, and must have been the focus of the early dispute between these cities, as well as a prime source for early Greek exploration and colonization. British excavations there have dramatically changed our view of the so-called Dark Ages of Greece, in the tenth and ninth centuries BC.

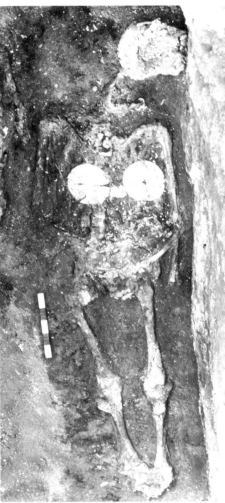

THE BURIAL OF A WOMAN AT LEFKANDI. She wore gold jewellery and an unusual gold brassière. Near her was the cremation burial of a warrior, his ashes wrapped in a cloak. Both were found in a great apsidal building over 45 metres long, with an external wooden colonnade. This is a striking demonstration of Lefkandi's wealth and industry, and a surprising discovery for a period in which Greece offers no other notable architecture. The burial, of the tenth century BC, is truly heroic, and seems to suggest a rich, dynastic society, with overseas connections.

Greater cohesion here encourages belief in greater cohesion elsewhere and poses questions about the political unification of Attica under Athens, about the relationship between Sparta and other communities in Laconia in the first two centuries or so after its Dorian foundation in the late ninth century, about the Theban expansion in Boeotia in the sixth century, and so on. Answers would be premature, but the questions are there.

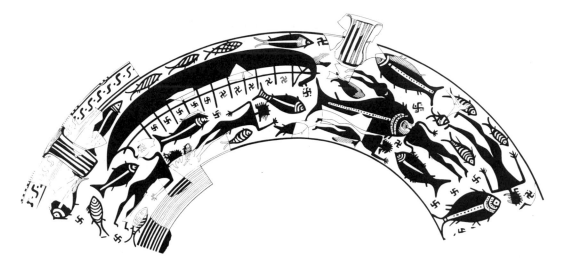

A SHIPWRECK. Drawing on a vase found on Ischia, near the Bay of Naples, site of the first Greek settlement in the west. It shows an upturned ship and men thrown into the sea—one being eaten by a fish; the record, it may be, of a disaster in waters far from the homeland. The style is Euboean (Ischia was settled by Euboeans), but made locally in the later eighth century BC.

More immediately relevant is the disintegration of the Euboean 'organization' in the late eighth century. By 800 some Greeks had begun to wander abroad, in the main, we suppose, in search of metal, and some even settled where they could find it, on the north-Syrian coast (before 800); in Italy a little later; perhaps on the south coast of the Black Sea. The chief operators were the Euboeans, still acting in concert; one of the chief profit-makers was Lefkandi. But about 730 Chalcis and Eretria quarrelled and started the so-called Lelantine War which, Thucydides said, ranged 'the rest of the Greek world in alliance with either side'. Historians have been puzzled. Why should old friends quarrel? Why should 'the rest' join in? What can be meant in such early times by 'alliance'? The puzzles remain real. But comparatively large-scale associations lead more readily to contacts, to friendships and enmities at a distance than do little city-like units; international interests can more readily cement or break such friendships or enmities. In the world sketched above, the hypothesis that some distant outbreak of trouble (say between Phrygia and Assyria, at war with each other about 720–710) raised tensions among interested Greeks, principally Euboeans; that one city broke with existing friends but kept or found others elsewhere, so that the 'rest of the Greek world' became involved—that hypothesis begins to make sense. Be that as it may, the war ended in Eretrian defeat, Lefkandi (which had probably been the site of early Eretria) was abandoned, the community had crumbled. The strains of war brought other readjustments elsewhere, and something more like the city-state structure of later centuries began to appear.

It would not be absurd to see these same strains as in some measure an explanation of the other phenomenon of the late eighth century, a second and much greater wave of emigration, from the mainland, from Ionia and the islands. The earlier adventurers will have brought home news of opportunities abroad that could tempt the less timid or the more desperate, in trade, in military service with foreign powers, above all in agriculture. If the war did not wipe out timidity, it must at least have increased desperation among the defeated or disrupted.

Already, as the war was beginning, Corinth had established a settlement on Corcyra, on the route to the riches of the West, and, in the midst of those riches, Sicilian Syracuse (733 BC); somewhat earlier still Euboeans were developing sites on the north-west coast of the Aegean. Thereafter, throughout the war and the century that followed, what we rather misleadingly call colonization went on in earnest—misleadingly because a 'colony', though a state-organized enterprise, often sent in a direction that would further the state's interests, became an independent unit, normally keeping no more than sentimental and religious ties with its mother city; colonists remembered more vividly and with more gratitude their founder, the man who had led them out, than their foundress city. Over-population, an occasional famine, political trouble, any of these could persuade a government to unload some of its unwanted and send them off, with of course its religious blessing, into the known or the unknown. Just as mixed were the motives for going; compulsion, desperation, ambition; to farm, to trade, to take a chance.

It is mistaken to draw too clear distinctions, between trade and agriculture for example. What part did trade play in Greek politics in general? With some few exceptions, the Greek trader was not a powerful man; respectable Greeks grew things rather than sold them; on the land, not in the market-place, were found Greeks who formed governments. But the Greek who grew things had to sell them or persuade traders to sell them for him. The element cannot be ignored, but we do not need to start talking of 'a powerful merchant class'. For instance, the founding fathers of Syracuse were farmers from an inland village near Corinth, scarcely entrepreneurial material. But they were led by a member of Corinth's ruling family—was he sent on a government-inspired mission or was he merely unpopular with his kinsmen? They settled at Syracuse, rich land, but with the finest harbour in eastern Sicily. Did they settle to survive or to sell? Whatever it was, there is no sign of any very significant relationship with the folks back home. Contrast contemporary Corcyra, surely strategic in intent and to acquire even more strategic importance when it found itself astride the route

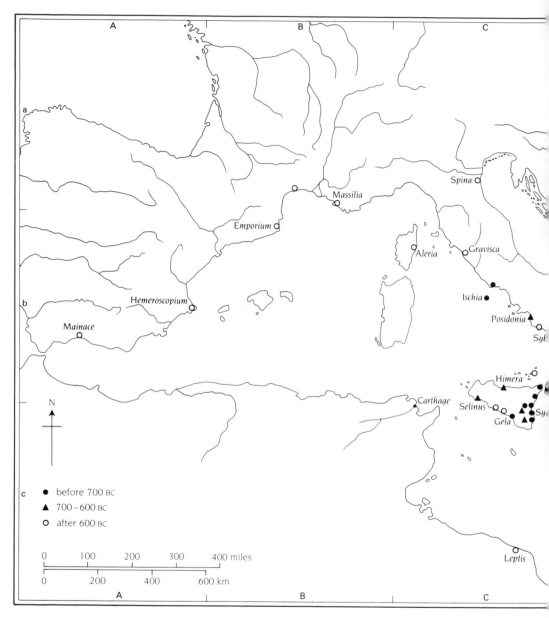

MAP 2. GREEK COLONIZATION. The earliest colonies were led by trade—to Ischia and Cumae in central Italy, close to Etruria. Consolidation soon followed in the agriculturally more promising areas of South Italy and Sicily. The Adriatic approaches were also explored, and the north coast of the Aegean (neighbouring the Thracians) from the later eighth century on. Early exploration of the Black Sea took Greeks to its farther shores, first (Olbia) where there was river-access to the hinterland, with later consolidation which gave access to the Caucasus (Phasis) and the corn-rich lands of the Danube valley (Istrus). The approach to the Black Sea was at the same time secured with cities on the Hellespont and Bosporus. On the east and south shores of the Mediterranean expansion was contained by the strengths of local kingdoms, but the south coast of Asia Minor was explored and Al Mina in Syria

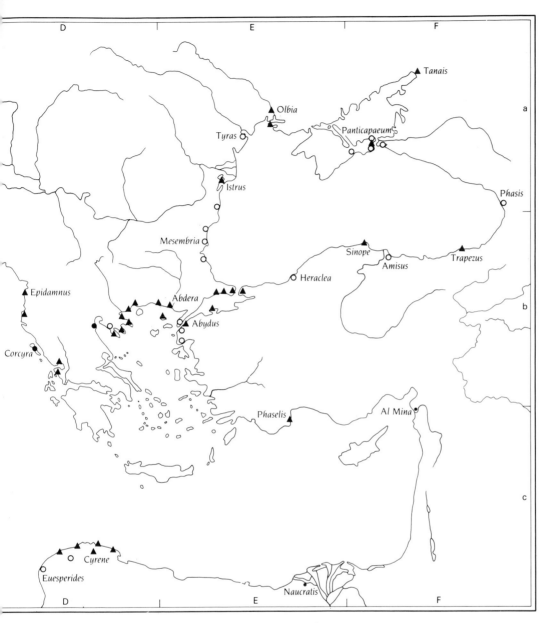

had served as a trading port for Greeks, apparently with Greek residents, from before 800 BC. Naucratis in Egypt served a similar function from the later seventh century on. Cyprus admitted substantial Phoenician (ninth-century) and Greek (eighth- to sixth-century) settlements, the latter becoming mainly Greek cities in later years. Most of the Libyan cities were settled by 600 BC, but further expansion to the west was contained by Phoenicians (in Carthage, Sardinia, and Spain), although in Sicily they had been confined by Greeks to the western end of the island. In Italy Spina and Gravisca were Greek settlements beside Etruscan towns. The principal colonizing cities were, in the eighth century, the Euboean Eretria and Chalcis (who had also opened trade through Al Mina), followed by Corinth in Sicily and North Greece (with Megara and Achaea), and Miletus and the Ionian cities in the Black Sea.

to Adriatic silver as well as western grain. There the story is one of repeated conflict between the 'maternal' interests of Corinth and the legitimate Corcyrean feeling that they had come of age. Contrast again Cyrene, established with no maternal guidance from drought-stricken Thera about 630 BC. The settlers were conscripted and warned clearly that their return would not be welcome.

These examples show how foolish it is to generalize about colonization. We must argue for confusion, a confusion which by about 600 BC found Greeks established in southern France, northern Africa, Egypt, the Black Sea and the entrance thereto, along the north coast of the Aegean, above all in Sicily and southern Italy. Similar confusion upset the established order at home and produced the political revolution to which we must now turn.

The Invention of Politics

Throughout the Mediterranean, eighth-century Greeks had absorbed new experiences: in Egypt wealth and civilization at a level they could not have imagined; in the Near East power and organization, in the west barbarism and potential wealth, in the north a mixture. Being Greeks, they exploited all to their profit and their progress. Artists were captivated by oriental motifs, arms makers by oriental weaponry, traders by hauls of metal, timber or grain, poor farmers by the chance to emigrate, richer farmers by the chance to grow crops that would sell abroad (wine and oil), the sophisticated by different kinds of political life, poets and thinkers and businessmen by the alphabet—above all, everyone by the dawning of the idea that other places existed and might have something to contribute, material or mental. In the late eighth century a peevish Boeotian poet and farmer, Hesiod (below, pp. 82 ff.) was making discontented, but unsatisfiable, noises about the narrow aristocratic society in which he lived, a society pictured, a few years before, from within by the first and greatest epic poet known to us, Homer (below, Ch. 2). The epic does not grasp a particular moment in history though it claims to describe one. It grows with the society for which it is performed, and we cannot now separate the stages of growth. But Homer's heroes at the siege of Troy in his *Iliad*, proud, brave, honourable, touchy, vengeful, were understood by his aristocratic audience, and their values cannot have been wholly dissimilar, nor can their total disregard for men like Hesiod be unreal. But by the early seventh century Hesiod's peers were claiming regard.

It is vital to insist that this opening of the Greek mind is much more important than the particular forms of government which were produced by the opening. Here there was 'tyranny'; there 'oligarchy'; here 'a constitution'; there 'anarchy'. Common to all of the more flexible societies is turmoil, and common to all is the achievement in the end of some sort of what we are prepared to describe as the constitutional government of the city-state.

But the routes were indeed diverse. In Sparta in the early seventh century a great lawgiver, Lycurgus, it was said, laid down the rules for a system of military training (one could hardly call it education) which turned Sparta into the most efficient military power in Greece, helping it to hold ruthless mastery over the southern half of the Peloponnese, and by stages to acquire a more subtle control over the rest of the peninsula. At the same time he formalized and thus reformed Sparta's social structure and produced a constitution which guaranteed to all Spartans some form of political equality the like of which had not been imagined by Hesiod and was not to be realized elsewhere for many a day.

Sparta's position as mistress of vast tracts of conquered territory and vast numbers of subjects, compared with her own population (the notional figure was 9,000 adult males, outnumbered seven to one), was rare, but not unparalleled; her solution was to expropriate the bulk of the territory for state-controlled, but privately managed, exploitation and enslave, but not quite enslave, the subjects. Again, the state 'owned' the slaves (called 'helots'), but the individual Spartan took half the production. The numbers of the breed and its real or imagined racial coherence established helot discontent, the danger of helot revolt, as the key to much of Spartan behaviour for centuries. At the same time a fair number of more significant communities in the subjected area were given special treatment and recognized as having some independence in their own domestic affairs. These were the *perioikoi*, the neighbours, who had much less to complain about than the helots, but were not always as docile as a Spartan might like.

It is against this background that we must see the development and, after Lycurgus, the freezing of Spartan institutions. If her position was rare, her solutions made her unique. Most Greeks retained some traces of a state-imposed military training for the young; in Crete, for example, many close similarities to Spartan customs can be seen. But only in Sparta, so far as we know, was a child completely robbed of home and family between the ages of five and thirty and even thereafter compelled to devote his days to military training and his evenings to the company of his messmates. Most Greeks entered the archaic age with aristocratic attitudes, and in most some faint elements of these attitudes long survived. But of the states that mattered it was only in Sparta that these were captured and preserved so early and with so little chance of change in the composition or the interests of the aristocracy. And there was the compounding factor that Sparta retained its hereditary kingship, no mere titular kingship, when others had or were in the process of losing theirs. More oddly still there were two kings, drawn from two great houses, who by their friendships or rivalries could only emphasize the basic aristocratic principle of dependence of the small on the great.

In its constitution Sparta also stood apart, but here in a different way. The kings were the military commanders; with the aristocratic council, the Gerousia, they initiated most political and took most judicial decisions. But there was also an assembly of all Spartan citizens which met at fixed times and passed final judgements on most things that mattered—all Spartan citizens, that is, as defined by the great Lycurgus, all who had survived their training, who had been allotted state land in the conquered territory with helots to work it, and who continued to obey the rules. They called themselves *homoioi*, equals, and by doing so not only registered discontent with their earlier status, whatever it may have been, but justify the use a few lines ago of the word 'citizens'. Equality was more a statement of a basic minimum than of any absolute standard, but it does not matter much that some Spartans were rich (private as opposed to state-allotted land existed), others comparatively poor; it does not matter that some Spartans were of noble birth, others ordinary people; it does not matter that in a militarily based society political independence is not encouraged or even tolerated. What does matter is that, by the assertion of the basic minimum, Spartans were beginning to grope towards a definition of the citizen as a member of a society who was automatically entitled to certain rights (however small), who had a sense of community (however much it was merely the product of a shared fear of helots or a shared desire to exploit those helots for their own profit).

To the mechanics of the Spartan revolution we shall return. Spartan aristocrats did not cede 'equality' with good grace, but they used little violence. Elsewhere the process was different. In Corinth, for example, control of the state and of the wealth that could be gained thereby had lain with one aristocratic clan, the Bacchiadae. In 657 a half-member of the clan, Cypselus, collected sufficient support to kill or expel them and to take over as what later Greeks call 'tyrant'. Of the nature of Cypselus' government nothing is known except that enough of his support came from people experienced and competent enough to provide the city with uninterrupted, indeed increasing, prosperity. Nor can we tell what Cypselus had promised to them except a share in government, or to the wider circle who followed, except that his propaganda used a word, *dikaiōsei*, which can mean anything between 'put [Corinth] to rights' through 'give [Corinth] a set of rules' to 'give Corinth justice'. Whatever the precise meaning, there is more than a hint here of that same desire for 'equality' which had excited Spartans, even if that equality was limited to equality before the law and, paradoxically, was to be won under that most unequal of regimes, 'tyranny'.

No doubt Corinthians had other reasons for supporting Cypselus, at the lowest level a simple desire to beat up the Bacchiads; and in other cities of which we know less, where tyrants appeared or tried to appear, their supporters will have had their private reasons. But a widespread phenomenon invites some general explanation, and the theme of justice in some form or other is alluded to often enough in the seventh century to suggest that it was the first constituent in the Greeks' slow and uneven expansion of the idea of what it was to be a *polītes*, a full member of a *polis*. It was the arbitrariness of what passed for justice that had irked Hesiod; 'Justice done and seen to be done' (in Sparta) won confident praise from the seventh-century poet, Terpander of Lesbos.

But what had happened to turn despair into confidence, to produce this first crack in the aristocratic fabric? And what tools were used to produce it? The answer to the second question has been thought to lie, and probably does lie, in the murky area of military history. The basic unit of an early Greek army was the aristocrat and his entourage, collectively a 'phratry', members of his family, lesser dependent nobles, richer farmers, and so down through the social scale. The spearhead, literally, of this unit was the aristocrat, well armed, well trained, standing out in front of the rest, which was itself protected as its affluence permitted, or unarmed as poverty dictated, giving its moral or physical support by whatever methods or with whatever weapons came to hand. The developed army, on the other hand, while it might still contain some elements of cavalry and more of light-armed troops, depended for its effect on some thousands of heavily, and more or less uniformly, equipped infantry called hoplites. The hoplites were still often brigaded by phratry, though there was a shift in some places towards more firmly defined geographical units; but success required cohesion of the whole force, a line usually eight deep, helmeted, corsleted, greaved, presenting a solid front of round shields and thrusting, no longer throwing, spears, winning by co-operative weight. As the mid-seventh-century Spartan poet, Tyrtaeus (below, p. 96), put it: 'Stand near and take the enemy, strike with long spear or sword, set foot by foot, lean shield on shield, crest upon crest, helmet on helmet . . . .'

This is hoplite fighting in spirit, but how sophisticated in form? Here we appear to be faced with a paradox. Some random elements of hoplite equipment were being fashioned as early as the eighth century, but the earliest representations

RANKS OF HOPLITE SOLDIERS depicted on a Corinthian vase of about 650-640 BC. They advance on each other, with a piper to help keep the step. This style of warfare replaced the Homeric duels of leaders supported by light-armed rabble, and was generally adopted in Greece during the seventh century BC. The men are well armoured, with helmets, shield clamped on to the left arm by two grips, corselet and greaves. The main weapon is a thrusting spear, and victory lay with the ranks that kept their order, were not out-flanked, and did not break.

of an organized phalanx in vase-painting do not antedate by much the middle of the seventh century. Yet an individual hoplite is a curious object to imagine in aristocratic battle, while the creation of the phalanx with its practised cohesion surely demands one moment of decision. But the puzzle is not, perhaps, too real. It is the result of too easy a slide from thoughts of the single champion to pictures of the massed infantry of later years; of failure to recognize that an easier supply of metal and more wealth to make use of it could gradually lead to a multiplication of 'champions'; of collaboration between small numbers of them; of not asking what minimum number might be needed to form an effective unit of hoplite type (surely some hundreds, not thousands). The change could well be in train and even far advanced in the first half of the century, years before the painters appreciated it or mastered the technique of depicting a hoplite army on a pot.

If this is so, it becomes easier to answer the more important question. What, if anything, did military innovation have to do with political revolution? In Corinth in 657 Cypselus had the army behind him; he expelled the Bacchiads by force and did not need a bodyguard. Earlier, in Sparta, the army and its structure was at the heart of the Lycurgan revolution. To put it crudely, if there were 300 Bacchiads armed as hoplites, it needed only 301 other Corinthians similarly clad and with the added weapon of revolutionary fervour to overthrow them. The much larger numbers involved in Sparta need not yet have acquired even the measure of cohesion that Tyrtaeus implies, so long as they had enough to make themselves felt.

But military change was in the main only one factor in the mechanics of revolution. It will have affected its course but not its substance. It guided, but it did not generate, except in so far as new conditions would, of course, help to create a sense of common situation, to bolster confidence; and the newer the conditions the greater would be the effect. The origins of the move against aristocratic monopoly lie further back, in the consequences of eighth-century adventure and expansion. Economic expansion, even if only agricultural, as in Sparta, relief of population pressure, the experience of different worlds (the word *tyrannos* was of eastern origin), these did not create a new 'middle class' of well-fed farmers, still less a party of rich merchants. But they did produce tensions, between aristocrat and aristocrat, lesser aristocrat and greater, with the odd successful trader or pirate thrown in to complicate things still further. The old rules were not flexible enough, or later clearly enough defined, to cope.

Some states tried a third route to the new world, constitutional, like that of the Spartans, but less idiosyncratic, very much more humane. The setting up of a colony invited, if it did not demand, some conscious thought about the character of the new settlement, some element of self-consciousness even where the desire may only have been to reproduce what had been left at home (a desire that cannot have been profound, since most colonists left home because they did not like what they had experienced there). Thus a new need was added to the new instinct for change, or at least dissatisfaction with the existing order, the need to formulate; and (yet again) eastern experience will have shown that formulation was possible. It is thus no surprise that Crete, a natural link with the East, should have become for Greeks the home of lawgiving, that Crete (according to one story) should have inspired Sparta, that a Cretan should have taught the earliest named colonial legislator, Zaleucus of Italian Locri (*c*.670), and that other Italian and Sicilian colonies should have become a lawgiver's paradise.

But this is all shadow. It is only in mainland Attica that the translation of the desire and the idea into fact can be followed. Attica had survived post-Mycenaean turmoil better than most, but here too there had been economic collapse and only gradual redevelopment. When things settled down the city of Athens was at the head of whatever association Attica may once have been, not, like Sparta, a city of 'equals' surrounded by *perioikoi* or helots, but the centre of an Attica riddled throughout with inequalities. There were aristocrats, free men, and dependents in and around the city as there were in Eleusis, Marathon, or Sunium. It is not the least of Athenian achievements that she contrived to diminish or delete the distinctions across the country while building up the city as acknowledged capital, preserving at once local pride, national identity and individual dignity.

Around 630 there was an attempt at tyranny; around 620 the response was a law-code, the work of Draco, of which we know virtually nothing beyond its severity. But to insist on the severity is to ignore the point that by the mere fact of definition it invited criticism and change, and that Athenians went on to accept the invitation. Zaleucus' code was also said to have been severe, but the Locrians too ultimately made changes. It is the sad thing about Spartans that what had been 'good enough for grandfather' remained 'good enough for me'.

In Athens the first changes came after some twenty-five years. There arrived a moment of crisis, or near-revolution, when it was decided to appoint an arbitrator to produce a second, very different definition. Out of the background of discontent with Draco and the aristocratic in-fighting it had generated came the choice of one revolutionary leader, Solon, who, fortunately for us, was not only a politician, but a poet, albeit a somewhat self-centred, self-righteous, and just a trifle pompous one.

Solon, elected chief magistrate for 594, had one weakness. He did not like killing people. He could have made himself tyrant, but, as he wrote, 'Tyranny is a very pretty position. The trouble is that there's no way out of it.' Given this fastidiousness, he had to persuade two sides, 'the people' and 'those who had power', to ignore 'those who were in the game for plunder' and agree on a Spartan-type equality which satisfied both. It was not an easy job. 'Those who had power' had exercised it socially through an Athenian version of the widespread share-cropping system, in which a large number of Athenians paid one-sixth of their produce to a superior individual, not to the state, in return for freedom to work their land, a system which grew around or upon the phratry system of dependence described above (p. 23). Politically they had exercised it by an automatic consequence of this; a monopoly of the important magistracies and of the council, the Areopagus, recruited from ex-magistrates, the only deliberative body in the state. There was a citizen assembly, but it is not likely to have played much part except in moments of crisis when public opinion had to be tested or in annual magisterial elections where at most it might occasionally be allowed to show preference for the candidates of one noble faction against another. The Areopagus and the magistrates, indistinguishable in class or interest, ran Athens.

Much of what Solon did, like much of what Draco had done, was merely to codify existing practice, but in his search for something that he could present as a fair compromise he made some astute moves. 'Those who had power' kept their property, much of their position and, more seductive still, their lives. In exchange 'the people' were given 'the dignity that was their due'.

How? All debts had been secured upon the person of the borrower, and so a defaulting share-cropper became a defaulting debtor. Now existing debts were cancelled and personal security was forbidden. Share-cropping ceased to exist ('I freed the soil of Attica that had once been enslaved') and no Athenian could henceforth suffer the indignity of enslavement for debt. The political propagandist added a nice touch: 'I brought back home many who had been sold abroad. . . . who had even forgotten how to speak their native tongue.' One wonders how many he could find.

Politically too some element of equality was sought. The assembly won new authority, perhaps in some ways of which we know nothing (regularity of meeting, possibly? definition of proper business or method of voting?) but certainly by the acquisition of a new directing body, a rival council to the Areopagus, a 'second anchor for the city'. It does not matter how this council was constituted or what wider powers of administration it may have had. It prepared the assembly's programme, oversaw the exercise of any further popular say in elections to office, and was a buffer against Areopagite interference. Such things make a difference. So too did Solon's assertion that the assembly was to be the ultimate court of law. An Athenian could appeal to the assembly or a committee of it against a magistrate's verdict in his court. In the first decades not many will have had the courage to appeal, but the right was there, and was to be exploited.

To each according to his deserts. All Athenians deserved freedom from the threat of slavery, a guarantee against legal oppression, some voice in the direction of the city. But some Athenians, chief among them Solon's supporters, deserved more in the way of real political power. Solon, no less than Cypselus, had had some big men behind him, and they wanted a reward. The solution was simple, but very radical. Access to major political and military office, the archonship, previously restricted by convention to a limited group of families, the Eupatridae (the 'well born'), was to be determined by wealth in land. All Athenians were divided into four classes. To the top class or classes went the top offices, to the lowest, the *thētes*, only membership of the assembly, with consequent judicial influence. So far as can be judged the potential number of 'those with power' was doubled—no mean change.

If there is a note of cynicism in this account of Solon, it is introduced only to remind that Solon was, and had to be, a practising politician, that he was not a sage of moderation called down from Olympus to settle Athens' ills, but a shrewd operator and a radical thinker, a very good and brave man who gave Athenians a chance of peaceful change which, as we shall see, they did not immediately take.

Revolution is rarely in itself a pleasant thing. Even without violence some nice people and nice things tend to get upset. It is comforting that Greek revolutions on the whole led to pleasant things. Under Cypselus and his son Periander Corinth extended and tightened her colonial enterprise, while Corinthian potters and painters made very pretty pots; in Athens a later awakening produced a more startling wakefulness (again reflected for us mainly in the arts) while the liberated share-cropper made the most of his 16-per-cent relief; even in Sparta an imported poet, Alcman (below, pp. 101 f.), talked happily of days, and nights, of pleasure by the banks of the river Eurotas. The distasteful martial spirit of Tyrtaeus was forgotten when Alcman wrote of food, admittedly not elegant food, of wines, and of girls who 'cast glances that are more melting than sleep or death'.

But, as Greeks were fond of saying, though they said it more gracefully, one can have too much of a good thing. Corinthians who had followed Cypselus could not see why they should follow his son or his descendants. Periander's successor was expelled, and Corinth lapsed into an undistinguished oligarchy. Spartans were so pleased with themselves that they turned to further expansion. Some leisure and some freedom made Athenians lust for more of both. The results were gradual decline for Corinth (very gradual—she was always there to be reckoned with), a chequered domination for Sparta, and ultimately democracy in Athens.

Ultimate democracy; first there was a half-century of intermittent tyranny. Solon had refused the role of tyrant and had hoped to inoculate Athenian society against the disease; a young supporter, worse still a relative, proved to be infected and after two trial runs put himself firmly in charge in 546, to be succeeded by his sons after his death in 528. It is not easy to say why Pisistratus was able to establish himself with popular goodwill. Attica had been divided between those who lived around the coast, land that might be generating new wealth in the shape of olive oil, and the outback, rich enough, but far from the centre of things. Pisistratus, though as blue-blooded as any, came from and led the outback. What made it possible? Were his clients in the plain of Marathon producing better oil? Were some of them beginning to exploit the rich silver deposits at Attica's south-east corner? Was there, as a result of economic development or just for its own sake, a feeling that further parts might reach for the centre?

However it came about, it is arguable that a generation of tyranny did more to encourage Athenians towards the three goals mentioned above, national unity, local pride, and individual dignity, than would a continuing adherence to Solonian constitutionalism. Attention was attracted to the city of Athens, not only by the fact that power now rested there, but by public works, temples, fountain-houses, even drains, which made it seem a worthy seat of power, by fostering the cult of the goddess Athena, patroness of Athens and (Pisistratus liked to claim) of Pisistratus himself, by the encouragement or creation of national festivals and games: the Panathenaea, at which (shrewd advertising) the prizes were jars of Attic olive oil; the Dionysia, where first moves were made towards one of Athens' greatest creations, the drama.

Local pride needed no encouragement, but at least the central authority could show that it cared: a panel of itinerant judges was established to settle local disputes, previously in the hands, no doubt, of the local aristocrat. And it is in and around the standing of these aristocrats that lies the solution of the paradox that an autocrat, a tyrant, could, in fact, promote individual freedom and individual dignity.

Solon had opened government to new men, but had done nothing positive to diminish the aristocrat at local level, beyond robbing him of legalized mastery over the poorer around him. Now he had either died in the last battle against Pisistratus or thought it prudent to go into exile or, even if he stayed, knew that he had to acknowledge the existence of someone more powerful than himself.

THE ASSASSINATION OF THE ATHENIAN TYRANT HIPPARCHUS IN 514 BC BY HARMODIUS AND ARISTOGEITON. This event was celebrated by the new democratic regime (after 510 BC) with a statue group which was stolen by the Persians in 480 BC. The group was replaced, and is known to us from copies of the Roman period. Soon afterwards (*c.*470–460 BC) an Athenian artist offered this version of the event with figures which are inspired by the statues of the replacement group without copying them, but he added the victim.

Thus the rest either lost their master or realized that he did not matter so much as before. To change allegiance from one master to another may not seem to us a momentous step, but it is the first step towards a sense of being one's own master.

Thus, when Pisistratus' sons were expelled in 510 by a combination of exile, intrigue, and Spartan arms (below, p. 30) and the old guard thought that they could resume old-style politics, they found that the audience had changed. One of them, Cleisthenes, head of the great noble house that had supported Solon, the Alcmeonidae, sensed this change sooner than his rivals and, in Herodotus' words, 'added the people to his faction, the people who had previously been ignored, now by offering them a share in everything . . .' Cleisthenes' own motives may have been selfish; some of the things he did may have been designed to secure his own or his family's political future. That is no matter. He offered and with popular support gave Attica a new socio-political structure which served it well for some 200 years.

The essence of the new system was the recognition that small local units, country villages or townlets, wards of the city, should control their own affairs independently of the local aristocrat. Each chose its mayor and its council, and minded its own business. Then, for state purposes, these 'demes' as they were called, were grouped into larger more or less coherent geographical blocks (there are some signs of gerrymandering here) and from these blocks were constructed ten new tribes, each with one block from what were called the 'Plain', the 'Coast', and the 'City'. Upon the tribes were then based not only the army, but other parts of the administrative system, above all the Solonian council, now fifty from each tribe, each contingent serving as a standing committee of the whole council for one-tenth of the year.

In this way an Athenian in his village could make use of whatever self-confidence he may have had; at the same time, at state level, he could develop that sense of nationality which the tyranny had begun to encourage. It is never easy to judge how far legislation promotes a change of attitude, how far it merely recognizes one. Of Athens we can only say that Cleisthenes' legislation came in time to avoid trouble and that it was enough in accord with what was wanted to allow Athenians to do what later they did. He did not tamper with existing social groups, with their cherished cults, or with their prestige. He had no need to: he merely created a new structure and gave it the authority.

The Leadership of Sparta

One thing Athenians did was to fight against the Persian invasions, and morally theirs was the credit for Greek victory. But technically it was taken for granted by the Greeks who chose to resist that Sparta should be their leader. Why? Thanks to the Lycurgan rules Sparta had the only professional army in Greece. She could field 5,000 or so hoplites of her own, backed by a similar number of adequately trained *perioikoi* and many more thousands of lightly armed helots. But this army had no great record of success in the sixth century, and it was as much or more due to diplomacy, given weight by the threat of that army, that she held the respect that she did.

Herodotus says that, thanks to Lycurgus, the Spartans, 'their soil being good and the population numerous . . . sprang up rapidly to power and became a flourishing people. In consequence they soon ceased to be satisfied and to stay quiet . . .' In other words, they were not content to enjoy the relaxed pleasures of Alcman but chose to try to extend their domination into northern Peloponnese. They were opposed by one major city, Argos, and a number of lesser cities, settlements, or tribal agglomerations. Against Argos they won, though in no decisive fashion; against the rest they failed. But failure taught them the lesson that expansion by annexation and enslavement could not work, that to subdue an immediate circle of hostile neighbours would only create a more distant circle of hostile neighbours. A wise Spartan (some Spartans were wise) saw that expansion by diplomacy could be cheaper and more effective.

This sage was Chilon who, in 556 BC, held the office of ephor, an office which had been created in the turmoil of the Lycurgan period for purposes which we cannot now descry, but basically to give the Spartan 'Equals' a chance through an annual election to have their immediate favourites in a position to assert themselves against kings or Gerousia, or to side with one against the other. Chilon is the earliest ephor upon whom we can focus and it is clear that, with the 'Equals' behind him, he transformed Spartan thinking.

The problem was racial as well as military. Out of the confusion of the post-Mycenaean world came a Greece divided between Dorians, Ionians, and others. All were Greeks, all spoke Greek, but very different forms of Greek, all accepted that the Dorians were intruders, though perhaps a rather superior kind of intruder. It is hard to judge what these distinctions meant in day-to-day practice, but they did mean something, and it was Chilon's genius to see that playing down Sparta's Dorianism could cajole hostile non-Dorian neighbours into alliance, with no less profit in the end for Sparta.

So treaties were made city by city, with Corinth, with Sicyon, with the communities of Arcadia, indeed with almost all except the old rival for Dorian hegemony, Argos. In some cases, to fix the alliance, Sparta had to take a hand in the internal affairs of the future ally, and in some cases, in Sicyon for example, this interference led to the expulsion of a tyrant, thus giving a start to Sparta's later reputation as an opponent of tyranny as such. Spartans were not opposed to tyranny as such, except in Sparta, but her expansionism in the next half-century or so (Chilon had changed Spartan methods but had not quenched Spartan ambition) brought her up against various powers which were under tyrants and for differing reasons these had to be removed, chief among them being the sons of Pisistratus in Athens whom, in 510, Sparta successfully attacked with the encouragement and support of Athenian aristocrats in exile.

CORINTH. The city site is in the foreground, dominated by the remains of the sixth-century BC Temple of Apollo. In the distance to the south rises the citadel, Acrocorinth, linked by long walls to the city in the fourth century BC. It is the most impressive of the *acropoleis* of mainland Greece.

Differing reasons. Some tyrants (the Athenian among them) had been friends of Argos, some had established links with a new factor in Aegean politics, the expanding Persian Empire. About 546 the Persians, having absorbed the greater part of the Middle East and Asia Minor, appeared among the Greeks of the Aegean's eastern coastline, who had previously enjoyed a comparatively unoppressive dependence on the non-Greek powers of the hinterland, especially Lydia, under its amiable King Croesus (*c.*560-546). The Persians believed in tighter control, and compliant tyrants were installed or supported in the Greek cities. In 525 the Persians took over Egypt and then moved along the coast of north Africa; in 514 they crossed into Europe and, in spite of a disastrous foray into southern Russia, maintained a presence in Thrace and influence as far as Macedon. Thus the Greek mainland and the islands were beset to north, south, and east, while even in the west another alien power, Carthage, was pressing on the opulent outposts of Hellenism, the cities of Sicily and southern Italy, which from their poor colonial beginnings were now often as rich and as sophisticated as any in the homeland. The Persians may not have had any immediate ambition to occupy Greece, but they were there and had to be reckoned with. All Greek states we know of were divided about their response. In some the majority, in power if not in numbers, felt that an offer of compliance or even subservience was the more profitable course; others thought that they should fight; in every case there was domestic disagreement, and in every case it was easy for domestic disagreements on other issues to become entangled with the Persian question. A political loser might look to Persia for support, even a political winner could feel more secure with Persian favour. So the surviving exiled son of Pisistratus found sanctuary in Persian territory, and the most powerful family in northern Thessaly, the Aleuadae, lent towards collaboration. It was no different in Sparta. Although for long aware of the problem she resolutely and consistently refused to become involved, but in the end even there a quarrel between the two kings in the late 490s drove one of the disputants, Demaratus, to the Persian court.

Demaratus' opponent, Cleomenes, was clever, over-clever. He was also devious, unscrupulous, ambitious, cruel, and, it was believed, mad. There is no reason to think that this belief was wrong. At any rate, forceful though he was, ingenious though he was, most of Cleomenes' schemes turned sour (in a fit of ultimate despair and lunacy he committed suicide). Yet, paradoxically, his failures strengthened Sparta.

The alliances we have mentioned were between city and city, but the standard formula of a Greek alliance, 'to have the same friends and the same enemies', raised a problem; who was to decide who was whose friend, who was whose enemy? Between Sparta and a tiny community in Arcadia the question was academic; between Sparta and a state such as Corinth it was more delicate; between Sparta and the host of entities large and small to whom she was now allied it was unanswerable. Consequently the system of separate associations, one with one, had to be modified. Gradually or suddenly the idea of a league of states was created or recreated. Sparta was the military commander and effective mistress, but others had a voice. Perhaps they looked back to those other associations we have mentioned. In what must have been a very hazy process one moment stands out. In about 506 Demaratus, supported by the Corinthians and other allies, refused to follow Cleomenes in an attack on Athens (his first interventions had not gone well). Thereafter the 'Peloponnesian League' met in congress and acted only after debate and vote. Sparta provided the military expertise; the rest gave support. And so was created the military organization on which was based the Greek resistance to Persia when in the end Persia decided to invade.

The Persian Wars

In about 500 BC Sparta was the recognized leader of an alliance which embraced virtually all states of the Peloponnese except Argos; neither she nor her allies had shown any commitment on the Persian issue, though she had inadvertently acted against some who found Persians sympathetic. Athens was free of her tyrants, and Athenians were slowly growing to appreciate the 'democratic' constitution that Cleisthenes had invented (it is to be remembered that the word 'democracy' itself had not yet been invented). They had no unanimous view on Persia. Other states were similarly divided, and Herodotus sums it up, cynically but effectively, when he says of the decision of the men of Phocis, a small community in central Greece, to fight: 'My guess is that they did so because they hated the Thessalians. If the Thessalians had chosen to resist the Persians, the Phocians, I think, would have collaborated.'

The first serious trouble showed itself in Asia Minor. There, in the city of Miletus, a Persian-installed tyrant, Histiaeus, who had been adopted as political adviser at the Persian court, and his deputy, Aristagoras, whom he had left behind to look after affairs in Miletus, found themselves at loggerheads with the official Persian authorities. They had believed that they could insinuate themselves into a role of authority; they were wrong, and their machinations produced what later historians have described as a great patriotic outburst, Greek against barbarian, what Herodotus more soberly calls 'the beginning of troubles'. In 499 some (not all) of the Ionian cities, some (not all) of the Aeolian states to the north, perhaps some of the Dorian cities to the south disposed of their tyrants and began open revolt against the Persians. Sparta refused to help. Athens chose—hesitantly, but with irrevocable results—to support the rebels.

So Athens was to be punished, and in 490, after the Ionians and their friends had been squashed in 494, a Persian fleet crossed the Aegean to land on Attic soil at Marathon. Their number is not known, but it was vastly larger than the 10,000 hoplites that Athens and one small friend, Plataea, could put into the field against them. Persians, it is to be remembered, were good soldiers and were commanded

BRONZE HELMET DEDICATED AT OLYMPIA BY MILTIADES in the early fifth century BC. The dedicator's name appears incised along the lower rim— 'Miltiades dedicated to Zeus'. It is difficult not to identify this Miltiades as the victor of Marathon. It was customary to dedicate spoils of the defeated (there is a Persian helmet dedicated at Olympia by the Athenians) so this is perhaps not from Marathon, but from some other encounter, with Greeks.

THE PLAIN AT MARATHON. In the decisive battle in 490 BC, in which the Athenians repelled the Persian invasion, the Greeks formed up in the foothills and the flow of the battle was, in this picture, from left to right. The tumulus covering the Athenian dead appears at the centre. This fertile coastal plain is typical of the shore line of central Greece.

by able generals. Yet, miraculously, the Athenians won. More than 6,000 Persians died; some 200 Greeks. The results were many. We note three.

Greeks had distinguished between themselves and 'those who spoke other languages'; other civilized societies had done the same. Now two notions were added to the factual description. One of hostility, the other of superiority. There was something indecent in the idea that a Greek should work on equal terms with a 'barbarian' (one who spoke another language). Practical Greeks did not allow the idea to affect their behaviour. But many exploited it in immediate propaganda, and in the end it was only one who had exploited it to the utmost, Alexander the Great, who began dimly to see that it was absurd.

But the military superiority was real. In some extraordinary way 10,000 or so Greek hoplites had routed a great mass of Persians. It did not need a sophisticated military mind to draw the conclusion that a hoplite phalanx, even if only moderately well trained, could win against cavalry, archery, or any other sort of infantry however armed or brigaded. Spartans were brought up to believe that they were the finest soldiers in the world, but even Spartans must have been encouraged by the Athenian success.

The third result was even more important. Cleisthenes had recognized a change in Athenian attitudes and exploited it against other aristocrats by devising a social and political system which, either by accident or Cleisthenic design, gave scope for further enormous changes of mood. But traditional habits of thought do not die ovenight; in 507 most aristocrats will still have been behaving as they had always behaved. More importantly, most ordinary Athenians will in many re-spects have continued to behave as they always had. Some few aristocrats and rather more ordinary folk felt otherwise. By 480 the army was still commanded and the city administered by the old ruling class, but its absolute control over Athenian minds was beginning—we stress 'beginning'—to be blunted. Such movements are subtle and hard to plot even when evidence is abundant; they are not only gradual, they are irregular. When evidence is sparse and the atmosphere at start and finish impossible to catch with any precision, when men do not talk explicitly about shifts of this kind, we can only register the fact and look for any clues there are. Aristotle, with characteristic shrewdness, remarks that victory at Marathon gave the Athenian people political confidence. His illustration is the fact that in the decade after Marathon the Athenians first made use of a curious institution, ostracism, another Cleisthenic invention, which allowed the assembly to decide every year to send, should it wish, one of its political figures into temporary ten-year exile without loss of property. The explicit reason for the first three ostracisms was suspicion of treachery in 490, but Aristotle is surely right to think that courage to exercise power is as significant as the occasion for its exercise.

Whether this same surge towards democracy lay behind another constitutional change of these years we cannot say. In 487 direct election to the archonship was replaced by a system which combined election with the use of lot. Was this a conscious 'democratic' move? (Lot was a great feature of the developed democ-racy.) In the long run the ten generals (normally elected one from each tribe) came to replace the archons as the chief officers of state: desire for elected efficiency overcame principle. But long-term results are frequently not foreseen. We can only note the coincidence of time. The issues are obscure, as are those of the following years, and not only in domestic politics. It would be wrong to assume that, as they saw the tail of the Persian fleet scurrying home in 490, all, or even many, Athenians concentrated on the likelihood that the Persians would return.

Boeotia, increasingly united under its leading city, Thebes, posed no problem. Persuaded by King Cleomenes to share in his unhappy campaign against Athens in about 506, the Boeotians had been soundly thrashed. Nor any longer did Sparta itself. During the nineties her preoccupation was with the Peloponnese, with Argos, on which Cleomenes inflicted a terrible defeat at Sepeia about 494, nearer home with her own helots, who attempted a revolt (of uncertain date and duration), and nearer still with the quarrel between her kings, which led to

Demaratus' withdrawal to Persia. Moreover, at some point she committed herself in principle to the anti-Persian cause and even sent out her army to Marathon—though it arrived only in time to congratulate the Athenians on their success.

But there was another enemy. The rich, commercial island of Aegina, its triangular peak clearly visible some 20 miles from Athens' harbour at Phaleron, was a hostile rival as soon as Athens turned her attention seriously to the sea. There had been one early war. Now, about 500, began a period of conflict or threats of conflict which lasted through the eighties. How many Athenians felt in 489 that Persian flight had left them free to deal with a more immediate enemy?

There is an interesting clue. In 482 an exceptionally rich vein of silver was discovered in the Attic mines at Laurium. There was debate on the use of the profits. One side, led very probably by Aristides, nicknamed 'the Just', a hero of Marathon (he was elected archon in 489), later to distinguish himself in the crisis of 480/79 and to organize the Delian League in 478, argued for a simple distribution among the citizens. Others, whose spokesman was Themistocles, felt otherwise. Themistocles was renowned for his cleverness (some did not use the word in a friendly sense) and foresight. Foresight he had certainly shown when as archon in 493 he had begun to fortify a new and safer harbour at Piraeus, and would show afterwards when he tried to warn and literally fortify Athens against the threat of Spartan jealousy. In 482 he argued that the windfall should be used, not for largesse but for the building of a fleet, 200 warships ('triremes'), which would, as it turned out, be the backbone of Greek resistance to the Persian navy. But that was not his point at the time. He urged instead that a fleet was needed against Aegina, a point which at least reveals the priorities among his audience. Was this deception, or may even his foresight have been a bit blunted by what Pericles later described as 'the eyesore of the Piraeus'—Themistocles' new Piraeus?

The Persians felt no need of foresight, only determination to get their revenge. The Great King, Darius, was fond of Greeks (witness Histiaeus; above, p. 33) but not of Greeks who defeated him, and immediately after Marathon he began to prepare for a greater onslaught. But the plans were thwarted by a revolt in Egypt (487) and Darius' death soon after. Revenge was left to his son, Xerxes. Egypt was brought to order in 485, and the great scheme could be resumed.

Let us remember the situation. Persia held North Africa as far as Cyrenaica, while beyond that was the friendly Phoenician colony of Carthage, itself pressing on the Greeks of Sicily. Persia held the north coast of the Aegean as far as Macedon. Persia held Asia Minor and the offshore islands of the Aegean. Mainland Greece was a very small nut between the teeth of a mighty nutcracker. It never ceases to amaze that it should have been thought to merit the attention it was given. Darius' pride had been injured (but it had already suffered once in southern Russia without similar reaction); his queen, Atossa, was said to have coveted the services of Greek handmaidens; Xerxes may have been touched with megalomania, but none of these things seems to justify the effort—or the risk.

The nut itself was not wholly sound. Greek attempts, once the imminence of

THE ATHENIAN TREASURY AT DELPHI. The Greek states dedicated treasuries at the major national sanctuaries, to house rich offerings and display their own wealth and piety. This stands just below the temple terrace at Delphi beside the Sacred Way, and was dedicated by the Athenians to commemorate their victory at Marathon (490 BC). It was rebuilt at the beginning of this century. It is a small Doric building, of Athenian marble, with sculptural decoration in the metopes, showing the exploits of Heracles and Theseus.

danger had been realized in 481, to find help at any distance, from Crete, Corcyra, and Syracuse, were refused or turned aside with equivocation. North of the Isthmus of Corinth only Athens and one or two small states, Phocis, Plataea, Thespiae, were prepared to fight; but neither Thessaly nor Boeotia had much enthusiasm for the cause. Inside the Peloponnese Argos was neutral. At the heart of Greek sentiment, Apollo's oracle at Delphi was counselling what at the most generous can only be called prudence.

When what Herodotus calls 'the Greeks who had the best thoughts for Greece' met at Sparta in 481 and then at Corinth in spring 480, they resolved to forget their differences (chiefly those between Aegina and Athens) and gave Sparta the command on land and, with no material but some diplomatic justification, at sea (though the voice of the new Themistoclean navy could never be ignored). The Spartan kings could muster some 40,000 hoplites and substantially more light-armed troops; the Spartan admiral (the kings rarely took to sea) something over 350 ships—fine forces in Greek terms, but puny in the face of the army which Xerxes had collected from all his empire and which was on its way towards the Hellespont and Europe as the Greeks were talking at Corinth, or in the face of the navy, drawn principally from Phoenicia and the subject Greek states of Asia Minor, which was to accompany that army along the coast of Thrace while it looked for a river that it would not drink dry. It is impossible to fix even approximate figures. Herodotus' 1,750,000 for the army is absurd; 200,000 might be nearer the mark. His 1,200 ships owes less to fantasy; let us say about 1,000. No matter—the Greeks should have been overwhelmed.

The only answer was to find a position to defend where Persian numbers would be of less account and which could not readily be turned by the Persian fleet (though many throughout seem to have been less aware of this than they should have been). The first choice was the Gorge of Tempe where the coast road to the south turns into north-western Thessaly, and a force of 10,000 was sent to hold it. But closer inspection either confirmed fear of Thessalian irresolution (one of Thessaly's leading families, the Aleuadae, was said to have been among the foremost in urging Xerxes to invade), or exposed geographical vulnerability (there were other routes from the north; naval landings were possible in the south). The Greeks retired south, and northern Greece was left to the Persian.

Two defensive lines remained, at the narrow coastal pass of Thermopylae where the fleet could block the adjacent north-Euboean strait, or at the Isthmus itself with the fleet a little to the north at Salamis. Against the latter was the abandonment of Attica, against the former a natural Peloponnesian reluctance to fight for anything but their own. There are signs of some indecision, but the choice fell on Thermopylae. Leonidas, who had succeeded to the Spartan throne after his brother Cleomenes' suicide, moved north with a small Peloponnesian force, including 300 Spartan 'Equals', and with a hollow promise of full reinforcement, collected willing contingents from some neighbouring states, with 400

Thebans more as hostages than troops, and occupied the narrow pass. The fleet settled off the coast by Artemisium.

Herodotus does not integrate the operations on land and sea that followed when the Persian arms arrived; nor, therefore, can we. But they were interdependent. The fleet, primarily Athenian, was there only to protect the army and, perhaps, to test its new ships against what its commanders must have known were the faster vessels and better seamanship of the Phoenicians and the other Asiatics. With some confusion, some panic, and much help from (it was believed) 'God', it achieved both aims. The serious naval engagements were indecisive, but even that was encouraging. Meanwhile storm had already wrecked many Persians on their way south and now wrecked as many more when Xerxes sent a squadron of 200 to encircle Euboea and catch the Greeks in the rear, 'God' thus doing his best, Herodotus says, to equalize the opposing forces.

In the pass Leonidas' men held out magnificently for two days against the best that Xerxes could send at them. But on the third the Persians found an ill-guarded mountain track and moved round on Leonidas' rear. Most of the Greeks were sent home, but Leonidas, his famed 300, and the men of Thespiae, who merit equal fame, remained; the Thebans stayed too—but not because they wanted to. All but the Thebans, who surrendered, fought and died. It was almost a victory.

Two lessons had been learnt, that Greek ships and sailors were adequate and that the Greek hoplite was supreme. The problem now was to apply those lessons. The second did not immediately arise. When Xerxes occupied an evacuated Attica, his first concern was, very properly, with the sea. It is a pity for him that he was not in a position to concern himself with one seaman, Themistocles, in command of the Athenian navy which he had created. It was he who saw that the only hope lay in battle not anywhere in the open sea, further south at the Isthmus of Corinth or elsewhere, but in the narrow strait between Salamis, to which the fleet had withdrawn, and the mainland where Persian numbers would not count, indeed would count against them. His problems were to persuade his allies that this was what they had to do, and persuade the Persians that that was what they wanted to do. A mixture of diplomacy and blackmail ('either you stay or we go and found a new city in the west') solved the former; a ruse, a secret message to the Persians, solved the latter. Early one morning the Persians rowed into the confusion of the narrows; by afternoon the survivors were struggling out again. The bravery of the Greeks, foremost the Aeginetans and Athenians but Corinthians and the rest as well, and the skill of Themistocles had broken Xerxes' fleet and his nerve. The fleet was sent home, and Xerxes with the bulk of his army painfully retraced the confident steps of a few months before.

There will have been some celebration on Salamis that night. There was cause for celebration in Sicily as well. Some said on the very day of Salamis, the Syracusans had crushed the Carthaginian advance at Himera. In east and west the pressure was off, or so it must have seemed.

THE SITE OF THE BATTLE OF SALAMIS (479 BC) seen from the Island of Salamis facing east across to the Attic mainland and Mount Aegaleus (on the sky line) where the Persian King Xerxes sat to watch his fleet. The Greek ships formed up just beyond the small island (Psyttaleia) and the Persians approached from the open sea, top right. They outnumbered the Greeks by three to one, but once they were drawn into the narrows, they were readily confounded by the greater manoeuvrability and enterprise of their opponents.

FOUR EARLY GREEK COINS (*facing page*). (a) is of electrum, a metal alloy of gold and silver readily obtainable in western Asia Minor where (in Lydia) coinage traditionally started. The dump of metal is struck into the decorated die by a broken metal bar, leaving the rough incuse square sinkings on the back. The example shown carries a stag and the name Phanes, perhaps a ruler or moneyer, and may have been struck in Ephesus in 600 BC. In the Greek homeland the first coinage is struck in silver, on Aegina, probably by the mid sixth century. The device (b) is a turtle and the markings on the punch at the back show that the pattern of the broken metal bar had been stylized into quarterings. Athens soon followed Aegina's lead and her early coins (e.g. c: second half of the sixth century) have heraldic devices—here a Gorgon head and, in the punch mark on the back, a lion's head and paws. From now on a reverse type such as this is a regular feature of Greek coins. Among the western Greeks a flatter coin was developed in the late Archaic Period, with the reverse bearing a hollowed and simplified version of the obverse type. The example from Caulonia (d), of about 510 BC, shows Apollo carrying a branch and a small running figure, with a stag before him. The top two coins are shown at three times actual size, the bottom two at twice.

(a) × 3

(a) × 3

(b) × 3

(b) × 3

(c) × 3

(c) × 2

(d) × 2

(d) × 2

But Xerxes had left behind his general, Mardonius, with a large force of his best soldiers, far more than the 35,000 or so that the Greeks could muster. In face of this the unity of Salamis began to look a little hollow. Quite simply, the Athenians wanted their homes back in security; the Peloponnesians felt happier behind the Isthmus wall. One wanted offensive war, the other did not. There was a winter of bitter argument before Athenian threats were again effective (Themistocles does not now appear by name; instead Aristides edges forward) and the Spartan Pausanias, regent for Leonidas' son, came out to face Mardonius at Plataea on Boeotia's southern border.

The battle, when it came, was more typical of battles in general than Salamis had been—it was a chaotic affair. Neither side, the Greek especially, knew what it was doing, but the Greek hoplites, primarily the Spartans, pushed their way out of the mess to complete victory. On the same day, it was said, the fleet, which had ventured hesitantly across the Aegean, landed on the Ionian coast at Mycale, routed the Persians who opposed them, destroyed much of what was left of their ships, and so cleared the Aegean and began the liberation of the Asiatic Greeks.

There is no one explanation of the outcome. That the hoplite phalanx was a superior military machine; that the Persians made more mistakes than the Greeks (not many); that the Persians were far from home while the Greeks were at home and fighting for their home; that those who fought willingly as free men, 'fearing the laws more than your [Xerxes'] subjects fear you', as the exile Demaratus had once boldly said to the King—all these things counted, and so did luck, or 'God'.

The results can be more clearly seen. The distinction between Greek and barbarian (foreigner) became one between Greek and Barbarian (national enemy), 'appeasement' became 'treachery'. Sparta had won on land, Athens at sea; were these two supremacies to continue, were they to merge or clash? Athens had won as a budding democracy, Sparta as a monarchic oligarchy; would the difference divide not only them, but other Greeks? So the pattern was set.

Further Reading

A. Andrewes, *Greek Society* (Harmondsworth, 1975) is the best general introduction to Greek history; O. Murray, *Early Greece* (London, 1980) is a good modern account of the period. A more detailed account will be found in the second edition of the *Cambridge Ancient History;* with vol. iii 3 (1982) it has reached *The Expansion of the Greek World, Eighth to Sixth Centuries BC.* C. W. Fornara, *Archaic Times to the End of the Peloponnesian War* (Cambridge, 1983) is a useful collection of sources in translation.

For dark age Greece see A. M. Snodgrass, *The Dark Age of Greece* (Edinburgh, 1971); V. R. D'A. Desborough, *The Greek Dark Ages* (London, 1972); J. N. Coldstream, *Geometric Greece* (London, 1979). For the historical value of Homer, discussion starts from M. I. Finley, *The World of Odysseus* (Cambridge, 1954). The hero's tomb at Lefkandi (Euboea) discovered in 1980 is described by M. R. Popham, E. Touloupa, and L. H. Sackett in *Antiquity* 56 (1982), 169–74.

For archaic Greece see W. G. Forrest, *The Emergence of Greek Democracy* (London, 1966); L. H.

Jeffery, *Archaic Greece* (London, 1976); A. M. Snodgrass, *Archaic Greece* (London, 1980). Two books by A. R. Burn offer an excellent longer account: *The Lyric Age of Greece* (London, 1960); *Persia and the Greeks* (London, 1962; 2nd edn., with an appendix by D. M. Lewis, 1984). Important works on individual topics are J. Boardman, *The Greeks Overseas* (3rd edn., London, 1980); A. Andrewes, *The Greek Tyrants* (London, 1956); C. M. Kraay, *Archaic and Classical Greek Coins* (London, 1976); H. W. Parke, *Greek Oracles* (London, 1967); W. G. Forrest, *A History of Sparta* (2nd edn. London, 1980); P. A. Cartledge, *Sparta and Laconia* (London, 1979); J. B. Salmon, *Wealthy Corinth* (Oxford, 1984); R. A. Tomlinson, *Argos and the Argolid* (London, 1972); T. J. Dunbabin, *The Western Greeks* (Oxford, 1948).

2

Homer

❧❧❧

OLIVER TAPLIN

Preamble

THE early Greeks envisaged the world as encircled by the mighty freshwater river of Ocean, and held that all springs and streams derived from him. Ocean became their image for Homer: all poetry and eloquence derived from him as he surrounded and encompassed their thought-world. (Among the literary papyri found in Egypt those of The Poet, as he was known, outnumber all the other authors put together.) Alexander Pope, Homer's greatest translator into English, found a different image: 'our author's work . . . is like a copious nursery, which contains the seeds and first productions of every kind, out of which those who followed him have but selected some particular plants . . .' Like all really great literature, it is fecund and inexhaustible, generous to all comers, and it may be cultivated in apparently limitless ways.

There is, in my view, no point in searching for 'Homer' by the marshlight of a pocket biography of the author. Even if this were a good way of approaching literature in general, we simply do not have the material. The many ancient accounts of his life ('. . . mother's name . . . Chios . . . blind . . . died, etc.') are largely, if not entirely, demonstrable fictions: he was given suitable lives, not a true one. The firm conclusions of modern research are meagre, and even then are disputed. Date—somewhere in the area of 750–650 BC; place—the northern-Aegean coast of Asia Minor in the Smyrna area; poetic art learned from other bards in a tradition of performed poetry. It will not do to try to fit these mighty poems to the little we know of the poet. Even if 'Homer' is taken less as a person than as a historical context for the poems, there is little to be gained: we have no firm external evidence of Homer's audience or circumstances of performance. It is inside out to speculate and build up an *external* mould or framework called 'Homer' and then to try to fit the poems to it. The poems themselves are our firm evidence and they contain everything worth knowing about 'Homer'. The poet and his audience must be reconstructed to fit around them. This *internal* approach from within the poems follows the motto of some ancient scholars,

Homēron ex Homērou saphēnizein, 'you should elucidate Homer by the light of Homer.'

'Homer' is, then, for our purposes, the *Iliad* and the *Odyssey*. And what are they? They are narrative poems; they 'tell a story'. But the interest lies not in the story, but in the telling, the way it is turned into literature. Rather than summarize the plot of the *Iliad*, I shall attempt some account of its thematic shape, of some of the fundamental concerns beneath the narrative, such as life and death, victory and defeat, glory and ignominy, war and peace. It is for these that the *Iliad* has won its fundamental place in European literature.

A further reason for not attempting to give yet another brief summary of the plots is that both poems are extremely long—several hundreds of pages of long lines, which would each take about twenty-four hours to read at conversation speed. Each of them is arranged in twenty-four books. While convenient and sensitively done, the division does not go back to the poet. (There is one book for each letter of the later Greek alphabet, and it is unlikely that Homer knew any alphabet, let alone one with twenty-four letters.) It goes against the very nature of the poems to be summarized. Yet this lengthiness is not the result of telling a long and eventful saga from beginning to end: on the contrary, both poems are highly selective. In fact there is reason to think that other epic poets composed poems which were shorter and yet which told of many more events in a much more summary way. While this would be in keeping with the performance of the bards whom we see in the *Odyssey*, the more direct evidence concerns other early epic poems which were around in antiquity, though they are now all but lost. These were known as the 'Cycle' and told other legends such as those of Thebes as well as stories connected with Troy, from the Apple of Discord right through to the death of Odysseus at the hands of Telegonus, his son by Circe. The 'Cycle' known to antiquity was clearly a response to the stature of the *Iliad* and *Odyssey*, since its poems were constructed around them.

One of the most famous poems of the cycle was the *Cypria*. It was apparently longer than most, yet rather less than half as long as *Iliad* or *Odyssey*. So the scant summary we have of its contents is revealing: 'Rivalry at the marriage of Peleus and Thetis . . . . the judgement of Paris on Mount Ida . . . Paris visits Sparta . . . elopes with Helen . . . sacks Sidon . . . Meanwhile Castor and Pollux . . . next Menelaus consults Nestor . . . the expedition is summoned . . . Odysseus feigns madness . . . At Aulis . . . Achilles on Scyros . . . Telephus at Argos . . . back at Aulis the sacrifice of Iphigenia . . . Philoctetes . . . Protesilaus . . .'—and there is still quite a lot to come.

The contrast between this skimming saga and the *Iliad* and *Odyssey* is the subject of some observations made by Aristotle which are extremely enlightening.

[Epic should be] about one whole or complete action with a beginning, middle parts, and end, so that it produces its proper pleasure like a single whole living creature. Its plots should not be like histories; for in histories it is necessary to give a report of a single period, not of a unified action, that is, one must say whatever was the case in that period about one man or more; and each of these things may have a quite casual interrelation.... Most epic poets do make plots like histories. So in this respect too Homer is marvellous in that he did not undertake to make a whole poem of the war, even though it had a beginning and an end. For the plot would have been too large and not easy to see as a whole, or if it had been kept to a moderate length it would have been tangled because of the variety of events. As it is he takes one part and uses many others as episodes, for example, the catalogue of the ships and the other episodes with which he breaks the uniformity of his poem. But the rest make a poem about one man or one period of time, like the poet of the *Cypria* or the *Little Iliad*. That is why the *Iliad* and *Odyssey* have matter only for one tragedy or only for two, whereas there is matter for many in the *Cypria*, and in the *Little Iliad* for more than eight . . . (*Poetics* 1459, trans. M. E. Hubbard)

The Iliad

This prompts me to approach the *Iliad* by considering its shaping of time and place. It is not my purpose to make great claims for these frameworks as such, but rather to use them to bring out something of the thematic moulding of the *Iliad*, its underlying geology. I shall try to give some idea how this has a large-scale artistry and coherence, whatever the problems, most of them trivial, of the narrative surface.

The *Iliad* picks a few days only out of the whole story: not the most obvious days (which might be the arrival of the Achaeans, or the wooden horse and sack of Troy), but almost the only days during the ten years when the Trojans had the better of the fighting. It does not matter exactly how many days pass during the poem; what matters is that about twenty-one days pass in the opening scenes and another twenty-one in the closing scenes, thus separating the core from the years that stretch on either side. A very short time passes in between. In fact almost everything from Book 2 all the way to Book 23 takes place during only four days and two nights. Within this very economical time-scheme there is a tight grip on the dramatic calendar.

Take, for example, the great central day which dawns with the first line of Book 11 and sets at 18. 239-40 (almost exactly one-third of the length of the entire *Iliad*). It is tensely awaited during the previous night in the last part of Book 8 and throughout Book 9. When the day comes it is Hector's: despite setbacks he storms the ditch and wall, reaches the ships, kills and strips Patroclus. Zeus explicitly lets him know: 'I guarantee power to Hector to kill until he comes to the benched vessels, until the sun goes down and blessed darkness comes over' (lines 192-4 = 207-9). Hector refers to this message when he rejects the cautious advice of the seer Polydamas (12. 235-6), and when he calls for fire by the ships—'now Zeus has given us a day worth all the rest of them' (15. 719). Zeus himself repeats the terms of his undertaking as he pities Achilles' immortal horses: he will let Hector kill 'until the sun goes and blessed darkness comes over' (17. 453-5). Surely we are to have this in mind when the sun does eventually go

THE MISSION TO ACHILLES, to persuade him to return to the battlefield, was described in *Iliad* 9. The scene becomes popular on Athenian vases in the early fifth century, when the story was also treated on the stage by Aeschylus. On the vases the heroes involved and Achilles' mood do not closely mirror Homer's treatment. On this vase Odysseus is seated arguing with the disconsolate Achilles. At the left is an old man, Phoenix (Achilles' mentor) and at the right Patroclus. The artist (the Cleophrades Painter) is particularly fond of Trojan scenes: the date is about 485–475 BC.

ACHILLES FIGHTS MEMNON, on a vase by the Berlin Painter of about 490 BC. At the left Achilles is encouraged by his mother Thetis, and at the right a distressed Eos (Dawn), mother of Memnon, gesticulates towards her doomed son. The duel did not appear in the *Iliad*, but is popular with artists. It was preceded by a weighing of the souls of the heroes before Zeus (*psychostasia*) such as was performed for Achilles and Hector in *Iliad* 22, and it was attended by their mothers, which is why they are often also shown attending the fight. Memnon was an Ethiopian prince, the most handsome man at Troy.

down in Book 18. Immediately after that Polydamas advises the Trojans to retreat inside the walls; and it is the subtle control of the time-scheme which give the point to Hector's deluded reply;

> But now, when the son of devious-devising Kronos has given
> me the winning of glory by the ships, to pin the Achaians
> on the sea, why, fool, no longer show these thoughts to our people.
>
> (18. 293–5)

'Now' is wrong: Hector's day is over, and the next will be his last.

But while the action itself is so tightly bound in a few days, the *Iliad* makes us feel the pressure of the time that has gone before and will come after. Much of the long span between the quarrels on earth and Olympus in Book 1 and the first full-scale battle well on in Book 4 is taken up in giving us some sense of the previous nine years. Agamemnon himself admits

> And now nine years of mighty Zeus have gone by, and the timbers
> of our ships have rotted away and the cables are broken,
> and far away our wives and our young children
> are sitting within our halls and wait for us, while still our work here
> stays forever unfinished . . .   (2. 134–8)

The frustration weighs heavy, and Odysseus has to remind the Greeks of Chalcas' interpretation of the omen at Aulis, that they would take Troy only in the tenth year (2. 299ff.). Then we have the marshalling of the Achaeans, the catalogues of Greeks and Trojans, and the advance of the two armies. In Book 3 we have Helen of Troy, the view from the walls which further introduces the Greek leaders, the attempt at negotiations, the single combat of Paris and Menelaus, and the repetition of the fatal coupling of Paris and Helen. In Book 4 the treachery of Pandarus re-enacts the guilt of Troy; and then at last battle is joined. The past of the war has passed fleetingly before our eyes.

The future is almost all concentrated into two momentous events of destruction: the death of Achilles and the sack of Troy. Though they will happen months after the end of the poem, both are made the inevitable consequence of events within it. The death of Patroclus means the return of Achilles to battle; that means the death of Achilles himself and the death of Hector; and that means the sack of Troy. We are made to anticipate and envisage these future events so that imaginatively they are part of the *Iliad*. Of the many previsions two of the most vivid come close to the very death of Hector. With his last words he warns Achilles of the threat of his doom, but Achilles knows it well already and replies: 'Die: and I will take my own death at whatever time Zeus and the rest of the immortal gods choose to accomplish it' (22. 365–6). And as Hector's corpse is dragged in the dust the lamentation goes through Troy—'It was most like what would have happened, if all lowering Ilion had been burning top to bottom in fire' (22. 410–11).

The poem is rounded off by the meeting of Priam and Achilles which leads to the burial of Hector 'and on the twelfth day we shall fight again, if so we must do' (24.667). The poem is opened by the visit to the Greek camp of another old man who comes to ransom his child; and the speculation that Chryses was invented to counterbalance Priam is hard to resist. The few days in between are in no way a snippet from the Trojan saga, but stand for the whole war from the crime of Paris to the ashes of Troy.

There is a comparable economy of place. In fact nearly all the *Iliad* is set in one of four places, distinct in topography and significance: the city of Troy, the Greek camp, the plain in between, and Olympus. The city is ringed by its great walls and gates. Within it has broad streets and fine houses built of ashlar blocks, dominated by the mighty palace of Priam (described at 6.242ff.). These houses contain fine furniture, clothing, treasures; but above all they contain the Trojans' old people, wives, and children. It is no doubt significant that the first Trojan home we are taken inside is the childless one of Helen and Paris; but when Hector comes back to Troy in Book 6:

> all the wives of the Trojans and their daughters came running about him
> to ask after their sons, after their brothers and neighbours,
> their husbands . . .   (283 ff.)

In peacetime, before the Achaeans came, Troy had been a prosperous city ornamented with all the features of a civilized society. The standard epithets of Troy ('with broad streets', 'horse-pasturing', etc.) act as a constant reminder, almost subliminal in effect, of the constriction of the siege.

For all its fine stonework Troy is vulnerable and may be burned. This is even more true of the Achaean camp, which consists of wooden ships and shelters. So far the Greeks have felt so secure that they have not even built defences. At 7.436ff. they build a wall and ditch in one day, and this is fought over and breached in Books 11-15. Unlike Troy, this temporary camp has no past; it had been mere beach, and it will in time disappear again (7.446ff.; 12.1ff.). Over the years the shelters have grown quite substantial, and Homer seems to have a clear 'map' of the different bivouacs along the beach, with Achilles at one end and Ajax at the other. They contain possessions and women taken from neighbouring cities, but they are not homes. The Greeks have left their wives and children and parents at home. Phrases about 'the ships' are everywhere throughout the *Iliad*. They are the 'subliminal' reminder that the Greeks are away from home in a setting which is not household or city.

For both sides there are turning-points in past and future connected in time and place. For the Trojans the crucial day was the day the ships arrived on the beach; in the future it will be either the day they depart or the day that the city is burned. For the Greeks the crucial past event was the day each left his home—an event often recalled; in the future it will be death or return to parents, wife, and children. This may help us see why Homer devotes so much trouble to the

THE DRAGGING OF HECTOR'S BODY BY ACHILLES. On this late-sixth-century Athenian vase the artist expresses several different aspects of the story. The hero leaps on to his chariot to which Hector's corpse is already attached. At the left Hector's parents (Priam and Hecuba) mourn in a setting which represents the Trojan palace. At the right the white mound is the tomb of Patroclus whose shade (the little winged warrior above it) is to be appeased by this act. The winged woman in the foreground is not easily identified, but may be Iris, who was sent by Zeus (in *Iliad* 24) to tell Priam to ransom his son's body (see next illustration).

delightful journey to the city of Chryse in Book 1 (430–80): it helps to establish the framework of time and place for both sides still at Troy.

The plain which lies between the two sides is much less specific in topography and in human associations. For much of the war it has been an empty no-man's-land, or it has been occupied by the armies in the morning and emptied again in the evening. After their victory in Book 8 it is the first time in nine years that the Trojans have even contemplated camping out in the plain; the next night in Book 18 is the second and last time. In peacetime the plain may have been the deep tilth and horse pasture of Troy's traditional epithets, but in the *Iliad* it is dusty and almost barren. It is simply the place where warriors win glory and get killed.

During the *Iliad* the gods travel far and wide, but they always converge on Mount Olympus. There they have their homes each built by Hephaestus, though they usually meet to feast and converse in the great palace of Zeus. It is an immortal world of feasting and splendour. The gods are deeply involved in the Trojan war and are not untouched by the sufferings of city, camp and plain below; but the contrast is still extreme. For the gods there are no crucial turning-points in past or future; their life is diluted by immortality.

Homer is abundant, and there are many aspects which I have scarcely touched on yet. The most pressing is perhaps the *Iliad*'s creation of memorable and persuasive human portraits. Quite apart from the scores of minor figures, there is a spread of some two dozen finely individualized major characters. I shall select only the two most important, Achilles and Hector. It would be too simple to claim Achilles as *the* hero (as was seen by whoever it was who early on titled the poem *Iliad—The Poem of Troy*). Achilles occupies the second half of the first line, but Hector occupies the same place in the last. The balance and contrast between these two connect revealingly with the underlying themes already sketched.

Thus Achilles is a young adventurer away from home, out to win loot and glory. His closest bond (apart from his parents) is with Patroclus, his fellow warrior who looks after his horses. Achilles sleeps with captured women—though there is a poignancy in the hints that had he returned home he would have properly married Briseis. Achilles' loyalties and responsibilities are only to those friendships and relationships which he chooses to stand by, and to himself.

Hector, on the other hand, is the greatest of Priam's sons—'but one was left me who guarded my city and people' (24. 499). He fights before the eyes of his parents, brothers, and whole family. His fellow citizens depend on him: if he falls, they all fall. As he makes clear in Book 6 (440ff.) and again in 22 (99ff.), it is his sense of responsibility for them that keeps him in the front line and in the end sends him to his death:

> Now, since by my own recklessness I have ruined my people,
> I feel shame before the Trojans and the Trojan Women . . .
>
> (22. 104–5)

His closest relationship is not with another man, but with his wife Andromache (she even looks after his horses—see 8. 185-90). Their meeting in Book 6, one of the great scenes, must also serve as their farewell, since they do not meet again in the poem. Their small son is the bond between them and their reason to look to the future; and yet he epitomizes the 'heroic paradox'. Hector prays for him:

> Zeus, and you other immortals, grant that this boy, who is my son,
> may be as I am, pre-eminent among the Trojans . .
>   . . . and let him kill his enemy
> and bring home the bloodied spoils, and delight the heart of his mother.
>
> (6. 476-81)

The urge to gain heroic glory kills both Hector and his son, for it demands a loser as well as a winner. The *Iliad* never shirks this two-sidedness.

Near the end of the poem Hera compares the two men:

> Hector was mortal, and suckled at the breast of a woman,
> while Achilles is the child of a goddess . . . you all
> went, you gods, to the wedding . . .   (24. 55 ff.)

Hector is a great man; Achilles is mortal as other men, but there are ways in which he is close to the divine. He has possessions which were presents from the gods—his spear, his horses, the great shield and armour which Hephaestus makes for him in Book 18. His mother Thetis, caught between the two worlds, can tell him more than other men know, and can give him special help. She can even gain him special favours from Zeus, as is shown in the first book. Even so Achilles is a man and cannot see everything that this means. Only too late can he see:

> My mother, all these things the Olympian has brought to accomplishment.
> But what pleasure is this to me, since my dear companion has perished . . .
>
> (18. 78 ff.)

There is one thing, however, which Thetis can tell Achilles for certain, while for all other men it remains the great unknown. He has a choice of long life or young death, which is also a choice between uneventful obscurity and eternal glory (9. 410-16).

So when Achilles decides, without hesitation ('then let me die soon', 18. 98), that he must return to the fight for vengeance on Hector, he does so without any doubt that his own death will follow soon after. Hector, on the other hand, must, like everyone else, hope against hope for a long and prosperous life. Even when the dying Patroclus prophesies his death (16. 843 ff.), Hector retorts:

> Patroclus, what is this prophecy of my headlong destruction?
> Who knows if even Achilles, son of lovely-haired Thetis,
> might before this be struck by my spear, and his own life perish?

Even when he faces Achilles he maintains that the battle is not a foregone conclusion; and it is only at the last minute that he realizes that this is indeed the

THE RANSOM OF HECTOR. From the left Priam approaches with attendants bearing rich gifts. Achilles, at ease on his dining couch beneath which lies Hector's corpse, turns away to tell a cup-boy to bring more wine (the boy carries sieve and dipper). The mood is one of supplication to an arrogant hero rather than the more sympathetic one of Homer (*Iliad* 24), but was long preferred in Greek art. This Athenian cup is by the Brygos Painter, of about 490–480 BC.

end (22. 296ff.). But it is then, when he knows he has lost and when he has no aid from god or man, that Hector shows his finest heroism:

> Let me at least not die without a struggle, inglorious,
> but do some big thing first, that men to come shall know of it.
>
> (22. 304–5)

Hector loses, and yet he still wins immortal fame. He wins it because of the quality of his life and of his death. The *Iliad* is not so much concerned with what people do, as with the way they do it, above all the way they face suffering and death.

Achilles is the greatest warrior, the greatest looter and killer of all. But what makes him great is not that, but the uniquely penetrating way in which he thinks matters through. He sees and expresses the human condition without evasion or periphrasis. We feel this quality when he refuses compromise in Books 1 and 9, and when he shows no mercy to Lycaon in 21 (34 ff.) nor to Hector in 22.

> For as I detest the doorways of death, I detest that man, who
> holds one thing in the depths of his heart, and speaks forth another.
>
> (9. 312–13)

But it is this same quality that leads to his treatment of Priam in Book 24, when, as Alfred Heubeck has put it, 'the image of the great man replaces that of the great hero.' Achilles sees, and brings the old father Priam to see, that it is the human lot to be bereaved, to endure—and as tokens of this to eat, drink, make love, and sleep. These things transcend the barriers which break men up into individuals and nations.

So Homer wins immortal glory in rather the same way as his finest characters, by going beyond the mere narrative achievements of killing and derring-do. He sets mighty deeds in a context of defeat as well as victory, woman as well as man, peace as well as war, doubt as well as confidence, feeling as well as action.

The Odyssey

Whether the *Iliad* and the *Odyssey* are by one and the same poet is one of the great unanswered questions of literary history. We should concentrate, without attempting here any answer, on the ways in which the two poems complement each other, helping to define each other's qualities. The obvious analogy—and one which is indeed directly related—is the complementary natures of tragedy and comedy. In the *Iliad* noble heroes move inexorably, by way of a combination of choice and of forces beyond their control, towards destruction and dissolution. We are left with mourning, honour, endurance, and pity. In the *Odyssey* a somewhat dubiously heroic hero wins his way through various fantastical hazards by means of trickery and ingenuity. The *Odyssey* is not exclusive; it has room for travel, for rustics and servants, for low life, and for dastardly villains. Its overall movement is away from war and from barbarity towards prosperity and peace, centred on the wife and a happy domestic scene. We are left with celebration and poetic justice, with loyalty and perseverance and intelligence rewarded. The beggar has turned out to be Odysseus in disguise, home at last. The tragedy–comedy dichotomy should not, however, be pushed too far. The *Iliad* has its humour especially, but by no means exclusively, at the funeral games in Book 23. The *Odyssey* contributes much to the future of tragedy: one only has to think of the recognition scenes, of the scenes of foreboding, and the tense planning of revenge.

The frameworks of time and place may again prove a way of bringing out some of the 'thematic geology'. The handling of the time-scheme is rather similar to that of the *Iliad*. Odysseus was ten years returning from Troy, but the poem picks up only the last forty days or so, and one-third of the poem (Books 16–23) takes only two days. Care is taken in the opening 100 lines of the poem to associate the taking up of the stories of both Odysseus and his son Telemachus, though they are worlds apart on anarchic Ithaca and the unreal island of Calypso. The number of days between then and their reunion in time and place at the shepherd's farmstead in Book 16 is carefully limited, though not precisely plotted. Odysseus' time on Phaeacia, however, is made to fit into three days (the middle one including the tales of his wanderings stretches from 8. 1 to 13. 17).

There is a certain symmetry to the two climactic days on Ithaca. At 16. 1 dawns the day which sees Odysseus enter his palace and endure maltreatment at the hands of the suitors and their minions. At the end of 18 the suitors go to their own homes for the night; but we are made to wait before Odysseus sleeps. First there is his long interview with Penelope, which is itself held in suspense when the aged nurse Eurycleia finds her master's old scar. Eventually Odysseus beds down in the opening lines of Book 20, only to hear his maidservants giggling on their way to join the suitors:

> He struck himself on the chest and spoke to his heart and scolded it:
> 'Bear up, my heart. You have had worse to endure before this,
> on that day when the irresistible Cyclops ate up
> my strong companions, but you endured it until intelligence
> got you out of the cave . . .'

The next day, however, gets off to a good start. Zeus thunders, and Odysseus overhears an old woman who is grinding corn:

> Father Zeus. . . . you show this forth, a portent for someone.
> grant now also for wretched me this prayer that I make you.
> On this day let the suitors take, for the last and latest
> time, their desirable feasting in the halls of Odysseus.
>
> (20. 91–121)

This is the day set for the contest of the bow and axes. It does not come to an end until Odysseus and Penelope have gone to bed, have made love, and have talked. (The strange episodes of Book 24 take one further day.)

Within these few days, however, the *Odyssey* knows scarcely any limits in place. This is very different from the *Iliad*. The *Iliad* looked outward from a narrow focus at Troy: in the *Odyssey* the journeys are converging, and converging from various places. It is a poem of the sea as well as of land, it reaches to the verges of the known world, and beyond into the realms of fable, and even ventures to the underworld of the dead (briefly in Book 24, as well as in Book 11). The opening lines of the entire poem prepare us for this broad geography:

> Tell me, Muse, of the man of many ways, who was driven
> far journeys, after he had sacked Troy's sacred citadel.
> Many were they whose cities he saw, whose minds he learned of,
> many the pains he suffered in his spirit on the wide sea,
> struggling for his own life and the homecoming of his companions.

It was a master stroke to devote the opening books of the poem not to Odysseus but to Telemachus. This gives us at the start a picture of the masterless palace on Ithaca and the unruly suitors who disrupt it. We then follow Telemachus on the relatively limited journeys he makes to Pylos and Sparta, to enquire after news of his father, journeys which are vital to his developing realization of what it means to be the son of Odysseus. He is also given the chance to see what stable and civilized households are like and to appreciate the worth of proper hospitality.

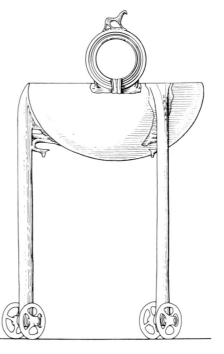

WHEELED BRONZE TRIPOD, found in a sea-shore cave at Polis on the island of Ithaca. Late eighth century BC. The cave appears to have housed a cult of Odysseus, which must have been inspired by the story of the hero's return home as told in the *Odyssey*, where he brings thirteen tripods (at least twelve were found) from Phaeacia and hides them in a cave near his landing place.

We first find Odysseus in Book 5 'suffering' the hospitality of the mysterious island-nymph Calypso. She has kept him as her lover for all the years since he lost his ships and men. Her island is paradisiacal (see the description at 5. 55–74) but it does not satisfy Odysseus: he is a man and longs for a proper home among men, and he longs for his mortal wife. After a vast and terrifying journey alone across the sea, Odysseus makes his vital landfall on Phaeacia. He kisses the soil and beds down under cover of a thicket of wild and cultivated olive (5. 463, 476ff.) Phaeacia is a land which is in several ways half-way between the real world and 'fairyland'. Demodocus, the bard at the court of King Alcinous, sings of one end of that world, the great deeds at Troy. Troy is Odysseus' departure point when he himself tells of his travels, and he is almost home (9.79) when he is driven away into the world of the 'traveller's tales'—the wanderings which may have made the word 'Odyssey' part of our everyday vocabulary. The lotus-eaters, the Cyclops, Circe, the Sirens, Scylla and Charybdis, and finally the cattle of the Sun—these are the archetypal adventures of the European consciousness, material for the imaginations of poets, painters, and children ever since.

By the time Odysseus leaves Phaeacia the *Odyssey* is just over half-way through, and Odysseus is about half-way from the fringe world of Polyphemus and Circe towards a homecoming. While he makes this last marine transition he sleeps (13.78–80):

> They bent to their rowing, and with their oars tossed up the sea spray,
> and upon the eyes of Odysseus there fell a sleep, gentle,
> the sweetest kind of sleep with no awakening, most like death . . .

On land Odysseus sleeps by an olive tree with his treasures, and when he realizes that this is Ithaca he kisses its soil (13.102ff., 120ff., 354). So the threads of the vast journey of Odysseus and the lesser apprentice voyage of Telemachus (with a last view of Sparta and Pylos at 15.1–300) are drawn together at the remote, yet very real, farmstead of the loyal swineherd Eumaeus, a straightforward dwelling free from strangeness, danger, and deceit.

The time comes for Odysseus to make his way from this outpost to his own palace in the town. It is a significant journey which culminates with the recognition by the old dog Argus (17.182–327).

> The doom of dark death now closed over the dog, Argus,
> when, after nineteen years had gone by, he had seen Odysseus.

The palace is the setting of the next six-and-a-half books, and attention is lavished on this setting, its rooms, corridors, stairways, and courtyards. But two rooms are given special significance: the great hall, which is the battlefield where the suitors feast and where they spill their blood in recompense; and the marital bedroom which Odysseus himself made immovable around the stock of a mighty olive. 'They then gladly went together to bed, and their old ritual' (23.296). The poem ends at the farm of Laertes, Odysseus' father, in the Ithacan countryside near by.

The first word of the *Odyssey* is *andra*, 'the man', and that man is far more directly the core of the poem than 'the wrath of Achilles' is of the *Iliad*. The first four books, the 'Telemachy', is the only substantial part in which Odysseus is not involved; and even that is very clear preparation for him. Telemachus finds out the nature of a properly civilized society, the sort worthy of that great friend and fellow fighter of Nestor and Menelaus, Odysseus.

Odysseus left Troy a great hero. We hear from Demodocus of his finest hour at the sack. But as his travels go on he loses his treasure and his companions. To escape the Cyclops he even toys with losing his name. As part of his plot to escape he gives his name as 'Noman'. Once at sea Odysseus cannot resist revealing his real name. Though this gives the Cyclops a name to curse, it also salvages Odysseus' heroic identity. But after many years of slothful obscurity with

Calypso (whose name is close to the Greek word for to 'conceal') what is there left of the celebrated Odysseus? On his journey to Phaeacia he loses even his clothes. He has no possessions at all, and to approach Nausicaa he has to hold a branch in front of his nakedness. Only his wits are left to him, and these he puts to good use.

It is not until he has proved himself in Phaeacia that he is ready to proclaim himself. Despite the urgent curiosity of his hosts, the moment is held back until Book 9 (19-28):

> I am Odysseus son of Laertes, known before all men
> for the study of crafty designs, and my fame goes up to the heavens.
> I am at home in sunny Ithaca . . .
> a rugged place, but a good nurse of men; for my part
> I cannot think of any place sweeter to look at.

To win on Ithaca he has to disguise himself and reveal his identity to as few as possible. But when the vital moment comes, there is no need for Odysseus to declare his name, and he identifies himself with great dramatic understatement:

> You dogs, you never thought I would any more come back
> from the land of Troy, and because of that you despoiled my household . . .
>
> (22. 35 ff.)

The *Odyssey* is not, then, only a journey of physical endurance for Odysseus; the survival of his heroic stature and his reputation are put to the test. He has to come back from the very verges of civilization and of humanity; and to do so he has to show patience as well as cunning. He must never give himself away until he is sure of the other party; and so again and again there are scenes of testing— Odysseus even tests his old father after the danger is past. He always keeps his guard up. The only time it fails is when his wife out-tests him with the secret of the construction of their bed: Penelope shows herself worthy of Odysseus (Book 23).

But it is not only loyalty which is tested in the *Odyssey*. It is an overtly moral poem in which villainy meets its just deserts. The villains are those who do not care for a secure and prosperous world; and it is especially by the testing of hospitality and inhospitality that the various societies visited by Odysseus are distinguished. It is, of course, the suitors above all who abuse all the rules of civilized behaviour. They ransack another man's property, try to murder his son, importune his wife, sleep with his servants, and use his house for their riotous living. Their insolence towards all comers is illustrated in such profusion that we hardly need the explicit moralizing of 22. 373-4:

> '. . . so you may know in your heart, and say to another,
> that good dealing is better by far than evil dealing.'

This clear pattern of crime and punishment is quite different from the tragic inscrutability of the *Iliad*. This is reflected on a divine plane also. The suitors offend the divine laws no less than the human—

'. . . fearing neither the immortal gods who hold wide heaven
nor any resentment sprung from men to be yours in future.'

(22. 39–40)

Odysseus is not only a man reclaiming his own, he is an agent of divine punishment. The way that he comes in disguise to test people, and then rewards or punishes their reception of him, draws on the perennial 'story-pattern' of the god or angel or fairy who visits earth in humble disguise. It is not only Odysseus' homecoming which is at stake, but our whole sense of whether the gods care about right and wrong in this world. As long as the suitors flourish, this remains in doubt. The delight we take in the outcome is voiced by the ancient Laertes when he exclaims

'Father Zeus, there are gods indeed upon tall Olympus,
if truly the suitors have had to pay for their reckless violence.'

(24. 351–2)

The pleasure we take in the *Iliad* is the pleasure proper to tragedy, the salvage of humanity amid destruction: the *Odyssey* indulges our optimism, our hopes that all will turn out to be well, that the strange beggar will set all to rights.

The Tradition

I have presented the *Iliad* and *Odyssey* as coherent works of art, held together on many levels by organic links both sweeping and intricate, 'like a single whole living creature', as Aristotle put it. But this view has been by no means an orthodoxy. I have up till now scarcely touched on the questions which dominated Homeric studies from 1795 for the next 140 years or more: the dispute between so-called 'analysts' and 'unitarians'. In 1795 F.A. Wolf published, with considerable misgivings, the first serious case for holding that the *Iliad* and *Odyssey* as we have them are compilations put together from the works of many poets.

Once the notion was established, scholars devoted themselves to analysing the poems into their constituent contributors, and to isolating the 'real' Homer among them. However much aesthetic intuition might feel the poems to be unities, the experts insisted that reason and science showed them on analysis to be many poems more or less incompetently combined. My own view is that, subject to some relatively minor reservations, the poems are in a better form as they are than they can have been at any earlier stage of development. Whoever put them in their present form was, that is to say, so much the best of the poets who contributed to them that he is The Poet.

In any case the great bulk of the arguments which the analysts brought to bear have been invalidated by the recognition in the last fifty years of the relation of Homer to his tradition, to the poets before him. We have come to see that there are ways in which many poets may have contributed to the *Iliad* and *Odyssey* other than by the editorial combination of separate and separable parts. Much analytic work was based on the unravelling of elements, often inconsistent with each other, which were claimed to come from different periods of history; these included linguistic as well as material and cultural elements. Most analysts also took verbal repetitions as evidence for their theories: only one occurrence was the 'original', and all others were later and derivative additions. All of this collapses once it is seen that the poetic tradition which Homer inherited would by its very nature have incorporated elements from different periods and even different cultures, regardless of technical consistency; and that it would have positively depended on verbal repetition. While this discovery did not come out of nowhere, the credit for its synthesis goes to the Californian Milman Parry (who died at the age of thirty-three in 1936).

Every work of art comes out of a unique interaction between tradition and the individual talent. But Homer's debt to his tradition is different, in both quality and quantity, from any kind familiar in the rest of European literary history. The key to this difference is that Homer learned to compose poetry *aurally*, by listening to more experienced bards. Whether he could himself write or whether he composed *orally* remains controversial. But the case—as near to 'proof' as can be expected—has been made that he is the beneficiary of a tradition passed orally from generation to generation.

ODYSSEUS AND CIRCE. Greek artists, like the playwrights of comedy, could take a relaxed view of mythical occasions. This cup is of a class well represented in the fourth century at the Sanctuary of the Cabiri near Thebes. It shows a puzzled, but determined, Odysseus with drawn sword, threatening Circe, who has left her loom to mix him the potion by which she hopes to turn him into an animal, as she had already his companions. The *Odyssey* enjoyed the attention of classical artists less than the *Iliad*, but there are some favoured scenes.

THE CYCLOPS' CAVE. A unique scene, on an Athenian vase of about 480 BC showing the giant Cyclops (Polyphemus) blinded by Odysseus, blocking the exit from his cave while his flock pass by him with Odysseus and his companions clinging on beneath their bellies—the story of *Odyssey* 9. About 480 BC by an artist who also left us a good study of Odysseus with the Sirens.

Parry worked from the ubiquitous verbal repetitions. The fixed epithets are the most obvious, with both proper names and ordinary nouns—'much-enduring Odysseus', 'wine-dark sea'—but there are also whole lines and even blocks of lines which come again and again. Virgil's 'pius Aeneas', like Tennyson's 'And answer made the bold Sir Bedivere', imitates this pervasive characteristic. Parry made the crucial connection between this 'formulaic' diction and the possibility, long speculated on, that Homer was an oral bard rather than a literate writer. He started from proper names and their epithets, and demonstrated how these constitute a remarkable system within the technically demanding epic metre, the dactylic hexameter. (Which like all Greek metres is based on certain combinations of long (—) and short (∪) syllables.) By means of this system Homer had at his disposal a noun–epithet combination to fit all forms of the names of all his main characters (as e.g. nominative *Hēctōr*, accusative *Hēctŏră*). What is more, he had a different noun–epithet combination to go in each of the main sections into which the line might be divided. For example, the last six or seven syllables of the line, $\underline{\cup\cup} - \cup\cup - \underline{\cup}$, often form a section after a verb (such as the very common *prŏsĕphē*, 'he/she said') which needs to be filled with a noun–epithet combination. On the other hand, while Homer has a formula ready for all these standard eventualities, he has by and large one, and only one, for each eventuality. Thus after *prŏsĕphē* Hector is *always kŏrŷthāiŏlŏs Hēctōr*, 'of the shining helmet'. The remarkable thoroughness of this system of 'extension' and 'economy', as Parry called them, must have been the product of an inherited tradition. The concomitant processes of enlargement and refinement must have taken generations, and must have been the product of composition by oral improvisation. The development of the diction, passed from master to apprentice over generations, was practical as well as aesthetic.

Once we have in mind this process of an oral tradition constantly acquiring attractive and useful new material and casting off outmoded or unpleasing or superfluous material, it may be extended beyond names and nouns to verbs and phrases and whole lines. For example, in the part of the line before the verb *prŏsĕphē* there is a whole range of formulae, mostly using participles, which give a tone or attitude to 'he said'—'in reply', 'standing near', 'greatly troubled', 'looking darkly', etc. It is rather like a system of chemical elements which can combine in all sorts of different ways to make up different molecules. There has been a tendency, however—partly due perhaps to the molecular or 'building-block' analogy—to reckon the range of combinations and possibilities of expression to be far more limited than they are. Parry and his successors may also have based too much on the analogy of still surviving traditions of oral verse-making, especially in Croatia; these have comparable formulaic systems, but they are far more limited and crude than those at Homer's disposal. The possibilities of his diction are amazingly rich, with an abundance of variation and flexibility and a huge range of subtly differentiated vocabulary and formulaic phrases. Homer never seems at a loss or stuck in a corner for the right means of expression. His formulaic diction increases rather than limits his poetic inventiveness.

But while the range and fecundity of the traditional oral language should not be underestimated, neither should its pervasiveness in the making of Homeric poetry. The inheritance of ready-made elements extends beyond phrases and lines to whole scenes. This is clearest in the scenes such as serving a meal or launching a ship, 'typical' scenes as they have come to be known, where whole blocks of lines are completely or nearly repeated verbatim. But the traditional 'formulaic' scene-shape can often be seen in sequences where there is little actual verbal repetition. This has been amply demonstrated by Bernard Fenik for the mass of battle scenes in the *Iliad*, material which one would expect to be highly traditional. But the same inherited shaping may be seen in recurrent sequences in the *Odyssey*. For example, the hero arrives in a strange place and is at a loss; he is met by a noble stranger who helps him and directs him to the royal palace. The outline provides a set of directions for the oral poet to work within.

Once more we should not assume that the traditional pattern is restrictive or inflexible. It creates expectations which as well as being satisfied may on occasion be varied or contradicted. Take, for example, the slight variation on the usual scene-sequence of the arrival of a stranger at a hospitable house, which we have when Telemachus arrives at Sparta at the beginning of *Odyssey* 4. Usually the host himself takes charge of the guest at once; but here there is a wedding feast in progress and Telemachus is met by Menelaus' henchman, who is not sure what to do and consults Menelaus while Telemachus waits outside. Menelaus is angry at this and insists that the strangers should be treated properly whatever the circumstances. The variation in the pattern shows the example of really noble hospitality. The pattern of a 'typical sequence' can also be carefully adhered to and thus create a sense of order and orthodoxy. A remarkable use of this possibility comes in the last book of the *Iliad*. Feasting in Homer, and no doubt in epic bards before him, is narrated with a set of procedures which include many recurrent formulaic lines. A sense of ceremony and normality is thus imparted to this daily social occasion which ratifies a communal bond. In *Iliad* 24.621ff., however, these regular procedures, told in the familiar way, take on a special colour and significance since the two parties are Achilles and Priam. The uniqueness of the occasion, and its boldness, gain greater depth from its typicality.

Parry's discoveries have, then, opened up new explanations and significances for the 'repetitiousness' of Homer. They also account for the strange linguistic phenomena of Homeric diction. His language is evidently nothing like the Greek that any native speaker ever spoke. Most of the word-forms are variants drawn from the dialects of different places and periods, but never spoken together in any one time or place. Some of the forms are even, it seems, completely artificial, the word-forging of poets, especially under metrical pressure. Philologists are largely agreed that, while the basic dialect of Homeric Greek is that of Ionia in the archaic period, there are many features quite foreign to that time and place. The most interesting is perhaps the occurrence of outcrops of so-called 'Arcado-Cypriot'. The evidence of Linear B tablets confirms that this is the Greek of the Mycenaeans some 500 years before Homer and on the mainland of Greece. The oral tradition can accommodate all this: travelling bards will over the years have picked up some phrases and discarded others according to their tastes and needs. Gradually a language comes into being which is special to epic poetry. Some phrases go back hundreds of years; others are recent acquisitions; others are new on the very day of performance. In this sense hundreds of anonymous bards may well have contributed to the *Iliad* and *Odyssey*, in that they will have contributed phrases, lines, or scene-sequences which became part of the tradition.

This 'artificiality' of epic language does not mean that it was precious or outlandish. Although it contained words and forms that the audience will never have heard outside poetry, it will have been a language made familiar by poetry and proper to it. It makes for pace and assurance infused with an epic and high colour. These qualities were well seen by Matthew Arnold: 'He is eminently rapid; he is eminently plain and direct both in the evolution of his thought and in the expression of it . . . he is eminently noble.' Colin Macleod has brought out the insights underlying these epithets: 'Arnold saw, with the acumen of the critic, that what is artificial in origin need not be artificial in effect ("rapid . . . plain . . .") and that judgements of poetic quality are vacuous if they take no account of moral quality ("simple . . . noble . . .").'

The idea that dozens of nameless bards have made their contribution to Homer is an attractive one. The poems become the achievement of a group or guild. But Milman Parry and some of his successors have been carried away by this 'folkist' romance, and have become so set on the notion of traditional poetry that they have denied all individuality to the bard within it, adding that such a tradition has no place or value for originality. For them 'Homer' is the tradition, handed down over the centuries. This runs into problems, if only because the tradition must somehow have developed and grown; it cannot have instantaneously sprung into mature existence. And, unless it is maintained that all of Homer's rivals, earlier or contemporary, all produced poetry just as good as his— in fact indistinguishable from it—then there must have been ways in which Homer was better. The ways in which he was better than the others constitute his originality. So, however much he was within his tradition, he must also have improved on it.

The question now is, how far was Homer the servant of his tradition, how much its master? Must he have worked entirely with it and within it, or might he have worked against it also? It is still an open question, indeed, whether very long epics were a centuries-old norm or an invention of Homer; whether or not something very like the *Iliad* or the *Odyssey* could have been heard generations before Homer.

We have not got any of the poetry of Homer's predecessors or rivals, and so nothing much can be said with confidence; that this or that was innovative or anti-traditional on the part of Homer must remain a speculation. There are those, for instance, who have claimed that Patroclus is a Homeric invention, and Eumaeus, and the pastoral element in the *Odyssey*. The hope for progress on such issues is one of the great challenges facing Homeric scholarship.

It seems to me more than plausible that Homer was doubly original, that he worked against the tradition as well as within it. Take as a test case the attitude of the *Iliad* towards Troy. The tradition seems to have been partisan in favour of the Greeks and to have supplied Homer with much more material for telling of Greek victories than of reverses. Although the Trojans generally have the better of Books 8 to 17, more Trojans are killed than Greeks, and there are constant Greek revivals, and—a telling detail—the left and right of the battlefield are always viewed from the Greek perspective. In creating a epic where the Trojans have the better of the battle for much of the time, and where the battle is in poetic terms seen from their side no less than from the Greeks', it looks as if Homer must have gone against his tradition. The challenge of doing so seems indeed to have been an essential poetic catalyst.

Long similes are one of the special glories of Homer and one of his distinctive contributions to the whole future of European poetry. They may be another example of an innovation or late development in tension with the tradition. It is widely supposed that long similes are a product of long epic, and that 'monumental' compositions like the *Iliad* and the *Odyssey* are a late development. On the other hand it would be no surprise to find the standard long similes of beasts of prey, especially lions, well back in the tradition of heroic epic. The philologists say that the language of the similes is notably non-formulaic and late: but this seems largely explicable by the non-heroic subject-matter of many similes. What seems to me most unlikely to be traditional about Homeric similes is the wide variety of relationships between the similes and their surrounding contexts. Each seems to set the audience a challenge in working out the connection. Some work by similarity, some by contrast, some concentrate on a physical comparison, others on comparison of tone or emotion.

An example from each poem will have to suffice. At *Iliad* 21. 342 ff. Hephaestus, helping Achilles against the river Scamander, burns the vegetation and corpses on the banks of the river:

> As when the north wind of autumn suddenly makes dry
> a garden freshly watered and makes glad the man who is tending it,
> so the entire flat land was dried up with Hephaestus burning . . .

Hephaestus and Achilles rejoice in the drying blast: on the other hand it is the river which keeps fertile the vegetation of Troy and which supplies irrigation for the gardens. The simile draws attention to the destructive reversal of nature when fire burns water. At *Odyssey* 5. 388 ff. Odysseus is lifted on a wave and sees the coast of Phaeacia in the distance:

> And as welcome as the show of life again in a father
> is to his children, when he has lain sick, suffering strong pains,
> and wasting long away, and the hateful death spirit has brushed him,
> but then, and it is welcome, the gods set him free of his sickness,
> so welcome appeared land and forest now to Odysseus . . .

This is indeed the first moment at which there is hope that Odysseus will survive after all, and will eventually live to see his family. When he is at last safe in the arms of Penelope it is a simile which reminds us of the feats of endurance that Odysseus has had to go through:

> And as when the land appears welcome to men who are swimming,
> after Poseidon has smashed their strong-built ship on the open
> water, pounding it with the weight of wind and the heavy
> seas, and only a few escape the grey water landward
> by swimming, with a thick scurf of salt coated upon them,
> and gladly they set foot on the shore, escaping the evil;
> so welcome was her husband to her as she looked upon him . . .
>
> (23. 233 ff.)

To regard the thematic interaction of these two similes as coincidence seems absurd; to attribute it to tradition seem scarcely less implausible.

In recent years there has been something of a reaction against Milman Parry and the approach to Homer through tradition that he opened up. There has been a feeling that this approach has failed to deliver the great insights it claimed it would reveal. It is true that it cannot resolve the sort of large questions about Homer's place within and against the tradition which I have been raising; it is still very important, however, and especially on the level of the formulaic phrase, the basic unit from which Parry started. The reason is not just that the exigencies and pressures of oral composition help to explain away the infelicities and inconsistencies that so exercise the analysts; this is a petty gain, merely making excuses. There are much more important insights to be won. The whole inimitable rapidity and directness of Homeric poetry may be seen as the benefit of the oral tradition. In a writing poet 'pius Aeneas' or 'bold Sir Bedivere' are in danger of becoming precious, but in Homer the unobtrusive reiteration of such characteristics seems perfectly natural. Thanks to the repeated phrases and scene-sequences we are in a familiar world where things have their known places. It is a world which is solid and known, and yet at the same time coloured by the special diction with an epic nobility. Robes, beds, sheep, springs, mountains—their constancy is conveyed by the traditional language. The sun rises each day in familiar terms; Achilles remains swift however inactive he may be. Set against this formulaic backcloth are the unique, terrible events. The sun sets as ever, but Hector is dead. In Homer we have a supremely pervasive counterpoint of static and dynamic, the constant and the ephemeral. This owes much to the essential style of the poetry.

Homer and History

The old question of whether Homer was one poet or many has, then, been largely displaced by the new question of Homer's relation to his tradition. The other great Homeric controversy, which goes back to even earlier than Wolf, is still as lively as ever, and has in fact captured more widespread interest than the scholars' obsession with multiple authorship. How 'true' is Homer? What is the relation of the *Iliad* and *Odyssey* to any historical reality? Was there ever a Greek siege of Troy? Did the Phaeacians exist, and if so where?, etc., etc. The issue of the 'truth' of Homer has often been connected with the question—in most respects a very different one—of the historicity of the Old Testament. This should sound the warning that we must ask questions appropriate to the work. Inappropriate questions will lead to false answers.

While there have always been a few who are happy to regard the events of the poems as fiction set in a world which is largely the creation of poetic fantasy, there have been many more who have passionately believed that Homer is, more or less, history. They seized on Robert Wood's reports in the eighteenth century that the topography and natural history of Turkey corroborated Homer's accuracy. They drew more comfort from the archaeological discovery in the late nineteenth century that there really had been a great Mycenaean civilization. The romantic fabrications of Heinrich Schliemann clearly satisfied a popular desire by 'verifying' Homer.

Most vindications of Homer's historicity have claimed him as an accurate record of the Mycenaean Age of about 1400–1100 BC. A few, however, have claimed him as a record of his own contemporary world (say ninth or eighth century). But, against this latter, it seems inevitable that a distant world of heroes calls for a way of life different from that of the audience (they eat roast meat every day, for example); and that it has to be free from blatant 'anachronisms' known to be recent innovations—hence, for example, the absence of literacy from the poems. The most influential modern claim for this historicity of Homer, M.I. Finley's *World of Odysseus*, looks neither to the Mycenaean past nor Homer's present, but the 'Dark-Age' Greece of about 1050–900 BC. He claims that Homer accurately records that world in such anthropological aspects as social and kinship structures, moral and political values, and general world-view.

Although archaeologists continue to dispute, it is now generally agreed that various elements of the material world of Homer are derived from different periods. Fighting weapons and armour, for instance, are all bronze, while iron is a rare metal: this preserves the metallurgy of the Mycenaean (Bronze) Age. On the other hand, the dead are cremated rather than buried, and this is a post-Mycenaean Iron Age practice. In some places the heroes carry huge Mycenaean shields, in others the smaller 'modern' sort. The material world seems to come from different times, spread over many centuries, and as likely as not from different places also. In this respect it is very like the language of the poems and the explanation must surely be the same. The oral poetic tradition has created, by a long process of addition and rejection, an amalgam. In matters of armour, burial, and so forth this amalgam, while historically impossible, is aesthetically coherent and convincing. What mattered to the poet was not that he should be accurate—why should that matter?—but that he should be plausible and enthralling, that he should create a past that was solidly imaginable and yet suitable for heroes.

Just as Homeric language included an element of poetic diction which no one had ever spoken, so there was surely a considerable made-up element in the world of Achilles or Odysseus. The twin springs of the river Scamander in *Iliad* 22.145–56 provide a good illustration since much of the topographical search for a real setting for the *Iliad* and the Trojan war has concentrated on them. There are two springs, one icy cold, the other steaming hot, and close by them are the stone-washing troughs where the Trojan women used to do their laundry. It is by them that Hector, after being chased three times round Troy, takes his final stand against Achilles. Needless to say, no explorer has managed to find such a hydrological curiosity outside the walls of any ancient city, though apparently there are springs of varying temperatures somewhere in the mountains of north-west Turkey. The springs are not there for the sake of descriptive accuracy, but for their dramatic and poetic topicality. Not long before, in Book 21, Hephaestus and Achilles defeated the Scamander, the river of Troy; now Hector, the protector of Troy, runs for his life past the springs of Scamander. The washing troughs stand for Troy's former delight and prosperity. Troy will never know that peace again, once Achilles has caught Hector. Its fine clothes will be taken as booty, and its women will labour at far-distant springs.

Could it be that, even if Homer's material world is mixed from different periods with a strong leavening of invention, its social structures and values are still drawn from the real world, indeed from a particular historical reality? Finley's case is that Homer is consistent and anthropologically plausible on such matters as Agamemnon's constitutional position, the inheritance customs on Ithaca, the status of wives and monogamy, the legal and social treatment of murderers, to give four examples. I would maintain that in all four cases the poems are in fact inconsistent, treating the issue differently in different contexts. There is no need, for instance, for the Achaeans to have a consistent constitutional procedure or a defined hierarchy of kings, elders, assemblies, etc., as long as their debates and deliberations convince the poet's audience on each particular occasion. It is, in fact, important for the *Iliad* that Agamemnon should not have a definite constitutional position.

When it comes to morality and values, it is also widely claimed that these are consistent and furthermore simple. The 'Heroic Code' consists of precepts such as that you must strive to be first, you must kill and humiliate your enemies, and you must preserve your honour, which is measurable in material goods. But much of the *Iliad* is spent in disputing and debating about these very precepts, and many others. One of the reasons why so much of the poem consists of direct speech is that so much of it is spent in argument about values. If the 'Heroic Code' were agreed and beyond dispute, there would be no real conflict. In fact the criteria for approval and disapproval are open for consideration; and much of the power of the *Iliad* comes from its lack of moral simplicity and consistency.

Scholars have been even more determined to impose a religious 'reality' on Homer (and here the Old Testament analogy may have been particularly influential). Out of all the variety of manifestations of the divine, they have laboured to produce theological consistency and system, the actual religion of an actual historical moment. Here again, in my view, they produce their theologies as the answer to questions of a sort which it is not appropriate to ask of a work of literature. They ask, for example, what kind of god is Fate (*Moira*), and is Fate more powerful than Zeus? When Athena intervenes in *Iliad* 1. 193 ff. is she merely a poetic personification of Achilles' better judgement? What is the function and power of non-Olympian powers such as Ocean, Sun, Scamander?

One illustration will have to suffice to suggest how the gods in Homer do not have a theological existence independent of particular poetic context. In *Iliad* 22 Achilles is pursuing Hector round Troy:

> But when for the fourth time they had come around to the well springs
> then the Father balanced his golden scales, and in them
> he set two fateful portions of death, which lays men prostrate,
> one for Achilles, and one for Hector, breaker of horses,
> and balanced it by the middle; and Hector's death-day was heavier
> and dragged downward toward death, and Phoebus Apollo forsook him.
>
> (22. 208–133)

It seems to me simple-minded to conclude from this that Fate is superior to Zeus because Fate must tip the scales. In the context it is clear that the scales do not determine who will win, but when Achilles will win. The outcome of the battle is already put beyond doubt by many other factors, human, divine, and poetic: the scales mark a dramatic turning-point. It is at this point that Apollo leaves Hector and Athena joins Achilles. But it would again be a theological over-simplification to conclude that the battle is merely divine puppetry without any place for human achievement. The gods do not change the outcome of the battle. Nor do they diminish the victory or the defeat; on the contrary their interest and participation elevate them. Great heroic deeds are marked by the attention of the gods. So the golden scales are neither a real theological belief nor mere picturesque ornament; they are the elevation of a turning-point.

The conclusion that the Homeric world is through and through on every level a poetic amalgam is in no way inconsistent with its having exerted a powerful influence on the real life of the Greeks over the next 1,000 years after its creation. Homer provided one persuasive, universally known, and inspiring model of heroism, nobility, the good life, the gods. Homer affected history. But it is not by being a faithful representation of history that his world-picture has captured the imagination of so many people for so long. It is much more memorable and universal than that.

There does remain, however, one time and place in history which Homer tells us about, though indirectly. There must have been an occasion for the creation of the *Iliad* and *Odyssey*. The very fact that they came into existence says a lot about the concerns and sensibilities of Homer's own audience. For I take it as axiomatic that these great works of art would never have come into existence without an audience. There must have been people who were willing to pay attention to these poems, to make the trouble worth Homer's while by listening to them properly—and quite likely by supplying his livelihood also. They must have been able to appreciate Homer: otherwise he would never have made the poems. And if the *Iliad* and *Odyssey* are the kind of works which I have argued for in this chapter then that is an important thing to know about some Greeks in the general area of Ionia around the date of 700 BC.

Further Reading

TRANSLATIONS

The translation of Homer into English, since the first by Chapman, epitomizes the development of national taste and letters. (It is no chance that Matthew Arnold made it the subject of one of the classics of literary criticism.) The greatest is surely that of Pope, which has laboured too long under the vacuous reproof of Richard Bentley—'a very pretty poem, Mr. Pope, but you must not call it Homer.' William Cowper's translation into Miltonic blank verse has been unjustly neglected. There are two good modern verse translations, both by Americans. Preferences will vary between the tough shorter lines of Robert Fitzgerald (New York, 1961, 1974; Oxford, 1984), and the more literary, close and slow-pace six-stress metre of Richmond Lattimore (Chicago, 1951, 1965)—the source of most of the translated passages in this chapter. There is also a fine *Odyssey* in high prose by Walter Shewring (Oxford, 1980), and an *Iliad* by Martin Hammond (Harmondsworth and New York, 1987).

INTRODUCTIONS

There is a variety of introductions to be recommended. Chapter 3 of A. Lesky's *History of Greek Literature* (translated by J. Willis and C. de Heer, London, 1966) is admirably catholic. Adam Parry's long Introduction to his father's work *The Making of Homeric Verse: The Collected Papers of Milman Parry* (Oxford, 1970) is an important evaluation of the achievements and shortcomings of the approach through the oral tradition. J. Griffin's *Homer* (Oxford, 1980) in the 'Past Masters' series aims to bring out the quality of Homer's thought and imagination. Michael Silk's *The Iliad* in the 'Landmarks of World Literature' series (Cambridge, 1987) is particularly strong on style and tone. The Introduction to C. W. Macleod's text and commentary on *Iliad*, Book 24 (Cambridge, 1982) is far more than is usually expected of that genre: it is a tragic, yet humane, interpretation of the *Iliad* of the kind intuitively glimpsed by Simone Weil (*L'Iliade ou le poème de la force*, trans. M. McCarthy, New York, 1940); and it is explored on the level of detailed phrasing as well as larger structure.

THE ILIAD

Among the more specialist works on the *Iliad* B. Fenik's *Typical Battle Scenes in the Iliad* (Wiesbaden, 1968) demonstrates how the oral tradition works on the scale of whole scenes. C. Segal, *The Theme of the Mutilation of the Corpse in the Iliad* (Leiden, 1971), traces the cumulative sequence of an important motif. J. M. Redfield, *Nature and Culture in the Iliad* (Chicago, 1975), while 'anthropological' in mode, makes many sensitive observations on the human stuff of the poem. J. Griffin's *Homer on Life and Death* (Oxford, 1980) is more perceptive about Homer's gods in the course of showing that the poem's fundamental 'subject' is mankind's state of mortality. S. Schein *The Mortal Hero* (Berkeley, 1984) is a good distillation of the revaluation of Homer's poetic quality which has gathered momentum since 1970.

THE ODYSSEY

The *Odyssey* has not yet inspired the same kind of new wave of interpretation as the *Iliad*. B. Fenik's *Studies in the Odyssey* (Wiesbaden, 1974) goes much further than his *Iliad* book, however, in showing how typical scenes contribute to the character of the whole poem. N. Austin's collection of essays *Archery at the Dark of the Moon* (Berkeley, 1975), while fanciful in places, is also a serious attempt to capture the *Odyssey*'s elusive allure. W. B. Stanford's *The Ulysses Theme* (2nd edn., Oxford, 1958) is a classic study of the archetypal character of Odysseus in the *Odyssey* and later literature.

BACKGROUND AND HISTORY

Most of the work in English for thirty years and more after Milman Parry's discoveries was on the background to Homer rather than the poems themselves. These studies concentrated on the development of the oral tradition and the relation of Homer to the Mycenaean age. They culminated in two wide-ranging books, *A Companion to Homer* (London, 1962), made up of chapters by many scholars edited by A. J. B. Wace and F. H. Stubbings; and G. S. Kirk's *The Songs of Homer* (Cambridge, 1962, also in a shortened version, *Homer and the Epic*, Cambridge, 1965).

The modern classic on Homer and history is M. I. Finley's *The World of Odysseus* (2nd edn., London, 1977), but this is an attempt to illuminate history by means of Homer, not the other way round. Homer's integrity as a creative artist is better respected by O. Murray, *Early Greece* (London, 1980), chs. 3–4, and A. M. Snodgrass, *Archaic Greece* (London, 1980), ch. 2. There are good essays on the relation of Homer to the real world in L. Foxhall and J. K. Davies (eds.), *The Trojan War* (Bristol, 1984).

3
Greek Myth and Hesiod

※

JASPER GRIFFIN

Myth

EVERYONE is familiar with some Greek myths: that Oedipus solved the riddle of the Sphinx and married his mother, that the Argonauts sailed away in search of the Golden Fleece. Many people know that there is a large modern literature about mythology, from Sir James Frazer's *Golden Bough* and Robert Graves's *Greek Myths* to the dense and complex accounts given by Claude Lévi-Strauss and the Structuralists. Myth is a very attractive subject, but the immense disagreements of the experts show that it is also a very difficult one. It was a brilliant stroke of George Eliot to show the learned Mr. Casaubon, in *Middlemarch*, struggling to write a *Key to all Mythologies*, swamped and overwhelmed by masses of material on which he could not impose any intelligible order.

Even to define myth is extraordinarily difficult, if it is to be marked off from legend, folk-tale, and other relatives. It will perhaps be best to settle provisionally for something like the modest definition of G. S. Kirk, 'A special sort of traditional tale', to suspend the search for a single source, and to offer, instead, a couple of examples of the typically mythical mode of thought, in contrast with something recognizably different.

In the fifth century, Greeks were struck by the fact that whereas their own rivers tended to flood in winter and dry up in summer, the Nile flooded in the summer and not in winter. Pindar, in a lost poem, told of a 'guardian daemon' a hundred fathoms tall, who caused the flood by the movement of his feet. Herodotus, by contrast, considers three theories (including the correct one of melted snow in the distant mountains), but settles for a theory of his own about the movement of the sun, which 'behaves as it normally does in summer', but is subject to deflection by storms at a certain time of year. He is anxious, that is, to give an explanation in terms of familiar natural laws, not fantastic personalities. Again, the old story explained why the Greek chiefs followed Agamemnon to Troy by saying that Helen's father made all her suitors swear in advance to come to the aid of her chosen husband, if her beauty should lead to her abduction. Thucydides rejects this story, replacing it with an explanation in terms of economic power: Agamemnon was the most powerful man in Greece as the heir of the wealthy immigrant Pelops, and he had 'courted the favour of the populace'; the chiefs followed him 'from fear rather than goodwill'. In these examples we see an older sort of explanation in terms of the free acts of striking individuals, succeeded by one in terms of rationalistic physical speculation, or of reflection on the real nature of political power. It is no accident that Thucydides' Agamemnon, wealthy, democratic, and master of a fleet, is so reminiscent of the Athens of the Peloponnesian War.

Until this century 'myth' virtually meant 'Greek myth', but now anthropologists and others have collected immense stores of myths from all over the world. It soon becomes clear that those of the Greeks are unusual in important ways. The great majority of Greek myths are concerned with heroes and heroines: that is, with men and women of a definite period in the past, who had greater powers and were more interesting than modern people, but who were not gods. The mythologies of Egypt and Mesopotamia are not much concerned with heroes. Very rare in Greek myths are talking animals; and in general, although there are many exceptions, the events of the myths are an exaggeration or heightening of ordinary life rather than the wholly bizarre and dream-like sequences found in so many of the world's traditional tales. This special character of Greek myth has proved a considerable stumbling-block to modern general theories of mythology.

Another way in which Greek mythology is a special case is its pervasiveness and importance, in a society more advanced than most of those in which modern missionaries and travellers have been able to interview native speakers. From Homer to Attic tragedy, it is in terms of the myths that poets work out their deepest thoughts; both history and philosophy emerge from mythical thought, and both poetry and the visual arts remained always attached to mythical subjects.

Greece did, of course, have its cosmogonies, myths which told of the creation of the world, and other stories which took place on the purely divine level. Hesiod, as we shall see, told in his *Theogony* of the coming into existence of Earth (Gaia) and her son-partner Heaven (Uranus), and how they were separated, and how Zeus came to be the ruler of the gods. That story has been heavily influenced by eastern sources, and it has little connection with real Greek cult or Greek religion. Another tale which is clearly early is that of the abduction of Persephone (or *Korē*, 'the Maiden', as she is more usually called) by the Lord of the Underworld. In anger and grief her mother Demeter made the whole world barren, and in the end Kore was restored to her for two-thirds of the year, but had to spend one-third of it under the earth. It is natural to connect her absence with the 'dead' time when the corn is in the earth, before it comes up.

One striking omission in the *Theogony* of Hesiod is any account of the origin of mankind; and early Greek thought had in fact no agreed account of it. Sometimes men are said to come from ash trees, or to be made from clay by Prometheus, or to have emerged from stones; in some sense Zeus is the 'father' of all men. The omission seems strange to readers of the Bible, which opens so memorably with Adam and Eve; but it is interesting that after the Book of Genesis Adam is barely named again in the Old Testament, in which 'in the beginning' is normally expressed by reference either to Abraham or to Moses. Early man is not as constantly aware of his ultimate origins as those who are brought up on the theory of evolution.

Another point worth making at the outset is that there was no standard or orthodox version of a myth. The fact that a story was told in one way in Homer did not prevent later poets from telling it very differently. To give a striking instance, the lyric poet Stesichorus, in the early sixth century, produced a celebrated poem denying that Helen ever went to Troy at all—which of course made nonsense of the Trojan War. Euripides exploited the ironic potential of that subversive tale in his *Helen*, and Herodotus, with delightful rationalism, says that it must be true, as otherwise the Trojans would obviously have given her up long before the destruction of their city. 'And I think Homer knew this story,' he adds, 'but because it was not so appealing a subject for poetry, he preferred the other': a good example of the judgement passed by fifth-century enlightenment on the historical value of the poets and their myths. Certainly we hear, from the beginning of Greek literature, protests at the mendacity of poets. 'We know how to tell many lies that look like truth,' say the Muses to Hesiod, 'but we know how to tell the truth when we choose'; and Solon, himself a poet, said (in verse), 'Poets tell many lies'. Each new poet had the right to interpret the tradition in his own way, and the audience did not feel committed to accepting what he said, however fascinating, as necessarily true.

Some myths are closely related to a ritual: for instance, the myth of Kore. When she disappeared, her mother wandered barefoot seeking her over the world, fasting; at Eleusis she was persuaded to smile, and to partake of a special barley drink, by the obscene jesting of a woman called *Iambē* (evidently a name related to the iambic metre often used for coarse personal attacks); she regained her daughter, and she gave blessings to men. All this was acted out by those who flocked to be initiated into the great Eleusinian mysteries. Fasting and abstaining from drink, they made their way in long procession from Athens to Eleusis. At a certain point on the pilgrimage obscenities were shouted. Initiates drank the *kykeōn*, the special barley drink, to break their fast. And the change of the goddess from gloom to gladness was echoed by the sudden blaze of light from darkness in the hall of the mysteries, followed by rejoicing. It is evident here that the worshipper is acting out the sufferings of the goddess—a comparison with the Stations of the Cross is not unnatural—and that myth and ritual are, on different levels, the same.

But the myth does more than that. The anger of Demeter plunged the world into an abnormal and horrible state, in which the earth's fertility failed, and it seemed that mankind would die out and the gods would cease to receive their cult and their honours. The idea that normal life might fail serves to add value to its continued existence; and the anxiety which naturally arises in the mind when the seed is sown in the earth—suppose it fails to grow?—is given form, removed to the past, and provided with a satisfying conclusion. There is another level, too. The seed dying and being reborn suggests the idea of rebirth and immortality: 'Except a corn of wheat fall into the ground and die, it abideth alone; but if it die, it bringeth forth much fruit' (John 12:24). The seed is sown, it disappears in the darkness, and yet it lives and will rise again; Kore was snatched away to the Underworld, and yet she comes back; and the initiates at Eleusis were promised a happier and more glorious life after death.

Some myths, like that of Kore, relate not only to ritual, but also to ideas of the reversal of ordinary civilized life. On the island of Lemnos once a year all fires were extinguished for nine days; family life ceased, and an atmosphere of grimness prevailed, as the women separated themselves from the men, who lay low. Then new fire was fetched from Delos, and new purified fires were kindled; there was a great festival of rejoicing, with laughter and sexual intercourse. The mythical counterpart of all this is the story that the women of Lemnos were once afflicted by Aphrodite with an evil smell, so that their husbands rejected their embraces; they then murdered all the men, and there were only women on the island until suddenly the Argonauts arrived. The women welcomed them, games and festivities were held, and the island was repopulated, Jason begetting twins on the queen Hypsipyle (the twins then had an eventful mythical career . . .). No doubt the women of Lemnos, in reality, ate garlic in the period of separation, as we know that the women of Athens did at the festivals of the Scira and the Thesmophoria, to mark their withdrawal from sexual activity. The nine days are a time of reversal: women are in the ascendant, unattractive and unapproachable; there is no cooking and no sacrificial ritual. Then normality is restored with exultation. Again we see the reinforcement of the value of ordinary civilization; and again we see a release of anxiety, this time the tension natural between the sexes. At regular intervals the women were violently released from their normal domestic round; and the men had their most horrid secret fears about the evil potentialities of their wives and womenfolk brought out into the open and, perhaps, disarmed.

Myths in which women reject their ordinary feminine role are numerous. Their natural role, their *telos*, was marriage. Those who reject marriage become, in the myths, hunters and outdoor girls—the outdoors belonging, in the normal way, to men. Girls such as Atalanta and Callisto chose that life, only to be overcome in the end and brought back to marriage. Others behave in an irregular manner within marriage. Fears about a wife naturally focused on sexual misconduct and disloyalty, and we find bad wives like Phaedra making advances to young men. The seer Amphiaraus knew that if he joined the doomed expedition of the Seven against Thebes, he would not return: his wife was bribed to make him go to his death. Agamemnon's wife Clytemnestra took a lover in his absence and murdered her husband on his return. Evil deeds or rejection of their role on the part of mythical women are a way of defining and endorsing that role. We shall find that the potential of men, too, is limited and clarified in myth in a similar way, when we turn to the aspirations of the hero.

A myth can have a political function ('charter myth'). In Cyrene a historian told the story that once the local Africans were plagued by a monstrous lion. In desperation their king proclaimed that whoever destroyed it should be his heir. The nymph Cyrene killed the lion, and her descendants, the Cyreneans, inherited after her. This tale legitimizes the Greek colony: not just invaders, the settlers inherited the land from a heroine who earned it as reward for a memorable action. Again, the Athenians got control of the island of Salamis in the sixth century. Not only did they make Ajax, the great Salaminian hero, the eponym and theoretically the ancestor of one of the ten tribes of Attica: they also, so other Greeks alleged, introduced a spurious line into the text of the *Iliad* to support the assertion that Salamis and Attica went together in the heroic period (*Iliad* 2.558). The Dorians, too, had an elaborate myth which presented their invasion of the Peloponnese, in which they were the last Greeks to arrive, as being in reality a return, to claim an inheritance which was their due: the children of Heracles, their ancestor, having been driven out and coming back several generations later. In the modern world we think of the many myths of nationalism, or of the importance to modern Israel of the possession of its land by distant ancestors.

The myths were all that later Greeks knew about their own early history, apart from a few striking remains such as the 'Cyclopean' walls of Tiryns and the citadel of Mycenae. Systematic excavation was neither a practical possibility nor an ideal. In the middle of the nineteenth century there was a fashion for saying that apparently historical myths contained no truth at all, being in reality disguised or allegorical statements about natural phenomena such as the sunrise or the coming of winter. Schliemann's discoveries at Troy and Mycenae, and those of Evans in Crete, showed that such radical scepticism was mistaken: Mycenae had been 'rich in gold', as Homer said, and at Cnossus there had been a great and complex building and some strange sport involving bulls—the originals of the Labyrinth and the Minotaur. Already in the fifth century the two possible ways of treating myth for the purposes of history were both understood. Thucydides, in the opening chapters of the first book of his *History*, gives a brilliant sketch of early Greece, reinterpreting the myths in the light of modern rationalism, with a heavy emphasis on economic factors. We have seen how he dealt with Agamemnon (above, pp. 72 f.). For Thucydides, King Minos of Crete was 'the first man we hear of to have a fleet'; ruler of much of the Aegean, he 'put down piracy, it is reasonable to suppose, so that his revenues would come in' (1.4). No mention, needless to say, of the Minotaur. Herodotus, on the other hand, at one moment at least envisages rejecting the myths completely, as being just different from history. He says of the sixth-century tyrant Polycrates that 'He is the first man we know of who set himself to rule the sea, except indeed

GOLDEN MASK FROM A TOMB AT MYCENAE. When Schliemann excavated this he declared it the 'Mask of Agamemnon'—a claim which would no doubt have been echoed by any Classical Greek who had come upon it. Although much older than the assumed period of Agamemnon and the Trojan War it is an example of a type of Bronze Age artefact which, with the great fortified citadels themselves, demonstrated to Classical Greeks the wealth and power of their heroic forefathers, the kings of Mycenae 'rich in gold', as Homer described it.

for Minos and anyone there may have been before him who did it; of what is called human lineage, Polycrates was the first' (3. 122).

Myth could preserve certain things from the past: names, great events, historical places. Of course it transformed and distorted them. Troy was once taken by storm, and there was a great king in Mycenae; but we cannot know how much truth there is in the story of a great expedition against Troy, and Achilles in his origins is clearly more akin to a saga-figure such as Siegfried than to a historical person such as Augustus. But another sort of survival in the myths is no less interesting: that of customs, and indeed of a picture of a society as a whole. As an example of the preservation in myth of an archaic custom, we can take the story of the adoption of Heracles by Hera. After his apotheosis,

Zeus persuaded Hera to adopt him as her son and henceforth for all time to cherish him with a mother's love. The adoption is said to have taken place in the following way: Hera reclined on a bed, drew Heracles towards her, and let him fall through her clothes to the ground, acting out what happens in real childbirth. This is what non-Greeks do to this day, when they carry out an adoption. (Diodorus Siculus 4. 39. 2)

It is clear that what is described is an archaic and rather naïve procedure: a child cannot be adopted without being, symbolically, born of his adoptive mother. The Greeks observed that many things which among them happened only in myths were regular in the society of contemporary 'barbarians'.

Myth could preserve features of archaic life and society. But it could also transform quite recent history for spectacular exotic potentates: Cyrus the Mede and Croesus of Lydia, historic personalities of the mid sixth century, were given in the fifth century strong mythical features. Cyrus was exposed at birth and brought up by an animal, like Romulus or Aegisthus; Croesus was carried off from death by Apollo and given eternal happiness among the Hyperboreans, because of his great offerings at Delphi.

That children exposed at birth might survive was a natural wish in a society in which such exposures were not uncommon, and in myth, as in comedy and in the novels, we find many examples. That a world-conqueror such as Cyrus, or a great figure such as Oedipus, should have risen to the zenith of prosperity from the desperate position of an exposed infant had the added appeal of a superlative 'log-cabin to White House' story. It is another sort of fantasy when, as in the myth of Anchises and Aphrodite, a beautiful girl drops from the sky to seduce a young man minding his flocks on the hills. Darker fantasies found cathartic expression in myth: every variety of incest, murder of kindred, cannibalism, sexual union with animals. The speculative imagination combined various creatures into compound monsters: man–horse centaurs, man–bull river gods, woman–bird harpies, the woman–lion sphinx, the winged horse Pegasus. Here the visual arts led the way for literature. Fantastic changes of scale produced giants and pygmies. The dog Cerberus had three heads, Geryon had three bodies; Argus had a hundred eyes, Briareus and his brothers a hundred hands. The whole natural world could be peopled with Pan and the satyrs, with Artemis and her retinue, and with nymphs in the trees, the streams, and the mountains.

We have seen (above, p. 75) how the myths helped to define the nature and position of women in relation to men. They also were the framework within which men were defined not only in relation to women, but also in relation to gods. The mythical period in Greece is not like the 'Dreamtime' of Australian aborigines, a remote and dateless past. It consisted of two or three generations, the time of the Theban and Trojan wars; and it could be dated and fitted in with history. Hellenistic scholars calculated that Troy fell in 1184 BC. What happened after that period was different: tragedies, for example, were not written about the colonizing period or about the tyrants, although some of the stories in Herodotus about Periander of Corinth might seem suitable material for one. No doubt this is due, at least in part, to the incalculable impact of the Homeric poems. The epic showed the heroic age as one in which gods intervened openly in human life, in a way in which later they did not. That in turn implied two things: both that the gods took the events of that age very seriously, and also that the events are transparent, allowing the hearer to discern through them the will and working of the gods, as he cannot in ordinary life. The few known historical tragedies, such as the *Persae* of Aeschylus, dealt with the Persian conquest and disasters, events on so vast a scale that they seemed to reveal the working of the divine in human history, and so to resemble myths. A final consideration is that everybody was familiar with the persons and stories which figured in the epic.

The total effect of all these considerations was to make the heroic period the natural setting for serious poetry. The Homeric epic handled the myths in one way, smoothing away the bizarre, the monstrous, the horrible; incest, killing of kindred, human sacrifice, are all reduced to a minimum or excluded altogether—Homer does not mention the sacrifice of Iphigenia, and though the *Odyssey* repeatedly dwells on Orestes' killing of Aegisthus, it never says that he killed his mother Clytemnestra. Homosexual love is also excluded from the epics. They do, however, deal with the position of men in the world, aspiring to be 'god-like', struck down by the gods when they attempt to go too far, and doomed in the end to die. The lyric tradition of Stesichorus was more picturesque, less tragic, sometimes pathetic. Pindar sheds radiance on his athletic victors by juxtaposing their triumph with some story from the career of a hero; the achievement of victory raises the athlete for a moment to a stature and significance which puts him beside the heroes, humdrum ordinary existence transfigured with the timeless splendour of the mythical world. Aeschylus is able to express his most profound broodings on the true nature of war in the odes in the *Agamemnon* about the fall of Troy, and Sophocles finds in the story of Oedipus a vehicle to represent a view of human life which is at once both bleak and terrifying, and also, as we experience the courage and resolution of the hero, and his capacity for suffering, strangely exhilarating. Epic had tended to purify the myth of precisely the things which tragedy emphasized in it, and almost every possible variety of incest, killing of kindred, and human sacrifice, is presented in the tragedies known to us. The dark colouring of tragedy as a form, with its ritual lamentations and masks of woe, explains this in part; but no doubt it is right to see also a new attitude, questioning and exploring, and delighting in extreme actions and painful conflicts.

In the myths men and gods were close. Heroes were sons of gods, greater than modern men, aspiring to fight with the gods themselves: Achilles says to Apollo in the *Iliad* 'How I would pay you out for this, if only I had the power', and both Diomede and Patroclus attack gods and are sharply called to order by Apollo: 'Remember what you are! Gods and men can never be equal' (*Iliad*, 21.20, 5.440, 16.705).

In the myths we constantly see men tempted to go beyond mortal limits: we feel pleasure as they enlarge our conception of human powers, and then a different pleasure at their inevitable defeat or destruction. Agamemnon walking on the precious tapestries, Ajax telling Athena he has no need of her, Hippolytus defying Aphrodite, the Greek commanders in the *Troades* behaving with arrogant cruelty in ignorance of the ruin the gods have planned for them, Achilles at the end of the *Iliad* forced to come to terms with the mortality which links him with his enemies—all these and many more are examples of a use of myth which became central to Greek culture. The same idea of human limitation is expressed in a less tragic way in the myths which say that life could indeed be what we wish it to be—peaceful, beautiful, eternal—only it must be somewhere cut off from us in time (the Golden Age), or in place (the Hyperboreans at the back of the North Wind; the Ethiopians where the sun rises and sets). The existence of such images is like the existence of the blessed gods: it defines by contrast the real lot of man.

Two outstanding questions remain. The first is that of the fate of myth in Greece after the rise of technical philosophy and history, prose and rationalism, in the late fifth century. The mythical genealogies gave place to a conception of history which tried to exclude the supernatural: Thucydides himself says, rather grimly, that 'the absence of the mythical element' may make his *History* less immediately enjoyable, but that it will be the more instructive. The cosmic speculations of myth gave place to philosophy, and the Presocratics, whose minds still naturally worked in a quasi-mythical way, are rejected for that very reason. Aristotle can say coolly that 'Hesiod and the theological writers were concerned only with what seemed plausible to themselves, and had no respect for us... But it is not worth taking seriously writers who show off in the mythical style; as for those who do proceed by proving their assertions, we must cross-examine them...' (*Metaphysics*, 2. 1000^{a}9). When we add to this the moral criticism of the content of the myths, which had been vocal for at least a century, and which led Plato to demand that the myths be radically censored, it is clear that time had run out for myth as the vehicle of serious thought. *Mythos* now becomes opposed to *logos*: a 'story', an 'old wives' tale', as opposed to a 'rational account', 'a definition'.

Plato invented his own myths. Some of them are indeed memorable, but they are radically different from the old ones, and carefully scrutinized by their inventor for impropriety or pessimism. The old myths were kept alive in local cults; they continued to haunt poetry, from the *Hymns* of Callimachus to the *Dionysiaca* of Nonnus in the fifth century AD, and to form the main subject matter of painting and sculpture; in Latin poetry, too, the Greek myths had a great future, from the frivolity of Ovid to the seriousness of the *Aeneid*. But the natural medium of serious argument is now prose; and mythology, and poetry with it, was more and more an ornament—admittedly a beloved and indispensable one— rather than the serious thing which it had been before 400 BC.

The second of our outstanding questions is that of the analysis of the myths. This chapter has been suggesting that myths are of different kinds and various origins, and that they did not all serve one purpose; that there is, in fact, no Key to all Mythologies. It still remains possible that some myths may be deciphered, analysed, and (in the structuralist phrase) 'decoded'. If we renounce the idea of one key to all myths, is it true that each individual myth can be definitively analysed?

The myth of Adonis will serve as a sobering example. His mother Myrrha fell in love with her own father and conceived a child by him. She was metamorphosed into the incense tree. The baby was very beautiful from birth, and Aphrodite herself fell in love with him. She gave him to Persephone in a chest, but Persephone too became enamoured of his beauty; the goddesses had to divide his favours. He was killed by a boar while hunting, and every year he is lamented by women. Such in outline is the myth. For Frazer, Adonis was a divinity of vegetation and fertility, dying every year and returning to life with the new crops; but it was pointed out that virtually no ancient source ever mentions a resurrection of Adonis. Recently, two interesting attempts have been made to unriddle the myth.

A structuralist analysis is given by M. Detienne. For him the myth is concerned with marriage, and with excess and mediation. Adonis, irregularly conceived, is precociously attractive and dies in adolescence. The 'gardens of Adonis' which were planted in his honour consisted of shallowly rooted plants which similarly were quick growing and sterile, soon withering. As his sexual career was opposed to the fruitful norm of marriage, so his gardens were the opposite of true agriculture. His festival was held in the sultry and sensuous Dogdays. The perfumed spices associated with his mother mediate between gods and men, in sacrifice-ritual; and also play a part in attraction between the sexes, which in marriage can be good, but which can also threaten to turn into mere sensuality. And incense is the food of the gods, on which men cannot subsist: the Phoenix is the creature associated with them, and it is solitary and sexless. Detienne finds four 'codes' in the story: botanical, zoological, alimentary, and astronomical. The whole account, to which so short a summary cannot do justice, is worked out with great brilliance.

W. Burkert has also analysed the Adonis myth. He begins, 'If we take the "Adonis myth" to be the story about his death by the boar . . .' This story is descended from a myth of the ancient Sumerians, about a hunter named Dumuzi. The contest between Aphrodite and Persephone for the boy is a conflict between love and death; Adonis is a hunter, and the mourning for him is in reality a means by which hunters work off their feelings of guilt and anxiety about killing animals.

We look at these two able and learned accounts of the same myth, and we see that they have nothing in common. They seem to be explaining two different stories, and to start from totally different positions, which reflect the interests of the two scholars. It is impossible to imagine a process of argument which would make one prevail over the other. That, of course, raises the question of the logical status of this sort of theory. What *are* these accounts of Adonis, if they are not really susceptible to argument? The answer, I think, must be that what we have here is two more myths. Frazer's Dying God had a great vogue in poetry and novels; although now despised and rejected by anthropologists, he was a powerful myth for modern men. Few scholars write as well as Frazer, but the mythopoeic faculty does live in some of them. Some myths are, I have suggested, simple to analyse; but others are elusive, complex, many-faceted. Different minds see different patterns in them, as they do in the interpretation of dreams. In antiquity itself the myths were often reinterpreted. For many myths we may indeed find suggestive and even poetical flashes of insight; but to grasp for 'the' meaning may be as hopeless as to grasp the evanescent shadows of the dead.

Hesiod

The first author of a systematic mythology is also the first personality in Greek literature, the poet Hesiod. It is likely that he was composing his poems about 700 BC. The impersonal manner of the Homeric epic admitted no personal revelations at all by the poet, but Hesiod goes out of his way to tell us a number of facts: that his father came from Cyme (on the coast of Asia Minor, slightly south of Lesbos), leaving home—

> Not running away from prosperity, nor from wealth and ease,
> But from the ills of poverty, which Zeus gives if he please.
> Near Helicon he stopped, in a poor place, the best he could:
> In Ascra, bad in winter, worse in summer, never good.
>
> (*Works and Days*, 637–40)

Ascra is in Boeotia, and Hesiod's father had settled far from home. Hesiod also tells us that he was made a singer when he met the Muses under Mount Helicon and they gave him a staff and breathed song into him; that he went to the funeral celebrations of one Amphidamas of Chalcis, on Euboea across the strait, and in the singing competition won a prize, a tripod, which he dedicated to the Muses; and that he had a brother named Perses. Perses, however, is a problem, and we shall have to come back to him. In addition to giving us these facts, Hesiod has a strong personality, which also marks off his work from the epic. In place of aristocratic withdrawal we find a speaker who is argumentative, suspicious, ironically humorous, frugal, fond of proverbs, wary of women.

His two poems, *Theogony* and *Works and Days*, are traditionally classed as didactic. They are in hexameters, like Homer, and Hesiod describes himself as a singer; it is natural to suppose that these poems, too, develop out of an oral tradition. Some think that Hesiod himself was the first to write his songs down. They contain highly poetical passages, but in general M. L. West's phrase 'Hesiod's hobnailed hexameters' is pretty fair. The *Theogony* was composed first. At the beginning Hesiod presents his credentials, telling how the Muses inspired him and told him to 'sing of the blessed deathless gods, and first and last to sing of themselves'. Hesiod fulfils this instruction by starting at the very beginning, with Chaos (something like 'Yawning Space', not 'Disorder)'), then Gaia/Earth, the broad seat of gods and men, and Tartara beneath the earth, and Love. Gaia/Earth gives birth to Uranus/Heaven—the double names are an attempt to convey the double aspect of these beings, who are both the natural objects and also anthropomorphic personalities. Thus Uranus is 'starry', but also he begot children on Gaia and then 'hid them away at their birth in a cleft of Earth and would not let them into the light; and he exulted in his evil-doing'.

The beginning of the gods is the beginning of the world, and theogony includes cosmogony. Earth is the first requisite, since everything else is placed by reference to it, either on it or under it. Heaven, as we have seen, is secondary to Earth, but is a good partner, being of comparable size; and since Earth, out of which things come to birth, is obviously a mother, Uranus/Heaven must be a father. The world is then built up and furnished by a series of sexual unions which produce offspring. That incidentally explains why Love is given such a very early position. Love has no children of his own, but he is the principle of procreation which is to create the world. The idea is a simple one, but we can see Hesiod developing it: one thing can be the 'offspring' of another in several different senses.

The children of Night will serve as an example. Night gave birth to black Doom and Death, and to Misery and Retribution and Strife (and other disagreeables), and to Sleep and the tribe of Dreams, and to Deceit and Affection, and to Day and Ether, and to the Hesperides. Death is dark and inactive, *like* night; misery and retribution are dark and deadly; sleep happens *in* the night; deceit perhaps started out as simply one of the unpleasantnesses, but suggested seduction—and love-play happens at night; day comes to birth, visibly, *from* night, and Ether is the sky left bright by night's departure; the Hesperides simply live in the west, where the sun goes down. Much of this, no doubt, is Hesiod's own invention. The purely mythological conception of genealogy has been half changed into an intellectual device to impose a different sort of order on the world.

The story opens with Gaia and Uranus. Zeus is not yet on the scene; in fact he is the grandson of Uranus/Heaven, and his father Cronos of the crooked counsels was supreme between them. Hesiod tells the story, known to Homer, of the succession of sky gods. First Uranus was supreme, but he suppressed his children, and Gaia encouraged his son Cronos to castrate him. Cronos in turn devoured his own children, until his wife Rhea gave him a stone to eat in place of Zeus; the child Zeus was brought up in Crete, compelled his father to disgorge his siblings, and with them and other aid defeated Cronos and his Titans and cast them down into Tartarus. This barbaric tale was always an oddity. Zeus' own name (akin to the Latin *dies*, 'day') meant 'sky', though classical Greeks had forgotten that; and it was strange that he should have a grandfather whose transparent name is the ordinary Greek word for 'sky'. Moreover, both Uranus and Cronos hardly existed as realities in cult. In this century the decipherment of a number of ancient Near Eastern languages has shown that the story is a version of a very archaic one, known to the Hittites by 1200 BC, to the Hurrians and the Phoenicians, and recited at Babylon annually in the poem known as *Enuma Elish* perhaps as much as 600 years earlier. Its ultimate origin seems to have been Sumerian. In these eastern stories we find a succession of gods, and the motifs of castration, of swallowing, and of a stone recur in ways which, though varying, show that the resemblance with Hesiod is no coincidence. And we see that while the predecessors of Zeus are shadows whose existence is virtually limited to this myth, in Mesopotamia one city did indeed rise and oust another from supreme power, and in turn give its own god the supreme position in Heaven: so Marduk of Babylon replaced Enlil of Nippur. The myth made sense on a Mesopotamian background as it did not in Greece.

ZEUS BLITZES A GIANT OR TITAN. From the corner of the pediment of the Temple of Artemis on Corcyra (Corfu), early sixth century BC. Apotropaic monsters such as the Gorgon (which figures at the centre of this pediment) or violent scenes of Olympian power such as this, are favourite themes for the decoration of early temples. Later the scenes are more closely related to local cult or history. The giant is here wholly human, Zeus naked as is common with gods and heroes, displaying their power and reflecting Greek acceptance of and pride in nudity.

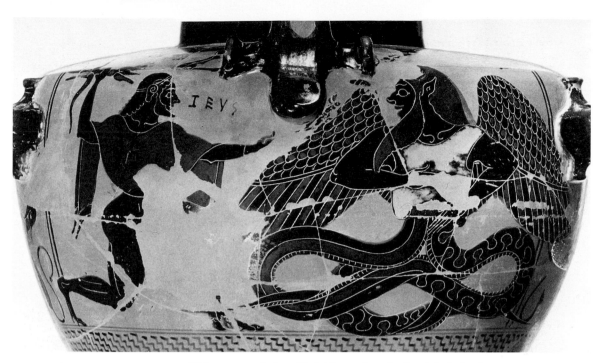

ZEUS BLITZES A MONSTER. This vase, made in a Chalcidian colony in South Italy in about 550–525 BC, shows Zeus attacking with thunderbolt a male monster with wings and snake-legs. Its identity is not certain, but it may be Typhon. In Hesiod this monster has a hundred serpent heads but artists seldom follow literary prescriptions for such creatures, and compound them from various sources, sometimes Near Eastern. Giants are often given snake-legs in later art but seldom wings.

Oriental influence, then, is certain for an important myth in Hesiod. That raises the question of the character of his poems as a whole; for both cosmogonical and what may be called 'wisdom' literature was widespread in the Near East. Apart from Mesopotamia, we find it in Egypt, among the Phoenicians and Canaanites, and of course among the Hebrews. Striking parallels to lines in the *Works and Days* can be found in the Book of Proverbs; Genesis opens with the creation of the world before going on to human genealogies and the origins of the different nations. The early Greeks found themselves in a world which contained ancient and impressive civilizations, which they were not yet ready to dismiss as 'barbarians'. Oriental influence, since the story of Zeus' succession is so firmly embedded in Homer and Hesiod, may well go back to the Mycenaean period.

The *Theogony* does not give any account of the creation of man. It does, however, like Genesis and other legends, imagine that there was a time when man existed, but woman did not. The creation of woman came about in the following way, as a consequence of the peculiarities of Greek sacrificial ritual. Once upon a time the clever Prometheus (a god, not a man: but his actions involve men for ever) tricked Zeus by cunning division of a slaughtered ox. In one pile he put the flesh, making it look meagre and unattractive in the animal's paunch: in the other he put the bones, covering them with a toothsome layer of fat. Zeus, remarking on the unequal division, seized the fat and bones; and that is why, ever since, bones and fat are what the gods get, while men feast on the meat. The original sense of the ritual of sacrifice was not of feeding the gods at all, but of offering them back the bones which are the basic structure of the animal, probably as a magical device to ensure that they in turn would not withhold animals in future from the hunters. Later, an explanation was felt to be necessary for a custom which gave the worshipper all the good bits. The explanation is older than Hesiod, who says:

> Zeus in eternal wisdom knew the trick, was not deceived,
> But planned for men disasters which should never be relieved.
> He seized the white fat with two hands: his wrath was very great
> To see the white bones underneath, Prometheus' clever cheat.
>
> (*Theog.* 550-5)

We see the attempt, quite in Hesiod's manner, to preserve the omniscience of Zeus, although the story clearly assumes that the god was really taken in.

Hesiod develops his story to deal with two other great features of the world: fire and women. In anger at his deception Zeus deprived men of fire, but Prometheus brought it back in a hollow tube. Angered still more, Zeus devised the first woman, the mother of the disastrous race of women, who live with men like drones with bees, parasitic and profligate; yet necessary, if a man is not to be without children to care for his old age. We see the contrast between this peasant misogyny and the tragic clear-sightedness of the *Iliad*, when we compare Achilles' description to Priam of the two jars of good and evil from which Zeus gives to mankind either a mixture of both or unmixed evil: 'So did the gods deal with my father Peleus . . . and you too, old man, we hear were happy once, before the Achaeans came . . .' (*Iliad* 24. 534 ff.), with Hesiod saying that if a man gets a good wife, then he has something to offset the bad; but with a bad one life is unbearable (*Theog.* 607 ff.).

The poem establishes Zeus as ruler, and runs out (the original end is lost) in a catalogue of the offspring of divine and human amours. In the fifth century Herodotus could say of Hesiod and Homer (in that order), 'They it was who composed the theogony for the Greeks, giving the gods their titles and assigning them their honours and their occupations.' To some extent Hesiod was an authority for later Greeks in such matters, but there was no question of universal acceptance. His count of nine Muses did not prevent different people from talking of them as three, four, five, seven, or eight in number; the Hecate of Hesiod is quite different from the goddess we find elsewhere.

The *Works and Days* is evidently a later work. In the *Theogony* Hesiod listed Strife as one of the horrid children of Night; but in the *Works* he has thought further, and now he finds that after all there are two kinds of Strife. One is bad, but a second, characteristically called 'the elder', meaning 'the better', is a healthy spirit of competitiveness, which makes men work. For brother Perses has been

BRONZE WARRIOR FIGHTING A CENTAUR, BOTH HELMETED. Geometric style of the later eighth century BC. The centaur need not be the creature fought by a Heracles or Theseus in later scenes, but a generalized monster of the wild, possibly a giant or Titan. Identities in this early period are not assured.

RELIEF VASE FROM BOEOTIA, of a type made both in Boeotia and the Greek islands in the mid seventh century. PERSEUS BEHEADS THE GORGON MEDUSA. Perseus wears his cap of darkness and magic boots, and carries a small bag in which to carry the head. He looks away since the head literally petrifies. The Gorgon has a horse body because her father was Poseidon, god of horses, and she will give birth to the winged horse Pegasus in her death throes. Later artists do not generally give her a horse's body, but a human one with wings, and a different lion-mask face.

THE DECORATION OF A HANDLE OF THE FRANÇOIS VASE, a large Athenian mixing-bowl (crater), 66 cm high, found in Etruria at Chiusi. It is one of the earliest Athenian vases devoted completely to figure decoration—270 human and animal figures with 121 inscriptions, painted about 570 BC. Artemis is shown here in her early guise as a mistress of animals, and winged, a form which may owe much to the Near East: later her relationship with the animals changes and she is a huntress. The warrior carried from the field of battle is a stock group, with the figures here identified as Ajax with Achilles, as commonly, but not exclusively, on other works.

behaving badly, demanding more than his share of the inheritance and bribing the local 'kings' to adjudge it to him. Instead of that sort of wickedness, he should work:

> Work, Perses, my fine gentleman, that Hunger may keep clear,
> But fair Demeter love you well and fill your barn with cheer.
>
> (299–300)

The poem opens with moral remonstrances, hammered home in every way that Hesiod can think of; it turns into a more or less systematic account of the farmer's year, as far as agriculture and vines go, with miscellaneous precepts and a long excursus on sailing. 'If you are taken by desire for uncomfortable seafaring', says the poet characteristically, '. . . I will tell you the ways of the sea',

HERACLES LEADS CERBERUS to the terrified king Eurystheus, on a vase by a Caeretan painter—an immigrant Ionian working in Etruria in the later sixth century BC.

FLORAL FANTASY with ostrich-riders, wildlife, and a Triton on the neck of the vase, made by an immigrant Ionian in Etruria in about 540 BC.

> Not as a seasoned mariner: I've never been on ship,
> Except indeed from Aulis to Euboea's nearest tip
>
> (649-50)

—a distance of perhaps 100 yards. Thoughts of morality, of right and wrong ways of getting a livelihood, and of the land of which Perses has robbed the poet, gradually crystallize into an account of the farmer's year; which was not what we expected at the beginning.

Perses, the bad brother, appears initially to have cheated Hesiod and to be living on the fat of the land: 'Let us settle the case afresh, with an upright decision' (35). But later on it appears that he is impoverished and scrounging on Hesiod. Strip to sow and strip to plough, says the poet, lest you be forced to go a-begging, 'as now you come to me: but I will give you nothing more' (396). The discrepancy has led some to think that Perses is a fiction, a mere peg to hang the poem on. It is indeed quite regular for works of moral instruction to have a narrative framework. The Book of Ecclesiastes is put into the mouth of a disillusioned old king of Israel; and in other Near Eastern literatures we find a Sumerian work in the form of a father's remonstrance with his prodigal son, Egyptian wisdom texts spoken by viziers or unfairly disgraced priests, and so on. The narrative is evidently meant to catch the reader's attention for the instructions.

But it is not easy to imagine that Hesiod could have travelled the countryside singing a song which accused the local magnates at Ascra of 'devouring bribes' and incurring the vengeance of heaven on the whole community, if everybody knew the case was a fiction. The details about the father, too, seem to be truthful: it is hard to see why Hesiod should have invented that sort of background for himself. So the explanation is probably twofold: the song went on forming and enlarging itself in his mind, so that the situation of Hesiod and his brother could develop and change; and also the changing focus and emphasis of the poem led the poet to make his brother, at moments, fit in with the things he wanted to say.

THE CALYDONIAN BOAR HUNT on the neck of the François Vase (see illustration on p. 88). An epic occasion introducing many important heroic figures. Atalanta (white-skinned, to the left) struck the first blow but Meleager, before the boar, kills it. The Dioscuri, behind it, share a spear.

Another thing Hesiod has continued to think about is the Prometheus myth. In the *Works* he wants a general explanation for the hardness of life and the necessity of work: that, too, is given by the same myth. This time the mood is even gloomier: the Father of gods and men 'laughed aloud' as he promised condign punishment for men (59), and the woman—Pandora is now her name—is not just a calamity in herself, concealing beneath her seductive appearance 'the mind of a bitch and a heart of deceit' (67); she takes the lid off a great jar in which diseases and ills of every sort had hitherto been locked away. So now the world is full of them. 'You cannot make a fool of Zeus' (105). We think of Eve, also saddled with the responsibility for all that is unsatisfactory in the world.

That story, though elliptically told at some points, goes with a swing. It is typical of Hesiod that at the end of it he is temporarily stuck for a way to go on with his poem, and can only say 'Now if you like I'll tell you another story', this time a version of the decline from the Golden Age of lost Paradise, by way of increasingly inferior Silver and Bronze Ages, to the awful Iron Age in which we have the misfortune to live. This is another eastern idea: Hesiod has rudely adapted it to Greek notions about the past by inserting the age of heroes, who could not be left out, between the Bronze Age and our own. The heroes are, as they have to be, 'better and more virtuous' than the berserkers of the Bronze Age, and that spoils the elegant shape of the tale; but Hesiod, we feel, finds it hard to force his thoughts into shape, and he has to accept such inconcinnities.

Also typical of Hesiod is the way in which, in the opening 300 lines of the *Works*, he wavers between addressing Perses and addressing the 'kings'. He has things to say to both. 'I will tell a fable to the kings', says he, and tells of the hawk who caught the nightingale.

> The nightingale wept piteously, but harsh was the reply:
> 'You fool, a stronger has you now; no use to wail and cry.
> You'll come where I shall carry you, for all you sing so sweet;
> And as I choose I'll let you go, or have you for my meat.'
>
> (205 ff.)

Having reached this point, Hesiod tells his brother 'Don't you try to behave violently: a small man can't get away with it'. That suggests the perils of wrong-doing in general, which extend to the whole community; so he addresses the kings, urging them to turn to justice (248 ff.); the eye of Zeus sees everything; then back to Perses—he should forget violence and be mindful of justice. 'For Zeus made it right for fishes and beasts and *birds who fly* to eat each other, for they have no justice; but to men he has given justice . . .' That, as the emphasis on the birds helps to show, is the moral of the fable: the kings have treated me as animals treat each other, without thought of right and wrong. But with the difficulty of managing both his targets, it is Perses in the end who gets the moral meant for the kings.

Some parts of the poem are more closely organized than others. There are passages in which Hesiod slides from thought to thought. 'Be pious and offer sacrifice—invite neighbours to eat of the meat—neighbours are important—invite those who invite you—give to those who give to you—giving is good, violent taking is bad—even in small things—small acquisitions do add up—it's good to build up stores—think ahead—but misplaced economy can be mean—don't stint on wages; trust and mistrust can each be fatal—don't trust a woman—as for having children, one son is best—but Zeus may provide for several and still make you rich—if you want to be rich, here is the Farmer's Year.' That would be a rough summary of the connections of thought from line 336 to line 383. They are there, but you can miss them.

Other passages are poetical in a more ambitious sense. The Prometheus stories in both poems are well told. The battle of gods and Titans, and Zeus' fight with the monster Typhoeus (*Theog.* 674-712, 820-68), aim at the grandiose; more attractive to most readers will be the description of winter (*Works* 504-35), with the wild animals cowering, the old man bent like a hoop by the wind, the young girl staying at home and protecting her beauty, and 'the boneless one gnawing his foot in his fireless house and gloomy lair' (a riddling allusion to the octopus); and of summer, when 'women are lewdest and men are feeblest', but one can enjoy a picnic in the shade of a rock (*Works* 482-96).

The poems are by their nature rather formless, and the end was especially vulnerable to addition. The *Works* peters out into a rather random list of taboos (724-59), then a list of lucky and unlucky days of the month (765-828), after which in antiquity there followed a treatment of bird-omens. It is hard to know how much of this is by Hesiod. The *Theogony* as we have it leads directly into the most important of the other works sometimes ascribed to Hesiod, the long *Catalogue of Women* or *Ehoiae*. We now have very considerable fragments of this poem, which organized the heroic Greek genealogies back to Deucalion and the Flood. It cannot be by Hesiod; for example, it includes the story of Cyrene, but Cyrene was not founded until 630 or so. Some passages are quite picturesque, but as mythical narrative it is no rival to Homer. Its subject-matter was in the fifth century turned into prose by mythical historians like Acusilaus and Phere-cydes. A short epic called the *Shield of Heracles* survives under Hesiod's name; it is a rather lurid production. Of the ten other poems ascribed to Hesiod by one ancient writer or another, none of them perhaps on any substantial grounds, we know too little to say anything significant.

Further Reading

MYTH

H. J. Rose, *A Handbook of Greek Mythology* (London, 1928: 6th edn., paperback, 1958) gives a reliable account of the main mythological stories. The Loeb edition by J. G. Frazer of the ancient mythological compilation known as Apollodorus' *Library* (2 vols., 1921) contains a mass of detailed information about them. A more amusing way of making the acquaintance of these myths is by reading the *Metamorphoses* of Ovid.

G. S. Kirk discusses the particular character of Greek mythology in *The Nature of Greek Myths* (Harmondsworth, 1974); his book *Myth: Its Meaning and Functions in Ancient and Other Cultures* (California, 1970: paperback) deals with the role of myths in different societies and with modern theories on the subject. Both books show a certain dissatisfaction with the 'rational' atmosphere of most Greek myths. M. P. Nilsson showed that many of the myths go back to the Mycenaean period: *The Mycenaean Origin of Greek Mythology* (California, 1932: paperback). C. Lévi-Strauss, in *Anthropologie structurale* (Paris 1958, 1973) and *Mythologiques* (4 vols.: Paris, 1964–71)—available in English as *Structural Anthropology* (Paris, 1972) and *Introduction to a Science of Mythology* (4 vols.; London, 1964–81)—applied a radical structuralist analysis to mythology, primarily that of South America. Structuralist works on Greek myth include M. Detienne, *Les Jardins d'Adonis* (Paris, 1972) (in English, trans. J. Lloyd, *The Gardens of Adonis*, Hassocks, 1977), and *Myth, Religion and Society*, Structuralist Essays edited by R. L. Gordon (Cambridge, 1981: paperback). W. Burkert, *Structure and History in Greek Mythology and Ritual* (California, 1979: paperback) criticizes such views from a standpoint closer to that of the zoological researches of Konrad Lorenz and the new science of ethology.

On the moral implications of myth, see H. Lloyd-Jones, *The Justice of Zeus* (California, 2nd edn. 1984: paperback). Bruno Snell, *The Discovery of the Mind* (Harvard, 1953: paperback), gives an idea of the uses of myth in literature—see especially chs. 2, 4, 5, 12. K. Schefold, *Myth and Legend in Early Greek Art* (London, 1966) discusses the visual arts; J. Seznec, *The Survival of the Pagan Gods* (New York, 1961: paperback) traces the myths through the Middle Ages to the Renaissance.

HESIOD

There is an English translation in the Loeb Classical Library volume (with the Homeric Hymns), and also one by M. L. West (Oxford, World's Classics, 1988). Modern text and commentary of great learning and interest are in the editions by M. L. West of the *Theogony* (Oxford, 1966) and *Works and Days* (Oxford, 1978). The oriental material is discussed in these two books; much of it is conveniently assembled by J. B. Pritchard (editor), *Ancient Near Eastern Texts Relating to the Old Testament* (Princeton: 3rd edn. 1968). A. R. Burn, *The World of Hesiod* (London, 1936), puts the poet in his historical setting. The third chapter of H. Fänkel, *Early Greek Poetry and Philosophy* (Oxford, 1975), is a valuable discussion of Hesiod.

4
Lyric and Elegiac Poetry

EWEN BOWIE

ONLY of hexameter poetry have we examples earlier than 700 BC. But many genres first known to us from the seventh century were certainly thriving long before—that century gives us our first elegiac, iambic, and melic poetry because by then writing was spreading, so that the works of celebrated poets could be recorded as those of their predecessors could not. Of our genres only elegiac significantly exploited those formulaic phrases which both aided the composition and recitation of epic and contributed to its oral preservation. Furthermore much of our poetry was composed with particular audiences and occasions in view, so that incentives to preserve it orally were fewer.

Also different from epic is the prominence given to the personality of the poet or singer. The first person becomes the focus of attention, and 'I' (occasionally 'we') tell of 'my' loves, griefs, hates, and adventures. This has sometimes misled scholars into seeing the seventh century as an efflorescence of individualism. Not only, however, did such poetry exist earlier, but the 'I' of a poem cannot unquestioningly be referred to the person of the singer or poet. As traditional folk-songs and modern popular songs show, 'I'-songs can be sung with feeling by many other than their composers. Rarely do we take such statements as autobiographical; sometimes indeed no composer is known. Hence we should hesitate to use fragments of such poets as Archilochus to ascribe strident self-assertion or to reconstruct biography.

Three more preliminaries. First, although what survives is ascribed to a few dozen figures, the genres exemplified, and many conventional themes and approaches, will have been attempted by hundreds over the Greek world. Most of our poetry was not, like epic, the virtuoso's preserve, but was designed for occasions where amateurs contributed. This is clearest in the tradition about after-dinner singing at Athens: a myrtle branch circulated, and with it the obligation to sing. The songs, Attic *skolia*, were short and simple; and some drew a distinction between these and songs sung by the 'more talented'. This relates to only one city, but much early poetry is designed for similar occasions, and we should not imagine *soirées* at which only one virtuoso sang while other people listened or chatted.

Second, relative importance of text and accompaniment. Melic and elegiac poetry was sung, usually accompanied respectively on the lyre and the *aulos* (an oboe-like wind instrument). For no song can we reconstruct the vocal or instrumental line, and indeed we have only a rudimentary understanding of what it might have been like. In many songs music may have contributed more to initial impact than text, in many more it was an integral part of the effect. Doubtless the texts selected for copying and transmission were those whose words were of greater moment than music: but never forget that, even reading these poems aloud, we gain access only to part of their intended effect, and before impugning deficiency of thought or skill, ponder whether modern song-writers would gladly be judged on 'lyrics' alone.

Third, the work of almost all these poets has survived only in shattered fragments, preserved by later quotation or on papyri recovered from Graeco-Roman Egypt. We have a few dozen elegiac poems arguably complete, but of melic poets other than Pindar and Bacchylides only half a dozen complete songs remain.

Some poets composed in several genres. Since many composed both elegiac and iambic poetry, I treat these genres together. They share numerous themes and stances and were probably intended for similar occasions. They also exhibit clear differences. Elegiac poetry alternates the dactylic hexameter (used line after line for epic) with a 'pentameter' built up from the same metrical unit, the *hemiepes*, giving

$$- \cup\cup - \cup\cup - \cup\cup - \cup\cup - \cup\cup - - \text{ (hexameter).}$$
$$- \cup\cup - \cup\cup - \| - \cup\cup - \cup\cup - \text{ (pentameter).}$$

Like epic, elegiac couplets were sung to an accompaniment, in elegy's case the *aulos*: being a wind instrument, this must have been played by someone other than the singer. Doubtless this relatively formal presentation and a metre accommodating to epic vocabulary invited a certain dignity of tone—neither theme nor language descends to the depths plumbed by iambic poetry. This seems to have been recited, not sung, and its rhythms (commonest the iambic trimeter) readily accepted everyday speech. Occasionally poets combine dactylic and iambic rhythms in a form often (confusingly) called 'epode'.

Archilochus (*c.*650 BC) used all these metres. Traditionally he was the son, albeit bastard, of the leader of the Parian colony to Thasos, and a high place in society is corroborated by some poems' address to Glaucus, also distinguished in Thasos' early history. His elegies were probably sung at *symposia*, post-prandial drinking parties which only wealthier male citizens are likely to have attended. Such men were also in the front line when Thasians fought Thracians or other Greeks, and the treatment of these struggles in some long iambic fragments suggests that Archilochus took them seriously. Serious, too, is a reflective elegy on friends lost at sea and man's need to endure what gods dispose (fr. 13). But he also played on the contrast between war and singing (fr. 1), and a song imitated by Alcaeus, Anacreon, and Horace shows how conviviality encouraged suspension or mockery of normal values:

> My shield delights some Thracian, for I dropped
> the blameless gear, unwilling, in a wood—
> but saved my skin: what is that shield to me?
> Stuff it! I'll get another just as good.

The pithiness and balance of this, perhaps complete, song foreshadow the elegiac metre's later use for epigrams. Some iambic poems were much longer. Themes of fighting and shipwreck may reflect Archilochus' own life, but in fr. 19, opening with a high-minded rejection of kingly wealth and power, the speaker emerges as not Archilochus, but a carpenter, Charon, and in another (fr. 122) a father commenting on his daughter's conduct. Both situations may be invented, but fr. 122 is often linked with Archilochus' supposed affair with Neobule, inferred in antiquity from his poems: when her father Lycambes ended it Archilochus' embittered iambics allegedly drove him and his daughters to suicide. Historical or invented, they figure in several poems, notably a fragmentary epode where the fable of the fox and the eagle warns Lycambes that betrayal doesn't pay. In another, discovered almost complete in 1973, Archilochus tells a male friend of his passion for Neobule's younger sister and how he seduced her in a flowery meadow. His 'reported' words criticize Neobule savagely:

> Let me tell you this. Neobule
> let another man have:
> ah! *she's* gone off—she's twice your age
> and all her young girl's bloom has flowed away
> and the charm she once had.
> (fr. 196A. 24-8)

But her sister's conquest is narrated tenderly and without coarseness:

> These were my words: and 'mid the blooming flowers
> I embraced the young girl
> and laid her down, and with a soft
> cloak covered her, her head clasped in my arms.
> a-trembling with fear
> just like a fawn [   ]
> and gently stroked my hands across her b[   ]s.
> (ibid. 42-8: square brackets mark gaps)

The poem extends Archilochus' known range of themes and tones. The scanty fragments of his near-contemporaries, Tyrtaeus, Callinus, and Mimnermus, who also composed poetry for the *symposion,* hardly suggest similar versatility, but their range may be inadequately reflected in what survives. Our only substantial elegy of Callinus of Ephesus exhorts young men to fight for their country; so too Tyrtaeus' elegies for Sparta, sung (according to fourth-century sources) at banquets during campaigns. Mimnermus of Colophon also sang martial exhortations (fr. 14), but it was songs on love, youth, and age that immortalized him. Tyrtaeus urged a warrior to

> hold his shield fast
> making his own life his enemy, and the black spirits
> of Death as dear to him as the rays of the sun.
> (fr. 11. 6–8)

Mimnermus turned this image to praise of youth and abhorrence of age:

> But we, like the blooms that blossom in the season of many flowers,
>   Spring, when they suddenly shoot, caught by the sun's bright rays—
> like these, for a cubit's length of time the flowers of youth
>   we enjoy, at the hands of the gods knowing not evil days
> nor good. But beside us there stand the black spirits of Death,
>   one of them holding an end in age with its dreadful pain
> and the other in death: but of youth only a short time lives
>   the fruit—for as long as the sun spreads itself over the plain.
> (fr. 2. 1–8)

Such themes suited *symposia*, but disclose little about Mimnermus' society at large. Even in warlike Sparta, after all, where Tyrtaeus demonstrates elegy's popularity, elegies praised drinking; and the Athenian lawgiver Solon's songs enthused over love and the good life (frs. 23, 25, 26). However, Solon's poems also exemplify lengthy treatment of political issues—doubtless common topics in after-dinner conversation, and so not surprising candidates for song in the same setting. A fanciful anecdote has Solon recite in the *agora* a 100-line elegy urging the Athenians to recapture Salamis; but, like other political fragments, this song is simply a particular form of elegy's reflective and exhortatory mode. Another (fr. 13) is our longest early elegy to survive. In its seventy-six lines (probably a complete poem) Solon prays for wealth—but justly acquired, for Zeus punishes evil—shifts to the emptiness of man's hopes, slides into a catalogue of different human activities, then returns to actions' uncertain outcome—uncertain save that greed attracts god-sent ruin. Despite loose construction the poem has power, momentum, and several striking images. Solon's iambics, apparently all political, exploit less poetic vocabulary, but here too is a moving personification of 'Black Earth, greatest mother of the Olympian gods' (fr. 36. 5–6), called to witness how Solon freed her, the soil of Attica, by abolishing serfdom. Note too that in such poems (fr. 33) Solon, like Archilochus, made others speak.

Alone of early elegiac and melic poets Theognis of Megara (*c.*540 BC) has had some poetry transmitted in a continuous manuscript tradition. Less fortunately for him, the 1,400 or so lines there ascribed to him are a mixture of his and others' elegies; and snippets, as naturally in an anthology, outnumber complete songs. Nevertheless the collection is priceless. First, much of Theognis' work is identifiable by being addressed to his boy-friend Cyrnus: we hear a sententious oligarch, bitter at his class's loss of power and distrusting all about him. Some songs are distinguished, notably 237–54 (probably complete), confidently promising Cyrnus poetic immortality, only to conclude:

> And yet I receive from you not even a little respect.
> But, as if I were a small boy, you deceive me with tales.

Secondly, that Theognis' platitudes on friendship, wine, or wealth became the core of a song-book exposes the general level of singing and the preferred themes of *symposia c.* 500 BC. Finally, several passages overlap quotations elsewhere from other elegists, augmenting their known work.

Although some fifth-century pieces survive, by then elegy, like aristocratic *symposia*, is in decline; by the fourth century it is dead. Iambic poetry also disappears, its metres annexed by Attic drama. Even for its acme iambic fragments are too sparse to allow confident reconstruction of the genre. Some poets other than Archilochus and Solon stand out. Semonides, who led a Samian colony to Amorgos *c.*630 BC, composed a witty male-chauvinist piece whose 118 lines compare women unflatteringly with various animals (fr. 7). Bitter invective marks one iambic fragment of Anacreon (fr. 318); another (fr. 335), addressing a reluctant girl as an unbroken filly in an extended *double-entendre*, exhibits the wit that dominates his melic poetry (below, p. 100). But the most colourful exploiter of autobiography and invective was Hipponax of Ephesus (*c.*540 BC). Prayers to Hermes, god of thieves, and sordid orgies with the mistress of the sculptor Bupalus, take us lower in society than Hipponax probably lived. Perhaps he carried Archilochus' mixture of fantasy and reality one stage further, and complete poems might show us an interesting coda to the iambic tradition.

Alongside iambic recitation and *aulos*-accompanied elegy, both composed for individual performance, there flourished singing to the lyre, 'melic' poetry. This was sometimes sung by individuals (like the songs of Sappho and Alcaeus) and sometimes by choirs (like those of Alcman and Pindar). Whereas elegy originated in Ionia and retained features of the Ionic dialect even in Dorian Megara and Sparta, melic poetry was at home everywhere. When individuals sang to the lyre, therefore, their vernacular was used, which aided the directness often praised in archaic monody. Apart from some work-songs, most monody seems, like elegy, to be intended for *symposia* or comparable female gatherings. Such gatherings existed, at least in Lesbos, since it is from Sappho of Lesbos (*c.*600 BC) that some of our masterpieces come.

Sappho's poetic personality is as clear as her life is obscure. The singer is forever in love: Aphrodite's patronage helps her win girls who reject her (fr. 1); for her the love-object outshines anything else mankind admires (fr. 16); desire precipitates complete physical collapse (fr. 31). Love is not simply the centre of Sappho's universe, it *is* her universe. When not creating song around 'her own' feelings she presents herself consoling a girl-friend leaving her in tears:

> 'and honestly I want to die'
> —so sobbing, many times, she left me
>
> and she said this [to me]
> 'My god! what awful things are happening to us:
> Sappho, I swear I am leaving you against my will.'
>
> And I replied to her in these words:
> 'Go with a light heart, and with memories
> of me, for you know how we cherished you.
>
> And if not, then I want to
> remind you [   ]
> [   ] and we had good times
>
> For ma[ny garland]s of violets
> and roses [   ] together
> and [   ] you put on beside me
>
> And many garlands
> woven from flowers about your soft neck
> [   ] fashioned
>
> And with m[uch] myrrh
> from rich flowers [   ]
> and royal you rubbed your skin
>
> And on soft beds
> tender [   ]
> you would satisfy desire [   ]
>
> And there was no [   ] nothing
> holy nor [   ]
> from which [we] kept away
>
> No grove [   ]
> [   ] sound
> [   ]'   (fr. 94)

These lines well illustrate Sappho's simple language and presentation. Recollections of shared pleasures demonstrate that, whatever roles (e.g. music teacher) are alleged on the scanty evidence of certain poems, she claimed that of lover of girls unashamedly and openly. Presumably audiences knew, and might include, her current flame, though in two songs (frs. 1, certainly complete, and 31) Sappho, in declaring love, names no beloved. Girls are named when Sappho's interest is less immediate: Anactoria, whose absence provokes the love-object's exaltation in fr. 16, or Atthis, recalled as a past flame in fr. 49. Atthis' part is different in fr. 96, consoling her for the departure of *her* lover. Solace is drawn from memory of mutual fondness (cf. fr. 94), but also from the lover's beauty:

> now she shines out among the women of Lydia
> as sometimes, when the sun has set,
> the rosy-fingered moon
>
> outshines all the stars: and its light
> spreads over the salt sea
> and alike over the many-flowered fields
>
> and the dew falls fair, and in full
> bloom are the roses ...   (fr. 96. 6–13)

Despite the image's ambiguous relation to the girl it evocatively conveys her beauty: with Sappho's rococo scene of Aphrodite's descent from Olympus (fr. 1) it attests her skill in vivid depiction. Of more formal poetry we have but scraps of wedding songs and thirty-five lines describing Hector and Andromache's wedding (fr. 44)—here myth is narrated not as illustration, but for its own sake.

Alcaeus, her contemporary from Mytilene, deploys the same language and metres on similar themes. Myth figures in hymns, and in two poems is narrated for its own sake. Like most personal poets, Alcaeus sang of love, but the songs most read later are political—one-sided views of aristocratic power-struggles in Mytilene *c.*600 BC. For Alcaeus success—such as one tyrant's overthrow, which evoked 'Now we must get drunk, since Myrsilus is dead' (fr. 332)—was rare and brief. Pittacus, once Alcaeus' ally, himself became tyrant, and his 'betrayal' of Alcaeus prompted his most vigorous poetry. One fragment (129) recalls oaths sworn together and calls upon Zeus, Hera, and Dionysus to succour Alcaeus and his exiled friends while an avenging Erinys pursues Pittacus. Another (130) voices despair at exclusion from the political life enjoyed by his ancestors. Elsewhere he suppresses his political message until another theme has captivated his listeners. Thus a long fragment (298 *Suppl.*) blames Ajax's rape of Cassandra in Athena's temple for the Achaeans' troubles returning from Troy: the rape fills four stanzas, then a storm punishes Ajax with death. This, we now discover, illustrates a community's need to destroy its sinners before gods act, a message presented as relevant to the Mytileneans harbouring the 'sinner' Pittacus. Two other vivid storm scenes, perhaps allegorical (frs. 6, 326), also have political contexts.

Many songs, like that on Myrsilus, take their cue from the drinking central to *symposia*. Like love, this theme can be given many twists. So, trite but apt, fr. 335:

> We should not abandon our hearts to our woes
>   for we gain not a whit by our moping;
> but, Bycchis, the medicine best for our case
>   is to pour out the wine and start toping.

More ingenuity goes into fr. 338 (imitated by Horace) where drink is invoked to combat wintry weather. Naturally summer heatwaves allow the same conclusion (fr. 347).

Wine and love were handled very differently by two poets whose careers crossed about 530 BC at the Samian court of Polycrates. Ibycus of Rhegium presumably became known in Italy and Sicily before attracting Polycrates' hospitality. Anacreon was from nearby Teos, and when Polycrates was murdered he moved to Pisistratid Athens, probably staying on after Hippias' expulsion. Both resort frequently to provocative imagery, often symbolic. But Ibycus' aim in accumulating images of passions seems to be to saturate one's mind by their intense lushness:

> In spring the Cydonian quinces bloom,
> watered from the rivers' streams,
> where lies the maidens' unplucked garden,
> and the vine-blossoms
> thrive, taking their strength
> beneath the vine's shady shoots:
> but my Love rests at no season;
> [but like] the Thracian North Wind
> blazing with lightning
> it darts from the Cyprian goddess
> with wasting frenzies
> dark and fearless
> and all-powerfully shakes
> my heart from its very roots.   (fr. 286)

Anacreon, by contrast, unfolds scenes swiftly, image by image, suddenly imposing a surprising and witty perspective by twists at the end. Thus fr. 358, probably complete:

> Once again his crimson ball
> Love, golden-locked, throws my way
> challenging me to play
> to a gaudy-sandalled lass's call:
>
> But she—from an isle with a touch of class,
> Lesbos—my hair (now turned
> white) has spurned
> and makes eyes at another lass.

Anacreon's songs also differ from Ibycus' in scale. Several of around eight lines look complete, a length typical also of his Hellenistic imitators. Ibycus is more problematic: fr. 286 and another about love could come from short poems, but quotations of mythological details suggest heroic narrative unattested for Anacreon. It may, of course, have served as illustration. Certainly in one forty-five-line fragment (282) Ibycus catalogues Trojan-war episodes and figures he will *not* sing of, using them as a foil to his concluding praise of Polycrates' renown, boldly linked to his own. Often he recalls Stesichorus in metre and language, and clearly stands close to that tradition of heroic narrative which Stesichorus alone represents.

Much about Stesichorus (*c.*560 BC) has become clearer from recent discoveries. His treatment was so expansive that Alexandrian editors gave songs individual papyrus rolls and titles. Thus *Geryoneis*, telling of Heracles' fight with three-bodied Geryon, exceeded 1,800 lines. *Oresteia* in two books must have been longer still. Other features too explain the ancient assessment of Stesichorus as 'most Homeric'. Many phrases evoke, without duplicating, Homeric formulae, and *Geryoneis* shows how Homeric motifs were transposed. At *Iliad* 12. 322 ff. Sarpedon urged Glaucus to fight, since even survivors of the battle would one day die. Geryon adapts this to answer a long speech counselling him not to face Heracles. 'If I am immortal it would be better to [   ]. But if I must grow old among mortals, far nobler now to face my destiny' (*Suppl.* 11). Later, when a poisoned arrow has cleft the last of Geryon's three heads, Stesichorus creates sympathy by developing an Iliadic simile (8. 306-8):

> and then Geryon's neck leaned over
> to one side, as when a poppy
> disfiguring its soft body
> suddenly casts away its leaves
> (*Suppl.* 15 col. ii, 14-17)

Stesichorus' metre, although dactylic, like Homer's, is different in important ways. Units of varying length form a strophe: this is repeated (antistrophe), then follows a shorter system (epode) giving a triadic structure (in *Geryoneis* twenty-six lines) repeated throughout the song. Ancients credited Stesichorus with this structure's invention and classed his songs as choral. This classification has been challenged, and it is disputed whether his songs were sung by choirs or, like Homeric epic, by the poet himself.

Before considering poets whose songs were certainly choral, we note another point that groups Stesichorus with them and not with Homer. Whereas Homer suppresses his personality, choral songs regularly highlight poets' views of life and their creative role. Thus Stesichorus' second *Helen*: his first told the *fable convenue*, but, doubtless eager to exploit a box-office success, he completely changed the story in the second, sending Helen to Egypt and only a phantom to Troy, and explicitly criticized Homer and Hesiod for their mistakes, claiming that his own information came from Helen's angry appearance to him in a dream (frs. 192-3).

Assertion of moral outlook and mythological variants becomes most prominent in Pindar. But already about 600 BC Alcman deployed maxims to point up narration of myth by his chorus of Spartan girls: 'Let none from mankind fly up to heaven' (fr. 1. 16) and, rounding off his myth, 'There is some punishment from gods: but blessed is he who in good heart weaves his day tearless' (fr. 1. 36-9). Fr. 1, once probably 140 lines, is Alcman's only substantial monument. Of its first part only scraps of thirty-five lines surrvive, glimpses of a myth involving sexual violence. The second, largely complete, turns abruptly to praise two girls, apparently chorus leaders: 'but I sing of the light of Agido: I see her like the sun, whom Agido calls to shine as our witness' (fr. 1. 39-43). Brilliant light yields to racehorses as the image compared, then returns with Hagesichora's golden hair and silver face. There follows praise of eight other singers, some merely named, all set clearly below the leaders. The last two systems of the poem, even if complete, would still leave puzzlement about the local deities alluded to and the ceremony being performed (simply a *rite de passage*?) in which girls sing of gods, heroes, and themselves. Puzzling too are innuendos of sexual attraction towards their leaders: 'Nor will you say "May I get Astaphis, and may Philylla look upon me, and Damareta, and desirable Wianthemis"—but it is Hagesichora who wastes me away' (fr. 1. 74-7). These go even further in another choral song enthusiastically praising Astymeloisa's charms (fr. 3).

Songs for girl choruses were still composed by Pindar. But the form which dominates his and Bacchylides' remains is the victory song, commissioned to celebrate competitors' successes at the great Panhellenic festivals. About the lesser poet, Bacchylides of Ceos (active *c*.485-450 BC), we knew little until in 1892 a papyrus yielded twenty poems, many almost complete. Its fourteen victory songs can be confronted with those of Pindar (active *c*.500-446 BC) to reveal common elements of the genre and each poet's individuality. Praise of the patron is naturally prominent—not only his recent victory, but other marks of excellence, including the now enhanced distinction of family and city. Equally mandatory was a myth, found in all but the shortest songs. Its bearing upon the victory varies: it brings victor and audience into the world of gods and heroes, but it can also underline man's limitations and constant risk of grief and pain. To emphasize such messages the poet plays the moral teacher, studding his composition with maxims, and since their worth and that of the whole song depends upon the poet's own distinction, he highlights his part in its creation and his poetic superiority.

In Bacchylides the relation between these elements is clearer and narrative of myth more straightforward than in Pindar. Language flows lucidly, metre is simpler. Aspects of the difference emerge from two songs for the victory of Hiero, tyrant of Syracuse, in the horse race at Olympia in 476 BC.

Bacchylides' *Ode* 5 opens with an address to Hiero, complimenting his literary taste and stating the poet's wish to praise him (1-16). An eagle, unfettered by 'the peaks of the mighty earth or the craggy waves of the tireless sea' (16-30) stands for the poet who has countless ways to praise Hiero (31-6). The horse Pherenicus has won, at Olympia as at Delphi—never yet, the poet swears, has he been defeated. Then a maxim: 'Blessed he to whom god has given a share of fine things, and to live a life of wealth with enviable fortune: for no one among earth-dwellers has been happy in all things' (50-5, cf. Alcman, quoted above). Now the myth: unconquered Heracles, braving the underworld to fetch Cerberus, 'encountered the souls of wretched mortals ... like the leaves that the clear-blowing wind ripples on the sheep-grazed ridges of Ida'. Amazed by Meleager's might, Heracles asks how he died: Meleager tells how the Achaeans at last vanquished the boar sent by a wrathful Artemis to ravage Calydon of the fair choruses, but how then he, embattled over the spoils with his mother's kin, died when she burned the magic log embodying his life (56-154). Then only Heracles wept, saying 'Best for mortals not to be born, nor to see the light of the sun; but since nothing is achieved by lamenting this tale, have you a sister alive whom I might wed?' Meleager names Deianeira; there Bacchylides leaves his myth (175) and we understand that Heracles (to be killed unintentionally by over-loving Deianeira) exemplifies, like Meleager, an unhappy end. Briefly Bacchylides hymns Zeus and Olympia, and, quoting Hesiod, defends unenvious praise of success (176-200).

Pindar opens *Olympian* 1 more obliquely. 'Best is water, and gold shines out like a blazing fire in the night beyond any proud wealth: and if you wish to sing of prizes, dear heart, seek no other bright star that is hotter in the day than the sun in the empty sky, nor shall we name a contest better than Olympia.' Thus Pindar introduces praise of Olympian Zeus for Hiero who 'picking the crown of all the virtues' glories in music (1-17). Pherenicus' renown in the Peloponnese leads to the myth—Poseidon's love for Pelops. Disparaging false tales and insisting that a mortal utter fair things about the gods, Pindar explains Pelops' disappearance as a Ganymede-like visit to an immortal lover, and tales of Tantalus stewing and serving him to the gods as a jealous neighbour's invention (18-51). 'But for me there is no way I could call any of the blessed ones belly-mad. I recoil. Loss has time and again been the portion of ill-speakers' (52-3). Tantalus, however, honoured by the gods, 'could not digest his great prosperity' and blindly stole divine food and drink to entertain his friends: 'if any man hopes to do something without god's notice, he is wrong' (54-64). Pelops, sent back to earth, obtained Poseidon's help in defeating Oenomaus, king at Olympia, in the chariot race required of his daughter's suitors (with certain death if they lost). Here again Pindar silently rejects discreditable stories of sabotage, giving Pelops a noble appeal to Poseidon: 'but for those who must die—who would simmer in vain an inglorious old age sitting in darkness with no portion of all that is fair?' (82-4). By Pelops' marriage, progeny, and tomb Pindar brings us back to Olympia, its contests, victory's lifelong reward, his own song and Hiero's pre-eminent taste and power (90-105). God cares for Hiero, and Pindar expects to praise even sweeter successes. But 'Peer no more into the distance. On this day may you step high, and may I have this commerce with victors, conspicuous for my skill among Greeks worldwide' (114-16).

Although the ingredients, and some images, recur in Pindar's forty-four other victory songs, each is rewardingly diverse, carefully matched to a different patron. Substantial fragments of his *Paeans* (hymns, especially to Apollo) and some of his *Dithyrambs* (associated with Dionysus) show similar complexity of thought and language: we glimpse what we have lost because these genres lack what illuminates victory songs, Pindar's continuous manuscript tradition and Bacchylides' long papyrus. That papyrus indeed contains six 'Dithyrambs'. *Ode* 17, more properly a Paean, narrates Theseus' quarrel with Minos: as in *Ode* 3, direct speech is prominent. *Ode* 18, probably for an Athenian festival, focuses upon Theseus' return to Athens. Its dramatic form is unique: four metrical systems are sung alternately by an unnamed questioner and by Theseus' father, Aegeus.

Transmission has been less generous to Bacchylides' uncle, Simonides of Ceos (active *c.*520–468 BC). Simonides composed in all the genres just mentioned, and probably even pioneered the victory song, yet of his melic poetry we have little. Tradition associated him with Hipparchus in Athens, the Scopads of Thessaly, and the Sicilian tyrants, making him the first to write for money and imputing avarice. In our longest fragment (542) Simonides addressed Scopas, arguing from maxim to maxim with un-Pindaric patience: only god, not man, can achieve a state of virtue; man can only *act* well, when circumstances permit—'I proclaim to you what I have discovered; and I praise and love all those who willingly do nothing shameful; but against necessity not even gods struggle' (26–30). As often, we can only guess at the song's genre and context. Simplicity could also mark his treatment of myth, as emerges from the narrative of Danae and Perseus drifting in their castaway chest: 'If for you the fearful had been fearful', she says to Perseus, 'then indeed to my words would you have turned your tiny ear. But I bid you sleep, my babe, may the sea sleep, and may our boundless trouble sleep; and may some change of heart come from you, father Zeus' (fr. 543. 18–23).

Antiquity admired Simonides' evocation of pathos. This was probably due less to such pieces as fr. 543 or his encomium of Leonidas and the Spartan dead at Thermopylae (fr. 531), than to his epigrams. The poetry hitherto considered was composed for singing or recitation, and certainly to be heard, not read. But from the seventh century dactylic verse—initially hexameters, then hexameters or elegiac couplets—was also used for inscribed dedications and epitaphs. The earliest distinguished poet known to have written these was Simonides. Because his epigrams became famous, many were later ascribed to him that cannot be his: of those that can only a few certainly are, like that on his friend Megistias, vouched for by Herodotus (vii. 228):

> Here famed Megistias is laid, whom once the Mede
> slew at the crossing of Spercheius' flood:
> this prophet clearly saw the Fates' attacking wings
> but did not stoop to leave the Spartan kings.
>
> (*Epigr. gr.* 6)

Possibly Simonidean is a couplet from a statue group commemorating the Athenian tyrannicides:

> Harmodius and Aristogeiton slew
>   Hipparchus, and brought Athens light anew.
>
> *(Epigr. gr.* 1)

But the puzzles that confront scholars in studying archaic literature are epitomized by this couplet's doubtful attribution, and by the fact that an inscribed version from the Athenian *agora* shows that there, at least, another couplet followed this one (previously known from quotation).

A great poet's attention to a written genre heralds a new literary epoch in which prose and poetry were composed to be read, not heard. Religious songs were still composed, although no great names succeed Pindar and Bacchylides. But by the beginning of the fifth century, secular, informal monody was in decline, and by its close the songs sung at *symposia* to *aulos* or lyre were not new compositions, but the heritage of archaic poetry already becoming classics.

Further Reading

Greek texts of the poets discussed in this chapter will be found in the following editions (whose numeration is used in references within the chapter). The elegiac and iambic poets in *Iambi et Elegi Graeci*, ed. M. L. West (Oxford, 1971-2), and in his OCT (which contains all fragments of importance and alone has the new Archilochus, 196A) *Delectus ex Iambis et Elegis Graecis* (1980). The melic poets in *Poetarum Lesbiorum Fragmenta*, edd. E. Lobel and D. L. Page (Oxford, 1955) for Sappho and Alcaeus, and *Poetae Melici Graeci*, ed. D. L. Page (Oxford, 1968) for the remainder—a selection containing all fragments of importance from both editions appears in the OCT *Lyrica Graeca Selecta*, ed. D. L. Page (1968), and more recent fragments in *Supplementum Lyricis Graecis*, ed. D. L. Page (Oxford, 1974). Epigrams in the OCT *Epigrammata Graeca*, ed. D. L. Page (1975).

Greek texts with facing page translations into English are available in the Loeb Classical Library *Greek Lyric*, ed. D. A. Campbell, vol. i *Sappho and Alcaeus* (1981, others forthcoming); this replaces the three-volume *Lyra Graeca*, ed. J. M. Edmonds (Cambridge, Mass./London, 1922-7), which is unreliable as well as outdated, but at present the only edition with translation of early melic poets other than the Lesbians; the iambic and elegiac poets are to be found in J. M. Edmonds's Loeb, *Greek Elegy and Iambus* (Cambridge, Mass./London, 1931). Selections of Greek texts with translation will be found in the *Penguin Book of Greek Verse*, ed. C. A. Trypanis (Harmondsworth, 1971) and in the separate volumes of the *Oxford Book of Greek Verse*, ed. C. M. Bowra (1930) and the *Oxford Book of Greek Verse in Translation*, edd. T. F. Higham and C. M. Bowra (1938).

The best commentary on the poets up to and including Bacchylides is that of D. A. Campbell in his selection *Greek Lyric Poetry* (London, 1967; 2nd edn. Bristol, 1981). For Bacchylides there is now a full commentary in German in the edition by H. Maehler (with German translation, Leiden, 1982); English translation by R. Fagles (New Haven, 1961). A. P. Burnett's *The Art of Bacchylides* (Cambridge, Mass./London, 1985) offers texts and translations of many poems and stimulating though sometimes speculative discussion. Useful, but very dated, literary discussion can be found in C. M. Bowra, *Early Greek Elegists* (Cambridge, Mass., 1935); id., *Greek Lyric Poetry*[2] (Oxford, 1961); G. M. Kirkwood, *Early Greek Monody* (Cornell, 1974); H. Fränkel, *Early Greek Poetry and Philosophy* (Oxford, 1975); and for a more recent conspectus see A. J. Podlecki, *The Early*

Greek Poets and their Themes (Vancouver, 1984). Fundamental points of text, language, genre, and interpretation of the elegiac and iambic poets are discussed by M. L. West, *Studies in Greek Elegy and Iambus* (Berlin, 1974). The most interesting assessment in English of Archilochus is that of A. P. Burnett, *Three Archaic poets. Archilochus, Alcaeus and Sappho* (London, 1983). For the Lesbians D. L. Page's *Sappho and Alcaeus* (Oxford, 1955) remains fundamental, but valuable perspectives can be obtained from Burnett, op. cit., and from the essay by R. H. A. Jenkyns in *Three Classical Poets* (London, 1982; also paperback). For epigrams see the commentary by D. L. Page in *Further Greek Epigrams* (Cambridge, 1981) esp. pp. 186–302 (on Simonides and *Simonidea*).

Pindar is much better served. The best text is the Teubner, edd. B. Snell and H. Maehler, 2 vols. (1971–5); OCT² (1947) by C. M. Bowra. Text with facing English translation in Loeb Classical Library, 2nd edn., ed. J. E. Sandys (Cambridge, Mass./London, 1919). Commentaries on Olympian and Pythian Odes by B. L. Gildersleeve (New York, 1890); on Isthmians by J. B. Bury (London, 1892); on all (with transl.) by L. R. Farnell, 3 vols. (London, 1930–2). Fundamental work for understanding the genre by E. L. Bundy, *Studia Pindarica* i–ii (Berkeley, 1962; Berkeley/Los Angeles, 1987: paperback); carried further by D. C. Young in *Three Odes of Pindar. Mnemosyne Supplement* 9 (Leiden, 1968). A useful introduction to the epinician genre in M. R. Lefkowitz, *The Victory Ode* (Park Ridge, NJ, 1976) and H. Lloyd-Jones, 'Modern Interpretation of Pindar', in *Journ. Hell. Stud.* xciii (1973), 109–37. C. M. Bowra, *Pindar* (Oxford, 1964) is still usable with caution. English translation by F. J. Nisetich (Baltimore, 1980). D. S. Carne-Ross, *Pindar* (New Haven, 1985) offers a good short introduction.

5

Early Greek Philosophy

❦

MARTIN WEST

IN the eighth and seventh centuries BC the Greeks appear as a lively and talented people, active in trade and exploration, endowed with no little skill and individuality in the visual arts, rich in heroic legend, and above all remarkable for a poetry in which a wide range of human experience and feeling was given highly articulate expression. If they had achieved nothing more than that, they would still claim our attention as the most interesting and sympathetic of ancient peoples. In fact they went on to add immensely to that claim. They added to it in many fields: art, literature, mathematics, astronomy, medicine, government, to name half a dozen. But the most significant single addition was perhaps philosophy. Its origins and development make an essential strand in the cultural history of the sixth and fifth centuries.

As in dealing with other aspects of archaic and classical Greek culture, it is important to remember that different towns and regions had their own traditions, and that initiatives taken in one did not necessarily affect others quickly or at all. We must not assume that each philosopher's pronouncements were public knowledge, from one end of the Greek world to the other, as soon as he made them, or that divergent pronouncements by subsequent philosophers were necessarily made in reaction or modification. Early Greek philosophy was not a single vessel which a succession of pilots briefly commanded and tried to steer towards an agreed destination, one tacking one way, the next altering course in the light of his own perceptions. It was more like a flotilla of small craft whose navigators did not all start from the same point or at the same time, nor all aim for the same goal; some went in groups, some were influenced by the movements of others, some travelled out of sight of each other. We run them together as 'philosophers', but they had no generic name for themselves. Philosophy is of course a Greek word—it meant originally something like 'devotion to uncommon knowledge'—but it did not acquire a specialized sense or wide currency until the time of Plato. It is not easy to draw a line between 'philosophers' and others. There were some for whom a philosophical theory, original or borrowed, served as a basis or buttress for something else—a religious or moral diatribe, a dissertation on some aspect of medicine, or an essay on the development of civilization. Some such writers are traditionally included among the philosophers while others are excluded. There were others again, especially poets, who made use of philosophical arguments or theses on occasion but in whose work this was no more than a minor element.

Some examples will help to make clear the variety of the subject. The first 'school' that we can identify is constituted by three sixth-century thinkers from Miletus, one of the principal Ionian towns on the coast of Asia Minor: Thales, Anaximander, and Anaximenes. Thales left no writings to posterity, though Aristotle, who regarded him as the first real philosopher, knew of certain doctrines which were ascribed to him. Presumably he expounded his ideas orally to those of his fellow citizens who were interested in hearing them, and certain of them were recorded as his by some early Ionian writer. In subsequent decades Anaximander and Anaximenes likewise gave discourses (Anaximander is said to have worn splendid clothes, as did later sophists and rhapsodes), and their books, which were among the earliest works written in Greek prose, were the record of their discourses. This Milesian phenomenon of the philosopher who discoursed before an audience and also issued a written account of his opinions presently became a wider Ionian phenomenon. But it may have been some while before readers outnumbered listeners. Heraclitus, about the beginning of the fifth century, refers to people hearing his discourse; and in alluding to other philosophers he does not say 'all those whose books I have read' but 'all those whose discourses I have heard'.

This, then, was one mode of philosophical expression. Less direct ones were employed by Pythagoras of Samos, who seems to have been part philosopher, part priest, and part conjuror. He too is said to have worn imposing costume, to wit a gold coronet, a white robe, and trousers. Instead of discoursing in reasoned prose he appealed to the authority of poems under the name of Orpheus, which he was suspected of having composed or at least doctored. He also bequeathed to his disciples in south Italy a quantity of brief maxims, catechisms, and enigmatic sayings, some expressing old religious taboos, others cosmological or eschatological dogmas. Some of his followers added to these, or composed new Orphic poems embodying a picturesque metaphysics. Others, taking their inspiration from Pythagoras' (probably mystical) interest in number and music, developed the study of mathematics and harmony in a more scientific spirit. 'Pythagoreanism' thus came to cover a strange gamut of different phenomena, and it became difficult to disentangle the master's own ideas and achievements from those of his successors.

There were others in the early fifth century, especially in the western colonies, who regarded poetry as a suitable medium for reasoned argument: Xenophanes, who, like Pythagoras, migrated from Ionia to the west; Parmenides of Elea; Empedocles of Acragas. Empedocles was another who dressed to attract attention, and besides expounding the nature of the world he claimed to impart cures for sickness or old age, and the ability to control wind and rain or raise men from the dead. People followed him in droves, he tells us, adorning him with ribbons and garlands, and asking for oracles and remedies.

Clearly the identification of 'philosophy' is a delicate task. Our primary concern is with the development in Greece of critical and constructive thought about the physical world, the place of gods and souls in it, the relationship between reality and appearance, the origins and nature of human society, and the principles which ought to govern it. But this process was concurrent with, and to some extent implicated in, the spread of untraditional doctrines derived not from pure reason but from oriental myth. The mind that was willing to question conventional assumptions was receptive to novel ideas from abroad; or perhaps the mind that was aware of alternative accounts of things was stimulated to think.

Thales taught that everything is derived from water and that the earth rests on water. Perhaps he was attracted to these tenets, as Aristotle conjectures, 'from seeing that the nutriment of all things contains moisture, and that heat itself comes from this and is sustained by it; and because the seeds of all things have a moist nature, and water is the basis of moisture'. At the same time it is hard to separate Thales' world picture from Egyptian and Semitic creation stories in which the initial state is a waste of waters, now covered over by the earth.

Anaximander taught that the world, and countless other worlds beyond our ken, came into being out of the Boundless and will eventually be absorbed back into it. He gave a detailed account of the stages by which the parts of the cosmos were differentiated, and of their shape and arrangement. What we see as the sun, moon, and stars are really, according to him, great rings of fire, respectively twenty-seven, eighteen, and nine times the diameter of the earth, and encircling it, but each concealed in a tube of mist except for certain holes through which the fire shines out. The earth, a drum-shaped body with its depth a third of its diameter, floats in the middle. The cosmos's existence is an imbalance in the Boundless, an 'injustice', which must in due course be corrected in accordance with an ordinance of Time. All cosmic change, in other words, has its appointed season. The Boundless itself is everlasting and inexhaustible, encompassing and directing all things. Now we may admire the grandeur of this system, and allow that it is in some sense philosophical. Anaximander attempts to explain the visible world as the product of orderly, universal processes, which, he infers, must continually be producing other worlds elsewhere. (As Metrodorus of Chios later remarked, you do not get only one ear of corn growing in a field.) But the system is only to a limited extent deduced from the visible world. Much is postulated that can have no basis in rational inference, and some of it is undoubtedly inspired by Iranian cosmology. The sequence earth-stars-moon-sun is distinctively Iranian, not Greek, and the Boundless that lies beyond the sun corresponds to the Beginningless Lights which are the abode of Ohrmazd and the highest paradise for the Zoroastrian. Ohrmazd created this world with the blessing of the unaging god Time, and a finite duration of 12,000 years has been appointed for it. Thus the 'ordinance of Time' in Anaximander's system was not a creation of his intellect but can be traced to barbarian theology. There, however, it is a single, non-recurrent act of will; Anaximander made it into something resembling a law of nature. This illustrates an important feature of the Greek philosophers' approach. They sought to eliminate the arbitrary events characteristic of mythical narratives; but this did not by any means incline them to eliminate divinity from the world. They preferred to depersonalize their gods and identify them with the unchanging forces that govern the working of the universe.

The third of the Milesians, Anaximenes, goes further in the direction of extrapolating from the visible world to what lies outside it. He holds that it is encompassed not by an undefined Boundless but by air, to which he gives the qualities of Anaximander's Boundless: infinite extent, immortality, and perpetual motion leading to the formation of worlds. Air surrounds and contains the world just as the soul, which also consists of air, holds the body together. All other substances are derived from air by condensation or rarefaction. The earth is flat and thin like a table and supported by air, as in Thales it was supported by water. Vapours rising from it become rarefied and form fiery discs which also float on the air, like leaves, and are the sun, moon, and stars. Among them, invisible to us, move certain solid bodies, probably intended to account for eclipses. It is difficult not to find Anaximenes' system somewhat crude after Anaximander's. Anaximander had made a tremendous imaginative leap forward by reducing the earth to a small body in relation to the cosmos and by dispensing with a material support for it; he apparently thought that equipoise was enough. Anaximenes reverted to more conventional presuppositions. At the same time his is a more economical construct. Nature does not change into something unimaginable at the edge of his cosmos. Everything, inside and outside the cosmos, is based on something we have experience of, air and its transformations. It is in a sense a materialistic cosmology. But Anaximenes does not conceive of his air as an inert substance which needs something else to set it in motion. He regards movement as an intrinsic property of air. It is, as it were, a *live* substance, and the parallel he draws between the cosmic air and the human soul implies an assumption that certainly became general in the fifth century, namely that the soul is not something apart from the material world but a natural part of it. It is tempting to see here an affinity with the Upanishadic doctrine of a universal wind or breath with which both the unchanging life-soul of the world and the individual self are identical, by which living things and worlds are held together, and which the whole universe obeys. Two details in Anaximenes' system which do not suit it very well, the dark bodies that cause eclipses and the notion that the heavenly luminaries circle round a great mountain in the north, seem to be of Iranian provenance.

The Milesians were unable completely to free themselves from the preconceptions of the myth-makers of the pre-philosophical age. Like them, they assumed that something so complex as the present world must have originated from something simple; that the earth is finite in extent and more or less circular, with something different underneath it; that the sky is a physical entity at a definite distance from the earth; that there are immortal sources of energy which are the moving or directing forces in the universe. Their new, philosophical assumptions were that these forces operate in a perfectly consistent way that can be observed in everyday phenomena; that everything can thus be explained from the working of a few universal processes in a single original continuum; and that there is no such thing as creation from nothing or decay to nothing, only change of substance. They tried to account systematically for all the most notable features of the world about us: the movements of the heavenly bodies, phases of the moon, eclipses; lightning, thunder, rain, snow, hail, rainbows, earthquakes, the annual inundation of the Nile.

One thinker who did succeed in breaking right away from conventional world models was Xenophanes. His independence of mind took him in a direction so contrary to the truth that he gets little but derision from modern writers; yet no one else so ruthlessly followed the rule of measuring the unseen by the seen. What he saw was earth stretching in all directions, with empty air above it. He accordingly declared that the earth was of infinite length, breadth, and depth, and that the air extended infinitely upwards. The disappearance of the sun and other luminaries beyond the western horizon he explained as an optical illusion: they were really continuing in a straight line, just getting further away. The sun that arrives in the east the next morning is a different one. There are, moreover, other suns and moons moving on parallel tracks over other regions of the earth, because the rising vapours form clouds which become incandescent, and this happens with strict regularity.

His theology also was radical, without being so eccentric. He was certainly not the first to reject the idea of gods having human shape or behaving as immorally as they do in Homer, but it was he who pointed out that the Thracians represent the gods as like Thracians, the Negroes as negroid, and if cows and horses had hands they would no doubt depict their gods as cows and horses. The late sixth to the early fifth century was a time when the Greeks were developing a particular interest in the beliefs and customs of other nations. As Xenophanes' argument illustrates, the effect was to make them aware how much their own beliefs and customs were based on mere convention, which might profitably be challenged. Xenophanes' god is equally suitable for Thracians or cows. He does not have eyes or ears: every part of him is sentient. He does not go about from place to place but stays still, effortlessly moving everything else by the power of his thought.

Heraclitus, who wrote in a particularly haughty and oracular manner, and was unusual among the early philosophers in criticizing others by name, castigated Xenophanes as one of several notable men to whom learning had not taught sense. Yet he shared some concepts with him, including that of a unique divine intelligence which governs everything. Both men accepted the existence of other gods, but looked for an overriding master purpose. Heraclitus said that the Intelligence 'does and does not want to be called Zeus'. This, he is saying, is what your 'Zeus' really is, but it is an inadequate name. He also speaks of the thunderbolt, Zeus' traditional weapon, as directing all things. He holds the cosmos to have always existed, and to be a fire which is never extinguished, though not all parts of it are alight at once. The parts that are not alight exist as other substances, convertible with fire at a measured rate, as goods are for money. So he finds unity in the apparent diversity of the world by regarding everything as participating in one great continuous process—a conception which a few centuries later was to form the basis of Stoic cosmology. This process is controlled by divine agents of justice, and perhaps given direction and momentum by the thunderbolt. It is characterized as 'strife' or 'war', because Heraclitus sees the continuance of the cosmos as dependent upon the sustained differentiation of opposites. But because of the underlying unity, apparent opposites are really aspects of the same thing. Heraclitus collected many quite dissimilar examples to illustrate this paradox. Hot and cold, wet and dry, living and dead, are not irreconcilable opposites, since things pass from one state to the other. The road up is the same as the road down. Sea water is simultaneously drinkable (for fish) and undrinkable (for men). A monkey may be at once handsome (by monkey standards) and ugly. In one extraordinary fragment Heraclitus identifies day and night, summer and winter, war and peace, famine and abundance, as different manifestations of God.

He did not offer answers to all the cosmological questions which exercised the Milesians—he had nothing to say, for example, about the shape or support of the earth, or what there was outside the cosmos—and there is reason to think that what lay at the centre of his interest was rather religion, morality, and the destiny of the soul. The cosmic stock exchange, however, is the setting in which this is seen. Souls die by turning into water, which dies in its turn by becoming earth; they thus participate in the cyclic transformation of elements which, starting from fire, continues throughout the world. To preserve one's soul one must keep it dry, especially by avoiding alcoholic and sexual indulgence. At death, according to a plausible reconstruction of Heraclitus' theory, souls rise into the air, the damper ones to the level of the moon, where they contribute to winter, night, and rain, drier ones to the purer region of the sun and stars; some particularly favoured ones become the watchers of living and dead that men call heroes. The cosmos is crowded with spirits. There is, moreover, a Great Year of 360 human generations in which the balance swings between the dominance of damp and bright—a concept which was to be developed further by Plato and the Stoics.

Heraclitus could not have arrived at such a system by pure reason, and it has many points of contact with Zoroastrianism and with the Upanishads. In the latter, souls which fail to pass the moon return to earth as rain and are reincarnated in whatever animal form is appropriate to their conduct in their last life.

The doctrine of reincarnation is not attested for Heraclitus, but it had gained a foothold in Greece in the mid sixth century, a century or so later than in India. Pythagoras believed in it, and it was taken up by Empedocles, who denounced the killing and eating of animals as murder and cannibalism, and implored men to abandon it.

Like Heraclitus, Empedocles endeavoured to integrate his teaching about the fortunes of the soul in a general theory of cosmology involving cyclical changes over vast periods of time. Everything in the world is produced by the mixture and separation of four elements, earth, air, fire, and water, which Empedocles identifies with certain of the traditional gods. Xenophanes, as we saw, rejected Homer's gods, so much prey to love and strife. At about the same period one Theagenes from Rhegium developed a line of defence that was to remain popular into the Middle Ages, interpreting the Homeric deities as allegories of the physical world. What Empedocles is doing is akin to this. He elevates the gods' love and strife into a pair of supreme powers who rule in regular alternation by the terms of a treaty. When Love's power is absolute, the divine elements are completely blended into a featureless, homogeneous sphere. As Strife gradually makes its way in, they begin to separate and form a cosmos. Eventually they will be four separate masses, a ball of pure earth in the centre with successive spheres of water, fire, and air surrounding it. We can see that the universe is on the way towards that state. Subsequently the reverse process will operate until the cycle is completed. Empedocles went into much ingenious detail in explaining astronomical and meteorological phenomena and the evolution and physiology of living creatures. He apparently found room for gods within the cosmos other than the elements themselves. They are presumably entities of a fiery nature. When one of them yields to the influence of Strife, he is torn away from the company of his fellows and forced to consort with the other elements for myriads of years, a soul going through countless animal and plant lives.

Empedocles has turned away from the idea held by some Ionians that one original substance can change into others. To account for the diversity of substances in the world he finds it necessary to postulate a set of contrasted primary elements which can be combined in countless ways. This pluralist approach was taken to an extreme by Anaxagoras, an Ionian who taught at Athens for many years in the mid fifth century. Like Empedocles, only without his cyclicalism, Anaxagoras begins his cosmogony from a state of perfect mixture which is then unbalanced by the operation of a divine force. But there is no limit to the number of ingredients in the mixture, and the separation process is never absolute. There always remains a proportion of every substance in everything; we name each thing according to what predominates in it, as if it were composed purely of that substance. This is why whatever Miss T. eats turns into Miss T. It always contained flesh (even the vegetables), and when she eats it a material rearrangement takes place making flesh the dominant constituent. The only thing not mixed with everything else, and therefore able to control everything else, is the finest and purest of all: Mind. This is the divine force that gives the cosmos its initial impulse and supervises the whole process of creative separation.

Socrates, according to Plato, read Anaxagoras' book and was disappointed that he still made so much use of mechanistic explanations instead of making Mind shape each detail of the world for an intelligent reason. Anaxagoras seems here to have fallen between two stools: the Milesian desire to explain the world as the natural product of certain given processes, and a new inclination (perhaps implicit in Xenophanes and Heraclitus) to see it as planned. Diogenes of Apollonia, a somewhat younger man who began his book on human physiology with a cosmology, argues explicitly that the balanced arrangement of the seasons, among other things, must be the work of intelligence. He identifies this divine intelligence with the material element air, which, like Anaximenes, he regards as the single substance from which all others are derived. Everything that breathes air partakes of intelligence.

A sense of proportionate arrangement, whether imposed by a divine Mind or resulting automatically from natural processes, had been a feature of cosmological thought since Anaximander. The discovery that simple mathematical ratios underlie the fundamental musical concords led some Pythagoreans to focus on number as the essence of the universe. One of them (perhaps Philolaus) formulated a theory according to which numbers are generated from an initial One as it 'breathes in' a portion of the adjacent infinity; this portion becomes finite and at the same time divides the one into two. The evolution of the cosmos from a primordial unity is simply an example of this process. Things are numbers, and their relationships (justice, for instance) are mathematical relationships. Aristotle's allusions to the theory hardly allow us to grasp its meaning, and he was doubtless justified in complaining that it left all sorts of questions unanswered. But it is regrettable that we do not understand more about a doctrine which threw the universe into such a novel perspective.

The thinkers so far discussed accepted that the material world is on the whole (allowing for certain misinterpretations on our part) as our senses represent it to us. Meanwhile Parmenides, at the beginning of the fifth century, had struck out along a path of logical reasoning about Being which threatened to undermine that assumption. To put the argument in a nutshell: only Being can exist; there can be no coming-to-be or passing-away, because they imply non-being; no gap or discontinuity in Being; no movement, for lack of space (=non-being); not even any qualitative change, for that would mean the not-being of what had been. *Ergo*, reality consists simply of indivisible, changeless, featureless, motionless, rock-solid Being. The whole phenomenal world with its colour, movement and impermanence must be a sham. It is of course a sham with a pattern, and Parmenides feels obliged to offer an account of it, while emphasizing that he is analysing an illusion or *fable convenue*. He reduces its diversity to a basic duality of light and dark, each of which subsumes a range of other qualities. He claims that this is the best analysis attainable by man, but, being unable to reconcile it with his account of the nature of Being, he has to say that it is ultimately false.

Parmenides' reasoning, though brilliant, is at the same time so artificial that we may suspect his conclusion of being preconceived, particularly as his vision of Being shows resemblances to a certain type of mystical experience in which space and time seem to lose all significance and there is an acute sense of the unbroken unity of all things with each other and with the self. He actually presents his philosophy as derived from a private divine revelation. But nothing is more significant of the intellectual climate in which he lives than the fact that he does not say 'the goddess showed me, and I saw', but 'the goddess proved it with the following arguments'. He is concerned to rationalize his vision.

Parmenides had two followers. Zeno also came from Elea, Melissus from Samos; by convention the three are collectively called the Eleatics. Zeno reinforced the case against plurality and motion with arguments and paradoxes of a mathematical nature, including the famous paradox of Achilles and the tortoise: Achilles can never overtake the tortoise because every time he reaches the point where it was, it has moved on. Melissus went beyond Parmenides in arguing that Being is infinite in extent (Parmenides had made it finite and spherical) and that it is incorporeal, because otherwise it would have parts, implying plurality. The divorce between the philosopher's 'reality' and the world of experience could not be made more complete.

Eleaticism was in one sense a dead end. But the concept of an unchanging reality beyond the material world endured in, and because of, Plato; and a passage in which Melissus argues that if there were after all a plurality of things, they would all have to be as unchanging as his One, points the way to the greatest inspiration of ancient physical theory, the atomism of Leucippus of Miletus. Leucippus follows the Ionian tradition for the general shape of his cosmos, and contradicts the central axiom of the Eleatics by asserting that Non-being (empty space) exists just as much as Being. But he reduces matter to minute particles which resemble the Eleatic One in being indivisible (*atoma*), indestructible, and qualitatively neutral; they differ from one another only in shape and orientation. Different rearrangements of them produce the effect of changeable qualities such as colour, heat, hardness, etc. There is no guiding intelligence, just the blind mechanical interplay of flying and colliding atoms.

The atomist system was appropriated by the prolific writer Democritus, perhaps to serve as the background to his account of the origin and development of civilization. This became a popular subject of theorizing in the mid fifth century. It quickly came to be common ground that primitive man was merely an animal, sheltering in caves and eating whatever grew wild, until gradually he developed his skills, built houses and cities, tamed animals, invented language, and so on. Socrates' teacher Archelaus gave an account (prefaced by a cosmology on Anaxagorean lines) designed to bring out the conventional nature of law and justice. The most influential of these reconstructions of prehistory may have been due to Protagoras, whose several visits to Athens (like Democritus, he was a native of

Abdera) attracted much attention. Protagoras stands at the head of that series of intellectuals whose discourses on a range of philosophical and technical subjects seemed so instructive that they were able to charge attendance fees, and who are called Sophists. They offered, among other things, stimulating reflections on the theme of nature versus custom, the bases of morality, the power of education; scientific treatment of subjects like grammar, metre, music; not least, displays of the adaptability of argument to support any conclusion, or either of two opposite conclusions. At this point we can no longer take it for granted that what appears to be a philosophical argument is meant seriously. Gorgias, an orator and essayist from Sicily notorious for his euphuistic style, published a lengthy proof that nothing exists. He was, no doubt, simply enjoying himself, as when he devoted another work to the defence of the infamous Helen of Troy, describing it as 'an encomium for Helen and amusement for me'. Socrates had some of this playfulness.

The early philosophers were aware that they were seeking answers to questions that lay beyond the bounds of possible human knowledge. 'No one has ever known or ever will know for sure,' says Xenophanes, 'for even if what he says is exactly right, he does not *know* it is—it is all a matter of opinion.' It was something of a commonplace that our senses are weak and easily misled, but that we must extrapolate from the observed to the unobservable. The Greeks were not as quick as they might have been to draw the inference that an accumulation of systematic scientific observation is desirable, though we do see something of the sort in the fifth century in the field of medicine. Some real ground was gained, though gradually, by astronomy. About 500 BC it was realized that the moon shines by reflected light, while by 400 the view that the earth is spherical was gaining adherents, and the planets had perhaps all been identified. In other areas unverifiability precluded consolidation. Atomism remained one theory among many. There was no agreement on which facts to extrapolate from. One seized on one physical phenomenon or logical formula as the key to the universe, another on another. What provokes admiration is the mental vigour and independence with which these people sought after coherent systems and did not shrink from following their lines of thought to astonishing conclusions. It may well be that contact with oriental cosmology and theology helped to liberate their imagination; it certainly gave them many suggestive ideas. But they taught themselves to reason. Philosophy as we understand it is a Greek creation.

Further Reading

The best introduction is E. Hussey, *The Presocratics* (London, 1972); while assuming no knowledge of Greek, it maintains close contact with the primary sources. A. Wedberg, *A History of Philosophy*, I *Antiquity and the Middle Ages* (Oxford, 1982), is very concise but lucid and well judged. G. S. Kirk and J. E. Raven, *The Presocratic Philosophers* (2nd edn. with M. Schofield, Cambridge, 1983), give a good selection of texts with translations and critical discussion. Translations are also available in J. Burnet, *Early Greek Philosophy* (4th edn, London, 1930) and in Kathleen Freeman's *Ancilla to the Presocratic Philosophers* (Oxford, 1948).

On an ampler scale are W. K. C. Guthrie, *A History of Greek Philosophy* (Cambridge, 1962–81; the first three of the six volumes cover the pre-Platonic period), and J. Barnes, *The Presocratic Philosophers* (London, 1979, 2 vols.). Guthrie is comprehensive and safe; Barnes is dense and dazzling, concentrating on philosophical interpretation.

The following are concerned with particular aspects of the subject: G. E. R. Lloyd, *Polarity and Analogy* (Cambridge, 1966: discusses in depth two of the main types of argument and explanation used by early Greek thinkers); W. Jaeger, *The Theology of the Early Greek Philosophers* (Oxford, 1947); D. R. Dicks, *Early Greek Astronomy to Aristotle* (London, 1970). Knowledge of Greek is required for C. H. Kahn, *Anaximander and the Origins of Greek Cosmology* (New York, 1960: wider in scope than its title suggests), and M. L. West, *Early Greek Philosophy and the Orient* (Oxford, 1971).

Useful collections of important, mostly rather specialized articles have been published in book form by D. J. Furley and R. E. Allen, *Studies in Presocratic Philosophy* (London, 1970–5, 2 vols.), and by A. P. D. Mourelatos, *The Pre-Socratics* (New York, 1974).

6

Greece: The History of the Classical Period

❧❧❧

SIMON HORNBLOWER

Outline of Events (479–431)

THE Athenians founded a naval empire in 478, thus replacing the Spartans as leaders of Greece. Their power expanded in the 470s and 460s, as they took the offensive against the Persians, the recent invaders of Greece. The climax of this offensive was reached in the early 460s when the Athenian commander Cimon won a battle in Pamphylia in southern Asia Minor, the battle of the Eurymedon. The suppression of a revolt from Athens by the northern Aegean island of Thasos in the mid 460s was another landmark: it led to a deterioration in relations with Sparta and her league, the Peloponnesian League. From *c*.460 to 446 a war, the so-called First Peloponnesian War, was fought between Athens and the Peloponnesian League; in the early phases of this war Corinth, not Sparta, was more obviously to the front in the fighting, though the Spartans did invade Attica in the last year of the war. Corinth's uncharacteristic hostility towards Athens was the result of the adhesion to Athens of Megara, the small state which separated Athens from Corinth geographically, but hatred of which had united Athens and Corinth politically up to now. In the 450s Athens, despite the warfare on her hands in Greece, fought in support of anti-Persian rebels in Egypt (a revolt which failed disastrously and cost many Athenian lives) and opened diplomacy with communities in Sicily. Formal hostilities with Persia ended in about 449 with the Peace of Callias. The settlement in 446 of the First Peloponnesian War recognized the existence of the Athenian Naval Empire and was thus a victory for Athens, although she had to abandon the mainland Greek territories which she had acquired in fighting, notably Boeotia. Athens was now free to expand to the north, where in 437 she fulfilled an old dream by establishing a settlement at the timber-rich site of Amphipolis; to the east, where she imposed her authority more firmly on Samos, which had revolted unsuccessfully in 440/39; and to the west, where she made a series of alliances, perhaps hoping for uninterrupted

THE ERECHTHEUM ON THE ACROPOLIS AT ATHENS. An unusual, asymmetrical building of the Ionic order, which housed the cults which were once served in the Archaic Temple of Athena. This had been burned by the Persians in 480 BC: its foundations lie in the foreground and were perhaps left exposed as a memorial to the Persian attack. The Caryatid porch, with statues of girls supporting the roof, overlaps these foundations; the porch itself is accessible only from within the building. The Erechtheum was built just after the Parthenon, and completed in the last years of the Peloponnesian War. It is the most sophisticated application of the Ionic order to any Classical building and elements of it—the Caryatid porch and the columns of the north porch—were often copied in antiquity and in nineteenth-century Europe.

supplies of the timber which she needed for her navy. This western and northern expansion, combined with renewed aggression against Megara, reawakened the suspicions of Corinth in the 430s, for Corinth had traditional ties with her colonies in Northern Greece and in Sicily. The result was the Second or Great Peloponnesian War of 431-404, which Athens lost.

The historian of this war, Thucydides of Athens, makes the great leader Pericles say that Athens will be remembered for having ruled more Greeks than any

THE ENTRANCE TO THE ACROPOLIS AT ATHENS SEEN FROM THE HILL OF THE AREOPAGUS. The small, late-fifth-century BC Temple of Athena Nike (Athena Victory) stands clear on a bastion beside the entrance, to the right. The dominant outline is of the Classical entrance-way, the Propylaea, which housed a picture gallery; but from this view the bulk and sheer sides of the rock demonstrate well the Acropolis' original role as a citadel.

other Greek state. Thucydides (or Pericles) was wrong; it is only specialist ancient historians who know about Athenian imperialism, but everybody has heard of the Parthenon, and of Greek tragedy. We ought rather to say Athenian tragedy, because Aeschylus, Sophocles, and Euripides were all Athenians. Specifically, the treatment by those tragedians of a handful of myths continues to provide the direct inspiration for modern thinkers (such as Freud), dramatists (Brecht, Anouilh), and novelists (Thomas Mann's *Death in Venice* is a variant on Euripides' *Bacchae*). These are the achievements which justify the intensive study to which ancient Greek culture, and especially its literature, have been exposed since the Renaissance. Thucydides was not alone in the lopsidedness of his judgement: Aeschylus wrote his own verse epitaph, boasting of his military service in the Persian Wars, and neglecting to mention that he was a playwright; Socrates, the great teacher and philosopher, features in the contemporary histories only for the stand he took over a piece of purely political injustice. It is even possible that Sophocles' Oedipus, a legendary king of Thebes, is meant as a portrait of imperial Athens: quickwitted, meddlesome, and doomed because of those precise elements in his greatness. An audacious anachronism.

But we should not be lopsided in the other direction, and neglect the military and political successes which underwrote fifth-century culture. First, it was the

AN OIL VASE (*lekythos*) made for an Athenian burial by the Achilles Painter in about 450–440 BC, showing a muse on Mount Helicon. The figures on these vases must resemble those of contemporary and earlier (Polygnotan) wall-paintings.

STATUE OF A GIRL (*korē*) dedicated on the Athenian Acropolis about 520–510 BC. Probably Ionian (Chian) work.

THE TEMPLE OF HEPHAESTUS IN ATHENS, SEEN FROM THE SOUTH-WEST. This is the best preserved of all Doric temples of mainland Greece; it owes its survival to its conversion to a Christian church. It was completed while the Parthenon was being built, in the third quarter of the fifth century BC, and dedicated to Hephaestus with Athena, as joint patrons of crafts in Athens. It overlooks the Agora, which lies to its south-east.

Persian Wars which, by worsening the political atmosphere in Ionia, filled Athens with a diaspora of intellectuals such as Hippodamus of Miletus who replanned the Piraeus, the harbour town of Athens; and Anaxagoras, the philosopher friend of Pericles. But above all, aristocrats such as Cimon and Pericles, by their political and military leadership, brought in the public wealth which subsidized the buildings and sculptures of Phidias, Ictinus, and Mnesicles on the Acropolis; and, by making available their private wealth for public purposes, they financed the festivals and dramatic productions which gave classical Athens its attractive power. (This was the liturgy system, a tax on the rich which conferred prestige when taken beyond what was obligatory.) Pericles' first known act was to pay for Aeschylus' great historical opera, the *Persae*. We know this not from Thucydides, who idealized Pericles, but from a list carved on stone. Such lists are the raw material of the present chapter, which is political and military. We should not forget that such evidence can help the literary student.

Empire: Athens and the Alternatives

'Shared blood, shared language, shared religion, and shared customs.' These, according to Herodotus, were the ingredients of *to hellēnikon*, 'Greekness'. This definition of nationality, which would not disgrace a modern anthropologist, proves that by the middle of the fifth century some Greeks recognized what they had in common. That common feeling had been most strengthened by the menace of the common enemy, Persia, in the wars of 499-479. However, the Greeks of the classical period never managed to translate their psychological awareness of their 'Greekness' into political unity. The history of the classical Greek city-states is a history of failure to achieve unity: Sparta would not, and Athens could not, impose it indefinitely by force as Macedon and Rome were to do. There is a way of achieving unity without force, namely by federalism, and this method was experimented with in the fourth century by a third great Greek power, Boeotian Thebes, which in the time of Epaminondas (below, pp. 143 f.) exported federalism beyond the frontiers of Boeotia (but not without a compulsion which was fatal to Theban popularity). The classical Greek cities valued their independent traditions too highly to be prepared to subordinate themselves to a system in which their vote would be one among several. (The Athenians and Spartans both found ways of controlling decision-making within their leagues so effectively that they might better not be called leagues at all.) We call this attitude 'valuing independence'; a candid Greek might have called it *phthonos*, envy. It is above all the *phthonos* felt by Sparta for Athens which determines the course of fifth-century Greek history. Unwilling, for reasons we shall discuss, to lead the Greek world herself, Sparta (or rather, some Spartans, some of the time) could not bear to see Athens do the job instead: the 'dog in the manger' is in origin a Greek story, one of the fables of Aesop. As Arrian makes the Spartans say at the beginning of Alexander the Great's reign, Sparta traditionally leads, she does not follow.

Greece, and especially the east-Greek islands still threatened by the Persians, needed a leader in 478. There were not many candidates. Sparta was the most obvious, because in the recent fighting she had led the Greek League against Persia, a temporary coalition distinct from any so far mentioned. Sparta was certainly unwilling to let Athens lead: the rebuilding of Athens' walls—a precondition of any active foreign policy—drew a protest from Sparta in the form of a delegation, which was nullified only by the wit of Themistocles. More positively, Sparta can be detected in pursuit of expansionist goals in the period after 479, but by land (in central Greece) rather than at sea, an element on which she had little experience. Thus her king Leotychidas intervened in Thessaly, resuming a line of policy begun, perhaps, by King Cleomenes I in the late sixth century. This interest in Thessaly on the part of Sparta and her rivals, including fourth-century Thebes and Macedon, will run right through our period; and it is worth noticing here what Thessaly had to offer. Thessaly was agriculturally rich and thus able to support horses on a scale well beyond what most Greek states could afford. So cavalry was the first of Thessaly's advantages. The second was her advantage of position, athwart the main land route to Macedon and Thrace, places to which Greeks looked for grain and ship-building timber; a stranglehold on eastern Thrace and the Hellespontine region would have an additional economic attraction: control of the Hellespont meant control of grain shipments from another main source of supply, namely south Russia (via the Black Sea). It was important for Athens to keep this supply line open, as it was for her enemies to close it. The third advantage of Thessaly was its excellent harbour at Pagasae (modern Volos), the best in central Greece. Finally, Thessaly controlled a majority of votes in, and traditionally supplied the president of, the Delphic amphictyony, the international panel which controlled the affairs of the shrine of Apollo at Delphi, seat of the most famous oracle in the ancient world. It was the amphictyony that declared the 'Sacred Wars', which throughout Greek history—there were no less than four between 600 and 336—were a device for mobilizing Greek opinion and Greek military forces against some real or alleged sinner. Control of the amphictyony thus had enormous propaganda and political value. Spartan interest in the amphictyony is specifically attested for the 470s, when she tried to get Persian sympathizers voted off the panel, thus strengthening her own hold; as with the attempt to prevent the rebuilding of Athens' walls, it was Themistocles who stopped this.

Nevertheless Sparta did pass up the hegemony after 478 and for the next fifty odd years (in Greek the *pentekontaëtia* of 479-431) was content, or obliged, to let Athenian power grow. Only on three occasions did Sparta stir against Athens: in 465 she promised, but in the event failed, to invade Attica as a way of relieving the pressure which Athens was applying to the wealthy island of Thasos; in 446, near the end of the First Peloponnesian War, the Spartan king Pleistoanax did invade Attica, but then withdrew; and in 440 Sparta voted to go to war with Athens who was disciplining another powerful subject ally, Samos. But again this did not come to anything because Sparta allowed herself to be outvoted by her allies at a second meeting, of her whole league. These three occasions have a common feature: Sparta ultimately draws back, just as she had drawn back after 478. If Sparta was an imperialist she was a singularly reluctant one.

The reasons for this reluctance lie in her domestic difficulties. Like all Greek states, Sparta had a population of slaves, but her slave problem was unique both because of the sheer numbers involved and because most of them, the helots, who approximated more closely to medieval serfs than to chattel slaves of an ordinary Greek type, were of one single nationality, Messenians. Because these Messenian helots all spoke Greek (unlike, for instance, Athens' slaves who were a wide racial mix and had no common language in which to articulate discontent), and had a national self-consciousness, they posed special problems of security for their Spartan masters, whose own numbers were constantly on the decline. Apart from the helots, a second set of domestic difficulties faced Sparta after 478, difficulties which had to do with the Peloponnesian League. There is evidence of serious unrest in one area in particular during the 470s and 460s, namely Arcadia, north of Sparta. There were several reasons for this. First, the Peloponnesian League had been called into existence in the first place by fear of

Argos; but Argos was now in low water as a result of her defeat by Cleomenes of Sparta in 494. The Arcadians may thus have felt that the league now lacked a justification. Second, Cleomenes' own suppression by the Spartan authorities may have caused disaffection among the Arcadians, whom he seems to have singled out with promises of a personal relationship with himself, perhaps involving lighter control. Third, there is the unsettling effect of Athenian democracy, which had, in the years after its establishment by Cleisthenes in 507, shown itself to be militarily capable as well as politically attractive: it was now no longer necessary for the Greek cities of the second rank to choose between tyranny on the one hand and Spartan-sponsored oligarchy on the other. A third possibility now existed, namely imitation of, or affiliation to, democratic Athens. It is likely that this possibility was made concrete by the presence in the Peloponnese of Themistocles in the late 470s and early in the 460s. Though he had fallen from favour in Athens, he continued to oppose Spartan interests on Sparta's own doorstep, by encouraging democrats in Arcadia and Argos.

So much for Sparta, and the domestic reasons which ruled her out as permanent leader. An additional worry, which may have been felt by her or her would-be supporters, was perhaps the thought that Sparta had little experience of naval warfare, or of overseas empire.

In this she was unlike Corinth. Corinth did have a naval tradition, and she had experience of administering distant colonial possessions, places like her colonies in north-west Greece, for instance Ambracia or in the northern Aegean, but Corinth had been too close to Sparta for too long to be able to contemplate defying or superseding her; and from the point of view of the other Greek states she lacked the ideological magnetism exerted by Athens or by Sparta, whose *agōgē* (military training and discipline) was not just an effective repressive device, but was thought of in many quarters as somehow admirable in a positive way.

That left only Athens; for the other main classical Greek states, Thebes and Argos, had disqualified themselves for the moment, as had Thessaly, by taking the Persian side in the Wars ('Medism'). Argos was in any case, as we have seen, in poor shape in the early fifth century. She was indeed to make a short-lived bid for power during a lull in the Great Peloponnesian War (the so-called Peace of Nicias of 421), when she attempted to revive the old Argive greatness of the heroic age: such nostalgic, but altogether sincere, attempts to capitalize on traditional or mythical periods of supremacy are characteristic of Greek politics and poetry. As for Thebes, her bid for hegemony was to be postponed still later, until the 360s; even Thessaly, so often the object of the avarice of other states, had a brief fling on her own account in the 370s, under Jason of Pherae who, like the Argives after 421, defined his aims in very ancient terms, levying the 'tribute of Scopas', and modelling his military reorganization on the army of Aleuas the Red. Scopas and Aleuas were figures of the dim past of Thessaly.

Athens in 478 had all the advantages, and none of the disadvantages, of the other claimants we have considered. She had no helots or discontented Arcadians to stab her in the back. She had (unlike Corinth) positive incentives to offer, in her democracy and her *paideia* (culture): thanks to the artistic and literary patronage of the sixth-century Pisistratid tyrants she was already a strong cultural magnet, to which many dispossessed Ionian intellectuals were drawn after 480. As for the claims of history, memory, and myth, Argos may have had her ancient kings, and Thessaly her Aleuas and Scopas; but Athens produced some of the ablest propagandists ever to advertise on behalf of an imperial power. Cimon was to justify coercion of the island of Scyros, in the early days of the Athenian empire, by discovering there the bones of Theseus, mythical king of Athens. The image of Athens as universal benefactor of mankind (and hence morally justified in her suzerainty) was propagated by means of the myth of Demeter and her gift of corn to man. This cult was centred on Eleusis, a great religious focus—but also a constituent village of Attica and so in the territory of Athens. The great Athenian leader Pericles, and his successors, took a leaf out of Pisistratus' book when they placed this emphasis on Eleusis; and there is a further explicitly Pisistratid reminiscence in the 'purification' of Apollo's sanctuary of Delos carried out in 426. The central-Aegean island of Delos was the spiritual heart of the Athenian Empire (and incidentally acted as the imperial bank where monetary tribute from the allies was stored until 454). That empire was, in racial terms, largely 'Ionian', and it was another brilliant coup of fifth-century Athenian propaganda to exploit and magnify, for imperial purposes, an undoubted historical fact: the part played by Athens in the colonization of Ionia in the Dark Ages. By posing as the 'mother-city' of all her subject allies, irrespective of the often hazy reality in particular instances, Athens could demand the religious homage which, according to Greek notions, a daughter city owed to the place which had founded her. Finally, the Athenians had—unlike the medizers of Argos, Thebes, and Thessaly—performed noble service to Greece in the most recent historical past, sacrificing their physical city to Xerxes. Athenian orators were still reminding each other of this well into the fourth century. And the theme was stressed in fifth-century architecture: the 192 figures in the cavalcade on the Parthenon frieze have been ingeniously interpreted as an attempt to represent the dead heroes of Marathon. The victory at Marathon was certainly in the mind of the architect of the mid-fifth-century temple of *Nemesis* (i.e. divine punishment of the Persians) at Rhamnous near Marathon. In fairness, not all this religious glorification of Athens was of her own manufacture: the oracle of Apollo at Delphi, which was to side with Sparta in the Great Peloponnesian War, nevertheless called fifth-century Athens an 'eagle in the clouds for all time'.

Above all, Athens had, like Corinth, a formidable fleet (above, p. 36). And Athens, like Corinth, had already had the beginnings of an overseas empire by the late archaic period; apart from her emotional and religious links with Ionia, there were her settlements at Sigeum near Troy, at the mouth of Hellespont, at the Chersonese and (nearer home) on the islands of Salamis and Euboea. One chief reason for this early transmarine activity is food: archaic and classical Athens needed the south-Russian grain which, as we have seen, came through the Hellespont. This gave Athens a special motive for responding to the appeal of the east-Greek islanders in the early 470s: economic necessity. To say, with one modern Marxist (de Ste. Croix), that fifth-century Athens 'pursued a policy of naval imperialism, but for this there were very special reasons', namely economic reasons, is therefore correct, but we need not follow this writer when he goes on to minimize the element of what he calls 'naked aggressiveness and greediness'. We shall see that individual Athenians, and not just hungry members of the poorer classes, stood to make economic gains from the empire which went well beyond the filling of their stomachs. As for aggression, many Athenian manifestations of it are remote from any immediate anxieties about the corn supply. We should at least expand the economic argument so as to include desire for precious metal for coinage (a supplement to the Laurium output), which goes far to explain the attack on Thasos in 465; and desire for ship-timber, which is relevant to Amphipolis in 437 and perhaps to the colony sent to Thurii in 443. Thurii is near the Sila forests in Bruttium (South Italy), and Thurian timbers are listed in Attic accounts in 407.

All that was in the future in 478; and even the wish for Black Sea grain is not formulated as a motive by Thucydides when he describes Athens' assumption of the leadership. Rather, the talk is of revenge and booty to be extracted from Persia, though in speeches we do hear of more high-minded motives of liberation.

SILVER COIN (TETRADRACHM) OF ATHENS, 440–430 BC. The types for Athenian coins, with Athena's head and the owl with olive twig, change only in style from the end of the sixth century through the Hellenistic period. Athens enjoyed her own supply of silver from the mines at Laurium and attempted to monopolize the coining of silver throughout her empire in the fifth century. The coin is shown at three times actual size.

'Revenge' is, however, stated to be a 'pretext' (rather than the whole story), and scholars have legitimately wondered what Thucydides took the whole story to be. Perhaps he meant that continued mobilization against Persia was a front for enmity directed against Sparta; or more likely he was thinking of the developed empire, whose activities were directed against the Greek world at large.

That the fifth-century Athenian Empire (despite the protection which it offered to the more uncomfortably placed Greeks against Persia and, we should add, pirates) was, or became, an oppressive instrument should not be disputed. The strongest argument, against desperate efforts to see it as a benevolent and generally popular institution, is to be found in an important inscription of the year 377, which sets out the terms and aims of a second Athenian naval confederacy and explicitly repudiates for the future a number of fifth-century practices—tribute, territorial encroachments, garrisons, governors, and so forth—which were clearly felt in retrospect to have been abuses. The only real argument is not over the adjective 'oppressive', but over the appropriate verb, 'was' or 'became'. That is, was the empire (always), or did it (gradually) become, oppressive? There is very little detailed evidence of any kind about the Athenian Empire before about 450, so that the appearance of qualitative change after that date may be a delusion. Nevertheless formulas do get more candidly imperialistic even in the period for which inscriptions survive in numbers, and from the Tribute Lists it is plausible to reconstruct a period of crisis after the Peace of Callias in 449. Late payment and non-payment of tribute in those years suggest disaffection due to a feeling that the originally anti-Persian organization had lost its justification. But whatever is taken to be the point of change, it is sure that there was one: the remark made in 411 by a speaker in the pages of Thucydides, that what the 'allies' really wanted was freedom from both Spartan-sponsored oligarchs and Athenian-supported democrats, could not have been made in the euphoric atmosphere of 478.

What forms, then, did Athenian interference and control, or (less neutrally) oppression, take? First, economic: obedient to the economic compulsion which we have noticed already, Athens used imperial institutions to make sure of her own corn-supply. We hear of 'guards of the Hellespont', who determined how much grain was permitted to consumers other than Athens; of 10-per-cent taxes levied on shipping there (grain bound for Athens herself was presumably exempt); and, in the fourth century at any rate, of laws restricting commercial transactions involving grain bound elsewhere than for Athens. More generally we have already noticed that desire for precious metal and ship-timber was part of the explanation for aggression against, and settlements at, Thasos, Thurii, and Amphipolis. Above all there was tribute, in ships or money (increasingly the second was preferred by all parties).

Second, administrative and military garrisons and garrison-commanders are amply attested, by no means all of them to be explained as present by invitation, like Russian tanks rolling into 'fraternal' Prague or Kabul. And the greatest weapon of all was the fleet.

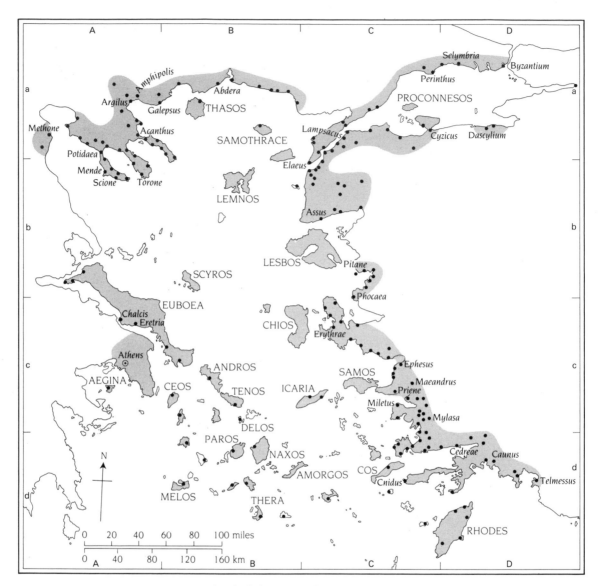

MAP 3. THE ATHENIAN EMPIRE. The shaded area on the map shows the maximum extent of the Athenian Empire: 'the cities which the Athenians rule' is how the Athenians themselves would have put it; alternatively, 'the islanders'. This map shows why the second description was appropriate. It should be remembered that some places in Asia Minor probably paid tribute to Persia as well as to Athens; that some strategically important and financially valuable possessions (such as Amphipolis in the north) did not pay tribute in a way which caused them to be entered on the so-called Tribute Lists at all; and that the Athenian Empire was not exclusively, though it was primarily, an 'Aegean', i.e., east Mediterranean affair. For instance, payments from some Italian and Sicilian communities in about 415 were handled by the *Hellenotamiai*, the imperial treasurers; and it has been suggested that Orchomenus in land-locked Boeotia paid tribute in the mid-century. The 'Tribute Lists', from which we learn details of the payments, were great marble stelae set up on the Acropolis which recorded that one-sixtieth of the tribute which was due to Athena; substantial fragments survive.

Third, judicial. Inscriptions show that serious cases were concentrated in Athens. Literary sources allege, no doubt truly, that the popular lawcourts (below, p. 130) were used for the persecution of anti-Athenian elements, a category which overlaps, but is not necessarily identical with, oligarchs. A final judicial shortcoming: Athenian law never anticipated Roman in developing a separate category of 'extortion' offences, specifically framed to protect oppressed provincials from the rapacity of governors.

Fourth, religious. Doctrinaire imposition of religious views was generally alien to Greek and Roman thinking, but we have noticed already the way in which Athens, the self-proclaimed metropolis of Ionia, exploited religious propaganda as a way of asserting her authority over her allies. A more concrete abuse of religion was the territorial encroachment on allied territory by the 'goddess Athena' herself, whose precincts were delimited by a number of surviving boundary-stones. Since this land might then be leased out to individual Athenians, this is really a subclass of our next category of interference.

Fifth, territorial. Settlements on allied or conquered territory brought obvious and immediate benefits to the lower classes; but recent work has rightly insisted that there were ways for the upper classes to profit too, and profit prodigiously. The chief evidence lies in the inscribed lists of the property of some Athenian aristocrats confiscated and sold as the result of an internal Athenian scandal half-way through the Great Peloponnesian War. These lists show that wealthy Athenian individuals owned holdings of land in allied territory, sometimes very large and valuable, in defiance of local rules about land-tenure (most Greek states confined land-tenure to their own nationals). This land-grabbing, which helps to explain why we hear so few voices raised against the morality of the empire by the representatives of any social class at Athens, was the major positive benefit which the rich derived from the empire. Their other chief benefit was negative: without a tributary empire the rich would have had to pay for the fleet themselves, as they had to do in the fourth century—with resultant class tensions absent in the fifth.

Sixth, social. A law of the year 451 restricted citizenship and thus its benefits—which, as the above discussion shows, were increasingly worth having as the century went on—to persons of citizen descent on both sides. It is surely not fortuitous that the law coincides with the planting of the first fifth-century settlements in allied territory. Athenian (and Spartan) stinginess with the citizenship was singled out by panegyrists of Rome as the chief cause of the brevity of their empires. Grants of privilege to isolated communities (Plataea in Boeotia, Euboea, Samos in 404) were made, but they were too late and too few to bridge the psychological gap between rulers and ruled.

Seventh and finally, political interference. The crucially important truth that Athens generally supported democrats against oligarchs was taken for granted in antiquity, but her occasional support of oligarchs was also noticed. She was not doctrinaire in her support of democratic factions, so long as the money flowed in. Even on the strategically and politically important island of Samos our two main literary sources disagree about whether the settlement imposed after the revolt of 440/39 took an oligarchic or a democratic form, and the text of a relevant inscription can be restored so as to yield either sense.

When Sparta, in 431, responding to pressure from Corinth, agreed to liberate Greece, we are told that the goodwill of the Greek world inclined to the Spartan side. The tight methods of control enumerated above show that there were indeed grounds for resentment of Athenian power.

Democracy

The connection between the empire and democracy was close, in that Athens usually supported democracies abroad. There was another connection, this time internal, between the democracy and the empire. It was the revenue from the empire, greatly increased as a result of Cimon's operations in the early 460s, which made possible the democratic changes at Athens of 462, associated with the names of Ephialtes and Pericles. These reforms increased the power of the popular assembly (*ekklēsia*). Solon at the beginning, and Cleisthenes at the end, of the sixth century had left Athens still in many respects an aristocratic state. In particular the introduction of 'appeal to the people', which the fourth-century thinker Aristotle regarded as one of the most 'democratic' things that Solon did, remained only potentially democratic until the introduction of jury pay in the 460s meant that large popular juries (*dikastēria* of hundreds or even thousands) could attend frequently without loss of income to the jurymen. Other kinds of democratic pay—pay for attendance at the council of 500 members which prepared the *ekklēsia's* business (the *boulē*), and at the city's festivals—were introduced over the next decades, and to this extent it is undeniable that the Athenian democracy was paid for by the allies. Attempts have been made to deny this, by arguing that after Athens was defeated in 404 and her empire brought to an end, fourth-century Athens went on distributing pay (and indeed she introduced a major new category of pay after 404, pay for attending the *ekklēsia*). Therefore (it is said) there was no necessary connection between democratic pay and the empire. The argument is politically naïve: once a vote-catching measure has been introduced—such as a new bank holiday in modern times—it takes a courageous politician to stand up and urge its abolition, at least in the kind of democracy which reserves to itself the right to sack its leaders instantly (Athens had nothing like the modern British notion of a five-year parliamentary term).

Democracy at Athens was both more and less democratic than in modern Britain or the United States; more, for the reason just given: the *ekklēsia* enjoyed more immediate power than a modern electorate, partly because the number of voters was so much smaller in ancient Athens; and less, for a reason also concerned with the number of voters: whole groups—slaves; women; the subject allies, whose lives were affected by many of the *ekklēsia's* decisions—were excluded from

FRAGMENT OF THE TRIBUTE LIST FOR THE YEAR 440–39 BC, recording 1/60 of the sums paid to Athens by contributing states of the Athenian League. The main headings here are for the Hellespontine District and the Thraceward District. The sums are in drachmae, written in Attic alphabetic numerals. The lists of payments were exhibited on the Acropolis.

the franchise. This left some 40,000 adult males who were eligible to vote. Of these perhaps as many as 6,000 (which is nearly the maximum seating capacity of the Pnyx, the *ekklēsia*'s meeting place, and was the quorum required for certain kinds of decision) may have attended for important debates.

The theory was that the *ekklēsia* was sovereign in Athenian political life, though it is hard to find a clear statement of this principle anywhere: the cry that 'it would be shameful if the people were not allowed to do what it wishes' is once raised—but to justify a piece of gross illegality. Aristotle perhaps puts it best when he says that the people would like to be sovereign. Actual popular sovereignty is best illustrated by the power which the people retained—and used—to depose and punish its servants, among whom the ten generals were conspicuous: they held the most important classical Athenian office to which appointment was by election, not by lot.

But there were various ways in which the sovereignty and importance of the *ekklēsia* were eroded in practice. The first limit on its importance was the vigour of deme life. The demes (there were 139 of them) were the constituent villages of Attica; each deme supplied a given number of councillors to the *boulē*, the numbers varying in proportion to the population of the deme. But that was far from being the only thing that demes did: like the democratization of Attica, the sixth-century centralization of Attica was a very partial affair, in that the city of Athens never absorbed all the political energies of the citizens of Attica; instead Attica was a kind of federal state in which local and national loyalties coexisted. Deme decrees, which survive on stone, are the best proof of this: they begin with formulas which closely echo the language of 'national' decrees ('it seemed good to the demesmen of ...', corresponding to 'it seemed good to the Council and People' of Athens), and cover such topics as the lending out of deme money, the leasing of a deme theatre, the construction of a deme 'civic centre' (*agora*), and the conferring of honours on men from other demes, and even on foreigners. The mention of theatres and *agora* (whose existence has occasionally been confirmed by archaeology) is itself suggestive: these buildings were characteristic of a developed *polis* and the Attic demes have been described in modern times as 'city-states in miniature'. A further proof of this is the intense religious life at deme level, which inscriptions attest, including long and complex cultic calendars (one inscription even shows an admittedly large and prestigious deme consulting the oracle at Delphi on its own initiative). Religion was central to the life of the *polis*, as to the deme. Naturally there were limits to the autonomy of demes: they had no 'foreign policy' beyond the right to honour foreigners, and in some respects their finances were subordinate to those of the city of Athens; for instance, the fortifications of militarily exposed demes were a state responsibility. But the absence of deme inscriptions after about 300 BC sadly illustrates the decline of one highly characteristic aspect of classical Athenian *polis* life, although, centuries after 300, Athenians still identified themselves by the old double system of father's name and deme.

The second limit on the *ekklēsia* was the *boulē* of 500 members, whose main function was to consider in advance everything which came before the *ekklēsia*. Like the Attic demes, the *boulē* has been described—this time by an ancient author—as a microcosm (*mikra polis*) of Athens, and the traditional view that the *boulē* was merely the agent and servant of the *ekklēsia* largely depends on this assumption that the *boulē* was socially representative and a 'cross-section' of the people. The assumption is not well founded. The *boulē* was elected and unpaid when Cleisthenes devised it in 507, and the first evidence for appointment of councillors (*bouleutai*) by lot from demesmen is about 450, and for pay no earlier than 411. That is not to say that these were the dates when those institutions were actually introduced (in both cases it is tempting to associate them with Ephialtes and the changes of 462), but it is important to remember that the change from an aristocratic to a democratic *boulē* was a gradual one. Actual evidence that the *boulē* was socially unrepresentative, in that wealthy and influential citizens preponderated, is harder to assess. There is practically no literary evidence; but by examining surviving lists of councillors, which begin in the fifth century, and checking them against independent evidence of wealth, we can see that membership of the *boulē* was associated with higher social rank than we should have expected had the system been really random. There are also allegations, in the writings of Athenian orators, that so-and-so wangled his way on to the *boulē* in a given year, and there are some striking coincidences—father–son or brother–brother teams serving together, or famous politicians who sit on the *boulē* in particularly exciting years for foreign policy—which all suggest that there were ways of circumventing the lot (which was supposed to ensure that *bouleutai* were supplied by demes in a random way). The most obvious method of circumvention was simple willingness to sacrifice time and therefore money when one's fellow demesmen were unwilling, but the 'wangling' allegations may imply that more positive pressures were applied by the ambitious, who could for instance have bribed fellow demesmen not to put their names forward at deme level. All this means that the *boulē*, as a collection of influential and self-confident semi-professionals, might be expected to lead the *ekklēsia*, not just to follow, and we do indeed find the *boulē* engaging in diplomacy which (judging from the formulas of the relevant inscriptions) was never ratified by the *ekklēsia*; moreover there is undeniable evidence of diplomacy being conducted, on occasion, in secret from the *ekklēsia*. There were of course limits to the *boulē*'s authority; for instance, membership lasted only a year, and nobody could serve more than twice (provisions which prevented the *boulē* from acquiring the hereditary prestige enjoyed by councils in some ancient states); but even this should not be exaggerated: a particular political group would surely take steps to see that it always had a representative, in an informal sense of that word, on the *boulē*. Mention of the formal rules about service in the *boulē* raises a fundamental question: were the lowest property group, the *thētes*, eligible for service? If not, that would be highly relevant to what was said above about the élite character of the *boulē*. But the evidence is unclear and the answer disputed.

Third, the generals. We have noticed that generals could be deposed, as even Pericles was, shortly before his death in 429. But common sense suggests that in ordinary conditions, and especially in wartime, the generals must have had great executive latitude: for instance, security considerations, although admittedly never a strong point with Greeks, must have made it undesirable to discuss detailed strategy in the full *ekklēsia*. And because it was an elected office, with no limit on re-election, the generalship enjoyed unusual respect.

Fourth, the 'demagogues', the popular leaders, such as Cleon in the 420s and Hyperbolus after him, who without necessarily holding any particular office nevertheless exercised great power by oratorical and persuasive skills. Vilified by the literary sources, men like Cleon can be partly rehabilitated by the help of inscriptions, which have shown not only that their social origins were not nearly so obscure as comic playwrights like Aristophanes say, but also that a Hyperbolus

THE FURNITURE OF
DEMOCRACY, fifth to fourth
century BC. The bronze
wheels are public ballots:
Aristotle tells us that those
with solid axles were for
acquittal, the hollow for
condemnation, and the voter
could conceal his vote by
holding the axle between his
fingertips. These were found
in a building at the north-east
corner of the Agora in
Athens, near a clay bin, which
might be a ballot box, and a
water-clock (*klepsydra*) for
timing speakers in the law
court. The fragmentary
inscribed plaque is an identity
card for a juror; the bronze
ball for use in a machine by
which jurors were alloted at
random to serve in different
courts.

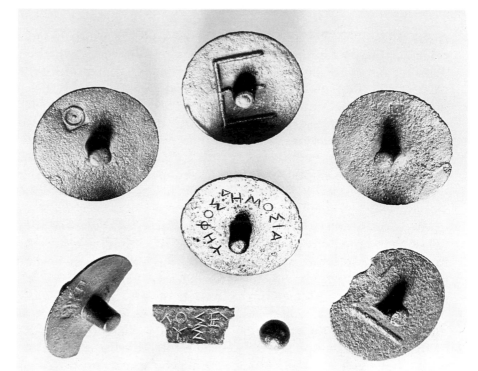

OSTRACA FOUND IN THE ATHENIAN AGORA. These are votes cast to choose a victim for ostracism—banishment from Athens for ten years. They are scratched on potsherds and the examples shown name four prominent politicians of fifth-century Athens—Aristides, Themistocles, Cimon, Pericles.

was capable of thinking out complex and sensible legislation. In fact the demagogues (and Pericles was himself only a grander kind of demagogue) owed their
positions of influence to a structural gap in the democracy: imperial administration meant an ever-increasing volume of work, and the Athenians, lacking a civil
service of a modern type, allowed such work to be done by politicians who
made detailed knowledge their business: knowledge was power. The sanction
against a Hyperbolus was ostracism, a way of exiling a man for ten years by a
kind of popular referendum (the word comes from the potsherds, *ostraka*, used
in the 'polling' process). In the fourth century there was a more sinister development: specialist politicians got a firmer grip on power by being elected, for
instance, to control state funds, jobs from which it was harder to unseat them.

Fifth and finally, there were features of the *ekklēsia*'s own procedure and
psychology which reduced its democratic effectiveness and independence. It met
much less often than the *boulē*, and infrequent meetings do not make for informed
debate. Its votes were not counted; opinion was manifested by show of hands
and this was then gauged impressionistically, as at a modern trade-union mass
meeting. And even as late as the end of the fifth century, the age of the demagogues, there is evidence that the democratic Athenian voter 'loved a lord': the
young aristocrat Alcibiades in 415 could still demand a high office of state on the
grounds that his racehorses had won at the recent Olympic Games. Such claims
show the enduring power of wealth, especially inherited wealth, which inevitably
militates against democracy. Despite all the blemishes and shortcomings of Athenian democracy, its long arm did act as a protector against arbitrary treatment
of the poorer classes by oligarchs throughout the fifth-century Aegean world,
and from the point of view of those classes it was a tragedy that that world
gradually lost faith in its protector.

War

The democracy just described was called 'generally acknowledged folly' by
Alcibiades; but we have seen that Alcibiades and his class stood to gain from the
combination of democracy and empire: magistracies and military commands
were conferred on them through the deference of their political 'masters' in the
ekklēsia, and the empire brought them territorial and other material benefits. They
were therefore ready to fight to preserve the 'acknowledged folly' when the
Great Peloponnesian War broke out in 431. But that war was to break the power
and influence of the Alcibiades class; virtually no Athenians entered chariot teams
at Olympia in the three generations after 400 (as opposed to twelve in the single
generation 433–400), and when the empire itself disappeared in 404 there disappeared also the motive for upper-class co-operation with what one oligarch's
epitaph called, with engaging frankness, the 'accursed people'; so that the rich no
longer splashed out on civic expenditure at home with their old panache. The
greatest change effected by the Peloponnesian War was an increase in profession-

alism generally, and naturally this was most conspicuous in the military sphere. Politician and general are henceforth separate callings in Athens, a development foreshadowed in the career of Pericles himself, whose first known activities (in the 460s) are purely political; only later came the great military commands. This professionalism meant that Alcibiades' horses, even supposing that the accursed *dēmos* had let him keep them in the more vindictive atmosphere of the fourth century, would not have sufficed to guarantee him political or military success. Such professionalism affected more than the officer class. The fourth century has been called the age of mercenary soldiers, but the change begins in the last decades of the fifth century: when in 400 the Athenian Xenophon helped to lead a paid army of 10,000 Greeks eastwards in support of a Persian pretender, Cyrus, the financial terms of mercenary service are already fixed and taken for granted. Persian satraps (provincial governors), and even the Athenians themselves, had been using mercenaries for two or three decades before 400.

The Peloponnesian War also brought changes in the methods of fighting. The traditional Greek infantry technique was hoplite fighting, which required heavy and relatively expensive armour, but during the Peloponnesian War we hear for the first time of experiments with lighter-armed troops (peltasts, named from their shields); they became fashionable partly because of their greater flexibility and partly because a peltast cost less to kit out. Although the peltast never replaced the hoplite in classical Greek warfare (most of the great set battles of the fourth century were hoplite affairs), the combination of heavy and light armed was specially formidable. The social effects of a diminished dependence on hoplites, who had tended to be citizens of the states they were fighting for, and of the increased use of peltasts and mercenaries, was to weaken the link between the *polis* and the men who fought to defend it. The numbers, and potential for damage, of the rootless 'men without a city' may have been exaggerated by the fourth-century writer Isocrates, who is a spokesman for the propertied class; but the problem certainly got worse as a result of the Peloponnesian War, if only because after 404 there was no single leading power to impose its own political order as Sparta and Athens had done at different times. This led to a general increase in political instability with violence. Hence the exiles of whom Isocrates complained.

Sea warfare and siege techniques also developed more quickly after 431. By contrasting the accounts of Athenian naval techniques in Books 1 and 2 of Thucydides we see that in just a year or so the Athenians under Phormio have acquired the courage and skill to manœuvre in the open sea. In siege warfare, the agent of change in the late fifth century was not the Peloponnesian War, but the contemporaneous warfare in Sicily against the Carthaginians: this led to the invention of non-torsion catapults about 400 BC (to be followed by torsion catapults, perfected—apparently in Thessaly—about 350). Though the defenders of cities were quick to adapt, with new kinds of wall circuit and more effective fortifications, it was now possible to take fortified cities by storm. Alexander in

DEPARTURE SCENE on an Athenian vase of about 450 BC. A hoplite warrior clasps the hand of his father, while his wife or mother stands with a jug and *phialē* cup for the ritual libation of farewell. These poignant scenes are characteristic of Classical art and a similar mood is expressed on the later grave reliefs.

the 330s succeeded in Western Asia, where the Spartan king Agesilaus in the 390s had failed, largely because of the presence in the Macedonian army of Thessalian siege engineers recruited by Alexander's father Philip.

Strategic thinking was the slowest department of classical Greek warfare to change, even under the strain of the Great Peloponnesian War. In tactics, the generals of most Greek states continued to be the servants of the political assemblies, who were reluctant to grant them more than the minimum of formal powers. But there were changes even here: at the battle of Delium in 424 we hear for the first time of a deepened file of troops on the Theban side: these extra troops are a kind of tactical reserve, of a kind later perfected by the Theban Epaminondas in the fourth century. Henceforth more was to depend on the judgement and timing of the general who had to decide when and where to deploy the reserve. Handbooks about, and the oral teaching of, tactics (both of which we hear of first in the late fifth century) announce the change of intellectual attitudes: if warfare is to be scientific it can be taught like any other science.

But strategy, in the sense of grand strategy—the achieving of political results by the best military means—was cautious to a degree in the early phases of the Peloponnesian War. The best strategy which the Spartans could think of at the beginning of the war was to invade the territory of Attica every year in the hope of making the Athenians submit. This was bound to fail because Pericles' strategy for Athens was to abandon the territory of Attica and concentrate the population within the walls of the city and its harbour town Piraeus 9 kilometres away (Athens was joined to Piraeus by a line of parallel walls, the 'Long Walls', so that the two places formed a defensible unit). Access to Piraeus meant access to the food and commodities which Athens' imperial possessions could provide. All Athens needed to do to win the war was to survive it: Thucydides uses the same Greek word for 'survive' and 'win'. She had the financial resources of the empire, capital accumulated over many years, to pay for any disciplining of her allies which might be necessary to ensure that essential supplies kept coming through.

Sparta's position was less easy: she had no reserves or tribute and so had to satisfy the military and political wishes of her allies, on whose human resources she was dependent for her levies. But those wishes included, above all, the 'liberation' which we saw the Greek world expected of her in 431, and liberation meant taking the initiative, taking positive steps to dismantle the Athenian Empire. But, for that purpose, Sparta needed extra manpower, which her social system was ill equipped to provide, and above all the money to pay for more audacious campaigning, possibly by sea (which would mean building a fleet, a costly business). There was one way out: to apply to the richest non-Greek power in the offing, namely Persia; but here the Spartan dilemma became acute because the 'liberation' of Greece from Athens, which Sparta's allies required of her, logically implied as the next step liberation of the east Greeks of Asia Minor from Persia—a point which Alcibiades makes to a Persian satrap in the final phase of the war. Before paying for the Spartan war effort, Persia would require guarantees about Spartan intentions in the east Aegean, guarantees which Sparta's obligations to her own League allies made it impossible for her to give. Nor did Persia have any special motive for disturbing the satisfactory relationship with Athens created by the Peace of Callias.

So Sparta must think of some way of striking a positive blow at Athens and her empire; and that blow must be struck without help from Persia—that is, without a fleet. The answer she hit on in 426 was the resumption of her old central-Greek aspirations. Much of Thucydides' account of the fighting in the middle years of the so-called Archidamian Wars of 431–421 is concerned with the northern activities of the Spartan commander Brasidas. But it is important to notice that the first step, the founding of a large-scale military colony at Heraclea-in-Trachis at the southern approach to Thessaly, was taken in 426, before Brasidas moved with his army to the north. So some Spartans other than the unusually energetic Brasidas were after all forcing themselves to think about grand strategy. It was, however, Brasidas' successful operations against Athens' Thracian and northern possessions (including Amphipolis, which he captured in 424), which made Athens happy to make peace by the end of the 420s; Sparta was equally ready to cease hostilities because Cleon, partly by chance and partly by a skill with which Thucydides does not credit him, had taken prisoner 120 full Spartan citizens at Pylos in the western Peloponnese. Full Spartan citizens in these numbers could not be spared; the result was that Brasidas' successes were cancelled politically by Cleon's, and the Peace of Nicias was made (421–415). Athens had kept her empire and won the Archidamian War.

Thucydides calls this peace a 'festering peace', and it is true that though there were no formal hostilities Athens, prompted by Alcibiades and perhaps by Hyperbolus, was energetic in stirring up anti-Spartan elements within the Peloponnese. This came to nothing because in 418 Sparta defeated a coalition of her enemies at Mantinea. But a far more important development than all this inconsequential diplomacy was a catastrophic error made by Athens at some point in the years of peace; she supported two Persian satraps in western Anatolia, Pissouthnes and then his son Amorges, who were in rebellion against the Persian King. It was this which gave the Persian King the motive for helping Sparta against Athens, which in the Archidamian War he had lacked. Hence when Athens sent a fleet against Sicily in 415, and this fleet was annihilated at Syracuse (413), with a consequent shaking of confidence in Athens within her empire, Persia at last seemed in a position to win the war for Sparta.

But, despite Sicily and despite a short-lived oligarchic revolution in 411 in the aftermath of Sicily, Athens fought on for a further nine years. Indeed as early as 410 she had scored one major naval success, the battle of Cyzicus, which actually caused the Spartans to sue for peace. Only when Persian money, supplied through the King's son Cyrus, began to pour in without stint, after 407, did Sparta under Lysander force Athens to capitulate, after the battle of Aegospotami (405)—and even then it was not the battle, but the subsequent blockade of the Hellespont, which was decisive. The war was lost; the empire was dissolved; the eagle had been shot down from the clouds.

Hegemony: The Fourth-Century Struggles

'Freedom, or rule over others' is a phrase which Thucydides puts into the mouth of one of his speakers. The equation is instructive about Greek attitudes: freedom to oppress others was valued at least as much as freedom from oppression. Sparta's behaviour, after she had finally 'liberated' Greece from the Athenian Empire, was to illustrate the positive, sinister side to the notion of liberation. A few years after 404 Sparta was to be engaged in war in Greece, the Corinthian War (395–386) against a coalition of Greek states: Boeotia, Corinth, Argos, and, remarkably, a revived Athens which had got rid of the oligarchic junta briefly imposed by Sparta after the Peloponnesian War. At the same time (400–390) Sparta was fighting in Asia against Persia. Alcibiades had been right: liberation of mainland Greece by Sparta did lead to her attempted liberation from Persia of the Greeks of Asia Minor.

How had this warfare come about? Spartan expansionism in this period is the answer, an unqualified expansionism to all points of the compass, which has to be connected with the personality of Lysander. But in some respects Lysander was only resuming in a more single-minded way Sparta's traditional, but intermittently pursued, policies, just as the Spartans who planned Heraclea in 426 were resuming the central-Greek policies of Leotychidas and Cleomenes I.

We may start with Heraclea and central Greece, for the renewal of Spartan aims here posed grave threats to Boeotia and Corinth—the risk of encirclement. Shortly after the end of the war Sparta reasserted her authority in Heraclea, which in the years since its foundation had oscillated between Spartan and Boeotian control. Moreover Sparta seems, on the evidence of an intriguing speech delivered by a Thessalian politician in 404, to have interfered in the politics of Thessaly proper, and she certainly threw a garrison into the Thessalian city of Pharsalus. This interference threatened to bring her into collision with the dynamic Macedonian king Archelaus (413–399), who also had Thessalian ambitions. The presence of Lysander in north and central Greece at the appropriate times is securely enough attested for us to associate him with these policies.

So much for the north. Then there is the west: in Sicilian Syracuse, at about the time that the Peloponnesian War was ending in Greece, the tyrant Dionysius I established himself in power—with Spartan help. Again we may suspect the hand of Lysander, who, according to an early chapter of his biography by Plutarch, paid a visit as ambassador to Dionysius. Here were grounds for unease in Syracuse's mother city of Corinth, especially since the help given by Sparta to the tyrant included the assassination of a Corinthian mysteriously described as a 'leader' of the Syracusans.

Then there is the south. Another of Lysander's attested visits was to the Egyptian oracle of Ammon at Siwah; and since Lysander's brother was called Libys ('the Libyan') this may indicate family links. Now Egypt, since 404, had been in revolt from Persia under a rebel native Pharaoh, and it is possible that Lysander was playing the same game in Egypt as at Syracuse—backing, and thus placing under obligation, a newly emergent power. Certainly both Dionysius and the new Pharaoh repaid the debt with concrete naval help to Sparta in the Corinthian War.

Finally and most important—since it concerned Persia directly—the east. Spartan involvement in Asia Minor after 404 begins surreptitiously, with the help to Cyrus, now in revolt against his brother the new King, given by Xenophon's 10,000 (above, p. 136): this force had official backing from the Spartan state, but that is an aspect which the pro-Spartan Xenophon is at pains to suppress in his account of the expedition, his *Anabasis*. Sparta acted more openly in Asia against Persia when appealed to directly by some Ionian cities: a series of expeditions sent between 400 and 396, the last of them actually led by a Spartan king, the newly acceded Agesilaus, crossed to Anatolia and campaigned there till recalled by the outbreak of the Corinthian War (395). But even a defeat (Cnidus, 394) at sea by a Persian fleet commanded by the Athenian admiral Conon was not enough to cause Sparta to renounce her Asiatic ambitions. That was only achieved (in 392) by the ravaging of the Spartan coast-line by Conon and a Persian satrap, for this raised the old possibility of revolt by helots who would be encouraged to see Spartan enemies so close. The result, after a few years more of desultory fighting, was the King's Peace (387/6), which finally settled that Asia Minor should be Persian and that the Greeks should be 'autonomous'. The delay between 392 and 387/6 was due partly to the need to starve Athens into submissiveness, but largely to the Persian King's hostility towards Sparta because of her help to Cyrus in 400.

IMPRESSION FROM AN ENGRAVED CHALCEDONY GEMSTONE FOUND AT BOLSENA IN ITALY. A Persian horseman attacks a Greek soldier. The style is 'Greco-Persian', current in the southern states of Asia Minor in the later fifth and fourth centuries BC, and serving Persian or Persian-dominated courts. The style and spirit of the subject matter, however, owe much to Greek art.

The 'autonomy' provision of the King's Peace was greatly to Sparta's advantage, for she could use it as a pretext to dismantle those of her enemies whose organization could be held to be a violation of internal 'autonomy': thus Mantinea, in Arcadia, a unified and democratic *polis* since Themistocles' day, was broken up into its constituent villages. It is doubtful, however, whether Sparta relied on legal technicalities about autonomy to intervene in Mantinea; the fact was that her prestige as a result of the King's Peace, of which she was appointed by Persia to be in some sense the guarantor, gave her the power to do what she liked. This was especially true since two of her main enemies, Thebes and Athens, were caught by the 'autonomy' clause: Thebes had to renounce her position of dominance over the Boeotian League, and Athens had to abandon for the moment her hopes of a revival of her old empire. There is no doubt that those hopes had revived, very soon after 404: an Athenian orator in 392 refers to the desire to recover the overseas possessions which Athens had lost by the war, and in the period after the battle of Cnidus Athens had revived the old 10-per-cent tax at the Hellespont. This hankering after empire on fifth-century lines, and especially the desire to recover another northern possession, Amphipolis, determined the course of Athenian foreign policy down to the age of Philip.

The King's Peace left Sparta free, not merely to coerce immediate neighbours such as Mantinea, but to go north again: in 383 she attacked Olynthus, in the Chalcidice. But *en route* for the north the Spartan commander Phoebidas was invited into Thebes by a pro-Spartan faction, and seized the Theban citadel, the Cadmeia. This blatant aggression was viewed by the pious Xenophon, for all his Spartan sympathies, as a piece of divinely sent madness, and certainly it created a mood of violent antipathy to Sparta in the Greek world at large, so that when some Theban exiles liberated their city in 379 they were able to call in help from Athens. Capitalizing on the anti-Spartan atmosphere, and perhaps fearful of Spartan reprisals for their part in the recent events at Thebes, the Athenians now (378) gathered together an alliance, the second Athenian Naval Confederacy, with Thebes as the most noteworthy ally. As we have already remarked, the new alliance was careful to abjure the most hated of the fifth-century imperial practices (tribute, garrisons, cleruchies); even so there was no immediate rush to join. Only when the new confederacy showed its effectiveness in practice by a naval defeat of Sparta off Naxos in the Aegean (376) did adherents flock in. Athens' new position was recognized in a renewal of the King's Peace in 375. The Athenian

THE ATTIC FORT AT PHYLE ON MOUNT PARNES. It was built in the early fourth century BC and guards the most direct route from Athens to Thebes.

eagle had taken wing again, though it was altogether a less plump and formidable bird. Despite the promises of 377 (above, p. 127), the energetic naval campaigning of the decade had to be paid for, and by 373 we hear for the first time of financial 'contributions'—the old fifth-century tribute under another name. And in the same year there is evidence of the first Athenian garrison, on the island of Cephallenia off the west of Greece.

Not only did Athens begin thus early to break her negative pledges; more important, the ideological justification of the new league—originally, a democratic freedom-fight against Sparta, with Athens and Thebes as joint leaders—was called into question by Thebes' own behaviour in the 370s. Soon after the liberation of the Cadmeia Thebes reclaimed her position within Boeotia, reviving the Boeotian League under Theban leadership. The recalcitrants among the smaller Boeotian cities were bullied and some even destroyed. At next-door Athens all this was watched with alarm. When at the battle of Leuctra in 371 the Thebans confronted Sparta and—to the amazement of Greek opinion, accustomed for generations to the idea of Spartan invincibility—defeated her, Athens received the herald who announced the Theban victory with arctic incivility, and henceforth moved closer to Sparta diplomatically, a shift which dismayed the other allies of Athens. The decade of Theban hegemony had begun.

Leuctra was a defeat for Sparta, but its most important consequence for her was the Theban refoundation of Messenia as an independent state after many centuries of helotage (369). Sparta now, deprived of the economic means to pursue the old *agōgē* on which her supremacy had rested, and which required the leisure which only massive dependent labour could bring, sank to second-class rank among the Greek powers.

This allowed Thebes and Athens to pursue their rivalry in the vacuum created by Sparta's disappearance. In Thessaly a third power whom we have already met, Jason of Pherae, destroyed the walls of Heraclea to prevent any enemy coming that way again. That was the end of Sparta's central-Greek ambitions. But Jason was assassinated, and Thessaly became once again, as the 360s opened, a passive object of the covetousness of others. Thessaly and Macedon, the latter at this time tormented by dynastic disputes, are the first main theatre of Theban activity in the 360s: it was the Theban Pelopidas who led this diplomatic and military penetration into Macedon and Thessaly. Here Theban interests clashed with Athenian, for one result of Leuctra was to reawaken serious hope at Athens for the recovery of Amphipolis and the Chersonese. All that either side was able to achieve in the north, however, was to prevent the other being successful without qualification, thus making easier the eventual task of Philip II of Macedon. Thebes did however gain one positive advantage; control via Thessalian votes of an outright majority on the Delphic amphictyony.

The second main area of Theban activity was the Peloponnese, where Epaminondas, the victor of Leuctra, followed the refoundation of Messenia with the creation of a new federal Arcadian state with a capital Megalopolis, the 'Great

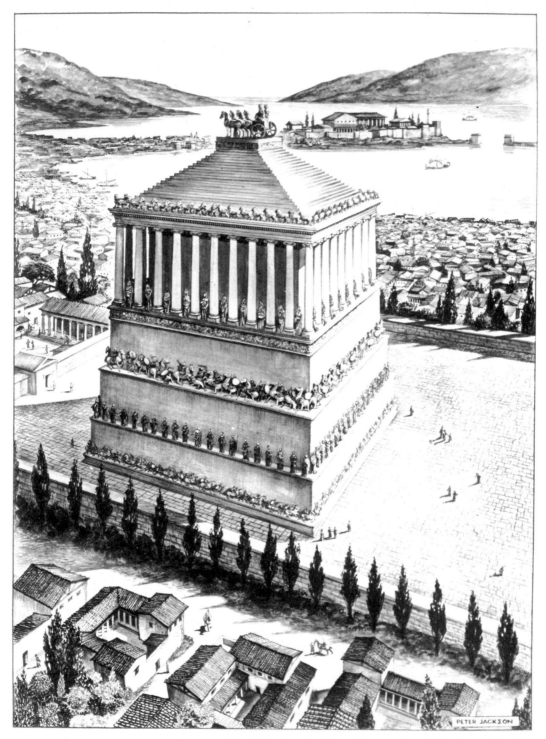

THE MAUSOLEUM AT HALICARNASSUS. Reconstruction by Peter Jackson. One of the Seven Wonders of the World, it was built in the mid fourth century for King Mausolus of Caria by his wife Artemisia, who was said to have employed the leading Greek sculptors of the day. The building is described by Pliny, but the site has been excavated and many pieces of the sculpture decoration recovered (see next illustration), mainly from their re-use in the castle of St Peter, built by the Knights of St John, overlooking the harbour of the modern town (Bodrum).

City'. Such foundations, like the export of federalism to Aetolia and the creation of a new Boeotian federation (distinct from the Boeotian League—which continued in being—and modelled on the Second Athenian Confederacy), represent Thebes' main legacy to Hellenistic Greece.

The third and final area of Theban expansion was by sea in the Aegean. Here again the enemy was Athens, who in 365 had overstepped herself in the eyes of her allies by sending a settlement to Samos, thus breaching another confederacy pledge. The breach was moral rather than formal since, first, Samos was not a confederacy member, and, second, the Athenian action was provoked by a Persian garrison, in violation of the King's Peace, which had granted Asia (but not offshore islands like Samos) to Persia. The violation was flagrant, and Athens was entitled, in view of the strategic strength of Samos, to react as she did. But her action, the installation of the settlement, was deeply and (as pro-Samian inscriptions show) widely resented. This resentment enabled Thebes to seduce some of Athens' most valuable allies out of the confederacy, notably Byzantium on the Hellespontine corn-route (also, temporarily, Rhodes). Epaminondas is in this respect the forerunner of Mausolus, the Persian satrap who further exploited allied grievances against Athens in the 350s, taking Rhodes and other places finally out of the Athenian camp in the Social War. This satrapal infiltration of the islands, which took an oligarchic form, starts as early as the 360s in some places (notably Cos). It did much to settle the 'class struggle' in the Aegean world between oligarch and democrat, tilting the balance against the democrats; but we

RELIEF SLAB FROM THE TOMB OF MAUSOLUS AT HALICARNASSUS (see last illustration). It shows Greeks fighting Amazons, who were skilful archers and riders (note the figure at the left, shooting from the saddleless horse).

IVORY HEAD, probably a portrait of Philip II of Macedon. Part of the relief decoration of a wooden couch found in the tomb of Philip II at Vergina, with other ivory heads, apparently portraits of other members of the royal family.

should remember that it was Athenian selfishness—the pursuit of private goals like Amphipolis—which led democrats such as the Rhodians to prefer even Mausolus to their fellow democrats at Athens.

When the 360s ended, feeling against Athens was running strong inside her own confederacy, Thebes was generally unloved, and Sparta broken. So when Philip II, whom a contemporary historian described with justification as 'the greatest man Europe had ever produced', succeeded to a debilitated Macedonian kingdom in 359, he was fortunate above all in the weakness of the states who should have been making it their business to confront him; otherwise that personal greatness would have remained merely potential. We can add that the Syracusan tyranny had ended after the second generation, true in this respect as in others to the pattern of the old archaic tyrannies of the Greek mainland; and that mid-fourth-century Sicily, anarchic and economically battered, was in no position to intervene against the new king in Macedon. A Corinthian called Timoleon was to restore and revive Sicily in the 340s, but it was not till the Hellenistic age had begun that a Sicilian ruler would again play a part in world politics. The problems of Athens, Sparta, and Thebes got worse in the course of the 350s: Athens' confederacy, as we have seen, was torn apart in the Social War of 357–355; Sparta's efforts to recover Messenia were futile, but consumed all her energies; Thebes picked a quarrel with neighbouring Phocis in the early 350s and induced her stooges on the Delphic amphictyony to declare Sacred War on Phocis. But the Phocians seized the Delphic temple treasures, hired mercenaries, and made such a good showing against Thebes that the war was ended in 346 only by Philip's intervention. The importance of the Sacred War, in thus bringing Philip into the heart of Greece, can hardly be exaggerated. But, to return to the 350s, Philip had been taking advantage of the disunity and the private preoccupations of the Greek states to seize a string of northern places, including Amphipolis, and to acquire control of Thessaly with all its assets. Olynthus succumbed in 348, unaided by Athens, despite the oratory of her great patriot Demosthenes, who in the late 350s had been slow to identify Philip (rather than Persia or Sparta) as Athens' real enemy, but rarely faltered after 349. By 346 Athens' military struggle against Philip had achieved so little that formal diplomacy was substituted, the so-called Peace of Philocrates, whose most important single clause

PORTRAIT HEAD OF DEMOSTHENES. Copy of a portrait made by Polyeuctus, forty-three years after Demosthenes' death in 322 BC. The original bronze stood in the *agora* at Athens and was a whole figure, dressed, with hands clasped before him.

from Athens' point of view was her acquiescence in the loss of Amphipolis. From Philip's point of view it may have mattered more that he had not only a peace but an alliance with Athens, since there is reason to think that he was already contemplating the war against Persia which his son Alexander the Great carried through: for that purpose he would need Athens' navy or at least her neutrality. The peace of 346 was, however, impermanent, and it is a question whether it was Philip or the endlessly provocative Demosthenes who willed that it should be so. Philip used the later 340s to strengthen his hold over Thessaly and Thrace, and to install (or perhaps merely encourage) his partisans elsewhere, for instance on Euboea. By Demosthenes the interval was spent rallying Greek opinion against 'the barbarian', as he unjustly and inaccurately called the Macedonian (the near-Greekness of whose culture is now revealed in a clearer light by such archaeological finds as the painted frescoes at Vergina, uncovered in 1977). That Demosthenes' propagandist and political efforts almost succeeded is shown by the closeness of Philip's final victory on the field at Chaeronea (338). The result of Chaeronea was diplomacy of a new kind: a settlement (the 'League of Corinth', which had little to do with classical ideas of federalism), with a king as its centre, and relying for its maintenance on the goodwill of the possessing classes whom it entrenched in power. They were never, either under Macedon or Rome, to lose that position of power; the classical class struggle had been decided: democracy and Athens had lost, as a result of Athens' own folly. Imperialism had after all proved incompatible with democracy.

Further Reading

The ancient sources for the period from the Persian to the Peloponnesian wars were collected in G. F. Hill, *Sources for Greek History 478–431 B.C.* (revised edn. Oxford, 1951 by R. Meiggs and A. Andrewes). The indexes are specially useful because they set out the ancient references under geographical and chronological headings. The fifth-century part of Fornara (above, p. 48) translates many of the items, literary and epigraphic, in Hill. The later part of the period is covered by P. Harding, *From the end of the Peloponnesian War to the battle of Ipsus* (Cambridge, 1985). There are good revised Penguin translations of Thucydides (revised by M. I. Finley) and Xenophon (revised by G. L. Cawkwell), *The Persian Expedition* and *A History of My Times*.

There are two recent histories of classical Greece: J. K. Davies, *Democracy and Classical Greece* (London, 1978), the subject-matter of which is broader than the title implies: this is a stimulating general history of the period; S. Hornblower, *The Greek World, 479–323 B.C.* (London, 1983), which gives fuller bibliographies than is possible in the present work.

On the Athenian Empire the major works of modern times are B. Meritt, H. T. Wade-Gery, and M. F. McGregor, *The Athenian Tribute Lists* III (Harvard, 1950) and R. Meiggs, *The Athenian Empire* (Oxford, 1972, with paperback reissue in 1979). (The same author's *Trees and Timber in the Ancient Mediterranean World* (Oxford, 1982) brings out the importance to imperial Athens of sources of timber supply.) An excellent brief survey is P. J. Rhodes, *The Athenian Empire* (*Greece & Rome New Surveys in the Classics* xvii, 1985). The relevant source-material is translated and commented on in M. Greenstock and S. Hornblower, *The Athenian Empire* (LACTOR 1³, 1983).

On Athenian democracy, much work and rethinking has been done since C. Hignett's conservative and sceptical *History of the Athenian Constitution* (Oxford, 1952) and A. H. M. Jones's still invaluable *Athenian Democracy* (Oxford, 1957). The most important books (though many of the major new theses have been advanced in articles) are W. R. Connor, *The New Politicians of Fifth-Century Athens* (Princeton, 1971); P. J. Rhodes, *The Athenian Boule* (Oxford, 1972) and the same author's magnificent *Commentary on the Aristotelian Athenaion Politeia* (Oxford, 1981); M. H. Hansen, *The Athenian Ecclesia: a collection of articles, 1976–1983* (Copenhagen, 1983) and *The Athenian Assembly* (Oxford, 1987); M. I. Finley, *Politics in the Ancient World* (Cambridge, 1983); and J. K. Davies, *Wealth and the Power of Wealth in Classical Athens* (New York, 1981: a supplement to his *Athenian Propertied Families*, Oxford 1971). On demes see D. Whitehead's splendid *The Demes of Attica* (Princeton, 1986).

On the Peloponnesian War, A. W. Gomme's *Historical Commentary on Thucydides*, completed after Gomme's death by A. Andrewes and K. J. Dover (Oxford, 5 vols. 1945-80) is fundamental. G. E. M. de Ste. Croix, *The Origins of the Peloponnesian War* (London, 1972, paperback 1982) is rich in discussions which go beyond the scope of the title; he returns to some relevant themes of classical Greek history in ch. 5 of his *Class Struggle in the Ancient Greek World* (London, 1981, paperback, 1982). On the final phase of the war, D. M. Lewis, *Sparta and Persia* (1977) ch. 4 and 5 are crucial.

The fourth century has been worked on more in articles than books until recently; but T. T. B. Ryder's *Koine Eirene* (Oxford, 1965) is useful on the complicated diplomatic history (especially relations with Persia) in the period. The second Athenian confederacy is re-examined with perhaps too kindly an eye in J. Cargill, *The Second Athenian League, Empire or Free Alliance* (California, 1981); J. Buckler, *The Theban Hegemony 371-362 B.C.* (Harvard, 1980) has much chronological and political detail; but it is still necessary to consult works like J. A. O. Larsen, *Greek Federal States* (Oxford, 1968) for the importance of federal developments in the 360s. For Thessaly, H. D. Westlake, *Thessaly in the Fourth Century B.C.* (London, 1935) is good and has not yet been surpassed. S. Hornblower, *Mausolus* (Oxford, 1982) discusses, in ch. 7, the Athenian and Persian aspects to the 370s and 360s and treats the Social War and (in ch. 6) the Satraps' Revolt in detail.

Philip II has been well served recently in monographs; the best is probably G. L. Cawkwell, *Philip of Macedon* (Faber, 1978); more detailed discussion of modern views in G. T. Griffith's contribution to N. G. L. Hammond and G. T. Griffith, *History of Macedonia* ii (Oxford, 1979).

Finally, a book which contains contributions of importance on several themes covered in this chapter: P. Garnsey and C. Whittaker, (edd.), *Imperialism in the Ancient World* (Cambridge, 1978); see especially Andrewes on Sparta, Finley on the fifth-century Athenian Empire (this is reprinted in his *Economy and Society in Ancient Greece*: London, 1981; Pelican edn., 1983), and Griffith on the second Athenian League.

7

Greek Drama

PETER LEVI

Introduction

THERE is plenty of drama in everyday life, and the experience of life is the source of everything that succeeds in the theatre. Almost every human society has formal drama of one kind or another, if we define the word loosely. We know the Greeks sat on theatre benches to watch sacred rituals. The ceremonies of state and of religion, and the moments of birth, death, marriage, harvest, and so on, have a great deal in common with theatrical drama, but we recognize drama strictly speaking because it uses actors, takes place in something like a theatre, an area defined by an audience, and probably has a plot, and more importantly an inner form, that we have learnt to expect. Once there is a theatre, there will be many other conventions: applause, competition, a style of speech, maybe the mask and the dance.

These conventions were not invented, though the Greeks believed that some of them were, but inherited and modified from social and religious ceremonies in which the drama began before it became theatrical. The obvious direct ancestor of theatrical choral lyrics is the dithyramb, which was a processional and choral lyric performance with narrative themes. When did the first actors step out from the chorus line? The history of the theatre, like all social history, is always the history of change; conventions may alter and then recur, but the inner form of theatrical performance, the skeleton of what is expected, becomes utterly transformed in time; this transformation is irreversible.

Then what about the origins, the very earliest adaptations? First one, then two, then three actors, always with the same choral background, though the chorus could be used in quite different ways.

Three kinds of plays—tragedy, comedy, and plays in which the chorus was the satyrs who belong to Dionysus. Music, with a history of its own. It is apparent that in the course of the fifth century BC, Athenian plays tended roughly to become more human and realistic, rather more secular and less religious, more fictional and less mythical, although none of these changes ever reached its final stage even in the fourth century, and tragedy with invented plots, as opposed to the wild and original adaptations of Euripides, was an innovation that had no future for many centuries. It was made late in the day by the sophisticated young poet Agathon who figures in Plato's *Symposium*; we know little about it.

The origins of Athenian tragedy are almost equally obscure. There is no doubt that dancers in animal masks performed in the sixth century in various parts of Greece. The origins of tragedy are certainly ritual and religious. The first tragedies in Athens were performed around a cart in the *agora*, which was mostly an open space. The actors probably came in from the country, perhaps from the sanctuary of Dionysus at Icaria or from Eleutherae. The fact that they spoke in verse should not surprise us: impromptu dialogue in verse between actors and audience could be heard at the Zacynthus carnival until the other day.

But beyond this we are in an area where the findings of modern folklore studies and social anthropology must be called in to cast their flickering and often misleading light. Occasionally, in a play we have, one seems to catch a whiff of origins, of a dying god or the rituals of initiation or the animal dancers, but these sensations are insecure, and the romantic arguments and general theories they have sometimes given rise to have been unsatisfactory. All the same, the English miracle plays, mystery plays, and mummers' plays, the goat dancers of Scyros, and the *commedia dell'arte* do throw some light on the nature of drama itself, and on the peculiar mixture of its origins.

The most important feature of early Greek tragedy that we should notice, apart from its extreme formality in performance and its slow, controlled progression like that of music (and determined in fact by music and ritual dancing) is that tragedy was a substitute for Homer. It was from Homer that tragedy took many of its themes, its irony, its preoccupation with justice, and the inner form of tragedy itself: the destruction of a hero or a superman: Homer is already tragic, and in everything but theatrical convention Homer in the first book of the *Iliad* is already the greatest tragic dramatist. Aeschylus was right to say 'We are all eating crumbs from the great table of Homer.' The influence of epic poetry on fifth-century Athenian theatre is vast and pervasive. Aeschylus in the *Oresteia* consumes some two-thirds of the *Agamemnon* in setting history in the context of epic. Even the fact that we are never given the precise origin of the curse on the house of Atreus can be seen as epic convention. True epic poetry is always an episode, the origins belong to another genre, to poems like Hesiod's *Theogony*, and even they are full of unexplained episodes.

Let us descend from these cloudy observations to what we know more exactly. The inscribed list of winners in Athenian dramatic festivals seems to have been begun or reorganized by the newborn democracy; they were festivals of the whole people. But the chief, and in the early fifth century the only, tragic festival was the Great Dionysia in spring, which was probably organized originally by the tyrant Pisistratus and remodelled by Cleisthenes. Clearly enough, the popularity of the tragic performances produced the development of the form and the extension of the set days. At first three poets presented three tragedies each, and one

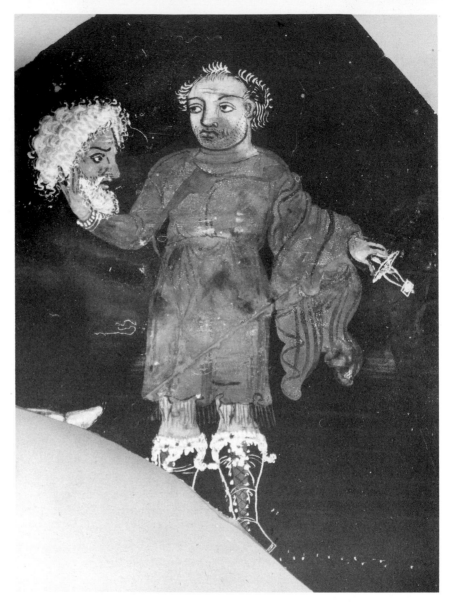

FIGURE OF AN ACTOR on a fragment of a vase from Tarentum, painted about 340 BC. He is shown holding a mask, as for a king, carries a sword, and wears elaborate stage buskins.

satyr play. For most of the fifth century, the staging of plays was very simple, even to naïvety, with two or three actors and a chorus of twelve or later fifteen.

In 488/7, comedies began to be organized at the Dionysia. Until then comedy was in the hands of 'volunteers'. It was a wilder growth, and it existed elsewhere in Greece; Epicharmus was composing comedies in Sicily in the early fifth century. At Athens, by 440 BC, comedy had spread to the Lenaea, a winter festival of the same god at which the weather cannot always have been clement (about 2 February). Tragedy spread to that festival about 432 BC: usually two poets with two tragedies each, it seems. Comedies were more numerous, five at each festival, except during wartime when the number was three. Were tragedies more expensive and grander? Or was comedy more popular? They were both popular, since in the fourth century they both spread through villages of the Athenian country-side at the Country Dionysia in autumn. As time went on they spread all over the Greek world, and travelling groups of players must have had trouble, as athletes did, in keeping their numerous appointments. The Athenian drama was never quite isolated: Aeschylus wrote plays in Sicily, and Euripides and Agathon were lured to Macedonia. At the Athenian Lenaea resident aliens were permitted to perform, though there is no doubt that both the tragedies and the comedies were great state occasions and popular national events. Phrynichus in his *Phoen-issae* and *Fall of Miletus*, his slightly younger rival Aeschylus in the *Persae*, and also much later writers dared to treat contemporary political themes directly in the theatre. Many other tragedies touched on the real world in a few verses or less directly. The *Oedipus at Colonus*, the last masterpiece of Sophocles, cannot be fully understood without the force of its real context, its first production as the city of Athens toppled to its fall.

AESCHYLUS

We have seven complete plays by Aeschylus, unless we accept the opinion re-cently accepted by many scholars that *Prometheus* is not his. But it is worth while noting at once that wonderful as the texts are that came down to us, they are a pitiful remnant of what once existed; their isolation from a huge context of similar works has surely distorted our judgement of them in many ways. The fragments we have of the lost plays of Aeschylus extend his range as poet and dramatist, and some of them are surprising. Who for example would have pre-dicted his humorous touch and gentle handling in satyr plays? But he was cham-pion of that genre. And who would have supposed that Aeschylus would present Achilles and Patroclus as full homosexual lovers? The fragments of religious sublimity are less unexpected, yet every new fragment of Aeschylus on papyrus as it turns up is always a surprise.

Only from Aeschylus have we a complete trilogy: that is, on at least one occasion his three tragedies were a coherent series, a continuous story. This is the Oresteia, of which the first play, the *Agamemnon*, has the most powerful impact of any ancient tragedy, grander and more thrilling even than the *Oedipus* of Sophocles, which Aristotle took to be *the* classic tragedy. The resolution of the *Oresteia* in the *Eumenides*, its third play, remains strangely moving to this day, and perhaps as close as we can come to intellectual understanding of the problems and solutions of the late archaic Greek world. It is a world utterly remote from ours, but the further one enters into it the more surely one realizes that we cannot afford to neglect it. Aeschylus is Blake-like, but without the obscurities or the divided mind of Blake. He is Shakespearean, but with a terrible concen-tration. His theatre is a circle of dead silence, and he used the form of his plays to the marrow of their bones.

Agamemnon begins quietly, with the Watcher on the roof. The chorus of old men is to come; this is the moment before daybreak, the opening of the theatre festival in 458, when Aeschylus was about sixty-seven. He had two more years to live.

> I ask the gods for relief of these labours,
> this watch from year's end to year's end, crouched
> on the roof of the Atreidae like a dog.
> I know the assembly of night stars
> the bright lords glittering in upper air
> that bring winter and summer to mankind.
> I attend for the signal light to burn
> and for the flame to blaze the news of Troy,
> the city fallen. We are mastered here
> by a woman's man-minded all-hoping heart.
> While my night-restless bed wettens with dew
> and no dreams ever watch over my sleep,
> because I must not shut my eyes and sleep,
> pounding out song for a drug against sleep,
> then I weep for the miseries of this house
> that lacks the good management of the past.
> O for lucky relief of these labours
> and the fire of good news in the darkness!
>
> O Hail bright shiner, daylight at midnight,
> beginning of dancing in all Argos!
> Yooo! Yooo!
> I signal clear to Agamemnon's wife
> to come quickly from bed and raise her cry
> in thanksgiving and welcome to this light,
> because the city of Troy has fallen,
> so says the messenger of fire at night.

It will be seen at once, even through the smoky medium of a modern translation, that this is a poet of brilliant and yet simple strokes. His images are very simple, his observation is acute, and he tells us far more than he says. His language has a stately formality but it moves swiftly and vividly. This is cumulative poetry; it builds on itself as music does. It is intensely dramatic. The special interest of this particular piece is that it begins from nothing, and from a minor character. But it leads into a magnificent set-piece, a long, very lively account of the chain of signal-fires on every mountain top and headland from Troy to Argos; spanning the whole of eastern Greece. It is curious and characteristic of Aeschylus, that he often highlights long geographical catalogues, real or half imaginary, and that this taste goes back to Homer and can be found after Homer, and (interesting to note) in each of the three long Homeric hymns, to Demeter, to Apollo, and to Hermes. It expressed one of the ancient purposes of poetry. Ancient Irish poetry has it; so has ancient French poetry.

Some scholars have spent time recently in tracing particular images through whole works of Aeschylus. I doubt whether those complex patterns have great significance. He works cumulatively, but quite simply. His thoughts are not hidden in the imagery, but stated in so many words, or stated and contradicted, as must happen in dramatic poetry. His mightiest strokes are often simply to turn a homely and familiar image inside out and make it terrifying: the friendly *kōmos*, for instance, which is a controlled alcoholic riot, and the visit from relatives, and the friendly dog a word or two turns sinister. In such simple terms Cassandra tells her vision of Agamemnon's house.

> I shall not speak in riddles anymore.
> Be witness that I smell out swiftly
> the tracks of evils that have long been done.
> There is a choir that never leaves this roof,
> unmusical, in concert, unholy.
> And it has grown drunken and overbold
> on human blood, it riots through the house,
> unriddable, blood-cousins, the Furies.

Most of what Aeschylus has to teach is dark, though the sublimity (simple once again) of his view of Zeus constantly bursts out, with the same naïvety as the psalms of David have, and a poetry perhaps nearer to our own expectations of poets. The force of the *Oresteia* is dramatic; the same lines would work much less well in an anthology, or if they were fragments. There is an important sense in which all this wonderful language is about the murder of Agamemnon by his wife. The scene of his death, which happens like nearly all horrors in the Greek theatre off stage, is well prepared at a conscious and an unconscious level; when it comes, the thud is terrible. What Aeschylus has done is to present a squalid and bloody killing, quite unacceptable in principle to Greek feelings about women, in such a way that one is awestruck rather than horrified by the character of Clytemnestra. Everything in the play, even Agamemnon's power and magnificence, is tailored to her appalling greatness. For her lover Aegisthus Aeschylus has nothing but scorn. The *Agamemnon* belongs to the theatre, though not alas in the hands of most modern directors. It is simple, bare, and forceful, and its pace is slow, its gestures slower than most dancing.

In the second play we have implicit compassion, ruthless action, and a long anguish with formal prayers. The queen and her lover are killed at last by Orestes, Agamemnon's son. Orestes is pursued by the Furies which rise from a mother's spilt blood. This is not really what Elizabethan scholars call a revenge tragedy; it is cumulative, but in its slow balance it says something dreadful about the justice of Zeus and the nature of the gods. The third play, which, most unusually, has a change of scene to accommodate Apollo at Delphi in a story which Aeschylus firmly transfers for its conclusion to Athens, brings good out of evil. The most venerable Athenian lawcourt is instituted by Athena and, by the reversal of what we know as a traditional cursing formula of great antiquity, the

Furies become the guardian spirits of Athens—Eumenides, the kindly ones. There are some lines that indicate a political message, not very clear to us, but the chief point that Aeschylus is making is a blessing on Athens that has the weight of the *Oresteia* behind it.

The *Persians* (472 BC) is based on an interesting device. The tragic hero has to be the Persian King, because there is no other way of showing the Athenian victory in the sea-battle at Salamis in a tragic form. Only losers can be heroes. Homer demands our sympathy for Troy partly because he has to make the Trojans talk like Greeks, but the lamentation for Hector is convincing because epic poetry was very closely bound up with lamentation. Aeschylus makes us feel, as Homer does, that war is terrible, and in his description of the battle of Salamis, of which he was very likely an eyewitness, nothing is spared. He sees it certainly as a great and inspiring Greek victory, but the battle is described by a loser; it is terrible, and the massacre in which it ends appalling. The whole action of this play is fascinating, but the battle scene stands alone. It does in verse what prose would take a long time to learn to do half as well. That is not only a technical device of tragedy. One must add that Aeschylus wrote his own epitaph, from which it appears he wanted to be remembered only as one who had fought in the infantry at Marathon.

THE *EUMENIDES* BY AESCHYLUS. Scene on a vase made in Paestum by the artist Python, about 350-340 BC. The fourth-century Greek vases of Italy often display scenes which seem to be inspired by stage presentations of tragedies by Athenian poets. Here Athena (at left) comforts Orestes who has taken refuge before the tripod and *omphalos* (navel-stone of the earth) at Delphi. Apollo stands at the right beside a snake-trimmed Fury (there is another over the tripod) waiting to wreak vengeance on Orestes for the murder of his mother. Apollo will purify Orestes, and Athena eventually rescue him while the Furies become the Kindly Ones (*Eumenides*).

SOPHOCLES

Sophocles used to be thought of as the most truly classic of the three great poets, the incarnation of tragic wisdom, a poet poised by a kind of controlled passion between the untrimmed grandeur of Aeschylus and the literary inventiveness of Euripides. That is probably because Aristotle took *King Oedipus* as the perfect example of tragedy. In Sophocles he thought the art of tragic poetry had 'attained its nature' and ceased to be capable of genuine development. Aristotle was looking back over many years, and in view of the extravagance of later productions and compositions it is not surprising that the clarity and austerity of structure of Sophocles' plays attracted him by comparison. The structure of *King Oedipus* in particular is as lucid as the skeleton of a fish; indeed its lucid structure contributes to its force. But the structures of the seven plays of Sophocles we have differ remarkably, the verse style of Sophocles is mannered in iambic passages and in choral lyrics often compressed and exotic.

Sophocles lived from about 496 to 406 BC, that is, nearly all the years of the fifth century. At the age of about twenty-eight he won a festival competition against Aeschylus, in 468. In the year of his own death he paraded his chorus in mourning for the death of Euripides. He was comparatively rich and several times took part in public life. He treated the gods with respect, and several kinds of pain, affliction, and horror with extraordinary directness. It is therefore all the more interesting that in real life he played an important part in the introduction of Asclepius to Athens, which effectively means the founding of the first public hospital. In the theatre he was particularly interested in consequences, and in the fulfilment of prophecy. The common ending of Athenian children's stories or folk-tales was apparently 'and so the story came true.' With his vigorous and memorable poetry one must beware of identifying what the chorus chants or what is spoken in passionate irony or grief with the wisdom of the poet himself.

The momentum of any tragedy leads to the end of the action. In Sophocles' *Women of Trachis* this is five minutes after the end of the play, when Heracles will be consumed by fire and rise out of it unconsumed to be a god. In the *Philoctetes* the end of the action is rather far in the future and involves the fall of Troy. Reconciliation is to come; the audience need not think much about it; the pain of the hero's wound is an unforgettable impression. In the Ajax the suicide of the hero is in a sense the end of the action, and it comes early, but the force of the play is in the consequences and in his burial. The *Electra* of Sophocles, which corresponds to the second play of the *Oresteia*, is like a frame with action at the start and finish, but its centre and substance is a play about women to which the thought of action gives great tension. The greatest set-piece in it is a long, thrilling story about a death, which the audience knows is a lie, a deceiving fabrication.

> Look, here Orestes is, who by device
> was dead, and by device was saved alive.

What all these varied structures have in common is their restrained clarity of line; the clarity in turn permits a quantity of formal embroidery in speech. In the *Antigone*:

> She howls in the sharp
> tongue of that bitter bird which sees the void
> bed of its marriage emptied of all young.

And again in the same play:

> we were two sisters of two brothers robbed
> killed on one day each by the other's hand.

There is a certain strength in these verses that flows into them from the very marrow of tragic form, the marrow of folk-tales. Their likeness to Elizabethan verse, which I do not think I have exaggerated in translation, is striking and may derive from the same cause. Sophocles is also capable of great and moving simplicity, yet again for a similar reason. Here, for instance, in a prayer, a lyric chant from the *Electra*:

> O Furies, dreadful children of the gods,
> who see all murders of the unjustly dead
> and see all beds of marriage that are robbed,
> come now, help now, avenge our father killed.
> Send me my brother home. I can no longer
> carry the weight of grief I am to bear.

For two plays by Sophocles we have the admirable translations of W.B. Yeats, with some interesting music he commissioned for the choral lyrics. They are the two Oedipus plays, which with the *Antigone* are probably the greatest and to most people the most living of Sophocles' works. *King Oedipus* is an expression of such passionate rage and grief that in modern production control of pace becomes a problem, and usually Oedipus rants. *Oedipus at Colonus*, the death of the old man, goes to the heart of that mystery by which, in Greek subconscious belief, punishment, affliction, plague, blindness, and madness are intimately linked to the special protection and the dreadful blessing of the gods for victims: that is, to what becomes, by the degree of its affliction and degradation, taboo and then holy, sacred, a source of benefits. This is a mystery without mechanical solutions, but one on which social anthropology can cast much light.

> Make way for Oedipus. All people said
> 'That is a fortunate man';
> And now what storms are beating on his head?
> Call no man fortunate that is not dead.
> The dead are free from pain.

That is how *King Oedipus* ends, with that slow drumbeat. In another final chorus Yeats makes the same point even more generally. Rather interestingly it was perhaps not really written by Sophocles; it looks like a distillation of many dark sayings from here and there in the play, strung together as the conclusion of a late production. By that time, if not earlier, the audience expected a message, almost a sermon of tragic wisdom. It is almost equally interesting that Yeats, who was not to know the technical arguments against the authenticity of these lines, later adapted and re-used them as tragic wisdom of his own, as the end of a sequence of lyrics called 'A man young and old'. They are worth quoting here as among the most Sophoclean lines ever written in English, in spite of pedantic arguments. Some very great scholars have believed they are genuine.

Endure what life God gives and ask no longer span;
Cease to remember the delights of youth, travel-wearied aged man;
Delight becomes death-longing if all longing else be vain.

Even from that delight memory treasures so,
Death, despair, division of families, all entanglements of mankind grow,
As that old wandering beggar and these God-hated children know.

In the long echoing street the laughing dancers throng,
The bride is carried to the bridegroom's chamber through torch-light and tumultuous
    song;
I celebrate the silent kiss that ends short life or long.

Never to have lived is best, ancient writers say;
Never to have drawn the breath of life—never to have looked into the eye of day;
The second best's a gay good night and quickly turn away.

Sophocles would not have given his thoughts the romantic touches that Yeats gives to these lines. If there is a perfect Greek tragic line in English it is probably one by Webster: 'the friendless bodies of unburied men'. Yeats is at his best in the play *Oedipus at Colonus*, but that is a strange and wonderful place. The play centres on a holy wood near Colonus, where Sophocles was born. In that wood the gods grant Oedipus his death; beyond it he vanishes. Theseus, who accepted him, tells us that the grave where Oedipus is buried, in a place no man knows, will have an infallible protective power between Athens and its borders. A great deal is made of the trees themselves, the wood is almost a character.

> Come praise Colonus' horses, and come praise
> The wine-dark of the wood's intricacies,
> The nightingale that deafens daylight there,
> If daylight ever visit where,
> Unvisited by tempest or by sun,
> Immortal ladies tread the ground
> Dizzy with harmonious sound,
> Semele's lad a gay companion.

Yeats has transformed his original, but not without tact, and much less wildly than most translations. His trees are splendid.

> . . . The self-sown, self-begotten shape that gives
> Athenian intellect its mastery,
> Even the grey-leaved olive tree
> Miracle-bred out of the living stone;
> Nor accident of peace nor war
> Shall wither that old marvel, for
> The great grey-eyed Athene stares thereon.

What Sophocles stresses, and what means less to a modern audience, is that Athenian olive trees have no rival in Asia or in southern Greece, and that no enemy can destroy them. But when this play was produced the Spartans and their allies were all round the walls of Athens; they were visible, very close to the sacred wood of Colonus. Sophocles was dead by then, the play was post-humous. And of course the trees were cut down in the end.

He is supposed to have written about forty-one series of three plays, won competitions twenty-four times, and never come lower than second place. He said of himself that his early style was full of Aeschylean grandeur, his second period developed a style of his own, which he came to feel was artificial and without sweetness, but his last period was suppler, better fitted to individual characters. No plays of his first twenty-five years in the theatre survived; in the *Ajax*, and a few years later in the *Antigone* (probably 441 BC), he was already moving into his final mastery.

In a way the *Antigone* is also the tragedy of Creon. Because Antigone insists after the Theban civil war on more than one attempt to bury her brother, which in Greek feeling and in the speeches that Sophocles provides was her absolute natural duty, the tyrant Creon condemns her to death. His own destruction begins from that moment, and the end of the play is like an avalanche. It is not that we underestimate Creon; the thrilling figure of Antigone belongs to a world of absolutes and consequences no political man could be at home in; Sophocles had little sympathy with any other. If there was one supreme hour in the fifth century BC, perhaps it was that of the *Antigone* of Sophocles, which was composed while the Parthenon was being built.

EURIPIDES

Euripides was country-born as Aeschylus was, quite early in the fifth century, in about 485 BC; that means he was no more than ten years younger than Sophocles, and was eighty when he died in 406. It is tempting to think of his work as a third chapter, a new generation, and it is true that he entered the theatre when Aeschylus was already dead; his first success was in 441 BC, when he was forty-four. We have seventeen complete tragedies by him, one satyr play, which is worth a separate discussion, and one, the *Rhesus*, wrongly attributed to him. It is as well to remember that this comparatively huge mass of poetry represents his popularity among poets, professional scholars, and teachers of the late Greek world, long after the collapse of Athens. He wrote something like ninety-two plays, but in his lifetime he won only four theatrical competitions. All the same, he is wonderful as a dramatist, full of originality at every stage of his development. His plays are remarkable for their range of tones and the gleeful inventiveness, which morose critics call cynical artificiality, of their construction. He is the master of the unexpected, and the building-blocks he uses are not so much characters as set scenes like the recognition scene, the scene of self-sacrifice, the furious quarrel, and so on. In his last plays the surprises are often hectic and elaborate, although the greatest of all his plays, the *Bacchae*, is the last or one of the last he ever wrote, and its construction is bold and simple, its colouring here and there Aeschylean.

The *Hippolytus* (428 BC) is dramatically exciting, very beautiful and harmonious, and tragical. It is one of his most satisfying plays, and one of his few successful ones with the contemporary audience. The hero is acceptably naïve.

> O Goddess, I bring you what I have made:
> a twisted wreath picked from pure meadow ground,
> where no shepherd ever pastures his flock,
> no steel has come, only the bee in spring
> passes across the untrodden meadows,
> Virginity keeps them with sprinkling streams.

The last of these lines I find untranslatable in verse. It means really that Shame, or Respect, the personified quality of youthful respect and restraint, which carries strong implications of virginity, is the gardener of the meadow, sprinkling it with the dew of rivers or streams. Maybe the lack of a precise English equivalent for the Greek *Aidōs* debars us from the world of Hippolytus. Here he is paying his tribute to virginal Artemis, and neglecting Aphrodite, who contrives his downfall through the hot passion of his stepmother, and then his death through his father's curse. In its terrible and effective alterations of tone, this play remains in tension with itself until the final scenes, one between Artemis and Hippolytus, in which the goddess speaks for the first time, and then a death scene which occurs uniquely in Greek tragedy on the stage.

> I shall be firm, I am dying, father,
> Cover my face up swiftly in your robe.

Euripides' other great masterwork about women's passion is his *Medea*, a tragedy so terrible that it can end only with the famous sorceress flying away in a chariot drawn by dragons. She has murdered her children out of a passionate hatred which is the dark side of rejected love, and out of insulted honour. The verses of this play are so convincing that it becomes easy to enter into these scenes even today; for whatever reason, the murderess and sorceress is more alive than the unhappy male characters in the play. Some of her speeches have that curious ring of modernity with which Euripides is sometimes rather mistakenly

THE *IPHIGENIA IN TAURIS* BY EURIPIDES. Scene from a vase made in Campania, about 330–320 BC. The stage building is shown with projecting wings, architecturally elaborated. The one at the left serves as the temple of Artemis, in which her statue is seen; the one at the right, the house of the priestess Iphigenia who emerges to speak to her brother Orestes and his companion Pylades who have come to steal the statue.

credited. It is only an uninhibited and passionate reasoning, but the passion, not the argument, is fundamental. Euripides picks the arguments and the point of view of each character with cool deliberation, and carries them through with great dramatic power. The theatre demands freshness; old stories demand intellectual versatility. But a passionate coherence and a passionate understanding of life underlie *Medea*.

In 415, the year of the expedition against Syracuse, the high tide of Athenian power-hunger and also a time of increasing superstitious fear, Euripides produced three tragedies on the Trojan war. The first showed the youth of Paris and the seed of destruction, the second dealt with Palamedes, the inventive Greek, but we know little of its plot. The third is the *Trojan Women*, a succession of tragic episodes under the walls of fallen Troy. In verse that differs with brilliant technical effect from one episode to another, Euripides delivers a series of hammer blows. They are linked only by black lamentation, with a faint spark of human compassion from the Greek herald, and a few strangely nostalgic lines about the holy land of Greece. Sometimes the magnificence of language puts fire and brimstone into the air, sometimes the formal clang of verses lends a sharpness, sometimes rhetorical patterns overspill like waterfalls.

> O throne of Earth and thou whose seat is earth
> hard to be known whatever thou mayest be,
> necessity of nature, mind of man,
> Zeus I pray to thee, who doest lead mankind
> in justice by a road not to be blamed ...
>
> O mortal fool who will pull cities down,
> temples and holy places of the dead,
> and make all those a desert, and then die ...
>
> To bring her where she shall be put on board ...
>
> Lead me, who walked soft-footed once in Troy,
> lead me a slave where earth fails sheer away
> by rocky edges, let me drop and die
> withered away with tears. Never say now
> that happy was happy until we die.

The cumulative effect of the *Trojan Women* is strong. This is not the formalized story of a legendary prince, it is more like history, more like the experience of life.

The *Bacchae*, the punishment of King Pentheus by Dionysus disguised as his own priest and then terribly revealed, may possibly be an adaptation from a lost work of Aeschylus. It is the most unforgettable play Euripides wrote, its poetry is towering; unlike the *Trojan Women*, if it had not been written it would have been unimaginable.

> I bring you him who put to ridicule
> me and my mysteries. Take your vengeance.
> And as he spoke one flash of dreadful light
> struck at the earth and struck against heaven.
> The air was silent. The wooded ravine
> held all its leaves silent. No creature called.

This language, which occurs just in the moment before the awful climax of the play, when Pentheus will be torn to pieces by his own mother and the other women, is nothing if not dramatic. The most dramatic verses and the most effective set-pieces in Greek tragedy are spoken by messengers; they describe action elsewhere. Tragic poetry is in this also an extension of Homeric poetry.

Tragic Poetry (Conclusion)

In the *Bacchae* of Euripides the chorus hardly speaks at all; it virtually confines its expressions to song. Is that a modern, that is, a late Euripidean device? Is it because he can no longer bear the intrusions of the chorus? In the earliest tragedies and in all Aeschylus, the chorus had an all-important function. It was as if the first actors had only just stepped out of its ranks, and lacked confidence. Even where the usual characterization of the chorus as old citizens, full of their proverbial wisdom and hopelessness, serves a purpose of mere contrast or transition between speeches, as similar utterances sometimes do in the choral lyric poetry of Pindar, their presence was significant to the unfolding of the plot. They are like those black-dressed women near a small harbour or those black-dressed peasants around a market square, who give sudden murder or the vengeance of the gods its social meaning. The tragic action fixes them like a photographer's flashlight.

> Many the transformations of the gods:
> and many things they judge as we do not:
> and what appeared was not what was fulfilled;
> the god found a way through the unlikely.
> And that was how this matter concluded.

These lines occur as conclusion of a number of Euripidean tragedies, including his *Alcestis*, and they do represent the stupefied, reverent, and somewhat dark attitudes of the chorus to events. One should be careful not to identify any chorus with the tragic poet, although there are times, for instance late on in *King Oedipus*, when they certainly speak for the audience. But the chorus can have many different functions. Sophocles varies the use of his chorus as he does the construction of his plays. In the *Prometheus* the chorus are Airs, Winds, divine beings. At the end of the *Agamemnon* they threaten violence. In another play they are *Suppliant Women*. Euripidean choral lyrics are often exotic and simple at the same time. Their geography and some of their other allusions are bizarre. Aeschylus is a great lyric poet in a more authoritative sense; he is Pindar's contemporary. But throughout its development the Greek tragic chorus was most austerely restrained, compared to later interpretations and revivals. It can never now be recreated. Even if all its conventions were rediscovered and re-enacted, they would not be conventional to us.

The text of tragedies was fixed by being written down and learnt by heart, though actors' interpolations do exist in tragedies, and much worse producers' interpolations. A stage direction survives from a late production of the *Agamemnon*: 'Enter the chariots, the army, and the spoils of Troy'. That is not the style of Greek tragic poetry, which was lavish only in messenger speeches, in conjuring the imagination of an audience, and in certain choral lyrics. The plots were given a new direction, a new meaning, quite boldly by every new treatment, and as much by Aeschylus and Sophocles as by Euripides.

The bones of the verses are what today we call rhetoric. Whenever we read the dialogue of tragedy, with its line-for-line correspondence and apparently artificial figures of speech, we should remember that this imitates a reality. Properly read aloud, it ought to sound like a quarrel between fishwives: I suppose I mean Greek fishwives. Both the continuity of the underlying rhythm and the sharp breaks, the mutual parodies and ironies, are precisely real. The fact that later teachers offered to classify every syntactic figure and every device of argument or persuasion should not affect our views. But ancient tragic poetry is rhetorical only in a subtle sense, and each of the great poets is his own rhetorician. The day of common rhetorical rules mechanically applied began in the fourth century BC, with its dead characters, its foolish plots, and its wooden tragic poetry.

A few marginal elements in tragic production in the fifth century are still important enough to merit some notice. One which is quickly disposed of has to do with the theatre of Dionysus at Athens. Leaving aside all the arguments about the raised stage and the stone house for actors and the high places where gods appeared, all of which are much later than people used to believe, we should consider a great rock that stuck out into the acting space until it was in the end removed on architectural grounds. How could the Athenians have permitted it? They accepted it tranquilly, they adapted it, and used it. It became the rock of Prometheus and other famous crags. They used it because it was to hand, just as their fathers would have done, acting round a cart in the *agora*. Of the original stones of the theatre of Aeschylus' time at Athens there are fewer than seven that still survive. They are hard to find and hard to recognize; only their simplicity makes them moving.

But in the course of the fifth century at Athens there arose an art of scene-painting which two or three centuries later, and perhaps elsewhere, was to produce elaborate perspective painting. It spread to the walls of houses, the house of Alcibiades first, and, like Oxford ragwort, which died out in the gardens, but was found flourishing centuries later in the walls, this new art of scene-painting survived a long time. Its theatrical origin explains the continual theatrical allusions in the wall-paintings of Pompeii, where fully developed perspective painting was several times imitated.

Satyr Plays

It is tempting to call the satyr plays simply pastoral plays, but they are not about nymphs and shepherds in idyllic countryside. They are usually set in wild countryside, with wild satyrs for a chorus, amoral, humorous, and pathetic creatures with human weaknesses for drink, sex, and the safety of their own skins. The chorus leader seems to be their father, but they are always lost, always in search of their master Dionysus. Otherwise there seem to be no rules about the plot. They receive the stolen fire from Prometheus, or they greet the infant Perseus, born in a chest floating out to sea, or the Cyclops has them as servants in the cave where he entertains Odysseus. The verse is somewhere between tragic and comic; it has a comic enchantment without being as boisterous as Aristophanes. The custom was to present one satyr play with three tragedies, and it is

SCENE FROM A SATYR PLAY, on an Athenian vase of about 470–460 BC. That these are not real satyrs is shown by the loin-cloth to which are fastened their tails and phalli, and the piper and bystander at the right indicate that this illustrates a stage production. The satyrs are carrying pieces of a throne which they are assembling, and we have the title of a satyr play by Aeschylus called *Thalamopoioi*, which might be roughly translated 'The Interior Decorators'.

very likely that they preserve something of the origins of Greek dramatic performance. Tragic solemnity could hardly have coexisted with an animal chorus.

The only complete satyr play we have is the *Cyclops* of Euripides, which is an interlude half the length of a tragedy, with tragic, comic, obscene, and religious elements curiously combined.

> I on the prow held a great fitted beam,
> while my sons were labouring at the oars
> whitening grey sea-water into foam:
> and all this in search of you my lord.
> We had sailed close in to the South Cape
> when a wind out of the sun's eye hit the beam
> and threw us up on the Etnaean rock
> among the one-eyed sons of the sea-god
> the murderous Cyclopes of desert rocks.

It is obvious at once that this kind of verse is intended as simple entertainment. If one spotted a *double entendre* in this or some other passage, one would not feel ashamed of oneself. Later, Euripides shows a flair for comedy of character at the same time. The Cyclops defends his cannibalism and his way of life.

Wealth, little man, is the god of the wise.
The rest is fine words and pretentiousness.
I bid my father's headlands of the sea
go fly away. Why should I pretend?
I don't fear Zeus' thunderbolt, my friend,
I don't see Zeus is stronger than I am.
That's all I care about; you want to know why?
Then listen. When he pours the rain down
I have a dry shelter under this rock.
I dine on a roast calf, I dine on game,
I lie back and I wet my belly well,
drink milk by the bucket, screw my cloak,
and make thunder as Zeus makes thunder.
And when the Thracian wind comes with the snow
I wrap my body up in pelts of beasts,
and make my fire up, snow doesn't worry me.
Earth produces grass by necessity
whether it likes or not, and fattens my flock.
I sacrifice to no god but myself
and to my belly here, to this great god.

The Cyclops is preposterous, and meets an unhappy end, of course, but the poet does feel some sympathy. At least he gives the Cyclops some good lines and some interesting arguments. It may be that the sudden excitement of the sophistic movement, the professional arguers and perverse philosophers who arrived in Athens during Euripides' lifetime, is nicely caught in this spirited composition. Plato is full of jokes and parodies; I do not think we are a thousand miles here from the kind of argument he deals with.

It is a pity we have no complete satyr play by Aeschylus. The fragments of his *Net-Fishers*, in which the satyrs fish up Danae and the baby Perseus, are very promising. It is hard to reconstruct the plot, but the characters include a king's brother called Net, and an old man of the island, possibly a god, just possibly the old Silenus, father of the satyrs. who will have owned the physical net and claimed what it netted. The island is Seriphos, and the character called Net is a traditional element in the story, which originally had no satyrs in it. He was the fisherman, and Aeschylus adopted him. The pleasantest surviving passage is a lyric fragment where the satyrs entice the child: 'Come along darling' (they use a Doric diminutive). There follows a whole line of that 'popopopo' noise which is still part of the Greek repertory of sounds. 'Come along quick to the children. Come nicely to my nursing hands, my dear. You will have weasels to play with and fawns and baby hedgehogs, and sleep in the same bed as your mother and father.' These words are not as innocent as they appear: Silenus appoints himself as father without consulting Danae. We know from another line that the baby was amazed by the erection which was part of a satyr's stage dress. 'What a cocklover the little fellow is', says the satyr. Unfortunately there is little more to be done with the fragments of this play; we must just hope that one day the goddess of papyri is merciful and we get the rest of it.

Comedy

INTRODUCTION

The main surviving mass of ancient Greek comedy begins only with Aristophanes, who was born within a few years of the mid fifth century, long after the great tragedians and too late to tell us much about the riotous early days of the comic chorus, before the state took it over. The consolation of this is the youth and zest of his work in the twenties of the century, and the fact that he worked on with great originality until 388 BC. In the early plays of Aristophanes, traditional Athenian comedy, the Old Style, as it came to be called, had already reached its full development; it has, as Aristotle remarked of tragedy, 'attained its nature'. The chorus was all-important, and the revelation of its dress and dances and music as the *Wasps* or the *Wine-bottles* or the *Clouds* or the *Caterpillars* was central to the competition. Not all the choruses were animal or even precisely humorous. The *Knights* and the *Towns of Attica* will not have been played entirely for laughs.

The comic theatre in the fifth century was directly political in a way that tragedy was not; its jokes had a bite and were often meant to be taken seriously. Aristophanes used his chorus at a certain moment in the play to address the audience directly; sometimes the chorus itself, the Birds or Clouds or Wasps or Frogs or whatever, seems to be speaking to us, sometimes the poet himself speaks through them. The connection of the Athenian political theatre with direct democracy is obvious. Its imaginative devices are bold and its characters are very plain-spoken. The Aristophanes who speaks in Plato's *Symposium* is surely very close to the real man, but the same cannot be said for the Socrates in Aristophanes' *Clouds*. The style of parody of individuals in the theatre is simple, vivid, and full of glee. It is not naturalistic.

All the same, real Athenians could be parodied by name or mostly thinly disguised, and plays could even be named after them. We know that the politicians resented this, which is hardly surprising, but there is no evidence that they ever managed to stamp it out under the fifth-century democracy. Maybe laughter really is like the crackling of thorns under a pot: hard to stamp out, and kicking only scatters it. Aristophanes attacks with joyful accuracy anyone and anything that strikes his fancy. As for his own political views, clearly enough they were democratic and patriotic. He was devoted to the Athenian democracy, and even more so to the comic theatre, perhaps the most characteristic of all its institutions. It was never a 'theatre of the common man'; it was nothing so safe. It was alive, part of a real democracy.

Comedy had its solemn as well as its political side. The plots were topsy-turvy. Right deserted to the side of Wrong, you could fly to heaven on a beetle, but

CLAY FIGURES OF COMIC ACTORS, both masked, and the one on the right wearing the characteristic short padded dress with phallus attached. Fourth century BC. These are from Attica, which is the principal source, but the types are met all over the Greek world and the masks shown on these and later figures can often be matched closely with those defined by the second-century AD writer Pollux for use on the Attic stage.

the bawdy irreverence with which gods and men were treated was somehow set in a frame, it was 'only a joke'. Serious things like peace, the city of Athens and her goddess and her physical beauty, were handled gently and beautifully. It is the few nostalgic verses, and those haunting lyrics in which poetry is suddenly set free from the comic action, which one never forgets. Aristophanes intended to give pleasure in as many ways as possible, and he still does so. Some of his allusive jokes that were meant to go fast raise only a gentle smile on the tired faces of scholars. Some of the puns and obscenities are only as memorable as their modern equivalent, for better and worse. But Aristophanes probably intended only his lyrics to be learnt by heart in Athens. Unfortunately they have never been successfully translated; almost no Aristophanes has been.

The greatest comic poet we know much about before Aristophanes is Cratinus. They overlapped; young Aristophanes attacked old Cratinus as a drunk who had given up poetry. Cratinus replied the next year, 423 BC, with a play in which the poet deserts his wife Comedy to go whoring after boys called Wine-bottles and a slut called Drunkenness. In that year's competition, Cratinus came first, and the

Clouds of Aristophanes came second. Since it was in the *Clouds* that Aristophanes attacked Socrates, one may hope that Socrates took it in the same spirit as Cratinus. We are told that the basic conception of plays was Cratinus' strong point. There is little to add except his vigorous obscenity, compared to which Aristophanes was a pale writer, and his uninhibited attacks on Pericles and his mistress Aspasia. It is probably true that vigour and obscenity and personal invective declined as the century wore out, though we shall see there are some exceptions.

The nearest contemporaries to Aristophanes in his working lifetime were Eupolis, who started producing comedies in 429 BC and died young in the course of the war, by drowning at sea, and a comic poet called Plato, younger than either of them, at work from about 410 to some time after 390. Eupolis presented Dionysus in the armed forces, subject to tough discipline, and in the *Towns of Attica* a scheme that was both solemn and humorous, and had a huge influence on Aristophanes' *Frogs*. In the competitive theatre of those years, it was inevitable that each year's plays, thirsting for an original idea, should often find it in last year's successes. Aristophanes and Eupolis shared some targets, and Aristophanes had already denounced Eupolis for plagiarism. In the *Towns of Attica* dead Athenians in the underworld argue about who should be sent back from the dead to put Athens in order; the Towns of Attica seem to be the chorus. In the *Frogs* the dispute is only over putting the tragic theatre in order.

The *Frogs* embodies a feature of comedy that is somewhat hard to explain: its parodying of tragedies, sometimes too self-consciously, as if comedy has to be a poor cousin of tragedy. Well, perhaps it was so. It is also true that the audience was the same for both, and the festivals came to be the same. Comedy was founded on mockery, and the stage mocked itself. But of all the elements in comic verse that meant most to an ancient audience, the one that most seldom amuses us now is the parody of tragedy—with the shining exception of the *Frogs*, which can be very funny indeed.

ARISTOPHANES

In the course of his career, Aristophanes spans the first two of the three phases or styles of Greek comedy. We must leave Epicharmus in Sicily out of account; Sicily and Athens in his day were separate planets. But starting in the twenties with vigorous and farcical burlesque, intermingled with savage onslaughts on politicians, he moved through the sadder, and in places more solemn, schemes of comedies such as the *Frogs* (405 BC) to the revival of comedy after the fall of Athens. If we believe that tragedy never did flower again, that may be because the fall of the city coincided with the deaths of Euripides and Sophocles, at about eighty and ninety years old. Comedy did reflower, perhaps because Aristophanes and the comic poet Plato survived.

Of the plays we have, the very first is like a bucket of cold water in the face.

It not only sounds, it trumpets the great themes of comic poetry: sex, life on the farm, the good old days, the nightmare of politics, the oddities of religion, the strange manners of the town. It is called the *Acharnians* (425 BC). The *Knights*, in the next year, adds to the old mixture some stern moralizing, some furious invective, and some lyrical patriotic politics. The quarrel with Cleon had begun earlier, in a severe onslaught in 426, in the *Babylonians*, Aristophanes' second play, which alas has not survived. Cleon was the leader of those who had wanted a year earlier to massacre the people of Mytilene, and he nearly brought that off. Aristophanes in the *Babylonians* showed cities of the Athenian League as slaves grinding at the mill.

We cannot avoid taking an interest in Aristophanes' attitude to slavery. Laughter without pity probably does not exist, but Aristophanes certainly introduces comic slaves. Yet racial comedy is not involved, because anyone could get enslaved, and it is noticeable that he shows his slaves with humanity, and with no more indignity than other characters. What he really hates, apart from such scum of the earth as Cleon, is charlatans and pretentiousness and pseudo-reform. But he differs from modern satiric writers in having a strong and passionately held moral standard, rooted in a society that he profoundly loves. Also, of course, in being a poet, perhaps a great poet, with a mind as open as daylight. Combine all these contradictions together and add a comic genius, and you will have Aristophanes, but only in the fifth century. What went to produce him is so many elements, so highly specific, they can never again be repeated. The most important is direct democracy in a traditional society.

His early comedies were political, his latest began to be social. In the second phase of Athenian comedy, to which Aristophanes is virtually our only witness, the chorus withered away to some musical interludes, plot knitted together into coherence, and a kind of realism took over. The early plots had been as wild as English pantomimes used to be. They were terribly spirited. The society they showed was diverse and in numerous ways eccentric: the overlap of generations, given the speed of change at that time, and the intermingling of types when Athens was under siege, produced plenty of paradoxes and comic fireworks. But in the fourth century something smoother, more like a bourgeoisie, began to emerge. It was mirrored, not very kindly, in the comic theatre. It was bourgeois in its morality, in its limited views of things, in its tastes and ambitions. No doubt such people can be justified by history. Aristophanes would not have liked them, nor would his Acharnian peasant. His *Wealth* (388 BC) reflects only the transition. What was coming was comedy as the modern world has known it, beginning with Menander.

As an imaginative artist, Aristophanes was fully developed by the end of the twenties, and already in *Peace* (421) he was driven to wild fantasies to express his longing for war to end. In 414 the heroes of the *Birds* are two Athenians who despair of the city altogether. He makes the point lightly, but make it he does.

> We're flying away from home with both our feet,
> not that we hate that city, not at all,
> that great city happy by nature
> and general provider for all men.
> But the crickets sit singing on the branches
> for one or two months; Athens does it for ever,
> singing away their lives in the lawcourts.

Life at Athens being no longer worth living, they go to consult a mythical hero who was turned into a bird. The plot of the play is the building of the city of the birds. One of its chief pleasures is a very long aria, a long lyric poem in a series of attractive metres sung by one character, the hoopoe, who calls the other birds with some bird-mimicry such as possibly a bird-snarer might use. Apart from the *Wasps*, who are melodious in Vaughan Williams but less so in Aristophanes, this is the first animal chorus we have from Aristophanes. The bird mimicry is remarkable. It is untranslatable, of course, because a lot of it depends on onomatopoeic words in Greek. For gaiety and lightness of touch, Aristophanes perhaps never outdid that scene.

The birds set up a blockade to cut off sacrifices from earth to the gods. The play ends as comedies were supposed to end, with a celebration. The gods make peace with the birds and mankind, and we have a marriage hymn with prayers to Zeus, shouts of victory, and the play disappearing in a shower of fireworks. At the festival of that year, the winning play was called the *Revellers*, this was second, and the third was called the *Solitary*; it was another escapist play. The *Birds* is crammed with comic inventions, including Prometheus hiding under an umbrella from the other gods, Iris captured in mid air by the birds, a Thracian god of extreme barbarity, and a poet who wants to be turned into a nightingale.

For a really funny play by modern standards we can turn to 411 BC, to the *Lysistrata*. By this time Aristophanes' despair about altering the course of events seems to have set hard. What he proposes is a conspiracy of women to refuse sex with their men until the men agree to make peace. This has to be world-wide within the Greek world, and the priestess of Athena, who seems to be based on someone real, has organized it. The characterization of women from all over Greece is hilariously funny, and so are the details of the plot as it unfolds. It is one of the few ancient comedies that entrances modern audiences. It is also the earliest in which one may suspect a touch of compassion in the rather vigorous treatment handed out to people. When the old men are grovelling, there is one case where one is almost sorry for the poor beast. Aristophanic comedy usually has a string or two strings of episodes in which various characters get attacked or seen off; one is not usually sorry for them. Maybe *Lysistrata* is close to the beginning of a new sense of laughing through tears, which made Menander possible and the old style impossible. We need not necessarily see this as a change for the better.

If we do not, we can be pleased that most of *Lysistrata* is splendidly heartless.

It is not Aristophanes' only women's play, but the only one in which they are really heroes. The other two are the *Thesmophoriazousae*, from the same year as *Lysistrata*, which is almost entirely based on jokes about Euripides, and *Women in Parliament*, an extravaganza of 392 BC, the year of an alliance between Athens and Sparta. Women take over the state in it and announce communism. The plot is incoherent because it lacks political drive: Aristophanes does no more than toy with his themes, and the political humour which once generated such alarming fantasies has sunk to a whimsical level. The *Lysistrata* is stronger because it deals with impossibilities as if they were real; it belongs to a year in which something was still possible, maybe everything.

The *Frogs*, in 405 BC, is in one way the saddest play of Aristophanes that we still have, because the only thing it puts right is the theatre. But there is no lack of brilliance in its verbal texture, and no weakness of construction. It does raise problems, since unless there were two choruses, which would be unique in our experience, then either the Frogs themselves or the choirs of the Blest never appear. The essential plot of the *Frogs* is the descent of Dionysus, a god with many human weaknesses, to the underworld, mocked by the Frogs as he learns to row in Charon's boat; he is searching for a great tragic poet, and chooses between Aeschylus and Euripides by a contest in which they destroy one another's lines with parody and mockery. This process is for once extremely funny, and (even more unusually) instructive, since it tells us something about the texture and technique of tragic verse. Still, the tendency of mockery is to suppress extremes, and the view of poetry that Aristophanes takes is too safe to be sound.

He does take his own calling as a poet most seriously, in a way unfamiliar in our times, but as a comic poet in the theatre of Athens his responsibility is greater than that of modern writers. He says 'We must indeed say things that are good, because to little children it is the schoolmaster who speaks, but to those past puberty it is poets'. From his very first play, which was about modern versus old-fashioned education, at least down to the *Frogs*, which contains strong moral views thinly disguised, Aristophanes writes as if the lines I have quoted here are important to him. Aeschylus wins the contest in the underworld, Sophocles being too peaceable to take part. At the very end we suddenly have these words:

> The graceful thing
> is not to sit
> by Socrates and talk
> and cast aside the Muse
> and all the great matter
> of the tragic art.

He wants more poetry and fewer philosophers; particularly he wants more Aeschylus. Dare one say he was wrong? Would Socrates say so?

His last surviving play, *Wealth*, was produced in 388 BC. Wealth is notoriously blind, and gives his benefits to the wrong people, so Apollo shows him how blindness can be cured by Asclepius at Athens. Wealth does recover his eyesight, but the resulting redistribution of money produces comic confusion. The old rich woman loses her gigolo, because now he has enough without her; Hermes reports chaos among the gods; Wealth gets enthroned in his home of the good old days, the national treasury inside the west end of the Parthenon. This play has no choral lyrics and hardly any chorus, its arguments are in social and philosophic, not in political terms, the humour is more often low than obscene, and even the most farcical episodes begin to be handled more gently.

MENANDER

Comedy never seems to have hardened or died on its feet as tragedy did, but the next substantial glimpse that we get of Athenian comedy in good health is many years after the deaths of Aristophanes and the comic poet Plato. A generation had passed, and few alive had any serious recollection of the fifth century, when Menander was born in 342 BC. He lived through the reign of Alexander and its aftermath. He was a baby when the freedom of Greece was lost, and by the time he was twenty Alexander was dead. His Athens was cosmopolitan, crowded, full of foreign business. But it could not take its fate into its own hands or alter its future. Even in private life fate was something that was done to you; it was what happened more than what you did. Great cities had their Lady Luck as well as individuals; in a world in which everything was uncertain, people concentrated on their private lives. Philosophy was some consolation; it implied an order of a kind.

    This state of things produced a comedy of manners, with social targets and an action of limited consequences. It depended on surprise piled on surprise by the turning wheel of fortune, and the guiding genius of the comic poet came to include some of the skills of the modern thriller-writer. Writing for the theatre became a sophisticated, technical matter. It was no longer a mystery or a matter of genius. And yet what was produced is astonishing. The numerous papyrus texts of Menander recovered in the last hundred, even in the last thirty, years, have heavily reinforced his reputation. He is funnier, faster, and stronger altogether than scholars used to expect. It is much better to emphasize heavily the intervening darkness between him and Aristophanes, to forget regret, and to see Menander's theatrical poetry as a new-created world. His work has not been successfully translated. He was a poet after all, and his subtly modulated verse demands more understanding of poetry than it has been offered.

    One could hardly go beyond the mythic hero and the comic type after all, in a theatre in which masks were still worn, though the masks were more realistic now, and so were the clothes and settings. Still, it is surprising how much can be done with type-cast characters. One may question whether Agatha Christie in our own times ever used anything else, though she was no poet, and not so great an artist as Menander.

    His world is one in which soldiers thought to be killed in some Asian battle turn out to be 'living and saved as never before', thus confusing people's hopes to inherit. A chest is fished out of the sea, the shipwrecked come to land, or a treasure gets dug up in a field. Intrigues between lovers and confidential slaves produce intricate crossed lines. Slaves turn out to be free-born, kidnapped in childhood. Families are reunited, and improper marriages become suddenly possible. The love interest is not dominant, though; it is largely secondary to the relationships and fortunes of the inner family, and a young man may as easily

THE NEW COMEDY POET MENANDER (who died about 292 BC). Mosaic portrait found in a Roman villa of the fourth century AD near the main town on the island of Lesbos (Mytilene). Other panels showed figures from the poet's plays, similar to that found at Pompeii and illustrated in Vol. 2, p. 62. These may derive from illustrations to manuscripts, possibly of Hellenistic date.

fall for a whore as for a character capable of a permanent romantic link. This is one inherited convention among others.

In the *Shield* Fortune herself appears after the first scenes to explain to the audience what really is going on. This too is a convention simply accepted and objectively treated. Choice between the delights of foreseeing and those of surprise seems to have been a consuming problem in Menander's theatre. At any rate the end of every play could be foreseen: it would be happy. It might recall ancient comedy by being a mildly riotous celebration. The *Difficult Man* ends with dancing to flute music at a picnic near the cave of Pan, who in that play represents the contriving and benevolent divine powers. In fact this pleasant ending, after which there is only an invitation to applause, is the most memorable feature of the *Difficult Man*. If one wants to laugh aloud one would do better to delve among the fragments for a scene of divine possession, possibly false, observed by two terrified Greeks. The play is *Theophoroumenē*, 'The Possessed Woman'.

Some of the plots are elaborately complicated; it would be hard to recount them in less length than that of the plays. They are like dances, with contrasted couples, ill suited and well suited, and a variety of interlocking opposites. The conclusions are also dance-like, shadow-footed, magical in a sense in which Aristophanes was not. Everything mysteriously falls out just right, at the very last moment and in spite of numerous unlucky strokes and incompetent intrigues.

All the same, the harmonious confusion and the mild violence within the magic circle of Menander's theatrical effects are meant to keep out the black outside world, just as the philosophers of escape tried to keep it out. It is even probable that Menander and Epicurus, who were exactly the same age, had done their Athenian military training together. There are touches of Epicurean pleasure and gentleness here and there in Menander. As for the outer world, we have very few dates for individual works of Menander, so it is hard to trace any development in his poetry or his invention, or any more precise relation with the events of history. His poetry is just a patch of sunlight moving over the grass. The famous humanity was only one of his qualities, but the more detail of plots and counterplots we recover, the more meaning his urbane and somewhat sweet-tasting philosophic remarks take on.

One very odd element in Menander's plots is moral reformation. Of course he inherits a morality from fifth-century comedy, in which characters get taught a lesson or won round by comic means. But he wants to philosophize and moralize these conversions, although at the same time he wants to characterize his people more fully and realistically. The result is a character like the Difficult Man, beautifully observed, perfectly convincing, who suddenly sprouts a lot of noble philosophic thoughts. The robust action is not enough: the old gentleman has just fallen down a well after all, and being rescued is what converted him. He still has to reason it out in noble sentiments. One is tempted to say that in the world of Menander poetry belongs to children; for those past puberty it is the moral philosopher who speaks.

In another play a shepherd and a charcoal-burner quarrel over a baby they find lying about abandoned with its few little treasures; they go to an old man for decision, but little does he know the baby is his grandchild; his daughter got into trouble at a night festival and threw away the resulting baby for shame. This is only one tiny area of an unbelievable web of intrigues; in the end the man who fathered the baby at the night festival turns out to be the girl's husband. One can sympathize with the German nineteenth-century scholar who remarked that the most immoral feature of such immoral plays as this was their happy endings. The Lord of Misrule had not lost all influence over the Greek comic theatre; the absurdity of the story-line of these plays, as well as their elegance of construction, was intended to give delight, and so it does.

A COMIC PRODUCTION WITH *PHLYAX* ACTORS (probably so-called for their padded costumes), on a vase made in Apulia about 375 BC. They resemble Athenian comic actors in their dress, masks, and prominent phalli. They do not act in a formal theatre but on a low wooden stage, with lean-to roof and steps up from the auditorium, seen here in profile. To judge from the vases the subjects were comic versions of Greek myth and some everyday situations recalling Athenian Middle and New Comedy. Here the old centaur Chiron (but shown as human) is helped on to the stage by Xanthias. Comic nymphs watch (top right), and standing at the right is a 'normal' youth, perhaps the stage-manager. This is a theatrical genre peculiar to South Italy in the fourth century BC. See also Vol. 2, p. 65.

The Results of Comedy

Without comedy, without the long development and the transformations of comedy at Athens, there would have been no invention of pastoral poetry or the fishermen's poetry that corresponds to it. The romance, and the novel that arose in the end from plays and romances, have their taproot in the comic theatre. They derive from Euripides as well, but only because comedy had shown how Euripides could be adapted and travestied. The oddest of all the survivals of Greek comedy was through its offshoot as Latin comedy, in the revived Latin and vernacular comedy of the renaissance. That line of descent is much more direct and easier to trace than the rediscovery of tragedy, which happened at many removes, partly through the blood-soaked exaggerations of Seneca, exaggerated still further in translation by Jasper Heywood, who became a Jesuit, was arrested, and died mad.

There is a sense in which Menander's comedies, filtered as they were through

Plautus and Terence, gave us our fundamental ideas about what human beings are like: not only through the refined and noble sentiments which spread like bindweed through the whole literate world, in books of sayings and copybooks of every kind, but our idea of urban man, and civilized man, and his limitations. That is surely because of Menander's apparent interest in individuals and his real handling of types. As the life of individuals and the ambition of families became newly interesting to the literate classes in the late Middle Ages, it was natural that ancient comedy should be their model. Menander was part of the culture of St Paul; his unassuming nobility, his humanist maxims, above all his universality and vague compassion had melted into the moral atmosphere. The urbanity and the liberty turn out to be inseparable. Medieval and Byzantine satire are the steam screaming out of an engine. Horatian satire is quiet and deadly; it derives from Athens, and runs through Voltaire and Diderot, nearly down to our own times. In Byzantium, what comedy could there be? Only a venomous courtly hissing, or a popular comedy so low it would escape notice: something like the shadow-theatre of Karaghiozis. Admirable as that is, it belongs to the comedies of the 'volunteers', before comic poetry became an art. One of the bravest, most inspired steps the Athenian democracy ever took was to make comedy a state event: for that to happen comedy had to exist already, and its audience had to exist.

Further Reading

Albin Lesky's *History of Greek Literature* (London, 1966) discusses all the Greek theatrical writers and the general problems that they raise. He is useful even when one disagrees with him. His *Greek Tragic Poetry* (Yale, 1983) goes into considerable detail about every play. More challenging is Brian Vickers, *Towards Greek Tragedy* (London, 1973), which uses both anthropological and Shakespearean material to illustrate the nature of myth and of suffering in tragedy.

A. D. Trendall and T. B. L. Webster, *Illustrations of Greek Drama* (London, 1971), has replaced all earlier works of this kind and presents the evidence of visual art extremely clearly. A. W. Pickard-Cambridge, *The Dramatic Festivals of Athens*, (2nd edn., revised by J. Gould and D. M. Lewis, Oxford, 1968) is a reliable guide to its subject.

O. Taplin, in *The Stagecraft of Aeschylus* (Oxford, 1977), has opened a new and much clearer way of reading and understanding Aeschylus; his *Greek Tragedy in Action* (London, 1978) effectively brings out the significance of performance and spectacle in Attic tragedy. There are particularly good books on Sophocles: Karl Reinhardt's *Sophocles* (English trans., Oxford Blackwell, 1978); *Sophocles: an Interpretation* by R. P. Winnington-Ingram (Cambridge, 1980) and B. M. W. Knox's *The Heroic Temper: Studies in Sophoclean Tragedy* (California, 1966). These works bring out well the nature of Sophocles' world and the stature and situation of his central characters. Gilbert Murray's classic *Euripides and his Age* (1913, Oxford; paperback 1965) is still worth reading. An excellent book in French: J. de Romilly, *L'évolution du pathétique d'Eschyle à Euripide* (Paris, 2nd edn. 1980). There is a paperback *Oxford Readings in Greek Tragedy* (1983) edited by E. Segal, which reprints many interesting papers, some of them translated from other languages.

Richmond Lattimore, in *The Poetry of Greek Tragedy* (Baltimore, 1958) and *Story Patterns in Greek Tragedy* (London, 1964), both brief books, does more than many longer ones to make plain the things we most want to know about the subject.

Hugh Lloyd-Jones in *The Justice of Zeus* (California, 2nd edn. 1984) and E. R. Dodds, in *The Greeks and the Irrational* (California, 1951) constantly discuss tragedy, and their work is an indispensable introduction to this as to other matters.

T. B. L. Webster's *Introduction to Menander* (London, 1974) makes many useful observations and is sound and thorough, though F. H. Sandbach's general book, *The Comic Theatre of Greece and Rome* (London, 1977), is more intuitive; sounder still, and easy to read, which Webster is not, K. J. Dover's reliable *Aristophanic Comedy* (London, 1972) is an admirably precise, if sometimes laconic, treatment. Kenneth McLeish's *Theatre of Aristophanes* (London, 1980), on the other hand, is a very lively book, brimming over with ideas and full of insights. It is appealingly unsober and romantic.

Hugh Lloyd-Jones's translation of the *Oresteia* (London, 1979) with new introductions to the three plays in this edition, is the best English version and literary interpretation that we have for any Greek play. The most successful versions by poets are the Oedipus plays by W. B. Yeats and the *Women of Trachis*, eccentric but brilliant, by Ezra Pound. No wholly satisfactory translations of most tragedies or any comedies exist in English, though Dudley Fitts has produced actable adaptations of Aristophanes of great interest, and the Penguin translations of Aristophanes have great merits (by D. Barrett and A. H. Sommerstein).

Impressive versions of tragedies by Louis MacNeice and Rex Warner can still be found in second hand bookshops.

8

Greek Historians

❧❧

OSWYN MURRAY

The Origins of History

MANY societies possess professional remembrancers, priests or officials, whose duty it is to record those traditions thought necessary for the continuity of social values; many societies also possess priestly or official records, designed to help regulate and placate the worlds of gods and men, but capable of being converted by modern scholars into history. Yet the actual writing of history as a distinct cultural activity seems in origin independent of these natural social attitudes, and is a rare phenomenon: it has in fact developed independently only in three very different societies: Judaea, Greece, and China. The characteristics of history in each case are distinct: history is not a science, but an art form serving the needs of society and therefore conditioned by its origin.

The Greek tradition of history writing is our tradition, and we can best see its peculiarities by comparing it with that other tradition which has so strongly influenced us, the Jewish historical writings preserved in the Old Testament. Greeks and Jews came to history independently, but at roughly the same time and in response to the same pressures, the need to establish and sustain a national identity in the face of the vast empires of the Middle East: just as the struggles with Assyria, the exile in Babylon, and the return to the promised land created Jewish historical writing, so the sense of national identity resulting from the defeat of Persia created Greek historical writing. But the presuppositions and the materials with which the two historical traditions worked are very different. For the Jews history was the record of God's covenant with His chosen people, its successes and disasters conditioned by their willingness to obey His commands. History was therefore a single story, belonging to God: the different elements and individual authors are moulded (not always successfully) into a continuous account. Greek history, while it could recognize a moral pattern in human affairs, regarded these affairs as in the control of man: history was the record, not of the mercy or wrath of God, but of the great deeds of men. Among those deeds was the writing of history itself: so a Greek historian is an individual who 'signs' his work in its first sentence—'Herodotus of Halicarnassus, his researches ...', 'Thucydides of Athens wrote the history of the war ...' The great exception to this rule serves to confirm it: those who, like Xenophon, sought to continue the unfinished work of Thucydides, chose not to reveal their identity: Xenophon begins his work, 'Some days later ...', and nowhere mentions his own name, although he is far freer than Thucydides with opinions delivered in the first person. We do not even know the name of the author of another (and better) continuation of Thucydides, partly preserved on papyrus, the 'Oxyrhynchus historian' (so called from the village in Egypt where the copy of his text was found). Later Christian generations in fact tried to transform this individualistic group of historical writings into a tradition of the Old Testament type, and succeeded through instinct or economy of effort in selecting a 'chain of histories', so that only one historical account now survives for each period, and these accounts give a relatively continuous narrative history of the ancient world. A proper history of Greek history writing must take due notice of what has been lost as well as of what survives.

A second difference between Jewish and Greek historical writing is in their sources and attitudes to the sources. The Jewish historical account is built on a multiplicity of evidences which would do credit to a modern historian, and are of three basic types—acts (customs, taboos, rituals, and their explanations), the spoken tradition (hymns, poetry, prophecy, myths, folk-tales), and the written tradition (laws, official documents, royal and priestly chronicles, biographies); it is prone to quote proofs and evidence such as documents. The source material used by Greek historians is initially far simpler and more rudimentary, and the Greeks were always more concerned with the literary, rather than the evidential, aspects of history; they therefore seldom quote documents. Paradoxically the Greek tradition remains superior to the Jewish in its ability to distinguish fact from fiction: God can falsify history far more effectively than the individual historian with his mere mortal bias. The Greeks indeed taught the West how to create and write history without God.

Both peoples learned the alphabet from the same source, the Phoenicians who invented it; writing came to Greece in the eighth-century BC, yet Greece long remained an oral culture in which men spoke in prose, but composed in verse. The distinction between poetry and prose was later a mark of the difference between myth and history, but the earliest known prose literary work was philosophical rather than historical, and related to the need to formulate and convey thoughts in a precise and accurate form; about 550 BC the philosopher Anaximander of Miletus wrote a book *On Nature*, which discussed both the basic structure of the physical world and its visible forms: it contained the first maps and descriptions of both earth and the heavens. Some fifty years later Hecataeus of Miletus similarly wrote a *Description of the Earth* accompanied by a map: it was divided into two books, one for Europe and one for Asia, and recorded the information he had gathered from his own and others' travels. Geography and ethnography are important components in the Greek view of history.

Another work of Hecataeus called *Genealogies* has often been thought to be the first to exhibit that spirit of critical enquiry which is characteristic of western history writing, for it began: 'Hecataeus the Milesian speaks thus: I write these things as they seem true to me; for the stories told by the Greeks are various and in my opinion absurd' (*FGH* 1, F.1). The book actually seems to have been a collection of heroic myths and genealogies of heroes, designed to reduce them into a pseudo-historical account by rationalizing them; it is a curious false start to history, on the one hand recognizing the need to understand the past in rational terms, but on the other hand using the fundamentally unsuitable material of myth. It shows both a desire to liberate history from myth, and an inability to distinguish between the two.

Herodotus

From time to time critics have tried to discover lost historians in the generation after Hecataeus to help explain the next development in the writing of history; but such theories are based on shaky evidence and a mistaken belief that local history or the monograph must come before general history with a grand theme. Herodotus of Halicarnassus in fact deserves his ancient title of 'father of history'. His work is the earliest Greek book in prose to have survived intact; it is some 600 pages or nine 'books' long. Its theme is presented in the first sentence: 'This is the account of the investigation of Herodotus of Halicarnassus, undertaken so that the achievements of men should not be obliterated by time and the great and marvellous works of both Greeks and barbarians should not be without fame, and not least the reason why they fought one another.'

The ultimate justification of the work is the account of the conflict between Greece and Persia, culminating in the Great Expedition of Xerxes to Greece in 480 BC described in the last three books: it is the story of how an army of (allegedly) one and three-quarter million men and a navy of 1,200 ships was defeated by the fragmented forces of the Greeks, who in no battle could muster more than 40,000 men and 378 ships; we may doubt the Persian numbers, but the strategy shows that we cannot doubt the fact that the Greeks were heavily outnumbered on each occasion (above pp. 38 ff.). A fleet from Herodotus' city had fought on the Persian side, and one of his earliest memories was perhaps of the setting out and return of that fateful expedition; he grew up in an Ionia suffering the joys and pains of its liberation and then subjection by the victorious Athenian navy (above, pp. 127 ff.). For the generation of Herodotus the epic achievements of their fathers had created the world in which they lived, as the return of the exiles from Babylon had created the world of Ezra. In his last books Herodotus sought to raise a fitting monument to the new race of heroes, using all the literary skills at his command, 'so that the achievements of men should not be obliterated by time'.

The central theme of this conflict requires Herodotus to go back to its origins:

'who was the first in actual fact to harm the Greeks'. So the work begins with the earlier struggles between the Ionian Greeks and the kingdom of Lydia, before passing on to the origins of Persian power and the story of Cyrus the Great, and then the further conquests of the Persians, in Egypt and north Africa, and around the Black Sea, until we see that the conflict was inevitable.

But this central theme is merely one aspect of the work; there is another, at least as important—'the account of the investigation' or 'researches' of Herodotus (this is in fact the original meaning and the first recorded use of the word *historiē*). Like Hecataeus, Herodotus was a traveller: in the first four books and often thereafter the theme of the conflict is subordinate, a thread on which to hang a series of accounts or stories gathered from different places. These range from individual stories about famous figures (the mythical poet Arion or the Persian court doctor Democedes of Croton, for instance) to substantial histories of the rise and fall of cities (Athens, Sparta, Naucratis in Egypt) and finally to full-scale geographical and ethnographic accounts of civilizations, the most extended of which, on Egypt, occupies the whole of Book 2.

The result is far more than an account of the causes and events of a mere conflict. It is rather a total picture of the known world, in which the geography, customs, beliefs, and monuments of each people are at least as important as their often tenuous relationship to the war. It is this which gives added depth to Herodotus' account, and makes it both a great work of art and a convincing history of a conflict not just between two peoples but between two types of society, the Mediterranean egalitarian city-state and the oriental despotisms of the Middle East. It also makes Herodotus more modern than any other ancient historian in his approach to the ideal of total history.

Herodotus' openness to other cultures indeed caused him to be called a 'barbarophile'. It reflects in part an older Ionian view from an age of exploration, reinforced perhaps by the traditions of Herodotus' own community of Halicarnassus, which was a mixed Greek and Carian city. But these attitudes have been systematized under the influence of the new sophistic interest in the relationship between culture and nature, *nomos* and *physis*; 'For if anyone, no matter who, were given the opportunity of choosing from amongst all the nations of the world the set of beliefs which he thought best, he would inevitably, after careful consideration of their relative merits, choose those of his own country.' Herodotus illustrates the point with a story of the confrontation between Greeks and Indians arranged by King Darius; the Indians were disgusted to hear that the Greeks burned the corpses of their dead parents, the Greeks appalled that the Indians ate theirs: 'One can see from this what custom can do, and Pindar, in my opinion, was right when he called it "king of all" ' (3. 38).

The two aspects of the work in one sense reflect the two main literary influences on it, Homer and the world of war and conflict, Hecataeus and the world of peace and understanding. They also probably reflect a chronological progression in the development of Herodotus' book. He seems to have begun as an expert on foreign cultures, a travelling sophist who lectured on the marvels of the world; only later did he arrange his researches around a unifying theme. Despite much modern controversy, that still seems the most satisfactory account of the various peculiarities in the book.

How did Herodotus acquire his information? Some information may have come from previous literary works; but Hecataeus is the only such author Herodotus mentions, and no convincing traces of the use of earlier written narratives have been detected. Herodotus can quote poetry and oracles, and occasionally gives information ultimately based on eastern documentary sources; but it is clear that he did not regard written documents as an important source of information, indeed that he knew no language but Greek. Herodotus' own characterization of his sources is always the same, and is consistent with the types of information he gives. He claims to practise that most modern of historical disciplines, oral history, the collection and interpretation of the living spoken tradition of a people: his sources are 'sight and hearing', what he has seen and what he has been told; the two of course interrelate, since monuments and natural phenomena preserve and call forth verbal explanations. His travels included Egypt and Cyrene in north Africa, Tyre in Phoenicia, Mesopotamia as far as Babylon, the Black Sea and the Crimea, and the north Aegean, apart from the main cities of Asia Minor and Greece, and ultimately (though this has left little if any trace in the *Histories*) south Italy where he settled. In each place he seems to have sought out 'men with traditions', particular groups, interpreters, priests, or leading citizens, and to have recorded a single version of the oral tradition available, a version which may of course often have been partial, biased or merely frivolous; he compares different versions only if they come from different places. The difficulties of writing oral history are well recognized today; yet on the main cultures such as Egypt and Persia, where Herodotus can be checked he is revealed to be remarkably well informed for someone working from such oral sources.

It is in his Greek history that Herodotus reveals the most important aspect of his artistic personality. For mainland Greece his information seems to come from the leading political groups in the cities. For Sparta he gives an official line, for Athens a version based at least in part on particular aristocratic traditions; the narrative is concerned with events and wars, rational in tone, without moral or religious colouring, and designed to enhance or justify the status of particular groups. At Delphi a different type of tradition was available, a series of stories told by the priests and related to the monuments and offerings at the shrine. These stories contain many folk-tale motifs and have a strong moral tone: the hero moves from prosperity to misfortune as a victim of divine envy—the ethical teaching is not aristocratic, but belongs to the shrine of a god whose temple carried the mottoes, 'Know yourself', and 'Nothing too much'. The same types of story pattern are dominant in Ionia: Herodotus' history of his home area is far less 'historical' and far less political than his account of mainland Greece. He is, for instance, often thought to have had particularly good sources for the history of Samos, where he spent much of his youth, yet his account of the tyrant Polycrates only two generations earlier has already turned into a folk-tale.

This characteristic of his Ionian sources suggests a popular, non-aristocratic tradition of story-telling which is directly related to Herodotus' achievement. For the overall shape of his history shows the same moral patterning as his Ionian and Delphic stories: the story of the Persian Wars is a story of how 'the god strikes with his thunderbolt the tall, and will not allow them to display themselves, while small beings do not vex him; you see how the lightning throws down always the greatest buildings and the finest trees' (7. 10). The message is created through a series of devices derived from the art of the folk-tale: the warning dream, the figure of the wise counsellor disregarded, the recurrent story pattern. Just as behind Homer there lies a long tradition of oral poetry sung by professional bards, so behind Herodotus there lies an Ionian tradition of story-telling of which he himself was the last and greatest master.

Thus Herodotus' collecting of information was not guided by any spirit of systematic enquiry, neither was it the product of random curiosity. It was informed from the start with the principle of the *logos*. Herodotus uses the word *logos* to refer to the whole of his work, to its major sections (the Egyptian or the Lydian *logos*), and to the individual stories within it: he surely regarded himself as a *logos*-maker in the same way as he regarded both Hecataeus the mythographer and Aesop the creator of animal fables; Thucydides indeed dismisses him as a '*logos*-writer'. The word *logos* in this context may very often seem to mean little more than the English 'story', as long as we remember that a story has a shape, a purpose: it is not an isolated fact preserved for its own sake; it may be true, but it must be interesting. The achievement of Herodotus was to harness the skills of the *logos*-maker to the description of human societies in peace and war.

From the evidence for his friendship with the poet Sophocles, Herodotus was already active as a lecturer in the late forties of the fifth century; the final version of his history was published shortly before 425 BC, when Aristophanes parodied his account of the causes of the Persian Wars in his comedy, *The Acharnians*. Already Herodotus seemed old-fashioned, for the wider Ionian responsiveness to the interplay of civilizations had been replaced by a narrower concern with the Greek city-state and its interests; history became the history of the *polis*, and took new directions.

Local History and Chronography

The first of these consisted in a fragmentation of the synoptic view of Herodotus into the systematic exploitation of local traditions, and more importantly local archives. These local or ethnic histories satisfied the interests of a local audience for the history of their particular city, and continued to be written throughout antiquity as long as the *polis* survived; all are now lost, but the Augustan critic Dionysius of Halicarnassus describes their general characteristics:

These men made similar choices about the selection of their subjects, and their powers were not so very different from one another, some of them writing histories about the Greeks and some about the barbarians, and not linking all these to one another, but dividing them according to peoples and cities, and writing about them separately, all keeping to one and the same aim: whatever oral traditions were preserved locally among peoples or cities, and whatever documents were stored in holy places or archives, to bring these to the common notice of everyone just as they were received, neither adding to them nor subtracting from them. (*On Thucydides* 5)

This movement for the first time in Greece set the written archive alongside oral tradition as a source for history; two figures from its earliest stages will illustrate its character. About the end of the fifth century Hippias of Elis, travelling sophist and lecturer on antiquities of cities, published the victor list of the Olympic Games, which took chronology back in a four-year cycle to 776 BC; this became the basis for Greek time-reckoning, just as the Romans counted from the foundation of their city, the early Christians from the birth of Abraham, and ourselves from the birth of Christ. Chronology, the dating and ordering of human events, is the basic grammar of history: Hippias began a tradition which continued through the Hellenistic period, to produce in late antiquity the surviving chronological tables of sacred and profane history compiled by the Christian writers Eusebius and Saint Jerome.

Hellanicus of Lesbos in the last third of the fifth century similarly published a whole series of local histories and chronographies (at least twenty-eight), based at least in part on archival research. Among these was the first history of Athens; and the discovery in Egypt of a papyrus of Aristotle's lost work on the *Constitution of Athens* (written in the late fourth century) enables us to reconstruct the development of one city history in some detail. The *Atthis* (or history of Athens) began with Hellanicus, a non-Athenian working in a wider tradition; later authors were mainly Athenian, often from priestly families (Cleidemus) or politicians (Androtion, the author on whom Aristotle largely relied) or both (Philochorus). Their works were characterized from the start on the one hand by a strong interest in local myth, on the other by the possession of a firm chronology: events were arranged (perhaps somewhat arbitrarily) in accordance with the Athenian list of their annual chief magistrate or *archon*. Fragments of such a list inscribed on stone and dating from the 420s BC have in fact been found in the Athenian *agora*: the public record is almost certainly evidence of state interest in the discoveries of Hellanicus, which stimulated the Athenians to set their archives in order. This is a good illustration of the interplay between civic pride and the writing of history; not surprisingly such a tradition is dominated by the interests of the *polis*, its local cults and its politics.

Thucydides

Thucydides too is a product of the world of the developed city-state, and belongs to roughly the same generation as the first local historians; but he proclaims himself a conscious rival of Herodotus in his first sentence:

Thucydides of Athens wrote the history of the war between the Peloponnesians and the Athenians, beginning it as soon as war broke out and believing that it would be a great war and more worthy of record than any preceding one, on the evidence that both sides went into it at the height of preparedness, and seeing the rest of the Greek world taking one side or the other, either immediately or after consideration.

The main themes emerge at once: the explicit rivalry with Herodotus in the description of a great war, the claim to contemporaneous recording, the emphasis on proving his views, the self-conscious assertion of being a writer not a performer in an oral tradition, all expressed in a prose of extraordinary density and sophistication. The war that Thucydides describes is the Great Peloponnesian War between Athens and Sparta, which lasted for a whole generation from 431 to 404 BC with only a short interlude of official, but broken, peace from 421 to 416, and ended with the defeat of Athens and the collapse of her empire. Thucydides did not live to complete his work; Book 8 breaks off in mid sentence in 411; and whereas Books 6 and 7 on the Athenian expedition to Sicily seem to be a polished work of art, there are signs of lack of finish in Books 5 and 8. Thucydides' own activities in the war are best described by himself:

I lived through the whole of the war, being of an age to comprehend events, and giving my attention to them in order to know the exact truth about them. It was also my fate to be an exile from my country for twenty years after my command at Amphipolis [in 424 he had failed to save the city from a surprise attack]; and being present with both parties, and more especially with the Peloponnesians by reason of my exile, I had considerable leisure to observe affairs. (5. 26)

Thucydides is first of all a historian's historian: he is obsessed with methodology. He sets out to prove the greatness of his war by a long excursus on earlier history designed to show the comparative insignificance of earlier wars and the poverty of earlier generations; and at the same time he offers a devastating critique of the standards of evidence employed by Herodotus. He establishes with precision the starting-point and the end of his war, and argues carefully that the so-called period of peace was really part of a single war. Like his contemporaries he is fascinated by chronology, but he rejects their lists of magistrates as unsuitable for military history; instead he dates by campaigning seasons, 'by summers and winters'. He attacks the lack of care others take in ascertaining facts, and asserts that he was not satisfied with any one eyewitness account, but took great pains to correlate and judge between the often differing accounts of different participants. Even for the speeches in his work, he claims in a famous problematical passage to give 'whatever seemed most appropriate to me for each speaker to say in the particular circumstances, keeping as closely as possible to the general sense of what was actually said'. These principles he recognizes will detract from the literary charm of his work: no matter, for its aim is scientific, to be 'a possession for all time, not a display piece for instant listening' (1.22). In such attitudes we recognize the first critical historian, the founder of the western tradition. It is perhaps curious that we do so, for Thucydides is not of course a historian at all. He claimed that it was impossible to write accurately about the past; his methods and his standards of proof are applicable only to the present. He is a social scientist, a student of the contemporary world, not a historian. It was not until the nineteenth century that the discovery of archives and the invention of the techniques of source criticism allowed historians of the past to believe that they could meet the standards demanded by Thucydides. And it was not until this century that these standards could even begin to be applied to the study of Greek history, with the publication by F. Jacoby of the fragments of the lost Greek historians.

One area illustrates well Thucydides' advance on Herodotus: his account of the causes of the war. Contemporaries found Herodotus' frivolous mythology of rape and counter-rape, from Io to Helen of Troy, hilarious, and failed to note the problem that a clash of cultures ultimately leads to a war whose causes are incapable of being isolated, inherent in the nature of the societies in question. In the case of Greek city-states, however, there were established rules of international relations: an act of aggression or the refusal of a just request were causes of war which had an overt political nature. It is to Thucydides' credit that he does not remain on this level of claim and counter-claim. Instead he argues in detail for two episodes as the generally accepted grievances which led to war, and for a 'truest cause seldom mentioned explicitly'. The two episodes were military adventures involving a clash of interests and of military forces between Athens and Sparta's leading ally, Corinth. The nature of 'the truest cause' is harder to define, and it is indeed described as a personal opinion—'the Athenians becoming great and provoking fear in the Spartans compelled them to fight' (1.23). Is this a statement about social psychology, or an assertion of inevitability? How unmentioned was it, and where does it leave responsibility for the war? These questions have been endlessly debated; here we need only note the sophistication of a view which goes behind the diplomacy, and asserts two types of forces at work, two levels indeed of causation. It is this abandonment of the obvious, and of the idea of a single cause or type of cause, which is the decisive step in our understanding of the idea of causation in human affairs.

Where did Thucydides learn his method? The theory of politics and society was still in its infancy, and there is nothing of comparable depth in any contemporary sophist. The medical writers operated with ideas of underlying disposition to illness, and active cause for it, not unlike those of Thucydides, and they had developed a science combining theory with practical insight which was analogous to his. But we have only to read Thucydides' account of the Great Plague at

Athens in Book 2 to see his superiority even in describing a medical phenomenon: no contemporary medical writer has his clear description of the two central medical concepts in disease of contagion and immunity. In fact we may say with confidence that Thucydides' conception of social and historical method is his own creation. The problem of Thucydides is essentially his isolation.

This conclusion is reinforced by consideration of Thucydides' literary style. It derives ultimately from the antithetic periods of contemporary sophistic orators; but these have been twisted to present a succession of broken opposites and ill-matched pairs, where no one word is the obvious word and each phrase is unexpected. Its vice is that the simple becomes tortuous, the complex incomprehensible; its virtue is not in its precision (for the precision is a false one), but in the way that it forces the reader—even the contemporary Greek reader—to consider the exact significance and placing of every word. No other Greek ever wrote or thought like Thucydides.

The result is, of course, that he has his limitations. The silences of Colonel Thucydides are impenetrable for us; we have no means of knowing why he does not mention what he does not mention, or how much he does not mention. We cannot construct history from him, we can only accept or reject his conclusions. This would not matter if he were as perfect a historian as some have believed. But there is good reason to suspect that he was sometimes swayed by personal bias: his account of Pericles is surely too favourable, his account of Cleon omits a number of vital facts. Again what ultimately do the speeches represent, if no one ever spoke like that, and word and thought are so closely connected? Where does this leave his account of decision-making? Moreover the very power of Thucydides' illumination throws into prominence the darkness around it: he systematically ignores the significance of Persia—the war is a war of Greek states. Would he ever have faced the fact that ultimately it was Persian gold which defeated the Athenians?

Many of these limitations reflect the aims of his work: 'it will be enough if it is considered useful by those who wish to judge clearly both what has happened and what will come about again in the future, in the same or similar fashion, given the nature of man' (1.22). Thucydides here asserts no crude theory of repetition, but merely the usefulness of the study of human society in action. But what sort of society? Obviously not Persian, yet equally perhaps not merely Greek—rather the self-conscious political society in which decisions are taken by rational and open discussion and in accordance with rational principles. That is why political scientists from Machiavelli onwards have taken Thucydides as their ideal historian: Thomas Hobbes called him 'the most politick historiographer that ever writ'.

The influence of the sophists on Thucydides' theory of politics is clear. Thucydides seems to accept as a general fact about human society that 'might is right'—societies are in fact organized in terms of self-interest, and states act in accordance with self-interest: appeals to sentiment are seldom made in his work, and when made are unsuccessful. Athens holds her empire as a tyranny 'which it may have been wrong to acquire, but is dangerous to surrender' (speech of Pericles, 2.63). The philosophical expression of such views is given most clearly by the sophist Thrasymachus in the first book of Plato's *Republic*. So in terms of social morality no one is ever in the right or the wrong: once Sparta's fear of Athens has been isolated, it is clear that the war is 'in accordance with nature'. We know that this view of society was not a universal view in the fifth century, and very probably not a majority view; nevertheless it was clearly an influential one, and Thucydides cannot be accused of solipsism or completely falsifying the nature of political debates. That he has not given a full account of the decision-making procedure is already obvious from the way that the speeches are offered as antithetical pairs, not as part of a general debate. Many of the speeches in fact serve more as a vehicle for exploring the consequences of the Thucydidean view of politics than as an accurate account of what was actually said. On the two occasions when Thucydides himself offers sustained political analysis he is less successful: the account of the development of political leadership at Athens after the death of Pericles (2.65) and the discussion of the nature of political revolution during the war in relation to the example of Corcyra (3.82-4) are both unsatisfactory in their attempt to impose a linear progression on complex phenomena.

Despite his acceptance of this type of social theory, Thucydides is deeply concerned with its consequences, and especially with the resulting problems of morality; he seems particularly interested in the effects of such theories on internal politics. The famous funeral oration of Pericles over the Athenian dead in Book 2 portrays a society without conflict or tension, united in pursuit of an ideal, in contrast to the pathological state of a city like Corcyra, torn apart by civil strife. In general he highlights the occasions which raise such questions in their most crucial form. In Book 3, for instance, there are three great set episodes, the question of how Athens should punish the Mytileneans for their revolt, the question of how Sparta should deal with the captured Plataeans, and the story of the revolution at Corcyra. In the first, the new morality of empire leads to the conclusion that it is more advantageous to rule by kindness than by terror. In the second, the representatives of the old morality reject an appeal to sentiment, and destroy the sacred city of the Persian Wars: they decide to liberate the Greeks through terror. In the third, Thucydides explores the breakdown of trust and social order when a society is entirely ruled by the new morality, and the only madness is to be a moderate.

Book 3 is the centre of the original history of Thucydides, which described the first part of the war and ended at 5.24. Already he has shown himself ambivalent about the desirability of the world he portrays as reality. In the second half of his work this unease, this sense of an 'anti-Thucydides in Thucydides', is magnified. The reason lies in the logic of events: if the laws of politics which Thucydides has accepted are laws of nature, then their full horror will be brought home in the greatest tragedy of all, the destruction of Thucydides' own city of

Athens; and the pessimism of the historian concerning human nature will be finally justified in that fall. There are strong signs that Thucydides began to articulate the second half of his history around the conception of a tragedy. In Book 5 the Athenians make an unprovoked attack on the small island of Melos, and the Melians challenge the morality of their action in a passage cast in dialogue form: the Athenians respond with the arrogance of a tyrannical city. The episode in Thucydides is deeply influenced by the literary forms of Greek tragedy, and it also embodies that deed of pride on the part of Athens which will lead to calamity in the Great Sicilian Expedition of Books 6 and 7; the story of that expedition itself is told with a passion and an artistry which show Thucydides' belief that it is the turning-point of the war: his own involvement in the telling of it is all the more effective for being disguised. We do not know how Thucydides would have ended his story; in particular we do not know how he would have explained why Sparta did not destroy Athens completely, as she should surely have done on his theory: the problem for the historian is that history is not capable of being an artistic unity, it is always being falsified by events. Thucydides' history demonstrates on the one hand the moral development of an author experiencing the events he describes as a contemporary, and on the other hand the impossibility of scientific history.

Thucydides' view of history was dominant in antiquity, as it is today. Each society gets the sort of history it deserves. Machiavellism or *Realpolitik* is still seen as the only rational response in politics, even when it leads to self-destruction. That is natural once Thucydides' characterization of history is accepted, as being the realm of politics and war. The lesson is already there in Thucydides himself, that a society which lives solely by such criteria will inevitably destroy itself.

Xenophon

History continues, and so must historians: that was the problem of the fourth century. The fact that Thucydides was unfinished at first made it easier, as the examples of his continuators showed: one could simply begin 'Some days later', at least attempting to reach the same standards of dispassionate accuracy. The Oxyrhynchus historian achieves this, Xenophon almost does in the first two books of his *Hellenica* or Greek History, which carry the story of the Peloponnesian War down to its end in 404 BC. But when later in life he came to continue the story to the battle of Mantinea in 362, covering the period of the Spartan leadership in Greece, its collapse, and the short-lived Theban leadership, he produced an account so careless, so lop-sided, and so prejudiced that it would not be taken seriously if it were not the only surviving contemporary account: even the claim that he was writing memoirs, not history, fails to excuse a work whose omissions are more interesting than its contents. The sadness is that Xenophon did fulfil the Thucydidean criterion of being an eyewitness and participant in these events, and yet missed completely the tragic theme of the failure of the

Spartan way of life which he was so well qualified to interpret. Nevertheless Xenophon's fresh and easy style, his simple view of virtue and vice, and his unqualified admiration for Sparta make a pleasant change from the rigours of his predecessor.

Style and a moral content suitable for schoolchildren made Xenophon popular throughout antiquity and ensured the survival of all his works. Many of these are on the fringes of history. The *Anabasis* is a boy's own adventure story of the march of 10,000 Greek brigands through the heart of the Persian Empire, told by one of its leaders; the *Agesilaus* is an obituary piece praising the record of Xenophon's lifelong friend and protector, Agesilaus, king of Sparta; the *Memoirs of Socrates* presents an intimate portrait of a famous man whom Xenophon probably never met, in the tradition of literary memoirs going back to the fifth century. Another work of Xenophon's, the *Cyropaedia*, can claim to be the first historical novel: it is a very long and completely fictitious account of the education and exploits of the founder of the Persian Empire, Cyrus the Great; its usefulness as a mirror for princes and its emphasis on moral leadership made it one of Europe's most popular books until kings went out of fashion. In antiquity it was responsible for a number of semi-historical accounts of the education of the hero from Alexander the Great onwards. But the East had more claim to be exotic than moral; and Ctesias of Cnidus, court doctor of Artaxerxes II in the early fourth century (who had actually been present at the same battle of Cunaxa as the Xenophon of the *Anabasis*, but on the other side) wrote an enormously popular and wildly fanciful (lost) history of Persia, which gave inside authority to a view of Persia 'breathing seraglio and eunuch perfumes, mixed with the foul stench of blood' (Eduard Meyer). Never trust a doctor: such writing derives from Ionian popular story-telling, and has its proper continuation in the romantic novels of the Hellenistic period.

Hellenica

The mainstream of Greek history-writing remained the Thucydidean history of city-states in conflict, but now standardized in a series of connecting and competing *Hellenica* or histories of Greece. Among the lost historians of the fourth century two stand out. Ephorus of Cyme wrote a Greek history in thirty books, which sought to replace all rivals by beginning at the beginning with the return of the sons of Heracles and ending in 341 BC. He is interesting for his attempt to delimit the sphere of history from that of myth, and for the way he justified his wider approach in a series of prefaces to individual sections which asserted the unity of history. As a pupil of Isocrates (below, p. 224), he began the dangerous relationship between rhetoric and history, with its tendency to sacrifice truth to effect. He also had other vices: he had a sharp eye for the use of poetry as evidence for history, but little judgement in exploiting it; and he sought to disguise his dependence on earlier historians by 'modernizing' facts and figures, and where necessary inventing circumstantial detail. His style and completeness unfortunately made him rather popular, but at least he stands out as one who had thought about the purposes that history should serve, and got them wrong.

To the modern eye another pupil of Isocrates, Theopompus of Chios is more attractive; he wrote a *Hellenica*, a continuation of Thucydides, and then a work which suggests by its title the new direction that history was taking, a *Philippica*, or history with Philip, king of Macedon, at its centre. These works gaily exposed both the deviousness and corruption of Athenian politicians at all periods and the drunken barbarism of the new Macedonian ruler of Greece. Anti-history, the exposure of vice and incompetence, is always fun, and Theopompus wrote to puncture the pretensions of the great. But he also foresaw the need for a new type of history, as the title of his *Philippica* shows—history for (or against) a world ruled by kings.

History for Kings

Alexander the Great was the first serious challenge, and, being a man who knew that he was making history, he was careful to take a historian along to record it. His choice was unfortunate; Callisthenes, Aristotle's nephew, after displaying a mixture of sycophancy and sullenness, began tampering with the Royal Pages and had to be disposed of. The actual Alexander historians are a motley crew, to judge from their fragments—for ironically no continuous account of this great event, the conquest of the world, survives from before the Roman imperial period. Our standard history, written more than four centuries later by Arrian, a Roman official, chose to use two eyewitness narratives which were certainly competent, one by Aristobulus, an architect, and one by Ptolemy, a junior commander who later became founder of the Egyptian successor kingdom. Other accounts such as that of Diodorus use a popular romantic version written by Cleitarchus, a shadowy figure of uncertain date and not necessarily a participant. Many who went on the expedition wrote their memoirs in different literary styles. The most genial is Nearchus, Alexander's admiral, who explored the Indus valley, the Punjab, and the desolate Makran coast to the mouth of the Tigris in 326-324, and wrote a Herodotean account of it which is an important source for Arrian's description of the Indian expedition. But the most lasting consequence of the career of Alexander the Great was the tradition of the Alexander Romance, perhaps the most popular book in world literature, compiled in late antiquity from various Hellenistic strands such as a fanciful biography and collections of forged letters and treatises: the result is sheer fairy-tale, with Euphrates and Tigris flowing into the Nile and Alexander born of an Egyptian snake, visiting men without heads and Indian brahmins (the last a true episode), descending to the seabed in a diving bell, and flying in a basket powered by griffins.

The Hellenistic Age

The challenge of the historical Alexander was therefore refused, and it is worth asking why neither the age of Alexander nor the period of the Hellenistic kingdoms produced a new form of political history, why no tradition of biographies of kings or dynastic histories emerged to cope with the great empires and kingdoms. One reason was the strength of the tradition of history-writing created by the city-state; another was the lack of a real biographical tradition in Greece. For such reasons it was left to the Romans to discover the fascinations of imperial history and of political biography; the most successful political historians in the Hellenistic age continued to write *Hellenica*, usually chronicles of their own day, merely incorporating the new Hellenistic kingdoms into the old framework.

The best of these histories was that which lies behind Books 18-20 of Diodorus, by Hieronymus of Cardia, an administrator of public affairs in various kingdoms, whose adult life covered three generations from Alexander to about 260 BC, when he died in full possession of his faculties at the age of 104; not surprisingly his history was so long that 'no one could read it through to the end', But it was also clearly a marvellously accurate and balanced account of an age when politics and war spanned the world from the Indus to the Nile and the Danube; in particular these books of Diodorus offer a version of military history better even than that in Thucydides. The lesson that Hieronymus learned from the dismemberment of Alexander's empire and the creation of the great successor kingdoms was perhaps that most important of all truths in history, that it is chance, not human skill, that rules human affairs. The goddess Tyche presides over his history and over that of his successors down to Polybius—chance both blind and yet capable of being used by those who understand her ways: 'there is a tide in the affairs of men'.

The other main development in political history is known largely through the polemics of Polybius against his predecessors: it is aptly named the 'pathetic school of history', in which rhetoric and history join hands, to recreate through pathos the sensations of the past. Whether this school, which only too easily sacrificed truth to effect, had a basis in an Aristotelian theory of 'tragic history' is disputed; the claims of these historians do, however, foreshadow some aspects of the theory of Benedetto Croce, that all history is contemporary history, the re-enactment of past experience relevant to the present.

The early Hellenistic period also saw the renewal of the Herodotean tradition. Already writers such as Nearchus had recognized the relevance of Herodotus to their experience; when the new kingdoms began to consider their native subjects, they felt the need to understand these alien customs, and to create some sort of identity for their kingdoms. The result was a revival of the Herodotean *logos* in a systematic form as scientific ethnography, often patronized by kings and written by experts who might be non-Greek, resting on records and inside knowledge, and arranged in a standard form—myth and religion, geography and natural history, political history, social customs. The earliest of these authors, Hecataeus of Abdera, wrote for Ptolemy I of Egypt, and is the source for Diodorus Book 1; in the next generation he was followed by the Egyptian priest Manetho, whose chronology is still the basis of Egyptian history. In the Seleucid kingdom, Berossus, a bilingual priest of Baal, wrote a Babylonian history, and Megasthenes, ambassador of Seleucus to the court of Chandragupta in India, wrote an impressive survey of the beginnings of the Mauryan empire. This renewal of the relation between history and geography in ethnography was undoubtedly the most important cultural result of Alexander's conquests. For a brief period once again the Greeks were able to stand outside themselves and their city-states, and wonder at the world around them.

The city-state rapidly reasserted itself and drove ethnography into the area of utopian philosophical romance, with the imaginary worlds of Euhemerus and Iamblichus. There continued to be good geographers like Eratosthenes and Strabo (whose work survives), and from time to time a figure of interest emerged to unite the main strands of history. The most important of these was Posidonius, philosopher and polymath, whose lost history continued Polybius and recorded the harsh realities of Roman imperialism in the late Republic. But it is Polybius who represents the way forward, as the emergence of Rome on the Mediterranean scene gave a new unity and direction to political history in the tradition of Thucydides. So the culmination of this tradition in Greek historical writing was in a history of Rome, whose importance must be explored in Volume 2, Chapter 9.

Towards the end of the millennium that encyclopedic tendency emerged which heralds the closing of a cultural tradition; for us the importance of the tendency is that many of these bulky works survived to drive out their predecessors, but also to offer the evidence for reconstructing the historical tradition. The late Hellenistic world is a world of big books and small men with big pretensions. Dionysius of Halicarnassus in his *Roman Antiquities* provided Rome with a respectable local history like a proper Greek city; in the same age the *Historical Library* of Diodorus is important, both for its attempt to improve on Ephorus by including all civilizations (not just all Greece) in the realm of history, and as a quarry for lost historians—for the work is genuinely a library, a succession of abbreviations of other people's books.

In the course of 350 years the Greek tradition of history-writing had invented most of the styles of history that we still practise, and tried to analyse most of the political and social problems that we still face. It had established standards of accuracy and a variety of approaches which make it clearly superior to any other historical tradition. If it had one defect, it was a defect we share, the inability to cope with the power of God in history; happy the age that can afford to ignore God. The end of the Hellenistic period saw the beginnings of a new religion, and the flowing together of the traditions of Greece and Judaea into a new form of history, the working out of God's salvation on earth. The Books of Maccabees and the works of Josephus are products of this fusion of cultural traditions which survive, to point the way forward to the *Church History* of Eusebius and the Christian world of Byzantium.

Further Reading

I

Of the main extant works, Herodotus, Thucydides, Xenophon's *Hellenica* and *Anabasis*, Aristotle's *Constitution of Athens* and Arrian's *History of Alexander* are available in good Penguin translations, with introductions by leading modern scholars; the best translation of Thucydides is however still that of R. Crawley (1876, often reprinted in Everyman's Library, London and New York). The lesser works of Xenophon and other authors (Diodorus, Dionysius of Halicarnassus, Josephus) are most easily found in the Loeb Classical Library, with facing text and translation; special mention should also be made of the new two-volume Loeb Arrian, with important introduction, notes and appendices by P. A. Brunt (Harvard 1976, 1983). *Aristotle's Constitution of Athens and Related Texts*, translated and with commentary by K. von Fritz and E. Kapp (New York, 1950) is excellent.

The fragments of the lost Greek historians have been collected by Felix Jacoby, who devoted his life to the task; his monumental *Die Fragmente der griechischen Historiker* (Leiden, 1923–58) in fourteen volumes is the most important work on Greek history of this century. Jacoby died before he could finish it; it is arranged according to types of history, and the main areas which remain to be covered are geography, and literary and philosophical history and biography. The work consists of the evidence for the life of each historian, the fragments of his works, and an often extensive commentary in either German or English. There is no translation.

II

The most illuminating modern work on Greek history-writing is that of A. Momigliano; his more important essays are collected in two volumes, *Studies in Historiography* (London, 1966), and *Essays in Ancient and Modern Historiography* (Oxford, 1977). For the relations between Greek and other historical traditions there is much of interest in Herbert Butterfield's unfinished *The Origins of History* (London, 1981). See also the survey of the Mediterranean and the Middle East in J. Van Seters, *In Search of History* (Yale, 1983), which is primarily focused on the Jewish tradition. The beginnings of Greek historical writing are surveyed by L. Pearson, *Early Ionian Historians* (Oxford, 1939, repr. Connecticut, 1975), and R. Drews, *The Greek Accounts of Eastern History* (Harvard, 1973, to be treated with caution). For the problems faced by Herodotus the best introduction is the general work by the anthropologist Jan Vansina, *Oral Tradition* (Harmondsworth, 1973); see also A. Momigliano, *Studies* chs. 8 and 11. The best recent general book is J. A. S. Evans, *Herodotus* (Boston, Mass., 1982); other books offer more partial insights.

The development of local history is discussed by Momigliano, *Studies*, ch. 1; for the local Athenian historians there is the masterly book of Jacoby, *Atthis* (Oxford, 1949), and his commentary in English on them in *FGH* III b Supplement; see also P. J. Rhodes, *A Commentary on the Aristotelian Athenaion Politeia* (Oxford, 1981). Three books on Thucydides stand out for their different strengths: F. M. Cornford, *Thucydides Mythistoricus* (London, 1907), J. De Romilly, *Thucydides and Athenian Imperialism* (Oxford, 1963), and G. E. M. de Sainte Croix, *The Origins of the Peloponnesian War* (London, 1972). Thucydides is also the subject of a great commentary in five volumes (Oxford, 1945–81), begun and planned by A. W. Gomme, and finished by A. Andrewes and K. J. Dover.

For Xenophon see J. K. Anderson, *Xenophon* (London, 1974), and the introductions by G. L. Cawkwell to the two Penguin volumes. For Ephorus see G. L. Barber, *The Historian Ephorus*

(London, 1935); for Theopompus, Gilbert Murray, *Greek Studies* (Oxford, 1946), ch. 8, and W. R. Connor, *Theopompus and Fifth Century Athens* (Washington, DC, 1968). All studies of Alexander the Great devote much time to the historical sources for his career; the most complete survey is L. Pearson, *The Lost Histories of Alexander the Great* (New York, 1960); the studies by W. W. Tarn, *Alexander the Great* Volume II: *Sources and Studies* (Cambridge, 1950), are controversial. For Arrian, see Brunt's Loeb (above); P. A. Stadter, *Arrian of Nicomedia* (North Carolina, 1980); A. B. Bosworth, *A Historical Commentary on Arrian's History of Alexander*, vol. I (Oxford, 1980).

Jane Hornblower, *Hieronymus of Cardia* (Oxford, 1981) is a brilliant recreation of that lost masterpiece, and the best general account of the working methods of Diodorus. For other early Hellenistic historians in the ethnographic tradition, see O. Murray, 'Herodotus and Hellenistic Culture', *Classical Quarterly* 22 (1972), 207 ff. For Josephus see T. Rajak, *Josephus* (London, 1983).

9

Life and Society in Classical Greece

❧

OSWYN MURRAY

Society

BY the classical period of the fifth and fourth centuries BC there were hundreds of communities of Greeks living scattered around the shores of the Mediterranean 'like frogs around a pond', as Plato put it. From the central sea of the Aegean, with its island communities, and the coastal towns of Turkey and eastern and southern Greece, they had spread to north Greece, the Black Sea coast and southern Russia, to Sicily and south Italy, and as far as Provence, Spain, and north Africa. These communities regarded themselves as basically similar, as living in a *polis*, the only form of truly civilized life. Of course many aspects of their social and economic life were different: some cities possessed large agricultural territories or serf populations, others were heavily engaged in trade in raw materials such as corn, olive oil, dried fish, wine, metals, timber, slaves, or in manufactured goods, whether made on the spot or imported from eastern and other cultures; there was also a huge outflow of Greek goods in certain areas, and of skilled labour such as doctors, stonemasons, and professional mercenaries. The economy of the cities varied enormously, and so did their functions: some were essentially fortresses, others based on a religious shrine; but most had ports, and all had some land and constituted an administrative centre. In principle it should be possible to reconstruct the social and economic life of a typical Greek city, much as Plato in the *Laws* and Aristotle in the last two books of the *Politics* believed it possible to discover an ideal city behind the unsatisfactory multifariousness of real cities.

The reason that we cannot do this satisfactorily is not so much the absence of evidence as its concentration on two unrepresentative examples. Only Athens offers a sufficient variety of material for us to be able to understand in detail the way people lived; and from that evidence we see that Athens was fundamentally untypical, in being more varied, and yet more systematic in its interrelations, in fact more advanced than most, if not all other, Greek cities. In contrast Sparta is described for us by Athenian writers as the opposite of Athens, so that we see only those parts of it which are different from Athenian institutions. Order and obedience are contrasted with anarchy and freedom, the agricultural economy with trade and manufacture, the freedom of women with Athenian restrictions. Where there is no opposition the sources fall silent: our main writer, Xenophon, in his little book on Sparta, forgets to mention the Spartan helot serfs, because slavery was universal; and we hear nothing of the massive armaments industry which must have provided the standardized weapons of the Spartan military caste. Outside these two cities we have only scattered information or chance finds, such as the great law-code of the small city of Gortyn in inland Crete.

So Athens must be the focus, in the knowledge that we are describing life in other cities only in so far as they resembled Athens, and in the belief that at least the basic social and economic relationships of Greek cities are more similar to each other than to the tribal and non-Greek areas which surrounded them. Yet even for a single society we must recognize that there is no one viewpoint: each individual witness will describe his world differently. Plato's dialogues portray Athens in vivid detail, as a world of young and godlike intellectuals meeting in private houses for conversation or social drinking, strolling in suburban parks or walking down to the Piraeus for a festival, listening to famous visitors skilled in rhetoric or philosophy from all over Greece. Even when Socrates is in prison under sentence of execution, the authorities allow large groups of his friends to visit him and discuss with him such questions as whether he should escape, and the nature of life after death. Finally Socrates drinks the hemlock, and his limbs slowly lose sensation as he converses peacefully and rationally.

Yet for most of the time which Plato describes, Athens was fighting a long and bloody war in which at least half the population died, many of them from a particularly horrifying plague which scarred even those who survived it, and which was partly the consequence of the unsanitary conditions in which vast numbers of citizens were camped, at first in the heat of the summer, and later all year, on every available space of open or sacred land within the city walls. In reality travel was dangerous and very much restricted; and the way down to the Piraeus must have been as filthy, as stinking, and as crowded as the slums of Calcutta. Nor were Athenian prison conditions as humane or as clean as Plato suggests; and the medical effects of hemlock are not mere numbness of the limbs—they include choking, slurring of speech, convulsions, and uncontrollable vomiting.

Plato's Athens is an ideal vision which reflects reality as much as the naked figures of the Parthenon reflect the pock-marked and poorly dressed peasants who stared up at them; yet we need to know the ideals which a society sets for itself. Attic comedy for its own purposes seized on certain aspects of daily life, to exaggerate them for comic effect; yet once again we may wonder whether the obscenities and the constant references to bodily functions are typical of a society

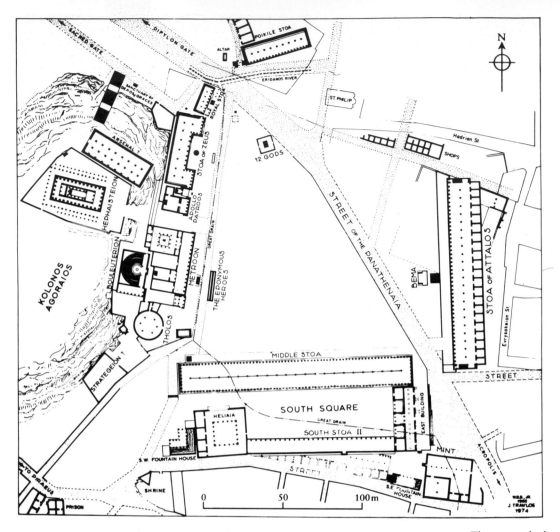

PLAN OF THE *AGORA* (MARKET-PLACE) IN ATHENS IN THE HELLENISTIC PERIOD. The square had been cleared early in the sixth century, then supplied with public buildings along its west side, behind which there later stood the temple of Hephaestus. Among the early buildings are the Royal Stoa, office of the royal archon (*archon basileus*) who saw to religious matters. There was also a council house (*bouleutērion*), archive (in the *metrōon*), and magistrate's club house (*tholos*), shown here in their Classical form. The Painted Stoa at the north held the early Classical paintings of Polygnotus and Micon. Across the square ran the Panathenaic Way which passed from a city gate (Dipylon Gate) to the Acropolis. At the south are sixth-century fountain houses and the state mint. The stoae—shops and offices—which close the square are comparatively late additions, the Stoa of Attalus, a gift of the Pergamene king, being now rebuilt to serve as museum and workrooms for the Agora excavations.

which kept its women in strict seclusion, rather than a form of ritual release reserved for the theatre: how regular was father-bashing or female drunkenness off the stage? Did women ever really dream of taking over the state? Again law-codes tell us only of the boundary areas where crime and punishment are thinkable, not of what is either normal or tabu. Then the speeches of Athenian lawyers concern a special group of the rich, and situations where there is an inherit-

MODEL OF THE WEST SIDE OF THE ATHENIAN AGORA IN THE LATE CLASSICAL PERIOD, seen from the south. Compare the plan, opposite.

ance to be disputed or a business interest to conflict; hidden behind them is a world of normal activity. For all the vividness of our evidence we are dealing with a set of stereotypes and partial views which inform us only indirectly of what it was like to be an Athenian.

The *polis* was essentially a male association: citizens who were men joined together in making and carrying out decisions affecting the community. The origin of this activity doubtless lay in the military sphere and the right of warriors to approve or reject the decisions of their leaders; the development of the *polis* is the extension of this practice to all aspects of social life, with the partial exception of religion. Politics, direct participation in the making of rational choices after discussion, was therefore central to all Greek cities. In Athens and Sparta all male citizens participated at least in principle equally; elsewhere particular rights could be confined to certain groups, richer or better born, thereby necessarily creating conflicts and a hierarchy of rights within the citizen body. Nevertheless the forms of political life, mass citizen assembly, smaller council, and annual executive magistrates were general, though the powers and attributes of the different elements varied widely.

It is already obvious that such a developed type of organization must relate itself to other more 'natural' and presumably earlier forms of association, of the kind generally described by modern anthropologists as kinship groups. Most Greek cities divided their citizens into hereditary 'tribes': Dorian cities traditionally possessed three, Ionian cities four, but political reformers were given to tampering with the organization, and Cleisthenes at Athens had changed the number there from four to ten (about 507 BC; above, p. 29). The lack of any organic connection between these city tribes and a real tribal past is shown by the fact that they only existed as social divisions in the *polis* communities, and are absent from the genuinely tribal areas of north Greece; they were in fact ways of dividing the citizen body for military and political purposes, sanctioned by tradition and reinforced by specially organized state religious cults.

In Athens the reforms of Cleisthenes had also reorganized the associations based on locality. The village or deme had become an administrative unit, with a local official and a local assembly to control all aspects of local government, and most importantly to maintain the citizen lists; there was a complex procedure for ensuring enrolment on the citizen list, and a legal machinery for appeal in the case of exclusion. Because of this connection with citizenship, membership of the deme remained hereditary, regardless of actual domicile, and every Athenian citizen was required to state his deme in any official transaction: so Socrates' official designation was 'Socrates son of Sophroniscus of the deme of Alopeke'. But however great the population movements, the deme remained a geographical focus for most Athenians because they lived there. Even more important to the ordinary Athenian than these central and local government organizations was the phratry (*phratria*), the group of *phrateres*. This is the sole context in Greek of the important linguistic root common to most Indo-European languages, found for instance in the Celtic *brathir*, German *Bruder*, English *brother*, Latin *frater*, or French *frère*; in Greek it designates the non-familial type of 'brotherhood' (there was a quite different word for the blood relationship of brother). These brotherhoods were originally perhaps aristocratic warrior bands, but once again the democratic state had reorganized them to make them open to all: every male Athenian belonged to a phratry, and it was his phratry which dominated his social life. Each phratry worshipped a male and a female god, Zeus Phratrios and Athena Phratria, at a general annual festival held in traditional localities and under local phratry control: the mixture of uniformity with a spurious diversity suggests strongly a remoulding of older institutions at a particular date. The various rites of passage of the young male Athenian were connected with this festival. At an early age he was presented to the *phrateres* by his father and relatives at the altar of his Zeus Phratrios, and the acceptance of his first sacrifice signified his acceptance into the community. In adolescence he was again presented and dedicated to the god his shorn hair; the *phrateres* then voted to admit him as a phratry member and inscribed his name on the phratry list. It was also the *phrateres* who witnessed the solemn betrothal ceremony which was the central public act of the Athenian marriage, and who celebrated with a feast paid for by the bridegroom its final consummation. Thus the phratry was involved in all the main stages of a man's life and was the focus of his social and religious activity; when in difficulties, for instance needing witnesses at law, he turned first to his *phrateres*. The only area in which the Athenian phratry was not concerned was death, though elsewhere this too was part of their functions.

This type of association was common in the Greek world, and had developed for different ends in different cities. Sparta is the most striking example: the male citizen body was divided into *syssitia* or mess groups on which the entire social and military organization of the state depended. Here the normal practices of the Greek world had been transformed to create a military élite. From the age of seven, boys were given a state-organized upbringing, and brigaded into age groups. They lived communally from the age of twelve, taught all sorts of skills useful to self-reliance and survival, and provided with inadequate clothing and food to toughen them. At twenty they joined the *syssitia* where they must live until the age of thirty, and even thereafter they were required to eat daily those common meals to which they had to contribute from the land allotted to them and farmed by state-owned slaves, who were in fact the enslaved descendants of neighbouring communities, constantly rebelling and requiring suppression. The theoretical elegance of this solution (soldiers make slaves, slaves make soldiers, slaves need soldiers to suppress them), and the way it built on traditional Greek social customs, much impressed ancient political thinkers, and offered a counter-ideal to the Athenian democracy. The two examples show how differently similar institutions could develop in different states, and produce societies with utterly opposed characteristics.

The need to belong remains, and in an open society like Athens it led to a multiplicity of social groups more or less integrated into the state. There were aristocratic religious groups called *gennētai* who claimed descent from a common ancestor and monopolized the priesthoods of the more important city cults. Lower down the social scale there were other religious groups centred on the worship of lesser gods and heroes, but with a strong social purpose in feasting and mutual help. There were aristocratic drinking groups, which might even on occasion be mobilized for political ends, but which were more often to be found indulging in mindless post-prandial destruction and the molesting of innocent passers-by; in the daytime the same young men would be found in other but overlapping groups associated with the various sporting complexes or *gymnasia* of the city. There were benefit clubs and burial clubs, and clubs associated with individual trades and activities. There were religious or mystical sects, and intellectual organizations such as the philosophical schools of Plato and Aristotle. Characteristic of these organizations are a cult focus, the ownership of property for the common benefit, the existence of a formal constitution with officers and a means of taking formal decisions, often recorded on stone, and a strong element of common feasting and drinking; characteristic too is the fact that these are all-male groups engaging in all-male activities. Occasionally we hear of equally exclusive female organizations, usually connected with specific cults confined to women, but these tend to be or to be seen as mere extensions of the male world. The range of such associations is shown by the Athenian law relating to them; 'If a deme or *phrateres* or worshippers of heroes or *gennētai* or drinking groups or funerary clubs or religious guilds or pirates or traders make rules amongst themselves, these shall be valid unless they are in conflict with public law.'

The developed Greek city was a network of associations: as Aristotle saw, it was such associations which created the sense of community, of belonging, which was an essential feature of the *polis*: the ties of kinship by blood were matched with multiple forms of political and religious and social groupings, and of companionship for a purpose, whether it be voyaging or drinking or burial. This conception of citizenship could even be invoked in time of civil war: when the democrats and the oligarchs of Athens were fighting in 404 BC, a priest of the Eleusinian mysteries, a man of noble family on the democratic side, made this appeal:

Fellow citizens, why are you driving us out of the city? Why do you want to kill us? We have never done you any harm. We have shared with you in the most holy rites, in sacrifices, and in splendid festivals; we have danced in choruses with you and gone to school with you and fought in the army with you, braving together with you the dangers of land and sea in defence of our common safety and freedom. In the name of the gods of our fathers and mothers, of the bonds of kinship and marriage and companionship, which are shared by so many of us on either side, I beg you to feel shame before gods and men and cease to harm our fatherland. (Xenophon, *Hell.* 2. 4. 20–2)

In such a world it might be argued that multiple ties limited the freedom of the individual, and there is certainly an important sense in which the conception of the autonomy of the individual apart from the community is absent from Greek thought: the freedom of the Greeks is public, externalized in speech and action. This freedom derives precisely from the fact that the same man belongs to a deme, a phratry, a family, a group of relatives, a religious association; and, living in this complex world of conflicting groups and social duties, he possesses the freedom to choose between their demands, and so to escape any particular dominant form of social patterning. It is this which explains the coexistence of the group mentality with the amazing creativity and freedom of thought of classical Athens: the freedom which results from belonging in many places is no less a freedom than that which results from belonging nowhere, and which creates a society united only in its neuroses.

Family

The Greek family was monogamous and nuclear, being composed in essence of husband and wife with their children; but Greek writers tend to equate it with the household as an economic unit, and therefore to regard other dependent relatives and slaves as part of it. The family fulfilled a number of social functions apart from the economic. It was the source of new citizens; in the classical period the state intervened to establish increasingly stringent rules for citizenship and so for legitimacy: ultimately a citizen must be the offspring of a legally recognized marriage between two Athenian citizens, whose parents must also be citizens; this increasingly sharp definition tended to exclude the more flexible unions of an earlier period. It became impossible for an Athenian to marry a foreigner or to obtain recognition for the children of any other type of liaison: the development is essentially democratic, the imposition of the social norms of the peasant majority on an aristocracy which had previously behaved very differently; for the aristocracy had often married outside the community and thereby determined its own criteria for legitimacy. Indeed Pericles, the author of the first of these

WEDDING PROCESSION on an Athenian vase by the Amasis Painter, about 540 BC. Bride and groom sit in a mule cart, accompanied by relatives and guests, on their way to their new home. The bride's mother leads them carrying torches, and in the house the groom's mother is also seen with a torch. The preparation of the bride, the procession, and special occasions for the receiving of gifts, were the main ceremonies of a Greek wedding, apart from the contract about property.

citizenship laws, demonstrates the painfulness of the process of adaptation; for, when his legitimate children died of the plague, he was forced to seek from the assembly permission for his children by Aspasia, his Milesian mistress, to be declared legitimate Athenian citizens. Other individuals, often of aristocratic birth, found themselves reclassified in this process as bastards, without either citizenship or rights of inheritance.

For a second function of the family, intimately connected with citizenship, was the inheritance of property. Greek society in general did not practise primogeniture, the right of the eldest son to inherit; rather the property was divided equally by lot between all surviving sons, so that the traditional word for an inheritance was a man's *klēros* or lot. This is one important reason for the instability of the Athenian family, for each family survived only as long as its head, and its property was redistributed on his death. There were of course countervailing tendencies. The common practice of burial in family plots gave a focus for a group of families over several generations, at least among those able to afford the considerable expense of the land and the impressive monuments which were a feature of these group burials: the phenomenon is perhaps a case of the wealthier citizens imitating aristocratic practices. Marriage, even at the highest levels, was endogamous, within a close circle of relatives, in order to preserve family property from fragmentation. More generally, for the same reason, it was common to limit family size; and that could often lead to the absence of male heirs through death, and the redistribution of the property among the wider group of relatives, who also had duties to prosecute a man's murderer. But in general there is little evidence for extended family groups being important in the classical age.

Another function of the family raises one of the central problems in our understanding of Athenian social values: the family clearly served as the means of protecting and enclosing women. Women were citizens, with certain cults reserved to them and not allowed to foreign women, and they were citizens for the purposes of marriage and procreation; but otherwise they lacked all independent status. They could not enter into any transaction worth more than one *medimnos* of barley; they could not own any property, with the conventional exception of their clothes, their personal jewellery and personal slaves. At all times they had to be under the protection of a *kyrios*, a guardian; if they were unmarried, their father or closest male relative, if they were married their husband, if widowed their son or other male relative by marriage or birth. At all times the woman belonged to a family and was under the legal protection of its head.

The two types of occasion when a woman could be involved in property transactions illustrate the nature of this protection. The first concerns the dowry: it was the duty of a *kyrios* to provide a dowry for all women in his family: the lack of a dowry demonstrated extreme poverty, and might even lead people to suspect that no legal marriage had in fact taken place. The formula in the betrothal ceremony was:

> I give this woman for the procreation of legitimate children.
> I accept.
> And (e. g.) 3 talents dowry.
> I am content.

Marriage was deemed to have taken place on receipt of the dowry. The dowry accompanied the woman, but did not belong to her: it was in the complete control of her husband; but in the case of divorce or the death of the husband it could be reclaimed along with the woman, and was only really transferred once the woman had a male heir to inherit, and to be her *kyrios*.

A woman could also be the carrier of property in the absence of a will and of male heirs in the appropriate degree. In this case the woman became an *epiklēros*, or heiress: her name was publicly proclaimed in the assembly, and she and the property were adjudged to the closest male relative of the deceased who was prepared to marry her, often her paternal uncle. This was a well-established procedure: soldiers were given special leave to press their claims; a claimant was entitled to divorce his wife in order to marry the heiress, and could even take the heiress from her husband if she were already married, provided the marriage was childless: 'many who were married have had their wives taken from them', says one orator in a speech in which he explains that his father did not claim an inheritance belonging to his mother, for fear that one of her relatives would then seize her in marriage.

A system of law and private property reflects the prejudices of the society which creates it; the Athenian system was unusual in ancient Greece merely in being more systematic; but it was possible for other cities to develop differently. In Sparta, for instance, the freedom of women was notorious, and much disapproved of by those very philosophers who idealized Sparta otherwise; in Sparta too women could inherit land in their own right, until by the third century the fact that two-fifths of the land was in their hands provoked a political revolution. The status of women in Athens does perhaps require explanation.

CLAY FIGURES OF A WOMAN KNEADING BREAD AND A COOK WORKING AT A GRILL. Fifth century BC. There are several of these Classical studies of work in the kitchen, mainly from Boeotia.

There are two different strands in the Athenian attitude to women. The first is the effect of democracy on the status of women. Aristocratic women at least had been freer in earlier times, but the coming of democracy meant the imposition of the social norms of the majority. Many peasant societies combine a high value placed on women with mistrust of them. Semonides of Amorgos in the sixth century described the appalling varieties of women that the gods had made to be a burden on men, in terms of their animal characteristics; only one type is any good, and she is like the bee: 'She causes his property to grow and increase, and she grows old with a husband whom she loves and who loves her, the mother of a handsome and reputable family. She stands out among all women, and a godlike beauty plays around her. She takes no pleasure in sitting among

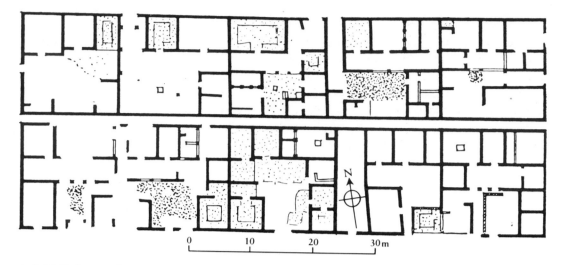

A STREET 'BLOCK' OF FOURTH-CENTURY BC HOUSES AT OLYNTHUS IN NORTH GREECE. There is some variety in the basic scheme of entrance to a courtyard from which there is direct access to living rooms, bedrooms (upstairs), and the men's dining room (*andrōn*). Compare the more elegant villa at Olynthus shown in the next illustration.

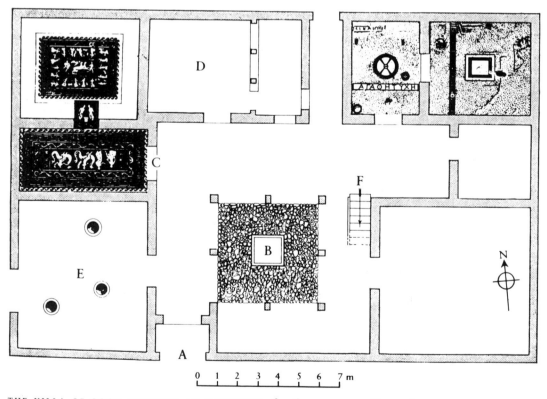

THE VILLA OF GOOD FORTUNE AT OLYNTHUS, fourth century BC. The main entrance (A) is into a verandahed courtyard with a central altar (B). The men's dining room (*andrōn*) is reached from it through an anteroom (C), both with mosaic floors. The kitchen is adjacent (D) and the sunken store-room (E) can also be reached from a side street. At the east are workrooms and the stairs (F) to the upper floor (bedrooms and women's rooms). This area also has access from a back door, while the main door leads directly to the dining room, leaving the women's quarters separate, though not secluded.

woman in places where they tell stories about love' (83–93). Such attitudes compound fear of the irrational and passionate nature of women with an exaggerated belief in their value and the importance of protecting them from the public eye. In agrarian societies these attitudes are held in check by the need for women's labour in the fields; with the advent of urban life the woman is confined to the house, and increased wealth brings with it aspirations to liberate her even from domestic duties. In a dialogue of Xenophon, Socrates confronts the problem of a friend who, because of the political turmoil, finds himself with fourteen female relatives living in his house, all well brought up and therefore unused to any form of work: Socrates persuades him that he should nevertheless provide them with suitable work such as spinning; their tempers are much improved, and the only problem is that they now complain of the idleness of their protector— but, says Socrates, his duty is to protect, as the sheepdog cares for the sheep (Xenophon, *Memorabilia* 2.7).

At a quite different level similar attitudes emerge among intellectuals. Philosophers (with the honourable exception of Plato) agreed that women are less endowed with reason than men—as Aristotle put it, 'the deliberative faculty is not present at all in the slave, in the female it is inoperative, in the child undeveloped'; the family is a natural relationship involving ruler and ruled and 'as regards male and female this relationship of superior and inferior is permanent'. Tragedians and comic poets may portray women with greater vividness and character than men: the most powerful figures in Greek tragedy are women. But the reason for this is precisely that women are believed to be more liable to extremes of emotion and to consequent violent actions. The tragedians show great insight into the predicament of women:

But now outside my father's house I am nothing; yes, often I have looked on the nature of women thus, that we are nothing. Young girls, in my opinion have the sweetest existence known to mortals in their fathers' homes, for innocence keeps children safe and happy always. But when we reach puberty and understanding, we are thrust out and sold away from our ancestral gods and from our parents. Some go to strangers' homes, others to foreigners', some to joyless houses, some to hostile. And all this, once the first night has yoked us to our husband, we are forced to praise and say that all is well. (Sophocles, *Tereus*, fr. 583)

But these very insights are embedded in stories of appalling violence: in this lost play of Sophocles, Procne is preparing to kill her son in revenge for her husband's seduction of her sister. In the religious sphere, too, women were seen as different from men in their suitability for the blacker, less rational, more orgiastic aspects of belief and ritual. Despite the many signs of empathy with the female condition, the result was a reinforcing of social attitudes that women needed protection from themselves and from the outside world.

Such attitudes relate only to Athenian women:

For this is what having a woman as a wife means, to have children by her and to introduce the sons to members of the phratry and the deme, and to betroth the daughters to husbands as one's own. Call-girls (*hetairai*) we have for the sake of pleasure, mistresses for the daily refreshment of our bodies, but wives to bear us legitimate children and to look after the house faithfully.

Thus did an Athenian speaker appeal to an Athenian jury to remember the distinction between Athenian women and others.

It is an outrage if a stranger enters a house where women are or may be present, unless invited by the master. The layout of Athenian houses in fact suggests even within the house a strict segregation between women's quarters and the public rooms for men: in larger houses the women's quarters are situated away from the street entrance which is well guarded by a slave porter. In the country the characteristic shape of the farmhouse is a courtyard where the women and children live during the day, surrounded by single storey rooms; in one corner stands a strong storage tower, into the upper floors of which the women retreat if strangers come. In smaller city houses the men's quarters are on the ground floor, the women's on the upper: in a famous murder trial the defendant claims that his young wife persuaded him to swap sleeping quarters so that she would be near the well to wash the baby—and so that her lover could visit her. But how had this lover even made contact with a married woman? He had noticed her at a funeral, he had bribed her slave-girl to run messages, he had met her under cover of the women's festival of the Thesmophoria: only on such occasions would she have left the house. It was of course legal for the husband with a gang of neighbours to kill the lover caught in the act: the prosecution could only claim that the murder was planned beforehand for other reasons. Women normally left the house accompanied; and the fact that a woman worked in public was either a sign of extreme poverty or evidence that she was not a citizen.

It is not easy to come to terms with such attitudes, however common they may be in peasant societies, if only because we idealize the Greeks as the originators of western civilization. But we should remember that (polygamy apart) the position of Athenian women was in most important respects the same as that of the 200,000,000 women who today live under Islam, and that in the history of the world only communism and the advanced capitalist societies have made any pretence of treating men and women equally.

The consequence of these attitudes in Athens, combined with the importance placed on male social groupings, was to establish public life as the centre of the *polis*: the balance in ancient Athens was shifted away from the family and towards the community: hence the magnificent festivals and displays, the great public buildings for religious and political purposes. It was surrounded by these buildings, in the *agora*, that the Athenian male spent his time. In contrast his home was mean and unimpressive: it was not safe in a democracy to display a lifestyle different from that of other citizens, and anyway a man's life was lived in public not in private. Here lies a fundamental reason for the achievement of Athens in exemplifying the ideal type of the ancient city; the erosion of the family was the price to be paid for her success in escaping from the ties of tribalism and kinship to create a new type of social and political organization.

Economy

It is all too easy to compare and contrast ancient economies with modern ones, and fall into the trap of believing that the ancient economy was primitive and agrarian, as if agrarian economies are naturally simple. The example of Athens is a useful corrective. The land of Attica is fundamentally unsuited to a simple economy: it consists of about a thousand square miles of mountain, upland forest and grazing, with only small pockets of cultivable land, most of that suitable only for olives; such geographical constraints imply a number of quite different and highly specialized agricultural activities, co-ordinated by a central settlement for exchange. One of the curious consequences of recent study of the political system established by Cleisthenes at the end of the sixth century is our ability to plot the population distribution in Attica at the start of the classical period, since each deme provided a number of city councillors proportionate to its population. The richest lands were the plain of Eleusis, the valley of the Cephissus river, and the plain of Marathon: here arable farming and viticulture must have been dominant; the next most fertile area of the Mesogeia is still the centre for *retsina* production. Not surprisingly these areas account for about two-fifths of the population. The city itself, where manufacture, trade, and service activities will have been concentrated, comprises a further fifth. What is perhaps remarkable is the evidence for large settlements in the uplands, and in the rocky Laurium peninsula: here the main activities will have been olive-growing where possible, but otherwise pastoral, centred on sheep and goats for wool and milk products (meat at all times in the Greek world being reserved for festival occasions and the eating of the sacrifice), and also forestry: even today Attica is still heavily wooded. As a result, although the overall population density is naturally lower in these areas, they contain many of the largest individual settlements; the largest of all, with roughly double the representation of other comparable demes and more than half that of the city of Athens itself, is Acharnae, famous for its charcoal industry: charcoal was, before coal, the main domestic and industrial fuel, required in huge quantities for smelting metal, and for cooking and heating under urban conditions. Nor should such activities as fishing in the coastal areas be forgotten.

There is no such comparable evidence for the classical period; but already, before the full development of urbanization in Attica, a complex and diversified agricultural economy existed. It is also clear that the conurbation of Athens required from a very early date the importation of cereals in large quantities; evidence of serious interest in corn imports goes back to the late seventh century, and the protection of the corn routes, especially from the Black Sea, was a major

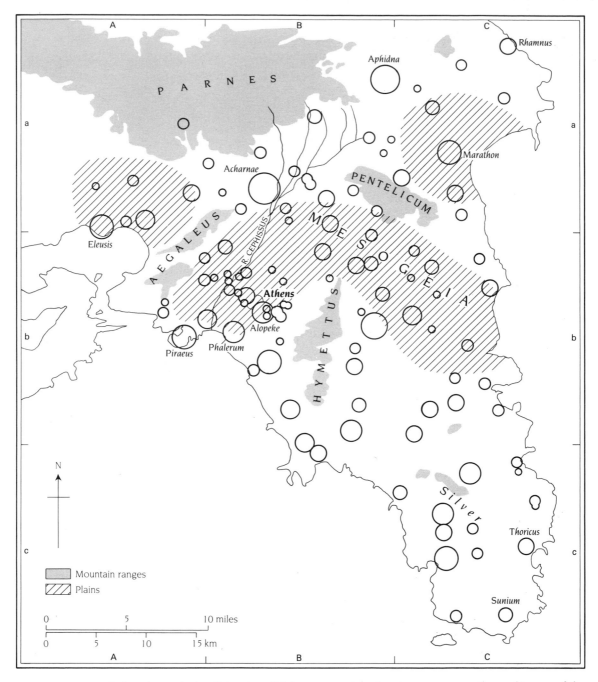

MAP 4. ATTICA. Attica, the territory of the city of Athens, comprises about 1,000 square miles, and is one of the largest city territories. The fertile agricultural areas are in the Cephissus valley and the Mesogeia, together with the plains of Eleusis and Marathon. Upland pastures and woodland cover the rest of the area, together with the bare mountain ranges of Hymettus, Pentelicum, and Parnes. This map shows the population distribution at the start of the Classical period (509 BC): the circles are graded according to the population of the settlements. Note how in the lowlands the villages are often located just off the plains, and also the evidence for large centres of population in the uplands.

determinant of Athenian public policy throughout the classical period. The adult male citizen population rose from about 30,000 to about 40,000 in the fifth century, and then dropped to the 21,000 shown in a census of 317 BC, largely during the Peloponnesian War; the same census reveals 10,000 resident foreigners. These figures may very approximately be multiplied by four to account for freeborn dependents, and we should add around 100,000 slaves. Figures available for the corn yield of Attica in the fourth century suggest that in order to feed this population at least half and probably nearer 80 per cent of corn, the staple food, had to be imported. Trade was therefore a vital component in the Athenian economy. The corn trade was strictly regulated: it was forbidden for Athenian residents to ship corn except to the Piraeus; there were laws preventing the re-export or stockpiling of corn, and special officials to regulate the market. The system of mixed loan, profit sharing and insurance, by which individuals lent capital at a very high rate of interest to shipowners for particular voyages, the loan to be repayable only if the voyage was successfully completed, seems to have been primarily designed for the corn trade. But Athens encouraged the development of other areas of trade by quick and easy access to her courts, fair treatment of foreigners, and encouraging foreigners to settle in Athens (below, p. 216). The basis for the trading supremacy of Athens was laid by Themistocles in the early fifth century with the fortification of the Piraeus and the establishment of a proper port; and the unification of the old city and the port was completed in 457 BC by the building of the Long Walls between them. By the end of the century Athens was the leading trade centre in Greece; her position was scarcely affected by her defeat in war and the collapse of her empire, and she began to lose it only with the shift of economic focus as a result of the conquests of Alexander and the unification of the eastern Mediterranean with the Middle East around the new Hellenistic city foundations.

A second type of economic activity in Athens resulted from the public works programme initiated by Pericles in the mid fifth century (below, pp. 292 f.). The records of accounts that survive relate to the later stages of building, the finishing work and the activities of skilled craftsmen on the sculptural decoration: it emerges that the labour force is mixed Athenian and foreign, free and slave, and that the wages for each type of work are identical regardless of social category. Earlier there must have been a large demand for unskilled labour in the digging of foundations, levelling of sites and the main stages of the building; equally the building programme itself used for the first time on a large scale the marble quarries of Mount Pentelicum, and created a great demand for labour both there and in the transport of stone to Athens (always the costliest part of an ancient or medieval building operation). In the absence of large gangs of slave labour it is virtually certain that the poor citizen population benefited most from this work. There is a well-established continuity between the public sculpture of the fifth century and the private grave monuments of the fourth century: when temple building stopped, sculptors moved either elsewhere in Greece or into the private

WORK IN THE CLAY PIT. A small clay plaque, one of hundreds dedicated at a shrine near the potters' quarter at Corinth in the sixth century BC. Many bear scenes of the potters at work, this one the quarrying for clay with refreshment being lowered to the workmen in the pit.

sector. Similarly with unskilled labour: it is noticeable that the democratic state at Athens at all times, except during war and periods of financial crisis, supported a major public works programme; the great frontier forts and the building programme of Lycurgus in the fourth century are the direct continuation of a policy of providing state employment on public works, which had begun as early as the sixth century under the Athenian tyrants.

Other economic activities rested mainly on craft skills, and did not therefore employ large numbers; nevertheless in total they were of considerable importance in creating a lively and varied market. Athens had become the main centre for high-grade painted pottery in Greece in the fifth century, and she remained dominant until the late fourth century, when the increased availability of precious metals from Alexander's conquests removed the need for art pottery. A famous part of the city was known as the *Kerameikos*, the Potters' Quarter. It has been calculated that the number of actual master vase-painters working at Athens at any one time was no more than a hundred, and some at least of these were also potters; nevertheless, taking into account every stage of the process, from the clay digging and fuel suppliers to the workshop staff, and finally the network of merchants who distributed the results as far away as Etruria and Spain, it is clear that this was a major economic activity.

Other crafts had developed beyond the workshop stage towards the factory, largely through the use of slave labour: the father of the politician Demosthenes owned two manufactories, one making swords with over thirty slaves, the other making couches with twenty; the shield factory of Lysias (below, pp. 216 f.) is the largest establishment known, with 120 slaves. A number of prominent politicians of the classical age seem to have drawn considerable revenues from such enterprises, to judge from remarks made in the comic poets about their professions (to the comic poets the wealthy Cleon, for instance, was a tanner); the development is to be explained in part by the existence of government contracts, espe-

THE SILVER MINES AT LAURIUM IN ATTICA. A view looking east over part of a fourth-century industrial complex at Agrileza, including a washery for silver ores uncovered in recent British excavations.

cially in the armaments sector, and in part more generally by the needs of a large city.

A final source of wealth must be mentioned, the mining of silver. In the early fifth century a new deep vein of silver was discovered in the Laurium hills, and silver mining continued intensively, with intermissions in times of disturbance, throughout the classical period. Concessions were leased by the state to Athenian entrepreneurs and syndicates, who worked them with slave gangs. The profits were enormous; the total state revenue was of the same order as the total cost of the corn trade, and individual concessions could make as much as 100 talents over three years. The fifth-century politician Nicias profited in a different way, by supplying the labour: he had a gang of 1,000 slaves whom he let out for work in the mines, drawing an income of 10 talents a year, a return of 33 per cent on his capital. Plato's *Protagoras* and Xenophon's *Symposium* are set in the house of the aristocratic Callias, who belonged to one of the most prominent political families of the fifth century, whose immense wealth was largely derived from the silver mines.

The rich have always preferred to live off rents and profits rather than engaging in direct economic activity; but it is only the prejudices of ancient philosophers which deceive us into thinking that the ownership of land was the only respectable source of wealth. The declarations for tax and inheritance purposes demonstrate a variety of sources; the categories are listed in a standard form: agricultural property, town property let out, manufactories and craft workshops owned, private possessions, money in hand, money deposited or out on loan. Those declarations known to us list capital and income in all or most of these categories.

Among ordinary Athenians, it is true that those who had land were primarily engaged in agriculture; but there were many at all levels of prosperity whose livelihood depended on other activities, and there is little evidence for social barriers: some of the most prominent dedications on the archaic Acropolis were those of craftsmen; potters and sculptors especially had a high social status. One prejudice did however exist: with the exception of state employment, wage labour was despised, and only under exceptional circumstances or in extreme necessity would Athenians work for others on a permanent basis. This was perhaps the chief consequence of the existence of slavery, that no man would willingly work for a master, since to do so was to put himself in the position of a slave; thus slavery both caused and filled a gap in the labour market.

One-third of the free population was non-citizen. The resident foreigner was called a metic (*metoikos*). At Athens he must find a citizen protector and register with the authorities, paying a small annual tax; in return he acquired effectively full protection at law and most of the duties of a citizen, such as contributing to public funds and financing expenses at festivals as well as military service: he was merely not allowed to marry a citizen or to own landed property in Attica. The boundary between citizen and metic was crossed only under exceptional circumstances, and later writers often contrasted the exclusiveness of Greek cities with Roman liberality, claiming that this was why Greek empires were so short lived and unpopular. However in practice, throughout the classical period, the metic population in Athens was large and prosperous, loyal to the city, and proud of its status; it was concentrated in the Piraeus, and its members were naturally especially prominent in the non-agricultural sectors, in manufacture, skilled crafts, trade, and commercial enterprises such as banking. One example will show how integrated the metic could become. Cephalus the Syracusan was invited to Athens by Pericles: he owned a large shield factory clearly fulfilling government contracts; his house in the Piraeus is the scene of Plato's *Republic*, and the dialogue begins with a discussion between him and Socrates on his attitude to his enormous wealth. His sons Polemarchus and Lysias were strong supporters of the radical democracy; Polemarchus was executed and they lost their property under the pro-Spartan oligarchy of 404 BC. Lysias fled into exile, and on his return was rewarded with citizenship for his loyalty, though the grant was soon annulled on legal grounds. Lysias then became the leading composer of legal speeches until his death about 380 BC; the fact that as a non-citizen he could not speak in court mattered little, since all litigants had to speak for themselves, and employed professionals merely to write the speeches. It is clear that Cephalus and his family mixed freely with the aristocratic and intellectual élite of Athens; they were themselves leading members of Athenian society and unswervingly loyal to it, even if they did not possess citizenship.

Unlike wage labour, slavery was a natural form of exploitation in the ancient Mediterranean; and, though we have no precise figures, it is likely that the number of slaves in Attica was roughly equal to the number of free inhabitants, or around 100,000. Slavery as a social status is unproblematic: the slave is in Aristotle's phrase 'a living tool' whom the master can treat as he wishes, though only a fool would maltreat his tools; damage to a slave by others involved compensation to the owner. It was, however, a rule of Athenian law that a slave's evidence was only admissible if procured under torture, for the obvious reason that, in order to liberate a slave from fear of his master, one must substitute a greater fear.

To begin with numbers, there is ample evidence that, while the very poor possessed no slave, this was considered a grave misfortune, and all aspired to own at least one slave: one might compare the modern European's attitude to owning a car. However, as with other consumer durables, possession increases the need up to the limit of what one can afford. Every soldier on campaign was accompanied by a slave, which would normally imply others left at home. Towards the top end of the scale a really rich man might own more than fifty slaves, and employ them in manufactories, as well as possessing household slaves. Larger numbers were exceptional outside the special case of the silver mining gangs. The evidence of the titles of the different jobs we find slaves performing (porter, nurse, tutor, maid, cook, and so on) suggests a comparison with the numbers of servants in Victorian households of various social classes. Agricultural slavery was limited by economic considerations: it is unlikely that the average peasant working his own land with his family could support more than one or two slaves; but those with enough land to choose to live without working would immediately require a slave overseer and a minimum of four or five farmhands, perhaps as many as fifteen.

The question of numbers is important, because it serves to demonstrate how, in most areas of the economy, slave and free worked alongside each other and under the same conditions: indeed one category of slaves actually worked independently as craftsmen, paying a part of their earnings to their owner. This working relationship explains why in many respects, while Athenian society was definitely a slave-owning society, it lacked the characteristics of a slave economy, in that special modes of exploitation had not evolved: in a real sense slavery was a substitute for wage labour, implying the same sort of social conditions. The situation is caricatured by a reactionary Athenian critic:

Now as for the slaves and metics in Athens, they live a most undisciplined life; one is not permitted to strike them there, and a slave will not stand out of the way for you.

Let me explain why. If the law permitted a free man to strike a slave or a metic or a freedman, he would often find that he had mistaken an Athenian for a slave and struck him, for, so far as clothing and general appearance are concerned, the common people look just the same as the slaves and metics. (Pseudo-Xenophon, *On Athens* 1. 10)

In only one area had a true slave economy developed: the silver mining gangs were organized to obviate the need for free labour in conditions which no free man would tolerate. The slave-owner's contract protected him against loss by insisting on the replacement of all slaves who died, but this scarcely offered much protection to the slave, for the owner's profit was such that he could afford a new slave after three years. The skeletons and evidence of living 300 feet under-ground in tunnels fed with air through downdrafts created by fires halfway up the shafts, the niche for the guard at the mine entrance, and the fact that the tunnels were so small that the face workers must have crawled and knelt at their work while all porterage was carried out by pre-adolescent children, reveal the truth. Few Athenians cared to visit their investments in the Laurium mines, and special overseers were employed; even on the surface miners were kept chained. It is indeed an appalling indictment of Athenian indifference that Nicias, whose money was made from child labour of this sort, could widely be regarded as the most moral and religious man of his generation.

Culture

Culture requires leisure and occasion: leisure is not usually a problem in the pre-industrial world, or where one works for oneself rather than another. There were two main types of occasion in the classical world, private and public, the *symposion* and the festival.

   The *symposion* or male drinking group belongs to the world of social groups already described, and embodies essentially an aristocratic form of culture still practised in the classical age, but no longer dominant. Earlier much of Greek poetry, Greek music, and Greek pottery had been created for such groups, whose character was remarkably uniform across the Greek world; if artistic creativity had diminished, the *symposion* was still a main focus of social life. The *symposion* took place in a room called 'the men's room' (*andrōn*), often specially designed, with the door off-centre to accommodate the couches on which the participants lay, one or two to a couch, propped on their left arm. Before them were light snacks on low tables. The size of the rooms varied from three to twelve or more couches, so the groups were relatively small. In the room stood a large *kratēr* or mixing bowl, in which the wine was mixed with water in proportions usually of two or three of water to one of wine: the alcoholic content was therefore less than that of modern beer; the wine-pourers were young male or female slaves, often chosen for their beauty. The participants drank occasionally out of metal, but more often out of the fine painted pottery which was an Athenian speciality,

SYMPOSION, on an Athenian cup by the Brygos Painter of about 490–480 BC. Reclining at a feast—an eastern habit—was adopted by Greeks before 600 BC. The furniture is as that for the bedroom, but often more elaborate, and the couches determined the size of the room in the house (the *andrōn*) set aside for banquet and *symposion*. Women attend only to entertain, boys to provide music or bring wine. The artists dwell on the lighter-hearted aspects of the *symposion*, but it could serve more serious social and even political purposes as a private gathering of men from different families—like a club.

and followed complex social customs in their behaviour, under the direction of a leader. Poetry continued to be performed; although there are no great names like Anacreon or Alcaeus, and those anonymous drinking rounds (*skolia*) which can be dated are mostly earlier, the collection of short elegiac poems attributed to Theognis seems to go back to sympotic song-books of this period. There were games (*kottabos*, flicking wine at a target, was one of the most developed), and increasingly professional entertainments performed by slave girls and boys. Our literary evocations of the classical *Symposium* by Plato and Xenophon illustrate two basic features. The first is the element of order and succession: the speaking, like the drinking, is ordered—each man talks in turn on a chosen theme. The second is the importance of love and sex: excluded from the family setting, these natural emotions found their place in the drinking group. Here is the main reason for the importance of homosexuality in ancient Greece; for the *symposion* provided the focus for liaisons of both 'earthly' and 'spiritual' type, whether in relation to fellow drinkers or the slave boys: the idealization of these emotions inspired some of the highest expressions of love in European literature. Athenian women never attended the *symposion*; but 'call-girls' or *hetairai* were common, slaves often owned by one or more men and accompanying them as part of the entertainment: 'the defendant Neaera drank and dined with them in the presence of many men, as an *hetaira* would do'—therefore she cannot be an Athenian citizen. Vase-painting illustrates most clearly the range of behaviour which resulted; in literature Xenophon is the best guide, with his informal account of conversations about love, of Callias' infatuation with the son of one of his guests, and of the entertainment provided by two professional slave performers, both acrobatic and erotic. After the evening was over, the party often ended with a drunken riot through the streets, in which innocent bystanders might get beaten up, or sinister events might occur, such as the smashing of the herms outside the doors of Athenian citizens one dark night in May 415 BC. It was even alleged that the Eleusinian Mysteries had been deliberately profaned behind closed doors at a number of parties.

These activities were aristocratic: the social gap is exemplified in the scene in Aristophanes' *Wasps* where 'aristocratic' son tries to teach his 'working-class' father how to behave:

> Come and lie down, and learn how to behave at *symposia* and parties.
>   How do I do it then? Come on, tell me.
> Elegantly.
> You mean like this?
> Oh *no*.
> How then?
> Straighten your knees and pour yourself over the cushions, flowing like an athlete.
> Then praise one of the bronzes, inspect the ceiling, admire the hangings in the hall.

Needless to say, the old man ends up behaving disgracefully, stealing one of the flute-girls and pursued by outraged citizens threatening writs for assault.

The *symposion* was part of a youth culture which also found its expression in the *gymnasion*. Greek society was the first known to us to take sport seriously. The circuit of international festivals where top athletes competed (the Olympic Games being only the most famous) was set up in the sixth century; and athletes were famous figures in their own cities, feasted and celebrated in victory odes by men such as Pindar: rather surprisingly, given the importance of the group in these and so many other activities, team sports did not exist. Young men spent much of their day at the *gymnasion* where they exercised naked, pursued their loved ones, or passed the time in conversation. It is no accident that two famous *gymnasia*, the Academy and the Lyceum, gave their names to two famous schools of philosophy, those of Plato and Aristotle; for these philosophers had established their activities deliberately in proximity to the exercising grounds.

Festivals were the focus of democratic culture, where the people could enjoy displays which were a combination of public feast, religious experience and great art. Other chapters explore the theatrical (Ch. 7) and religious (Ch. 11) aspects of the festival; here it is enough to remember that the different aspects cannot be separated. At the Great Dionysia the theatrical performances were preceded by a day in which perhaps as many as 240 bulls might be ritually slaughtered and eaten, there was drunken revelry, and many people spent the night sleeping in the streets: part of the experience of the tragic audience must have been the reek of dried blood and a monumental hangover. In cultural terms the important aspect is the shift in patronage that public festivals imply. It is no longer the tyrant or the aristocrat who commissions great art, but the *dēmos* as a whole. The art produced responds to the demands for a more public, more colourful display: building on the traditions of choral dance appropriate to religious festivals, it creates a truly public art. But there was still a place for that close relationship between artist and patron which seems essential to great art, for the people 'realize that, where it is a matter of providing choral or dramatic festivals or athletic contests or of equipping a naval trireme, it is the rich who put up the money, while the common people enjoy their festivals and contests and are provided with their triremes.' The rich were in fact required by law to undertake these public 'liturgies', and competed to display their generosity before the people.

Education

The Greek alphabet, which is essentially our alphabet, was adopted from the Phoenicians in the eighth century, and created the preconditions for widespread literacy. By the fifth century the ability of male citizens to read and write is taken for granted, which makes it difficult for us to determine how widespread literacy actually was. But certain facts are clear. Literacy in Greece was never a

A READING LESSON. On the interior of an Athenian cup of about 430–420 BC. The boy stands reading a folding wooden tablet, the leaves of which would have been waxed, while the man reads from a scroll. The scene is contemporary Athenian, but the figures are given mythical identities with the names Musaeus and Linus, a poet and a teacher of the Heroic Age.

craft skill, possessed only by experts; from the start writing was used for a great range of activities, from composing poetry to cursing enemies, from displaying laws to voting, from inscribing tombstones or dedications to writing shopping lists. To be completely illiterate was to be ignorant, uncultured; but our evidence shows that there existed all levels of skill in writing, spelling, and grammar: only a society in which literacy is widespread can offer such a range of evidence from semi-literacy to illiteracy. There is of course no sign that women were expected or encouraged to read, though many of them could. To be cautious, we may say that in a city like Athens well over half the male population could read and write, and that levels of literacy in the Greek cities of the classical and Hellenistic periods were higher than at any period in western culture before this century. Yet it is important to remember that for many purposes Greek culture remained an oral culture, in which the preferred forms and means of communication were oral not written.

Widespread literacy implies widespread schooling: organized schools are first heard of at the end of the sixth century. Education had to be paid for, but the cost was low, since schoolteachers were generally despised. Athenian law laid down the hours of opening and closing of schools, the numbers of boys permitted and their ages, and established state supervision of teachers, apparently in the interests of the moral protection of the children from their teachers; those who could afford it were accompanied to school by a slave. Schooling began at the age of seven, and doubtless for many did not continue beyond the three or four years necessary to learn the basic skills. But the next stage in life was thought of as starting about eighteen, so we must assume that many had as much as ten years of schooling. Education was traditionally divided into three areas, under three different types of teacher: literature, physical education, and music. Literature began with reading and writing, grammar and language work, and included learning poetry by heart (especially Homer), imbibing its moral content, and discussing a limited range of literary and other questions raised by the authors; there was a great deal of emphasis on mechanical exercises and rote learning, and teachers made up for their low social status by imposing discipline through corporal punishment. Prose authors were not studied, nor were mathematics or any technical subject: the general Greek view of the usefulness of the poets for practical instruction and their moral value reflects their educational practice. Physical education was carried out at the *palaistra*, some at least of which were public, under special teachers, and included the basic sports practised in Greece, which were again individual rather than team sports. Music seems to have been losing ground in the classical period; it included choral dancing as well as performing on instruments.

It is easy to see that this education is essentially aristocratic in origin, providing the basic cultural and physical skills needed to shine in the *gymnasion* and the *symposion*; but in classical Athens there are signs that it was being made available to a far wider group, which may explain some of the tension between styles of education evident in Aristophanes' *Clouds*. Towards the end of the fourth century the Athenian system was sufficiently standard and universal to be completed by a state system of youth training, in which all young men from the age of eighteen spent two years in the *gymnasion* and in military training under specially appointed officials: this institution, called the *ephēbeia*, became in the Hellenistic period the mark of a Greek city, and the chief distinction between citizen and non-citizen.

The main point of Aristophanes' *Clouds* is, however, a different conflict, that between lower and higher education. By the 420s, when that play was written, there was becoming available a systematic form of higher education intended to train young men for public life. The travelling lecturer, displaying his knowledge of esoteric subjects such as antiquities, anthropology, mathematics, or linguistics, and more especially his skill at public speaking, was an established part of fifth-century life, reflecting ease of communication and a premium on intellectual showmanship; the development of Athens caused these lecturers to converge on the city, and Plato captures well the excitement caused by the visits of men such as Gorgias of Leontini, Protagoras of Abdera, Prodicus of Ceos, Anaxagoras of Lampsacus, Hippias of Elis, or (we may add) Herodotus of Halicarnassus. Plato also sets up an antithesis between these figures, the so-called 'sophists', and Socrates the Athenian: they profess knowledge of all sorts, he professes ignorance; they parade skill in public speaking, he can only ask questions, and rejects the elegant prepared answer; they offer to teach, to make men better, he merely offers to confirm man's ignorance; they charge high fees, his teaching is free. But the great confrontations in such dialogues as the *Protagoras* or the *Gorgias* do not reflect contemporary opinion, which did not distinguish the activities of Socrates from those of the sophists. Sophistic ideas are discussed elsewhere (below, p. 230); but to Aristophanes, reflecting the prejudices of the ordinary Athenian, these men were all pretty similar in their scepticism and moral relativism, their love of money and pretentious intellectual claims: they made people question the basic values of society like the existence of the gods and the duty to obey the laws; some of them even seemed to encourage their pupils to think that the political constitution was a matter of indifference. If they taught anything useful, it was 'the ability to make the worse seem the better cause': skill in public speaking implied the development of a rudimentary theory of argument and an understanding of the psychological springs of persuasion, together with a willingness to regard the art of rhetoric as separable from belief in truth. The results of this set of techniques might seem mildly useful, as for instance the lists of arguments and counter-arguments in the anonymous late-fifth-century text called the *Dissoi Logoi* (Opposite Arguments), or Antiphon's *Tetralogies*, pairs of speeches on opposite sides of imaginary murder trials; but if a man learned to argue both sides of a case, how would he know which was right?

The impact of the sophists on the aristocratic youth of the late fifth century was enormous: a whole new generation of politicians emerged, more sophisticated and more cynical, to counter the plebeian attitudes of the demagogues; their involvement in the various oligarchic coups of the period discredited the attempt to claim politics as an art, at least in the practical world. But the sophistic educational system developed in two directions, notably under the two great fourth-century educators, Plato and Isocrates. Behind the informal fifth-century world of Plato's dialogues lies an increasingly efficient fourth-century educational establishment attempting to create leaders for a new philosophical age, and studying more or less systematically the various branches of what we know as philosophy, from mathematics to metaphysics. Isocrates was a born educationalist, the most tedious writer Athens ever produced, who unfortunately lived to the age of ninety-eight. He took the sophistic movement forward to offer a training in technique without content: rhetoric became a universal art, suitable for all verbal occasions, not just public speaking. He also offered an education in general culture, and numbers of competent speakers and literary figures are said to have studied under him; but his theories lacked any incentive to serious thought. They were therefore eminently suited to become the standard pattern for organized higher education. This conflict between Plato and Isocrates developed the systematic theories of logic and of rhetoric which we find in Aristotle; it also developed a polarity between philosophy and rhetoric as two forms of mental activity suited to the adult mind, which was to dominate culture for the rest of the ancient world.

The development of the profession of medicine is a phenomenon parallel to the development of rhetoric and philosophy, and subject to many of the same tendencies. Greek doctors were already famous for their skills in the sixth century, and could command high salaries at the courts of Greek tyrants or the Persian king, or significantly as publicly paid city doctors; their scientific theory was drawn from the Ionian philosophers, their skills were acquired by apprenticeship, heredity, and practice. In the fifth century more stable identifiable groups begin to emerge, in south Italy, and in the two Ionian cities of Cos and Cnidus; by the end of the fourth century these last two had become established medical schools with specific traditions: the parallel with the contemporary development from itinerant sophist to philosophical and rhetorical school is plain. The process can be followed in the so-called *Hippocratic Corpus*, a collection of medical treatises attributed to Hippocrates of Cos, contemporary of Socrates, and mostly belonging to the period 430 to 330 BC. These works reveal already an established body of empirical data on most aspects of medicine—anatomy, physiology, gynaecology, pathology, epidemiology, and surgery; most of the observations are related to general physical theories such as that of the four humours. There is a lot of emphasis on diet and regimen, not surprising in a science where pharmacology and surgery necessarily played a smaller role. Many of the early treatises show attempts by doctors to distinguish their profession from the activities of natural philosophers, sophists, and 'irrational medicine'—magicians, sorcerers, and quacks; although they regarded themselves as a guild under the protection of

AN EAST GREEK GRAVESTONE FOR A DOCTOR, about 500 BC. Two metal 'cups' hang in the background. Heated and applied to the flesh, they drew evil humours and pains from the body: a commonly applied remedy in antiquity and not forgotten to the present day.

Asclepius, there is virtually no recourse to divine explanations for illness or cure, and one is left puzzled about the relationship between the medical profession and the various healing cults (involving incubation, dream therapy, incantation, prayer, holy water, and various non-rational types of cure), which are usually associated with Asclepius or other healing gods: perhaps the two attitudes to medicine coexisted in much the same way as orthodox medicine and homeopathy today—the more rationally, since it is surprising that scientific medicine could survive at all in a world where it must have seemed so much less effective than belief.

The Hippocratic Oath embodies the principles of that new medicine, and reveals its organization:

I will pay the same respect to my master in the Science as to my parents and share my life with him and pay all my debts to him. I will regard his sons as my brothers and teach them the Science, if they desire to learn it, without fee or contract. I will hand on precepts, lectures, and all other learning to my sons, to those of my master, and to those pupils duly apprenticed and sworn, and to none other. . . .

The conception of medicine as a craft to be learned by apprenticeship or heredity has fused with the conception of medicine as a body of scientific knowledge and as a moral way of life; it is not surprising that this oath and the attitudes it enshrines have remained central to the practice of medicine down to our own day.

Society is composed of interrelating phenomena, and there is a fascination in seeing how they fit together; perhaps that aim is sufficient justification for this chapter. But social history may also be seen as the background against which man creates his art, his literature, and his systems of thought; it is essential to understanding them, and yet it does not explain them. What is unique about the classical Greek world is its cultural achievements. If we may pause to ask how these came to be, I would suggest that there was, at least in the case of Athens, a crucial conflict between a traditional society and the complexities of its public and private life, which can be traced in the social, economic and cultural developments of the classical age; these complexities liberated the individual from the constraints of tradition without causing him to lose his social identity. The conflict is potentially present in the Greek city-state, and actualized in the case of Athens: Athens is the paradigm of the latent forces of the *polis*.

Further Reading

The various authors mentioned are available in the Loeb Classical Library; the most interesting individual texts are Xenophon's *Symposium* and *Oeconomicus*, the first book of Aristotle's *Politics*, the murder trial in Lysias, *Oration* 1, and Demosthenes, *Oration* 59 (against Neaera). The Gortyn Law-code is discussed in R. F. Willetts, *Aristocratic Society in Ancient Crete* (London, 1955). For the evidence of Aristophanes see V. Ehrenberg, *The People of Aristophanes* (2nd edn. London, 1951). The death of Socrates and the evidence for the effects of hemlock are discussed in C. J. Gill, 'The death of Socrates', *Classical Quarterly* 23 (1973), 25–8.

There is a lively general account of *Athenian Culture and Society* (London, 1973) by T. B. L. Webster. For Spartan society the best discussion is W. Den Boer, *Laconian Studies* (Amsterdam, 1954), part III; see also E. Rawson, *The Spartan Tradition in European Thought* (Oxford, 1969).

H. W. Parke, *Festivals of the Athenians* (London, 1977), describes the Athenian religious year; D. M. Macdowell, *The Law of Classical Athens* (London, 1978), is the best introduction to the complexities of Athenian law. Athenian social values are described in K. J. Dover, *Greek Popular Morality in the time of Plato and Aristotle* (Oxford, Blackwell, 1974). On kinship, women, and the family see W. K. Lacey, *The Family in Classical Greece* (London, 1968); S. C. Humphreys, *The Family, Women and Death* (London, 1983). On women the best general book is Sarah B. Pomeroy, *Goddesses, Whores, Wives and Slaves* (New York, 1975); see also *Images of Women in Antiquity*, ed. A. Cameron and A. Kuhrt (London, 1983: essays by Ruth Padel and Susan Walker); David M. Schaps, *Economic Rights of Women in Ancient Greece* (Edinburgh, 1979).

On the economy of Athens the best general account is S. Isager and M. H. Hansen, *Aspects of Athenian Society in the Fourth Century B.C.* (Odense, 1975); for a very different account, see M. I.

Finley, *The Ancient Economy* (London, 1973). On special topics see A. Burford, *Craftsmen in Greek and Roman Society* (London, 1972); J. S. Boersma, *Athenian Building Policy from 561/0 to 405/4 B.C.* (Groningen, 1970); C. Conophagos, *Le Laurium antique* (Athens, 1980; an excellent account by a professional mining engineer who has also excavated); D. Whitehead, *The Ideology of the Athenian Metic* (Cambridge, 1977). For slavery the only up-to-date general account is in French, Y. Garlan, *Les Esclaves en Grèce ancienne* (Paris, 1982); there are excellent essays in *Slavery in Classical Antiquity* ed. M. I. Finley (Cambridge, 1960), and in his own collection on the history of modern scholarship, *Ancient Slavery and Modern Ideology* (London, 1980).

For sport see H. A. Harris, *Greek Athletes and Athletics* (London, 1964), and the same author's *Sport in Greece and Rome* (London, 1972). There is an interesting lecture by Michael Vickers on *Greek Symposia*, published by the Joint Association of Classical Teachers, London, no date. Homosexuality is discussed by K. J. Dover, *Greek Homosexuality* (London, 1978). On education see H. I. Marrou, *History of Education in Antiquity* (English trans. New York, 1956); G. B. Kerferd, *The Sophistic Movement* (Cambridge, 1981). The extent of literacy in Athens is discussed in an important article by F. D. Harvey, 'Literacy in the Athenian Democracy', *Revue des Études Grecques* 79 (1966), 585-635. For the consequences of the change from oral to literate culture, see J. Goody (ed.), *Literacy in Traditional Societies* (Cambridge, 1968); E. A. Havelock, *The Literate Revolution in Greece and its Cultural Consequences* (Princeton, 1982). There is an excellent collection of the *Hippocratic Writings* (Penguin, London, 1978), ed. G. E. R. Lloyd; see also his essays, *Magic, Reason and Experience* (Cambridge, 1979); E. D. Phillips, *Greek Medicine* (London, 1973).

Any discussion of the fundamental questions of freedom of thought and religious belief in ancient Greece begins from the work of E. R. Dodds, notably *The Greeks and the Irrational* (Berkeley, 1951), chs. VI and VII; *The Ancient Concept of Progress and other Essays* (Oxford, 1973).

IO

Classical Greek Philosophy

❧❦

JULIA ANNAS

Background: Philosophy in the Fifth Century

WHEN Plato began to write, philosophy in Greece already had a long and striking history—a history against which Plato himself in his early dialogues rebels. It is tempting for us to take Plato as marking a fresh start in philosophy, and we are encouraged in this by the fact that his are the first complete works that we can discuss philosophically without the preliminary labour of piecing out fragments and disentangling later reports. But Plato's work as a whole is best seen against the background of the philosophical tradition that he found; and this is even more true of Aristotle, who indeed largely charts that tradition for us, and whose work is deeply marked by his continued engagement with, and responses to, previous thinkers.

Plato's dialogues, written in the fourth century, are for the most part set dramatically in the fifth. Socrates, whom they depict, was then doing philosophy in Athens, at the time when it had become the intellectual centre of the Greek world, and philosophical activity had become exciting and diverse.

Philosophy in Greece had begun as cosmology, explanation of the universe in terms of unifying and simplifying principles which render intelligible a wide variety of phenomena. By the fifth century we find that this activity continues, but its status has changed. There are figures such as Diogenes of Apollonia and Archelaus of Athens, who produce traditional cosmology after giving perfunctory attention to newer metaphysical concerns; but they now represent only one option, one way of doing philosophy in a world conscious of alternatives. The explanation of nature is on its way to becoming only one part of philosophy.

We can see from Plato's *Theaetetus* 179d–180c that in the fifth century philosophers were aware of another tradition of philosophy also, a quite different one going back to Heraclitus. In that passage Heraclitus' followers are berated as arrogant, unco-operative individualists: a recognition, though a hostile one, of a tradition exalting self-understanding and the importance of turning inwards to seek it, something each of us can only do in our own case. Heraclitus despises conventional ways of looking for truth, including cosmology as done by others;

by his pronouncements and his enigmatic style he tries to prod each of us into a personal search for inner enlightenment, a search that will also lead to the excellence (or 'virtue', *aretē*) of *sōphrosynē* or soundness of mind, the state of the person whose clarity about himself leads him to act appropriately towards others. According to Plato, Heraclitus' followers degenerated into pretentious would-be gurus; none the less by Socrates' time thinkers had been introduced to the idea that human excellence, intellectual and other, lies not in curious exploration of the world around us but in a right use and ordering of our own rational faculties.

More striking and widespread than the effects of Heraclitus, in fifth-century philosophizing, were the effects of the arguments propounded by the Eleatic thinkers Parmenides and Melissus. They proved, by an argument that nobody could fault, a conclusion that nobody could believe: that although it appears to us that we refer to a plurality of qualified and changing objects, in reality there is only one thing to be referred to, and to conceive of this as qualified, divided, or pluralized in any way is to imply absurdities. Until Plato and Aristotle nobody challenged the actual arguments, but the conflict they forced between the results of reasoning and the assumptions of experience was taken to heart in two ways. First, traditional philosophizing, mainly occupied with explanation of the world, was jolted into self-consciousness about the issues of reality and appearance and, relatedly, of reasoning and experience. Fifth-century cosmologies show continued confidence in our reasonings about explanation and the ultimate constituents of things; but confidence in the phenomena to be explained has gone. In deference to the Eleatic arguments the world of our experience is thought of as mere appearance, and theories become, for the first time, reductive: they tell us what is really there (atoms and void, for example) and the world of our experience is consigned, mysteriously, to mere convention. Anaxagoras criticizes as wrong the common-sense belief that things come into being and perish; the truth is no longer available to us without philosophers' theories, and it comes to be taken for granted that philosophical thinking reveals a contrast between reality, displayed by theory, and the world as it appears to us, which we pre-reflectively accept. But we find a record of puzzles on this topic rather than solutions; it is not a primary interest for any thinker until Plato.

The outrageousness of the conclusions of Eleatic argument produced another striking development: a new awareness of argument itself, and its use and abuse. It was a novelty when Zeno of Elea, in defence of Parmenides, produced a whole book consisting solely of arguments. It was even more of a novelty when Gorgias of Leontini (*c*.485–*c*.380) produced a book proving by argument that there is nothing, that if there were we couldn't understand it, and if we could we couldn't communicate it. We admire the ingenuity of Gorgian argument while remaining unsure of his commitment either to its validity or to the truth of the conclusion.

At a time when such detachment was new, this could easily strike people, and did, as disturbing and irresponsible. By the time of Aristophanes' *Clouds* cleverness in argument is feared, but it is perceived as a dubious talent, likely to go with indifference to the truth of what is in dispute. This was a sad state of affairs, largely due to confusions about the nature of argument which were not definitively cleared up till Aristotle. But that the suspicions were often deserved can be seen from such a text as the fifth-century *Dissoi Logoi* or 'Double Arguments'. In it arguments are listed pro and con a number of theses; interesting arguments and feeble fallacies are indifferently lumped together; and there is no attempt to understand the grounds or point or mutual relations of any of the theses.

Gorgias was one of the first of the 'sophists', teachers who went round various cities offering, for a fee, the only available 'higher education'. Other famous sophists were Protagoras (*c.*490–421), Prodicus (*c.*460–390s), Hippias (roughly contemporary with Prodicus), Antiphon and Thrasymachus (both difficult to date but active in the late fifth century), Alcidamas and Lycophron (late fifth century, the former a pupil of Gorgias). As well as further instruction in subjects like mathematics, the sophists taught 'rhetoric', the art of arguing convincingly, irrespective of subject-matter. Their services were welcome because the art of arguing other people down was useful in the highly public arena of city politics; thus they tended to pride themselves on skill in arguing, without being clear what in this was due to rhetorical tricks and what to serious philosophical points. Plato depicts them as pretentious, but with little understanding of the techniques and arguments they manipulated; and although we are at a disadvantage because of our dependence on the indirect tradition, we certainly get the impression that they enjoyed the sheer exercise of raising logical puzzles and paradoxical statements without any strong drive to get systematic understanding of them.

Their contribution was not all negative, however; they developed what had hitherto been marginal in philosophy: the study of ethics and politics. People making their livings by teaching the means of success in a number of places were bound to pay attention to the differences between the political institutions and ethical codes of various cities. Protagoras was most famous for drawing relativistic conclusions from this; Plato in the *Theaetetus* presents the relativism of 'Protagoras' as undifferentiated and confused, but we have no way of knowing how fair this is. It became also more and more fashionable to claim that human institutions are a matter of *nomos* (law, rule, interpreted increasingly as arbitrary convention) and not of *physis* (nature). The general idea is clear: human institutions, unlike the laws of nature, can be changed to serve different purposes. But so many different notions were brought under the alluringly vague contrast that it came to bring more confusion than illumination. Callicles in Plato's *Gorgias* is put forward as an example of someone who parades the contrast without meaning anything clear by it. Callicles illustrates also the widespread tendency to draw (largely unjustified) amoralistic conclusions about *nomos* from its vaguely specified contrast with *physis*, and to reject not only inherited customs but any kind of laws or norms as being merely arbitrary and deserving no respect.

Socrates was thus aware of a philosophical tradition that had already become diverse and pluralist. Traditional cosmology continued alongside the newer developments of ethics and the art of reasoning, with some interest in metaphysics and the theory of knowledge. And, especially at Athens, personal certainties had been shaken: not so much by awareness of alternative ways of life, which was hardly new, but by a growing feeling that inarticulate tradition now needed reasoned defence. Respect for the powers of argument created a demand that what was valued be argued for; but the respect was indiscriminate, the nature of argument ill understood, and the result often confusion. Such was the state of philosophy when it was, for a time, revolutionized by a powerful personality.

Socrates

Socrates (470–399) was an ordinary Athenian citizen belonging to no philosophical school; he may have had an early interest in cosmology, but if so, he abandoned it. He wrote nothing, and our reports of him come from sources (Plato, Xenophon, Aristophanes) that give widely divergent pictures. If our interest is philosophical, however, we have no choice but to follow Plato; and although we have always to remember that the Platonic Socrates is Plato's creation, we can form some idea of what it was about the historical Socrates that led Plato to use him as the main spokesman for Platonic ideas. The most important facts about Socrates were that he lived, uncompromisingly, for philosophy; and that he was put to death on anti-intellectual grounds, the charges being that he introduced new divinities and corrupted the youth. It is plausible that behind this lay unspoken political motives, since Socrates had associated with many of the aristocrats who had overthrown the democracy, but the dislike was in part genuinely anti-philosophical. Socrates remained for Plato the prototype of the person unconditionally committed to philosophy; his conception of philosophy changed, but never his conviction of the importance of Socrates' example.

The later cliché about Socrates was that he turned philosophy from science to ethics; but there had already been plenty of ethical and political enquiry. What he did was to make philosophy personal again. He ignored Protagoras' theories about society as much as Anaxagoras' theories about matter, and instead went around picking on individuals and addressing to each of them the disconcerting and unpopular question, 'Do *you* understand what you are talking about?' This naïvely direct refusal to take at face value claims to philosophical and other expertise marks a return to Heraclitus' kind of concern: scientific and sociological enquiries are rejected until we have the self-knowledge to understand the proper use to make of the results. Until we do, the most urgent task for each person is to turn inwards rather than outwards; and in keeping with this Socrates refused to write down any teachings or speechify in any way. Whereas Heraclitus did think he had access to the truth, Socrates represents himself as ignorant, superior only in argumentative technique and self-awareness; he is, he says, merely the gadfly that stings people out of their complacency. But he has a much more intellectual conception of understanding and its requirements than Heraclitus. He argues people into realizing what an undefended mess their views are. He insists that his questioning will only be halted by a rational defence of the interlocutor's views, when he can 'give an account' of them. Indeed, we can see a tendency on Socrates' part to demand a more intellectual articulation than is actually appropriate in the case of the ethical and practical matters on which his interest centres. He demands that practical capacities, including the virtues, be utterly transparent to the agent in a rationally articulated form which he can produce and defend, and this seems a dubious demand. The biographical tradition reinforces our unease by depicting Socrates as in many ways a weird and inhuman person making excessive demands on human nature in both himself and others. (But we have little chance of finding out what, if any, historical reality lies behind these stories.)

Plato

Plato (*c*.427–*c*.347) was an aristocratic Athenian who followed Socrates' example in devoting his life to philosophy, but did not follow him in his rejection of the permanent written word in favour of personal encounter. However, although he did write, a great deal, he retained some Socratic suspicion of writing: *Phaedrus* 274 b–277 a is a famous passage where he warns us that written words are dead and cannot answer back, whereas true philosophy is always a live activity and interchange of thought. Plato's early writings are designed to avoid these dangers; he rejects the established media of prose (or verse) exposition for what must have seemed at the time an amazing choice—the dialogue, which had hitherto been used only for fairly low-grade entertainment. Some of Socrates' other followers, such as Antisthenes and Aeschines of Sphettus, wrote Socratic dialogues, but only with Plato can we see the form put to philosophical use. He employs it to present philosophical arguments in a way that ensures that the listener is stimulated to participate and continue, rather than passively learning off doctrines. Plato never speaks in his own person, and this makes a certain detachment inevitable; we have to make what we can of the picture of Socrates arguing. No message is forced on us, but we are made aware of a problem, and of the need for argument and thought to get further with it.

The dialogues that have these characteristics, and are traditionally accepted as early, are: *Apology* (a monologue), *Crito, Euthyphro, Ion, Lesser Hippias, Greater Hippias, Laches, Lysis, Menexenus, Protagoras, Euthydemus, Charmides, Lovers, Hipparchus, First Alcibiades.* (The last three have been excluded from the Platonic 'canon' since the nineteenth century, but for no good reason; so have a number of others whose authenticity is more doubtful.)

Usually grouped as 'middle' dialogues are *Gorgias, Meno, Phaedo, Symposium, Republic, Phaedrus, Cratylus.* With these some would put *Timaeus* with *Critias*; others would place these with the dialogues usually grouped as 'late': *Theaetetus, Parmenides, Sophist, Statesman, Philebus, Laws.* The dialogues are often 'placed' chronologically by the prominence of certain stylistic features, such as the avoidance of hiatus; but this is a very fragile aid in the case of a conscious literary artist who revised his works. In any case we do not yet possess an adequate statistical analysis of Plato's style. But a rough grouping of the dialogues forces itself on us: the middle and late dialogues are radically different from the early ones. They are much longer, mostly undramatic, especially in their use of Socrates, and above all are didactic. The stylistic changes reflect a shift away from the personal urgency of Socratic enquiry: from the middle dialogues on, we are in no doubt that Plato does have views of his own which the figure of Socrates serves merely to present. When he gives us a theory of society (in the *Republic*) or a cosmology (in the *Timaeus*) or a long set of arguments about the Eleatic One (in the *Parmenides*) the dialogue form is serving merely to make the argument more accessible. Often it does not succeed in this; and sometimes it produces an unsuitably casual drift in the argument or exposition. The dialogue form, and the use of Socrates, become strained to breaking-point as Plato becomes ever more engaged in straightforward philosophical debate, often with contemporary positions. All the same, Plato never wholly abandoned dialogue, and clearly continued to value its detachment, and the avoidance it necessitates of more than a mild degree of technicality and systematization of different positions.

His followers and interpreters (with a few exceptions such as the sceptical New Academy) have mostly displayed a different spirit. The dialogue form has usually been taken as a way of communicating different parts of a single system of ideas, a purely literary device which philosophers can safely ignore. Such an approach is unsubtle and risks insensitivity to differences between different dialogues each of which is self-contained. We can readily find in Plato continuing preoccupation with certain themes; but to build a system of Platonic doctrines is to do what he never did. He never commits himself *in propria persona* to any of the doctrines commonly thought of as Platonic; still less does he tell us which of the ideas he discusses are most basic for him and what their relationships are. There are dangers also in trying to go behind the elusive dialogue form to a supposedly more solid historical development of Plato's thought and personality. The 'biographical' tradition is untrustworthy, going back to later interpretations of the dialogues. There are several 'Letters' purporting to be by Plato, of which the Seventh is often claimed as genuine. But forgery of 'letters' was quite standard with famous figures; the 'Seventh Letter' is so peculiar philosophically that it would be perverse to use it as a basis for interpreting the philosophy in the dialogues; and it is as a whole such an unconvincing production that its acceptance by many scholars is best seen as indicating the strength of their desire to find, behind the detachment of the dialogues, something, no matter what, to which Plato is straightforwardly committed. Plato himself thought it important to frustrate just this desire.

A search for the factor, whatever it is, that distinguishes *knowing* from other states, has preoccupied many philosophers, and preoccupies Plato, in changing form. In the early dialogues his concern is the individual agent's understanding of what he is doing. Socrates picks on people whose reasons for acting are second hand, picked up in an unreflective manner, who do not realize that tradition (even a good one) if followed passively will leave one acting in a way which one does not oneself fully understand and cannot defend. Ion, a famous performer of Homer, Laches, a brave general, Euthyphro, a religious expert, and many others are brought to see that they do not really have any idea of why they act as they do. The early dialogues are in this respect variations on a single theme, and leave many dissatisfied, since we get little indication as to what further we are to do. But possibly Plato thought that beyond this there was nothing general to say, that once shorn of pretensions each person must achieve understanding for and by himself. This fits well with a cryptic insistence in some early dialogues on the importance of coming to know oneself. In the *First Alcibiades* the stage after the victim's conviction of his own lack of knowledge is followed (132 ff.) by an exhortation to look at his own inner self, his soul, to find understanding there. It is assumed without argument (in a way recalling Heraclitus) that each person must achieve self-knowledge in his own case, that this self-knowledge amounts to the virtue of *sōphrosynē*, and that having this soundness of mind ensures that one will have a proper appreciation of one's relations to others (indeed in the *Lovers* (138 b) it is identified with the virtue of justice).

The emphasis on self-knowledge as the basis of one's understanding of others is suggestive, but not followed through. One reason can be found in the *Charmides*, where discussion of self-knowledge peters out because no coherent sense can be made of it. The problems seem to lie in the assumption that knowledge must have an independent object, which 'self-knowledge', however interpreted, is unable to provide; and the appearance of this assumption is of great importance. Concentration on individuals' self-understanding turns out to have been a false start, and the model of attaining knowledge comes to be quite different: a grasp of a systematic body of truths which is objective, independent of the individual agent, and capable of being imparted.

In a famous passage in the *Meno* (82 b–86 c) Socrates takes a slave boy ignorant of geometry through a proof, in such a way that he becomes able to see what the right answer is; he has become able to work out for himself why the result must be the way it is. Socrates draws from this the optimistic conclusion that knowledge is really 'recollection' of what our souls know already (hence, knew before our present embodiment). Here we see clearly that knowledge involves having rational grounds in argument and proof (so that it becomes unclear how we can have knowledge of something we simply find out from experience, such as the road to Larissa). Plato has no doubt that such reasoning is objective; it reveals what is really there, just as a geometrical proof does. And our reasoning capacity, identified with the soul, is sharply separated from our empirical means of cognition. The *Phaedo* develops this conception in two ways. The soul, the reasoning ability which grasps reality, is even more drastically separated from the body, understood as everything in us that is not pure reasoning. And Plato is more aware of the need to systematize reasoning, making suggestive, but obscure, remarks about the organization and testing of arguments (100 a, 101 d–e.)

In the central books of the *Republic* this model of knowledge, which clearly owes much to mathematics, is fully displayed. Now knowledge is acquired only after years of preliminary training in mathematical disciplines (inculcating the need to rely on argument rather than experience) and in 'dialectic' or philosophical reasoning, in which 'hypotheses' about the nature of reality are put forward and exhaustively tested by questioning until they can be fully and explicitly defended. Knowledge is systematic and hierarchical: one's beliefs are understood only when one comes to see where they belong in a system of truths where some are basic and some derived. Knowledge so conceived has two further features: it can be imparted, and it requires time and effort, being achieved only by those who have actually come to understand in context what others appreciate only in unintegrated fragments. Unsurprisingly, knowledge will be something only few can attain, and most people's beliefs, however individually well qualified, will not count. It does not follow from such a view that we cannot have systematic understanding of the physical world we experience, but (with a few lapses) Plato's stress on pure reasoning leaves no room for this.

The more emphasis is put on knowledge as grasp of an objective, shared, impartible system of hierarchically ordered truths, the more we wonder what has happened to Plato's original concern to wake each of us up to personal understanding as the basis of our actions. In the *Republic* Plato still insists on the importance of the individual's own insight, and also insists that knowledge culminates in and flows from the Good, and thus has practical import; but most readers are rightly not satisfied that Plato has retained good grounds for this insistence. The original problems about knowledge that come alive in the context of Socratic refutation have got lost.

In the later dialogues we find that, although Plato continues to assert that knowledge requires a rational basis, he seems to have lost confidence in the middle-dialogues model. It is never explicitly argued against or replaced, but it is not put to any use either, and Plato's last thoughts on knowledge are inconclusive ones—the brilliant dialogue *Theaetetus*, where instead of giving us a model for knowledge Plato turns at last to asking what knowledge actually is, and finds the answers, as many have since, persistently elusive.

But the *Republic* model remains pervasive in interpretations of Plato, partly because it is impressive, though vague and never given precise application, partly because it goes naturally with a similarly impressive though vague conception of the reality that corresponds to knowledge.

The knowledge that interlocutors in the early dialogues lack is a grasp of the basis of whatever virtue is in question. They cannot 'give an account' of it which will define the real nature which underlies its various manifestations, and which explains and corrects our ordinary beliefs. What marks off the person with understanding is grasp of what there is real and objective to know about bravery or beauty or justice, or whatever is in dispute. This is what Plato calls (untechnically and with a variety of vocabulary) the Form, the real basis of qualities like the virtues, which can be grasped only by people who have thought and reasoned and is not accessible to those who wrangle blindly about their experience without reflecting on it. Corresponding to the way that knowledge comes to be seen more and more as systematized pure reasoning, the Forms come to be conceived of as objects of pure thinking, cut off in a mysterious way from our experience.

It is often said that Plato has a 'Theory' of Forms and even that it dominates his entire work. In fact Forms appear rarely and are always discussed untechnically; they answer to a variety of needs which are never systematically brought together; and they are prominent only in the early to middle dialogues, which progress towards an ever more grandiose and all-embracing conception of them. They are objects of pure thinking, and thus separate from our experience; yet in a strange fashion they motivate us to grasp them in a way that lifts us out of our everyday individual concerns. In the *Phaedo*, *Symposium*, *Republic*, and *Phaedrus* Plato gives famous poetic expression to the thought that the reasoning part of us is drawn to the Forms in a way that is both rigorously argued and a kind of mystical communion; and that by comparison the rest of our life is worthless and a mere distraction.

If we ask 'What are Forms?' we find a variety of answers. They are objects of knowledge (and hence, as we have seen, of reasoning). A central thought is that the Form F is what has the quality F essentially; this is the heart of the most extended argument for Forms, which recurs in different guises (*Phaedo* 74-6, *Republic* 475-80, 523-5). When we say of things in our experience that they are just, or equal, we can equally well ascribe to them the opposite of that quality, for a variety of reasons, such as applying a different standard. This possibility, it is claimed, shows that in our experience there are no beautiful things that are not also ugly, no just actions that are not also unjust. So (unless we are to infer, which Plato never does, that the use of these terms is always relative to some standard) they cannot be applied without the possibility of the opposite also applying within our experience, but only to the Form, the Form of F which is essentially F and never not-F, and which the F things and actions in our experience 'partake of' (in so far as we can correctly call them F) but also 'fall short of' (in so far as we can also say of them that they are not F). This argument applies only to terms that have opposites, and so, while it will serve for terms that exercise Plato in the early dialogues, such as *just*, *beautiful*, and *equal*, it will not show that there are Forms of Square or Triangle, or of substances such as men or artefacts such as tables. It is disputed whether Plato ever seriously wanted there to be Forms for these cases, and, if so, what his motivation could have been. In *Republic* 10 we find the notorious Forms of Bed and Table, but at *Parmenides* 130 b-d young Socrates is made to say that he is unsure whether there are Forms even for substance terms. Plato never gets to the root of another problem, either: why, given the argument, he concludes that they are Forms for the good opposites only and not for *ugly*, *unjust*, and so on. Mostly he ignores these, though in one passage (*Theaetetus* 176-7) he allows that there are evil and negative Forms, which the evil and ignorant person comes to resemble.

The role of Forms as essential bearers of qualities which in our experience always turn up contaminated by the possible application of their opposites explains some of the uses to which they are put: for example, in the *Phaedo* (100 ff.) they figure as preferred explanations for why things in our experience have the qualities they do. But some of the Forms' roles are less clearly motivated; sometimes, for example, they are taken to be stable and unchanging objects as opposed to the changing objects in our experience; occasionally we find Forms to be models for artefacts. Most centrally, Forms are contrasted with the supposedly defective way in which particular objects have certain qualities: but sometimes it is types of object or action that provide the contrast. However, sometimes they are contrasted with particular objects themselves, whose supposed fault is that they change, or even that there are many of them and not one. Because of the dialogue form, Plato never has to say which of his arguments for Forms is fundamental, and what their relations are; and because the arguments and contexts of discussion differ so widely in point and result, it is never made clear what the basic motivation for Forms is, nor what the range of Forms is, nor what it is (particulars, types, instantiation of qualities) that they are primarily opposed to. The 'Theory' of Forms is not a theory at all, but an imaginative holding together of different ideas which we glimpse in different contexts, without getting the chance to demand answers to questions about the overall structure of the ideas. The 'Theory' appeals to those who can enter imaginatively into the spirit of it without worrying too much about these questions. It has also been found fascinating precisely by those who want to press these questions and see whether a single coherent theory survives when they are made rigorous. The first of these is Aristotle, who in a work *On the Forms* distinguishes different arguments for Forms and their implications, and concludes that Plato has no single coherent theory of Forms (though he finds them compelling enough to develop his own theory of form).

One of the most disputed questions in recent Platonic scholarship has been whether Plato himself came later to criticize his earlier indiscriminate acceptance of Forms. In the first part of the *Parmenides* young Socrates puts forward what looks like the middle dialogues' conception of Forms, only to have it torn to shreds by the unhistoric, but symbolic, figures of Parmenides and Zeno. And in other late dialogues there are many arguments which do in fact undermine some of Plato's earlier uses of Forms. This certainly looks like self-criticism; but Plato draws no explicit morals. The ideas which for a time he held together in passionate conviction are quietly allowed to fall apart again, and in the late dialogues he pursues different interests for their own sake without over-ambitious synthesis.

The late dialogues are a disparate collection of often unattractively written works. In them we no longer find powerful overall ideas such as Forms or the middle dialogues' model of knowledge; what we do find are detailed and rich investigations of particular themes, which do not lend themselves to synthesis, or to individual summary. These dialogues have always been found most rewarding by philosophers, and this is surely largely due to the fact that in them we find Plato returning to traditional philosophical concerns which he had earlier impatiently rejected. (It is as true now as when they were written that the early dialogues appeal to non-philosophers, whereas only a philosopher will get through the *Parmenides* and the *Sophist*.) Not only is Plato taking traditional philosophical questions more seriously, it is probable that these dialogues were written at a time when Plato had founded a philosophical school, the 'Academy', and come to accept the idea of philosophy as something that could be imparted, as a co-operative and developing endeavour rather than a matter of intense personal insight. As Plato engages more and more in the tradition of cosmology, study of society, and investigation of argument, particularly Eleatic argument, Socrates becomes an increasingly inappropriate and anachronistic representative of his views.

Repeatedly in these dialogues we find that earlier intransigent attitudes have become modified, and that Plato is more willing to discuss and take seriously others' philosophical views. Socrates in the *Phaedo* sees cosmology merely as a mistake, but in the *Timaeus* Plato accepts that it is a legitimate part of philosophy and produces his own (very bizarre) explanation of the physical universe. In the *Gorgias* rhetoric is angrily rejected; in the *Phaedrus* it is an area where superior philosophical understanding can be advantageously applied. In the *Parmenides* and *Sophist* Plato gives careful attention to the structure and sources of the Eleatic problems which he had hitherto tried to solve by his ambitious theory of reality. In the *Cratylus* (which shares many characteristics with the late dialogues) he discusses current theories of language and word-meaning. Most strikingly, perhaps, the nature of his interest in ethics and politics changes considerably. In the early dialogues he is concerned with the personal achievement of virtue, and this is still the theme of his most famous middle dialogue, the *Republic*. In that dialogue his interest has spread sufficiently to society for the account of the just person to be placed against a background of the just society; but it is made clear that this is a society which is *ideally* just, an ideal which has no practicable political application. However, in the late dialogues we find Plato returning at length and several times to ethical and political questions from a changed perspective, one that has much in common with the formerly despised approach of Protagoras and the other sophists. In the *Statesman*, the *Critias*, and the *Laws* he returns to fifth-century questions about the origins of society, takes history and prehistory seriously, and investigates from several angles the issue of what social arrangements actually work and produce a stably functioning real society. The study of ethics and politics is no longer seen from the viewpoint of the individual concerned to become just, but is carried out from the external viewpoint of the investigator, impersonally and historically. (As we would expect, the result is much duller, though more solid and doubtless more useful.)

The late dialogues show a fairly comprehensive reversion to traditional issues which Socrates had swept aside: cosmology; concern with the Eleatic arguments; interest in reasoning and in rhetoric; and the historical and political study of society. Further, the late dialogues are the product, most probably, of teaching and discussion with pupils, in the established forum of the philosophical school. We even hear that Plato came to propound 'unwritten doctrines' of a Pythagorean-sounding kind, a bizarre mathematical metaphysics in which the contents of the universe were 'derived' from the One and the Indefinite Two. (The chief interest of this lies in Aristotle's criticisms of it in *Metaphysics M* and *N*.) Plato has travelled a long way back from Socrates to rejoin the tradition.

It would be wrong, however, to see this as a failure of nerve, or of originality. Plato's ambivalent relation to philosophy as he found it brought it about that he enriched and transformed the tradition to which he returned. Like his ambivalent relation to writing, it produced a corpus of work unparalleled for its variety of appeal, and one in which discussions of contemporary issues are never conventional or derivative. Plato would not have been the great philosopher he is if Socrates had not influenced him, or if he had influenced him more consistently.

Aristotle

Aristotle (384–322) was a product of the Academy; he came there when he was eighteen and stayed there till Plato's death. He came from Stagira in the north of Greece, from a medical family with connections at court in the increasingly powerful state of Macedonia. After he left the Academy he spent some time at the court of Assus in Asia Minor, and then acted as a tutor to Alexander the Great—an episode that made remarkably little impact on either of them. About 335 he returned to Athens and set up his own philosophical school, the Lyceum. In 323 he fled to escape the hostility to pro-Macedonians that was set free by Alexander's death, and he died in Euboea the following year. We know as little about him personally as we do about Plato, and in his case the 'biographical' tradition is even more untrustworthy; it has been infiltrated by hostile and interested sources. We do get the impression of an attractive personality from his will, preserved in the *Life* by Diogenes Laertius.

Aristotle wrote a great deal, and like Plato produced many works in dialogue form for the general public. These survive only in fragments, and what we read as the 'Corpus Aristotelicum' consists of lectures and notes on courses within his school. Later these were grouped by an editor into the books we now read as the *Metaphysics*, *Physics*, *Organon*, and so on; but there are many signs that these unities are factitious. We find different treatments of the same issues; puzzling cross-references; later insertions; and a very uneven level of stylistic finish. The argument is usually very dense, and was clearly used as a basis for discussion; the reader can seldom coast along, and has to pause and work slowly through the thought. Aristotle has been found defeating by those who look for purely literary appeal; but he is an exciting and rewarding author if one has the right expectations of hard work and co-operation.

Unlike Plato, Aristotle never leaves the tradition in which study of the natural world, and its systematic explanation, are normal philosophical tasks. The *Physics*, the *De generatione et corruptione* and the *De caelo* explain natural events in terms of highly theoretical principles, and give an account of the structure and physical constitution of the universe. But Aristotle's energetic appetite for explanation does not stop there; it comes down to more mundane levels. In the *Meteorologica*, for example, he produces an (understandably primitive) geology, meteorology, and chemistry: in the *De sensu*, ch. 3, we find a theory about colours. But it is living things that absorb Aristotle's interest to the greatest extent. The *De anima* and *Parva naturalia*, essays which create the science of the psychology of living things, are followed by massive studies of various aspects of the animals (including humans): the *De generatione animalium* discusses their reproduction, the *De motu* and *De incessu animalium* their modes of movement, the *De partibus animalium* their parts and structure. The *Historia animalium* is a record of animals' behaviour and habits, a record that must have been compiled in collaboration with others and that, although often wrong and sometimes credulous, is a famous historical monument of empirical science. Aristotle was the first biologist and is still respected by biologists. Instead of haphazardly using available reports, he made great efforts to observe many creatures for himself, seeking data and observations relevant to his enquiries. It is characteristic of Aristotle to devote energy both to theoretical physics and to empirical biology, valuing both with a width of vision impossible to recapture today.

Of all beings naturally composed, some are ungenerated and imperishable for the whole of eternity, but others are subject to coming-to-be and perishing. It has come about that in relation to the former, which possess value—indeed divinity—the studies we can make are less, because both the starting-points of the inquiry and the things we long to know about present extremely few appearances to observation. We are better equipped to acquire knowledge about the perishable plants and animals because they grow beside us ... Both studies have their attractions. Though we grasp only a little of the former, we gain more pleasure than from everything around us ... (but because the latter) are closer to us and belong more to our nature, they have their own compensations in comparison with the philosophy concerned with the divine things ... Even in the study of animals unattractive to the senses, the nature that fashioned them offers immeasurable pleasures ... to those who can learn the causes and are naturally lovers of wisdom ... For in all natural things there is something wonderful. (*De partibus animalium* 1. 5, Balme translation)

Aristotle's methods are, of course, unlike any in modern science (for which he has received rather disproportionate criticism). Although interested philosophically in mathematics he does not apply it systematically to the study of physical reality; qualitative change is basic in his physics and he makes no attempt to give a more basic quantitative analysis of it. But he had no good reason for so doing; the mathematical models of physics that he knew, from Plato and the Pythagoreans, were fanciful and unrealistic. He does in fact apply mathematical models, especially geometrical ones, in particular areas where this can illuminate; to analyse the colour spectrum or to reduce to essentials the patterns of animal movement. Another frequent charge is that he does not employ experiment; certainly he shows no interest in systematically varying the conditions under which a phenomenon is studied. But this is surely due to an assumption not queried until fairly recently: that items display their real natures in their customary environments in the actual world, not in artificially created ones. In fields such as physics and chemistry, where this assumption has been found unfruitful, Aristotle's work has only museum status; but it retains real interest in areas such as zoology and ethology, where a modern scientist still thinks that lions reveal the nature of the species better in their natural habitat than in laboratories or zoos.

Aristotle is a collector of facts; but he is far from being just that. In all his major works his treatment of the facts is informed by consciousness of philosophical issues, and it is here that he is most aware of belonging to a long tradition of philosophy and developing it further. He collected books and read them thoroughly and repeatedly; he worked in close familiarity with the works of his predecessors (including Plato) and usually this resulted in close criticism. Often he will illuminate and expand a discussion by referring to some treatment of it from the history of philosophy; and it is standard for him to begin a discussion by running through previous positions, and pointing out what in them is systematically promising or mistaken. He has been attacked as though this were arrogant cannibalizing of previous philosophy in the interests of his own ideas, but this is mistaken. His attitude in fact shows profound intellectual humility:

No-one is able to attain the truth adequately, while, on the other hand, we do not collectively fail, but everyone says something true about the nature of things, and while individually we contribute little or nothing to the truth, by the union of all a considerable amount is amassed. (*Met.* 993^{a}31–^{b}4, Ross translation)

Aristotle never tries to make a radical break either in style or in aim with the cumulative and developing body of philosophical thought available to him (indeed, his treatment of Plato is often insensitive to the extent to which Plato begins by making such a break). He sees himself as a partner in a joint enterprise, able to advance as he does thanks to the spade-work of others. Original achievement consists not in pushing forward unaided but in making intelligent use of what others have provided:

We must first consider what is said by others, so that, if there is anything which they say wrongly, we may not be liable to the same objections, while, if there is any opinion common to them and us, we shall have no private grievance against ourselves on that account, for one must be content to state some points better than one's predecessors and others no worse. (*Met.* 1076^{a}12–16, Ross translation)

Aristotle's philosophical methodology is subtle and avoids the trap of applying in one area an approach suitable only in others. ('It is the mark of an educated mind to look for precision in each class of things just so far as the nature of the subject admits' (*Nic. Ethics* 1094^b 23–5).)

In both the *Physics* and the *Ethics* he is explicit that a good treatment of an issue will do justice to the appearances or 'phenomena', where these cover both 'the facts', the way the world appears to us, and the observations and explanations that it prompts us to. He does not have uncritical respect for the phenomena, but he feels no urge to find theories that explain them away: long familiarity with the history of philosophy shows that such theories are likely to lead to dead ends. He begins by laying out various views that recommend themselves to us about time, say, or space, or weakness of will; then he analyses problems and conflicts that these produce. His own answer tries to understand and rationalize this material, showing why we are inclined to certain views, or why we tend to go wrong in accepting others. This does not mean that his own answers will be conservatively respectful of common sense: often they are highly technical and imply that our beliefs are largely mistaken. (We are, for example, tempted to the belief that there is such a thing as 'void' or empty space, but Aristotle's analysis shows us, surprisingly, that there cannot be, and that our concept of it is radically confused.) What is important is that his analysis should explain the phenomena: he aims to show us not just what the right answer is, but why we make both the advances and the mistakes that we characteristically do.

Aristotle's works are characterized by the kind of answers this methodology produces. He is subtle and nuanced, often introducing technical terms to gain precision. The course of his thought may be difficult to follow because he prefers inconclusive discussion of problems to the manufacture of speciously clear solutions. All his writing is marked by a balance between doing justice to observed complexity and bringing to our puzzlement the clarity of philosophical explanation. He strives always for the appropriate level of generality which will illuminate without over-simplifying.

The *Physics*, one of his most attractive works, displays this concern perfectly. It is not 'physics' in the modern sense. Rather it is the book where he argues for, and refines, the analytical concepts with which we understand the physical world, notably time, space, infinity, process, activity, change. Pre-reflectively, for example, we find it unproblematic that things change; but making philosophical sense of change runs up against what seem to be impossible philosophical difficulties. Aristotle analyses the sources of difficulty and shows them to be uncompelling in the light of his analysis of change, which focuses on the central case of an object coming to have a property that it formerly lacked. Arguably his paradigm is too restricted and blinds him to the importance of other kinds of changes, where we cannot plausibly find an object with properties. But is is an analysis that gives us a deepened view of what we naturally perceive as basic examples of change; it gives us theoretically grounded insight into the reason why we were right to find the world intelligible that way.

Equally characteristic is his analysis of explanation itself (the so-called doctrine of 'four causes'). Where Plato, in the *Phaedo*, impatiently rejected all other kinds of explanation (*aitia*) for Forms, Aristotle, in *Physics* 2, gives a careful analysis of four mutually irreducible types of explanation: 'form' or defining characteristics; 'matter' or constituents; source of movement (the nearest to our 'cause'); and end or aim (teleological explanation). The history of philosophy is full of (failed) attempts to reduce all kinds of explanation to one favoured kind; Aristotle is notable in his firm refusal to over-simplify and to rush to elegant, but falsifying, unification of phenomena which remain stubbornly complex. There are many kinds and levels of explanation, and they do not exclude one another. Aristotle can be systematic. His most systematic work is the *Posterior Analytics*, an ambitious classificatory structuring of the different branches of knowledge into what seems like a Platonic hierarchy, in which from basic truths are derived ever more specialized truths in various fields. But Aristotle's system is more realistic. The sciences each have their own basic axioms and are not derived from a single source; and the system itself serves as a regulative ideal, a representation of the ordered state of completed science, which we do not, of course, possess now.

Aristotle's 'metaphysics' is in many ways a continuation of his 'physics'. He develops his concepts of form and matter, actuality and potentiality, substance and attribute, as tools of explanation, used very much like those of process and change. He does believe that some items are metaphysically fundamental, independent of, and basic to, an explanation of the rest; and his views on this undergo change. In the *Categories*, usually accepted as an early work, concrete individuals such as Socrates and Coriscus fill this bill, and are called 'first substances'. In the *Metaphysics*, especially the difficult central books, substance appears to be not the individual but its form, and difficulties arise which are not clearly solved, given some of the other metaphysical roles that form plays. Aristotle's views here have been very variously interpreted and estimated; and it is more obvious here than in other parts of his work that what matters for him is getting properly to the roots of a difficulty rather than coming up with simple answers to the problem as originally posed. On one point he never wavers: hostility to Plato's Forms (or numbers or other abstract objects) conceived of as separate from the world we experience, existing independently of it. It is crucial that we do have understanding of the world; a theory must be wrong that cuts us off from what is supposed to make the world intelligible.

A most striking advance on his philosophical inheritance, and the only case where Aristotle consciously claims to innovate, is his great clarification of the nature of argument. The *Topics* and *Sophistical Refutations* are early records of his study of 'how to argue effectively'; but his real breakthrough is marked by the *Prior Analytics*, the first work of formal logic, where by the use of schematic letters he first isolates the notion of logical form and systematically classifies the forms of valid argument. Having made it possible for the first time to distinguish the soundness of an argument from its power to persuade Aristotle also, in the *Rhetoric*, performs the complementary task of classifying the various sources of persuasion in argument. To sort out so rigorously and definitively the various aspects of the 'art of argument' from its muddled state in the fifth century, and even in Plato, was an amazing achievement, displaying both the powers of Aristotle's intellect and his concern not to lose any aspect of the subject he is analysing. The logical and rhetorical works remained more prominent in estimations of Aristotle until the twentieth century; new developments in logic have shown the limitations of Aristotelian logic rather strikingly, and rhetoric is no longer a serious study. As a result it is easy for us to undervalue what appeared to Aristotle's contemporaries (and rightly to Aristotle himself) as an unparalleled achievement.

Aristotle devotes a large proportion of his philosophical energy to the study of people in society and to various phenomena of social life. Sometimes these are activities which Plato had attacked, such as drama and the arts, and Aristotle's subtle and complex theory of various literary genres in the *Poetics* can be seen as rescuing them from Plato's needlessly intemperate attacks. But mostly Aristotle carries on from Plato fairly directly; one such area is that of the monumental studies of society in the late dialogues. We have a number of works now grouped as the *Politics*, and three works on ethics; the *Nicomachean* and *Eudemian Ethics*, and the *Magna Moralia*. (The relation of the first two is very disputed, and so is the authenticity of the third.) Aristotle also deepens and carries further Plato's later interest in history as casting light on present political arrangements: he organizes research into the histories of the institutions of a large number of Greek states (one of these, the *Constitution of Athens*, survives) and makes chronological improvements to the important public records of athletic victors. The distribution of his interests reflects closely what we find in the physical works: thorough research is vital, but it is guided always by a concern for theoretical clarity. (Historians' appreciation of his work has thus varied a great deal, depending on how theoretical their own conception of their subject has been.) Aristotle is not philosophically interested in history for its own sake, as we can see from a famous aside in the *Poetics*: poetry is 'more philosophic and of graver import' than history since it is not concerned with mere brute facts. But history, and other forms of human practical activity, contingent and particular though they are, can still be usefully clarified and analysed by the philosopher. The *Nicomachean Ethics* in particular has deservedly attracted lasting detailed concern because in it the concerns of practical life—excellence, the best life, practical reasoning—are analysed with a beautifully appropriate degree of rigour and abstraction. The theory that 'virtue lies in a mean', for example, shows us the structure of our dispositions to action, and clarifies them to us without forcing them into over-simple, artificial moulds. On practical reasoning, a topic on which few philosophers have said anything both true and illuminating, Aristotle's account is still arguably the best in the field, showing us the structure in what looks like the chaos of everyday deliberations without implausibly reducing all our reasonings about action to a single form of calculation about how to achieve a single fixed end. The project of explaining rather than rejecting the appearances appears here in its most accessible and still relevant form. The ethical works display in a particularly happy way Aristotle's talent for applying the appropriate method, for producing the explanation which clarifies the subject, but clarifies it in such a way that we do not lose touch with our original view of the subject-matter and the difficulties it gives rise to.

Aristotle has throughout appeared as belonging to the more outward-turning philosophical tradition focused on explanation of the physical world and human society from the observer's viewpoint. It may seem that he lacks Plato's, and Heraclitus', concern for the inner, the search in philosophy for personal enlightenment. In fact it is easy to overdraw this contrast; there is in Aristotle a strong mystical streak. But it finds expressions that are impersonal. In short, difficult, and undeveloped passages in *De anima* 3 and *Nic. eth.* 10 he presents the peak of human achievement as abstract thinking which is a unity with its object. And the first mover of Aristotle's universe, established through remorselessly technical argument in *Physics* 7 and 8, is in *Metaphysics* 12 identified with god, and, in difficult and intense passages, with thinking of this abstract kind, which is, in the case of god, 'thinking of thinking', a thinking that escapes the mundane limitations of our cognitive activities, which always require a distinct object. It is clear that these short and cryptic passages contain ideas of considerable importance to Aristotle, but he presents them with no personal urgency, and, perhaps because he suspects it, none of Plato's appeal to the reader's imagination.

It soon became standard to contrast Plato and Aristotle and to claim that their 'systems' were opposed in every way. (A minority tradition claimed that they merely had different approaches to the same truths.) There are obvious contrasts between them, beginning with their styles, but these are not easy to characterize in general terms, if we give due attention to Plato's late dialogues and bear in mind the long period of their common philosophizing in the Academy. Plato was always to have the wider appeal throughout antiquity, partly because of his literary skill, partly because in the middle dialogues he attracts the part of us that loves exciting generalizations. Despite Plato's more vivid depictions, it is Aristotle who is concerned not to lose the complexity and delicacy of everyday experience; but this can be done only at the cost of hard and detailed work not lending itself to popularization or literary glamour. Typically, Aristotle's discussion of the soul or *psyche*, in the *De anima* and other works, is both careful in its study of human and other animal physiology, and suggestive in its theorizing; philosophers find it exciting but it is too difficult to have wider appeal. Plato writes about the soul in a way that is lofty and inspiring, and has appealed to poets and religious thinkers and many people not otherwise interested in philosophy; but philosophers have found it less satisfying, and have often been frustrated by the way Plato fails to distinguish importantly different ideas in his contrast of body and soul.

'Platonism' as a set of doctrines extracted from the dialogues had much wider appeal than Aristotle's ideas. Plato's school was luckier also, though partly by historical accident. The Academy and the Lyceum both became respected educational institutions. But whereas the Academy, under Plato's successors Speusippus and Xenocrates, concentrated on mathematical metaphysics, and later, under Crates, Crantor, and Polemo, on ethical instruction, the Lyceum had made a commitment to scientific research, and it suffered both from a narrowing of interests and from war damage to its records, equipment, and buildings, which were more exposed than the Academy's. The Academy continued, to be rejuvenated as the New Academy; but Aristotle's school, as the active and developing philosophical community he represented in spirit, soon petered out. His successor Theophrastus produced distinguished work in many fields, and his successor Strato was well known for his scientific enquiries; but after that the headship of the Lyceum passes to a string of unoriginal nonentities. Interest in Aristotle's ideas survived, but more and more in the unhelpful form of finding in him a set of doctrines to be mechanically applied. In this form 'Aristotelianism' was to have a long life, but of a kind most inappropriate to Aristotle.

Further Reading

THE SOPHISTS AND THE BACKGROUND

A good full account: W. K. C. Guthrie, *History of Greek Philosophy*, vol. III (Cambridge, 1971): available in two paperback volumes as *The Sophists* and *Socrates*. G. B. Kerferd, *The Sophistic Movement* (Cambridge, 1981) is less massive.

The Greek texts and translations are printed, with a helpful commentary, in G. S. Kirk and J. E. Raven, *The Presocratic Philosophers*, 2nd edn, by M. Schofield (Cambridge, 1984): available in paperback.

PLATO

A large volume, *The Collected Dialogues of Plato*, ed. E. Hamilton and H. Cairns, Bollingen Series 71 (Princeton, 1973) contains almost all the dialogues in good translations. The dubious works which it omits are included in the volume in the Loeb series which contains also the *Charmides*, *Minos*, and *Epinomis* (ed. W. Lamb, London and Cambridge, Mass., 1964).

Secondary literature on Plato is enormous. The following works will guide the reader to particular areas of it: I. Crombie, *An Examination of Plato's Doctrines*, 2 vols. (London, 1963); G. Vlastos, *Platonic Studies*, 2nd edn. (Princeton, 1981).

There are some good collections of articles: R. G. Allen (ed.), *Studies in Plato's Metaphysics* (London, 1965); G. Vlastos (ed.), *Plato* I (articles on Metaphysics and Epistemology) II (on Ethics, Politics, Philosophy of Art, Religion) (London, 1972).

The fourth and fifth volumes of Guthrie's *History of Greek Philosophy* deal with Plato and the Early Academy in detail.

ARISTOTLE

The Oxford Translation of Aristotle, revised by J. Barnes, 2 vols. (Princeton, 1984), contains translations of all the complete extant works and some of the fragments of lost ones.

J. Barnes, *Aristotle* (Oxford, 1982: in the Past Masters series) concentrates on the scientific and logical works. G. E. R. Lloyd, *Aristotle: The Growth and Structure of His Thought* (Cambridge, 1968: paperback) reconstructs Aristotle's intellectual development. On the ethics: A. Rorty, *Essays on Aristotle's Ethics* (California, 1980).

There is a good set of collections of articles: J. Barnes, M. Schofield, R. Sorabji (eds.), *Articles on Aristotle* (London, 1975–9): 1. Science; 2. Ethics; 3. Metaphysics; 4. Psychology and Aesthetics.

The sixth volume of Guthrie's *History of Greek Philosophy* (the last to be completed) deals with Aristotle.

11

Greek Religion

ROBERT PARKER

Gods and Men

GREEK religion belongs to the class of ancient polytheisms: one can in very general terms compare the religions of Rome, of Egypt, of the ancient Indo-Iranians, and most of the religions of the ancient Near East. The gods of such a polytheism have each a defined sphere of influence. The balanced worshipper does not pick and choose between them but pays some respect to them all. To neglect one god (Aphrodite, for instance) is to reject an area of human experience. Individual Greek communities paid special honour to particular gods (put the other way, gods 'took most delight' in particular sanctuaries), but not to the exclusion of others. Athena, for instance, was the divine patroness of Athens, and Hera that of Samos; an Athenian decree of 405 BC which celebrates Athenian-Samian co-operation is topped by a relief showing the two goddesses clasping hands; but Hera was also an honoured goddess in Athens, and vice versa.

The number of principal gods was always quite restricted. Homer shows ten important gods in action (Zeus, Hera, Athena, Apollo, Artemis, Poseidon, Aphrodite, Hermes, Hephaestus, and Ares) and these, together with Demeter and Dionysus, made up the 'twelve gods', the conventional total recognized from the fifth century onwards. Alongside them, there were innumerable lesser figures, some quite obscure, but others, such as Pan and the Nymphs, just as important in cult as the junior partners among the twelve, Hephaestus and Ares. Genealogies varied, but the twelve were all often said to be either siblings or children of Zeus, 'the father of gods and men'. Most of them could be conceived as living, a sprawling family, in Zeus' palace on the heavenly mountain Olympus. (At other times they were imagined as dwelling in their favoured cities.) They were thus the Olympians. Contrasted to them was a less clearly defined group of chthonians (from *chthōn*, earth), gods of the earth and the underworld, grouped around Hades, the god of death, and his luckless spouse Persephone. Since crops spring from the earth, the chthonians were not merely a negative counterpoise to the gods of heaven, and even the lord of the Olympians had also, as 'Zeus under the earth', a chthonic aspect.

BRONZE WARRIOR, found in the sea off Riace in south Italy. About 450 BC.

IRON CORSELET with gold attachments from the tomb of Philip II of Macedon (died 336 BC) at Vergina (ancient Aegae).

This restricted cast of principal gods could be made to play an almost infinite number of roles in cult practice by the addition of specifying epithets. A single cult calendar from Attica prescribes offerings on different days for Zeus as 'Zeus of the city', 'kindly Zeus', 'Zeus who looks over men', 'Zeus of fulfilment', 'Zeus of boundaries', and 'Zeus of mountain tops'. He had, in fact, several hundred such epithets. The epithet sometimes indicated the power in virtue of which the worshipper was appealing to the god: Zeus 'the general' evidently did not have in his gift the same benefits as Zeus 'of property'. Sometimes it seems that the epithet's main function was merely to introduce local discriminations within the pantheon common to all Greece. Villagers no doubt took pleasure in knowing that their Zeus or Athena was not quite the same as the one worshipped in the next village over the hill.

'There is never equality between the race of deathless gods and that of men who walk the earth', says Apollo in Homer. The gods had human form; they were born, and they might have sexual contacts, but they did not eat human food, and they would not age or die. Pindar tells how the two races both spring from Mother Earth but 'are kept apart by a difference of power in everything: the one is nothing, but for the other 'the brazen heaven is a fixed habitation for ever.'

ATHENA SHAKES HANDS WITH HERA. The goddesses symbolize the states of Athens and Samos. The relief crowns an inscription which records Athens' gratitude to Samos for loyalty even after the defeat at Aegospotami in 405 BC. The decree begins with the name of the officiating registrar, then an address 'to those Samians who stood with the Athenian people'. The *stele* was found on the Acropolis at Athens.

The gods were 'blessed', 'best in strength and honour'; men were 'wretched', 'powerless', 'creatures of a day'. In the golden age, men had dined with gods, but the two races were later 'divided'; this division occurred at the time of the first sacrifice, and each subsequent sacrifice was a reminder to man that he no longer dined with the gods but made offerings to them from a distance. Again, it was (with very rare exceptions) only in a greater and more glorious time that gods had visited mortal women to sire godlike sons.

Alongside men and gods there was a third estate, that of heroes. The term 'hero' had a technical sense in Greek religion: a hero was a figure less powerful than a god, to whom cult was paid. He was normally conceived as a mortal who had died, and the typical site of such a cult was a tomb. But various kinds of minor supernatural figure came to be assimilated to the class and, as in the case of Heracles, the distinction between a hero and a god could be uncertain. From Attica alone several hundred heroes are known; some have names and even legends, while others are identified merely as 'the hero beside the salt-pit' or the like. (In such a case it was presumably the existence of a conspicuous tomb that evoked the cult.) These heroes of cult were not identical with the heroes (this is Homer's word) of epic poetry, Achilles, Odysseus, and the rest, but the classes were not altogether distinct. Many of the poetic heroes did receive cult, and one reason for worshipping heroes must surely have been the feeling that they had been beings such as Homer described, stronger and altogether more splendid than the men of today. Large Mycenaean tombs, visible tokens of an ampler past, were often centres of hero-cult. Even historical individuals who displayed outstanding powers—warriors, athletes, founders of colonies—could become heroes. Above all, perhaps, it was the restricted and local scope of the heroes that made them popular. The hero retained the limited and partisan interests of his mortal life. He would help those who lived in the vicinity of his tomb or who belonged to the tribe of which he himself was the founder. Gods had to be shared with the world, but a village or a kinship group could have exclusive rights in a hero. (Heracles with his Panhellenic scope was a rare exception.) Thus hero-cults were the best focus for particular loyalties; and heroes were in general the great local helpers, particularly in battle, their natural sphere.

Greek religion had no single origin. The Greeks were an Indo-European people who settled in the non-Indo-European Aegean basin; they thus came into contact with the many advanced civilizations of the ancient Near East. Elements from all these sources contributed to the amalgam. Only one god bears a name that can be interpreted with certainty: Zeus *patēr* ('father') is the equivalent of Roman *Diespiter* (*Juppiter*) and Indian *Dyaus pitar*, all descended from the Indo-European god of heaven. Similarities, not of name, but of attribute, suggest the Indo-European origin of certain lesser figures, Sun, Dawn, and above all the Dioscuri, Castor and Pollux, who strikingly recall another pair of heavenly twins particularly associated with horsemanship, the Asvin of early Indian poetry. The closest equivalents to Aphrodite, on the other hand, are found in the love god-

THE TEMPLE OF APOLLO AT DELPHI, showing the foundations and restored columns and looking south-east over the lower sanctuary terrace (Marmaria), with a Temple of Athena, and to the pass leading east to Boeotia. The other approach led up from the Gulf of Corinth, at Itea, from the south west. The dramatic sanctuary site is built on a steep slope beneath the gleaming cliffs (Phaedriades) on the flanks of Mount Parnassus. At the left is the gully with the sacred spring of Castalia.

desses of the Near East, the Sumerian Inanna and the Semitic Astarte/Ishtar. This may mean, though, that Aphrodite has acquired oriental traits rather than that she is wholly oriental by origin: the individual gods often appear to be composite no less than the pantheon as a whole. Artemis too belongs in part to a near eastern type, that of the 'Mistress of Animals', while there are non-Indo-European traits in Apollo and Hephaestus. And the 'Kingship in Heaven' myth told by Hesiod is a particularly clear case of borrowing from the Near East in mythology (above, pp. 83 f.).

Thanks to the decipherment of the Linear B script in 1952, we can give some

MODEL OF THE SANCTUARY AT OLYMPIA. At the centre is the temple of Zeus and to its right the ash altar and the smaller, older temple of Hera. The small buildings at the right are treasuries dedicated by Greek states, beside the tunnel leading to the stadium, bottom right. The area before the temple was closed by a stoa. At the left are administrative buildings and beyond a big guesthouse and exercise areas. The columnless gabled building is Phidias' workshop in which the gold-and-ivory Zeus was made.

account of the state of Greek religion in the period 1400–1200 BC. The Linear B tablets reveal that the pantheon of this Minoan–Mycenaean civilization was already to a large extent that of classical Greece. Of great gods, Zeus, Hera, and Poseidon are certainly attested, and also, with varying degrees of probability, Artemis, Hermes, Ares, and Dionysus. A 'Lady of Athana' is doubtless a precursor of Athena, and several lesser figures appear—Eileithyia, the goddess of birth, Enyalios, a god of war who declined into an epithet of Ares, and Paiaon, a healer who was similarly absorbed by Apollo. Aphrodite, Apollo, and (except very questionably) Demeter are so far unattested, but they were not necessarily unknown. There is also, certainly, much that is unfamiliar, both among the gods (who is 'Drimios son of Zeus'?) and in cult practice and organization. The impression that the art of the period conveys, of a religion still dominated by pre-Greek goddesses of nature, is perhaps partly confirmed by a series of anonymous divine 'Ladies' who appear in the texts; but in general the Minoan–Mycenaean divine world now seems much more Greek than it did when only the artistic evidence was available.

With the fall of the Mycenaean civilization around 1200, Greece relapsed into illiteracy. When writing revived with the introduction of the Phoenician script in the ninth or eighth century, the crucial transition from Mycenaean to Greek religion had already occurred. The new script was used to record the poems of Homer and Hesiod, the earliest documents of true Greek religion, but for the preceding centuries we have only the fragmentary and ambiguous evidence of archaeology. Very few Mycenaean holy places continued to be used for cult throughout the Dark Ages. There is a growing body of evidence for oriental influence during the period, perhaps transmitted first through Cyprus and later through the trading post of Al Mina in Syria. From the eighth century, for instance, a typical religious site consisted of a free-standing temple, a cult image inside it, and a fire-altar in front of it; there are Near Eastern, but not, it seems, Mycenaean, antecedents for such a complex. Apollo and Zeus could be portrayed in the eighth century in the guise of the Hittite–Syrian war god. It was perhaps not until early in the Dark Ages that the cult of Aphrodite was introduced from the East (or took on eastern characteristics) and not till the end of them that the Kingship in Heaven myth was translated into Greek. It was almost certainly in this period that two foreign gods won a place on the fringe of Greek religion, Adonis the lover of Aphrodite (compare the Semitic word *adon*, 'lord') and the mountain mother *Kybelē/Kybēbē* (*Kubaba* is known as an Anatolian goddess). There is also a striking 'hymn to Hecate' in Hesiod's *Theogony*. Hecate seems to be a goddess of Asia Minor by origin, and Hesiod's hymn perhaps reflects the propaganda of a cult that was newly entering Greece. (Greek religion never lost this openness to foreign gods: at the end of the fifth century, for instance, two new gods arrived in Athens, Sabazius from Phrygia and Bendis from Thrace, and, though the cult of Sabazius was confined to private associations, Bendis found a place in public religion.) On the more important theme of religion's internal development in the period in response to social change we can say little. The cult of heroes seems to have had its origin in these centuries, beginning possibly in the tenth century and becoming more widely diffused (perhaps under the influence of epic poetry) in the eighth. To judge from epic, communities of this period were heavily dependent for their defence on individual warriors such as Homer's Hector, who 'alone kept Troy safe'. This prominence of the aristocratic champion in life may well have helped to foster the cult of heroes who continued to guard their people from the grave. But the archaeological evidence alters at the moment from year to year, and theories to explain the innovation (if such indeed it was) proliferate.

To understand the place of religion in Greek society we must think away the central religious institution of our own experience, the Church. In Greece power in religious matters lay with those who had secular power: in the household with the father, in early communities with the king, in developed city-states with the magistrates or even with the citizen assembly. At Athens it was a magistrate who impersonated the god Dionysus in an important ritual of 'sacred marriage', and decisions about the use of sacred moneys or land were taken by the democratic assembly. (As a result the gods found themselves willy-nilly financing Athenian efforts in the Peloponnesian War.) Individual gods had their priests, but to hold

a priesthood was a part-time activity which normally required no special qualification or training. There was no institutional framework to unite the priests
into a class with interests of its own. The only true religious professionals in
Greece were the seers. They were important figures, because omens were taken
before many public activities, such as dispatching a colony, beginning a military
campaign, or joining battle. As interpreters of the divine will, seers could come
into conflict with generals and politicians and their secular plans. There are several
reflections in literature of this tense relationship (Hector and Poulydamas, Agamemnon and Calchas in the *Iliad*; Teiresias and various kings in tragedy). These
were not, however, disputes about the rival claims of piety and patriotism, since
there could be no conflict of interest between the good of the city and of the
'city-keeping' gods, but about the best means to secure the agreed end of the
city's welfare. And such turbulent seers had no actual powers behind which to
take their stand. In high literature the seer is always right (for 'the mind of Zeus
is ever superior to that of men'), but the theme has tragic potential precisely
because he cannot enforce his view. The seer knows, but the ruler decides. In life
a layman could even challenge and defeat the experts on their own ground.
When the Delphic oracle in 480 BC advised the Athenians to 'put trust in their
wooden walls' against the Persian threat, the professional interpreters understood
this as a warning to remain within the city walls. The politician Themistocles
argued against them that the god was referring to the fleet. Themistocles' interpretation prevailed because the final decision lay not with the seers, but with the
citizen assembly.

There was, therefore, no religious organization that could spread moral teaching, develop doctrine, or impose an orthodoxy. In such a context a creed would
have been unthinkable. In a famous passage Herodotus casts two poets as the
theologians of Greece:

Not till the day before yesterday, so to speak, did the Greeks know the origin of each
of the gods, or whether they had all existed always, and what they were like in appearance.... It was Homer and Hesiod who created a theogony for the Greeks, gave the
gods their epithets, divided out offices and functions among them, and described their
appearance. (2.53)

It is, no doubt, true that the prestige of Homer's and Hesiod's poetry did much
to stabilize the Greeks' conceptions of their gods. But everyone knew that the
Muses who inspired epic poets told lies as well as truth, and in many details of
divine genealogy Homer's and Hesiod's accounts were in fact contradictory. Such
discrepancies caused no anxiety, and there was no need to question one's conscience before doubting or disputing a traditional myth. There were no heretics
because there was no Church. The only religious crimes were acts or attitudes
that caused general public resentment. The most obvious was sacrilege in all its
forms (including, for instance, the profanation of Mysteries). Another was the
crime that Socrates was charged with, 'not recognizing the gods that the city
recognizes'. This was to put oneself outside the norms of society in a way that

might be found intolerable. Both the flexibility and the sticking-point can be seen in Euripides' *Bacchae*. King Pentheus is here urged by his advisers to recognize Dionysus, and they offer the god to him in a variety of guises: if Pentheus doesn't believe the myths about Dionysus, can't he think of him as the divine principle in wine? And if not that, wouldn't he at least like people to believe that his aunt Semele had given birth to a god? But Pentheus refuses accommodation on any terms, and so he is destroyed by the god.

Cult

'Recognizing the gods' was principally a matter of observing their cult. Piety was expressed in behaviour, in acts of respect towards the gods. (A sociologist would be liable to say that the Greeks valued 'orthopraxy', right doing, rather than 'orthodoxy'.) Religion was not a matter of innerness or intense private communion with the god. This does not mean that strong feelings of loyalty, dependence, and even affection were impossible. Zeus was a 'father' as well as a 'king'; appeals to 'dear' gods are commonplace, and in literature we often find close and relaxed relationships between men and particular gods (Odysseus and Athena in the *Odyssey*, Sappho and Aphrodite, Ion and Apollo in Euripides' *Ion*, Hippolytus and Artemis in Euripides' *Hippolytus*). But piety (*eusebeia*) was literally a matter of 'respect', not love, and even the warmest relationship would quickly have turned sour without observance of the cult. Religion was never personal in the sense of a means for the individual to express his unique identity. No Greek would ever have thought of keeping a spiritual diary. Indeed many classes of person had much of their religion done for them by others: the father sacrificed and besought blessings 'on behalf of' the household, while the magistrates and priests did the same for 'the people' ('and its wives and children', the Athenians eventually added). In all of this religion reflected and supported the general ethos of Greek culture. It discouraged individualism, a preoccupation with inner states and the belief that intentions matter more than actions; it emphasized the sense of belonging to a community and the need for due observance of social forms.

What, then, of right conduct? To those used to Christianity Greek religion often seems a strangely amoral affair. Man was not for Greeks a sinful being in need of redemption; piety was not a matter of perpetual moral endeavour under the watchful guidance of conscience. The gods excelled in strength and skill more obviously than in the quieter virtues. Indeed their behaviour in myth was often scandalous:

> There might you see the gods in sundry shapes
> Committing heady riots, incest, rapes.

But even these easy-going rulers insisted (Zeus in particular) on certain standards of behaviour without which life would have dissolved into barbarism. They punished offences against parents, guests/hosts, suppliants, and the dead. They

SACRIFICE TO APOLLO, on an Athenian vase of about 440 BC. The statue of the god, holding bow and laurel branch, and laurel-crowned like his worshippers, stands on a pillar at the right behind the bloodstained altar. The priest is offering on it the offal and bones due to the gods. The edible meat from the sacrificed animal has already been cut up and wound on to the spits carried by the boy behind the priest, to be cooked.

particularly abhorred oath-breakers, destroying them 'with their whole stock'; such a man might seem to have escaped, but never did—his children would suffer, or he himself in the Underworld. Since oaths accompanied almost all of life's most important transactions (contracts, marriages, and peace-treaties, for instance), Zeus of Oaths was also inevitably a guardian of social morality. Zeus was in fact often said to care for justice in general, and it was a basic presumption of popular belief that, at bottom, the gods were on the side of good men. 'The gods exist', the simple Greek exclaimed when a villain came to a bad end. The Greek was not in danger of slipping inadvertently into sin, as the rules of conduct were clear. But if he broke these rules he forfeited 'good hopes' for the future.

All this, however, was a prerequisite for winning divine favour by ritual, not a substitute for it. Formal cult remained essential. Its most important form was the sacrifice. The typical victim was an animal, but there were also 'bloodless' or 'pure' sacrifices of corn, cakes, fruit, and the like, sometimes offered in addition to animals and sometimes in place of them. A Greek religious calendar was a list of sacrifices; several such survive, indicating what god or hero was to receive what offering on what day. In the commonest form, the thigh-bones of the slaughtered animal, wrapped in fat, were burnt on a raised altar for the gods; the meat was then cooked and eaten by the human participants. Such a sacrifice was a 'gift to the gods'. The gods had to receive their share of all human goods—first-fruits of harvest, libations at drinking parties, tithes of hunting catches, of spoils of war, and the like. In this case it was rather a meagre share, since they were given only the inedible portions of the carcase. Comic poets joked about this unequal division, and it was already a puzzle to Hesiod, who tells a myth to explain it: when gods and men first divided out the sacrificial portions, man's helper, Prometheus, tricked Zeus into taking the wrong share. None the less, by a convenient fiction, these useless parts were deemed an acceptable gift for the gods. Thus a basic form of human festivity, the communal banquet, was sanctified and became a means of approach to the gods.

Sacrifice was a theme on which subtle and expressive variations could be played. Sex, age, and colour of the victim varied with the god or festival concerned; there were rules governing who might participate and what portion of the meat fell to each. In an important alternative form the animal was held close to the ground while its throat was cut, so that the blood would drip into the earth. The carcase was then, it seems, normally burnt whole close to the ground. This ritual was used in particular in the cult of heroes and of powers of the earth (though they also received sacrifices of the other form); it probably derived from the cult of the dead. The antithesis between Olympian sacrifice and this earth-bound form was marked in various ways: on the one side a high altar, smoke rising to heaven, light-coloured victims, libations of wine (the drink of normal civilized life), sociable sharing of meat; on the other a low altar or pit, blood dripping down to 'glut' the powers below, dark victims, wineless libations, destruction of the victim uneaten. (Such wanton annihilation is a funerary practice, seen, for instance, at Patroclus' funeral in the *Iliad*.) And because the killing of animals was the central religious act, there were further rituals that exploited this source of power even though they were not sacrifices to any god: to purify a murderer, for instance, to solemnize an oath, or to take the omens before battle, the parts of slaughtered animals were manipulated in various symbolic ways. Human sacrifice, by contrast, was unknown in the historical period. It is common in mythology, but that is not good evidence even for prehistory, since the horrors that stories postulate to thrill us need not ever have occurred. They may have done, however; what had been the fate of a woman who was recently discovered, laid out with a sacrificial knife beside her head, in a warrior's tomb of the tenth century at Lefkandi in Euboea (above, p. 15)?

One should not be misled by the goriness of the ritual and the savagery of certain myths into thinking that this was a religion of horrors, of self-torment, and of perpetual confrontation with the unspeakable. Certainly, a few rituals were deliberately uncanny; a few festivals or parts of them had a gloomy or penitential tone. An Athenian festival of Zeus, the Diasia, was performed 'with a certain gloominess', and the Panhellenic women's festival of the Thesmophoria involved a day of fasting. There was even in many Ionian cities a ritual expulsion (though not killing) of human scapegoats that must have involved real cruelty. But the dominant tone of Greek ritual was one of festivity and celebration. Herodotus expresses this when he speaks of a group who spent their days 'sacrificing and having a good time'. Processions were very common, ranging from those of a single household (there is one in Aristophanes' *Acharnians*) to those such as the Panathenaic procession that involved the whole city. We can see from the Parthenon frieze or the end of Aeschylus' *Eumenides* what splendid occasions these were. The gods loved beauty: one dedicated to them the loveliest objects that one could, and the word for cult-image, *agalma*, means 'thing to take delight in'. The gods were happy too to see performed in their honour many of the activities that humans most relished. Singing and dancing in a chorus was one basic form of worship, and competing at athletics was another. The great Panhellenic games and the great Athenian dramatic festivals had moved far from their origins, but remained religious ceremonies. One had to put on a good show for the god. When the Thracian goddess Bendis was received in Athens late in the fifth century, she was honoured not by a relay race of torch-bearers on foot (old hat by now), but by a special torch relay on horseback. It never occurred to anyone to object, as did Newman of the Neapolitan carnival, that 'Religion is turned into a mere occasion of worldly gaiety'. At the festivals of country gods such as Demeter and Dionysus the fun did not even have to be kept clean. There were obscene jokes, gestures, and objects (although not normally acts)—the whole range of what scholars term 'ritual obscenity' (as if that made it less fun). The gods were lustrous, graceful, carefree beings, and a shoddy or joyless performance would not fulfil a festival's proper function of 'delighting' them.

Ritual was accompanied by prayer. It was unusual to pray seriously without making an offering of some kind (a sacrifice, a dedication, or at least a libation) or promising to make one should the prayer be fulfilled. By his gift the worshipper established a claim to the counter-gift that he requested, according to the notorious principle of 'do ut des', 'I give so that you will give.' In their prayers Greeks often alluded explicitly to this nexus of mutual benefit and obligation between man and god:

If ever I burnt the rich thighs of bulls and goats in your honour, grant me this prayer.

Maiden [Athena], Telesinos dedicated this image to you on the acropolis. May you take delight in it, and allow him to dedicate another [by preserving his life and wealth].

Protect our city. I believe that what I say is in our common interest. For a flourishing city honours the gods.

Mistress [Athena], Menandros dedicated this offering to you in gratitude, in fulfilment of a vow. Protect him, daughter of Zeus, in gratitude for this.

The gods were thus brought within a comprehensible pattern of social relations. As an old tag said, 'Gifts persuade the gods, gifts reverend kings'; gift-giving was

A RUSTIC PROCESSION FOR DIONYSUS, on an Athenian cup of about 550 BC. The image of a large, hairy satyr holding a massive phallus erect, is carried by a group of village boys, one of whom has climbed on to the satyr's back. Ivy tendrils and ribbons add a festive air to what was probably a ribald occasion celebrating the god of wine and fertility. The satyr, attendant of the god, is a fine creation of the Greek artist's imagination, horse-tailed and horse-eared, often depicted as a randy coward, but here in effigy on a mortal occasion of worship.

perhaps the most important mechanism of social relationships in Homeric society. It might seem to follow that the richest men could secure the most divine favour, and that punishment for crime could be bought off by gifts. The rich and the villainous were certainly free to nourish such hopes. Their subjects and their victims, though, might take a different view. There were always those who insisted that the gods 'rejected the sacrifices' of oath-breakers, and that the modest offerings of the innocent were more acceptable than hecatombs slaughtered by the lawless rich. One offered what one could from what one had. A Greek was not ashamed to mention to the gods that if he were a little richer (wealth being a gift of the gods) he could bring larger offerings. The real psychological significance of 'do ut des' was not the hope of bribery, but the fact that it allowed the worshipper to feel that he had established an ordered, continuing, two-sided relation with the god.

Religion and Society

Economic historians have found that the modern notion of an autonomous 'economy' is inapplicable to ancient societies, where economic activity was influenced by innumerable social constraints. To describe ancient conditions they have developed the concept of the 'embedded' economy. We need for the Greeks a similar concept of embedded religion. It was a social, practical, everyday thing. Every formal social grouping was also a religious grouping, from the smallest to the largest: a household was a set of people who worshipped (in the Athenian case) at the same shrine of Zeus of the Courtyard, while the Greeks as a nation were those who honoured the same gods at the Panhellenic sanctuaries and festivals. To belong to a group was to 'share in the lustral water' (used for purification before sacrifice). The Panhellenic sanctuaries were the great meeting-places, where one could swagger before an audience from all Greece. Perhaps the most important was Delphi, perched above a majestic valley on the slopes of Mount Parnassus in central Greece; it owed its original fame to the oracular shrine of Apollo, already mentioned by Homer, but also became the site of a great athletic festival. Its rival in importance, Olympia in the territory of Elis in the Peloponnese, sacred to Zeus, was home of the original and always most prestigious games, the Olympics.

Since religion was thus embedded, social and religious history are virtually inseparable. At Athens, for instance, the growth of the democracy involved a transformation of the forms of religious life. Cults that had been controlled by aristocratic families were absorbed into the public calendar of the city; new public cults were established, free from aristocratic influence; alongside the traditional groupings, based on kinship, the local group of the deme or village gained importance in religion just as it was doing in politics. Even associations that one entered by choice (the clubs of the Hellenistic period, philosophical schools) were normally dedicated to the cult of particular gods. Since slaves, by contrast, had no social identity as a group there was no distinctive slave religion. Such as it was, their religious life was conducted as humble participants in the cults of their masters' household and in a few public festivals that derived from household cult.

The goals of religion were practical and this-worldly. One important function was of course to steer the individual with appropriate rites of passage through the great transitions of birth, puberty, marriage, and death. Many public festivals throughout Greece had to do with preparing boys to be warriors, girls to be mothers. Another numerous class, including most of the many festivals of

THE ORACLE AT DODONA. After Olympia Dodona was the principal shrine of Zeus, where he gave oracles through the rustling of leaves of his sacred oaks, or the booming of his bronze cauldrons. These needed interpretation by priests. A more direct approach was to write a question on a lead tablet, such as the one shown, and receive the answer inscribed on the back— often just a 'yes' or 'no'. On this sixth-century example the writing is *boustrophēdon* ('as the ox ploughs'), running in lines alternately to left and right. Hermon asks which god he should approach in order to beget useful children by his wife Cretaea.

Demeter, goddess of corn, and Dionysus, god of wine, related to the events of the agricultural year. Others celebrated the political order; so, for instance, the Panathenaea (the 'all-Athenians' festival) and the Synoecia (the festival of synoecism, political unification as a single city) at Athens. Dangerous activities such as seafaring and warfare required especial protection from the gods; there were clusters of rituals associated with them, and even in the historical period gods or heroes were often thought to have intervened to save a ship or support a hard-pressed army. Craftsmen appealed to their divine patrons, and it was a common event in social, judicial, and even commercial life to summon the gods, by sacrificial ritual, to witness an oath. There were above all two practical goods that every Greek desired from the gods, prophetic advice and healing. Prophecy was obtained from oracular shrines, such as Apollo's at Delphi, from wandering oracle-mongers with their books of prophecies, or from seers who drew omens from the entrails of sacrificial animals and the flight of birds. It had, as we saw above, an important role even in public life. For the kind of enquiry that a private individual might make we have good evidence from the oracle of Zeus at Dodona, since some of the lead question-tablets survive:

Heracleidas asks the god whether he will have offspring from the wife he has now.

Lysanias asks Zeus Naios and Dione [Zeus' consort at Dodona] whether the child Annyla is pregnant with is his [often it was the obscurity of the present rather than the future that the god was asked to illumine].

Cleotas asks whether it would be beneficial and advantageous for him to keep sheep.

As for healing, there were healing gods and heroes throughout Greece, their shrines bedecked, like those of Catholic saints, with the votive offerings of grateful patients (often clay images of the affected organ). The commonest technique of healing was by incubation: the patient spent a night in the temple, and the god appeared to him in a dream to perform a miraculous cure, or at least to prescribe a treatment. The most successful such cult was that of Asclepius at Epidaurus, from which there survives an inscription recording miraculous cures. A typical specimen runs:

A man came to the god as a suppliant who was so blind in one eye that he only had the eyelids left and there was nothing between them, but they were wholly empty. Some of the people in the shrine made fun of his folly in thinking that he could see when he had no trace of an eye but only the place for it. He went to sleep in the shrine and a vision appeared to him. It seemed to him that the god boiled up a drug, drew apart his eyelids, and poured it in. When day came he went away, able to see with both eyes.

All this was practical religion. There were few expressions of unpractical religion, of concern for a world other than this. After death, according to Homer, a kind of wraith of the dead man vanished to the underworld, there to lead a joyless, eventless, meaningless shadow existence. (Bliss and punishment were re-

DIVINE HEALING. A relief dedicated about 370 BC by Aeschinus to the hero healer Amphiaraus. The relief is in the form of a building, with the god's all-seeing eyes shown on the roof. At the right the patient sleeps in the sanctuary and is visited by the divine snake which licks his wounded shoulder. At the left the god himself operates. Incubation in the sanctuary brought psychologically reassuring dreams of healing, and this, with more practical assistance, may sometimes have effected cures.

served for a few select heroes.) Nothing therefore of any value persisted beyond the funeral pyre. In classical times it was normal to bring offerings of food and drink to the dead (indeed at Athens this was a condition of inheritance; when an inheritance was disputed, unseemly competitions in mourning took place), but there was no clear theory about the afterlife to justify them and no substantial hopes were based upon them. We often find in Athenian orators the cautious formula, 'The dead, if they have any perception, will think . . .' Stories about punishment and reward in the underworld were in circulation, but were only half believed. The whole question was an open one, as Socrates' remarks in Plato's *Apology* (41) show. Firmer claims were made in connection with certain 'mysteries' or secret rites, entry to which was by 'initiation' (not an ordeal, but a spectacular and moving ritual lasting several days). The most important mysteries were those of Demeter and Persephone at Eleusis near Athens, which promised a better lot in the afterlife (eternal feasting perhaps), while for non-initiates 'everything there would be bad' (by the fifth century specific torments had been devised for them). The Eleusinian cult was famed throughout the Greek world, and it is spoken of with a reverence, tinged with moral awe, which shows that initiation was somehow much more than a technique for purchasing such felicity as might be available in the afterlife. But Greeks did not allow such an experience to inspire them with more than, at most, 'good hopes'. Even though many Athenians had been initiated, the normal attitude to the afterlife at Athens remained, as we have seen, one of uncertainty.

The Eleusinian cult was incorporated into the public religion of the Athenian state. Other more radical religious movements of the archaic age defied assimilation. Late in the sixth century Pythagoras taught that souls migrated after death into other bodies, both human and animal. Meat-eating was therefore an abomination, a form of cannibalism. As vegetarians, his followers were excluded from the principal institutions of social life; they lived in closed communities of their own, subject to strict rules of conduct. Probably in the same period poems began to be composed that bore the name of Orpheus, the mythical singer. 'Orpheus' taught that man was a guilty and polluted being. The human race as a whole was descended from 'unjust ancestors', the wicked Titans who dismembered and ate the young god Dionysus. For Orphism, as for Pythagoreanism, meat-eating was a further pollution, repeated day by day. The soul required 'purification' from these taints, or it would pay the penalty in the next incarnation or the next world. In these two interconnected movements (best illustrated for us by Empedocles' poem *Purifications*) we find a series of phenomena untypical of Greek religion: ascetism, preoccupation with the afterlife, rejection of profane society, the concept of a special religious way of life, doctrines of guilt and salvation. Herodotus believed that Pythagoras had imported his doctrines from Egypt, and external influence is not to be excluded; another important factor was doubtless the growing individualism of archaic Greek society, which loosened the traditional ties of kinship and encouraged the quest for individual salvation. Some of these ideas seem to have affected the Eleusinian cult, and there was an important Pythagorean influence on Plato. But it was on the outskirts of the Greek world, particularly in Italy and Sicily, that such movements had most adherents, and they remained marginal phenomena.

An abnormal approach not to the next life but to this one was offered, in particular to women, by certain forms of the cult of Dionysus (best illustrated by Euripides' *Bacchae*). In myth and literature Dionysus is represented as an outsider, a stranger from Lydia, and scholars used to believe that his cult had indeed been introduced to Greece at some date within folk memory. The decipherment of Linear B showed that he was almost certainly already known in Mycenaean times, and it now seems that the myth of Dionysus' arrival is not a reminiscence of historical fact but a way of saying something about his nature. Dionysus Bacchius had to be a stranger because the ecstatic irresponsibility that he offered to women was unique in Greek religion. All women's festivals were a release from domestic confinement, and most of them entailed a kind of temporary repudiation of male authority (the fantasy of Aristophanes' *Women at the Thesmophoria* has a real basis); but their content was often austere, and they normally related in some way to woman's proper function as a fertile being (which allowed her to promote the fertility of crops too, by sympathy). The votaries of Dionysus Bacchius, by contrast, laid down their weaving and abandoned their children to follow the handsome god to the mountains. There as 'maenads' they would dance, revel, and even (so it was said) tear apart live animals and eat them raw. Even in Greek states where such a flight to the mountains was not practised, some form of ecstatic dancing by women in honour of Dionysus certainly took place. But if this was a liberation it was only a temporary one, and indeed in an important sense it tightened the chains, since it confirmed the belief that woman was a volatile and irrational being in need of close control. Maenadism could thus be readily accommodated within public religion. Male bacchic ecstasy, on the other hand, seems to have been long confined to disreputable private associations. (It was in time taken up by Orphism, another fringe movement, and given a novel eschatological meaning.)

It is hard to summarize Greek attitudes to their gods. Much depends on the kind of evidence that one selects. The high literary genres tend to offer a pessimistic view. They often stress the unbridgeable gulf between blessed gods and

DANCING FOR DIONYSUS, on an Athenian cup by the painter Macron, of about 490 BC. The god is worshipped as a pillar, dressed, with a head carved atop and sprouting vines with odd globes attached. The women perform the ecstatic dance of maenads—one on the right holding the thyrsus wand of fennel with ivy leaves wrapped around its tip.

A HERM FROM SIPHNOS, of the later sixth century BC. Herms are stone pillars, topped with the head of the god Hermes and commonly with an erect phallus carved on the front. On the block-shoulders wreaths or clothes could hang. They were set up by roads, at street corners and in other prominent public places to solicit worship from, and offer protection to passers-by. The type of mount is later used for other deities (Heracles, Dionysus, Pan) and in the Roman period for portrait busts.

puny, doomed, suffering man. The gods' concern for mortals, creatures of a day, is necessarily limited, and they rule the universe for their own convenience, not for ours. Sufferings come even to the strongest, wisest, and most pious of men; one scarcely knows why, but 'nothing of this is not Zeus'. Poets who wrote so were not trying to do down the gods but to describe what, at the limits, human life is like. The gods can appear comfortless beings because life itself is brutal, and there was for the Greeks no power distinct from the gods, no devil, to be blamed for the wrongness of things. But since not everyone cared to look into life's worst possibilities so closely there was always room for a more optimistic view. According to Zeus in the *Odyssey*, men are responsible for their own misfortunes; far from hurting them the gods do what they can to save them from themselves. This comfortable doctrine was taken up by the Athenian statesman-poet Solon and became a keynote of Athenian civic religion. Whatever he might hear in the tragic theatre, the Athenian in daily life did not normally doubt that the gods were on his side. For their own Athena the Athenians clearly often felt a genuinely warm affection. Comic poets could even make good-humoured fun of certain gods. How indeed could one help being amused by Hermes, in myth a merry thieving rogue, in image little more than a huge erect phallus? There was nothing irreligious about such laughter, the expression of a relaxed and unthreatened piety. As we have seen, the mood of cult was normally one of festivity, and dedications express gratitude and faith: one of the seventh century, for instance, from the precinct of Hera on Samos was set up 'in return for great kindness'. The divine lustre, which is emphasized in high literature to bring out by contrast the murkiness of man, was also available to be admired in itself. It is clear from art and poetry (particularly the *Homeric Hymns*) that Greeks rejoiced in the grace and radiance of the immortals. They were marvellous figures; their deeds and their loves were as fascinating as those of film stars. Tragic literature was not, therefore, a simple expression of a generally shared tragic world view. (And there is, of course, much variety of attitude even within tragedy.) On the contrary, it often gained its effects by putting optimistic popular beliefs, such as that in the justice of the gods, to the test of extreme cases. The chorus in Euripides' *Hippolytus* comments, when faced by the downfall of a most virtuous man: 'To think of the gods' care for men is a great relief to me from pain. Deep within me I have hopes of understanding; but when I look around at what men do and how they fare I cannot understand.'

Traditional, local, mythological religions such as that of Greece are thought to have little power of survival. The proselytizing international religions based on books and doctrines mop them up. Greek religion, however, lasted for more than a thousand years, and it was able to do so largely because of its very lack of doctrinal precision. Criticism had begun in the sixth century with Xenophanes, who said that 'Homer and Hesiod ascribed to the gods everything that among men is a shame and disgrace: theft, adultery, and deceiving one another.' But it was easy to counter the objection, by rewriting embarrassing myths (as Pindar did in *Olympian* 1), interpreting them allegorically, or simply refusing to believe them (so Plato). Xenophanes went on to criticize anthropomorphic conceptions of deity: Ethiopians made their gods black and snub-nosed like themselves, and if cows had hands they would represent the gods as cows. He declared that god was in truth a single disembodied mind. Other pre-Socratic philosophers had already by implication banished anthropomorphic gods—for them the divine was some first force or principle of the world—and were ready to explain all observable phenomena in terms of natural laws: thus Zeus was robbed of his thunderbolt. No philosopher henceforth seems to have believed in the literal reality of deities such as those of Homer, human in form and erratic in conduct. There is, however, no evidence that, when first advanced, such ideas caused scandal. But late in the fifth century there was a kind of religious crisis at Athens. Protagoras the sophist announced: 'About the gods I cannot declare whether they exist or not'; other sophists speculated about why men had ever come to believe in deity, and it is possible that Anaxagoras, the leading scientist of the day, was an atheist. Men began to notice the moral implications of the scientists' physical explanations of the world, which left the gods powerless to intervene in defence of their ordinances. It is clear from Aristophanes' *Clouds* that traditional religion was felt to be under threat, and with it, crucially, traditional social morality. Late sources tell of a persecution of intellectuals at this time; details are very uncertain, but it is symptomatic that one of the charges brought against Socrates was that of 'not recognizing the gods that the city recognizes'.

But—we do not quite know how—the crisis was surmounted. Explicit atheism remained virtually unknown. Scientific enquiry ceased to be seen as threatening: even if Zeus did not hurl the thunderbolt with his own hand, might he not be working through the mechanisms postulated by the physicists? Philosophers could not accept the riotous Olympians of mythology, since it was now axiomatic that any god must be wholly wise and good, but they had no wish (least of all the influential and conservative Plato) to dispense with the divine. A compromise was therefore possible. One might not believe in the traditional gods exactly as they were described and portrayed, but one believed in the divine and in piety, and there was no reason not to pay homage to the divine principle through the forms of worship sanctified by tradition. Many philosophers even came to terms with a traditional belief as problematic as that in divination.

The institution of ruler-cult has often been seen as a symptom of a religion in decay. It was first paid, to our knowledge, to the Spartan general Lysander by the Samians late in the fifth century, and subsequently to Alexander and many Hellenistic kings. This was certainly a radical change, but the real precondition for it was a loss not of faith but of political freedom. In an autonomous democracy or even oligarchy there had been no room for men-gods. The divine kings did not supplant the old gods but took their place alongside them; they had little in common with, say, Asclepius, but were not so different from Zeus the King or Zeus the Saviour. The gods lived on. The traditional religion could still in the second century AD win the earnest devotion of a man as cultivated as Plutarch. It was still the old religion that was vanquished in the end by Christianity.

Further Reading

Fortunately the whole subject has recently been treated in a masterpiece of lively learning, W. Burkert, *Greek Religion*, trans. W. Raffan (Oxford, 1985). This is much the best starting-point on almost all the topics discussed here. A shorter general study is W. K. C. Guthrie, *The Greeks and their Gods* (London, 1950); there are concise introductions to particular aspects in M. P. Nilsson, *Greek Popular Religion* (Columbia, 1940: issued in paperback as *Greek Folk Religion*); H. W. Parke,

Greek Oracles (London, 1967). P. E. Easterling and J. V. Muir (eds.), *Greek Religion and Society* (Cambridge, 1985), is an attractive collection of essays.

Source books: D. G. Rice and J. E. Stambaugh, *Sources for the Study of Greek Religion* (Decatur, 1979); for the post-classical period F. C. Grant, *Hellenistic Religions* (Indianapolis, 1953). Two important texts, Hesiod's *Theogony* and the *Homeric Hymns*, are available in prose translation in H. G. Evelyn-White, *Hesiod, the Homeric Hymns and Homerica*, Loeb Classical Library (Harvard, 1914, and many reprints).

Some works that are especially provocative in approach or perspective are: W. Burkert, *Structure and History in Greek Mythology and Ritual* (Berkeley, 1979), on the psychodynamics of ritual, seeking parallels with animal rituals; E. R. Dodds, *The Greeks and the Irrational* (Berkeley, 1951), wide-ranging; a classic; P. Friedrich, *The Meaning of Aphrodite* (Chicago, 1978); J. Griffin, *Homer on Life and Death* (Oxford, 1980), chs. 1, 5, 6; H. Lloyd-Jones, *The Justice of Zeus* (Berkeley, 2nd edn., 1984); W. F. Otto, *The Homeric Gods*, trans. M. Hadas (London, 1955), a vigorous assertion of the truth and value of Greek religion; and a collection (ed. R. L. Gordon), *Myth, Religion and Society: Structuralist Essays by M. Detienne, L. Gernet, J.-P. Vernant, and P. Vidal-Naguet* (Cambridge, 1981) and other works of the same school listed there. E. Rohde, *Psyche*, trans. W. B. Hillis (London, 1925) on the soul, immortality, Dionysus, is now largely outdated in theory, but unsurpassed in learning and vigour. Two recent works valuable for full and alert descriptions are J. D. Mikalson, *Athenian Popular Religion* (North Carolina, 1983), on attitudes rather than acts, and W. K. Pritchett, *The Greek State at War*, Part iii, *Religion* (Berkeley, 1979). The best introduction to attitudes to divination is A. D. Nock, 'Religious Attitudes of the Ancient Greeks' in his *Essays on Religion and the Ancient World,* ed. Z. Stewart (Oxford, 1972). On science and religion there is a brilliant study by G. E. R. Lloyd, *Magic, Reason and Experience* (Cambridge, 1979). B. F. Meyer and E. P. Sanders (eds.), *Jewish and Christian Self-Definition* iii: *Self-Definition in the Greco-Roman World* (London, 1982) contains expert essays on the Orphic/Pythagorean movement and on Dionysiac cult.

On particular topics there are:

J. Bremmer, *The Early Greek Concept of the Soul* (Princeton, 1983).

W. Burkert, *Homo Necans*, trans. P. Bing (Berkeley, 1983), on sacrifice.

E. R. Dodds, edn. of Euripides, *Bacchae* (Oxford, 1960²) (on Dionysus).

E. J. and L. Edelstein, *Asclepius* (Baltimore, 1945).

L. R. Farnell, *The Cults of the Greek States*, 5 vols. (Oxford, 1896–1909), and *Greek Hero Cults and Ideas of Immortality* (Oxford, 1921) are still valuable works of reference.

A.-J. Festugière, *Personal Religion among the Greeks* (Berkeley, 1954).

W. K. C. Guthrie, *Orpheus and Greek Religion* (London, 1935).

D. C. Kurtz and J. Boardman, *Greek Burial Customs* (London, 1971).

I. M. Linforth, *The Arts of Orpheus* (Berkeley, 1941).

G. E. Mylonas, *Eleusis and the Eleusinian Mysteries* (Princeton, 1961).

M. P. Nilsson, *The Minoan-Mycenaean Religion* (Lund, 1951²), is comprehensive, but prior to the decipherment of Linear B.

M. P. Nilsson, *Cults, Myths, Oracles and Politics in Ancient Greece* (Lund, 1951).

H. W. Parke and D. E. W. Wormell, *The Delphic Oracle* (Oxford, 1956²).

H. W. Parke, *Festivals of the Athenians* (London, 1977).

Robert Parker, *Miasma: Pollution and Purification in Early Greek Religion* (Oxford, 1983).

H. S. Versnel (ed.), *Faith, Hope and Worship. Aspects of Religious Mentality in the Ancient World* (Leiden, 1981), includes essays on prayer and votive offerings.

G. Zuntz, *Persephone* (Oxford, 1971), on eschatological beliefs of Greek Italy and Sicily.

Le Sacrifice dans l'antiquité, Entretiens sur l'antiquité classique, xxvii, Fondation Hardt (Geneva, 1981); several essays in English.

12
Greek Art and Architecture

❦

JOHN BOARDMAN

Introduction: Greekness

THE arts of the western world have been dominated by the art of the Greeks. Even the alternative arts of Celtic Europe or the Asian steppes were infiltrated by classical imagery. Although this record makes it easy for us to isolate those characteristics which distinguish Greek art from the arts of other cultures, contemporary or later, it has probably also made it the more difficult to assess on its own terms, to judge its role and the response of those for whom it was practised, and to value justly its profound innovations. And the attempt to define its characteristics may also do less than justice to that other remarkable phenomenon, the rapidity of its evolution from virtual abstraction to realism; while if its history *is* defined in such bald terms we may also miss other fundamental qualities—its unusual (for antiquity) subject-matter and its preoccupation with form and proportion.

The subject-matter of Greek art was essentially man (and to a lesser degree woman). Even when he worked in near-abstract, geometricized forms the artist's prime subjects were human, and this remains true when his skills allowed him to imitate closely, or even to improve upon, nature. Man's actions and aspirations are performed in Greek art by the figures of gods or heroes more often than of mortals, and often in settings, which, though dressed and furnished by their own world, belonged to their heroic past. The gods and heroes were their ancestors; they looked like men and behaved like men. A picture of heroic myth carried a simple message of narrative, but might equally reflect mortal and contemporary problems or successes, as surely as the Attic playwrights explored problems of contemporary society through their dramatized versions of tales of Troy or the heroes. A god in Greek art had the body and carriage of a perfect mortal athlete: a goddess, that of a beautiful, or at least a determined, maternal and wise woman. Supernatural features—breathing fire, multi-limbed, hybrid—are generally abjured except in stories and depictions of what is virtually timeless folk tale. Monsters are remarkably plausible: we can believe in centaurs. And, however horrific, they are there to be beaten, rather than to threaten or terrify. The petrifying Gorgon head evolves from an eastern lion mask to the head of a beautiful woman with snake locks, no less deadly. Animals are subordinate, decorative, or at best an expression of man's dependence on the fertility of his beasts, or they are used in parables for mortal behaviour—the concept of Achilles as a lion and of Aesop's talking creatures is as familiar in art as in literature, though less readily recognized. In such an art landscape is no more important than furniture. Set all this beside the art of Egypt and the Near East, obsessed with the demonic or the ritual of court, temple, or tomb, and judge the difference.

By about 500 BC, in little over 200 years, the Greek artist's presentation of man had progressed from a composition of geometricized parts to an image as detailed and plausible as any in Egypt or the Near East. To this image he added life, and the image based on pattern and on what he knew or had been taught about the representation of man was transformed by what he now looked at and deliberately sought to copy. The art that had offered symbols of the natural world, now by choice imitated it. Illusion began to replace the conventional symbol: the artist began to create replicas of man as skilfully as the poet explored his fears and hopes—to the distress of some philosophers who detected a desire to deceive.

The images were of man, the male body, and generally naked. In classical Greece athletes exercised naked, warriors could fight near-naked, and in everyday life the bared young male must have been a fairly common sight. Artists did not need to look for naked models of their idealized athlete figures; they had grown up in a society in which male nudity was commonplace and a well developed body was admired. The foreigner found this behaviour disgusting, and the foreign artist depicted nudity mainly for religious, erotic, or pathetic appeal. The Greek artist's interest in the naked male may have exaggerated what he saw in life, but it was not to him a conscious aesthetic device. The image of the 'heroic nude' may stem from classical Greece, but the concept does not. Later Greeks, and Romans, used Greek nude types for heroized or deified mortals, and the genre is familiar enough to us since the Neo-classical Revival, in subjects which range from Voltaire to Napoleon, from Beethoven to Mussolini. For us it is unnatural in life, but we have learnt to accept it in art. In classical Greece it was not unnatural in life, and in art it required neither excuse nor explanation.

We measure the world around us, ourselves included, in feet. The human body is the natural, common reference point for measurement, and the non-Greek world had devised complicated systems of measurement interrelating width of finger, of palm, length of forearm (cubit), foot, and so on in proportion and multiples that approximated to nature. Before life became the model, if an artist wished to draw a human figure at any scale, preparing to sculpt it, for example, he would have recourse to the hierarchy of measure, and in Egypt this was rationalized into a simple grid on which the human body could be drawn in a plausible form. This appealed to the Greeks, but they were soon concerned less with absolute ideal measurement than with proportion, and sought to express a

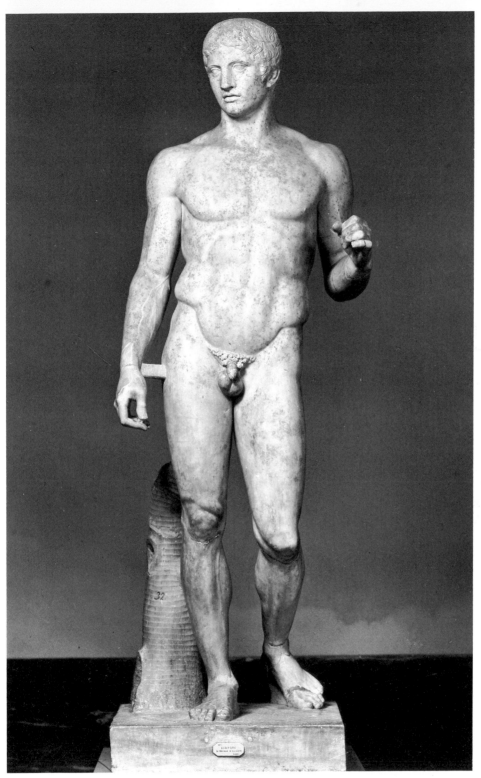

THE IDEAL MAN. The Doryphorus (spear-carrier) by Polyclitus. Roman marble copy of a Greek bronze original of about 440 BC. The original was known as the 'Canon' and had been used by the artist to display his views about the ideal proportions for the human figure. The type differs from the Phidian (as on the Parthenon) and was on the whole more influential in antiquity. The tree trunk and struts are the copyist's additions.

theoretical basis for this ideal. Polyclitus, the fifth-century sculptor, wrote a book on the subject which he illustrated by a statue (his Doryphorus or Canon—'rule'). It expressed his views on *symmetria*, the commensurability of parts of the body. The notion seems mechanical, but his figures, known to us only in copies, were clearly no less life-like than those of his contemporaries. This controlling principle in Greek art appears with no less subtlety in architecture. It is demonstrated by the shapes of vases, by the articulation of the decoration upon them, by the suiting of a subject's size and pose to its field. It determined the shape and decoration of an eighth-century Geometric vase no less than it did the Parthenon pediments. The challenge in Greek art which guaranteed movement and progress was the desire to reconcile what might seem uncompromising opposites, the instinctive sense of pattern and proportion, and the growing awareness of what might be expressed through a more accurate representation of natural forms.

Stimuli and Origins

The greatest stimulus to progress and belief in a future is knowledge and under-standing of a past. The Greek of the ninth century BC, living in a sparsely populated country, in a manner seldom rising above the austere, had around him the evidence of the civilization of his predecessors, the Bronze Age Mycenaeans and Minoans. The massive stones of their citadels were built by giants. The gold and ivory on their deserted sites and cemeteries showed where gods had walked with men, and where gods should, therefore, still be worshipped. The techniques of the past were lost when the Bronze Age palace societies crumbled. There was physical survival, and some cultural survival, notably in areas less disturbed by the break-up of the old world, as in Crete, but on the whole this evidence of their past stood more as a challenge than as a model to be copied, and although we may discern in the Mycenaean something of those qualities which later distinguish Greek art, physically there is virtually a new start, a renaissance. It was bred on formal patterns which mainly derived from the older repertory, but were executed with a new discipline and balance. Greek art had been given a false start in the Bronze Age by the dominant modes of the non-Greek Minoans. Fortunately, the new Geometric arts of Greece could respond differently and profitably to foreign inspiration.

The style is best expressed on painted vases, but can be seen on metal-work as well. Proto-Geometric artists (mainly of the tenth century) had subjected the free curvilinear patterns of the past to the authority of the compass. Rectilinear patterns—the meander, zig-zag, swastika—provided the main themes in Geo-metric art (ninth to eighth centuries) and beside them crept in simple figure subjects—a mourner on a grave vase, the prestigious symbol of a horse, pattern bands of animal bodies. After barely a generation of experiment with scenes of human figures, some in action, the Athenian Dipylon Master was able to offer on his vases the classic statement of Geometric art, panels of pattern which are

PROCESSION TO THE TOMB, drawn on an Athenian Geometric vase of about 740 BC. With the simplest conventions of drawing the artist conveys a complicated scene of women mourners (below the handle and behind the cart), males and a child above, with the chequered shroud raised over the dead man on his funeral bed which rests on the cart for its journey to the grave. In front of the horses are warriors. This was a grand funeral, and it decorates a large vase (in all 123 cm high) which served as a grave marker.

resolved into figures of mourners and the dead in the ritual of laying out (*prothesis*) and burial. The scenes are not demonstrably other than of contemporary practice. The silhouette figures, composed of geometric patterns, can step beyond being symbols for man to some expression of his behaviour, by nuances of gesture or drawing, but something more was needed to translate this art into a medium for greater narrative expression.

Contact with the eastern shores of the Mediterranean had never, perhaps, quite been broken. The Cyprus-Crete route seemed well established, and via Cyprus, no doubt, the Levantine prospectors brought the exotica which began to appear even in Proto-Geometric Greece. In the ninth century the Phoenicians founded their city on Cyprus, Citium, but it seems to have been left to the Greeks, from Euboea and the islands, to guarantee trade with the Aegean by planting their own emporium at the mouth of the Orontes in Syria (Al Mina) by the end of the century. This model for trade they followed in succeeding centuries on Ischia in Italy and at Naucratis in Egypt.

Eastern goods and eastern craftsmen (for sophisticated techniques cannot be learnt by mere observation of their products) brought to Greece foreign styles and long-lost techniques of handling precious and foreign materials like ivory. Through the eighth century the orientalizing crafts in Greece, notably in Athens and Crete, were practised alongside the native Geometric, with little cross-fertilization. But gradually the orientalizing bronze shields made for the Idaean Cave in Crete admitted Greek motifs; gradually the jewellery of Attica and Crete geometricized its shapes and patterns; gradually eastern techniques and patterns were admitted to native forms, while eastern subjects were Hellenized, like the naked ivory goddess (Astarte) who in Attica acquired a meander-patterned cap and a trim Greek physique.

The gifts of the East to the Greek artist were manifold. The mere example of an art devoted to figure and animal decoration may have encouraged him to develop figure decoration in his native, Geometric idiom, though even these angular forms were by no means alien to eastern arts. The incised eastern bronzes and ivories showed how detail could be added to silhouette figures, bringing the possibility of closer definition of dress and action, and eventually differentiation of the figures which went beyond differentiation of sex. In vase-painting this produced the incising miniaturist black-figure technique of Corinth by the end of the eighth century, but some studios, in Attica and the islands, clung to larger outline-drawn figures with linear details, products mainly of the seventh century.

The animals and animal-frieze decoration of the easterners were not unfamiliar to the Greeks, and in some centres they became dominant at the expense of human figure or abstract decoration. Animal friezes long remained a hallmark of the orientalizing style, even long after their source was forgotten. The creatures patrol Corinthian, later Attic, and east-Greek vases well into the sixth century. The wildlife was not unfamiliar, either, but some had slipped from the repertory since the Bronze Age. Lions were not to be seen in mainland Greece, except perhaps in the very north, and could be treated as monsters, like sphinxes or griffins, both well known to Bronze Age Greek artists. A Greek hybrid too, the centaur, could be added, and new monsters for myth created from eastern models—the chimaera, the Gorgon—to depict creatures of sung story who had no image.

Where the Greek preferred Geometric friezes or panels the East had curvilinear or floral patterns. This new, rank growth never quite ousted the Geometric, and was itself subjected to Greek discipline through the seventh century until the friezes of lotus and palmette, overlapping leaves (becoming egg and dart) and cable, became an integral part of Greek Classical design at any scale, from jewellery to temple architecture. More importantly, new techniques allowed action scenes of narrative to be created which could depict more than mortal rituals or adventures, and they opened the way to pictorial narrative of myth.

Orientalizing stimuli continued with distinctive, if diminishing, effect through the seventh and sixth centuries, the role of the Phoenicians and what they carried

Stimuli and Origins   275

from further east being taken over by the example of Egyptian, Assyrian, Babylonian, and Persian arts. They sometimes led nowhere or served to stereotype rather than quicken new forms, but they were more than mere catalysts, and in this formative period the coherent and natural characteristics of Greek art are demonstrated most clearly by what their artists chose and what they rejected in the many new models, techniques, and materials with which they became familiar.

The Archaic Style

Archaism in Greek art ran to the early fifth century. Down to that time its course was swift but, except in some exploitation of unusual media, such as vase-painting and architectural sculpture, it was not very dissimilar to that of other cultures, and it held little obvious promise of what was to follow. With hindsight we may try to claim the inevitability of the revolution which the fifth century ushered in. The seeds were there, but so were they in the arts of the Assyrians and Egyptians. In other arts the Greeks had already explored new fields in narrative and lyric. The artist, it may be, lagged behind the poet and philosopher, but was inspired by the same spirit of enquiry, and whether his dismantling of Archaic convention was inevitable or accidental, it was clearly something that is less surprising in Greece than it would have been elsewhere in the ancient world.

Archaic Greek art was highly conventionalized, and most of its conventions depended in varying degrees on foreign arts. It is generally in these strictly orientalizing essays that progress was slowest and the incentive to change least urgent. One example is metal-work: the type of full-rounded Eastern cauldron, with cast animal attachments, had a longer vogue than its Geometric predecessors, the big tripod cauldrons (yet it was the Geometric shape that survived in Greece for prestigious votive offerings or prizes). The griffin heads that decorated many of the cauldrons, which became favourite dedications at Greek sanctuaries, may have acquired a new serpentine elegance in Greek hands, but they are still recognizably the creatures introduced from the East at the end of the eighth century. These vessels, however, had encouraged Greek artists to develop other types of cast attachment for vases and utensils, and although these too owe something to the foreigner, this was a genre with greater possibilities.

A sculptural type, characterized by frontal features and wig-like hair, misleadingly called Daedalic by modern scholarship, also derives from the East. With it was introduced the use of the mould for mass production of figurines and plaques, another instrument inimical to change. Even so, it was a style which the Greeks exercised with imagination in different media—usually clay, for figurines, plaques, or on vases, but also up to lifesize in limestone, and in miniature in gold or ivory.

The third gift from the East, incising on silhouette figures, was practised on pottery (as it had not been in the East) as well as on metal-work. Black-figure

THE AUXERRE STATUETTE (*left*). Seventh-century sculpture is four-square, with emphatic, angular forms. Only in the second half of the century was marble used, and on life-size or colossal figures. This is one of the latest (about 625 BC) of the smaller (65 cm high) figures in the 'Daedalic' syle, cut in soft limestone. The cast shown here has been painted with what is believed to be the original colouring. There must have been much wooden sculpture of this style in this period.

A *KOUROS* (*right*)—grave-marker of about 530 BC from Keos. The *kouroi*, and their lady counterparts, the *korai*, could serve as grave-markers or votive offerings. The boldly patterned anatomy recalls nature without copying it and the figure stands squarely balanced, one foot before the other.

vases began to be made in Corinth in the seventh century, and at the end of the century the technique was adopted in Athens. Other Greek studios followed their lead in the sixth century. There is something uncompromising about silhouette, especially when executed in brilliant black gloss on a pale clay (buff in Corinth, orange in Attica), and the incised line which reveals the clay through the black is crisp but generally unsubtle. Colour additions are no more than dabs of white and red—real polychromy was for the early Archaic Island schools, and rare in black-figure, being technically difficult, although artists brought up in areas where panel- or wall-painting (commoner than the scant surviving examples would lead us to believe) was practised were bolder: for instance, the east-Greek painters who emigrated to Etruria in the sixth century. The Eastern animal-frieze style too long obsessed the painter, but later some artists were able to rise above the limitations of their technique and produce works whose quality of mass, line, and mood anticipate the Classical. Here Athens leads.

In sculpture it was a different overseas source that inspired change, replacing one convention for another, but offering new possibilities for progress. In Egypt Greeks of the mid seventh century and later saw colossal works of hard stone, learnt the techniques of laying out figures at such a scale (the tools they had already: better than the Egyptians who used no iron) and returned to exploit the fine, hard white marble of their island quarries on Naxos, and then Paros. In later Greek art the truly colossal was generally reserved for cult statues, but in the early years the new marble workshops produced massive works which served as dedications and grave markers. The standing naked male, the *kouros*, was the most important of the new types to emerge. At first the figures are carefully, but rather dully, cut four-square, with a pattern of surface detail for anatomy. Experiment, and a natural selection of the more lifelike forms, led the artist, by the end of the Archaic, to figures which are superficially realistic, though still the slaves of pattern in faces, hair, muscles, pose. The addition of colour, now lost, would not have made them much more real, but they were proud, imperishable statements of man's place in the world—not kings, priests or viziers, but citizens serving a god or commemorating the dead.

Their female counterparts, the *korai*, were dressed, and the pattern of their dress exercised the artist as did the anatomy of their brothers. Again, interest in pattern defied reality and dress-making. If we replace the lost colour, we see them as rather garish compositions of line, fold, and zig-zag. The *korai* serve sanctuaries rather than graves.

Egypt also taught the Greeks about the use of stone for columns and architectural ornaments. Until the later seventh century the Greeks built in brick, wood, and mainly undressed stone. Only in the seventh century had fired clay tiles begun to replace thatch or mud for roofs, and the only major buildings were temples, *oikoi* (houses) for the god's image. The need to create an image for a god had slight effect on the early development of sculpture, but the requirements of his house dictated the development of architecture, and only in the sixth

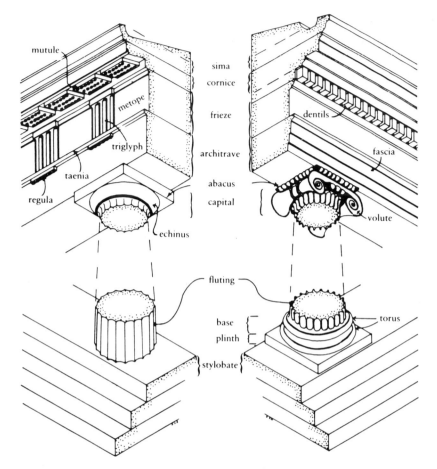

THE ELEMENTS OF THE CANONIC CLASSICAL DORIC (*left*) AND IONIC (*right*) ORDERS OF ARCHI-
TECTURE.

century did other public buildings begin to attract the architectural elaboration
otherwise reserved for temples. The Greek response to the use of dressed and
carved stone was, predictably, the establishment of new conventions. In plan this
meant the regularizing of the earlier, basic type of deep hall and porch, which
had already in places been provided with encircling colonnades. In elevation it
meant the creation of decorative schemes for these colonnades and the upperworks of the buildings. By the end of the seventh century the Doric order
emerged in mainland Greece, its intricate but austere patterns based on the tim-
bering of earlier structures. Soon afterwards the east-Greek world contributed
the Ionic order, based on orientalizing patterns of flower and scroll. As in sculpture, the colossal was not shunned, and some of the largest temples of the Greek
world, double-colonnaded, were planned in the sixth century by Ionian tyrants,
in Samos, Ephesus, Miletus, Didyma. In both orders development was slow, and
it is in some respects easier to judge the date of a building by the proportions of

its overall plan and elevation, of its columns and friezes, than from the detail of its mouldings and capitals. For decoration the temples were provided with sculpture: *akrotēria* for their roofs; relief or figures in the round for the low Doric gables—a dire challenge to the artist's skills in space-filling; reliefs in the Doric metope panels, or on Ionic friezes. These proved important fields for the display of religious and state propaganda, as had the very differently disposed, wall-covering reliefs and paintings of Near Eastern palaces and temples.

The intractable character of black-figure for vase-painting was resolved in about 530 by the invention in Athens of a new technique, red-figure. The

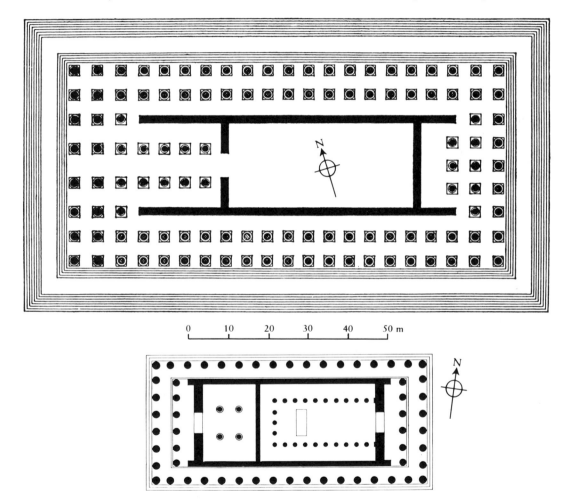

0   10   20   30   40   50 m

THE FOURTH-CENTURY TEMPLE OF ARTEMIS AT EPHESUS (*top*), AND THE FIFTH-CENTURY PAR-THENON AT ATHENS (*bottom*). Plans to scale. The gigantic Ionic temples, like the Ephesian, with their forest of columns, were no smaller even in the sixth century (this plan is of the replacement of the burnt Archaic temple). They dwarf even the Parthenon, the largest Doric temple of the Greek mainland of its day (exceeded only by temples built for Sicilian tyrants). Ephesus, like most Greek temples, had open porches. The Parthenon has shallow porches and a closed back room which was the Treasury. (For a reconstruction of its interior see illustration on p. 299.)

drawing was now done in outline, the background blacked in and the figures reserved in the clay ground with detail painted on where before it had been incised. Replacing the graver with the brush gave the artist a subtler line and a new range of linear expression. There was soon to be less colour, and the old sex differentiation of white = woman, black = man was lost, but by the end of the century the Pioneer Group of painters was experimenting with a rendering of anatomy which the sculptor was only later to emulate in three dimensions. The style was certainly closer to that of painting on wall or panel, but this seems not to become a major art form until the fifth century.

Athens figures large in this account of the Archaic, but it was a period in which virtually every major city in Greece had its own studios for most media. Regional styles are most readily distinguished on vases, but in sculpture too east Greece had its own way both in patterning the *korai* and in giving *kouroi* a fuller, fleshier physique, or even dressing them. Colonial Greece played its part too. The West had no white marble but developed skills in terracotta statuary or made do with limestone. Styles could travel with their artists. Persian pressure on east

HERACLES WRESTLES WITH THE LIBYAN GIANT ANTAEUS, on a vase by the Athenian red-figure Pioneer Euphronios about 510 BC. A fine display of precise anatomical detail. The kempt Greek hero with his curls rendered in low relief, is contrasted with the wild hair, beard and appearance of the giant, which closely resembles some representations of Libyans in Egyptian art. Notice the giant's grimace of pain and limp hand.

THE ATHENIAN ACROPOLIS (*above*); THE FOURTH-CENTURY THEATRE AT EPIDAURUS (*below*).

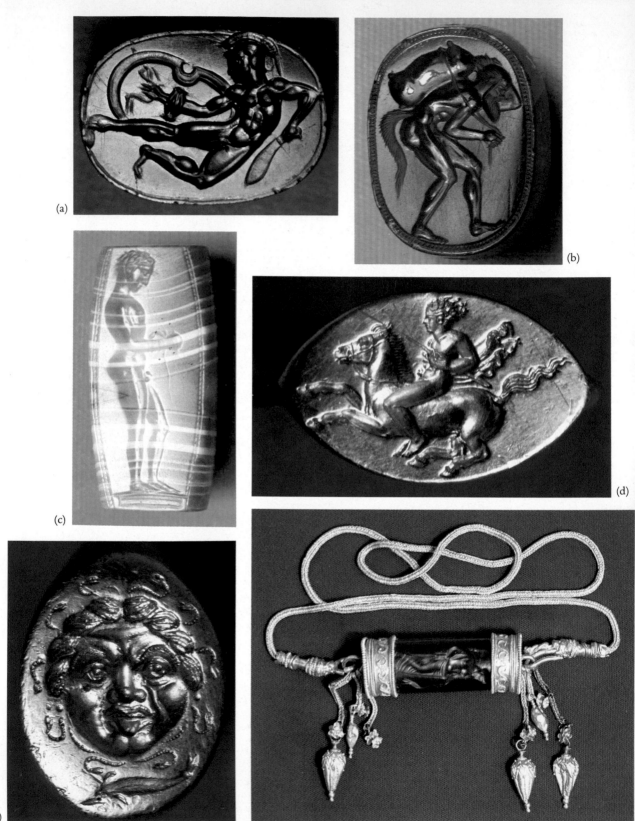

ENGRAVED GEMS, FINGER RINGS, AND JEWELLERY: (a) and (b) are of around 500 and 470 BC; (c) and (d) are Classical; (e) and (f) are of the fourth century BC.

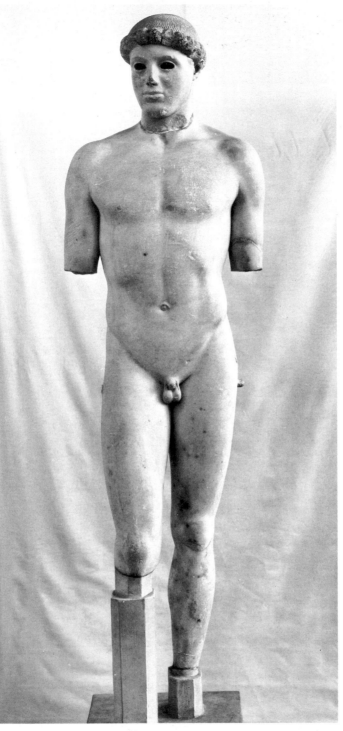

THE 'CRITIAN BOY'. Marble statue (height 85 cm) found on the Athenian Acropolis with debris from the Persian attack of 480/79 BC. The earliest near-complete example surviving of the new style which breaks with the rigidity of the Archaic *kouroi* and shows the weight of the body shifted on to one leg, with the corresponding adjustment of hips and shoulders—trivial features, but a landmark in the history of western art.

Greece in the mid-sixth century led to a diaspora of artists which brought Ionian styles to Attica, and to Etruria where they determined the course of late Archaic Etruscan art.

Athens was the home of the best black-figure, and the inventor of red-figure, vase-painting. Its sculpture was of high quality and more familiar to us through the Attic practice of using *kouroi* and relief gravestones in their cemeteries, and through their burial of the overthrown marble monuments of the Acropolis after the Persian sacks of 480/79. Among these sculptures is one which vividly demonstrates the sculptural revolution which had already taken place and which the vase-painters had presaged. The 'Kritian boy' has abandoned the four-square stance of a *kouros*. He stands in a natural, relaxed posture, weight mainly on one leg, his hips, trunk, and shoulders shifting to adjust to the stance. This is a vital novelty in the history of ancient art—life deliberately observed, understood, and copied. After him all becomes possible.

The Classical Style

The sculptor's new understanding of what he could achieve once he had decided to *look*, continued to be expressed in the standing male, and the succession is clear, from the early Classical Apollos, to Polyclitus' Doryphorus, and, in the fourth century, Lysippus' athlete Apoxyomenus. These were still commemorative statues, not (as the Archaic *kouroi* had been) to mark a tomb or serve a sanctuary, but more explicitly of individuals—athletes or warriors—to be dedicated for success in games or under arms, or more self-consciously (as by Polyclitus) to demonstrate proportions and technique. Progress was slow but certain in rendering the effect on the body of a shift in its weight and balance, or of partly resting on a separate support. This may seem little enough, but it was novel and could have appeared grotesquely inadequate in the hands of the incompetent or imperceptive. Fighting or exercising figures are often less subtle but no less accurate in the observation of life which they display, but there is an age of experience between Myron's discus-thrower who is virtually a freestanding relief, and Lysippus' who seems to pull the viewer round to admire him from any angle. Frontality came naturally to an Archaic artist and was encouraged by architectural sculpture and the setting of most statues. The abandonment of the implied frame or backdrop in statuary was answered in painting by a new sense of space which had also to be balanced in the composition.

Sculpture remains the senior art. Our knowledge of it is poor. Few of the finest works, generally bronzes, survive, and little architectural sculpture (but, luckily, that of the Parthenon) is of prime quality. Other original works are decorative or commemorative, like the grave reliefs, and seldom of high quality. And we have Roman-period copies of Classical works, identified for us with their artists from the texts of later writers. These may reveal little more than

IAMOS, from the east pediment of the Temple of Zeus at Olympia, completed in 546 BC. The artist has carefully observed the flaccid, ageing body, and in the gesture and features he expresses the old seer's anticipation of disaster.

subject and general appearance, and we rely on them for what we think we know of the style of a Myron, Polyclitus, or Lysippus. But when original works of the first rank do appear, like the Riace bronzes from a shipwreck off Italy (plate facing p. 248) we begin to sense how much we are missing, how less than perfect such familiar masterpieces as the Delphi charioteer may be.

Many think that the Riace bronzes are from a dedication set at Delphi in the mid-century by the Athenians to celebrate their success at Marathon. We can read what we will into the extrovert young male and his quieter more mature companion (and there must have been more to the group). Apart from such works, an Athens which had stopped decorating its tombs around 500 and had decided not to rebuild the temples destroyed by the Persians, offers us little for some fifty years. But at Olympia a new temple of Zeus was being built, and a sculptor imposed a style on his team which typifies for us the early Classical of roughly the second quarter of the fifth century (the temple was dedicated in 456). Of the two pediments the western offers Archaic vigour (the centaur fight), the

BRONZE ZEUS FROM ARTEMISIUM, recovered from an ancient shipwreck, no doubt en route to Italy. Made about 460–450 BC. A prime example of an early Classical bronze (as the Delphi charioteer, or the slightly later Riace bronze—plate facing p. 248). He held a thunderbolt (some have thought him Poseidon with a trident; far less probable).

GODS FROM THE EAST FRIEZE OF THE PARTHENON. Hephaestus, Apollo, and Artemis are seated with their fellow Olympians, awaiting the procession of the Panathenaic festival, which occupies most of the 160-metre-long frieze, in honour of Athena (who sits with them).

eastern Classical calm which is also a pregnant silence of reflection and foreboding. While the masons had yet much to learn of anatomy or the proper lie of dress, they succeeded in rendering nuances of age and mood with a subtlety far removed from the rather theatrical conventions of the Archaic.

Their successors include in the Peloponnese Polyclitus, with his essays in human proportions and, in an Athens which under Pericles had decided to revoke its decision not to rebuild its temples, Phidias. The Phidian school we judge from its architectural sculpture for Athens and Attica. It did not pursue the nuances of expression of the Olympia Master. Without the obsessions of a Polyclitus, it evolved a pure Classical style which idealized rather than individualized. At no time in the history of Greek art was the image of the divine so human, the human so divine. The placidity of the figures, even when represented in acts of vigour or high emotion, is not empty-headed, but other-worldly. As the body was understood so too was dress, and it can play its part in conveying the forms of the figure beneath, its action or inaction. Indeed, towards the end of the century there was a fashion for wind-blown or 'wet' dress, pressed against the body and contrasting with the deep shadows of the free-hanging or flying folds. With its 'Classic' style the Phidian studio became more than the school of Greece, since it was the style against which later sculptors' work was ever judged, and which was consciously recaptured by the artists of early Rome.

In the other arts vase-painting began its decline into fussiness or banality, but still attracted some fine draughtsmen, and the Attic red-figure style, transplanted to the Greek colonies of south Italy, enjoyed an Indian summer. Wall-painting of the early Classical period we have to judge from descriptions. On the walls of public buildings at Delphi and Athens Polygnotus painted great friezes with figures set up and down the field, though without perspective, and presented epic scenes of Troy and the underworld, and Micon the more recent, but heroically conceived, struggle for freedom at Marathon. The manner must have been sub-Archaic and, though much admired in later centuries, it was not copied. Their successors experimented at last with perspective and, more importantly, with realistic shading and coloration, and preferred the smaller panel to the great wall compositions which were the closest Greeks had come to the treatment of eastern or Egyptian walls. The anecdotes told about the realistic work of a Zeuxis or Apelles—the birds that pecked at the painted grapes, the painted curtain which could not be pulled—show that this is where the true tradition of western painting begins. It is the style copied on Roman walls, and the few original examples

ARTEMIS AND APOLLO SHOOT DOWN THE CHILDREN OF NIOBE, on an Athenian vase by the Niobid Painter of about 460 BC. The way in which the figures are set up and down the field, and not on a single ground-line, must be inspired by the new wall-painting compositions by Polygnotus which were appearing on public buildings in Athens.

HADES CARRYING OFF PERSEPHONE IN HIS CHARIOT. Painting of the second half of fourth century BC, on the wall of the small tomb within the great tumulus at Vergina (the Macedonian Aegae), which also covered the famous tomb of Philip II, discovered in 1977. The colours are red, yellow, violet, brown, orange (in Hades' hair). A very rare example of original Classical painting of high quality.

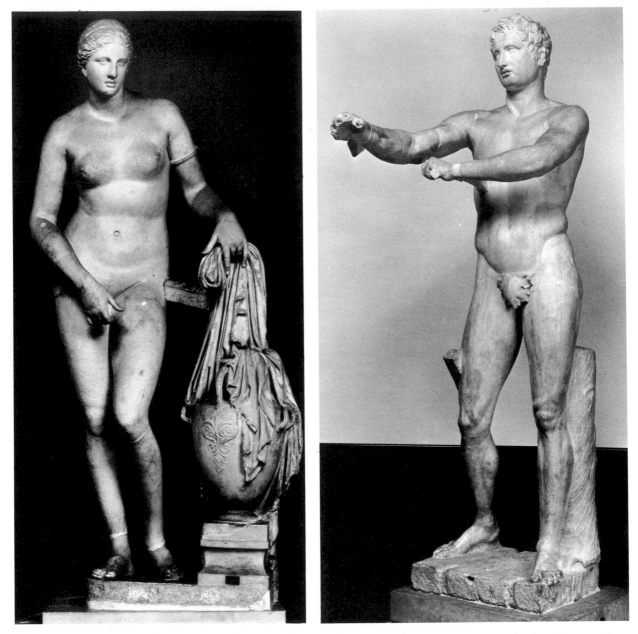

THE APHRODITE OF PRAXITELES (*left*). Roman copy of a marble original of about 340 BC. It was displayed in a temple at Cnidus in virtually peep-show conditions and widely held to be the greatest statue of antiquity. It is also one of the earliest female nudes in which the flesh-like qualities of marble must have been well exploited by the sculptor (earlier, major free-standing figures were usually of bronze). The type was endlessly copied, at various scales, in antiquity, and still is. No copy does more than hint at what must have been the quality of the original.

THE APOXYOMENUS (SCRAPER) OF LYSIPPUS (*right*). Roman marble copy of a bronze original of about 325 BC. The figure is of a young athlete scraping his forearm after bathing. The more relaxed, twisting pose offers a figure which claims no single optimum viewpoint, unlike Polyclitus' Doryphorus (illustration on p. 271). This is a new trait in sculpture, and Lysippus introduces also new ideal proportions, with a relatively smaller head.

which we have from the end of our period bear an uncanny likeness to styles of the Italian renaissance.

In the fourth century, until the patronage and aspirations of Hellenistic kings changed the focus of Greek life, thought, and art, the sculptors modestly explored beyond Phidian or Polyclitan Classicism. Praxiteles perfected the more feminine line of sinuous grace, and the female nude at last enters the history of western art. The louring brows of Scopas' heads marked a clear step towards the exaggerated expressionism of the Hellenistic. Lysippus had new views on ideal human proportions and could conceive and execute his figures in a fully three-dimensional manner, which must have revolutionized the setting of figures as well as the reaction and behaviour of viewers. All this amounts to further exploration of the possibility of realism, *pari passu* with the painters and, inevitably, of the realistic presentation not merely of specific types or age or mood, but of named individuals. Earlier commemorative statues of athletes or generals normally presented them in an idealized form with minimal personal traits. It is perhaps surprising that it took so long for observation and expression of the type to turn to observation and expression of the individual, especially since dedicatory practice and Greek personal pride gave every opportunity and encouragement. There must have been latent inhibitions about imposing personal features on generalized or idealized figures which were models for both men and gods. But the Greeks were becoming more aware of the divine in man, heroizing their dead and soon to declare divinity in certain favoured or powerful living. Thus, true portraiture of the contemporary, rather than idealized character studies of the dead, was another gift of the fourth century to western art.

Praxiteles was an Athenian, but Scopas was of Paros, the marble island, and Lysippus of Sicyon. Greece no longer had a dominant school or showplace. The masterpieces of the fourth-century artists are lost to us, and even the Praxitelean Hermes at Olympia no better than an excellent copy. We have to judge minor arts (minor in size only), or works commissioned for the barbarians such as the tomb of Mausolus in Caria with its colossal figures and relief friezes, or in areas where conditions of burial have ensured survival, as in Philip II's tomb at Vergina in Macedonia. The last provides the clue to the new patronage which dictated the future of Greek art.

Patronage, Private and Public

In Egypt and the East most works of art were commissioned for temples, palaces, or royal tombs. Decorative arts for the pleasure of most of the populace were thinly spread, though there was some elegant furnishing in the Levant, and engraved seals or scarabs and similar trinkets were fairly common (plate facing p. 281). In Greece there was no palace society in our period, but there were many state or religious projects to occupy the artist. A very high proportion of what survives was designed for the use of a wide spectrum of society. Many

GRAVESTONE FOR A YOUNG MAN, from near the River Ilissus, Athens. He is characterized as an athlete, accompanied by a weary child, his dog, and a pensive old man, perhaps his father. About 340 BC. The youth's proportions are Lysippan (see illustration on p. 288 right). The Classical gravestones of Athens commonly carry quiet contemplative groups of this type, recalling the dead in life. Few, however, are of this exceptional quality.

NIKE (VICTORY) BUILDS A TROPHY. Blue chalcedony gemstone, carved in intaglio, shown here at three times actual size. Victory, like Aphrodite, invites nude statues from the fourth century on. These hard-stone gems offer masterpieces of miniaturist art and must have been cut by major artists of their day. A big fourth-century stone such as this would have been set on a pendant since the practice of setting such stones in finger rings was still quite rare.

painted vases served the *symposion*, the drinking-party feast which played as important a social role as it did an entertaining or nourishing one. Others were used in ritual, often domestic, or were destined for dedication or grave furnishing. Most, in fact, survive thanks to the brisk export trade to Etruria and to Etruscan burial customs which guaranteed the preservation of so many intact. A private person could commission a dedication, paying for it with a tithe from some successful transaction or as a thanks-offering for some benefits thought to be divinely bestowed. If not a painted vase, there could be a bronze vessel of types which also served as prizes and might be dedicated after success in games or in the theatre. For poorer folk clay or wooden figures sufficed. At best a statue or group might be commissioned, like the athlete statues at Olympia, and a statue or relief for a grave monument.

Wealth acquired in the form of precious metal might be converted into jewellery for wear or silver plate for use, but in temple inventories the value of such dedications is reckoned as bullion without regard to the added value of workmanship. Greek jewellery was generally plain in colour and seldom even juxtaposed gold and silver, but it was technically perfect, and not the least of the peculiarities of Greek art is its display of both brilliant miniaturism (jewellery, engraved gems) and sheer monumentality.

State patronage was concerned principally with public buildings and their decoration, with commemorative dedications, usually at the major national sanctuaries such as Olympia and Delphi which thus became showcases of Greek art, and with coinage. A classical democracy could prove no less ambitious in promotion of its image at home and elsewhere than an archaic tyrant. Sources of funds were roughly similar—booty, taxes, ownership of mines—and the line was thinly drawn between expenditure on public works, even fleets and armies, and religious ones. Indeed the resources, including works of art, of the latter, could be called upon by the state to finance the former in times of crisis.

Temples were the prime demonstration of state wealth, to say nothing of piety (the backroom of the Parthenon was the treasury). They were also, in their way, the first museums, being display places for precious booty and for interesting bygones (Heracles' cup, the Amazon queen's belt, and so on). The tyrants of archaic Ionia went for sheer size with no little element of competition in overall dimensions (the late Archaic Artemisium at Ephesus measured 115.14 × 55.10 m.). This was a tradition sustained by the nouveaux riches tyrants of the western colonies as at Syracuse or Acragas, but the Parthenon shows that a democracy too could aim to impress by bulk (69.50 × 30.88 m.). The logistics of these undertakings probably presented more problems of personnel than of finance. Slaves might be hired for haulage, but for the finer work Pericles had to drain Greece of masons to rebuild Athens, though there seems to have been a remarkable reservoir of citizen talent.

Even with a democracy it was open to prominent private citizens to promote building. After the Persian invasion Cimon and his kin in Athens appear to have been responsible for the creation of a shrine for Theseus (which he endowed with a prize exhibit, the bones of the hero himself) and of the gallery which became known as the Painted Stoa for its panel paintings, which combined mythological narrative with state propaganda.

Pericles' decision to use League funds, contributed for the war against Persia, for the rebuilding of Athens (above, p. 213) heralded the most important programme of state patronage to have been seen in Greece, only to be rivalled later in the capitals of the Hellenistic kings. Work was not completed until the end of the century, the last phase being undertaken despite the distractions of a crippling and unsuccessful war. But even these latest additions can be seen as necessary parts of the overall programme. The Acropolis was to have a new, or rather redesigned, temple to replace the incomplete one overthrown by the Persians. The Parthenon was less a cult place than a war memorial, dedicated as much to the glory of Athens and Athenians as to the city goddess Athena. While it was building other temples were planned and under construction in Athens and in the Attic countryside, some not to be completed until later in the century, when also the Acropolis received its new monumental gateway (Propylaea, in the 430s) and the Erechtheum (mainly 421–406), to house its oldest cults. The architects, Ictinus, Mnesicles, and whoever planned most of the countryside temples (with the Hephaesteum in Athens) refined principles of proportion and detail for the Doric order, introducing new subtleties of line to distract the eye from the possible deadening effect which the comparatively primitive engineering of the structures could induce. The highest standards of design and execution were applied at every stage, from overall plan to the detail of a ceiling coffer. An infinite ability to take pains has not always been a characteristic of major art, and in some arts it proves positively hostile, but it is part of the essence of Greek art and architecture, an enhancement not a distraction.

The state too took a hand in the construction of other public buildings, the colonnaded stoas which served administration or commerce, council halls, theatres whose function was social as well as religious. Away from home a tyranny or state advertised itself by expensive dedications in the national sanctuaries. In the Archaic period these might take the form of treasuries, elaborate architectural and sculptural pavilions. At Delphi we should single out that of Siphnos (about 525 BC) with its proliferation of sculptural ornament, a tithe from a lucky strike of gold and silver in the island; and at Olympia the series of treasuries dedicated by prosperous colonies in south Italy and Sicily. At Delphi Athens set the bronze group which celebrated the victory at Marathon, but many a state dedication was for success over other Greeks, and the sanctuaries commemorated inter-state conflict far more often than any co-operative efforts against foreign aggressors.

Coinage from the start generally carried a state blazon for identification and as guarantee. Once devices were set also on the reverses of coins they could carry

SILVER COIN (DECADRACHM) OF SYRACUSE (*left*), of about 395–380 BC, showing the head of the local nymph Arethusa, and signed by the artist Euainetus. One of the largest and finest of Greek coins. Three times actual size. SILVER COIN OF ELIS (*right*), of about 350 BC, showing the head of Zeus. These fine issues were probably associated with Olympic festivals, controlled by Elis. Three times actual size.

other emblems of political or religious importance, and once the coins were in common inter-state use rather than for local exchange (for services, fines, taxes, etc.) they became as much ambassadors of the issuing city as its dedications might seem to be at Olympia or Delphi, and dies were commissioned from artists of quality, some of whom even signed their work.

Much of Greek art was, in the broadest sense, functional. Artists were commissioned for works which had a fairly clearly defined purpose, so it is important to understand the motives and resources of those who stimulated production of the objects and buildings which we tend to view and judge in a far more disinterested manner.

Narrative in Art

The art historian's view of Greek mythology is subtly different from that of the student of Greek literature. Most of the mythological scenes which have survived, and they are myriad, appear on objects of ordinary use, or at least not of extraordinary use like temple sculptures. Most Greeks learnt their myth-history from a rich and infinitely varied oral tradition. Our classical studies start from texts: theirs did not, and we exaggerate their literacy (there are more outward signs of literacy in the Indian subcontinent today than there were in ancient Greece, yet well over 70 per cent of the population cannot read or write). Most of the artist's stories were closest to those understood by everyman, often just as illogical, contradictory, and distorted or improved in the telling through generations. The poet's stories were more consciously adapted to the context of his poem or play, to the patron or society for which he was writing or for the moral he wished to draw from his use of myth as parable. Sometimes art follows texts, sometimes texts follow art: there are some scenes of our period which deliberately follow texts, though probably fewer than is generally thought. The artist had the same freedom as a writer to adjust his story, but he was more restricted even in the content of what he portrayed by the formulae of his craft. He could not, for instance, offer continuous narrative and there was a limit to what could be explained by inscription. He was also in many respects more conservative than the poet. He was not in our period guided by pattern books, but clear conventions for particular subjects and for generic scenes were established. Nevertheless, all but the veriest hacks avoided repeating themselves line for line, not deliberately, but because there was no need or compulsion to do so.

The earliest pictures are symbols for contemporary events, of burial or battle, and the example of the East led the artist to an idiom in which more specific detail of a historical (to us, mythical) story could be expressed. The first myth-scenes are prompted by formulae suggested by orientalizing arts. They have virtually nothing in common with the rich visual imagery of Homer, least of all in his Ionian homeland, beyond sharing the same traditional oral sources and, more tentatively than he, employing the same language of metaphor.

Abjuring the strip-cartoon system of narration the Greek artist was obliged to encapsulate the narrative and message of a story in a single-scene. The Archaic artist generally chose a moment of maximum action: the Classical, relying on his viewer's knowledge of the story, could sometimes dwell on proem or aftermath, which might be psychologically or dramatically more telling. Both relied for the identification of their figures on conventional dress, attributes, and poses. Few scenes are helped by inscriptions, and figures are more often allowed interjections than conversations. Reliance on detail of pose or attribute also enabled the artist to introduce an element of continuous narrative by allusion to past and future. Latter-day theorists devise imposing names for this process, as though it was a deliberate invention and not inescapable in a period in which the 'camera-still' was unknown and the media offered single panel or frieze compositions, not acres of temple and palace walls as in Egypt and the Near East.

THE DEPARTURE OF AMPHIARAUS FOR THEBES. Drawing from a Corinthian vase of about 560 BC (see text for description and commentary).

A classic example is the Corinthian crater of about 560, showing Amphiaraus departing for his doomed expedition (with the Seven) against Thebes. His wife Eriphyle stands off to the left, holding prominently the necklace with which she had been bribed to persuade the King to go to war. Behind him is his son Alcmaeon who will avenge him. To the right his seer whose gesture shows his foreknowledge of the outcome of the expedition. And there is a plentiful animal presence, no doubt omens. More subtly, in the east pediment at Olympia, the remorseless vengeance of Zeus on oath-breakers, which pursued the house of Atreus, is recalled not by any major episode of action but at the moment of the oath-taking, before the race between Pelops and Oinomaos. Juxtaposition of scenes involving the same figure, though not in episodes of the same story, seems to have been introduced with the new Theseus cycle in Athens at the end of the sixth century, and is taken up to better effect for the series of Heracles' Labours.

In the popular arts such as vase-painting the choice of subject seems generally

THE DEEDS OF THESEUS, on the interior of an Athenian cup of about 430 BC. It is unusual in being decorated around its central medallion with a frieze (which is repeated on the outside of the cup). In the centre Theseus pulls the dead Minotaur from the Labyrinth. In the frieze are six of Theseus' exploits on the road from Troezen to Athens, and his subsequent encounter with the Marathonian bull. Episodes of this type from a single cycle are run together on painted vases, kept discrete on temple metopes.

that of the artist who, of course, knew his market, and specially commissioned pieces for dedication or other occasions can generally be identified in an artist's work by their (for him) uncharacteristic subjects. He was influenced in his choice mainly by tradition. In some periods, as in fourth-century south Italy, stage subjects seem deliberately sought, and there is sometimes the echo of the stage on fifth-century Athenian vases. New stories, such as the Theseus cycle, or an emphasis on certain myths which answered state propaganda, were quickly mirrored in the popular arts. Theseus' role in the new Athenian democracy is clear enough in literature as in art. Before him it is in art that we most clearly observe a new treatment of Heracles with his patron Athena as symbol of the Athenian state and especially of its tyrant family. New cults too—Athens' adoption of Eleusis or the arrival of an Asclepius—are reflected in the popular arts. Certain almost ritualized aspects of everyday life, presumably of a significance which goes beyond mundane interest in the world around them, also occupied artists and were blessed with their own iconographic conventions, like myths: the symposium, courting of youths, athletics, wedding preparations.

In the major arts, wall-painting and temple sculpture, there were other considerations, not least the fact that they were for public display, not ephemeral
consumption, and that these expensive and lengthy projects were not appropriate
fields for experiments. The Parthenon is unusual in having its sculptural themes
all closely related to Athena, Athens, its glorious past, both mythical and recent,
and Athenians. On other temples the relevance of the subject is sometimes less
apparent, and we may imagine that the decisions were those of a committee of
magistrates and priests rather than of the artists. Many demands, of patronage,
politics, and religion might need to be answered.

While individual figures of myth, monsters or heroes, may seem to serve
mainly decorative functions, generally Greek art is telling a story or setting a
scene. The student of style may find the subject-matter irrelevant, and the mythographer may discount the power of tradition or of what, in terms of technique
and convention, was possible in the representation of myth. But a study of Greek
art can no more ignore its subjects than its style or purpose.

Religious Art

Most of Egyptian or Indian art and a large proportion of the arts of Mesopotamia
were religious: that is to say, they were designed to attract or appease a deity, to
inspire or intimidate worshippers, to guarantee a life beyond the grave. Hardly
any of this is true of Greek art, which may reflect upon man's relationship to his
gods but is seldom dictated by exclusively religious requirements. At a fairly low
level some degree of near-magical use of art is seen in the apotropaic devices,
usually animals or monsters, sometimes the human eye or male genitals, on
various objects, but Greek art was not dominated by such crude symbolism. The
sphinxes or lions on grave monuments no doubt did guard the grave, just as the
Gorgon head in early pediments guarded the temple (but from what?). There
must have been no less of the irrational in the thought of ancient Greece than in
that of other cultures, but it was expressed in literature, and hardly at all in art,
where even the monsters and demons have a stunning plausibility.

The artist was virtually never called upon to exercise his skills on objects
destined only for the grave. The oil flasks (white-ground *lekythoi*) made for some
two generations in Athens deliberately as grave furniture were placed on as well
as in tombs. The Archaic grave monuments idealized the dead in an anonymous
way, and the Classical ones expressed no more than a calm confrontation of the
live and the dead, as if both were alive: no demons, no gods of the Underworld,
no threats, no violent grief, more expressions of human dignity or even pride
than of desolation or dumb acceptance. The idealizing qualities of Greek art abet
these attitudes magnificently.

Dedications could flatter a deity with his image or a portrayal of his power in
scenes of action, but they were as often images of mortal attendants for the god
(the Archaic *korai* and *kouroi*), and if they portrayed the dedicator himself it is

not in a servile manner, but in the pride of his profession—soldier, athlete, or citizen. Remarkably, it became possible for a votive relief to depict the worshipper and his family in the presence of the deity, with only their smaller size to indicate the profound difference in status.

Scenes of cult and sacrifice were simple statements of the act, and the deity was often shown virtually as a mortal onlooker. The orgiastic rites of Dionysus, on which ancient literature is reticent, were ritualized into dance and myth by the artist. The god himself was wrested from his role of rustic fertility spirit into joining the Olympian family where his appearance and behaviour were made by the artist to conform with his new setting. But he rubbed shoulders with humanity more than most, mainly through his gift of wine, and this was well expressed on the clay vases, many of which were designed for the symposium. On them his maenad-nymphs impersonate his ecstatic mortal followers, while the satyrs, nature demons recruited into his troupe, act out mortal aspirations which wine, women, and song can promote, and become one of the most engaging creations of the Greek artist. Other mystic religions or beliefs, the Pythagorean or Orphic, found as little response in Greek art as did Hellenized foreign goblins such as Lamia.

Cult statues had a more clearly defined religious purpose, as symbols of the god's presence in his house. The earliest acquired their sacred power from their antiquity ('fallen from heaven' or the like), not their appearance, and were sometimes barely shaped logs which could be decked out on festive occasions with dress or weapons. When the old images had to be replaced or supplemented by new ones, the artist could have sought through his art to express something of the same magic power. But apart from attributes or dress or sheer size the cult statues are indistinguishable in appearance from statues of mortals. With the fifth century they sought to impress more through size—the Zeus at Olympia would have gone through the roof if he stood up—and material, the chryselephantine with beaten gold dress and ivory flesh. The setting, in the columned interior of a temple and barely lit from the doors or windows before them and, at Olympia and in the Parthenon, by the light reflected up from a broad shallow pool before them on the floor, will have enhanced their appearance. It was for much later writers to dwell on the spiritual aspects of Phidias' Zeus at Olympia. In its day his Athena Parthenos seems to have excited more concern over the accounting for her materials, and Pericles could point out to the Athenians that her gold was removeable and could help pay for war. Experience of the theatre, and of art for the theatre, may have had its effect on the artist's designs and settings for his works, but he made no special provisions for imbuing them with the numinous.

Even in his execution of religious subjects the Greek artist worked within the confines of his training, but could exercise imaginative invention to the full. The restraint was technical rather than psychological, and his choice of image did not depend, as in other periods and places, on prayer or meditation. Poets, actors, musicians, dancers, even historians had their Muse, but not artists.

RECONSTRUCTION IN THE ROYAL ONTARIO MUSEUM, TORONTO, OF THE INTERIOR OF THE PARTHENON, WITH THE GOLD AND IVORY STATUE OF ATHENA PARTHENOS BY PHIDIAS. The architectural setting is certain and the statue can be restored from numerous reduced copies. A shallow pool of water before her reflected light on to the statue (and kept the atmosphere humid for the ivory). She stood some 40 feet tall.

Decoration in Art

Nothing, except perhaps the heroic nude, provokes recognition of Greekness more readily than ornaments such as meander, egg-and-dart, palmette friezes. Subsidiary ornament was subjected to the same discipline as major designs, and in some periods and media we find objects devoted wholly to pattern. The need to articulate and frame friezes or panels allowed the development of orientalizing florals which adopted the rows of palmettes and lotuses of eastern art, created new and less botanically correct patterns, and established a decorative scheme that only in the fifth century gave way to more realistic florals with some observation of live forms, and the evolution of leafy, but strictly controlled, arabesques. Many patterns belong to woodwork, but have become more familiar translated and enlarged on to stone architecture. Care was taken to see that the profile of a moulding and its decoration were matched. The Eastern volute-trees could become adjusted in scale or use to Ionic columns or to decorative details of furniture or utensils.

Many arts have sought to animate objects by introducing human or animal features to otherwise functional forms. The Greeks were not obsessive about this, nor did they let it dominate what they made, and there are a few Archaic vessels in the shape of whole animal or human figures. But handles could be created from the curving body of an athlete or a leaping lion, human heads could spring from handle attachments, feet become lion paws. Curly extremities grew snake heads: Athena's aegis, Hermes' caduceus, the Chimaera's tail. The Greeks spoke of parts of the vase as parts of the human body, just as we do (lip, neck, shoulder, foot, ears = handles) and, mainly in the Archaic period, allowed this conceit expression by painted or moulded additions—eyes under arched handles, or on eye-cups where, with the ear-handles and trumpet foot (like a mouth), the whole vessel can look like a mask when raised to the drinker's lips.

The question of colour in Greek art is a difficult one. Architecture under a Mediterranean sun tends to simple, clear, bright forms, with colour in detail, not mass. On Greek architecture the colouring of details in the upperworks of buildings could have done little more than help articulate the sharply carved forms. Only in the clay revetments of Archaic roofs does there seem to have been a positive riot of colour. On sculpture it seems that colour was used to lend verisimilitude, but we know too little about how intense the colours were when applied. Neo-classical versions of Greek statues, with colour supplied, are disturbing, and we have become so used to judging form without colour that it is distracting. The few coloured marbles left from antiquity, as at Pompeii, look like rather crude dolls. There seems no indication of coloured outer walls for buildings, and for any painting on interior walls, figural or decorative, we have no evidence. New discoveries could dramatically change our view. Scraps of painted plaster show that the seventh-century temple of Poseidon at Isthmia near Corinth had somewhere upon it large (though not life-size) figures of animals.

We may, then, underestimate the value of colour in Greek art, but in their language they are strangely vague in defining colours, their jewellery long abjured settings of coloured stones, and the modest use of dark stone in architecture is in marked contrast with Rome's addiction to variegated marbles. Their vase-painting evolved from four-colour black-figure to two-colour red-figure, while their most famous Classical painters were said (as seems true, to judge from near-contemporary mosaics) to have worked in four colours only.

If not in colour, in form at least there was a tendency to what we would regard as the over-ornate. When execution and design is perfect a degree of elaboration is acceptable—I think of the finely chased and cast bronze and silver

BRONZE CRATER (MIXING BOWL), from Derveni, near Salonica, found in 1962. Late fourth century BC. The most elaborate of its type preserved (most must have been claimed by the melting pot in antiquity), with Dionysiac relief scenes on the body and figures in the round seated on its shoulders. It stands 90.5 cm high and had served as a funerary urn.

vessels of the later Classical period; where workmanship is poorer, or the medium less inspiring, it would become difficult to admit the products to one's drawing room—I think of the large, over-decorated, clay vases of south Italy in the fourth century. Knowing where to stop is the hallmark of the great artist. Not all Greek artists were sublime, nor their customers always impeccable in their taste.

The Artists

Greek art was not the big business in antiquity that it is today. Some portable works, jewellery and plate, were expensive, and it is notable that we have learned most about these from finds made outside the Greek world, where they appear as gifts or booty in native kingdoms, or as court furniture, from the Seine to Persepolis. Even the finer red-figure vases passed for hardly more than a worker's day wage. Some potters, especially in sixth-century Athens, observed the export market to Etruria closely enough to specialize in export models designed to attract by their familiar shapes or acceptable styles of decoration: the so-called Tyrrhenian amphorae and the products of Nicosthenes' workshop. The returns were no doubt gratifying, and some potters or pottery-owners could afford sculptural dedications on the Acropolis. In the Classical period the big names in sculpture and wall-painting could command high fees and provoke competition for their services, but these were men who travelled freely and worked wherever employment was offered. Only in the Athenian pottery trade and probably in metal workshops elsewhere (Corinth, Sparta) do there seem to have been industries which came to serve more than the local market. Specialized local industries for the national or international market were uncommon in Greece, and artists were in no different position in this regard from shoemakers or carpenters. Indeed, no distinction was drawn in antiquity in favour of those whom we designate artists—it was all craft (*technē*). Only with Phidias, and then increasingly with his successors, did any special social status appear to have been accorded to successful artists, although they had been housed at the courts of the Archaic tyrants, like musicians, entertainers, and doctors.

There was a tendency for crafts to be practised in families: a master's natural apprentice would have been his own son. There is evidence for this in pottery and in sculpture, but there was versatility too. Some of the finest vase-painters, known to us from only one or two vases, may also have been panel-painters. A sculptor might prefer modelled bronze to carved marble, but most could work in either and at any scale. He might also be an architect (Scopas) or painter (Euphranor). Some crafts were easily mobile—the jeweller, die-engraver, indeed even the sculptor who had to travel from home to quarry to finishing workshop on the site of his commission. While the family businesses helped to establish local styles and traditions, mobility meant rapid dissemination of new ideas and techniques, and the major sanctuaries served as galleries for both masterpieces of the past and novelties.

More than half the sculptors named in the Erechtheum accounts were Athenian citizens, but in earlier years the potter and painter signatures on Athenian vases reveal a high proportion of non-Athenian, or even non-Greek names, or nick-names which conceal nationality. In simpler crafts the immigrant Greek (metic) or non-Greek no doubt played an important role in the workshops and in a state like Sparta his role must have been a major one, but this did nothing to weaken the strong local character of Spartan art in the Archaic period. In Athens Solon is said to have encouraged the immigration of artists in the early sixth century and this, followed by the patronage of a tyrant court, may do much to explain Athens' busy record in the arts thereafter.

The number of artists' signatures from the Archaic and Classical periods is another peculiarity of Greek art. They appeared by around 700 and were by no means confined to major works or major artists. The desire of the vase-painter to sign his work might seem unusual, and the practice was fairly haphazard: for some we have only one extant signature on some fifty vases, and for most none at all. As advertisement it could have done little, and simple pride was probably the motive. The signature was often discreet, but not always: on Archaic grave monuments the artist's name may be as prominent as the deceased's. On late sixth-century Athenian red-figure vases the so-called Pioneers are free with challenges to their fellows' work or mottoes naming them. From their vases and inscriptions alone we can reconstruct a lively and very self-conscious artistic community. It was unusually literate too and may have had social pretensions, although inscribing references to handsome well-born youths of the day (the *kalos* inscriptions; irrelevant to the scenes they accompany) need not always imply close familiarity, and was as much practised by lesser artists on poorer works. The competitive spirit between artists seems also to have been exploited by patrons, but our record of these competitions, like that for the Amazons at Ephesus where each artist put his own work first and the prize went to the agreed second, Polyclitus, may have been distorted by the promotional tales of local guides who tend to be free in their use of great names and good stories.

The singular physical character of Greek art, when compared with those of other ancient cultures, was remarked at the beginning of this chapter. Its pre-occupation with the human and with the gods' proper place in the world of men (rather than vice versa) was also the concern of Greek writers. The Greek artist served the society in which he lived by answering the requirements of a far wider range of the community than its priests and governors, and he demonstrated for the first time in the history of man the potential of a truly popular art in reaching beyond the demands of magic or display of status. In such service the concept of art for art's sake was unknown and unnecessary.

Further Reading

A comprehensive and well-documented account of Greek Art from Bronze Age to Hellenistic is M. Robertson, *A History of Greek Art* (Cambridge, 1975), with his *Shorter History of Greek Art*

(Cambridge, 1981). Shorter handbooks are G. M. A. Richter, *Handbook of Greek Art* (London, 1974) by subject, and J. Boardman, *Greek Art* (London, 1985) by period.

For period studies there are J. N. Coldstream, *Geometric Greece* (London, 1977); J. Boardman, *Greeks Overseas* (London, 1980), and *Preclassical Style and Civilization* (Harmondsworth, 1967); J. Charbonneaux, R. Martin, and F. Villard, *Archaic Greek Art* and *Classical Greek Art* (London, 1971, 1973).

Sculpture. G. M. A. Richter, *Sculpture and Sculptors of the Greeks* (Oxford, 1971) for a detailed survey, and her comprehensive *Portraits of the Greeks* (Oxford, 1984). B. Ashmole, *Architect and Sculptor in Ancient Greece* (London, 1972) for important essays on Olympia, the Parthenon, and the Mausoleum, and *Olympia* (with N. Yalouris; London, 1967). J. Boardman, *Greek Sculpture: Archaic Period* and *Greek Sculpture: Classical Period* (London, 1978, 1985), heavily illustrated handbooks. J. Boardman and D. Finn, *The Parthenon and its Sculptures* (London, 1985). R. Lullies and M. Hirmer, *Greek Sculpture* (London, 1960) with fine pictures. C. Rolley, *Greek Bronzes* (London, 1986).

Architecture. There is no modern handbook, but W. B. Dinsmoor, *The Architecture of Ancient Greece* (London, 1952), is still useful, if taken with A. W. Lawrence, *Greek Architecture* (Harmondsworth, 1957). For other aspects, J. J. Coulton, *Greek Architects at Work* (London, 1977); R. E. Wycherley, *How the Greeks built Cities* (London, 1962) and A. W. Lawrence, *Greek Aims in Fortification* (Oxford, 1979).

Vase-painting. R. M. Cook, *Greek Painted Pottery* (London, 1972), a basic handbook. For pictures, P. Arias, M. Hirmer, and B. B. Shefton, *History of Greek Vases* (London, 1961). Period studies with full illustration are J. N. Coldstream, *Greek Geometric Pottery* (London, 1968); J. Boardman, *Athenian Black Figure Vases* and *Athenian Red Figure Vases: Archaic Period* (London, 1974, 1975). A. D. Trendall, *South Italian Vase-painting* (London, 1966), is a valuable brief survey.

Other Arts. R. A. Higgins, *Greek Terracottas* and *Greek and Roman Jewellery* (London, 1963, 1961); J. Boardman, *Greek Gems and Finger Rings* (London, 1971); D. Strong, *Greek and Roman Gold and Silver Plate* (London, 1966); C. M. Kraay and M. Hirmer, *Greek Coins* (London, 1966).

Many of the works named here relate also to the Hellenistic period.

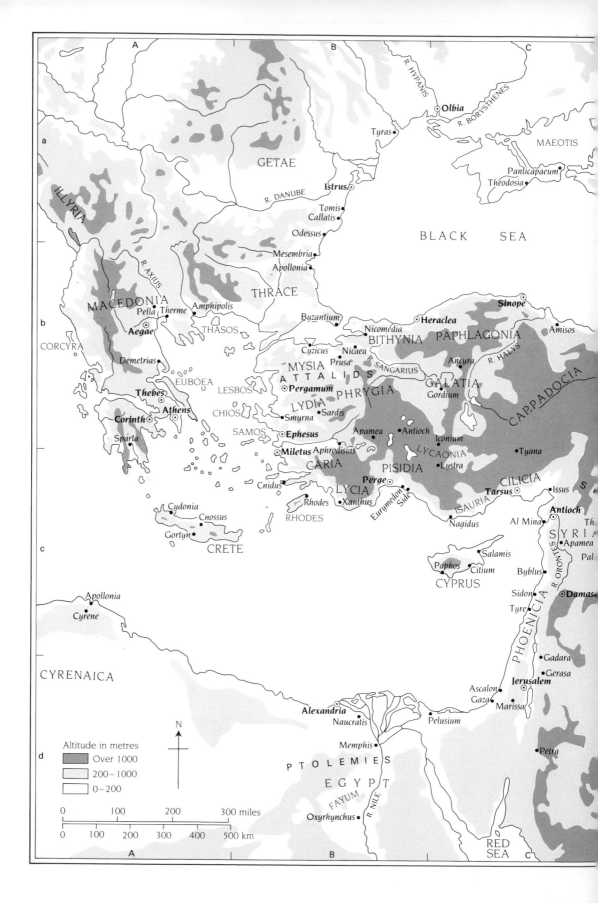

A

B

C

a

R. HYPANIS

Olbia

R. BORYSTHENES

Tyras

MAEOTIS

GETAE

Panticapaeum

Theodosia

R. DANUBE

Istrus

Tomis
Callatis

BLACK   SEA

Odessus

Mesembria

Apollonia

THRACE

Byzantium

Sinope

Heraclea

PAPHLAGONIA

ILLYRIA

Nicomedia

Amisos

BITHYNIA

R. AXIUS

MACEDONIA

Cyzicus

Nicaea

Pella Therme

Amphipolis

MYSIA

Prusa

R. SANGARIUS

Ancyra

R. HALYS

b

CORCYRA

Aegae

THASOS

ATTALIDS

GALATIA

CAPPADOCIA

Demetrias

EUBOEA

LESBOS

Pergamum

PHRYGIA

Gordium

LYDIA

Thebes

Athens

CHIOS

Smyrna Sardis

Apamea

Antioch

Iconium

Tyana

Corinth

SAMOS

Ephesus

LYCAONIA

Sparta

Miletus Aphrodisias

Lystra

Cnidus

CARIA

PISIDIA

CILICIA

Perge

Tarsus

Issus

LYCIA

S

Cydonia

Rhodes Xanthus

Eurymedon Side

ISAURIA

Antioch

Cnossus

RHODES

Nagidus

Al Mina

Th

c

Gortyn

SYRIA

CRETE

Salamis

Apamea

Paphos Citium

Byblus

Pal

CYPRUS

Sidon

Damas

Apollonia

Tyre

Cyrene

PHOENICIA

Gadara

Gerasa

CYRENAICA

Ascalon

Jerusalem

Gaza

Marissa

Alexandria

Petra

Naucratis

Pelusium

Memphis

d

Altitude in metres

N

Over 1000

PTOLEMIES

200–1000

EGYPT

0–200

FAYUM

R. NILE

Oxyrhynchus

0   100   200   300 miles

RED
SEA

0   100   200   300   400   500 km

A

B

C

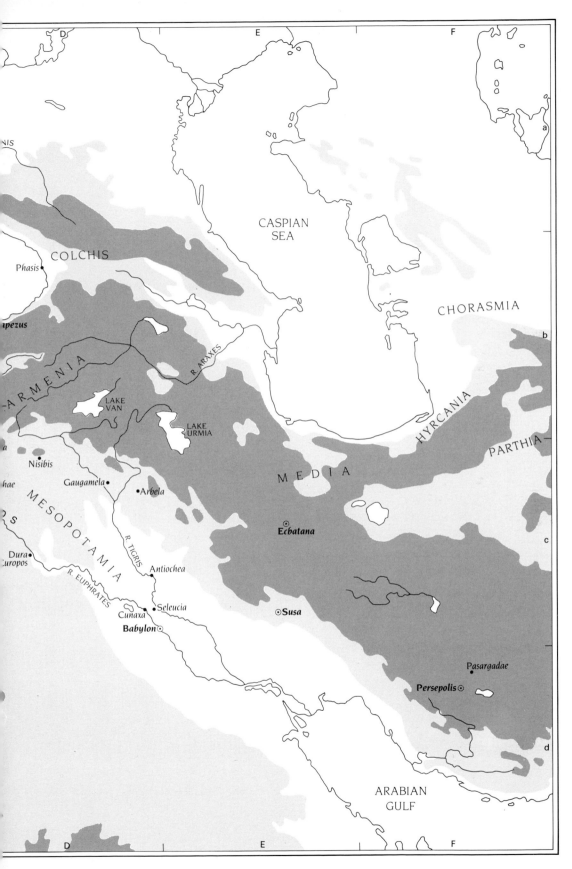

D   E   F

NIS

COLCHIS

Phasis

CASPIAN
SEA

CHORASMIA

pezus

b

A R M E N I A

R. ARAXES

LAKE
VAN

LAKE
URMIA

HYRCANIA

PARTHIA

Nisibis

Gaugamela

Arbela

M E D I A

c

hae

M E S O P O T A M I A

R. TIGRIS

Ecbatana

Dura
Europos

Antiochea

OS

R. EUPHRATES

Seleucia

Susa

Cunaxa

Babylon

Pasargadae

Persepolis

d

ARABIAN
GULF

D   E   F

MAP 5. THE HELLENISTIC WORLD

13

The History of the Hellenistic Period

❦

SIMON PRICE

THE Hellenistic period, the 300 years between the reigns of Alexander the Great of Macedon (336–323 BC) and Augustus, the first Roman Emperor (31 BC–AD 14), is often seen as an uninteresting and incoherent part of Greek history. Falling between the two 'central' periods of classical Athens and Ciceronian or Augustan Rome, the period seems to be merely the melancholy story of the decline of the Greek city, subjected first to Alexander and his successors and then to the Romans.

In fact the period has both internal coherence and topical interest. Its central feature is the establishment of Greek monarchies by Alexander and his successors which together controlled the area from Greece to Afghanistan. The impact of these monarchies on the Greek world is the theme of this chapter. I shall start by outlining briefly the reign of Alexander and the history of the four main Hellenistic kingdoms. In the wake of Alexander's conquests the new kingdoms consolidated the expansion of the Greek world: the kings founded new cities which ensured the dominance of Greek over native cultures. The connection visible here between political power and cultural dominance has an interesting analogy in the spread of European culture to our colonies. The needs of the competing kingdoms led to important administrative and military developments, which underpinned royal power. The kings ruled over numerous Greek cities, but what sort of impact did they make on them? What was it like to be subordinate to a super-power? Finally, within the cities themselves, civic life changed as a result of the growth of monarchy.

The Hellenistic Kingdoms

Alexander the Great is one of the archetypally romantic figures, as is shown by the vitality of the Alexander legend from antiquity to Mary Renault. Emulating the Homeric Achilles, he won a reputation for military genius and personal

BUST OF ALEXANDER THE GREAT,
the so-called 'Azara herm': a Roman
copy thought to be based on a bronze
statue, possibly showing the king in
heroic nudity holding a lance, by the
court-sculptor Lysippus (c.330–320 BC).
The tilt of the head and the mane-like
hair were standard features of
Alexander's portraits.

prowess. To him were attributed extraordinary tales: for example, Callisthenes, one of his court historians, recounted how once the sea had retreated from Alexander's path and bowed in homage before him. Though many of the stories, like this one, are at best dubious, their circulation as early as the lifetime of Alexander reflects his almost unthinkable achievements.

When Alexander succeeded to the throne of Macedon after the murder of his father Philip, he inherited a kingdom which had just come to dominate the affairs of mainland Greece. With enormous energy Alexander launched a crusade, long called for by Greek propagandists and indeed begun under Philip, to punish the Persians for Xerxes' invasion of Greece, almost 150 years earlier. Within a year Alexander had won control of the Greek cities of western Turkey, and he pressed east to Gordium. Here story told of an oracle that the person who loosed the knot that tied the yoke to the chariot of the ancient king of Gordium would become master of Asia: Alexander cut the knot. A romantic tale and possibly true. Only a month or two later he defeated Darius the Persian King at Issus (333 BC). Darius escaped, but Alexander was able to turn south and take control of Phoenicia and Egypt. From there he made an extraordinary expedition out west through the desert to the oracle of Zeus Ammon. No strategic purpose was served by this long march, but Alexander had a question to put to the god. We know neither the question nor the answer, but he was greeted at the oracle as 'son of Ammon', one of many intimations of his divine status. Thus encouraged, he marched north and east into Mesopotamia, where at Gaugamela (331 BC) he defeated Darius again, this time decisively. The Persian Empire, which had been a threat to the Greeks for more than 200 years, was now in the hands of Alexander.

Alexander did more than simply take over the Persian Empire. He continued his campaigns into the eastern part of it, putting down revolts and founding cities. In the far north-east, in Sogdiana, resistance was fierce, but Alexander captured the final stronghold, and an unbelievably beautiful woman, Roxane. He fell in love and married her. There was also other business in hand. He crossed from Afghanistan into the Punjab where he defeated the Indian king. Only a revolt of his troops prevented him from going further east, and he returned west via Baluchistan, a disastrous journey reminiscent of Napoleon's retreat from Moscow. Two years later, in 323, he died at Babylon, aged only thirty-two.

Alexander left behind not only conquests, but also monarchy. Monarchy, a traditional part of the Macedonian state, had been peripheral to the Greek world until the reign of Philip. Alexander succeeded in making it central. He provided a model for the series of Hellenistic kings that followed. The diadem, the plain headband worn by Alexander, became the standard symbol of monarchy; the title 'king', which Alexander had probably begun to use when addressing the Greeks, was employed by all the Hellenistic rulers and, as we shall see, there were generally accepted conditions for the assumption of the title. Stories about Alexander no doubt established the expectation that kings should have a striking personal appearance and a dignified bearing, or, less favourably, that they had arrogant pretensions and an offensive and haughty manner of dealing with visitors. Like it or not, the model of kingship was established.

Alexander's followers aspired not only to his ideals but also to his lands. The twenty years following his death saw tortuous struggles between his kin and his generals as each attempted to establish himself as his sole successor. The attempts failed, and by about 275 BC there had emerged the three kingdoms which were to dominate the eastern Mediterranean until the Romans came. First, Egypt. Ptolemy, who was granted Egypt at the death of Alexander, succeeded in founding a dynasty which ruled the country until his most famous descendant, Cleopatra, was defeated by Augustus (31 BC). The Ptolemies also at various times controlled lands outside Egypt: Libya, southern Syria, Cyprus, parts of southern Turkey, and the Aegean islands.

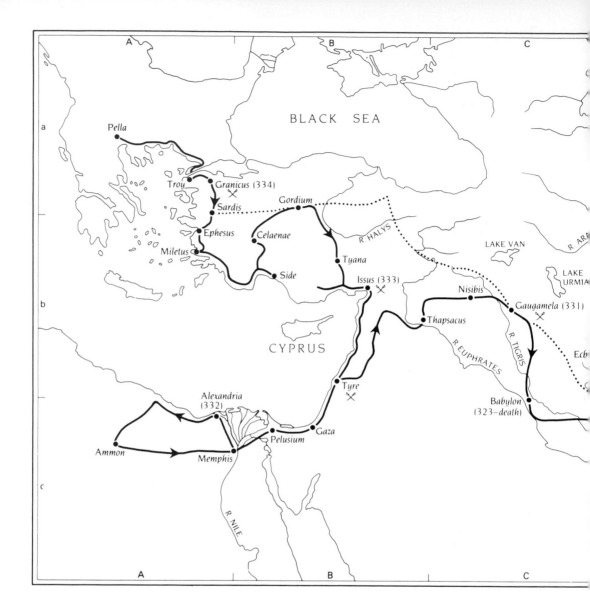

Secondly, the eastern conquests of Alexander. The capture of Babylon in 312 by Seleucus marked the foundation of the Seleucid dynasty. Seleucid territory at its greatest extent was by far the largest of any of the Hellenistic kingdoms; with its centre in Syria, it ranged from western Turkey through to Afghanistan. But it lost territory, both in the East and in the West. In the East there were two problems. The mountainous province of Bactria (Afghanistan) was turned into an independent Greek kingdom (256 BC), and there also emerged the non-Greek kingdom of Parthia (c.238) which effectively blocked the Seleucids from the east. In the West the Seleucids also lost ground. A new Greek kingdom of the Attalids with its capital at Pergamum was carved out of Seleucid territory in western Turkey. Though the first two Attalids (283–241) had been only partially

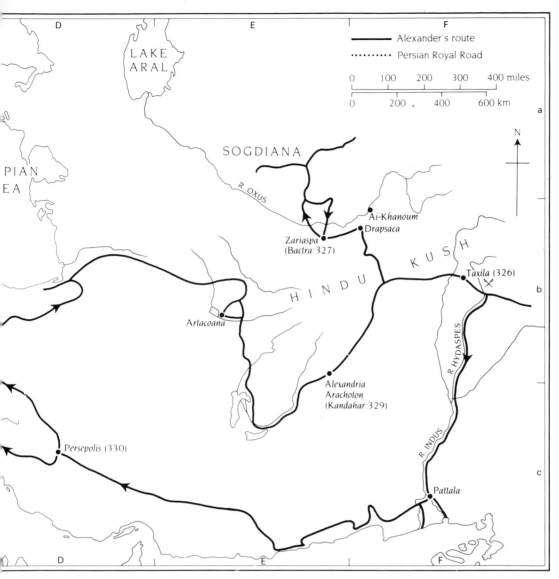

MAP 6. ALEXANDER'S JOURNEYS

independent of the Seleucids, the victory of Attalus I over the Galatians (*c*.238) allowed him to assume the title of king. In the second century Attalid power was further increased by Rome, to whom the kingdom was bequeathed by the last king (133). The Seleucid kingdom itself by the first century BC had been reduced (partly because of internal dissension) to a small area of northern Syria, and it finally fell into the hands of Rome (64 BC).

Thirdly, Macedon. The ancient dynasty from which Alexander himself came was exterminated, and possession of the land was fiercely contested, no doubt partly because it was Alexander's country, until in 276 Antigonus Gonatas succeeded in establishing himself securely in power. His heirs, the Antigonid dynasty, ruled the country until it was conquered by Rome in 168 BC.

STATUE OF A GAULISH CHIEFTAIN, the so-called Ludovisi Gaul, thought to be a copy of a bronze original which formed part of a monument set up in Pergamum in the late third century BC to commemorate Attalus I's victory over the Galatians. Various elements, including the arms of the warrior and the left arm of his dead wife, are modern restorations.

The Limits of Hellenism 315

The Limits of Hellenism

Within the boundaries established by the conquests of Alexander there were dramatic cultural changes as Hellenization spread thousands of miles over the whole of the Middle East. This process used to be seen through rose-tinted spectacles as the innocent gift of civilization to the benighted barbarians; after all the British were doing precisely the same thing in their empire. No doubt the Greeks themselves saw matters in this way. But our own post-colonial age is more aware that culture is intimately bound up with politics: we can see that Greek culture dominated other, ancient cultures, and that this process of Hellenization was in part a product of the power of the kings.

The creation of new Greek cities was fundamental to the process of Hellenization (for their design see below, p. 386). Alexander himself was reported to have founded over seventy cities (the actual figure may be half that), while the Seleucids created over sixty new settlements in the area from western Turkey to Iran. Some of these 'new' cities were in fact old settlements with a new, dynastic name and a Greek constitution. Others were in areas previously not highly urbanized. For example, the second Seleucid king founded a new city on the

AERIAL VIEW OF ANTIOCH ON THE ORONTES (modern Antakya, in south-eastern Turkey). Founded by Seleucus I in 300 BC and named after his son Antiochus, this new city became the capital of the Seleucid Empire. It shows the typical gridiron plan of the Seleucid foundations, with five avenues running south-west to north-east and at least twenty streets running cross-wise.

Persian Gulf, naming it Antioch after himself, and later took steps to increase its population by 'inviting' Magnesia on the Maeander, an old city in western Turkey, to send out colonists. New cities were founded even where there were perfectly adequate existing settlements. Thus in Egypt two Greek cities were founded, of which one, Alexandria, replaced the old Pharaonic city of Memphis as the Ptolemaic capital; while the ancient city of Babylon was superseded by the new Seleucid capital Seleucia on the Tigris, some 50 kilometres away. There could be no clearer illustration than these two cities of the dominance which the Greeks were to exercise over the non-Greek populations.

The new settlements varied enormously in size and status. First, there were the military colonies founded by the Seleucids in various parts of their kingdom, from western Turkey to (it seems) Kurdestan. These settlements might be small, with only a few hundred men, and they had few autonomous institutions and little independence from the king. Their purpose was to act as a safeguard against disaffection and their inhabitants were obliged to serve in the king's army (below, p. 321). Secondly, there were the new, independent cities with populations of several thousands, ranging up to Alexandria, a great cultural centre, which in the first century BC was reckoned to be the largest city in the (Mediterranean) world.

The culture of these cities was strongly Greek. At the most obvious level there developed a new Greek language, the *koinē* or common language, which transcended the divisions of the old Greek dialects (Dorian, Ionic, and so on). There is generally nothing in the language or the script of a document to indicate from which part of the Greek world it comes. In addition, the political institutions of the cities were closely modelled on traditional Greek practices. Susa, for example, one of the four Persian royal centres, was refounded in the late fourth century as Seleucia on the Eulaeus. Over 300 years later the city, by then in the Parthian Empire, still had a constitution which would have been familiar to a Greek of the classical period; the council proposed and scrutinized candidates for public office, who were then elected by the full body of the citizens. There was a treasurer and a college of magistrates, of whom two gave their name to the year. Seleucia illustrates both the 'exporting' of Greek constitutions and the tenacity with which they were maintained in an alien world.

One of the key institutions which supported the Greek culture of the cities was the *gymnasion* (above, p. 220). This was not just a place for a casual work-out; it was an educational institution promoting both physical and intellectual culture. The building itself was often centrally placed and at Alexandria, for instance, was reckoned to be the most beautiful building in the city. More importantly, all full members of the city were expected to belong to the *gymnasion*. Strict rules governed eligibility for admission. In mainland Greece we hear of the exclusion of (among others) slaves, freedmen, their sons, and those practising vulgar trades. It is likely that in the new foundations such rules effectively excluded those who were deemed not to be Greek. But those natives who did succeed in proving their eligibility had to exercise in the *gymnasion* naked—an abomination to

The Limits of Hellenism 317

non-Greeks. Stripping naked marked their alienation from their native background and their incorporation into the Greek world.

The remarkable cultural achievements of the Greeks must not blind us to their exclusivity against indigenous cultures. For example, the population of Seleucia on the Eulaeus remained exclusively Greek. Even 300 years after its foundation there is no known case where a person with a Greek name did not have a father with a Greek name. That is, there was no Hellenization of the native population, which remained excluded from the civic institutions. Similarly in Egypt there was a sharp divide between Greek and native culture. The Egyptians continued to build temples on the traditional model and to produce a lively and diverse literature of their own (there are as many Hellenistic papyri in demotic Egyptian as in Greek). But the Greeks commissioned sculpture which shows no points of contact with Egyptian art and resolutely read literature of the classical period. In the field of law too, there were separate Greek and Egyptian courts administering different law-codes, while the law of Alexandria itself was modelled in part on that of Athens.

The continuing coexistence of cultures is not an indication of liberal pluralism. Greek culture was dominant, even if kings did sometimes show respect for native cultures and were happy for their rule to be honoured in native contexts (the Ptolemies, for example, were depicted like the Pharaoh in Egyptian temples). The only way to gain entry to the new system of power lay in the adoption of Greek culture. One of the key strategies was to claim ancestral Greek connections. Thus about 200 BC a leading citizen of Sidon, an ancient Phoenician city, was able to compete in (and win) one of the 'Panhellenic' competitions in mainland Greece open only to Greeks; his eligibility was proved by the 'fact' that Thebes in Boeotia was founded by the son of the first ruler of Sidon. When it was convenient the Greeks themselves employed the same strategy to integrate outsiders into the Greek world. The city of Lampsacus in north-west Turkey appealed to the Romans for their help against the Seleucid king Antiochus III on the ground that they were kinsmen: Lampsacus was near the site of Troy, the home of Aeneas the founder of Rome. Lampsacus could not foresee how momentous the subsequent involvement of Rome would be for the history of the Greek world.

Conflict over non-Greek communities' adoption of foreign ways did sometimes arise; the interaction of Judaism and Hellenism in the second century BC is the best-documented example. The leader of one faction of Jews in Jerusalem succeeded in becoming High Priest with the backing of the Seleucid king Antiochus IV and immediately set up a *gymnasion* (174-171). To the horror of the rest of the Jews, the priests ceased to show any interest in the divine services and hurried off to take part in the unlawful exercises on the training ground at the earliest opportunities. Some even gave up circumcision. Though the subsequent events are obscure (we are dependent almost entirely on 'orthodox' Jewish sources, especially the first two Books of the Maccabees), opposition both to the Hellenizing party and to their backer Antiochus grew. This reached crisis point

HEAD OF A PTOLEMY IN THE GUISE OF
AN EGYPTIAN PHARAOH. The dichotomy
in style between the official portraits of the
Ptolemies, produced by Greek artists, and their
portraits in Egyptian contexts, which
continued the Pharaonic tradition, reflects the
dichotomy between Greek and native cultures
in Hellenistic Egypt.

when Antiochus stripped the Temple of its treasures and ordered the Jews to give
up their distinctive ways, replacing Jewish with pagan cults. Open insurrection
followed, which soon led to the restoration of Temple cult, but the conflict
between the Jews and the Seleucids continued until the Jews gained their independence in 141 BC.

This affair illuminates the relationship between Hellenism and the power of
the kings. The Greeks believed in their cultural superiority over 'barbarians', and
for them this belief justified political dominance. We, however, need to look
further at the political function of Hellenism. The populations of the new cities
were, at least initially, drawn largely from the old Greek world, and the culture
of the cities remained resolutely Greek. The Greek inhabitants of a new city on
the shores of the Persian Gulf were tied to their king by both culture and self-
interest, needing support from the king in an alien world. Through the cities the
kings could control their territories without the need for a substantial royal
bureaucracy. Antiochus IV would naturally help the Hellenizing party in Jerusalem, especially as it probably intended to transform Jerusalem into a Greek city
named after him. Active resistance to Hellenism was strong only in three areas,
Egypt, Persia, and Judaea; all three had firm traditions of indigenous monarchy,

and all three formulated their resistance in religious terms. The Book of Daniel, composed at the time of Antiochus IV, foresaw the further extension of his rule:

Yet he will come to his end—there will be no help for him. At that time Michael will stand up, the great prince who mounts guard over your people. There is going to be a time of great distress, unparalleled since nations first came into existence. When that time comes, your own people will be spared, all those whose names are found written in the Book. (12:1)

Courtiers and Soldiers

The king was the key figure in the royal administration. To him were addressed petitions by individuals and communities, and all major decisions were represented as emanating from the king himself. Not that the king stood alone. The Seleucid king had an official in charge of the royal finances and also one general aide 'in charge of affairs'. To return to the Second Book of the Maccabees, the successor of Antiochus IV decided to reverse his father's policy of forcible Hellenization of the Jews and wrote to 'his brother Lysias' to that effect. Lysias was not in fact the king's brother, but his assistant, holding various titles: 'brother', 'cousin', and 'in charge of affairs'.

Outside the court the king could act through a hierarchy of officials. The Seleucid kingdom was divided into a number of provinces (seventy-two in the time of Seleucus I), each under a governor; Lysias, for example, was governor of southern Syria and Phoenicia when Antiochus IV died. Through the governors the king could carry out plans, specific or general. Antiochus III was responsible for initiating a cult of himself and his ancestors throughout his kingdom; he later wrote to the governors of each province, informing them of the appointment of high priestesses of the queen in each province and instructing them to make the necessary arrangements. (There happen to survive three copies of Antiochus' letter, from western Turkey and Iran. For the very different royal cults organized by cities see below, p. 330.) The governors then issued instructions to their deputies to carry out the royal provisions.

In Egypt the royal administration was larger and more elaborate; the Ptolemies, in contrast to the Seleucids, had only three Greek cities in Egypt to provide a basic administrative framework. They therefore adopted the Pharaonic organization of the country: Egypt was divided into about forty 'districts', each subdivided into 'areas' and 'villages'; each unit of each tier was the responsibility of a specific official. The Ptolemies added to this Pharaonic system a new military organization with soldiers stationed throughout Egypt and a more complex taxation system.

The administration of both the Ptolemies and the Seleucids was staffed largely by Greeks, not by natives. The Seleucid ruling class completely excluded subject populations for about two generations; even after that it never included more than about 2.5 per cent of non-Greeks. One exception shows how non-Greeks might be admitted in peculiar circumstances. The First Book of the Maccabees recounts how two rivals for the Seleucid throne (Demetrius I and Alexander

Balas) contended for the support of Jonathan, the Jewish leader. Alexander gave Jonathan a whole series of titles normally accorded only to Greeks—'friend of the king', 'brother', 'first friend'—and finally a gold brooch 'of the kind customarily presented to the cousins of the king'. Jonathan thus reached the highest grade of court dignitaries, and for a time he did indeed support Alexander Balas. Similarly in Egypt the forms and language of the administration became Greek, and Egyptians were employed only so long as they learned Greek. The systems of royal administration thus served to reinforce both the dominance of Greek culture and the power of the king. But courtiers and administrators stood on the backs of the soldiers.

Warfare was basic to the Hellenistic world, in two ways. First, the legitimacy of the Hellenistic king rested in part on his military prestige (contrast the individual city-state where authority rested on tradition). The king, like Alexander and the Homeric heroes, was expected to take part in the hardships of campaigns and even in the dangers of combat. On one occasion the appearance of the king in battle inspired his men with courage and struck terror into the enemy. Victory also justified the assumption of the title of king, as we have already observed. A successful military expedition to the East even allowed the Seleucid Antiochus III to be called 'the Great King'.

Secondly, the scope of warfare was enlarged. When conflict was simply between two neighbouring cities over disputed territory the implications of warfare were limited; by contrast, in the Hellenistic period there was everything to fight for. Huge areas of land were regularly in dispute, even if the heartlands of each of the kingdoms remained secure throughout the period. The whole of mainland Greece, the Aegean islands, western Turkey, and southern Syria were fought over by various kings. The greater scale of the prizes, in comparison with the classical period, was responsible for an increased brutality. The total destruction of cities and the enslavement of their citizens by the kings became more common; the scale of Roman brutality towards Greece was even greater. The actual size of battles also increased. Whereas the decisive battle of Philip of Macedon against the Greeks at Chaeronea saw forces on each side of about 30,000, the Hellenistic kings could range 60,000 to 80,000 troops against each other. This was the maximum size of army thought possible as late as the eighteenth century.

The fundamental importance of warfare for the kings entailed major changes in military organization. Even those features of warfare that went back into the fourth century were given a new importance. (See above, pp. 136 f. for the earlier developments.) Heavy-armed infantry (hoplites) had long been the basic fighting force of Greece; Philip's reorganization of the Macedonian army created an improved heavy-armed infantry (the phalanx) which differed from the old primarily in replacing the short thrusting spear with a long pike (about 5.5 m. in the time of Alexander; about 6.5 m. a century later). This type of force, along with an important cavalry arm, formed the core of the Hellenistic armies.

The kings also made novel arrangements to ensure an adequate supply of men

ALEXANDER IN THE VAN OF BATTLE, detail of a figured frieze on a sarcophagus from the royal cemetery at Sidon (Phoenicia) (*c*.325–300 BC). The great king's exploits in battle cost him several wounds but set an example for his successors to imitate. On horseback at the left, he is shown wearing the heroic lion's-scalp helmet which likens him to Heracles.

for their forces. Ordinary cities seem to have supplied few men for the royal armies; special arrangements had to be made. The Seleucids, as we have already seen, established numerous military colonies, whose landholders were obliged to serve in the army; their sons had the option of forming the Guard, another part of the regular army. The Ptolemies followed a slightly different policy of granting scattered landholdings which were in principle revocable. In contrast to fifth- and fourth-century Athens, where war orphans were given public financial support until they came of age, in Egypt one official could write to another: 'the cavalry men listed below have died; therefore take back their holdings for the crown.' This is the world of professional, not citizen, soldiers.

The kings supplemented their basic fighting force by employing mercenaries. Mercenaries were not new in this period (above, p. 136), but their importance increased greatly. Alexander had tens of thousands in his service and they formed an important element in the Hellenistic armies, sometimes in the phalanx, but more often as light-armed troops. Mercenaries generally have a bad reputation (down to Shakespeare's braggart soldier and beyond), but this is largely unjustified. As professional soldiers, they were concerned about their pay, and on one occasion they abandoned a defeated king and went over to the other side. But mercenaries did not betray their king for gold. After some difficulties with one of the Attalid kings, his mercenaries even took a solemn oath of obedience to him and his descendants. The king did not have the unquestioned allegiance which a general of the classical period could assume from his own citizens, but equally disloyalty was rare.

The techniques of combat of these armies, despite the continuing reliance on heavy-armed troops, became more sophisticated. The most extravagant novelty was elephants. Five hundred were given by the Indian king to Seleucus I in 302 in return for a cessation of hostilities. Four hundred of them were able to fight on his side and played an important part in securing him a crucial victory the following year.

Many of these elephants continued in Seleucid service, and, despite attempts to breed elephants in Syria, fresh supplies were called for occasionally; an astronomical tablet in cuneiform records the sending from Babylon to Syria of twenty elephants which had been delivered by the governor of Afghanistan. The Ptolemies also had war elephants; the first Ptolemy had a force of Indian elephants, but the Seleucid kingdom later cut off the supply from India and the Ptolemies had to use the smaller African variety ('forest' elephants), which they went to considerable lengths to capture. Unfortunately elephants were cumbersome—soldiers learned to sidestep their attacks and then stab the elephants' flanks or even to hamstring them—and they did not transform the patterns of warfare.

A comparable phenomenon is the competition between the major kingdoms in building ever more elaborate and impressive ships of war. Down to the time of Alexander the standard Greek warship was the trireme, a ship whose design

TERRACOTTA STATUETTE FROM MYRINA, showing an Indian war-elephant crushing a Celt, perhaps a reference to Antiochus I's victory over the Galatians about 272 BC. Elephants, often described as the tanks of ancient warfare, were an important element in the armies of Hellenistic times, notably in the Seleucid army, which secured them from India, and that of the Ptolemies, which got them from north Africa.

ROUNDED TOWER IN THE WALLS OF ASSOS (north-western Turkey). Built in ashlar masonry in the Pergamene style of the second century BC, this tower bears witness to Hellenistic developments in siege warfare—slit windows for bolt-projecting catapults are set half-way up, and broader openings for stone-projectors at the top.

is much disputed (it either had three banks of oars or three men to an oar). From the end of the fourth century onwards the standard warship was the quinquireme, rowed with five men to an oar. There were also prestige ships which reached fantastic sizes in the third century: we hear of a 'seven', 'eleven', 'thirteen', 'sixteen', 'twenty', 'thirty', and even a 'forty'. It is not clear how these ships actually worked, and their limited usefulness is indicated by the fact that the Romans never found it necessary to employ such showy vessels. But this ancient naval arms race, along with the trouble taken to maintain a supply of elephants, are vivid tokens of the dependence of the kings on military prestige.

Changes in siege techniques were of greater importance militarily. In the classical period good walls had been impregnable; the Spartans never even threatened the Long Walls which connected Athens to the sea. However, the development of the torsion catapult, probably by Philip, tilted the balance decisively away from the besieged in favour of the besieger. Alexander's use of the catapult and of siege towers enabled him to capture every city he assaulted. In response walls were made more sturdy, but further improvements were made in catapults. The patronage of Ptolemy II resulted in the discovery of formulas which enabled a precise calibration of the weight of missile against desired range. Some cities did still make successful resistance, but by now no individual city could feel secure when faced with an assault by a king. This crucial fact underlies the dominance of kings over cities.

The Kings and the Cities

Reconciling the power of the kings with the traditions of the cities was a recurrent problem of the Hellenistic period. The kings had overwhelming superiority over almost all individual cities, while the cities possessed the ideal of political independence. In the face of this contradiction, how could the kings wield their power and the cities maintain their dignity?

The problem was eased because the kings did not set out to impose positive policies on the cities. Like the early Roman Emperors, they were an essentially passive force, interested primarily in hegemony. They did not on the whole issue direct instructions to their subject cities. There were, however, ways of ensuring that the royal will was followed. For example, Alexander wanted to have exiles restored to their cities, but he had no need to issue orders directly to the cities. He had a letter read out at the Olympic games informing the assembled exiles that he would ensure their return. The operative legislation was carried out by the cities themselves. A decree of Mytilene which was probably passed after this announcement happens to survive in part; it makes detailed arrangements for the restoration of exiles, but merely refers to 'the settlements which the king [Alexander] has determined' and establishes a celebration of the king's birthday.

Without making crude interventions in cities, the kings infringed the freedom of cities both externally and internally. Externally they constrained the scope of a city's foreign policy, without having to direct it explicitly. Thus Antioch on the Persian Gulf agreed to participate in the new games of Magnesia on the Maeander (a non-political act), but carefully avoided a direct response to Magnesia's request for special diplomatic status ('holy and inviolate'). Despite its gratitude to Magnesia for having provided colonists, Antioch knew that this was a matter for the Seleucid king to decide.

Internally, the kings infringed civic freedom by raising large amounts of money from the cities. In principle all cities subject to particular kings were liable to pay them tribute, though the picture is obscure and we cannot quantify total royal revenues. But the imposition of tribute on individual cities might be a heavy burden. Miletus, for example, once had to borrow money from another city in order to pay its annual tribute of 25 talents. The scale of the tribute is clear not only from Miletus' difficulties but also from a comparison with the fifth century when the maximum Miletus is known to have paid Athens was only 10 talents. The kings also made special levies in case of war and controlled certain local taxes.

Some cities were able to gain exemptions from these royal controls. Politically the king could permit a city 'freedom and autonomy', that is, the ability to determine its policies both internally and externally. 'Freedom and autonomy' was a privilege, which the king could always rescind, but it should not therefore be seen as meaningless. The slogan, proclaimed by the immediate successors of Alexander, remained a potent political ideal, and cities treated it very seriously. Indeed one city (Colophon), when given its freedom at the end of the fourth century, decided to build itself fortifications, a vivid token of independence within the framework laid down by the kings.

Exemptions from financial obligations were also made. Tribute was the most resented royal imposition on the cities, as it had been in the fifth-century Athenian Empire, and some cities were fortunate enough to gain remission. Miletus, when it passed into the Ptolemaic sphere of influence, was able to gain the remission of 'harsh and oppressive taxes and tolls which certain of the kings had imposed'. While some remissions were made by the kings as a matter of principle, often they occurred in order to alleviate particular distress. Thus when the Seleucid king Antiochus III took over Teos in Ionia from the Attalid kingdom (in the words of a Tean decree), 'he saw that we were exhausted both in our public and in our private affairs because of the continual wars and the great burden of contributions we were bearing ... He therefore granted to our city and territory to be holy, inviolate and free from tribute, and undertook to free us himself from the other contributions we were paying to King Attalus [I].'

Subtle forms of indirect control over the cities also existed which helped to ensure peace and public order. First, in regulating the relations between two cities the kings adopted the traditional practice of appointing a third city as an arbitrator. For example, when Antigonus wanted to ensure peaceful relations between two cities (Teos and Lebedus) which he wished to unite into one city, he appointed a third city (Mytilene) to settle any disputed lawsuits between the members of the two cities.

Secondly, the kings or their officials used indirect means of ensuring harmony within cities. The judicial apparatus of individual cities often broke down because of internal political tensions; the problem was not new, but there developed in the early Hellenistic age the practice of requesting another city to provide an impartial panel of judges. Such requests, particularly in the early part of the period, often originated with the king or one of his agents; for example, a Ptolemaic official 'wishing the city [of Samos] to be in a state of concord, wrote a letter requesting the people of Myndus to send a panel of judges to settle the contracts in suspense.' The growth of this practice is probably due to the concern of the kings that their cities be docile. Both practices, that of arbitration and that of foreign judges, were convenient devices enabling the kings to secure harmony between and within cities without involving invidious direct interventions.

Civic Life Transformed

Royal control, even if mediated indirectly, had important implications for the internal politics of the subject cities. It underlies the paradox that, while democracy was accepted by all as the ideal civic constitution, in practice real popular participation in government declined in the Hellenistic age and dominance by the wealthy increased.

Democracy was espoused by the kings from Alexander onwards. Alexander himself established democracies in place of tyrannies and oligarchies in the Greek cities of Asia Minor which he freed from Persian rule; this gross interference with their internal affairs was presumably a popular move. His successors on the whole pursued the same policy. Thus the new cities established by Hellenistic kings were all, it seems, based upon democratic principles; all had magistrates, a council, and a popular assembly. The old cities also continually asserted the desirability of democracy against oligarchy or tyranny. Citizens newly incorporated into the city of Cos had to swear the following oath:

I will abide by the established democracy . . . and the ancestral laws of Cos . . . I will also abide by the friendship and alliance with King Ptolemy and the treaties ratified by the people with the allies; I will never set up under any pretext an oligarchy or a tyranny or any other constitution apart from democracy, and if anyone else establishes such a regime I will not obey, but will prevent him as far as possible . . . (Austin, no. 133).

Such measures helped to ensure that actual oligarchies were confined to the fringes of the Greek world. Tyrannies did sometimes arise, but the real danger lay in the informal monopolization of power by the wealthy. The kings could pose as democrats while being indirectly responsible for the growing power of the rich.

In the Athenian democracy of the fifth and fourth centuries a delicate balance had been established between the power of the people and the power of the rich. The rich served the community by paying for religious festivals and for the maintenance of the fleet, and in return gained great prestige. But the people did not allow individuals to gain too much honour; they turned down the offer made by Pericles and his sons to pay for some building works, in favour of expenditure from the tribute money. But by the end of the fourth century the balance between the power of rich and poor had shifted in favour of the rich. Cities became dependent on the rich for their very survival.

Wealthy individuals now played a crucial role in mediating between their city and the king, thus gaining power over the city. One rich Athenian, the comic poet Philippides, over a twenty-year period (301–283/2 BC) was able to confer great benefactions on his city. Being at the court of King Lysimachus, he could gain from the king gifts of wheat, money, and other supplies; he buried Athenians who had died in battle, and gained the release of others who had been taken prisoner. In the past officially appointed civic ambassadors, rather than informal 'friends' of the king, had performed the task of diplomacy; the cities had not needed to depend on their own citizens for favours. The danger which the cities felt about the new situation is captured by one phrase in the decree honouring Philippides: 'and he has never said or done anything contrary to the democracy'. It might have been otherwise.

The wealthy also now began to deploy their wealth within the city in a more blatant manner, and gained overwhelming prestige. Though in many places the change from the classical system was gradual, as the cities became accustomed to dependence, in Athens a specific reform was carried out by a tyrant backed by Macedon. The new system, which gave the rich much greater prominence within the city, is well illustrated by Philippides.

When he was appointed agonothete [in charge of the city's competitions, in 284/3 BC] he complied with the will of the people voluntarily from his own funds, offered the ancestral sacrifices to the gods on behalf of the people, gave to all the Athenians (presents) at all the contests and was the first to provide an additional contest for Demeter and Kore [Persephone] as a memorial of the people's liberty, and augmented the other contests and sacrifices on behalf of the city and for all this he spent much money from his own personal resources and rendered his accounts according to the laws. (Austin, no. 43).

The cities devised a whole series of honours designed to recompense the rich for their services. Thus the Athenians voted Philippides a gold crown and a bronze statue in the theatre and for him and his descendants free public meals and a seat of honour at all the contests organized by the city. Honours, rather than laws, now formed the framework which defined the relationship of wealthy and city, and honours inevitably left the power with the rich.

This transformation of the relationship between rich and poor is linked to a decline in real democracy, that is, genuine popular control over political life. Popular assemblies continued to meet and to pass decrees, but the power of magistrates and council over them was greater than in the radical Athenian democracy. Magistracies themselves became the preserve of the rich, in part because of the growing expectation of considerable private expenditure from them. Aristotle in his *Politics* had already offered advice to oligarchs on how to control a state which prefigures Hellenistic practice: 'Those who enter into office may also be reasonably expected to offer magnificent sacrifices and to erect some public building, so that the common people, participating in the feasts and seeing their city embellished with offerings and buildings, may readily tolerate a continuation of this constitution [oligarchy]' (*Politics* 6.1321ᵃ).

In addition to the *de facto* restriction of office-holding to the wealthy, the popular courts, which had underpinned the Athenian democracy, also fell into their hands. In early-third-century Ptolemaic Egypt an uproar in council and assembly was quelled by the magistrates, who 'then voted that the council and the lawcourts should be recruited from pre-selected men.' Preselection would help to end uproar, that is, popular participation. Local courts were also circumvented by the use of judges from other cities for particularly sensitive cases, who were all well-to-do. Rome then consolidated the *de facto* power of the wealthy by instituting technical wealth qualifications for office-holding. But the assemblies continued to be open to all citizens, and so the constitutions were still 'democracies'. The political cant of the period strikes a curiously modern note. Today too we are all 'democrats': the western democracies, the Union of Soviet Socialist Republics, the People's Republic of China, and Democratic Kampuchea alike.

The decline in popular power was not, however, a peaceful process. There was always the danger of revolutionary activity. The citizens of one place in Crete were obliged in the third century BC to swear an oath of loyalty to the city, which included the following revealing clause: 'and I will not initiate a redistribution of land or of houses or of dwelling-sites or a cancellation of debts.' The fear of the two revolutionary demands, the redistribution of land and the cancellation of debts, does not often come to the surface of Hellenistic history. But it helps to explain, for example, an otherwise peculiar clause in a loan contract between Praxicles, an individual from Naxos, and the city of Arcesine on Amorgos at the turn of the fourth and third centuries: if the city did not repay the money, Praxicles was entitled to exact it by any means he chose from both the public and the private property of the Arcesineans and those living in Arcesine. Such a clause was the only protection for Praxicles against a legal cancellation of debts by the city.

The tensions between rich and poor were aggravated by the advent of Rome, and there was popular agitation, which the Romans naturally portrayed in the worst possible light. A Roman governor at the end of the second century BC sentenced to death those responsible for the burning and destruction of the town hall and the public records and the drafting of laws contrary to the (oligarchic) constitution given by the Romans to the Achaeans: 'those who carried out these things were to my mind manifestly laying the foundations of the worst state of affairs and of disorder for all Greeks—for not only are these things in keeping with a state of mutual disaffection and cancellation of debts, but they are also at odds with the freedom returned in common to all the Greeks and with our policy.' Roman freedom did not include the freedom to re-establish true democracies.

As these 'disturbances' indicate, the Greek city was far from dead in the Hellenistic period. There is no sign that people in general began to feel lost in the new world or to retreat towards quietism (below, p. 365). The cities, rather than the Hellenistic kingdoms, continued to provide the basic focus of attachment for their inhabitants and to have much vitality; in illustration of this point, I close by considering two types of civic response to royal power.

First, leagues of cities, which were a feature of mainland Greece in the Hellenistic period. In contrast to the classical leagues dominated by a single city (Athens or Sparta) these new leagues were an attempt by a number of small cities to group themselves in the face of the threat of royal power. The Achaean League, centred in the northern Peloponnese, is our best example. By the early part of the third century this ancient league had fallen into disarray; some of the cities had garrisons imposed on them by the Macedonians, others tyrannies. In the 280s and 270s some seven small cities came together to form the new Achaean League, expelling their tyrants and garrisons. Under the leadership of their great statesman Aratus, the league continued to pursue a single goal, 'the expulsion of the Macedonians from the Peloponnese, the overthrow of tyrannies, and the guarantee for each city of their common, ancestral freedom'. The institutions of the league—a primary assembly, a council and elected magistrates—formed, in theory, a democratic constitution which enshrined the equality of the member states. The competence of the league was limited to foreign policy; it, like the kings, passed a decree recognizing the special diplomatic status requested by Magnesia on the Maeander. There was no intervention in the internal running of the cities. Until Aratus turned to the Macedonian king to save the league from Sparta and perhaps also to ward off popular revolution in the Peloponnese (227-224), the league succeeded in preserving civic independence from royal power.

COINS OF THE ACHAEAN LEAGUE (after 280 BC). The idea of confederacy is emphasized by the silver coinage, which employs a common obverse type, the laureate head of Zeus, but varies the details of the reverse according to the city of issue. Within a wreath, tied either above or below, is set the Achaean League monogram (based on the Greek letters A and CH) and different letters and symbols, here a flying dove for Sicyon (*left*) and a winged horse for Corinth (*above*).

Secondly, civic cults of kings. It is a striking feature of the Hellenistic (and Roman) cities that they established cults of their rulers. Some see these cults simply as political honours, which are a mark of the decline of the traditional civic cults. I suggest on the contrary that cults of the gods were not in decline in the Hellenistic period (the special diplomatic status which Magnesia on the Maeander sought was because of her cult of Artemis), and that the royal cults were an attempt to relate king and city by incorporating the king within the main symbolic system of the city.

The cult of Antiochus III at Teos offers a good illustration. Teos had been captured by Antiochus from the Attalids and gained certain privileges (*c.*204), as we have seen (above, p. 325). In return the city established a cult which related Antiochus and his wife to Dionysus, the chief god of the city. Cult statues of the king and queen were dedicated beside the cult statue of Dionysus in his temple. There was also a cult statue of the king in the council house, and each year an offering of the first fruits was placed before this cult statue, which was also crowned with the produce of the seasons. The king, like Dionysus, is associated with the fertility of the crops; in particular, the Teans explained, his benefactions to the city had made agriculture more profitable. The cult of Antiochus allowed the citizens to represent the power of the king to themselves in a comprehensible and acceptable form. But Antiochus was shortly afterwards defeated by Rome. Perhaps only a decade or two after the cult of Antiochus was established, the neighbouring island of Chios established a cult of Roma, the personification of the power of Rome. There was a festival with a procession, a sacrifice, competitions, and a dedication probably showing the wolf suckling Romulus and Remus. With that the Greek cities entered a new period of their history.

Further Reading

The best general account of the period in English is F. W. Walbank, *The Hellenistic World* (London, 1981), with a good bibliography. See also W. W. Tarn and G. T. Griffith, *Hellenistic Civilisation*[3] (London, 1952); P. Grimal *et al.*, *Hellenism and the Rise of Rome* (London, 1968); C. B. Welles, *Alexander and the Hellenistic World* (Toronto, 1970). For more detail see the classic work of M. I. Rostovtzeff, *The Social and Economic History of the Hellenistic World*, 3 vols. (Oxford, 1941), M Cary, *A History of the Greek World from 323 to 146 B.C.*[2] (London, 1963), and the new edition of the *Cambridge Ancient History*, VII.1 (Cambridge, 1984). The key sources, including most of those that I discuss, are translated in M. M. Austin, *The Hellenistic World from Alexander to the Roman Conquest* (Cambridge, 1981), with a useful supplement in R. S. Bagnall and P. Derow, *Greek Historical Documents: the Hellenistic Period* (California, 1981). For the historians see Ch. 8.

Alexander has found numerous biographers. R. Lane Fox, *Alexander the Great* (London, 1973) is lively, J. R. Hamilton, *Alexander the Great* (London, 1973) more balanced; R. Lane Fox, *The Search for Alexander* (London, 1980) includes excellent photographs. The political histories of the individual kingdoms are listed by Walbank (above). G. J. D. Aalders, *Political Thought in Hellenistic Times* (Amsterdam, 1975) includes kingship theory, and some texts on this subject are translated by J. F. Gardner, *Leadership and the Cult of the Personality* (London and Toronto, 1974).

On the Greeks in India see R. Thapar, *A History of India*, I (Harmondsworth, 1966), V. Dehejia, *Early Buddhist Rock Temples* (London, 1972), J. W. Sedlar, *India and the Greek World: A*

Study in the Transmission of Culture (Totowa, 1980). For Afghanistan see F. R. Allchin and N. Hammond (eds.), *The Archaeology of Afghanistan from the Earliest Times to the Timurid Period* (London, New York, and San Francisco, 1978), which includes Ai Khanoum, and J. M. Rosenfield, *The Dynastic Arts of the Kushans* (Berkeley, 1967). For the Parthians see M. A. R. Colledge, *Parthian Art* (London, 1977), and G. Herrmann, *The Iranian Revival* (Oxford, 1977), both well illustrated. For the limits of Hellenism see S. K. Eddy, *The King is Dead: Studies in the Near Eastern Resistance to Hellenism 334–31 B.C.* (Lincoln, Nebraska, 1961), M. Hengel, *Judaism and Hellenism* (London and Philadelphia, 1974) and A. D. Momigliano, *Alien Wisdom* (Cambridge, 1975).

W. W. Tarn, *Hellenistic Military and Naval Developments* (Cambridge, 1930), G. T. Griffith, *Mercenaries of the Hellenistic World* (Cambridge, 1935), and B. Bar-Kochva, *The Seleucid Army* (Cambridge, 1976), survey different aspects of the military history.

A. H. M. Jones, *The Greek City from Alexander to Justinian* (Oxford, 1940), is basic to this and the next section. See also V. Ehrenberg, *The Greek State*[2] (London, 1969), P. M. Fraser, *Ptolemaic Alexandria* (Oxford, 1972).

A. R. Hands, *Charities and Social Aid in Greece and Rome* (London, 1968), discusses civic benefactors, and includes a dossier of texts in translation. G. E. M. de Ste Croix, *The Class Struggle in the Ancient Greek World* (London, 1981), documents the decline of democracy. S. R. F. Price, *Rituals and Power: The Roman Imperial Cult in Asia Minor* (Cambridge, 1984), includes Hellenistic ruler cults. Religious history may be approached through A. D. Nock, *Conversion* (Oxford, 1933), or H. I. Bell, *Cults and Creeds in Graeco-Roman Egypt* (Liverpool, 1953); sources are translated in F. C. Grant, *Hellenistic Religions, the Age of Syncretism* (New York, 1953).

14

Hellenistic Culture and Literature

᭬

ROBIN LANE FOX

Introduction: The World after Alexander

AFTER Alexander the horizons of the Greek world extended as far as India. Even Alexander had been surprised by the size of it all: he wondered if the Caspian Sea was the outer ocean of the world, and in India he began by thinking that the River Indus ran cosily round into Egypt's Nile. The new horizons were not altogether lost on those whom the Greeks bordered. Around 260 BC the Indian king Asoka dispatched an edict for inscription throughout his realm which referred to the 'world my children'. It listed exactly the Hellenistic kings from his Asian border through Egypt and Macedon to Cyrene in north Africa. A copy stood in Greek near the Greek and Macedonian settlement at Kandahar.

In the West, meanwhile, intriguing discoveries had been made by Pytheas, a ship's captain from Marseilles who sailed north past Scotland in, or shortly after, the age of Alexander. Noting the midnight sun, he continued north 'until there was no proper sea, land, or air, but a sort of mixture of all three like a jelly-fish, in which one can neither walk nor sail ...': anyone who has sailed in the Arctic will recognize the clamminess of the northern fog-bank. Afterwards, the best Greek geographers never made sense of Europe above and along the line of the Danube. The Celts were indiscriminate barbarians, and nobody bothered with inland Spain until the Roman conquests.

In the East, were the new settlers equally uninfluenced by their findings? At a great banquet Alexander had prayed for 'partnership' in rule between Macedonians and Persians: his partnership, however, required its orientals to speak and learn Greek. In a good story, he is said to have arranged Greek lessons for the captive women of the Persian King's family. In the East Greeks kept on exercising in Greek *gymnasia* from the Oxus to the Persian Gulf and explaining the peoples around them by their own culture's myths: the Armenians, they thought, descended from Jason, while 'Bouddhas' had followed their own Dionysus. In a world where it became usual to be bilingual, Greeks spoke and read Greek only. They imported vines into Egypt and Babylonia: wherever possible, they grew their olives. For most of them culture and politics still centred on the 'city' or *polis*, and on the disruptive power of kings who took Greece and the Aegean very seriously. The court and the city, not Persia or India, were the setting for Hellenistic culture and literature.

At the major courts the kings and their top friends had the money to be spectacular in open defiance of reason. The difference in style between a major and minor court was that the major had a bigger store of precious metal. On one winter's day in Alexandria during the 270s Ptolemy II staged a grand procession whose central section honoured Dionysus. Mechanical statues processed on huge floats; wine ran freely over the streets from vast pitchers; sweet refreshments were given out to the spectators. Actors and masses of women joined officials who had dressed as satyrs in a show which included scenes of Dionysus' drunken return from India, the figure of Alexander, and an enormous gold phallus, 180 feet long, covered with ribbons and tipped with a large gold star. The Morning Star led the way; the Evening Star brought up the rear. Between marched 2,000 oxen smothered in gold, 2,400 dogs, some giraffes, antelopes, Indian parrots, elephants, a gnu (or a hartebeest), ostriches pulling carts, and a 'white she-bear' which was not, alas, from the Arctic. The figure of 'Corinth' led a parade of women named after the cities of Ionia and the islands; she was a clear allusion to

INSCRIPTION OF ASOKA FROM KANDAHAR (Afghanistan). The great Mauryan king Asoka (*c.*268–232 BC), ruler of an empire covering much of the subcontinent of India, was converted to Buddhism about 257 and set up a number of inscriptions exhorting his subjects to lead lives of tolerance and self-sacrifice. Most were written in the native Prakrit, but in the north-west some were in Aramaic and/or (as here) in Greek.

EXEDRA IN THE *GYMNASION* AT AÏ KHANOUM, Afghanistan (late second century BC). Such recesses, equipped with benches against the walls, served as meeting-places where philosophers and other teachers gave instruction to the young men who frequented Greek *gymnasia*. The presence of a *gymnasion* at Aï Khanoum is a vivid testimony to the spread of Greek culture to the remote corners of the Hellenistic world.

the League of Corinth and the Ptolemies' concern for Greek freedom. Slaves dragged the carts and the military processed in thousands.

This extraordinary show combined artistry and free drink, the wonders of the world and a mobile zoo, the political themes of the dynasty's care for Greece and the power of a modern march-past. The elements differed in degree, not in kind, from the style of a royal wonderland which attaches to so much of the court culture in this period. It is matched by the taste for books on unscientific marvels among the literary scholars. It also shows in the royal mania for books themselves.

All the courts had libraries, even on the Black Sea, but Alexandria's are the most famous. Followers of Aristotle had settled in that city with memories of their master's learned society and great collection of books. Probably they suggested the ideas of a royal museum and library to the first Ptolemy. The royal library was probably attached to the colonnades and common room of the museum and served more as a vast arsenal of books than as a separate set of reading rooms. Nearly half a million book-rolls are alleged to have been stored inside, while another 42,000 are said to have lived in a second library attached to the temple of Serapis. Texts became hot royal property. When ships landed in Alexandria they were searched for books. Any found on board had to be surrendered for royal copying in scrolls stamped with the words 'from the ships'. The 'borrowing' of the master-scrolls of the great tragedians from the Athenians was one of the sharpest coups of Ptolemaic diplomacy. Pirating, in our modern sense, was a Hellenistic invention. As demand was insatiable, supply rose to meet it, aided by plausible forgery. Texts were faked and 'flogged' to the kings, until Aristotle had been credited with all sorts of interesting, if little-known, titles.

Why did the kings bother? As the Aristotelians had no doubt explained to a willing Ptolemy I, libraries and scholarly studies kept a king abreast of man's understanding of the world. The Ptolemies had had good tutors and they did not lose interest in learning. Ptolemy IV built a temple to Homer and wrote a tragedy on which a courtier politely wrote a commentary; rancorous Ptolemy VIII argued that the flowers in Calypso's garden were water parsnips, not violets. One of the last Seleucids wrote on snake-bites in verse. Royal extravagance inflated these tastes, and when others entered the race, book-collecting became a mad competition. To hinder the Attalid kings in Pergamum, the Ptolemies are said to have cut off the export of Egypt's papyrus. Thereupon, the Attalids pioneered parchment, or 'pergamene skins'. It is a good story, but fine parchment already existed.

Competition promised well for literary culture. In a court epigram Ptolemy

MAIN HALL IN THE LIBRARY AT PERGAMUM. Founded by Attalus I (241–197 BC), the library has been identified in a group of first-floor rooms behind the north portico of the sanctuary of Athena. It has been suggested that the line of holes visible in the walls may have helped to support book-cases, but the room was probably surrounded by statues of poets and historians.

III was honoured as a man 'good at battle and the Muses'. It was important to be both, for the kings were also competing for a pool of talent from the older Greek cities. Many of these men were exiles who found a better home as advisers and men of letters at the new courts. Museums and libraries were unquestioned goods to a Ptolemaic agent like Zeno. From his papyri we know this estate manager as the probable owner of a lovely, early text of Euripides' *Hippolytus*, the patron of epigrams for his hunting dogs, and the orderer of books and speeches on embassies which were to be sent from Alexandria to his brother, no doubt to polish him up. The ethical ideals of school philosophy were urged on the kings and repeated in the praises and edicts of their officials and agents. Like books, they made the kings more attractive.

Through these migrant courtiers the kings kept contact with the culture and education of older Greek cities. There was a reverse traffic, too, as part of their covert political publicity. They sent royal architects to the cities, encouraged participation in royal festivals, gave generous buildings, including libraries, and paid big sums for the education of the cities' youth: in the late 220s, Athens received a 'Ptolemaeum', a *gymnasion* for her young citizens which also housed books and hosted lectures. These gifts were apt attempts to influence and impress, for the grossness of the royal wonderland did not stifle keen, civic education. In Greek cities children now began to learn at the age of seven in privately funded schools, assisted sometimes by an individual's benefaction. They learnt to read and they practised writing in sentences, some of which, as known on papyrus, have an extreme anti-feminine and anti-barbarian content. Discipline was maintained by flogging. Aged fourteen, they passed on to a secondary stage which

DETAIL OF A SCHOOLTEACHER'S MANUAL from the Fayûm in Egypt. Dated to the last quarter of the third century BC, this papyrus scroll gives an idea of the somewhat artificial nature of many aspects of Hellenistic education. It begins by listing notional monosyllables and obscure, tongue-twisting words, then proceeds (here) to names from geography and mythology.

was dominated by literary exercises, the names of Greek rivers, and quizzes on Homer's Trojans. The old gap before the 'ephebe' stage, at the age of eighteen, was filled for many Hellenistic men with studies of the classics, including older poetry, and school composition. Then future citizens passed to the *gymnasion*, which was funded under civic control by a rich official. The hard core of its training was sport, but some *gymnasia* had libraries and held lectures too. Richer young men aspired further, to a private teacher in rhetoric or philosophy. The rhetorical training was very mechanical. By the later second century BC there are signs that more and more formal grammar was being taught in the earlier stages and that, overall, the studies were becoming ever more literary. There had never been lessons in law, while mathematics, for most men, was alarmingly elementary. As music became specialized, it withdrew from general schooling.

In every city the culture of the ephebes continued to be valued highly. Fathers troubled to put their sons down for a good *gymnasion*, and in later life the *gymnasia* looked to their 'old boys' for financial support. By the later second century BC Athens, the smartest centre of all, was admitting rich foreigners among her ephebes. In turn, they helped to keep up the idealization of the city. What, though, was the social value of all this Homer and arduous listing of Spartan rivers? It has been explained as a 'culture of reinforcement' to keep up Greek morale abroad and to keep out barbarians. That purpose is not convincing: the same studies flourished in old Greece where nobody risked being swamped. More relevantly, it marked social divisions between Greeks themselves. Vulgar people could not enter *gymnasia*. The parents were usually rich: in later third-century Athens there were scarcely forty new ephebes each year. This exclusiveness worked wonders for the city's international image. In the mid second century a recently found decree from a Macedonian city excluded slaves and freedmen, their children, those who had not attended wrestling school, anyone who had practised a trade in the *agora*, anyone who was drunk or mad. It also banned paederasts. *Gymnasia* were scenes of the golden years of romances between young men, but they were for 'amateurs' only.

Extravagant royal culture, therefore, was only the icing on a dry and well-established cake. Financed by their richer citizens, the cities set men's cultural horizons. Their speakers and antiquarians were not 'irrelevant'. They served on the vital embassies, while historians and local experts played a fascinating part in local boundary disputes and the many boards of arbitration. History had urgent public uses. At their own level cities also remained lively centres of shows and recitals, games and drama. They were served by wandering poets and musicians and the troupes of professional actors who were declared 'inviolable' on their travels through warring Hellenistic kingdoms.

A huge theatre has been unearthed at Aï Khanoum beside the Oxus river, and it is possible that the forms of Greek drama influenced the emergent theatrical art of India. The Hellenistic age also saw the flowering of many small societies in which members used to dine and patronize recitals. Non-citizens in places such as Rhodes or Delos found a focus for their loyalties in these groups, which were often organized with titles from civic life. By 300 BC they were joined by the foundations set up to honour a dead man's memory. Below the city's public patronage these groups all multiplied the centres of local cultural life.

Across such an area, how far was there a single culture? In the cities there was no common calendar and no common body of law. But there were broad similarities in civic life and the many sets of athletic games. At court, the kings used the 'common Greek' prose, or *koinē*, which developed from Attic origins and gradually pushed the older dialects in Greece itself into retreat. A measure of linguistic unity thus emerged around official, Hellenistic Greek. A common feeling was also aroused by the threat of barbarians, best seen in the sigh of Hellenic relief which followed the repulse of the Gauls from Greece and Delphi in 279 BC. Culturally, the kings all respected Athens' legacy. She had invented the theatre which every good city now imitated. Her fourth-century prose and her past record against Asian barbarians combined with the prestige of her former philosophers and dramatists. Together they kept up her appeal.

If there was a measure of common culture, how did it differ in the cities from fourth-century culture, except that we happen to know more about it? The differences were more of degree than of kind, and they are best brought out by some Hellenistic improvements. Closer contact with eastern spices transformed the industry of female scents and soaps. Make-up is thought to have been improved by Near Eastern skills, not least in the art of eye-shadow. There had never been such prostitutes as the great Attic mistresses of the Macedonian generals: the loose women of Alexandria were famous. The game parks and wild animals of Asia made the old Greek hare-chasing seem as tame as beagling. Indian blood bred newer and better hounds for spectacular hunting across Asia. The cooking, surely, improved: Alexandrian sauces for fish and gourds passed into Roman cook-books; the best banquets were spectacular, and although one of the Ptolemies kept pheasants without eating one, he crossed them with guinea-fowl and ate the result instead. Egypt's cabbage was so bitter that seed was imported from Rhodes to combat it. For one happy year it worked, but then the old bitterness emerged again. Greeks introduced chick-peas from Byzantium into Egypt, and a better wheat almost drove out the old, husked grain. An experiment was made with palm-trees in Greece, and estate owners in the Near East struggled to produce frankincense. We know too little about royal gardening, but there is an ominous hint in a letter from a Ptolemaic minister to his agent, telling him to plant 300 fir trees in the park on his estate, not just for ship-timber but for the 'tree's striking appearance': did other Greeks spatter Egypt with conifers? In places they greatly extended the area and yield of cultivable land. In Egypt's Fayum basin they are thought to have trebled it; the plain behind their city on the Oxus was never better irrigated or more densely worked. At Olympia we find baths with under-floor heating in the early second century, surely before any Roman influence. The Hellenistic *gymnasia* invented the detailed health exercises

REMAINS OF HYPOCAUST IN THE GREEK BATHS AT OLYMPIA. This underfloor heating system, dated about 100 BC, foreshadows the subsequent developments of thermal architecture in Roman Italy. The flue in the foreground leads into the heated room at the rear, with its floor supported on brick pillars.

which passed into the handbooks of the second century AD. Distinct from mere sport, they were planned as a 'work-out': jogging was said to be good for sexual diseases.

Most of this cultural life was restricted to the very few who could afford it. On the reverse side of Alexandrian elegance lay a battery of royal taxes and dependent workers and the appalling inhumanity of gold-mines. By the 150s they were manned by political prisoners and their innocent families. When Alexander founded cities beyond the Oxus he gave a horde of rebellious Asiatics to one of them, presumably as slaves. The huge benefactions of a rich citizen in a late-third-century city on the Black Sea have been shrewdly related to profits in the local slave trade. In the ancient economy people lived well only at the glaring expense of others.

To participate in cultural life natives had to Hellenize, and in a fascinating aspect of the period we see them doing just that. The kings settled colonies of native soldiers who spoke Greek in royal service and thus left signs of their Hellenization at unlikely spots in Asia. At Marissa, scarcely 30 miles across the

Jordan from Jerusalem, the burial ground produced handsome tombs and paint-ings in a Greek style. One of them had a frieze of wild animals, matching the African species known in the orbit of the Ptolemaic court. On its wall a Greek poem was beautifully inscribed, telling how a woman took temporary leave of one of her two lovers. At Marissa the Ptolemies had settled troops from Sidon: in the poem the woman keeps her lover's coat as a pledge, a theme which has been traced to old Semitic culture.

Greek culture was not always imposed: it could exert its own fascination. Among the Jews we know of voluntary Hellenizers who wished to go over to Greek ways and religion. They were only stopped after a bitter war, and Jewish culture emerged into the Maccabean age (175–63 BC), essentially resistant to the hard core of Hellenism. The Romans were far more flexible, and the Parthians, too, picked up the fashion: at their early capital instructions have been found for making a Greek actor's mask. Greek culture was so lively and such fun. It had

THE STADIUM AT PERGE IN SOUTHERN TURKEY. Though the present seating is Roman, the stadium was certainly laid out in Hellenistic times. Such stadia, designed to accommodate the running and field events of a local athletics festival, are one of the hallmarks of the Greek way of life which was carried into the newly conquered regions of the Hellenistic world.

PAINTED ANIMALS IN A TOMB AT MARISSA (Marêshah) in Jordan (second half of the third century BC). The creatures represented were all native to north Africa or believed to be such; here we see an elephant and a rhinoceros, both identified by tiny labels. The larger letters painted over the frieze refer to a subsequent burial.

theatres and athletics, some fascinating books, and a refined style of dining, the symposium. In response to it, a mid-second-century Jew turned the story of the Exodus into a Greek tragedy. By comparison it must have been rather dull to be a Jew in the evenings before the Greeks came. In their trading and art, their warfare and intellectuality, their literature and culture, the Greeks towered over their Asian subjects. In reaction, only Jews wrote anything literary, but it was minor stuff, largely taking refuge in divine revelation and sacred 'wisdom'. It is surely only a second-century-BC legend that Ptolemy II patronized the literal, clumsy Greek translation of Jewish Scripture, the Septuagint. Although some believe this story, it was probably attached to the translation later to give it prestige.

What, in return, of the Greeks? Like Alexander, the vast majority were not bilingual, and their schooling still absorbed them. Beside the Oxus, the wall which appears to divide the Hellenistic city has been proposed as a wall to divide the Greeks from the natives, as in old Massilia (Marseilles). But there is more to be said here. The rulers were often more open in their patronage than the cities: court Jews and a few Egyptians served several of the early Ptolemies. Alexander's associates did not at once forget his ambition; the army needed good men, especially Iranian horsemen; Ptolemy invented a new god, Serapis, which was indeed a fusion of Greek and native forms. True, the Attalid kings at Pergamum celebrated themselves as the defenders of Greek culture from the raids of barbarian Gauls. In Egypt, however, the earlier Ptolemies set Greek culture beside and above the customs of their new kingdom. A man such as Eratosthenes, the polymath, had an openness to people of all native origins, underpinned by his general theory of climatic 'zones' and geography. Clearchus, who walked to the

HEAD OF SERAPIS IN GREEN BASALT, now in the Villa Albani in Rome. This Roman copy probably reflects the cult-statue made (third century BC) by Bryaxis for the temple of Ptolemy I's new god in Alexandria. Serapis was created by grafting Greek elements on to the old Egyptian god Osor-Apis; but this image is very much in the Greek style, with a head closely related to depictions of the Greek gods Zeus and Asklepios. The corn-measure (*modius*) on the head is a symbol of fertility.

Oxus river from Delphi, also compared the wisdom of the Jews, the Brahmins, and the Magi. A Seleucid envoy to India, Megasthenes, left a fascinating mixture of observation and venial misunderstanding from his journey to the Indian court of the Maurya king on the Ganges. Greek education and theory did not entirely distort the value of the lively account of the Red Sea tribes which was written by a secretary to an official of the later Ptolemies, the appealing Agatharchides (flor. 170–145).

On one cardinal point, Greek observers of foreign peoples were more sharp-eyed than a whole generation of their modern historians. Intelligent men were quick to spot the lethal designs of Roman power, the 'cloud in the West' which menaced their freedom. Certainly the war with Hannibal was not far gone before mainland Greeks saw that Rome, not Carthage, was the threat, exemplified already in Sicily. They had not learned Latin, but they were already more perceptive than scholars who have learnt it since. By 146 Corinth was sacked and Agatharchides was remarking how the remote Sabaean Arabs owed their luxurious survival 'until our time' to their distance from 'people who turn their powers against every place'. He was referring, surely, to the Romans.

Literature and Patronage

Between 300 and 145 BC, how does the best Hellenistic literature fit into this context of lavish kings and a tenacious city culture? We have lost so much, especially in prose, that judgements are all provisional; might there be a master to our taste among the 130-odd names who wrote Hellenistic tragedy? It was an exciting time to be a man of talent, for new forms emerged from the old conventions in prose and verse. Every author of high quality came into contact with the patronage of kings of royal cities. Do the kings, then, take the credit for this new liveliness?

Only an exile, a gaolbird, or a starving man, said a character in late fourth-century comedy, would bother to resort to a king. Authors saw their chance. They were always claiming to be hungry and often they took up writing when exiled from their homes. Although Menander refused to leave Athens, subsequent literary men headed freely for the royal cities. At the courts, literary life was not too awkward. There are no stories of official works which the poets were asked to write, but refused. There was no need for a tactful intermediary to guide relations between the kings and their authors. The Attalids received their celebratory prose, the Seleucids their verse epics, but these works were not the sum of their authors' interests. In Alexandria poetic compliments to the dynasty were often paid in a witty and oblique style, and the best of them attached to the queens, not to the kings. At Pella, too, there are hints of give-and-take.

What studies, however, did the kings patronize with any permanency, beyond the occasional hand-out for good verses? We know most about patronage in Alexandria, where the Ptolemies' record was limited: the literature they patronized did not produce major talents in history and philosophy. They had an alphabetical list of pensions, a museum, and two libraries. They had a serious need for a royal tutor to teach the little princes and a royal librarian to preside over the growing arsenals of books. Long-term patronage was for useful industry: tutoring, science, the library, and textual scholarship. At first the tutors and librarians included men who also wrote excellent poetry. In the second century BC they were critical literary scholars, not original authors.

Poetry, except drama, was incidental to their patronage. Poets moved freely from king to king, whereas textual scholars were less mobile. The poetry which we still have and admire was not popular. Major Hellenistic poetry survives on only two papyri before about 100 BC. One was probably a manual for school-teachers; the other included a paraphrase in prose of the many verses which were too difficult. On prose, too (except history), the kings' persons weighed less than heavily. Just as the development of monarchy in twelfth-century Europe encouraged a better fund of royal stories, so the new age of kings and courtiers developed into a golden age of recorded gossip. Some of the best attached to the kings themselves: in his memoirs, even Ptolemy VIII ran through the fascinating list of Ptolemy II's mistresses a century or so earlier. An upper class reveals itself by its gossip, and to judge from theirs, the Hellenistic courts were elegant, ironic, and not overawed by royalty. Gossip crossed the literary boundaries: in Alexandria Machon, the comic poet, published witty verses on the dealings of great men and prostitutes, while later in Pergamum good anecdotes seem to have been a mainstay of Carystius' *Historical Notes* in prose. High society liked to read how the tireless Hippe called Ptolemy II 'Daddy' in private, and how King Demetrius the Besieger did and said the crudest things while asking Lamia ('Vampire') to choose from an array of scents and ointments. In Antioch the popular nicknames of the later Seleucids were bestowed in a similar irreverent spirit.

The libraries proved more of a dead weight. Scholarship had been the invention of fourth-century authors, and royal patronage merely gave it its head. Literature was prized for being antiquarian, and in royal circles its scope (excepting history) bears a striking resemblance to titles produced later by the scholars and courtiers in the equally polished society of ninth- and tenth-century Muslim rulers. It extended to brief biographical dictionaries, lists and catalogues, lively works on natural curiosities, and a long chain of titles on the wonders and marvels of the world. Like the Muslim courtiers, Hellenistic authors had an encyclopedic range and an interest in the fabulous and the exotic, which made better reading than a brilliant scientific tract by Archimedes in 'peculiarly rusty Doric'. These books were works to dip into, in search of something odder than Aristotle knew. They were totally unscientific, but they made for good conversation, like the popular lists of the world's biggest rivers and most impressive sights. We should remember this saving grace. Very little survives from the laborious volumes in which prose authors showed off so cheerfully, but the titles tell their own story, none more clearly than the works of Callimachus. His *Table of the Rare Words and Compositions of Democritus* was for enthusiasts only, but readers may have found more in his *Customs of Barbarians*, his *Collection of Wonders of the World*, and his books *On the Rivers of Europe, On Birds, On Winds*—but perhaps not so much in his monograph *On Changes of Names in Fish*.

The most punishing endeavour of Hellenistic learning was better directed. The first librarians in Alexandria were scholar poets, and from this combination grew the science of specialized scholarship which was at its peak from the 220s onwards. The poet's role in its origins is explicable. Prose used the common Attic dialect of the courts and did not react against its growing colloquialism until the classical revival of the first century BC. All Hellenistic poets, however, ignored the spoken dialects and looked back to the language and metre of the old classics. Difficult metres were revived or applied to unlikely subjects: Callimachus added a new one, by copying the hardest of all forms, the staccato galliambics which were used in one type of cult-hymn. Scholar poets set out to enrich the language by their own researches. In our own age W.H. Auden allotted poets the duty of legislating for language and guarding its purity. Hellenistic poets laid down the law too, but on dead, literary words. Much of their poetry is very difficult to translate, as it is packed with their sub-Homeric coinages, puns and glosses on obscure phrases in the classics, and an extravagant love of synonyms. On a mid-third-century papyrus we have a piece of a poetic 'vocabulary' which lists rare compound words. When searching for the *mot juste*, lesser poets could look at these handy catalogues. By the early second century, Aristophanes, the librarian in Alexandria, had compiled a big work called *Words*, perhaps the same as his *On Words Suspected of Not Being Used by The Early Writers*. By 200, literary scholarship had its own specialists who were no longer poets.

In the service of Philip and Alexander, the royal tutor Aristotle and his kinsman Callisthenes had worked on the text of Homer, whom their great pupil loved. In Alexandria scholarship became a science, spearheaded by the royal librarians from about 201 to 145 BC. Callimachus had already published a famous catalogue in 120 books, the *Tables of Persons Conspicuous in Every Branch of Learning and a List of Their Compositions*. Future scholars did more to swell libraries than reduce them. No critical work on forgeries is attested, and as scholars declared the old texts to be unsatisfactory, kings had to acquire their works and the new texts too. The master of the art was Aristarchus (*c.*215–143). Both tutor and librarian, he taught the best critics of the next generation and was distinguished by his flashes of historical sense, his caution, and his sane theory of regularity in grammar. The conjectures and deletions which these critics proposed have had less influence than their arrangement of the texts we now read.

The great age of scholarship ran from the later third century to the mid second, and afterwards, like philosophy, it lapsed into the industrious synthesis of rival views. As in philosophy, so in criticism: this synthesis followed an age of fierce dispute between sects, the second-century 'analogists' of Alexandria and the 'anomalists' at Pergamum. These subjects were best learnt by personal contact and thus among grammarians the ties of master and pupil were drawn very tightly. What exactly had Aristarchus said? There were no mass copies of his teaching, and a familiar industry developed in the circulation of first-hand lecture notes. Inevitably scholarship began to be practised on the scholars' works themselves. Ammonius, librarian and pupil of Aristarchus, wrote that jewel of Hellenistic piety, *On The Fact That There Were Not More Than Two Editions Of Aristarchus's Recension Of The Iliad*.

Royal men of letters did not only have to live with their texts. They had to live with each other. How did a man prove himself more learned than some wretched contemporary, except by compiling more information and attacking other men's views? An apt legend later credited the Alexandrian scholar Didymus with 3,500 books, justifying his nickname 'Brass Guts'. The remarkable

Eratosthenes spanned a range which few have matched since, writing well on geography, chronology, astronomy, on *Good and Bad Qualities*, and adding some notable poetry, including a brilliant epigram on the method of doubling a cube. A host of lesser minds ranged almost as widely and at similar length.

The quarrels, at first sight, are more depressing. The Museum was once described as the 'bird-cage of the Muses', and its subjects saw some spectacular cock-fights. They were led by Callimachus' attacks on poets and critics who did not share his taste and aims. On the topic of textual scholarship, Alexandria and Pergamum staged their own minor Hellenistic war. Literary critics throve on attacks: Aristarchus attacked Zenodotus, Demetrius and Crates attacked Aristarchus, Polemo attacked Eratosthenes, and so forth. One-upmanship made a man's name: Aristophanes even wrote a book *Against Callimachus' Library Lists*. Yet it is a dead subject which does not cause scholarly dispute. The personal tone was frightful, but on inspection these quarrels were not mere fights for promotion or the savage reaction of the old to the young. The competitors believed that principles were at stake. Callimachus, not unjustly, thought one wing of poetic taste entirely misguided. In scholarship it mattered greatly if a man was sensible and an analogist, or irresponsible and an anomalist, with a faith in allegory as a device to make the poets 'mean' things quite remote from their manifest meaning. Through the grammarians' invention, the worst-attested personal quarrel has become the most notorious. The two Alexandrian poets, Callimachus and Apollonius, were later alleged to have fought bitterly, perhaps because Callimachus' pugnacity was well known and, as master and supposed pupil, the two seemed inevitable enemies to later scholars who cast them in their own image. Modern scholars have given the legend a new twist, alleging that Callimachus abused his pupil for taking his material without acknowledgement. That is an amusing comment on scholars, but not on poets, who are happy to be imitated. The 'quarrel' lacks any good evidence.

In this atmosphere of industry and competition, where is good, readable writing still to be found? In the little which we still know of prose, new forms and a new emphasis show through, but they owe nothing directly to royal patrons. The earlier forms of biography blossomed in this age of individuals and educated interest in great men of the past. It was feeble, however, because it lacked a sense of social and psychological context and tended to be static and anecdotal. The germs of romantic fiction also hatched generously. The Alexander Romance excelled them all, beginning within a decade of the great man's death. Popular novels were matched by a new form of popular moralizing, cast in prose as the 'diatribe' and attached to the name of the itinerant Bion. The scholar Eratosthenes dismissed him as a fraud decked out in the flowery dress of a harlot. We know too little to decide, but there was some originality in the satirical mixtures of prose and verse invented by his near-contemporary Menippus. These pieces made fun of philosophers and their double standards, and later they interested Roman satirists. The best may have come from that sympathetic figure, Timon. One-eyed, he was remembered for many virtues, his love of gardens, his skill at avoiding pupils, and his hatred of interruptions from dogs and servants. In satirical sketches he took off the philosophers and made fun of contemporary geographers. He called the inmates of the Museum 'cloistered book-worms' and deflated the literary scholars, saying that the best texts of Homer were the old ones, before the poems had been altered out of recognition. It would be good to know more of this man who began by earning his living as a dancer.

Less attractively, the decade after Alexander's death saw the extension of school declamation with its mock speeches on particular dilemmas and legal decisions: we first hear of them in the early years of the New Comedy which shared something of their spirit. We also know of a taste for rhythmical, inflated rhetoric which became known as the Asianic style. Critics in the Augustan age gave Romans the credit for ending this extravagance and returning prose to a sober classicism by their steadying, moral influence. This view is questionable. Oratory had not declined into bombast, for it remained central to the cities' endless embassies to the kings and, later, to Rome. We have lost this practical oratory, and already in the 140s the master of 'Asianism' was being criticized by Agatharchides, whose own prose style earned high praise later for its dignity and nobility, its clarity and artistry with words.

Hellenistic Poetry

Poetry, however, is the form in which surviving Hellenistic literature excels. Of the classic styles of poetry, lyric was the obvious candidate in the wake of Aristotle and Alexander. The days when an aristocrat could advise or abuse his fellow citizens on politics were gone, but men still died and fell in love, wined and dined and pursued their ever-elusive boys. The traditional drinking party, or *symposion*, flourished among citizens and courtiers and remained a natural setting for polished poetry. Without any royal encouragement, the first Hellenistic poets saw their chance and returned to the themes, metre, and manner of older lyric masters. Like the early poets, they also attended to lower, popular songs. They twisted these themes to suit new settings and added the learning, wit, and urbanity which befitted true 'old boys' of a civic education.

We know so little of poetry in the fourth century that we may miss the roots of lyric's rediscovery. For us its impact is plainest in the epigram, which enjoyed a golden age between about 300 and 240 BC. Its masters filled it with their personality and literary tastes, capping one another's poems and contriving *doubles entendres* so neat that they are still being unravelled with pleasure. In Alexandria, especially, the epigrams convey the impression of a coterie of intimate and free-living friends, revelling in the polish of their new device. They give us more poems with point and dialogue, and they cast them in enigmatic settings. They convince us of their self-awareness and their life among wine and women, *symposia* and fickle boys.

The earliest master was Asclepiades from Samos, a respected poet who survives for us largely in his love poems. There is point and a genial self-awareness in his poems on favoured courtesans and on themes made familiar in the setting of the *symposion*. The relations of love and wine are his main subjects, with an awareness that if one love fails there is always another for another day. Posidippus covers similar ground and has also left us some pleasant epigrams on major buildings in the city. Scholars found it hard to separate Asclepiades' poems from those of a fellow Samian, Hedylus, and perhaps they were close companions. Hedylus' epigrams survive as poems against gluttons and gross banquets; they remind us that a good *symposion* was an expression of taste and civility. This trio were followed by the ornate and appealing Dioscorides, who takes us out of this small urban world in his epitaphs for a Persian and for settlers in the Egyptian country-side. A series of poems on past and present dramatists raise tantalizing problems of literary history, while his florid phrasing sits well round the pudgy, hospitable figure of Doris, his bed-fellow.

The master of the epigram was Callimachus, the royal tutor. He knew the others' work and attacked them for their taste in longer poems. In return, they took one of his best lines and reset it in an obscene context. If Callimachus' epigrams were all we had of his work, how differently we would picture him. In them his language is clear and fluent, while his grasp of the verse form remains the envy of all composers of Greek elegiacs. In his epigrams we meet Callimachus, the unhappy lover of boys, prey to passions which he cannot control and others will not oblige. He is Callimachus who 'knew how to have fun while the wine passed round', Callimachus who can chide the judgement of the gods. Nothing defies his art. He can construct good puns on a salt-cellar or defend his own refined literary tastes. The self-awareness is sharper, the emotions deeper than the themes to which our poems of Asclepiades are now limited. The royal tutor and cataloguer could also be playful. He addressed a perfect set of verses to his friend Philippus the doctor, to assure him that while poetry was one cure for the love of boys, hunger could prove as effective: the poet and his friend can defy love, as they possess both remedies. The reference to poetry possibly alluded to a poem by the great Theocritus. The epigram's language had a medical tone which suited a doctor.

More profoundly, Callimachus has left us a group of the best epitaphs in Greek. These themes were traditional for the epigram, and flowered again for several lost friends, among them poor, talented Heraclitus who 'tired the sun with talking' and left us one subtle funerary poem as his memento. These are great poems: simple, well angled, and profoundly moving. Epigrams, however, were incidental to Callimachus' patronage. No king gave long-term support to the other masters as poets only. Their debt was to the wonders of the city and the court society on which they touched. Two of the major poets came and went from Alexandria, while other good epigrams were written away from kings altogether. They lacked, however, the tone of the big city.

From Tarentum in the Greek west came Leonidas, whose major gifts lay with the scenes and objects of rural life and verses on his own simple, impoverished existence. In a similar style, we hear from two talented women, Nossis of Locri and her poems on female domestic life, and Anyte from little Tegea, whose charming poetry conveys a strong sense of a pastoral setting. To Anyte we owe the first known epitaphs for favourite animals, a genre which quickly extended to poems on the dogs of Ptolemaic 'top people' and on animals killed more nobly in hunts in Egypt or Afghanistan. The tone of these 'western' epigrams is lost by translations which turn them into rhyme. Generally, they die away, ending 'not with the thud of the hammer on the anvil, but the dying notes of a guitar'. This mood of a serene and wistful still-life has to struggle with elaborate language and the lack of perfect metrical polish, but at times it wins the battle.

By the 240s, the first age of invention and rivalry was fading. The style was imitated sweetly, and its centre shifted from Alexandria to the Syrian cities. The Syrian Meleager included the work of some fifty epigrammatists in his great anthology, the *Garland* (*c.*100 BC). In its first flush the epigram takes us to the frontiers of the new poetry. Its poets drew the new contemporary interests into their polished elegiacs: the mime and the pastoral, the enlarged iambic, and the taste for wit and pathos. Faced by a classic tradition, the early Hellenistic masters did not rebel against form and rules. There were no Vorticists and Imagists. Instead, they perfected form and multiplied metrical rules and archaism. Greek artists were particularly effective when particularly constrained by their own limits.

Dioscorides' epigrams honour the new dramatists, but nothing survives by which to judge them. At a lower level, however, there was a sudden new interest in the mime. This coarse, popular sketch had flourished in Doric prose, and its Sicilian master, Sophron, had once impressed Plato. Characteristically, it was given a literary twist and polish by the Hellenistic poets, Herodas and Theocritus. Herodas' talent has been underestimated. His poetry only reappeared on a papyrus in 1891, and it was wrongly identified with the contemporary style of 'realism'. Critics mistook his form and language. He revived the limping iambic metre and the old Ionic dialect of sixth-century-BC poetry, and attached this learning to the lowly mime. His surviving sketches are lively and give a wicked glimpse of social history. The best concern women, though seldom in a favourable light. One woman attempts to persuade another whose husband is away in Egypt that she must follow her instincts and have an affair. A cross mother takes her dissolute son to his schoolmaster for a thrashing: best of all, a woman who has been making love to her slave decides to have him flogged for his infidelities, then moderates her rage at the plea of a fellow servant. There is no reason why a good actor could not have performed these sketches on the stage. Herodas had his critics, and there is a strong case for connecting one of his sketches with the island of Cos, bringing him within the Ptolemies' inner political orbit, and attaching him to high literary culture. Certainly he left one of the most mischievous Hellenistic jokes: when one of his women sings the praises of a dildo which she has found in her friend's house, she is told that it once belonged to 'Nossis and Erinna'. These two names refer to famous poetesses. Herodas is surely having fun with two staid ladies of the literary world.

Our other mime-poems, written by Theocritus, are equally learned in tone and language. He cast them in hexameters, a grand metre for a low subject, producing a calculated incongruity. The best tells of the visit of two Syracusan ladies to a royal festival in Alexandria. The dialect, the irony, and the sense of simple visitors' wonder as they struggle through the crowds, are a brilliant sketch of the big city. A drama of magic and teenage first love is nearly as good, while a dialogue between two poor fishermen should be better known, whether or not Theocritus wrote it. He is the one consistently fine poet of this period. He was born in Sicily, probably in Syracuse. In the 270s he flattered Ptolemy II and then, or later, King Hiero in his own war-torn Sicily. Once he alludes to the Alexandrian masters, and two of his best poems are set in Alexandria's orbit, one in the city, one on the island of Cos. There is a slight bias towards the flora of the east Aegean, not Sicily, in the many plants he mentions. Otherwise, he is a mystery to us, although a good short epic-sketch in a hymn to Pollux shows that he understood boxing. Here he excelled the contemporary librarian in Alexandria.

Theocritus' good poems are varied, but his fame rests on his invention of pastoral poetry. From his example began the tradition which has given us Virgil's *Eclogues*, Spenser's shepherds, Handel's *Acis and Galatea*, and Shakespeare's *Winter's Tale*. He is the one Hellenistic poet to have been translated internationally: he even left a direct influence on nineteenth-century Russian poetry. The ancients themselves were puzzled where pastoral had come from. They guessed, probably wrongly, that it arose from choir-songs at various festivals of Artemis. A better guess may be the shepherd-songs of herdsmen with time enough to while away. In many cultures shepherds are associated with song.

Readers have long been bothered by widely differing aspects of his pastoral form: that point, said Sir Philip Sidney, 'where the hedge of poetry is lowest'. Some have regretted his realism, others his artifice. How could shepherds talk like that? Equally, how could Theocritus make his shepherds quite so coarse? Eighteenth-century pastoral preferred Virgil. 'I do not look on Theocritus as a romantic writer', Lady Mary Wortley Montagu told Alexander Pope, himself a pastoral poet in his youth; 'he has only given a plain image of the way of life among the peasants of his country ... I do not doubt, had he been a Briton, that his *Idylliums* had been filled with descriptions of threshing and churning ...'

In fact, the charm of Theocritus is that he keeps a foot in both camps. His shepherds still abuse each other with coarse jokes and hiss at their flocks. The feel of the Greek seasons and insects is still there, along with an eye for plants so precise that one critic has argued he studied botany with the doctors on Cos. At the same time he teases us with his urbanity and his uses of the set themes of early lyric poetry. Theocritus' shepherds meet, then challenge each other to sing.

PAINTING OF POLYPHEMUS AND GALATEA from the villa of Agrippa Postumus at Boscotrecase, near Pompeii (*c.*10 BC). The whimsical tale of the brutish Cyclops who fell in love with a
sea-nymph inspired two of Theocritus' *Idylls* and appealed to the educated taste of the Roman
nobility of the early Empire.

Their songs enchant us with their refrains and repetitions, a style which may derive from real songs in the hills. But they also weave together the themes of excluded lovers and revellers, poems for departing and returning travellers, which we find so often in past elegy and lyric. There is wit in the ugliness of the characters who love, the 'urban' laments of a Cyclops by the seaside, and the playfulness of the girl whom he woos among barking dogs and armfuls of apples. In one of its forms, the elegy, pastoral poetry has pleased almost every taste. In Theocritus' hands it gained form and pathos. All nature joined in the lament for a dying shepherd-poet, echoed by a polished use of the refrain. The pastoral elegy for the shepherd Daphnis developed into elegies for a dead poetic friend or master. In the touching lament for Bion it gave us the finest Greek poem to survive from the years around 100 BC. Writing in Italy, its unknown author contrasted the yearly renewal of nature and the death of man for ever. Directly from these elegies we derive three great poems, Milton's *Lycidas* (for his undergraduate friend Edward King), Arnold's *Thyrsis* (for the poet Clough), and the *Adonais*, or lament for Keats, which was the triumph of Shelley. His friend, Leigh Hunt, had introduced him to Hellenistic pastoral in autumn, 1816: 'like the odour of the tuberose,' he later wrote, 'it overcomes and sickens the spirit with excess of sweetness.'

The birth of pastoral has been misunderstood against the rise of the Hellenistic city. There is a pleasant story that Ptolemy II, when suffering from gout, once looked out of his palace window and envied the lives of simple Egyptians, seen picnicking on the banks of the Nile. That feeling was not the origin of pastoral. It took no interest in the foreign inhabitants of the new cities' territories. Theocritus' pastoral poems are not demonstrably linked to Alexandria, and in all but this huge city men walked easily into the fields near by, like the characters on Cos in his seventh *Idyll*. Town and country ran into each other everywhere, and nobody suffered from urban suffocation. The division, rather, was cultural. Pastoral transposed extreme urban wit and refinement on to those who owed least to urban values. Pastoral has always flourished in periods of an exquisite, urban culture, Spenser's England or Watteau's France. In Greece it arose from the same values of polish and technique and the reflective study of a classic tradition. These tastes had been bred by civic culture of the later fourth century BC, not by early Hellenistic 'urbanism' or by royalty.

Like the literary mimes and the epigrams, the pastoral combined learned language and metre with urbanity. Urbanity won, helped by the example of earlier lyric. In Alexandria the same values were pursued in bolder forms by the two top scholars in residence, the royal tutor and the royal librarian.

The librarian, Apollonius, was the younger, and his one known poem was audacious. He attempted an epic on the much studied adventures of the Argonauts, in an age when the social context and oral culture of the great epics had long since vanished. The ancients alleged that Apollonius wrote the poem as a young man, retired to Rhodes after a poor first reception, and then returned with a revised version. This 'second edition' seems correct, but the range of reading behind it suggests that the lure of the royal library came into the story, whether before or after Apollonius' appointment. The ancient commentators were stretched to the limit by his learning. Behind his language we can suspect the arguments of contemporary Alexandrian scholars on the precise meaning of particular words. Behind his content, prose-works on local antiquities kept company with subtle Homeric word-play and allusions to more recent poets. Among the full range of his references, the obvious allusions and debt to Callimachus have been greatly exaggerated. There is no reason, either, why the librarian and the tutor could not have read similar books on this familiar subject independently.

The poem's weaknesses are obvious. It has no balance, and it ends with a bump. One moment we are meeting Circe in the west, beset by her dreams of foreboding. 200 lines later we are sweltering on the sands of Libya while Medea's maids sing their swan-song, fearing death. From our point of view some of his learned passages have rather the air of versified footnotes, and the treasures of the royal library were a constant temptation to the poet. The story itself is intrinsically episodic—a long journey to Colchis (Books 1–2), events at Colchis (Book 3), a long return home (Book 4). Apollonius has not overcome this unsatisfactory structure, and in some ways his four books are less an epic than an intermittent display of gifts common in the best Hellenistic poets. In spirit, if not in form, he is often Theocritean.

At his best Apollonius can be excellent. His most famous scene is the epic's third book, which develops the love of the young Medea for Jason. Aphrodite inspires this passion by the arts of her mischievous child, Cupid, but we see it through Medea's own thoughts and emotions: how could she prefer a stranger to her parents? why should her parents come first? She longs to see him; when she does, she blushes and can hardly speak. They face each other like oaks or pines, silent till the breeze stirs them. This book is the Greeks' most brilliant portrayal of a girl falling passionately in love. Throughout the poem Apollonius placed Homeric similes, seventy-six in all, which developed odd perceptions or scenes from daily life. For Medea, his comparisons hit the mark. Her heart melts like 'the dew round roses warmed by the morning light'; her mind wavers like sunlight reflected on the wall of a house from a freshly-poured pail of water. Virgil, a careful reader of Apollonius, was quick to see the charm of this episode and take it as his starting-point for his deeper and more mature meeting of Aeneas and Dido.

The episode of Jason and Medea had already been foreshadowed by the excellent encounter of Jason with Queen Hypsipyle in Book 1, a scene worth reading for the same qualities. It was not lost on Virgil, either, as he brought his Trojans to the Queen of Carthage. Yet Apollonius retains a certain detachment from the adventures he relates. He is witty and ironic. He has the light touch and pictorial gift of a Sebastiano Ricci, and when he tells how the sea-nymphs tossed the good ship Argo to and fro for a whole day, like girls playing ball on the beach with

EUROPA AND THE BULL, Pompeian painting from the House of Jason, or of the Fatal Loves (first quarter of first century AD). This genteel version of one of Zeus' best known zoomorphic seductions nicely catches the romantic spirit of Hellenistic poetry, as represented by Moschus' *Europa*.

their skirts tucked up, we can see him smiling at his own rococo imagination. Over the sands of Libya the good ship Argo is led by the prow like a trusting horse in a head-collar. Apollonius loves the witty reversal: at heart he is an early Hellenistic master, as we begin to see the type.

His epic was not, then, such an anachronism. It veered between the two extremes of Hellenistic culture, and it shone wherever it escaped the one and approached the other. It almost avoided the dry learning of lesser authors in the 'didactic' style, poems like Aratus' on the stars, whose 'Hesiodic' quality and 'sleepless' effort were admired by Callimachus. These poets wrote a mass of versified learning on topics from cooking to farming. What survives is hard to admire: Nicander wrote a poem on *Antidotes to the Bites of Wild Creatures* which is as deadly as the hazard he professed to cure.

Conversely, Apollonius came very close to the charming epic sketches which focused on a lesser figure, often a female, and an unfamiliar incident in myth. These shorter poems were composed independently, as 'tiny epics' or *epyllia*. Court scholars such as Callimachus and Eratosthenes wrote them too, and we have a splendid example from Moschus (a pupil of Aristarchus) on the topic of Europa, crossing the sea on the back of Zeus as a bull. They are witty and often romantic, and their high colours conjure up a fine Tiepolo fresco. It took Virgil to tease and transform the grimmer, didactic poets and pass on their genre, through his *Georgics*, to its golden age among the Augustan poets of Georgian England. But the epyllion was transferred, not transformed. It passed first to Rome, then to Elizabethan poets, its aptest heirs at a moment when learning competed once more with playfulness. Though directly inspired by Ovid, Marlowe's sensuous *Hero and Leander* is in many ways a Hellenistic pearl.

Could a royal tutor escape the faults of a royal librarian? Like Apollonius, whom he may have taught, Callimachus could write fine, uncluttered verse. His epigrams were exquisite. He had thought seriously about poetry's options and asserted his choice against what he calls the 'envy' of his critics in epigrams, iambics, and a famous 'second Prologue' to a late, collected edition of his more experimental work. He exalted 'technique' and 'skill', the 'slender' Muse, the 'untravelled road', the waters from pure, unvisited fountains. Hesiod was a possible model, Homer an irrecoverable genius. He refused to write a long, continuous poem of epic proportions on a single subject of myth or ancient history. 'A big book', he wrote, 'is a big pest.' If he differed from Apollonius, it must have been on this point. In his forceful iambic pieces he defended his own versatility and his readiness to range between different genres, metres and dialects. With the help of ancient commentators we can put names to his dislikes. His bugbear was 'the fat woman', a long poem by Antimachus, the *Lyde*, which the great epigrammatists had admired, incurring his attack. He also opposed a critic who was probably Aristotelian. The issue, perhaps, was Callimachus' dislike of 'continuous' plot.

To Roman poets no name was weightier to drop than that of Callimachus, and Virgil made famous use of his Prologues in a poem on poetry's predicaments. Talk of 'new' poetry strikes home to readers in the wake of Pound and Eliot. Callimachus' learning and range were powerful, but what of their results?

Unfortunately, his most original works are known only in fragments; new ones are still being discovered, and a major new piece was published from papyrus in 1977. His iambics widen the range of the metre's subjects, but the surviving pieces are very difficult, written in a style which is oblique and highly erudite. Posterity respected his four books *On Origins* (*Aetia*) but they are an odd collection. In the first two books Callimachus asks puzzling questions, usually of the Muses, once of a stranger whom he had met and befriended at a coarse symposium which is described in a flash of oblique liveliness. Here is the 'new' poetry, the 'untravelled way': questions on why the people of Paros do not use flutes at sacrifices, or why the Icians are connected with Thessaly. The origin of a noble family on Ceos is the peg on which he hangs a witty and allusive account of a mythical wooing (Acontius and Cydippe, frs. 67–75): he explores local cults whose origins were linked with the Argonauts, handling prose sources which he and Apollonius could both read, but using them more tersely and subtly. The virtues of this poetry defy translation. Callimachus found much of his material in scholarly prose works, and strung it together with an abruptness which tested his readers. His vocabulary was very recherché indeed. In the poem's last two books Callimachus seems to have worked in witty praises of Queen Berenice, her chariot-victory in Greece, and her lock of hair, set among the stars as the *Coma Berenices* (the 'Lock of Berenice').

Like other Hellenistic poets, Callimachus ranged between the different genres, and some of his most appealing work belongs in forms which he shared with contemporaries. Like them, he tried a 'little epic', the *Hecale*. Its occasion was a heroic exploit of the young Theseus, but typically the poem dwelt on accompanying scenes, on Theseus' reception, the night before his ordeal, by the poor, but hospitable, old woman Hecale; on her simple entertainment, her reminiscences, even a dialogue between a pair of birds.

Of his six Hymns, which survive complete, the best three are set in the cities of Cos, Argos, and Cyrene. They combine the spectators' vivid sense of the gods' presence at their festivals with a playful excursus on relevant myths of their encounters with men. Are they proof of Callimachus's own sincere piety? Rather, the poet amuses himself and us by playing with the simple faith of the uneducated, in a style which presupposes high sophistication.

Born in Cyrene, Callimachus had taught as a school-master before coming to the Alexandrian court. Like many lyric poets and most Greek historians, he was an exile. In his surviving love poems he writes wittily of his loves for boys, but never of women. However, this taste was common among his contemporaries. His exile and his homosexuality have been curiously emphasized as forming his horizon, but his most obvious debt is to his days as a schoolteacher. He recalls the strengths and vices of the literary education of his age: the Homeric quizzes, the antiquarian catechisms, the sexual crushes, and the concern for rare words. Like so many schoolmasters, Callimachus was most successful when most conventional, in his funerary epigrams and classic hymns.

On one point Callimachus was proved right. His *Origins* and *Iambics* claimed to be poems for the refined few. The new papyrus of his *Origins'* third book was handsomely copied within a generation of the poet's death. Already it needed a literal prose paraphrase for many of its lines. In the Roman age Callimachus' 'new path' became an acknowledged model for the great Augustan poets. It is not altogether clear how much they read of it. Callimachus' poems survived to the end of antiquity, the delight of scholars and *érudits manqués*: we know of a tax clerk in Egypt in the 170s AD who amused himself by translating the name of an Egyptian on his register by Callimachus' rare word for 'mousetrap'.

Like Apollonius, Callimachus had enjoyed the direct patronage of kings and access to the great royal libraries. Like Apollonius, he had a playful, Hellenistic talent, immortalized in his epigrams and hymns, but he dressed it in learning and rare language. The library, one feels, was at times his worst enemy. Between 300 and 240 BC the most fruitful impulse for poetry belonged elsewhere, in the use of archaic lyric. So far as patronage helped, it was as a source of leisure and as the setting for secure life in a great capital city. To that degree, there is a connection between literature and the political fate of the monarchies. Stable kingdoms meant stable cities, in which poets could mature and practise, and court societies in which they could experiment and come and go. The earliest Hellenistic poets grew up in the city-states before Alexander and moved into the range of the kings while their courts were still young. By the 270s the new monarchies seemed settled: these are the years in which poets write of the 'calm weather' of the Alexandrian court. That serenity was never repeated. Failures abroad, internal squabbles, the rise of the new barbarians, Rome and Parthia, and the savagery of the Egyptian crowds whom Alexandria had simply excluded and exploited: the Hellenistic poets did not have the talent to make art from anarchy, and by the 240s the best was done. After the 240s the new excitement of Alexandria wore off, and poets were left to imitate the previous age's inventions. Scholarship emerged as a specialized art, and poetry, by the second century BC, relapsed into provincial sweetness. In 145 Ptolemy VIII drove the scholars and intellectuals out of Alexandria and scattered them like sparks across the Aegean. Writers of pretty Greek verses reached Roman patrons in the first century BC, but Catullus, Horace, and Virgil were right to look back and pick their models with such taste.

The great poetry had been wholly divorced from politics. It was witty and ironic, urbane and perceptive, yet aware of the sadness in life. It delighted in scenes of emotion which it found in odd episodes of myth, in the child and the old, the housewife as well as the heroine. Like much poetry of seventeenth-century Europe it drew an image or two, no more, from the sudden horizons of new science and travel. It preferred rococo wit and colour and the world of the older Greek city. We might long to tug Callimachus east to look for Zoroastrians or hear the minstrels of east-Iranian nobles. But he and his contemporaries had the polish of excellent 'old boys', brought up in a school and a civic culture which no eastern peoples matched. A host of unacknowledged schoolmasters had done far more for this last age of poetry than any well-intentioned king.

Between us and their playful urbanity lies the barrier of Romantic taste. The contrast brings out the best in these first, Hellenistic minds. In his fine *Sonnets on the River Dudden*, Wordsworth used an art which Callimachus would have applauded. The poems were short and their topic was a river and its origins. They were abrupt in their changes of tone and subject and were packed with learning and local legend. As the river ran into the sea, Wordsworth turned to Hellenistic pastoral:

> We, the brave, the mighty and the wise,
> We men, who in our morn of youth defied
> The elements, must vanish: be it so!

The lines were based on the Lament for Bion. But, he concluded,

> "enough . . . if, as toward the silent tomb we go,
> Through love, through hope, and faith's transcendent dower
> We feel that we are greater than we know".

In the wake of Aristotle, the best Hellenistic minds had had no room for such feelings. From Egypt to India, Greek culture made sense of human life; the marvels of the world made excellent reading, but its elements ran by natural rules; and third-century men of taste, through their schooling and philosophies, were neither less nor greater than wit and reason knew.

Further Reading

There are full, international bibliographies of Hellenistic culture in C. Préaux, *Le Monde hellénistique* (Paris, 1978), and C. Schneider, *Kulturgeschichte des Hellenismus* (Munich 1967), while P. M. Fraser, *Ptolemaic Alexandria* (Oxford, 1972) is a fundamental collection and discussion of evidence. H. I. Marrou, *History of Education in Antiquity* (London, 1956) is a classic study, although the English translation is erratic. A. Momigliano, *Alien Wisdom* (Cambridge, 1975), R. Pfeiffer, *A History of Classical Scholarship*, vol. I (Oxford, 1968), W. S. Ferguson, *Hellenistic Athens* (London, 1911), and M. Hengel, *Hellenism and Judaism* (London, 1978) are also indispensable. The range of M. I. Rostovtzeff's *Social and Economic History of the Hellenistic World* (Oxford, 1941) has not been surpassed. On the geographers, M. Cary and E. H. Warmington, *The Ancient Explorers* (London, 1963) give a lively introduction. P. M. Fraser, 'Eratosthenes of Cyrene', *Proceedings of the British Academy*, lvi (1970), 175–209, is a vivid portrait. Robin Lane Fox, *Alexander the Great* (London, 1973) and *The Search for Alexander* (Boston, Mass., 1980) describe and illustrate the first conquests and their impact. Hellenistic literature is surveyed by A. Lesky, *A History of Greek Literature* (London, 1966), pp. 642–806. P. M. Fraser's *Ptolemaic Alexandria* (Oxford, 1972) discusses the Alexandrians' literary achievement, and more particularly, a view of Callimachus. A selection of epigrams are translated in *The Greek Anthology*, ed. Peter Jay (London, 1973); Herodas was translated by his editor, W. Headlam (Cambridge, 1922); Apollonius is translated in the Penguin Classics series, by E. V. Rieu (Harmondsworth, 1958).

15

Hellenistic Philosophy and Science

❧❦

JONATHAN BARNES

GREEK philosophy has a continuous history. The death of Alexander the Great heralded no intellectual revolution, and the Hellenistic thinkers placed themselves in the tradition of Thales and of Socrates. But after Aristotle the emphasis changed: Hellenistic philosophy—in its scope, its aim, its self-understanding—differed somewhat from the discipline practised in earlier centuries.

Philosophy became an Art of Living. The pursuit of scientific knowledge ceased to be the defining mark of the philosopher. Rather, a man's philosophy was something that he lived by, and a philosopher's task was to discover the 'best life', to teach it, and to live it. Ethics, or practical philosophy, emerged as the regent part of the subject.

Practical utility determined the philosophical curriculum. As ethics rose, so metaphysics descended. More significantly, science divorced itself from philosophy and became the pursuit of professionals. The divorce was confirmed by geographical dislocation: Athens remained the chief centre of philosophy, but science migrated to Egyptian Alexandria and the financial subventions of the Ptolemies. Philosophy retained indeed a part called 'physics', and the general understanding of natural science never lost its importance; but Hellenistic philosophers did not care to describe the organs of the octopus or to chronicle the movements of the stars.

On the other hand, the Hellenistic period was marked by a passionate concern with the theory of knowledge. The art of living must rest upon a firm knowledge of the nature of things, and the foundations of knowledge must be philosophically secure. The challenge of scepticism was accepted by the Hellenistic thinkers: some of the subtlest work of the age was provoked by the debate over doubt and dogmatism.

For the Hellenistic philosophers wrote against one another. Philosophy became sectarian, and the sects squabbled. There was, to be sure, dispute within the

IMPRINT OF A GREEK PAPYRUS found in the palace at Aï Khanoum, Afghanistan. The papyrus has perished, leaving only the traces of ink preserved in reverse on the fine earth formed by decomposed mud bricks where they had fallen on the floor. Certain words which can be deciphered suggest that the text belonged to a dialogue of philosophical, and more specifically Aristotelian, character.

schools: thought did not ossify into doctrinal inflexibility. But variation was held within limits. A man would be characterized as a Stoic or an Epicurean or an Academic: he would be thought of primarily as a member of a school, devoted to its theories and to the art of living which those theories supported; only secondarily might he be regarded as an ingenuous seeker after truth.

The sects did not form exclusive or esoteric clubs. Men might study under several masters and migrate from school to school. Philosophy was both esteemed and popular. The Hellenistic monarchs solicited the presence of philosophers at their court. The city of Athens voted public honours to the Stoic Zeno. Nor was the subject limited to a rich or intellectual clique: Theophrastus attracted as many as 2,000 students to his lectures, and when Stilpo visited Athens men left their workshops and ran to see him. Far from Athens, in a remote garrison town in Afghanistan, archaeologists have recovered evidence of an interest in Aristotelian philosophy.

To those generalizations let there be added a puff. Scholars sometimes dismiss the Hellenistic philosophers as *epigoni*, men of a silver age whose lustre could not match the golden gleam of Plato and Aristotle. That is mistaken. The gleam did not fade; in some parts it glowed more brightly than before. The period produced work of the utmost brilliance.

After Plato's death in 347 the Academic coterie continued to philosophize, under the successive guidance of Speusippus (d. 339), Xenocrates (d. 314) and Polemo (d. *c.* 276). Aristotle's school likewise survived: Theophrastus (d. *c.* 287) carried on his work, and Theophrastus was followed by Strato of Lampsacus. But on Strato's death (c. 269) the school ran out of power, and for most of the Hellenistic period Aristotelian philosophy was a thing of the past—a thing of influence, but devoid of life.

Platonism too died. The Academy lasted as a school until the first century BC, but the Hellenistic Academicians, although they claimed to be the true heirs of Socrates and Plato, maintained none of the doctrines which we take to be constitutive of Platonism. When Arcesilaus of Pitane (d. *c.* 242) became head of the school in about 270 he converted the Academy to scepticism. The New Academy was a new school. Under its two greatest leaders, Arcesilaus and Carneades of Cyrene (*c.* 219-129), it developed a wholly negative and critical mode of philosophizing.

Constructive philosophy in the Hellenistic age was located neither in the Lyceum nor in the Academy but at two new sites, the Garden of the Epicureans and the Porch of the Stoics.

Epicurus was born of Athenian parents on the island of Samos in 341. He eventually settled in Athens in 307, where he taught until his death in 271. The philosophy to which he gave his name can be summarized thus: in ethics, hedonism—pleasure is the sole good; in physics, atomism—the universe consists of minute corpuscles moving in empty space; in logic, empiricism—all our knowledge is grounded ultimately on experience and perception.

Epicureans were notoriously conservative: they did not slavishly repeat their master's words, yet they refrained from doctrinal innovation. In the first century BC the Roman poet Lucretius (Vol. 2, pp. 101 ff.) composed his *De rerum natura*, an exposition of Epicurean thought. In his eyes Epicurus was 'the father, the discoverer of things', and his poem follows Epicurus with fidelity. Lucretius was not resuscitating a superannuated philosophy: the system he admired and delineated was still vividly alive.

The Porch, like the Garden, was at Athens, but none of its major figures was Athenian. Zeno (*c.* 333-262), the founder of the school, hailed from Cyprus. He came to Athens in *c.* 310, where he established a school in the *Stoa Poikilē*—the 'Porch'. His mantle was assumed, and his views were developed, by Cleanthes of Assus (d. *c.* 232); and Cleanthes' successor Chrysippus (d. *c.* 206), who also came to Athens from Asia Minor, transmuted Stoicism into a comprehensive and systematic philosophy—it was said that 'if Chrysippus had not existed, the Stoa would not have existed either'.

PORTRAIT OF EPICURUS (341–270 BC), based on a commemorative statue of the mid third century BC. The founder of the Epicurean school of philosophy taught that pleasure (that is, freedom from pain and peace of mind) was the goal of life. His 'atomic' theory of the universe inspired Lucretius' great poem *De rerum natura* in the first century BC.

The Stoics were not traditionalists. The school's long history divides into three phases, Old, Middle, and Late. The Middle Stoa, whose chief ornaments were Panaetius of Rhodes (*c.* 185–109) and Posidonius of Apamea (135–51), substantially altered the emphasis of the school. So, too, did the Late Stoa, which is represented for us by Seneca (Vol. 2, pp. 253 f.), Epictetus (Vol. 2, pp. 298 ff.), and Marcus Aurelius (Vol. 2, pp. 301 ff.) from the first two centuries AD. Nor was the Old Stoa marked by doctrinal uniformity. There were renegades, of whom the most important was Ariston of Chios. He limited his concerns to ethics, rejecting physics and maintaining that 'dialectical reasonings are like spiders' webs—they seem to display some artistry but are in fact useless'. Chrysippus himself 'differed on many points from Zeno and also from Cleanthes, to whom he would often say that he only needed to be taught the theories and would discover the proofs for himself'.

None the less, the central tenets of the Old Stoics remained firm. In ethics they rejected hedonism and counselled a life of 'virtue'; in physics they accepted a form of materialism but denied atomism; in logic they were empiricists, but they assigned a major role to reason in the development of knowledge.

Philosophy was pursued outside the main schools. Pyrrho of Elis (*c.* 365–*c.* 270) adopted an extreme scepticism, holding that our senses are unreliable, that we should commit ourselves to no judgements—and that tranquillity of mind will

THE STOIC PHILOSOPHER CHRYSIPPUS (d. between 208 and 204 BC): a seated statue reconstructed with the aid of a body in the Louvre and a cast of a head in the British Museum. It may be based on a statue in Athens mentioned by Cicero which showed the philosopher sitting with hand extended (a typical gesture of philosophical disputation).

supervene upon such a practice. Pyrrho was perhaps influenced by the Indian ascetics whom he encountered as a member of Alexander's expedition to the East. In his turn he influenced the Academic scepticism of Arcesilaus. The Cyrenaic sect, founded by Aristippus (*c.* 430–*c.* 350), was also of a sceptical inclination: 'they abstained from physics, because its subject-matter was evidently unknowable; but they studied logic because of its utility'. Their chief doctrine, however, was ethical: they maintained a radical hedonism, according to which bodily pleasure was the supreme good. The affinities between Aristippus and Epicurus were often remarked upon.

Aristippus was a pupil of Socrates. So too was Euclides of Megara (*c.* 435–*c.* 365). Euclides and his followers, of whom the most eminent was Stilpo (d. *c.* 300), were celebrated in their day. They had views on ethics and on various topics in logic, but little is now known about them. Allied to the Megarians was a group called the Dialecticians, whose interest centred upon logical paradoxes. Diodorus Cronus (d. *c.* 284), the leading Dialectician, had an importance we can only dimly discern.

Antisthenes (*c.* 450–*c.* 350) was another pupil of Socrates. He and his follower Diogenes of Sinope (d. 323) were the founders of Cynicism. Cynicism was a way of life rather than a theoretical philosophy. Cynics proclaimed the supreme importance of individual freedom and self-sufficiency; they preached the 'natural' life and rejected with contempt the customs and conventions of society, thinking

DIOGENES IN HIS STORAGE JAR, as depicted on an engraved gem-stone of the Roman age. The story that the Cynic philosopher (414-323 BC) lived in a jar reflects the ascetic manner of life which he and his followers favoured. He is shown with the stick and dog of a beggar, debating with a seated disciple who holds a scroll.

nothing of wealth, position, or reputation. They also affected to despise pleasure ('I would rather go mad than enjoy myself', said Antisthenes). Their ostentatious asceticism was a common spectacle, admired or ridiculed according to the spectator's taste.

Arcesilaus and Carneades wrote nothing, but their thoughts were recorded by their disciples. Epicurus wrote at huge length, and so did the Old Stoics. Of that massive volume little has survived. Epicurus has come off best: three introductory essays, in the form of letters, are preserved, substantial fragments have been recovered from the ruins of Herculaneum, and in addition we have Lucretius. For the Old Stoa and the New Academy we are obliged to rely almost entirely on second-hand sources—on quotations, paraphrases and allusions in later writers. Much of the testimony comes from hostile or tendentious witnesses. The difficulty of assessing such reports exacerbates the problem of piecing together a coherent system from scattered and fragmentary evidence.

Ethics

Philosophy was customarily divided into three parts: logic, physics, and ethics. Hellenistic ethics, like the ethics of Aristotle, turns on the notion of *eudaimonia*— of well-being, welfare, flourishing. The task of ethics is to analyse human welfare and to determine the conditions under which it may be attained. There was some measure of agreement among the schools at the most general level. According to Epicurus, we should 'refer all choice and avoidance to health of the body and tranquillity of the soul, since that is the goal of a happy life'. Tranquillity or *ataraxia* ('untroubledness') had been similarly exalted in the old Academy of Xenocrates, and it was to become the watchword of the Pyrrhonian sceptics. The Stoics, too, acknowledged the same ideal; for 'they expel from mankind all the passions by which the mind is disturbed—desire and delight, fear and grief'.

In order to achieve tranquillity and to calm what Epicurus called 'the storm of the soul', we need only take thought. It is an assumption implicit in Epicureanism that fears will dissipate once the beliefs on which they are grounded are shown by philosophy to be false. Chrysippus explicitly contended that the passions were themselves beliefs of a sort, and hence subject to rational control. Such optimistic rationalization is no less foreign to the philosophy of Aristotle than the ethical quietism which it subserves.

That quietism is sometimes represented as a disengagement from social and political life, and it is interpreted as a reaction to the tumultuous and troubled world of Hellenistic Greece. The interpretation is implausible: life in Hellenistic Greece was no more upsetting, no more at the mercy of fickle fortune or malign foes, than it had been in an earlier era. Nor does *ataraxia* imply a withdrawal into the self or an obsessive individualism. Epicurus abjured the political life ('You must free yourself from the prison of politics and the daily round'), but he placed happiness in friendship and society—and an Epicurean 'will cultivate a king when it is opportune'. The Stoics valued social life, and they urged an involvement in politics. According to Chrysippus, a wise man 'will willingly assume a kingship and make money from it—and if he cannot be king himself he will live with a king and accompany a king to war'. *Ataraxia* was not to be achieved by shunning the world.

Within that broad area of agreement, Epicurean and Stoic ethics are regularly presented as antithetical: if both sects sought contentment, they sought it in contrary directions. For Epicurus, the direction was determined by nature:

You need only possess perception and be made of flesh, and you will see that pleasure is good.

I summon you [he wrote to Anaxarchus] to continuous pleasures—and not to virtues which are empty and vain and which hold out troubling expectations of rewards.

We say that pleasure is the beginning and end of a happy life; for we recognize it as a primary and innate good, and from it we begin all choice and avoidance, and to it we return, judging every good thing by the standard of that feeling.

In his own lifetime Epicurus was vilified as a crude and unlettered sybarite. But although he held that 'the beginning and root of every good thing is the pleasure of the belly', his hedonism is not an excuse for sensual indulgence. First, Epicurean pleasures are rationally selected, and the Epicurean is aware that today's delights will be paid for by the misery of the morrow. That is why 'sometimes we pass over many pleasures when greater discomfort follows for us as a result of them'. In fact, calculation reveals that 'the pleasant life is produced not by a string of drinking-bouts and revelries, nor by the enjoyment of boys and women, nor by fish and the other items on an expensive menu, but by sober reasoning'. Secondly, Epicurus has an idiosyncratic account of the nature of pleasure. 'When we say that pleasure is the goal, we mean ... being neither pained in the body nor troubled in the soul.' Pleasure is construed negatively, as the absence of pain, and 'the limit to the magnitude of pleasures is the removal of everything that pains us'. Thus the pleasures of a sensualist are inferior to those of a sober reasoner: the sensualist's pleasures are followed by pain, and in any case the sensualist can never achieve more than that total freedom from pain which is equally within the grasp of the reasoner. 'True pleasure is a serious business', as the Stoic Seneca put it.

An Epicurean hedonist is virtuous as well as sober. For 'it is not possible to live pleasurably without living sensibly and nobly and justly'. 'A just man', for example, 'is least troubled but an unjust man is loaded with troubles', for 'up to the time of his death it is not known if he will go undetected'. Epicurus' invitation to Anaxarchus was disingenuous: an Epicurean will pursue virtue, and he 'revels in the pleasure of the body—on a diet of bread and water'.

Nature led Epicurus to pleasure, the Stoics to virtue. According to the Old Stoa, 'the goal is to live in agreement with nature—which is the same as to live in accordance with virtue, since it is virtue to which nature leads us'. But the road along which nature directs us is long and difficult to follow.

We are led first to ourselves. Chrysippus insists that 'the first thing congenial to any animal is its own constitution and its awareness of that'. But an initial egocentricity naturally develops into altruism: as a later writer puts it, man 'is a social animal and requires others. That is why we live in cities; for every man is part of a city. Again, we readily form friendships ...' Thus we come to do what is 'appropriate' for us (*kathēkon*). 'An appropriate act is one which, being consistent with the agent's mode of life, can be reasonably defended.' The reference to reason is not casual: indeed, it can be said that 'appropriate acts are those which reason selects—for example, honouring parents, brothers, country; consorting with friends'.

The performance of appropriate acts is a sign of progress, but it is not a mark of success. According to Chrysippus, 'a man who is progressing to the summit certainly performs all appropriate acts and omits none; but his life is not yet a flourishing one'. For he has not yet achieved virtue, and 'a flourishing life is found only in a life in accordance with virtue'. Virtues are mental states or dispositions—indeed, they are cognitive states. The 'perfect' virtues (i.e. the four 'primary' virtues of good sense, justice, courage, and temperance, together with the virtues subordinate to them) are forms of knowledge and 'consist of theorems'. An appropriate act, when it is performed virtuously, is perfect; and perfect acts are 'successes' (*katorthōmata*). The good life, according to the Stoics, is a sequence of successes, of appropriate acts virtuously performed, of acts in conformity to nature performed in full knowledge of their conformity.

Stoic ethics forms a rich and complex system. It is sometimes decried as being paradoxical and grim. That it was paradoxical the Stoics themselves allowed, and they revelled in remarking that 'all mistakes are equally bad' or 'only a wise man is rich'. Yet on inspection the paradoxes turn out to be verbal rather than real. As for grimness, the Stoics certainly deny that pleasure is a good thing; but they give a welcome to what they call joy: 'they say that joy is the contrary of pleasure, being rational elation'. In fact, we are told that a Stoic will like horses and hunting, that he will go to parties, that he will fall in love with beautiful young men; and 'what adornment', the Stoics asked, 'can a household enjoy to compare with the companionship of a man and his wife?' A Stoic is not debarred from the pleasures of life: he may enjoy them all—provided that he does so virtuously.

Nor is the Stoic maxim that 'virtue alone is good' a confession of moral severity. Its force is best shown by reference to the Stoic account of 'indifferents' or things neither good nor bad. 'Of indifferents they say that some are promoted, some demoted, some neither promoted nor demoted'. Things are said to be promoted 'not because they contribute and work towards welfare but because we should choose them rather than what is demoted'. Health is thus promoted, for plainly we should prefer it to illness; but health is not good—for 'what can be used both well and badly is neither good nor bad, and all foolish men use wealth and health and bodily strength badly'. Health is not good in itself; but health well used is good: health—and everything else—is advantageous only when it 'participates in virtue' or is wisely used. That is the sense in which virtue is the sole good.

There are differences, both theoretical and practical, between Epicurean and Stoic ethics. But the popular picture of a sybaritic Epicurean confronting a puritanical Stoic is a caricature: to an external observer there would in truth be little difference between members of the two sects.

Physics

Physics is subordinate to ethics. According to Chrysippus, 'the study of nature is to be undertaken for no other end than the discrimination of good things and bad'. Epicurus asserted that 'you must first realize that knowledge of celestial matters, like other branches of study, has no other goal but tranquillity and firm conviction'; and 'if we were not at all disturbed by our apprehensions concerning celestial phenomena and death ... and by our failure to understand the limits of pains and of desires, we should have no further need of natural science'.

The first theorem of Epicurean physics maintains that 'the nature of things consists of bodies and void.' Epicurus commends the theorem by urging that 'perception in itself universally testifies that there are bodies ... and if place, which we call void or space or intangible substance, did not exist, then bodies would have nowhere to be and nothing through which to move'. Bodies are either composite or simple. The simple bodies are atoms: indivisible, changeless, microscopic; infinite in number and roaming in infinite space; possessing size, shape, weight, mobility, but devoid of colour, taste, smell, and the like. The moving atoms sometimes collide. As the hooks of one atom chance to catch the eyes of another, macroscopic bodies are formed: the furnishings of the world—sheep, horses, chariots, and the souls of men—are congeries of atoms, their sensible forms and qualities determined by their corpuscular structures. Atomism is thoroughly mechanistic. Everything is explained by the laws of atomic motion. Lucretius instructs us to 'avoid the error of thinking that the bright orbs of the eyes were made in order that we might be able to see', or that any natural phenomena are amenable to teleological explanation in terms of goals or purposes.

Atomism has two profound implications. First, the heavenly bodies are not divine intelligences: according to Epicurus, 'since they are aggregates of fire, we should not suppose them to possess happiness and pursue their courses voluntarily'. There are indeed gods in the Epicurean universe, admirable beings who live a life of tranquillity far off in intergalactic space. But those gods are not to be feared. 'What is happy and indestructible neither is troubled itself nor causes trouble to others—hence it is moved neither by anger nor by gratitude.' Thus the heavenly rumblings at which the superstitious quake are purely material events, and the real gods have no interest at all in life on earth.

Secondly, 'those who say that the soul is incorporeal are foolish; for if it were it could neither act nor be acted upon—but in fact both those properties are plainly observed to belong to the soul'. The soul is a body within the body, 'composed of fine particles spread all through the structure, most like wind with an admixture of heat'. Thus 'when the whole structure is dissolved, the soul is dispersed and no longer retains its powers'. It follows that 'death is nothing to us; for what is dissolved has no perception, and what has no perception is nothing to us'. It is as absurd to fear the time after death as it would be to fear the time before birth. Lucretius makes the point vividly:

Just as in time past we felt no disquiet when the Carthaginians arose on all sides in conflict and all was shaken by the fearful tumult of war ... so when we shall no longer exist, when the body and soul from which we are compounded shall have separated, then nothing at all can happen to us, who then shall no longer exist; nothing will stir our senses, though the earth mingle with the sea and the sea with the heavens.

True physics dispels both the grosser fears of Hell and the more sophisticated inquietude aroused by the anticipation of future non-existence.

If we are fearless of the gods and of death, may we not still be troubled by pain and by the desolation of frustrated desires? Epicurean physics includes a psychological analysis of human desire. 'Of desires, some are natural, others empty; and of natural desires, some are necessary, others merely natural.' Non-natural desires—such as the desire to be honoured or to be commemorated— 'depend upon an empty opinion' and depart once the opinion is seen to be false. Similarly, 'those natural desires which bring no pain if they are not satisfied [a desire for roast beef, say, or for claret] ... depend upon an empty opinion'. There remain natural and necessary desires, such as the desire for food or for drink. Those desires cannot be eliminated, for the opinions on which they rest are true; yet they are also easily satisfied. As for pain, Epicurus is brusque: 'All pain is to be despised; for pains which hurt sharply remain briefly and those which endure in the flesh are blunt.' Moreover, pain is counterbalanced by pleasure. Epicurus himself, dying of strangury and dysentery, wrote 'on this happy day' to his friend Idomeneus that all his agonies were 'balanced by the joy in my soul as I recollect the conversations we have had together'.

Physics produces tranquillity by proving our fears to be groundless. To achieve that end, Epicurus believes that he must establish the fundamental truths of atomism. But he does not think it necessary to provide detailed explanations of natural phenomena—'the investigation of risings and settings and solstices and eclipses makes no contribution to happiness'. Indeed, such knowledge is unattainable: in the case of the first principle of physics, 'there is only one explanation which harmonizes with the phenomena, but that is not so in celestial matters: they admit more than one explanation of their happening and more than one account of their nature which harmonizes with perception'. Epicurus' scepticism is amateur, and the truth is that he does not care to know. 'If we recognize that an event can happen for a variety of reasons, we shall be as tranquil as if we knew that it happened in precisely *this* way.' At bottom one thing matters: 'only let superstition be absent'.

The Stoics, like the Epicureans, were cavalier about particular scientific theories but intensely concerned with the foundations of physics. 'They hold that the first principles of things are two in number: what acts, and what is acted upon. What is acted upon is qualityless substance, which is matter; what acts is reason in matter, which is god.' Since 'Zeno thought that nothing could in any way be caused by anything incorporeal', the active principle is itself material, and the Stoic universe is as thoroughly corporeal as the Epicurean. But the Stoics admit no empty space into the world, and do not suppose that matter comes in atomic parcels. Rather, the world is a continuous mass of stuff, gapless and infinitely divisible; it is a blend of the two principles, 'the mixtures of which' according to Chrysippus, 'are through and through ... and do not occur by way of circum-location or juxtaposition'.

The active principle, sometimes characterized as fire or 'breath', fashions the world, first creating the four elements of fire, air, water, and earth, and thence forming the structures of the cosmos. The universe 'is governed by reason and providence', for the active principle 'is an immortal living thing, rational, perfect in felicity, admitting no evil, providing for the world and the things in the world'—and it is called Zeus and Hera and Athena and the like. The world is not a machine, unthinking and purposeless: it is imbued with intelligence, and any explanation of its functionings must be primarily teleological.

We are little parts of the cosmic animal, having a proper place in its natural economy. Like Epicurean souls, Stoic souls are corporeal. They are fragments of the active principle, and a later writer explains that the soul 'is not contained in the body as in a vessel—like liquid in a cask—but is wonderfully blended and mixed throughout the whole of it, so that not even the smallest part of the mixture fails to have a share of each constituent'. Chrysippus agrees with Epicurus that the soul does not survive the dissolution of the body, but he can offer us a sort of spasmodic immortality: 'after our deaths, at a certain period of time we shall again come to be in the state in which we now are'. For the cosmos enjoys a cyclical history. At fixed intervals, the world is consumed by fire: after the conflagration, a new world, just like its predecessor, is formed, itself doomed to fiery destruction. Each world contains us: we shall live again, infinitely often— and we have already enjoyed infinitely many lives, each identical in its biography.

But man's place in the world is in one respect problematical, both for Chrysippus and for Epicurus. For men can act freely, and free action is not easily contained in a rule-governed universe.

Epicurus' world, though mechanistic, was not determined by iron necessity.

The atoms sometimes deviate from their normal trajectories by a minute amount: and the deviation, or swerve, has no cause. 'If the atoms do not swerve and thereby produce a sort of beginning of motion which breaks the bonds of fate so that cause does not follow cause everlastingly, what is the source of the free will which living things possess throughout the world?' Freedom implies the absence of external necessitation, and the postulated swerves ensure that necessity is not ubiquitous. Free actions are determined by the agent's will. And the will, thanks to an uncaused deviation in the atoms of the soul, is not wholly dependent on external events.

The Stoics thought little of that device to save free will: 'they do not allow Epicurus to swerve his atoms a jot, for he thereby introduces an uncaused motion', Chrysippus insisted that, 'since universal nature extends to everything, it will be necessary for everything whatever to occur in accordance with nature and with its rational principle, in due order and ineluctably'. Fate is the name the Stoics gave to the chain of causes and effects which binds the universe together: 'everything happens in accordance with fate'.

The Sceptical Academy launched a major attack against this Stoic position. One of their arguments—the 'Lazy Argument', probably formulated by Arcesilaus—ran as follows: 'If it is fated for you to recover from this illness, you will recover whether you call a doctor or not; again, if it is fated for you not to recover from this illness, you will not recover whether you call a doctor or not; but one or the other is fated: therefore it is pointless to call a doctor.' Carneades produced a different line of thought: 'If everything comes about by antecedent causes, everything comes about in a web or net of natural interconnections; if that is so, necessity causes everything; if that is true, nothing is in our power.'

The debate between the Academy and the Stoa was long and intricate. Chrysippus had a subtle reply to the Lazy Argument, but his most interesting manoeuvre depended on a distinction among types of cause. 'Some causes are perfect and principal, others auxiliary and proximate. Thus when we say that everything happens by fate in virtue of antecedent causes, we wish to be understood to mean not perfect and principal but auxiliary and proximate causes.' An example makes the point clear. A man places a cylinder on a flat surface and gives it a push: it rolls. 'Just as the man who pushed the cylinder gave a start to its motion but did not make it such as to roll, so an object that appears to us will impress us and as it were seal its form in our mind, but assent will be in our power; and, as we said in the case of the cylinder, assent, though pushed externally, will for the rest move by its own force and nature'. The antecedent cause—the man's push— makes the cylinder move; but it does not determine the cylinder to roll rather than to slide. That the cylinder rolls is due to its own nature, not to external circumstances. Similarly, Chrysippus urges, the antecedent cause—the impression of an external object—causes the mind to move; but it does not determine the direction of the movement. That the mind assents to or dissents from the impression is due to its own nature—it is something within our power.

That ingenious comparison did not end the debate. Chrysippus' successors elaborated his classification of causes, and the attempt to reconcile freedom and fatalism exercised the Stoa for the whole of its history. Whether or not the attempt succeeded, it inspired the subtlest analysis of the notion of causation in the history of philosophy.

Logic

Physics will succour ethics only if it is grounded in firm knowledge. Here the logical part of philosophy enters; for, according to the Stoics, 'everything is discerned by way of logical study—both what falls within the province of physics and what falls within the province of ethics'. Now things are either 'evident' or 'unclear'. If evident, they are grasped 'immediately' or 'directly'; if unclear, they are grasped indirectly and by the mediation of other things. Thus logic will have two main aspects: it will provide a 'criterion of truth', as the Hellenistic philosophers called it, by which we may judge what is evident; and it will offer a theory of inference, by which we may attain knowledge of what is unclear.

The Stoic theory of inference—Stoic logic in the narrow sense of the term—rests upon a detailed theory of language. It begins with the conception of an *axiōma* or proposition, 'something which in itself denies or asserts something—e.g. "It is day", "Dion is walking"'. Propositions are either simple or non-simple, the non-simple being 'those consisting of a repeated proposition or of several propositions' joined by a connecting particle. (Stoic theory concentrated on three connectives: 'if', 'and', 'or'.) An argument is 'a system of premisses and a conclusion', where premisses and conclusion are all propositions, simple or complex.

Like Aristotle, the Stoics recognized that a logician's business is with forms of argument rather than with particular inferences; and like Aristotle they achieved the generality which the business requires by the use of schemata. Again like Aristotle, the Stoics were systematic: 'there are certain arguments which are non-demonstrable (for they do not need to be demonstrated)'—Chrysippus lists five such arguments, others list others; and every argument is constructed by way of those. The five 'indemonstrables' play in the Stoic system the part played in Aristotle's syllogistic by 'perfect' syllogisms: they are basic, and other argument forms are derivable from them.

In content, Stoic logic is very different from Peripatetic. It corresponds roughly to what modern logicians call propositional or sentential logic. The foundation of Chrysippus' system consists of the following argument-schemata, the five indemonstrables: (i) If 1, then 2; but 1: therefore, 2. (ii) If 1, then 2; but not 2: therefore, not 1. (iii) Not both 1 and 2; but 1: therefore, not 2. (iv) Either 1 or 2; but 1: therefore, not 2. (v) Either 1 or 2; but not 1: therefore, 2. The logic which Chrysippus erected on that modest base was powerful and sophisticated.

Logic is the servant of knowledge, and its service consists in the provision and ratification of proofs. Not all arguments are proofs. Rather, 'a proof is an argument which, by way of agreed premisses, reveals by deduction an unclear conclusion'. The notion of 'revelation'—of uncovering or explaining—is crucial to the closely connected concept of a 'sign'. The world is full of signs—clouds signify future rain, scars are signs of past wounds—and signs are appropriately expressed by way of conditional propositions; indeed, a sign was loosely described as 'an antecedent proposition in a sound conditional which reveals the consequent'. Consider, then, a standard example of a proof: 'If sweat permeates the skin, the skin has imperceptible pores; but sweat permeates the skin: therefore the skin has imperceptible pores.' The argument has the form of the first indemonstrable; both its premisses are true or 'agreed'; its conditional premiss expresses the fact that perspiration is a sign of perforation; its conclusion is 'unclear' (the pores are not available to direct inspection). Thus by virtue of inference we advance from evident facts to a knowledge of what is unclear.

'Many people believe that if the gods studied logic it would be the logic of Chrysippus.' The Epicureans dissented—indeed, 'they reject dialectic as redundant' and they preferred to call the third part of philosophy 'canonics' or the theory of judgement. But they still required some account of how we might come to know 'unclear' facts. The later Epicureans, whose arguments are preserved in Philodemus' treatise *On Signs*, disputed the Stoic theory of signs and substituted an account of their own. Epicurus himself spoke not of proof and signs but of 'confirmation' and 'disconfirmation': 'if judgements are not confirmed or are disconfirmed, falsity arises; if they are confirmed or not disconfirmed, truth'. A later author illustrates the notion: 'when Plato is approaching from far off, I conjecture and judge because of the distance that it is Plato; after he has approached and the distance is reduced, it is testified and confirmed by direct evidence that it is Plato'. The ideas of confirmation and disconfirmation are relatively plain, but non-confirmation and non-disconfirmation produce puzzles: those puzzles may have spurred Epicurus' successors to develop their own theory of signs.

What, next, of the 'criterion of truth' by which we judge what is 'evident'? In general, 'the old philosophers say that there are two kinds of evident things, those which are discerned by one of the senses ... and those which strike the mind with a primary and non-demonstrable impression'. According to Epicurus, all objects are continuously emitting effluences of various kinds. When the effluences strike an appropriate part of a sensitive body—the ears or the nose, say—their parent object is perceived. The effluences which affect the eyes and cause the parent object to be seen are *simulacra* or replicas—thin skins which preserve the contours of the object as they speed through space. Thought is analogous: Lucretius states that 'the mind is moved by replicas of lions and of everything else it grasps in just the same way as the eyes are—except that it perceives more flimsy replicas'.

Such effluences supply us with the concepts we employ and form the basis of our knowledge. Moreover, the impressions they make on us are in some way infallible: 'whatever impression we grasp directly by the mind or by the sense-organs, whether of shape or of other properties—*that* is the shape of the concrete body . . . Falsity and error always depend on a superadded opinion.'

The Stoics agreed that our conceptual resources and our knowledge are founded upon direct impressions from external objects. They differed over the physics and physiology of cognition. But their most important difference from the Epicureans lies in their assessment of the impressions themselves. For the Stoics held that our knowledge rests upon one special type of impression. These 'apprehensive impressions' were defined as impressions 'deriving from an existing object, signed and sealed on the mind in conformity with the existing object itself, of a sort which could not derive from anything other than the existing object.' The impressions of a madman may be mere figments, deriving from no existent object; an impression may derive from a real object and yet misrepresent it; an impression may represent an object correctly, yet fail to record its peculiar individuality. No such impression is apprehensive. 'For they require that apprehensive impressions genuinely grasp their objects and imprint exactly all their individual characteristics.'

Epicurean impressions are all true: falsity enters only when we misinterpret our data. The Stoics allow that the data themselves are often distorted: in order to avoid falsity we must scrutinize and select. But both schools insisted that we do obtain knowledge from our impressions, and each faced challenge from the sceptics of the Academy.

The Epicurean dogma appeared easy to attack: there are familiar perceptual illusions, and the senses sometimes offer conflicting testimony—how, then, can all impressions be true? The Epicureans were well aware of the phenomenon of illusion, for which they offered physical explanations. Lucretius knows that a square tower when seen from a distance may be judged round. The replicas which leave the tower have sharp edges, but 'as they travel through a large space of air, the air by frequent collisions blunts them' and they become rounded. Even so, the tower does not *look* round: 'the stone structures look as though they had been turned on a lathe—yet they do *not* look like stones which are nearby and genuinely round, but seem to be, as it were, sketchy likenesses of them'. Again, 'Timagoras the Epicurean denied that when he pressed his eye he ever seemed to *see* two little flames in the lamp—the falsity belongs to opinion, not to the eyes.' Careful attention to the exact content of our impressions will show that illusions are due to the mind's misreading, not to the eye's misleading.

As for conflicting perceptions, each is true—but true of only a part of the object perceived. 'Since everything is mixed and compounded, and different things naturally fit different people . . . people encounter only those parts with which their senses are commensurate.' The water feels cold to me, warm to you. We are both right, or partly right; for the water contains cold elements and warm elements, the former affecting me and the latter you. Perception does not err.

The Epicurean defence of impressions was not mere quixotry. Epicurus asserted that 'if you reject absolutely any perception ... you will confound your remaining perceptions too with that empty belief, so that you will reject every criterion'. If any perception fails, all fail—and knowledge is lost. The Academics were not satisfied, but they were more interested in the Stoics than in the Epicureans.

The focus of the dispute was the final clause in the Stoic definition of apprehensive impression: the impression must be 'of a sort which could not derive from any other existing object'.

There are four points which imply that there is nothing that can be known, grasped or apprehended ... First, some impressions are false; secondly, they cannot be apprehended; thirdly, if there is no difference between two impressions it cannot be that one of them can be apprehended but the other not; fourthly, for any true impression derived from the senses there is another adjacent impression which does not differ from it at all and which cannot be apprehended.

If Chrysippus claims to possess a true impression, the Academics will offer him another impression which is false but which Chrysippus cannot distinguish from the impression he claims to be true. Hence his impression is not apprehensive; for it could have derived from something else, namely from the object from which the indistinguishable false impression derives. The Academics produced pairs of eggs, identical twins, real and wax apples, in an attempt to substantiate their claim that for every true impression there was an adjacent false impression indistinguishable from it. The Stoics made defensive manoeuvres. They claimed distinctions where the Academy saw none, they added an extra clause to their definition of apprehensive impression.

Moreover, they took the battle into the Academic camp. Without belief, life is impossible; for we lose all reason for action. The Epicureans made the same point. According to Lucretius, 'life itself is immediately ruined if you are not prepared to believe your senses—and to avoid precipices'.

Science

Even if scepticism does not subvert life, surely it will subvert science? The Hellenistic period was the golden age of Greek science, and it is natural to wonder whether the scientists noticed the concerns and perplexities of their philosophical contemporaries.

Euclid's *Elements* are perhaps the most celebrated product of the period. Euclid (*fl. c.* 300) 'composed his *Elements* by systematizing much of the work of Eudoxus and completing much of that of Theaetetus, putting into irrefutable demonstrative form propositions which had been somewhat loosely proved by his predecessors'. Euclid's achievement lay in form rather than in content: he insisted on a rigorous and systematic presentation of mathematical theorems. Archimedes of Syracuse (287–212) and Apollonius of Perge (*fl. c.* 200) opened up new areas of mathematical knowledge. 'His contemporaries called Apollonius a great geometer because of the remarkable features of the theorems on cones which he proved,' and modern scholars judge his work on conic sections one of the masterpieces of Greek geometry. Archimedes' was a more universal talent: he did original work in astronomy and engineering as well as in mathematics. Within mathematics he excelled in geometry (where he calculated the approximate value of pi), in mechanics (where he developed statics and invented hydrostatics), in arithmetic (where he discovered ways of calculating with very large numbers).

Astronomy is a mathematical science, and both Archimedes and Apollonius were astronomers. Early in the third century Aristarchus of Samos (*fl. c.* 275) 'hypothesized that the fixed stars and the sun stay motionless, and that the earth moves in a circle about the sun which lies at the centre of its orbit.' But Aristarchus' innovative hypotheses were not developed by his successors, who returned—in part for good scientific reasons—to a geocentric model of the universe. Apollonius was the first to devise a system of epicycles and eccentric orbits: the system was elaborated by Hipparchus of Nicaea (*fl. c.* 135), the second astronomer of the age, and it reached its zenith of sophistication in the work of Ptolemy

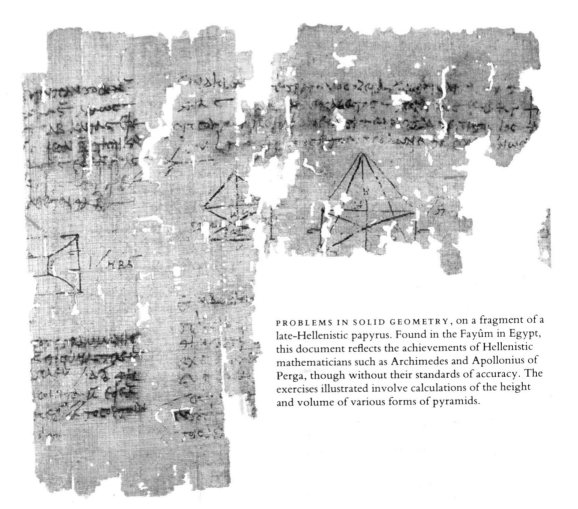

PROBLEMS IN SOLID GEOMETRY, on a fragment of a late-Hellenistic papyrus. Found in the Fayûm in Egypt, this document reflects the achievements of Hellenistic mathematicians such as Archimedes and Apollonius of Perga, though without their standards of accuracy. The exercises illustrated involve calculations of the height and volume of various forms of pyramids.

some three centuries later. Hipparchus was also an empirical astronomer: he invented or improved various optical aids; he produced a star-map; he discovered the precession of the equinoxes. Beside Hipparchus, the polymath Eratosthenes of Cyrene (*fl. c.* 225) cuts a small figure—indeed, 'because he was second best in every branch of study ... he was nicknamed Beta'. But he merits mention here for his calculation of the circumference of the earth: his method was sound, and his result was astonishingly accurate.

Eratosthenes had studied under Zeno and Arcesilaus, and the scientists doubtless knew, or knew of, the philosophers. Equally, some of the philosophers were aware of scientific speculations; thus 'Cleanthes thought that the Greeks should indict Aristarchus of Samos for impiety, inasmuch as he set the hearth of the world in motion'. But there is little evidence of any interdisciplinary influence or understanding. Problems of perception engaged the philosophers, and observational difficulties troubled the astronomers: the two areas did not overlap. The scientists discussed questions of method, and the philosophers speculated on the foundations of knowledge: the two enquiries were separately conducted. Astrology has been thought to link science and philosophy inasmuch as the astronomers may have regarded their science as a servant of astrology while the Stoics' fatalism made them likely to succumb to that occult science. But the link is tenuous. Hipparchus is said 'to have shown that we are related to the stars and that our souls are a part of the heavens', but that report is vague, and it is unlikely that the Hellenistic astronomers anticipated Ptolemy's addiction to astrology. Moreover, there is little evidence for any interest in astrology on the part of the Old Stoa.

In truth, the philosophers did not care for mathematical arcana, and the mathematical scientists ignored philosophy—they were more interested in the technological applications of their studies than in any theoretical speculations. Thus engineers such as Ctesibius of Alexandria (*fl. c.* 270), Philo of Byzantium (*fl. c.* 200), Hero of Alexandria (*fl. c.* 60), and Archimedes amused themselves and diverted their masters by inventing new machinery—water-clocks and mechanical puppets, fire-pumps and steam-toys, and many engines of war.

Hellenistic astronomy was rivalled only by Hellenistic medicine, the protagonists of which were Herophilus of Chalcedon (*fl. c.* 270) and Erasistratus of Ceos (*fl. c.* 260). Both men were practical physicians. Herophilus had an interest in new drugs, and he also developed a diagnostic technique which relied upon distinguishing different types of pulse. Both men were also interested in the theoretical aspects of medicine. Herophilus was the first scientist to describe the structure and function of the duodenum, an organ which is still known by the name Herophilus gave it. He also examined the brain. Erasistratus developed a physiological theory which rested on mechanical principles. The theories had an empirical base:

Herophilus and Erasistratus ... were given criminals from the prison by the kings <of Egypt> and dissected them alive: while they were still breathing they observed parts

MECHANICAL GADGETS described by Hero of Alexandria (first century AD) in his *Pneumatica* and *Auto-matapoeica*. (*Left*) Steam from a cauldron of boiling water is forced into a hollow sphere from which its only escape is via two small hooked pipes placed opposite each other; the result is that the sphere rotates. (*Right*) An automatic libation. The heat of the altar-fire forces hot air down into a tank of oil contained in the platform; the oil in turn is forced up through tubes within the bodies of the two statuettes and drips out from vessels held in their hands.

which nature had formerly concealed, and examined their position, colour, shape, size, arrangement, hardness, softness, smoothness, connection . . .

Nor is it cruel, as most people allege, by causing pain to guilty men—and only a few at that—to seek out remedies for innocent people of every age.

Such bloody researches may seem far removed from the contemplative arm-chair of the philosopher. But Greek medicine had a long association with philosophy, and the philosophical interests of the Hippocratic writers of the fifth and fourth centuries were inherited by their Hellenistic successors. Erasistratus was said by his followers 'to have associated with the Peripatetic philosophers', and his physiological theory betrays the influence of Epicurus and of the Stoa. He wrote a work *On Causes* which appears to have been primarily philosophical in tone. Herophilus too was exercised by the notion of causation: he 'cast doubt on all causes by many powerful arguments', and came to a sceptical conclusion: 'whether or not there are causes is by nature undiscoverable, but in opinion I hold that I am made hot and cold, and am filled by food and drink'. Herophilus was the first of a long line of medical sceptics which culminated in the second century AD in the figure of Sextus Empiricus, physician and Pyrrhonist.

Epilogue

To some degree the doctors preserved the Aristotelian ideal which the Hellenistic philosophers had generally discarded: science and philosophy, for them, were complementary aspects of a unified search for understanding. At the end of the Hellenistic age that ideal was briefly revived by an eminent philosopher.

Posidonius was an admired figure in his day, a friend of Cicero and of Pompey. In philosophy he was a Stoic, and though he was no blind follower of Chrysippus his Stoicism was heterodox only on the periphery. What was unorthodox about Posidonius was his voracious appetite for learning of every kind. He was a voluminous historian, who undertook a continuation of the work of Polybius; an original ethnographer, who described the manners and *mores* of the Celts; a travelled geographer, who propounded a theory of the Atlantic tides; a student of logic and mathematics, of botany and zoology, of seismology, geology, and mineralogy. In sum, as one ancient admirer put it, 'he Aristotelizes'. But Posidonius was a giant apart. He had no followers. Polymathy was outmoded, Aristotelian man extinct.

The river of philosophy ran a clear course for some two centuries, its two main channels, the Stoic and the Epicurean, being clearly marked. In the first century BC the waters became turbid. The Middle Stoa relaxed the canons of Chrysippus and advanced a more eclectic philosophy. The New Academy passed out of existence when the last proponent of scepticism, Antiochus of Ascalon (*fl. c.* 85), became a Stoic in all but name (Vol. 2, p. 293). Even Epicureanism altered, as the writings of Philodemus of Gadara (*fl. c.* 55) demonstrate. Pyrrhonian scepticism was rekindled by Aenesidemus (*fl. c.* 90). Platonism received fresh attention and attracted new followers. The edition of Aristotle's treatises by Andronicus of Rhodes (*fl. c.* 50) revived interest in the philosophical parts of the Peripatetic system.

The face of philosophy changed, but the Hellenistic age had left its mark. The systems of the Porch and the Garden never lacked adherents, and modern philosophy has been influenced as much by them as by the Lyceum or the Old Academy. Moreover, the conception of philosophy—of its scope, its subject-matter, its methods—which we have inherited from Greece is not the generously ambitious ideal of Aristotle but the narrower and more introspective notion of the Hellenistic schools.

Further Reading

Systematic accounts of Stoicism and Epicureanism can be found in Books 7 and 10 of Diogenes Laertius' *Lives of the Philosophers* (Book 10 includes the three *Letters* of Epicurus). For the New Academy the most useful single text is Cicero's *Academica*. The works of Sextus Empiricus—*Outlines of Pyrrhonism* and *Against the Mathematicians*—contain a mass of further material. All those texts are available in English translation in the Loeb Classical Library. Much of our information, however, comes in fragments. For Epicurus the indispensable aids are: G. Arrighetti (ed.), *Epicuro—Opere* (Turin, 1973²); H. Usener (ed.), *Epicurea* (Leipzig, 1887). The fundamental work for Stoicism is H. von Arnim (ed.) *Stoicorum Veterum Fragmenta* (Leipzig, 1903-24). There is nothing comparable for the New Academy.

The best English introduction to the subject is A. A. Long, *Hellenistic Philosophy* (London, 1974). Modern research can be approached by way of two collections of papers: M. Schofield, M. F. Burnyeat, J. Barnes (eds.): *Doubt and Dogmatism* (Oxford, 1980); J. Barnes, J. Brunschwig, M. F. Burnyeat, M. Schofield (eds.): *Science and Speculation* (Cambridge, 1982).

16

Hellenistic and Graeco-Roman Art

❧❦

ROGER LING

Introduction

HELLENISTIC art is an unfashionable field. To the *aficionados* of the Archaic and Classical periods it seems a bewildering farrago of divergent styles, at one extreme bloated and showy, at the other flaccid and derivative: it is almost as though Greek art, hitherto carried forward in a relatively comprehensible and consistent pattern of development, loses its way and threshes around without a sense of purpose. To the students of Roman art, with its clearer chronological framework and (in the mainstream at least) its firm political thrust, the Hellenistic age is the shadowy and half-understood background out of which emerge the technical know-how and many of the stylistic features which go into the making of the Roman state tradition. These attitudes of course do scant justice to the achievements of Hellenistic art. The period 323–31 BC saw the creation of some of the greatest of Greek masterpieces—masterpieces which have exercised considerable influence on the artists and art critics of recent centuries, especially the seventeenth and eighteenth.

The main reason why Hellenistic art has been neglected, if not denigrated, is the difficulty of studying it. The new political situation, in which Greek culture was brought into contact with various alien traditions and at the same time diffused over areas too vast for effective communications to be maintained, inevitably led to regional variations: there is no single current that can be traced. More serious are the problems of dating and attribution, due chiefly to the shortage of written evidence. After the comparative abundance of literary and epigraphic testimonia for the Classical period, our sources for Hellenistic art are exiguous. The Elder Pliny, previously our main support, provides no more than a few scattered and barely datable references for the 150 years between the early third and mid second centuries BC; and fragments of Hellenistic authors quoted by Athenaeus in his *Deipnosophistae* (*c.*AD 200), together with isolated snippets of information in the architectural treatise of Vitruvius and in the histories of Diodorus and Valerius Maximus, do very little to fill the gap. Archaeological associations are also less helpful for dating than in the previous period. The works of art which can be connected with precise historical events are few and far between: the Romans left very little behind when they destroyed Corinth in 146, and it is not always clear whether the abandonment of buildings on Delos is to be attributed to the sack by Mithridates in 88, to the pirate raid of 69, or to a later turn of events. There are in addition relatively few Hellenistic buildings which are closely dated by inscriptions. Nor do any classes of Hellenistic ceramics supply dating evidence comparable to that offered for previous centuries by Athenian black-figure and red-figure: only lately have more rigorous pottery studies sharpened the cutting edge of this particular chronological tool.

All this has contributed to an inextricable confusion surrounding Hellenistic art; but nonetheless certain generalizations can be made. First, the artistic centre of gravity in the Greek world shifted eastwards. While Athens remained an important focus of patronage and production, the great centres of Hellenistic times were in Asia Minor and the eastern Mediterranean: Pergamum, Rhodes, Antioch, Alexandria. Secondly, the type of patronage changed. Whereas in Classical times Greek artists had worked primarily for cities and private citizens, now they found themselves receiving commissions from all-powerful kings and their ministers; and the old ideals of civic pride and religious reverence which had inspired the great works of the Classical period gave way to the personal whims and propaganda of the new ruling classes. These circumstances, combined with the development of science and humanism, account for several aspects of Hellenistic art which will be illustrated below: the broadened range of subjects, a trend towards the secularization of art, the emergence of academic and ostentatious work, generally the tendency of art to entertain rather than to elevate the viewer. Ultimately, with the encroachment of Roman power upon the Greek stage, the focus of attention moved westwards and new patrons appeared: the merchants, magistrates, and military potentates of Rome. This ushered in a new phase of classicism and eclecticism and began the process whereby Greek artists were schooled to interpret the imperialist ideologies of the new world-power.

Architecture

In architecture the Hellenistic age saw an increased loosening of the rules which had governed Classical design, a fuller and more flamboyant use of surface decoration, often at variance with the interior structure, a gradual development of new structural forms and techniques, and the creation of the first truly homogeneous planned complexes in which each individual building was designed to fit in the ensemble.

The rules of Classical design had centred upon the two architectural orders, Doric and Ionic. In Hellenistic times not only were the rules of each order relaxed, but we find the two orders more freely combined within one building, for example in the superimposed storeys of a portico (*stoa*), or even elements of the one grafted on to the other to form a kind of hybrid order. In Doric there was a tendency for columns to become slimmer and more widely spaced, with three or four metopes and triglyphs per intercolumniation in place of the 'canonical' two. The lighter, more spacious effect was more in harmony with the aesthetic of Hellenistic times, which found traditional Doric too severe and heavy. At the same time the Doric triglyph frieze could be inserted in an Ionic order, as in the Sanctuary of Athena at Pergamum, and conversely the dentils of Ionic could be combined with Doric columns and entablature, as in the north *stoa* of the *agora* at Priene. A certain amount of mixing had taken place especially in the western colonies as early as the Archaic period, but the thoroughgoing hybridization of Hellenistic times betokens a new attitude in which the traditional orders lost much of their independence and became a common repertory of ornament to be dipped into almost at will.

This new flexibility is symbolized by the progress of the Corinthian order. Used in the fourth century for interior columns in such buildings as the temple

PORTICO OF THE SANCTUARY OF ATHENA AT PERGAMUM, built by Eumenes II (197–159 BC). Characteristic of the Hellenistic age are the combination of a Doric colonnade in the lower storey with an Ionic in the upper, and the relaxation of the rules governing the syntax of the orders (including the insertion of a Doric frieze within an Ionic entablature).

COLUMNS OF THE OLYMPIEUM IN ATHENS. Begun by Pisistratus in the sixth century BC probably as an Ionic temple, this most ambitious of all religious buildings in European Greece was resumed by the Seleucid King Antiochus IV (176–165 BC) in the Corinthian order. It was not completed until the time of the Roman Emperor Hadrian (AD 117–38).

of Athena at Tegea and the *tholoi* (rotundas) at Delphi and Epidaurus, this ornate subform of Ionic had hitherto seemed too avant-garde for exteriors except those of baroque follies such as the monument of Lysicrates in Athens. But the rich taste of Hellenistic times and the greater adaptability of the Corinthian capital, which, unlike the Ionic, can be viewed to good effect from all angles, led to increasing popularity during the third and second centuries, culminating in the adoption of Corinthian capitals for the main order of one of the most prestigious of all building projects, Antiochus IV's revival of work on the temple of Olympian Zeus in Athens.

The Corinthian style may have enjoyed particular favour in the Seleucid area, but florid decoration, in which relatively naturalistic vegetal forms played an important role, occurs widely in the Hellenistic world. Good examples can be seen in the massive new temple of Apollo at Didyma, begun about 300 BC and still incomplete 700 years later; a beautiful frieze of foliate scrolls and heraldic pairs of griffins which ran round the interior court is dated to the first half of the second century BC. Foliate decoration was especially popular in Pergamum, from where it was carried to Rome during the late second and first centuries.

This sort of surface decoration fits within the confines of columnar construction, but another Hellenistic trend sees the columnar orders themselves used increasingly in a decorative fashion, applied in a non-structural role to walls and façades. The exterior wall of the *bouleutērion* (council-house) at Miletus, built between 175 and 164 BC, was divided into two storeys, of which the lower was treated as a plain podium, while the upper was decorated with engaged columns. Here at least the horizontal moulding dividing the two storeys corresponded to a structural division in the interior, namely the top of the semicircular auditorium; but elsewhere the articulation of exterior walls responded to no internal logic. For example, the façade of the Great Tomb at Levkadia (*c*.300 BC) is decorated with an engaged Doric order surmounted by a continuous frieze of stucco reliefs, surmounted in turn by a small Ionic order carrying a pediment; but behind this pseudo-structural screen is a plain vaulted antechamber rising to full height: apart from the spring of the vault there are no internal caesuras to justify the external show. Such display architecture is epitomized by the mausoleum at Belevi, near Ephesus, perhaps intended as the tomb of Lysimachus, where the monumental masonry and elaborately carved mouldings of the great cube containing the burial chamber are merely a surface dressing for a massive outcrop of living rock. The divorce between structure and decoration is one of the important Hellenistic legacies to the Roman age.

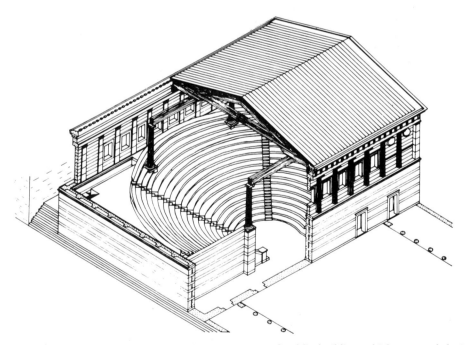

COUNCIL CHAMBER AT MILETUS (*c*.170 BC). A new type of public building which emerged during the fourth and third centuries BC was the concert or assembly chamber with a semi-circular auditorium like that of Greek theatres set within a great rectangular hall. Here an additional feature of interest is the use of engaged semi-columns as a purely decorative device on the exterior.

CRYPT OF THE SO-CALLED
ORACLE OF THE DEAD AT
EPHYRA, in western Greece
(third century BC). It is typical
of Greek architecture that the
vault is used in an
underground structure. The
principle of the arch and vault
was known to Democritus in
the fifth century BC, but
surviving examples date to the
second half of the fourth
century or later.

New structural forms and techniques did not make enormous headway east of the Adriatic. Post-and-lintel construction remained the basis of architectural form, and dressed stone, timber, and mud brick the staple constructive materials. In the time of Alexander, however, perhaps as a result of experience gained by his engineers in the East, vaults and arches became more common in the Greek world. Vaults were used to span the tomb-chambers of Macedonian nobles, and isolated examples are found in later buildings, generally in an inconspicuous or subordinate role. Sloping vaults covered the narrow passages leading to the interior court of the temple at Didyma, and barrel-vaults met at right angles in various Pergamene buildings. Elsewhere arches were used in subterranean structures to support stone paving above or (in the crypt of the third-century Nekromanteion at Ephyra) to bear the weight of a barrel-vault. In all cases the construction was carried out in stone, even though this might lead to structural weakness, especially where vaults intersected. The octagonal Tower of the Winds in Athens, an elaborate water-clock and planetarium built by Andronicus of Cyrrhus in the mid first century BC, was roofed by a series of long wedge-shaped blocks bearing upon a central keystone. Only with the development of concrete construction in

Italy (below, pp. 401 ff.) did vaulting become a fundamental component of architecture, destined to open up undreamt-of possibilities in the expansion and manipulation of interior space.

One final general aspect of Hellenistic architecture is the composition of ensembles which were visually unified, whether by the use of recurrent motifs or by the setting of one building as a foil to another. The urban foundations which Alexander and his successors planted in the newly conquered areas were a good testing ground for the planners. Most of them were laid out in accordance with the traditional Hippodamian, rectilinear grid, and, though development could be piecemeal and incoherent, as it had often been in the past, there was increasing concern to relate buildings to one another and to frame and define space by means of the ubiquitous *stoa*. The best-known examples are the monumental piazzas of Miletus and Priene, both pre-Hellenistic chequerboard cities which experienced major programmes of building during the third and second centuries BC. Even the chaotic sprawl of the *agora* in Athens had some order imposed upon it at this time with the construction, at right angles to each other, of the Middle Stoa along the south side and the Stoa of Attalus on the east. In another pre-Hellenistic city, Rhodes, unknown planners stacked buildings on the acropolis in a masterful exercise in giving architectonic shape to a sloping terrain. It was from beginnings such as these that the great terraced complexes at Lindus and Cos, with their broadly axial layouts and monumental stairways, evolved. But the finest architectural composition of the age dispensed altogether with orthogonal patterns. The upper city of Pergamum (first half of the second century) grew organically out of the landscape in a series of terraces climbing fan-like up a crescent-shaped hill in which the auditorium of a steep theatre formed a kind of valve. At the foot of the theatre, providing a firm visual basis for the great ensemble, ran a horizontal esplanade supported by a high retaining wall whose massive buttresses took root in the lower slopes. Throughout the composition Doric stoas acted as a leitmotif, both defining and unifying the different spaces. They also masked changes of level, being two-storeyed on one side and single-storeyed on the other.

Among individual building types in Hellenistic architecture most had existed before, but many now assumed more monumental form. Great altars with colonnaded enclosures approached by broad stairways were built at Magnesia, Pergamum, and Priene; in each of them sculpture played an integral part in the overall effect, statues being set between the columns at Magnesia and Priene, and high reliefs taking over the podium at Pergamum (below, pp. 394 f.). The huge *tholos* of Arsinoe at Samothrace dispensed with internal and external colonnades but incorporated an open gallery at the top of the wall. Stone theatres became a characteristic feature of Hellenistic cities and were now endowed as a matter of course with architectural stage-houses, including a high proscenium which encroached upon the circular space formerly allotted to the orchestra. In utilitarian building an important step was the introduction of heated baths: simple hypocaust

MODEL OF THE ACROPOLIS AT PERGAMUM, a *tour de force* in the adaptation of urban planning to the configuration of the land. At the bottom, the Theatre Terrace leading (at the left) to the small temple of Dionysus; above this, the fan-like auditorium of the theatre; round the theatre, from right to left, the court of the Great Altar (*c.*166 BC), the sanctuary of Athena (late third to early second century BC); and the second-century AD temple of Trajan.

systems are attested at Piraeus, at Gela in Sicily, at Gortys in Arcadia, and about 100 BC in the small Greek bath-suite at Olympia. Residential buildings too began to acquire some architectural pretensions, as the rise of officials in the new kingdoms and the emergence of wealthy merchant classes in the commercial cities created a demand for better-quality housing. Focused upon a small court, the typical middle-class house in cities such as Priene and Delos boasted at least one large reception room, frequently opening from the north side of a peristyle or a two-columned antechamber to catch the sun in winter; its interior surfaces were protected and enhanced by mosaic pavements and painted stucco wall-decorations; and quite often there were statues or marble furnishings set in the colonnades. A fine example is the House of the Hermes on Delos, terraced into a hillside on four levels, with a peristyle court rising through three of them.

Sculpture

For free-standing statuary there is a rather better survival rate in Hellenistic times than in the preceding period. This is partly because the major artists, following the lead given by Praxiteles, were less disdainful of marble as a sculptural material than had been Lysippus and, before him, many of the great fifth-century sculptors, whose massive output of works in bronze finished up in the melting-pots of the Middle Ages; and partly because several of the principal centres of patron-

PERISTYLE COURT IN THE HOUSE OF THE DIONYSUS ON DELOS (late second century BC). Such courts were the normal focus of the well-to-do houses in the Athenian colony of the second century BC. One portico was often deeper, and sometimes taller, than the others, in order to protect and enhance the entrance to a large reception room (here at the rear). A well-head (here in the right foreground) covers the opening to the cistern which provided the Delian house with its water-supply.

age now lay east of the Aegean and in the Levant and were not subjected to the wholesale plunder suffered by Corinth and other cities of European Greece in the wake of the Roman conquest. At a minor level there are large series of terracotta figurines, produced in factories such as those of Taranto, Tanagra in Boeotia (demure ladies in their Sunday best), Myrina in Asia Minor (characters from New Comedy), and Alexandria (ethnic and genre types).

Despite this relative abundance of evidence the problems of dating already mentioned make it well-nigh impossible to establish any sort of stylistic framework for the period. The most widely accepted schema is that of the German art historian Gerhard Krahmer, who postulated three main phases: a severe style distinguished by 'closed form', that is, by statues or statue-groups whose structure leads the eye into an inner focus (c.300–c.240 BC); the High Hellenistic phase, characterized by grandeur and pathos (c.240–c.150 BC); and the Late Hellenistic phase, in which open form and one-sided compositions reminiscent of earlier styles prevailed (c.150–c.100 BC). This and similar systems are however dependent upon a few datable works, chiefly from one or two main centres, and make too many presumptions about works for which the dating evidence is slim or non-existent; so they can at best be regarded as no more than a broad guide. It remains safer and more satisfactory to review the achievements of Hellenistic sculpture in general terms, category by category.

One category in which distinctive trends were developed was the draped figure. Alongside the high-waisted, narrow-shouldered look of the Tanagra ladies and many full-size statues, a look which was a condition of contemporary *haute mode* as much as of sculptural style, there are works which show a conscious virtuosity on the part of the sculptor. A favourite device was the stretching of

NIKE (VICTORY) FROM SAMOTHRACE
(*c*.200 BC), a statue set up in the sanctuary of
the Great Gods in commemoration of a naval
victory, perhaps by the Rhodians. The
goddess is shown alighting on the prow of a
ship, which was originally set in a rock-filled
pool—the kind of landscape composition
which seems to have been especially popular
in Hellenistic Rhodes. She probably held a
bronze victory-wreath in her right hand.

TERRACOTTA FIGURINE OF LADY WITH
DOVE from Tanagra (late fourth or third
century BC). Wrapped in a voluminous cloak
(*himation*), with a fan in her left hand, and her
hair centrally parted and gathered in a
chignon at the back of her head, she is the
height of early Hellenistic fashion. Such
figurines were highly popular trinkets at the
time.

the drapery across the body to create a pattern of taut and loose folds almost independent of the form beneath: good examples are provided by the statue of Tyche of Antioch (soon after 300 BC), known only from Roman copies, and a bronze statuette of a veiled dancer in the Metropolitan Museum of Art, New York. Another device, cultivated especially in the cities of western Asia Minor during the last two centuries BC, was the exploitation of different textures, and especially the rendering of the mantle to produce the effect of a silken shawl, through which the folds of the dress are clearly visible. But the finest of Hellenistic draped statues, the Nike (Victory) of Samothrace, employed a more traditional style, contrasting clinging folds over the breasts, abdomen, and left leg with deep-cut swathes in other areas. Here, however, the contrasts are more exaggerated than they had been in fifth-century Athenian sculptures, and the folds over the advanced right leg are used in an impressionistic manner, swinging this way and that without rhyme or reason to suggest the force of the wind as the winged goddess comes in to land. It is characteristic of the Hellenistic age that the Nike served a semi-decorative role as the crowning ornament of a triumphal ship-monument and that this monument was merely the centrepiece of a landscaped composition of rocks and water: more varied functions and more pictorial settings were one result of the new kinds of patronage.

Another important category of statue was the female nude. Praxiteles' much admired Aphrodite of Cnidus (above, p. 288) was the forerunner of a long series of Hellenistic Aphrodites, including a beautiful statue from Cyrene and the self-conscious *poseuse* commemorated in the Capitoline Venus. An interesting variant is the crouching goddess attributed by some to a Bithynian sculptor of the third century: the thrusting knees, the raised right and lowered left arm, the sharply turned head, and the torsion about the waist, accentuated by unflattering folds of flesh, produce an effect of tension and imminent movement which would have been inconceivable in any statue before the time of Lysippus. Equally restless, but much more subtle, is the majestic Aphrodite from Melos (Venus de Milo), a late-second-century work. Here the slightly twisting torso and the broad mass of drapery clinging precariously to the hips and sweeping over the raised and advanced left thigh were merely part of the complex composition: one has also to imagine the missing arms, which must have been extended to the side, perhaps holding a bronze shield in which the goddess admired her reflection.

A whole range of themes which would have been considered undignified or demeaning in the art of previous centuries now entered the repertory of sculptors: sleeping figures, drunks, cupids, old hags, thugs, hermaphrodites. Some of the more playful subjects, such as the delightful sleeping cherub in New York, the famous boy-and-goose composition of Boethus, and the various tussles between nymphs and satyrs, have reminded commentators of the rococo of the eighteenth century; and they indeed betoken the same sort of light-hearted, almost frivolous taste. Many must have been designed for the amusement of wealthy private collectors. So too may some of the more ugly and horrific subjects. They tend

APHRODITE FROM MELOS (VENUS DE MILO), the finest of all surviving nude female statues (late second century BC). It is normally argued that she held her drape with the right hand and rested the left on a pillar at her side; but the old view that she was looking at her reflection in a shield (like her prototype, the so-called Capua Aphrodite) is still attractive.

to be characterized as examples of Hellenistic 'realism'; but a glance at the bronze boxer in the Terme Museum in Rome, with his ostentatious wounds, exaggerated musculature, yet artistically ordered hair, will show that even now Greek sculptors were more concerned with types than with real appearances.

One area where types were less important was portraiture. Here, partly inspired by the activity of Lysippus and his school, including his brother Lysistratus who is said to have invented the practice of taking casts from the human face, sculptors broke new ground in the characterization of the individual. A fine example is the statue of the orator and statesman Demosthenes set up in Athens about 280 BC and known to us from copies (above, p. 147). The severe expression, furrowed brow, and stooping shoulders correspond well enough to the description given in Plutarch's biography, and the eloquent gesture of the clasped hands expresses something of the tragedy of Demosthenes' hopeless struggle against Macedonian imperialism. Replicas of other fine portrait-statues include the seated philosopher Chrysippus reconstructed in the Louvre (above, p. 363). But most

STATUE OF A CHILD PLAYING WITH A GOOSE, a Roman copy of a Hellenistic composition dated to the third century BC. A passage in Pliny's *Natural History* refers to a work by one Boethus which showed an infant strangling a goose (perhaps 'by embracing it', but the reading is uncertain); it may be the source of this type.

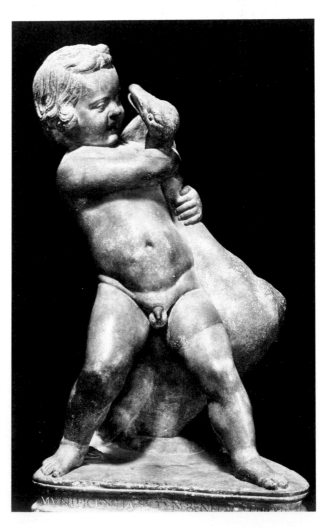

noteworthy were the long series of royal portraits running from the romantic Lysippan Alexander (above, p. 310), with tilted head, upturned eyes, and flowing hair, to the nice blend of realism and idealization found in heads of the Bactrian and Indian kings, known chiefly from their coins. As in earlier times, the Greek portraitist felt that the whole figure was essential to convey the character of the sitter, and therefore sculptured portraits were always full statues; but as time went on there was an increasing emphasis upon the expressive quality of the face and an increasing readiness to show wrinkles, creases, and other features which artists of the fifth and fourth centuries would have glossed over.

COIN PORTRAITS OF BACTRIAN KINGS: (*Left*) Antimachus (*c.*185 BC), (*right*) Eucratides I (*c.*165–150 BC). The portraits of this remarkable dynasty on the far-eastern fringe of the Hellenistic world show a degree of individuality never matched by the often bland depictions of their royal contemporaries further west. Eucratides is helmeted; Antimachus wears the Macedonian royal beret, or *causia*.

Another sculptural genre which owed much to the influence of Lysippus was the figure-group. Lysippus' exploitation of the third dimension, and no doubt the famous multi-figure compositions in bronze with which he and collaborators had commemorated the exploits of Alexander, paved the way for a whole range of virtuoso statue-groups, in which two, three, or more figures were arranged in complex relationships which required a new attitude on the part of the viewer. The wrestlers in Florence, the Ludovisi Gaul in the Terme Museum (above, p. 314), and the elaborate Rhodian composition showing the punishment of Dirce, reflected in a Roman copy in Naples, cannot be fully appreciated from any one viewpoint, but demand to be studied from all angles. The Ludovisi Gaul, whose prototype, together with that of the dying Gaul in the Capitoline Museum, formed part of a larger aggregation of bronze statues set up in Pergamum to commemorate the victories of Kings Attalus and Eumenes, also illustrates further facets of Hellenistic group composition, in particular its love of drama and of studied contrasts. The act of the Gaulish chieftain who has killed his wife and plunged the sword in his own breast rather than surrender might have seemed theatrical were it not for the impressive nobility of the warrior's face and figure. At the same time the artist makes great play of the contrast between the vigorous action of the Gaul and the limpness of the dead wife, between the muscularity of his virtually naked body and the lifeless fall of her drapery. Yet the two figures are artistically united in a favourite pyramidal structure by the left arm of the warrior supporting his wife's collapsing form. It is significant that this Hellenistic victory-monument expressed its message in more human terms than its great Classical predecessors: not only were the actual Gaulish foes of Pergamum represented where Classical sculptors would have chosen some remote mythological allegory, but they were also rendered with sympathy both for their distinctive physiognomy (broad cheeks, chunky hair, the man's moustache) and for their great courage and dignity. Other groups showed an increased emphasis on horror. For example, the old myth of Marsyas, hitherto represented in its earlier, milder stages, the discovery of the flutes and the musical contest between the satyr and Apollo, now moved on to its gruesome climax: a number of copies attest the existence of a group, again probably Pergamene, consisting of the terrified Marsyas strung up on a tree, a brutal, balding Scythian slave sharpening the knife with which he is to be flayed alive, and (no doubt) a pitiless seated Apollo.

In relief sculpture the Alexander sarcophagus (above, p. 321), apparently carved for Alexander's client king in Sidon, reveals a number of important developments of the early Hellenistic period. The representation of actual events involving living or recently dead personages (hunting scenes and episodes from Alexander's battles) and the portrayal of precise details of national costume and armour look forward to the Pergamene Gauls and ultimately to the historical reliefs of imperial Rome; while the complexity and interlocking of the main battle relief mark a complete break from the well-spaced duels which prevailed in fifth- and fourth-century sculpture. One effect here was a diminution in importance of the background, which had always been the essential foil to reliefs of the Classical period. This development reached a climax in the sculptures of the Great Altar at Pergamum (second quarter of the second century BC). The larger frieze, situated on the exterior of the podium, depicted the time-honoured subject of the battle of gods and giants, but did so with a bravado and grandiloquence never equalled in ancient art. Almost every inch of the available surface was covered with a writhing mass of bodies, wings, drapery, coiling snakes, and animal forms, all rendered with a loving attention to texture which can distinguish, for example, between the nap and plain surfaces of the same piece of cloth. The effect was to destroy the visual function of the podium and to leave the superstructure of the altar floating, as it were, above the cosmic tumult of the sculptures. A particularly good example of the ambivalent relation between architecture and decoration was the group of giants which rested hands, knees, and snake-coils directly on the steps of the monumental entrance stairway, as if trying to crawl out of the frieze. Along with the technical brilliance went a typically Hellenistic academi-

DETAIL OF THE BATTLE OF GODS AND GIANTS: frieze of the Altar of Zeus and Athena at Pergamum (*c.*166–159 BC). Athena seizes the giant Alcyoneus by the hair and wrenches him away from his mother Ge (Earth), while Victory flies in to place a wreath on Athena's head. A good example of the bombast and virtuosity of this most extravagant of ancient sculptural creations.

cism: in addition to the twelve Olympian gods, the artists had introduced about seventy-five lesser deities and personifications, all of whom, like the giants, were labelled with inscriptions for the benefit of passers-by. It is difficult to remember that all this, like most Greek sculpture in stone, must originally have been coloured.

While the great frieze denied the existence of the background, the smaller frieze of the interior court turned it into real space. This frieze, which told the story of Pergamum's legendary founder Telephus, a romantic tale of a type much favoured among Hellenistic court poets, employed a continuous narrative technique in which the same characters appeared again and again at different moments of time. Each episode ran on from the previous one without a break, but the shifting setting was indicated by landscape elements: the sacred laurel tree of Delphi, hangings in Aleos' palace, the oak forest in which Heracles seduced Auge. More striking, the figures occupied only two-thirds of the height of the frieze, so that the upper third was available for rocks, foliage, architectural members, and so forth, or could alternatively be left free to suggest sky. Sometimes a hint of perspective was conveyed by the placing of certain figures above those in the foreground: that they were not merely conceived as at a higher level is indicated by their slightly smaller scale. This 'activation' of the background, which surely owed much to the influence of painting, was echoed, in more tentative fashion, on a number of minor Hellenistic reliefs but was to be more fully exploited only in Roman times.

Painting and the Other Arts

Pictorial reliefs bring us naturally to painting. Here, however, much less can be said, because there is almost no direct evidence apart from funerary paintings in one or two Macedonian chamber tombs and on gravestones from Alexandria and Demetrias in Thessaly.

Major paintings probably continued to be carried out mainly on wooden panels. Alexander's reign was evidently a highpoint in the history of pictorial art, to judge from the literary references to the work of his court painter Apelles, at least three of whose famous masterpieces were later displayed in Rome. This golden age of painting continued at the courts of the Successors, who commissioned various works to commemorate the achievements of the great Macedonian. We hear of at least two multi-figure paintings of Alexander's battles (by Philoxenus of Eretria and a Graeco-Egyptian paintress Helen) and get hints of others. If, as seems likely, one of them was reproduced three centuries later in the famous mosaic pavement from the House of the Faun at Pompeii (Vol. 2, photo facing p. 24), the artists of this time were capable of highly complex compositions with a full mastery of foreshortening and of modelling by means of deep shadows and strong highlights: see especially the horse shown in back view in the foreground. They also conveyed a degree of emotion in the faces of the figures: Alexander's grim determination is contrasted with the alarmed expressions of Darius and the other Persians. In colour, though obviously the mosaicist was to some extent restricted by his materials, the copy seems to reflect a deliberate limitation of the painter's palette to red, yellow, black, white, and tones available from combinations of these, an aesthetic device whose popularity in the works of Apelles and his contemporaries is recorded by Pliny. Blue is absent and green confined to inconspicuous details.

The action of the Alexander mosaic takes place on a shallow stage between a brown foreground and a white sky, the effect of space being achieved principally by spears on the skyline. The only true landscape element, forming a counterbalance to the prominent figure of Darius in his chariot, is a dead tree. It has often been claimed that landscape was used sparingly in Hellenistic painting and always in a subsidiary role to human figures, much as it appears in the Telephus frieze. But a painted frieze above the entrance of a recently excavated tomb at Vergina dated as early as the fourth century shows a hunt scene in which landscape plays a larger role; the mounted huntsmen move in and out among trees as in a real environment. How far landscape settings had developed by late Hellenistic times is shown by the *Odyssey* paintings from a first-century house on the Esquiline hill in Rome, almost certainly adapted from a Greek frieze of the previous century. Here the story of Odysseus' adventures was told with small figures set within a vast unfolding scenario of trees, cliffs and water. Even so there is no evidence that landscape as a subject in its own right, that is, with the figured element reduced to staffage, was developed before the Roman period.

Among the other funerary paintings some interest attaches to the figures on the façade of the Great Tomb at Levkadia, representing a soldier, Hermes the guide of souls, and two judges of the dead, and to the interior scheme of the tomb chamber of Lyson and Callicles, also at Levkadia, which already in the second century offers a foretaste of the *trompe l'oeil* architecture to come in mural painting, albeit in a very simple form (shaded pilasters linked by hanging festoons). The painted gravestones are of limited interest, for they show mostly simple one- or two-figure commemorative subjects, like their Classical predecessors; only the *stēlē* of Hediste from Demetrias (third century) gives an indication of the kind of elaborate architectural interiors which may have occurred as backdrops in more monumental art. Otherwise our knowledge of Hellenistic painting is confined to little more than literary references (mainly lists of artists'

PAINTING OF ODYSSEUS IN THE LAND OF THE LAESTRYGONIANS, part of a frieze depicting scenes from Homer's *Odyssey* found in a house on the Esquiline Hill, Rome (*c*.50–40 BC). Such friezes, as Vitruvius tells us, were a popular feature of Roman wall-decorations in the first century BC. Some of the figures are labelled with their names in Greek.

DETAIL OF A PEBBLE MOSAIC AT PELLA in Macedonia (*c*.300 BC). The mosaic, which formed the centrepiece of a floor in a grand town-house, depicted a lion–hunt, a subject which became popular in the arts following Alexander's conquest of the Persian kingdom. The figures were carried out in natural pebbles of various colours; salient details were outlined with thin strips of terracotta or lead.

names) and tantalizing echoes. We know from Pliny that the period saw the emergence of new genres, such as caricature, everyday life, and still life, but there are no surviving examples before Roman times. The mythological scenes in Pompeian wall-decoration may in many instances go back to 'old masters' of the Hellenistic period; but it is rarely possible to determine the date and location of the prototypes or the degree to which the Roman painter adapted them to contemporary taste and to the decorative context.

Echoes of panel-painting in other media vary in value. A small group of polychrome vases manufactured in Centuripae in Sicily during the third and early second centuries carries figures in naturalistic colours, but compositions are simple and backgrounds a uniform reddish pink. More important, as we have seen, are floor mosaics. From the pebbled pavements of Pella, dated round the turn of the fourth and third centuries, through to the tessera *emblēmata* (inserts) of Delos and other cities in the second century, we have an impressive sequence of mosaic pictures in which pictorial devices such as modelling in light and shade were freely exploited. The early examples are subject to certain conventions which were probably rare in painting, notably an undifferentiated blue-black background (paralleled, however, in the frieze of a newly excavated tomb at Vergina); and the placing of these pictures at the centre of a floor, framed by bands of abstract pattern, scrollwork, or simply a patchwork of stone fragments set in mortar, produces a totally different aesthetic effect from that of a painting hung on a wall; but many of the later examples, such as the little New Comedy tableaux of Dioscurides of Samos from the so-called Villa of Cicero at Pompeii, achieve a remarkable fidelity to the brushwork of the painter. Particularly famous in antiquity was a pavement by a certain 'Sosos' at Pergamum in which an *emblēma* representing doves perched on the edge of a bowl was set in a surround decorated to suggest litter from the dining-table. This 'Unswept Saloon' demonstrates that mosaic pictures were usually intended to be viewed by diners reclining on couches placed on the more plainly decorated outer edges of the floor. The transference of pictorial emphasis from vertical to horizontal surfaces is also partly explained by the contemporary vogue for masonry-style wall-decorations in which there was little room for representational art. But the idea of decorating a pavement with refuse reflects a more general aspect of Hellenistic times: a tendency towards the 'trivialization' of art. It is the same spirit which produces sleeping hermaphrodites, drunken fauns, and playful centaurs in sculpture, and which concentrates upon technical tricks and virtuosity at the expense of depth of meaning.

Other art forms may be briefly mentioned: ceramics (often decorated in relief), glassware (including *millefiori* and vessels with gilded ornament, both produced in the factories of Alexandria), gold and silver plate, gem engraving, and jewel-

RECONSTRUCTED WALL-DECORATION FROM THE HOUSE OF THE DOLPHINS AT DELOS (late second century BC). This type of decoration, used in the more important rooms of Hellenistic houses, is sometimes referred to as the 'Masonry Style', because of its use of plaster raised in relief to imitate ashlar masonry. The blocks were brightly coloured and sometimes, as here, a figured frieze was included.

lery. The importance of these last three arts is attested by the fact that famous artists were engaged in them: Alexander, for example, issued a patent for royal portraits to Pyrgoteles the gem-cutter just as he did to Lysippus for portraits in bronze and to Apelles for those in painting; and Pliny seems to place all three artists on a par. Alexander's conquests opened up new resources of gold and introduced the Greeks to new kinds of precious stone, such as garnets, with the result that work in costly materials enjoyed something of a new lease of life. In gold jewellery the new technique of inset gems was added to the long established ones such as filigree and granulation. Alongside the surviving items, which are often of great beauty, we hear from ancient writers of much more ambitious products of the luxury arts. The most lavish and brilliant of all was Alexander's funeral carriage, elaborately decorated with gold and studded with jewels. It took nearly two years to construct.

The Transition to Roman Art

The transition from Hellenistic to Roman art was, of course, a gradual one, and we must distinguish between East and West. While the old styles and traditions remained firmly rooted in the eastern half of the Mediterranean, new aims and ideals, and above all a new patronage, sprang into existence in Italy.

Southern Italy and Sicily were always part of the Hellenistic world; and central Italy, by osmosis, acquired its own provincial-Hellenistic culture. Rome itself, as it gradually absorbed the Greek world, could hardly remain immune. In fact a passion for Greek art, along with Greek literature, swept the Roman nobility: already the capture of Tarentum and Syracuse in the third century brought works of art and artists pouring into the new metropolis, and in the second century, with Roman arms established east of the Adriatic, the tide grew to a flood. It became regular practice for Roman generals and provincial governors to bring back statues, paintings, and reliefs to decorate their Italian villas; and Greek artists found themselves working full-time to satisfy the demand.

In architecture the meeting of Greece and Italy produced a vigorous new tradition. Among its products were new types of building: the well-to-do Roman town-house combining Italic *atrium* with Hellenistic peristyle (Vol. 2, 308 ff.); the aisled basilica, an administrative building evidently descended from the Greek *stoa*; and the Roman temple. The latter inherited Italian features, notably a high podium and a strong frontal emphasis (much more pronounced than in the east); there was normally no access save by a monumental stairway leading up to the façade. But the decorative detail, and especially the use of Corinthian columns, was imported from the Greek world; and, once the Italian quarries at Luni had been opened in the third quarter of the last century BC, marble became the standard building material, as it had been (where possible) in Greek temples. The last step of significance in the evolution of the temple was the creation of the fully fledged Corinthian entablature, complete with modillions on the underside of the cornice; this had happened by the time of the Second Triumvirate and should perhaps be credited to the unknown architect of the temple of Venus Genetrix in Julius Caesar's Forum.

But more important than purely formal changes was the emergence in Italy of a new technique: concrete construction. This began to appear in the late third century and perhaps resulted from experimentation with *pisé* (rammed clay) building of the type previously used in Punic Africa; at all events it rapidly developed once architects discovered the remarkable cohesive strength and hydraulic properties of mortar made with the central-Italian volcanic earth known as 'pulvis puteolanus' (pozzolana). Concrete replaced ashlar as the logical medium for vault-construction. Not only did it enable buildings to be put up more economically, since materials were cheaper and the bulk of the work could be carried out by mass unskilled labour (readily available in the form of slaves and prisoners of war), but the results were also stronger and more adaptable: a well-built concrete vault, once set, is monolithic and can be used to roof much larger spaces than any form of stone construction. The new technique ultimately enabled the Romans to develop their great imperial edifices of mass circulation: the amphitheatres and public baths.

In the early stages concrete was used for types of building which had no tradition of columnar or trabeated construction, notably market- and store-buildings. The Porticus Aemilia, a huge warehouse in Rome's dockland, constructed in 193 BC and rebuilt or restored in 174, provides a precocious example, 487 m. long, 60 m. wide, and divided by 294 pillars into a grid of 350 vaulted bays. Its walls were faced with carefully fitted pieces of rubble (*opus incertum*), a style which remained in vogue throughout the second century. To the latter years of the century belongs the first great monument in the new technique, the sanctuary

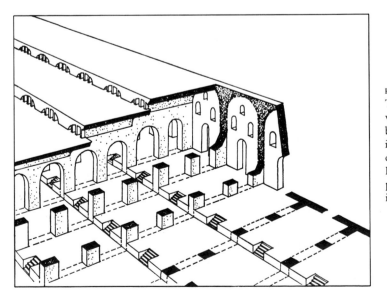

PORTICUS AEMILIA IN ROME (193 BC). The reconstruction shows how the gigantic warehouse consisted of a series of vaulted bays connected by transversal archways. It is the earliest surviving large-scale example of concrete vaulted architecture in the Roman world. The new technique provided greater floor-space, allowed better illumination, and reduced the risk of fire.

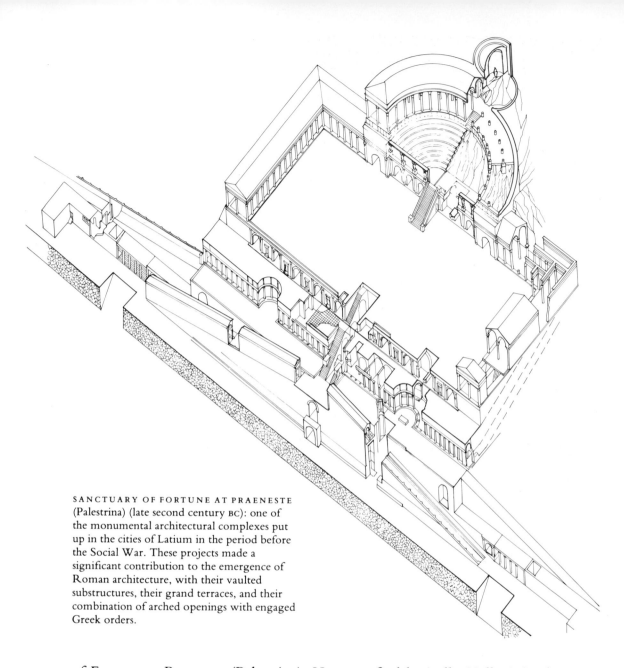

SANCTUARY OF FORTUNE AT PRAENESTE
(Palestrina) (late second century BC): one of
the monumental architectural complexes put
up in the cities of Latium in the period before
the Social War. These projects made a
significant contribution to the emergence of
Roman architecture, with their vaulted
substructures, their grand terraces, and their
combination of arched openings with engaged
Greek orders.

of Fortune at Praeneste (Palestrina). Here we find basically Hellenistic elements, such as an axial layout, open terraces, and arcaded retaining walls, employed on an unprecedented scale, thanks to the use of concrete. At the same time traditional Greek colonnades were incorporated in façades to support the front half of a longitudinal vault, or engaged in wall-schemes as a purely decorative framing for arched openings. The latter device, which was picked up by Sullan architects a few decades later, was destined to become a great favourite on Roman exteriors and serves almost as an epitome of the fusion of Italian techniques and the Hellenistic formal vocabulary.

THE BORGHESE CRATER (late second century BC): a fine example of the grand marble garden-ornaments produced by Neo-Attic workshops for the wealthy villa-owners of Roman Italy. Over five feet high, it is decorated with reliefs of Dionysus and his maenads and satyrs in a conventional classicizing style. Further, almost identical objects were found in a ship-load of *objets d'art* wrecked off the Tunisian coast soon after 100 BC.

On certain types of building concrete had a profound generative or regenerative effect. In domestic architecture it lent itself to the high-rise tenement blocks with which Roman speculators sought to capitalize on an urban population explosion in the late second and first centuries: the eventual conversion of rubble wall-facing into standardized pyramidal blocks laid in regular diagonal courses (*opus reticulatum*) was part of the same trend, for its purpose was to streamline the building process. Concrete vaults were also readily adopted in the architecture of baths, being both damp-resistant and fire-proof. Most important, concrete determined the transformation of the theatre from its Greek form, set in a hillside, to the complete structural independence of the Roman version. This process was gradual, and we know many examples of intermediate phases, with auditoria constructed wholly or partly on artificial mounds, or supported by substructures which were filled with earth; but by 55 BC the mature type, in which the substructures formed a network of passages to facilitate the circulation of the audience, was embodied in the first stone theatre in Rome, that of Pompey (Vol. 2, p. 95).

If contact between the Italian and Hellenistic traditions spawned a golden age in architecture, the situation is less clear-cut in sculpture. Much of the effort of sculptors from the mid second century onwards was devoted to producing

'PSEUDO-ATHLETE': statue of an Italian merchant or official from the House of the Diadumenus on Delos (early first century BC). A good example of the unfortunate effects which could result from the practice of adding contemporary portrait heads to mechanically reproduced bodies based on classical athlete statues.

classicizing work for the Roman art market. In Athens the so-called Neo-Attic school developed a popular line in marble garden ornaments (great fountain-basins and craters, candelabra, and the like) decorated with reliefs of elegant nymphs, satyrs, and maenads, beautifully carved, but devoid of all feeling. In southern Italy the school of Pasiteles concentrated upon eclectic statuary in the Classical manner, often amalgamating a Polyclitan or Praxitelean pose with an early Classical head: surviving works include stylistically improbable pairs of figures engaged in conspiratorial conversation. Along with these pastiches went the production of more or less mechanical replicas of famous statues. The earliest specimens, including a fine copy of Polyclitus' Diadumenus found on Delos, date from about 100 BC and are thought to be the result of improvements in the pointing technique; they represent the beginnings of a major industry, a vivid testimony of which are the plaster casts of parts of famous Greek statues excavated in the 1950s at Baiae near Naples. Not all such copies were intended for collectors. An important aspect of the industry was the reproduction of statue-bodies to carry contemporary portrait heads, a practice which did not always yield harmonious results.

This sort of arid Classicism continued well into the Imperial period and often found new roles for itself, particularly in the manufacture of pairs of statues in mirror image for the decoration of the niches which were a popular feature in Roman architecture. Alongside it another current, associated as far as we know primarily with Rhodian sculptors, created baroque masterpieces in the style of the Great Altar at Pergamum. The *Laocoon* and the Homeric compositions in Tiberius' grotto at Sperlonga are the main survivors of this mode, designed largely for the private delectation of emperors (Vol. 2, pp. 256, 377).

More original work was produced when Greek artists were asked to tackle unfamiliar themes. A good example is the census relief from the so-called Altar of Domitius Ahenobarbus, a statue base probably made for the temple of

A ROMAN MILITARY CENSUS: detail of a relief from the so-called Altar of Domitius Ahenobarbus (actually the base of a statue-group from a temple). This earliest known example of the representation of a Roman religious ceremony in sculpture poses serious problems of dating and attribution; but the most likely date-range is between *c.*120 and *c.*50 BC.

Neptune in Rome and datable some time between the late second and mid first centuries. Three faces of the base were decorated with conventionally florid Neo-Attic reliefs, now in Munich, showing the marine *cortège* of Poseidon and Amphitrite; but the fourth side (in Paris) carries a specifically Roman subject, the taking of a census and the associated ritual sacrifice of a pig, a sheep, and a bull (*suovetaurilia*), all rendered in a harder, more matter-of-fact style. Despite uncertainties in scale and a lack of fluency in composition, this scene takes its individual figure-types from the Hellenistic repertory and is unquestionably the work of a Greek artist, probably the same man as carved the other three panels. There he was reproducing a well-tried theme; here he was tackling one for which a new iconography must be created. For all its stumblings, his effort is an important pointer towards the future: the commemoration of Roman ceremonies and events, enhanced by attendant divinities (here Mars) and personifications, and rendered in a broadly Classical style, was to be one of the mainsprings of Imperial relief sculpture, brought to maturity in the finest state monument of the Augustan age, the Ara Pacis (Vol. 2, pp. 370 f.).

Another unfamiliar kind of commission was the Roman-style portrait. The Romans, under the influence of their native tradition, preferred portraits which concentrated on the face at the expense of the body and put a premium on maturity and experience rather than good looks; and, since Greek sculptors always responded well to the challenge of depicting foreign physiognomies, the outcome was the marvellous series of expressive portrait heads and busts which is perhaps the highest achievement of Late Republican sculpture. These shrewd, uncompromising faces, with their close-cropped hair, firm-set mouths, and deeply creviced cheeks, are more reminiscent of modern American financiers than of the philosophers and statesmen of the Hellenistic world; they provide a fine insight into the qualities of ruthlessness and hard-headedness which carried Roman rule to all corners of the Mediterranean. At times, as in the coin portraits of C. Antius Restio, the no-holds-barred, warts-and-wrinkles approach is carried almost to the point of caricature, and it has been attractively argued that such ruthless realism was in some measure inspired by the Greek artists' dislike of their Roman patrons. (For Republican portraits see Vol. 2, pp. 77, 87, 90.)

Finally painting. While the Greek tradition of panel pictures continued in both East and West (Caesar paid huge sums for two mythological paintings by Timomachus of Byzantium), a significant new development was the appearance of illusionistic murals in Italy. Inspired partly by Hellenistic stage-painting and partly by actual architecture, both past and present, wall-painters soon after 100 BC broke away from the stucco work of the so-called First Style (the Italian version of the Hellenistic fashion of masonry-style wall-decoration) to evolve a purely pictorial style which dissolved the wall into an illusion of three-dimensional space. Invariably this space was defined by an environment of simulated architecture. In the finest decorations the Italian villa-owner gave his rooms an exotic, quasi-palatial splendour, with schemes of marble columns tricked out with gilded

CORNER OF A PAINTED BEDROOM IN A VILLA AT BOSCOREALE, near Pompeii (mid first century BC),
a classic example of the Second Style of wall-decoration, in which the painter used architectural forms to
open up illusions of space beyond the wall. Passages in Vitruvius suggest that painted stage-sets were a
source of inspiration.

ornament, glimpses of colonnaded courts receding in both linear and aerial perspective, and grand historical or religious figure-compositions set out on a
podium or within a portico. Later, in the 40s and 30s, the architecture tended to
become a framework for a central picture, conceived like a window opening
upon another world, and occupied by sacred landscapes or mythological figure-
scenes. The pictorial emphasis which in the Hellenistic world had been largely
confined to the floor now returned to the wall, leaving pavements decorated
simply with abstract patterns in various mosaic or mosaic-related techniques. The
importance of these developments has often been underestimated, because much
of our evidence comes from the bourgeois houses of small towns such as Pompeii;
but remains of frescoes from imperial residences in Rome and elsewhere during
the Augustan period, combined with information in the literary sources, especially
Pliny, confirm that there was a clear shift in prestige from panels to murals in
the late Republic and early Empire. The imitation architecture of this Second
Style therefore marks the beginning of a new chapter in ancient painting, a

chapter which was to see such masterpieces as the garden paintings from Livia's villa at Primaporta and the magical landscapes of the Villa of Agrippa Postumus at Boscotrecase (Vol. 2, pp. 372 f.).

Further Reading

There is a shortage of good books in English dealing specifically with the art of this period, and in particular of books which effectively study the transition from Hellenistic to Roman art. By far the best and most up-to-date is J. J. Pollitt, *Art in the Hellenistic Age* (Cambridge, 1986). Another general book, though highly personal in approach, is T. B. L. Webster, *Hellenistic Art* (London, 1967); while good overviews of architecture and sculpture are given respectively by D. S. Robertson, *A Handbook of Greek and Roman Architecture* (2nd edn., Cambridge, 1943) and A. W. Lawrence, *Greek and Roman Sculpture* (London, 1972).

From the Greek end see the general works on Greek art and architecture cited in the bibliography to Chapter 11. Specifically on the Hellenistic period, J. Charbonneaux, R. Martin, and F. Villard, *Hellenistic Art* (London and New York, 1973) provides a broad survey in which the section on architecture is better than those on sculpture and painting. C. M. Havelock, *Hellenistic Art* (London, 1971) is more detailed on individual works but adopts heretical views on dating from Rhys Carpenter. On Hellenistic sculpture the standard book is M. Bieber, *The Sculpture of the Hellenistic Age* (2nd edn., New York, 1961), but the author tends to be too dogmatic about dating and provenance; otherwise there are only monographs on specific works such as E. Schmidt, *The Great Altar of Pergamon* (London, 1965). On the luxury arts an excellent study is H. Hoffman and P. F. Davidson, *Greek Gold: Jewelry from the Age of Alexander* (New York, 1966).

For the Roman Republic see the opening chapters of the general works cited in the bibliography to Chapter 15 of Vol. 2; the only book in English which concentrates on the period before Augustus is A. Boethius, *Etruscan and Early Roman Architecture* (Harmondsworth, 1978). G. M. A. Richter, *Ancient Italy* (Ann Arbor, 1955) deals with art in Italy in general, studying the impact on it of Hellenistic art and carrying the 'Greco-Roman' tradition through into imperial times. The Etruscan background can best be studied in O. J. Brendel, *Etruscan Art* (Harmondsworth, 1978).

TABLES OF EVENTS

TABLES OF EVENTS

Before about 600 BC most dates are approximate

THE MEDITERRANEAN WORLD

The Age of Palace Cultures

3000   Beginnings of Minoan culture in Crete

2200–1450   Middle Minoan palace culture in Crete

2100   Probable arrival of Mycenaean Greeks in Greece

1600–1200   Development of a Mycenaean palace culture in Greece, initially dependent on Cretan models

1450   Mycenaeans take over the Cretan palace settlements and dominate the Aegean area; palace settlements develop at Mycenae, Tiryns, Thebes, Pylos, Cnossus, and elsewhere; this culture is the historical reality behind the Greek heroic myths

The Dark Age and the Period of Migrations

Between 1250 and 1150 there was a breakdown of settled conditions in the eastern Mediterranean and Asia Minor.

1220   The destruction of Troy VIIa may be the historical event behind the legend of the Trojan War, and perhaps the last major enterprise of the Mycenaean Greeks

1200   Widespread destruction of Mycenaean sites in Greece

1184   Traditional date for the destruction of Troy worked out by later Greek writers

1150   Final destruction of the citadel of Mycenae

1100–1000   Invasion of the Dorian Greeks into mainland Greece (in myth 'the return of the sons of Heracles') usually placed in this period

1050–950   Migration of Ionian and other Greeks from the mainland to the Aegean islands and the coast of Asia Minor

1050   Beginnings of widespread use of iron in Greece, and the renewal of contacts with Cyprus

THE NEAR EAST

2700–2200   Old Kingdom in Egypt

2700–2000   Sumerian period in Mesopotamia

2130–1800   Middle Kingdom in Egypt

2000–1700   Old Babylonian period in Mesopotamia

1575–1100   New Kingdom in Egypt

1460–1200   Hittite Empire dominates central Anatolia

1400   Beginning of Assyrian domination of central Mesopotamia

1230   First settlement of the Israelites in Canaan

1200   Hittite Empire destroyed by peoples from south Russia, who include the Phrygians. The 'peoples of the sea' (perhaps marauders and refugees) repulsed from Egypt

1100   End of the New Kingdom in Egypt and of the centralized Pharaonic state

1050–900	Proto-geometric pottery
975	Hero's tomb at Lefkandi

1000–960	David King of Israel
960–931	Solomon King of Israel
910	Beginning of the expansion of Assyria, opposed by Urartu and later by the city and tribal cultures of Syria and Palestine

1000–750	Age of Phoenician prosperity and expansion overseas
814	Traditional date of foundation of Carthage

744–612	Assyrian Empire at its height

The Age of Euboean Expansion

In the period from 825 to 730 the Euboean cities of Chalcis and Eretria are the leading settlements in Greece, responsible for overseas foundations for trade and the early developments of the colonizing movement. The leading artistic centre in Greece until about 730 is Athens.

875–750	Geometric pottery
800	Foundation of Eretria and gradual decline of Lefkandi
	Euoboeans and Cypriots establish a trading post at Al Mina on the mouth of the Orontes river (north Syria) on an important route for eastern exports to the Greek world
776	First Olympic Games: the four-year cycle of games became later the basis for dating historical events in the Greek world
775	Euboeans establish a trading post on the Bay of Naples (Pithecusae, Ischia); beginning of contact with Etruria and the west
753	Traditional date of the foundation of Rome
750–700	Greek alphabet created on Phoenician models and rapidly diffused in varying forms throughout the Greek world
	New heavy ('hoplite') armour development in the Greek world
735	Foundation of the first Sicilian colony, Naxos
734–680	Lelantine War between Chalcis and Eretria, involving much of the Greek world, and resulting in the end of Euboean influence

THE GREEK WORLD

The Orientalizing Period

From about 730 Corinth emerges as the most advanced city in Greece, both culturally and politically; but other cities also became important, notably her neighbours around the Isthmus (Sicyon, Megara), Aegina, Samos, Miletus, Athens, and Sparta. Eastern influences begin to affect Greek art and life.

POLITICAL EVENTS

733	Foundation of Corcyra and Syracuse by Corinth
730–710	Spartan conquest of Messenia
720	Sybaris (south Italy) founded; Colonization of Chalcidice (north Greece) by Chalcis and Eretria; Greeks begin to move into the area of the Hellespont
700–650	Diffusion of hoplite tactics
683	Athenian archon list begins
675	?Lycurgan reforms at Sparta
670	Zaleucus of Locri, earliest lawgiver in western colonies
668	Argive defeat of Sparta at battle of Hysiae
664	Greeks begin to penetrate Egypt as mercenaries and traders
657–625	Tyranny at Corinth under Cypselus

CULTURAL DEVELOPMENTS

750–700	Homer and Hesiod
725	First stone temple of Artemis Orthia at Sparta
720–690	Early Proto-Corinthian pottery
720	Orsippus of Megara runs naked to win an Olympic victory; nudity becomes the rule in sport
690–650	Middle Proto-Corinthian pottery
675–640	Archilochus of Paros active as poet
655	Chigi vase

THE NEAR EAST

720	Sargon of Assyria conquers Cilicia and Syria; fall of Israel (722)
700	Cimmerian invasion from south Russia into Asia Minor; destruction of Phrygian kingdom of Midas; Median monarchy founded
696	Sack of Tarsus by Assyrians
687	Kingdom of Lydia founded by Gyges (687–652)
670	Assyrian power begins to decline
664	Foundation of Saite dynasty in Egypt under Psammetichus I (664–610)

650–620	Sparta fights second Messenian War	650	Terpander of Lesbos, Callinus of Ephesus, Semonides of Amorgos, Tyrtaeus of Sparta active as poets	650	Rise of Media under Phraates (650–625)
650	Tyranny of Orthagoras at Sicyon Foundation of Thasos Beginnings of Greek settlement in the Black Sea	650–630	Late Proto-Corinthian pottery		
640	Tyranny of Theagenes at Megara				
632	Attempted tyranny at Athens by Cylon				
630	Foundation of Cyrene in north Africa				

The Early Archaic Age

This period sees the rise of dominance first of Sparta and then of Athens in mainland Greece.

625–585	Periander tyrant of Corinth	630	Mimnermus of Colophon and Alcman of Sparta active as poets	626	Independence of Babylon from Assyria under Nabopolassar
625–600	Thrasybulus tyrant of Miletus			625	Naucratis established as main Greek trading post in Egypt
621	Draco promulgates Athens' first written laws	625–595	Early Corinthian pottery First marble *kouroi*		Coinage invented in Lydia
620–570	Period of tyrannies at Mytilene	610	Attic black-figure pottery begins	612–09	Fall of Nineveh: division of Assyrian Empire between Babylon and Media
600–570	Cleisthenes tyrant of Sicyon	610–575	Alcaeus and Sappho active as poets on Lesbos		
600	Smyrna destroyed by Lydians Foundation of Massilia by Phocaeans Athens wins Salamis from Megara	600	Temple of Hera, Olympia		
595–586	First Sacred War for control of Delphi	600–560	Solon active as poet	591	Expedition of Psammetichus II of Egypt to Nubia: Greek mercenaries write their names at Abu Simbel
594	Solon, archon at Athens, promulgates new law-code, and institutes social and political reforms	585	Thales of Miletus predicts eclipse of sun	587	Capture of Jerusalem by Nebuchadrezzar of Babylon; exile of Jews
		582–573	Establishment of cycles of games (Pythia 582, Isthmia 581, Nemea 573)		
583	End of Corinthian tyranny	580	Temple of Artemis at Corcyra; first major temple of Athena at Athens		

THE GREEK WORLD (cont.)

POLITICAL EVENTS

560	War between Sparta and Tegea, ending in alliance; First tyranny of Pisistratus at Athens (560–556)
556	Chilon ephor at Sparta; End of tyranny at Sicyon

The Late Archaic Age: the Conflict with Persia

546 was 'the year the Mede came' (Xenophanes): the arrival of the Persians on the Mediterranean shore was a turning-point, and the conflict with Persia dominates the next fifty years.

546	Sparta defeats Argos at the battle of the champions; Pisistratus establishes his tyranny at Athens with the battle of Pallene
545	Conquest of Ionian Greeks by the Persians
540	Battle of Alalia; Carthaginians and Etruscans check Greek expansion in the western Mediterranean
535	Polycrates tyrant of Samos
528	Death of Pisistratus; Athens ruled by Hippias
525–3	Spartan expedition to Samos; fall of Polycrates

CULTURAL DEVELOPMENTS

570–550	Anaximander of Miletus active as philosopher
566	Reorganization of Panathenaic festival at Athens
560	Sicyonian treasury at Delphi; Stesichorus of Himera active as poet
548	Temple of Delphi burned
570–475	Lifetime of Xenophanes of Colophon (philosopher and poet)
550	Anaximenes of Miletus active as philospher
540	Theognis of Megara, Hipponax of Ephesus, and Ibycus of Rhegium active as poets
535–490	Anacreon of Teos active as poet
535	Attic red-figure pottery begins
534	First tragedy performed at City Dionysia in Athens
530	Pythagoras active in south Italy as philosopher
525	Siphnian treasury at Delphi

THE NEAR EAST (cont.)

570–526	Amasis Pharoah of Egypt
560–546	Croesus king of Lydia
559–530	Cyrus founds Persian Empire
550	Cyrus conquers Media
550–480	Lives of Buddha and Confucius
545	Persian capture of Sardis; end of Lydian Empire
539	Persian capture of Babylon; return of Jews from exile
530	Death of Cyrus; accession of Cambyses (530–522)
525	Death of Amasis of Egypt; Persians conquer Egypt and north Africa

524	Etruscans defeated at Cumae	
520–490	Cleomenes king of Sparta	
519	Alliance of Athens and Plataea	
514	Harmodius and Aristogeiton murder Hipparchus at Athens	
510	Expulsion of Hippias from Athens	
508	Reforms of Cleisthenes at Athens	
506	Abortive Spartan invasion of Attica; Athens defeats Chalcis and Boeotians	
505	Tyranny begins at Gela	
499	Ionian Revolt	
498	Athenians and Eretrians help to burn Sardis	
494	Battle of Lade; sack of Miletus and end of Ionian revolt; Spartans defeat Argos at battle of Sepeia	
493	Themistocles archon at Athens; establishment of port of Piraeus	
491	Gelon becomes tyrant of Gela	
490	First Persian expedition to mainland Greece	
490	Death of Cleomenes of Sparta Destruction of Eretria Battle of Marathon	
487–483	Ostracisms at Athens War between Athens and Aegina	
485	Gelon becomes tyrant of Syracuse	
482	Discovery of silver at Laurium in Attica, spent on the fleet of Athens	
480	Great Persian Expedition by land to Greece; battles of Artemisium, Thermopylae, and Salamis; Athens sacked by the Persians; Carthaginians invade Sicily and are defeated at the battle of Himera	
479	Battles of Plataea and Mycale	

520–468	Simonides of Ceos active as poet	
510–490	Temples at Agrigentum (Sicily) built	
500	Alcmaeon of Croton (doctor), Hecataeus of Miletus (historian), and Heraclitus of Ephesus (philosopher) active	
498	Earliest surviving poem of Pindar (*Pythian* 10)	
490	Statues on the temple of Aphaea at Aegina Parmenides of Elea active as philosopher	
487	First comedy performed at City Dionysia at Athens	
485–450	Bacchylides of Ceos active as poet	
484	First victory of Aeschylus	

521	Darius seizes power in Persia
520–519	Darius recaptures Babylon
518	Darius' Behistun inscription
514	Darius' Scythian expedition
512	Darius conquers Thrace
509	[Traditional date of foundation of Roman Republic]
487–485	Revolt of Egypt
486	Death of Darius; accession of Xerxes

THE GREEK WORLD

The Classical Age: The Fifth Century

In this period Athens developed her empire out of the league against Persia, and expanded it to cover the Aegean area; conflict between her and Sparta began in 461, and culminated in the Second Peloponnesian War (413–404), in which Athens was finally defeated and lost her empire. Economic activity became centred on the Piraeus; and culturally this was the golden, Periclean age of Athens, as the imperial city became 'the education of Greece' (Pericles), and evolved the most extreme democratic government the world has known.

	POLITICAL EVENTS		CULTURAL DEVELOPMENTS
478	Foundation of Delian League against Persia with Athens as leader	478	The Charioteer at Delphi cast
	Refortification of the city of Athens		
477–67	Death of Gelon tyrant of Syracuse; Hiero succeeds him	476	Pindar's First *Olympian Ode* and Bacchylides' Fifth *Ode* for victory of Hieron at Olympia
	Naval campaigns of Cimon, culminating in the battle of Eurymedon (467), which effectively removes the Persian threat	472	*Persae* of Aeschylus
474	Syracusans defeat Etruscans at battle of Cumae	470	Pindar's First *Pythian Ode*
471	Ostracism of Themistocles, and subsequent flight to Persia	470–430	Career of sculptor Myron
466	Death of Hiero and end of tyranny at Syracuse	468	First victory of Sophocles over Aeschylus
465	Revolt of Thasos from Delian League	467	*Seven Against Thebes* of Aeschylus
464	Murder of Xerxes; Artaxerxes I succeeds as King of Persia		
	Earthquake at Sparta and revolt of Spartan helots		
462–454	Revolt against Persians in Egypt, supported by Athens	464	Anaxagoras of Clazomenae (philosopher) arrives in Athens
461	Cimon ostracized; radical reforms at Athens under Ephialtes; murder of Ephialtes. Pericles' supremacy begins (461–429)	460–420	Career of sculptors Polyclitus and Phidias
461–451	War between Athens and Spartan alliance; First Peloponnesian War		
458	Building of Long Walls from Athens to Piraeus; battle of Tanagra; Athens conquers Boeotia	458	*Oresteia* of Aeschylus
		456	Death of Aeschylus
			Completion of Temple of Zeus at Olympia
454	Treasury of the Delian League moved to Athens	455	First production by Euripides
451	Five year truce between Athens and Sparta		
	Thirty Years Peace between Sparta and Argos		
	Pericles' law defining citizenship		

Date		Date	
450	Cimon's return from exile and death on campaign against Persia in Cyprus	450	Zeno of Elea and Empedocles of Acragas active as philosophers
449	Revolt against Persia in Syria		
447	'Peace of Callias' ends hostilities between Athens and Persia	447	Building of the Parthenon begins
	Loss of Athenian land empire in Boeotia at battle of Coronea		
446	Revolt of Euboea	446	Pindar's last ode (*Pythian* 8)
445	Thirty Years Peace between Athens and Sparta	445–426	Herodotus of Halicarnassus active
	[Ezra and Nehemiah active rebuilding walls of Jerusalem]		
443	Athenian foundation of Thurii in south Italy		
	Ostracism of Thucydides son of Melesias, Pericles' last opponent	442–438	Parthenon frieze
440	Revolt of Samos from Athenian Empire	440	Leucippus invents atomic theory
			Temple of Poseidon at Sunium
		438	*Alcestis* of Euripides
			Statue of Athena dedicated in Parthenon
437	Athenian foundation of Amphipolis	437–432	Work on Propylaea of Acropolis and Parthenon pediments
		436	Birth of Isocrates (educator)
435	War between Corinth and Corcyra over Epidamnus	435	Work begins on Erechtheum
433	Athenian alliance with Corcyra		
432	Revolt of Potidaea from Athens		
431	Start of Second Peloponnesian War	431	Thucydides begins his history
430	Plague at Athens		*Medea* of Euripides
		430	Democritus of Abdera (atomic theorist), Meton of Athens (astronomer), Hippocrates of Cos (doctor), Socrates, and Protagoras of Abdera (philosophers) active
429	Death of Pericles		Phidias' statue of Zeus at Olympia
	Siege of Plataea		
428	Revolt of Mytilene	428	*Hippolytus* of Euripides
			Birth of Plato
427	Capture of Plataea by Spartans and Mytilene by Athenians	427	Embassy of Gorgias of Leontini to Athens begins the formal art of rhetoric
	First expedition of Athenians to Sicily		
425	Fortification of Pylos and capture of Sphacteria by Athenians	425	*Acharnians* of Aristophanes
	Cleon dominant at Athens		Hellanicus of Lesbos (historian) active
424	Boeotians defeat Athenians at battle of Delium	424	*Knights* of Aristophanes
	Peace conference of Sicilians at Gela		Thucydides the historian exiled from Athens
	Death of Artaxerxes; accession of Darius II in Persia		
423	Armistice between Athens and Sparta for a year	423	*Clouds* of Aristophanes

THE GREEK WORLD (cont.)

POLITICAL EVENTS		CULTURAL DEVELOPMENTS	
422	Brasidas and Cleon killed in north Greece	422	*Wasps* of Aristophanes
421	Peace of Nicias between Athens and Sparta	421	*Peace* of Aristophanes
418	Spartan defeat of Athenian–Argive coalition at battle of Mantinea; Thirty Years Peace between Sparta and Argos	420–400	Temple of Apollo at Bassae built
416	Athenians attack Melos and enslave its inhabitants		Hippias of Elis (antiquarian and polymath) active
415	Athenian expedition to Sicily; affairs of the Mutilation of the Hermae and Profanation of the Mysteries; Alcibiades exiled	415	*Trojan Women* of Euripides
413	Sparta renews the war and establishes a permanent fort in Attica at Decelea	414	*Birds* of Aristophanes
	Athenian expedition destroyed in Sicily		
412	Revolt of Athenian allies; Persia enters the war	412	*Helen* of Euripides
411	Oligarchic revolutions at Athens	411	*Lysistrata* and *Thesmophoriazusae* of Aristophanes
410	Battle of Cyzicus; democracy restored at Athens		
409	Carthaginian expedition to Sicily; destruction of Selinus and Himera	409	*Philoctetes* of Sophocles
407–406	Alcibiades' return from exile	408	*Orestes* of Euripides
406	Athenian defeat at Notium and victory at Arginusae	406	Deaths of Euripides and Sophocles
405	Battle of Aegospotami; siege of Athens	405	*Frogs* of Aristophanes
	Dionysius becomes tyrant of Syracuse; peace between Syracuse and Carthage		*Bacchae* of Euripides performed
404	Capitulation of Athens; installation of regime of the Thirty		
	Democratic exiles seize Phyle		
	Death of Darius II; accession of Artaxerxes II in Persia		
403	Fall of the Thirty; restoration of democracy at Athens		

The Classical Age: The Fourth Century

Politically, the fourth century saw a series of attempts to establish dominance by Sparta, Athens, and Thebes, with Persia holding the balance of power, helping Athens at first, but ending as guarantor of a Spartan-imposed peace. In the 370s Thessaly became important, and from the 350s onwards Macedon under Philip began to expand; in 338 Macedonian overlordship was finally established. In Sicily the Deinomenid dynasty controlled Syracuse and led the struggle against Carthage, until Timoleon created a Greek revival in the late 340s. Athens remained the dominant intellectual centre; with the schools of Plato, Isocrates, and Aristotle, philosophy, rhetoric, and prose in general become the main forms of literature.

410–387	Careers of Andocides and Lysias as speech-writers
401	*Oedipus Colonus* of Sophocles produced posthumously
400–360	Antisthenes (cynic), Aristippus of Cyrene (hedonist) and Euclides of Megara, pupils of Socrates, active
399	Trial and execution of Socrates for corrupting the youth of Athens
397–338	Isocrates (educator and writer) active
396–347	Plato (philosopher) active
395	Thucydides' *History* published Antimachus, epic poet, active
392–388	Last plays of Aristophanes
390–354	Xenophon (historian and essayist) active
387	Plato founds the Academy
384	Aristotle and Demosthenes born
373	Earthquake destroys temple at Delphi
370–330	Praxiteles and Scopas (sculptors) active
367	Plato visits Syracuse to educate Dionysius II Aristotle joins the Academy
361	Second visit of Plato to Sicily
360–315	Lysippus (sculptor) active
360–323	Diogenes (cynic philosopher) active

401	Expedition of Cyrus and 10,000 Greek mercenaries against the Persian king; battle of Cunaxa (subject of Xenophon's *Anabasis*)
398	Agesilaus succeeds as king of Sparta
396–394	Campaigns of Agesilaus to free the Greeks of Asia Minor from Persia
395–386	Corinthian War; Sparta against Corinth, Thebes, Argos, and Athens backed by Persia
395–393	Athens rebuilds her Long Walls
394	Persian fleet under an Athenian defeats the Spartans at Cnidus
390	Gauls sack Rome
387	Dionysius I captures Rhegium
386	Peace of Antalcidas or King's Peace imposes Persian-backed control by Sparta on Greece
382	Spartan troops seize Theban citadel
379	Liberation of Thebes
378	Alliance between Athens and Thebes Foundation of Second Athenian Confederacy
377–353	Mausolus dynast of Caria
375–370	Rise of Thessaly under Jason
371–362	Domination of Thebes under Pelopidas and Epaminondas
371	Thebes destroys Spartan power at battle of Leuctra
369	Foundation of Megalopolis and liberation of Messenia
367	Death of Dionysius I; Dionysius II becomes tyrant of Syracuse
366–360	Satraps' Revolt from Persian king
365	Athens expels Samians and colonizes Samos
364	Thebes destroys Orchomenus; death of Pelopidas
362	Thebes defeats Sparta at battle of Mantinea; death of Epaminondas
360	Death of Agesilaus
359	Philip II becomes king of Macedon

THE GREEK WORLD (*cont.*)

POLITICAL EVENTS		CULTURAL DEVELOPMENTS	
357	War between Athens and Philip; Philip captures Amphipolis	358–330	Theatre of Epidaurus built
357–355	Social War between Athens and members of her confederacy		
356–354	Dion, uncle of Dionysius and pupil of Plato, controls Syracuse		
356–352	Phocians seize Delphi and provoke Sacred War, bringing Philip into central Greece against them		
356	Birth of Alexander the Great	355	Literary and political careers of the orators Demosthenes (died 322) and Aeschines (left Athens 330) begin
		353	Death of Mausolus; Mausoleum begun
		350–320	Apelles (painter) and Theopompus (historian) active
		350–300	Stilpo (philosopher) active at Megara
348	Philip seizes Olynthus	348	Death of Plato; Speusippus becomes head of the Academy
346	Philip and Athens make peace (Peace of Philocrates) Second tyranny of Dionysius II		
344–338	Timoleon arrives in Sicily, ends the tyrannies, and defeats the Carthaginians at Crimisus (341); revival of Greek Sicily	343–342	Aristotle in Macedonia as tutor to Alexander
		342	Menander born
		341	End of *History* of Ephorus
		339	Xenocrates becomes head of the Academy
338	Philip defeats Athens and Thebes at Chaeronea; end of Greek independence Murder of Artaxerxes III	338	Death of Isocrates
337	Philip founds Corinthian League of Greek states, which declares war on Persia	338–324	Lycurgus in charge of finances of Athens, inaugurates major public building programme

THE HELLENISTIC WORLD

Alexander the Great

War against Persia had long seemed a means of recreating Greek unity, and events since 400 had shown both the wealth and the military weakness of the Great King. Alexander took up Philip's plan to invade the Persian Empire; within twelve years he had conquered as far as the steppes of Russia, Afghanistan, and the Punjab. These conquests created the Hellenistic world.

POLITICAL EVENTS		CULTURAL DEVELOPMENTS
336	Accession of Alexander	
335	Alexander sacks Thebes	335 — Aristotle begins teaching at Athens and founds the Lyceum (Peripatetic school)
334	Accession of Darius III of Persia	
	Alexander crosses into Asia	
	Battle of Granicus; conquest of Asia Minor	
333	Defeat of Darius at battle of Issus	
332	Sieges of Tyre and Gaza	
	Alexander enters Egypt	
331	Foundation of Alexandria	
	Alexander defeats Darius at battle of Gaugamela, takes Mesopotamia, and enters Babylon, Persepolis, and Pasargadae	
330	Burning of palace of Persepolis	330 — Aeschines and Demosthenes defend their political careers in the two opposed speeches *Against Ctesiphon* and *On the Crown*
	Darius murdered by his supporters	
330–328	Alexander campaigns in Bactria and Sogdiana	
327	Marriage of Alexander and Roxane	327 — Callisthenes (historian of Alexander and nephew of Aristotle) executed by Alexander
	Alexander enters India	The philosophers Pyrrho (sceptic) and Anaxarchus, accompanying Alexander, meet Brahmins
326	Alexander crosses the Indus and wins battle of Hydaspes. Conquest of Punjab. Alexander sails down the Indus to the Indian Ocean	

ROME

Early Rome

The dates and the reality of events in early Roman history are quite uncertain. Rome began as a community on the fringes of Etruscan culture; under the later kings she was in effect an Etruscan city dominating Latium. The establishment of the republic (509) caused a decline in her power as she fought for survival against the Etruscans and sought to re-establish her dominance in Latium. The fifth century was a period of acute social tension. The destruction of Veii (405–396) ended the Etruscan threat, and the sack of Rome by the Gauls (390) proved only a temporary setback. By 338 Rome had incorporated Latium and moved into Campania.

THE HELLENISTIC WORLD (*cont.*)

POLITICAL EVENTS

325	Alexander returns through Baluchistan, suffering great hardship in the desert
324	Alexander at Susa
323	Death of Alexander, aged thirty-two

Age of the Successors

The struggles of the generals who divided Alexander's empire centred on the attempts of first Perdiccas and then Antigonus the One-Eyed to maintain the empire's unity. By 306 the family of Alexander had been eliminated, and the contenders felt sure enough to claim the title of king in their own areas; by 276 the three great powers of the Hellenistic world, Macedon, Egypt, and the Seleucid Empire were firmly established.

323–320	Perdiccas tries to maintain unity through his regency, but is killed in Egypt
323–322	Athens and her allies attempt to free themselves from Macedon in the Lamian War
320–301	Antigonus the One-Eyed aims at universal empire
317–289	Agathocles tyrant of Syracuse
317	Philip III half-wit half-brother of Alexander murdered
315	Olympias mother of Alexander murdered

CULTURAL DEVELOPMENTS

326–324	Voyages of Nearchus, admiral of Alexander, down the Jhelum and back to Mesopotamia through the Persian Gulf
325–300	Pytheas of Massilia circumnavigates Britain
322	Deaths of Aristotle and Demosthenes Theophrastus becomes head of Lyceum
321–289	Career of Menander (poet of New Comedy)
320–05	Hecataeus of Abdera writes first Hellenistic cultural history of Egypt
317–07	Demetrius of Phaleron (Peripatetic philosopher) is Macedonian governor of Athens
317	*Dyscolus* of Menander performed End of Attic gravestone series

ROME (*cont.*)

The Colonization and Conquest of Italy

The period from 334 to 264 saw the gradual expansion of Rome to control by colonization, conquest, and alliance of all Italy, south of the Po valley.

327–304	Second Samnite War against Samnites in the central Apennines

Date	Political and Military Events	Date	Cultural Events	Date	Roman Events
315–311	Coalition of satraps against Antigonus	314	Polemo becomes head of Academy on death of Xenocrates	310	Roman advance into Etruria
312	Seleucus captures Babylon; beginning of Seleucid era				
311	Peace between the successors recognizes in effect the division between Antigonus (Asia), Macedon/Greece (Cassander), Thrace (Lysimachus), Egypt (Ptolemy), and by omission the eastern satrapies (Seleucus)	310	Clearchus of Soli (Peripatetic philosopher) visits Aï Khanoum in Afghanistan(?)		
311–306	War between Agathocles and Carthage; invasion of Africa	310	Zeno of Citium establishes the Stoic school in *Stoa Poikilē* at Athens		
310	Murder of Alexander IV, son of Alexander the Great and last member of the dynasty	309	Philitas of Cos (scholar and founder of Alexandrian poetry) appointed tutor to future Ptolemy II		
307	Demetrius the Besieger, son of Antigonus, 'liberates' Athens	307–306	Exile and recall of Theophrastus from Athens		
306–304	Antigonus, Ptolemy, and Seleucus call themselves kings	307	Epicurus establishes his philosophical school at Athens		
305–304	Siege of Rhodes by Demetrius	302–290	Megasthenes (author on India) at court of Chandragupta		
303	Seleucus cedes Indian territories to Chandragupta founder of Mauryan dynasty for 500 war elephants				
301	Destruction of power of Antigonus and Demetrius at battle of Ipsus; Antigonus killed	300	Ptolemy I founds Museum of Alexandria on advice of Demetrius of Phaleron; Zenodotus royal tutor and first head of the library Euhemerus writes his utopian romance Euclid (mathematician) active		
297	Death of Cassander ruler of Macedon				
297–272	Career of Pyrrhus of Epirus	295	Tyche of Antioch; Colossus of Rhodes	298–290	Third Samnite War

THE HELLENISTIC WORLD (cont.)

POLITICAL EVENTS	CULTURAL DEVELOPMENTS
	290 Berossus (Babylonian priest) writes history of Babylonia
285 Demetrius the Besieger captured by Seleucus, dies of drink in 283	287 Theophrastus dies; Strato head of Lyceum
283 Ptolemy I Soter dies; Ptolemy II Philadelphus succeeds	
281 Lysimachus killed	
Seleucus assassinated; his son Antiochus I succeeds	280 Duris of Samos (leading exponent of 'tragic history') active
Foundation of Achaean League	Bion of Borysthenes (satirist) active
279 Invasion of Macedon and Greece by Gauls	
276 Antigonus Gonatas, son of Demetrius, defeats the Gauls and becomes king of Macedon, founding the Macedonian dynasty	276 Death of Polemo, head of the Academy
	271 Death of Epicurus
	270–242 Arcesilaus converts the Academy to scepticism
	270 Callimachus, Theocritus, Lycophron (or a century later), Aratus, and Posidippus active as poets

The Balance of Power

The third century saw the creation of an uneasy balance of power between the great kingdoms, with conflict confined to disputed areas: the Ptolemies and the Seleucids fought over Syria and Palestine, while the Greek cities of the Aegean area sought to manipulate the great powers in order to achieve independence. This was the great age of Hellenistic culture: philosophy was centred on Athens, while the patronage of Ptolemy II created Alexandrian literature and science. From the 230s there are signs of the re-emergence of non-Greek forces on the political scene.

274–271 First Syrian War between Ptolemy II and Antiochus I

ROME (cont.)

280–275 Pyrrhus of Epirus crosses into south Italy to help the Greek cities against Rome, and is defeated by the Romans

Earliest Roman coinage

272 Surrender of Tarentum; alliance with Greek cities in south Italy

272–215 Hiero, lieutenant of Pyrrhus, elected general and then king (270) at Syracuse; Syracusan age of prosperity and building

Manetho (historian and Egyptian priest) lays foundation of Egyptian history

Ctesibius of Alexandria (engineer) and Herophilus of Chalcedon (doctor) active

Aristarchus of Samos proposes heliocentric theory of universe

269 Death of Strato, last head of Lyceum

265–235 Archive of Zeno illuminates economic life of Egypt

262 Cleanthes succeeds Zeno as head of Stoics

260 Hieronymus of Cardia (historian of the Successors) dies aged 104; Timaeus of Tauromenium (historian of the west) dies aged ninety-six

267–262 Chremonidean War: Ptolemy unsuccessfully supports Greek independence from Macedon. Antigonus Gonatas enters Athens

263–241 Eumenes ruler of Pergamum founds independent power and begins building programme

261 Antiochus II succeeds to Seleucid kingdom

260–253 Second Syrian War between Ptolemy II and Antiochus II

The First Punic War

Rome begins to emerge on the western Mediterranean scene with her expansion into Sicily, Corsica, and Sardinia, and her response to the Carthaginian expansion in Spain

264 First gladiatorial show at Rome
Roman army enters Sicily to help Mamertines against Carthage: First Punic War begins

263 Hiero of Syracuse becomes ally of Rome

THE HELLENISTIC WORLD (*cont.*)

ROME (*cont.*)

256–255	Expedition of M. Regulus to Africa ends in disaster
255–249	Series of Roman naval disasters
247	Hamilcar Barca begins Carthaginian offensive in Sicily
241	Roman victory off Aegates Islands; end of First Punic War
240–207	Livius Andronicus (earliest Roman poet and playwright) active

CULTURAL DEVELOPMENTS

260	Apollonius of Rhodes writes *Argonautica* (epic) Herodas (author of mimes) active Erasistratus of Ceos (doctor) understands action of heart and distinguishes motor and sensory nerves
260–212	Archimedes (mathematician and inventor) active
256	Asoka, king of Mauryans (269–232), proclaims his Buddhist mission to the Greek world
250	Ariston of Chios (Stoic philosopher) active at Athens
246	Eratosthenes becomes head of Library at Alexandria; literary scholar and pioneer of scientific geography, he calculates the circumference of the earth correctly

POLITICAL EVENTS

251–213	Career of Aratus of Sicyon statesman and general of Achaean League
246	Ptolemy III succeeds to kingdom of Egypt Seleucus II succeeds to Seleucid kingdom
246–241	Third Syrian War between Ptolemy III and Seleucus II
244–241	Agis IV attempts to reform Sparta and is executed
239	Demetrius II succeeds Antigonus Gonatas as king of Macedon War between Macedon and the Achaean and Aetolian Leagues
239–130	Independent Greek kingdom established in Bactria
238	Emergence of Parthia
238–227	War of Attalus of Pergamum against Galatians; he becomes master of Asia Minor and takes royal title

237	Roman occupation of Corsica and Sardinia Hamilcar begins Carthaginian expansion in Spain, followed by Hasdrubal Naevius' first play produced
236	
228	Rome establishes protectorate over the Illyrian coast
227	Sicily and Sardinia are made provinces
221	Hannibal, aged twenty-five, takes command of Carthaginian forces in Spain Rome allies with Saguntum in Spain
219	Siege and capture of Saguntum by Hannibal

235	Apollonius of Perge (mathematician) active
232	Chrysippus succeeds Cleanthes as head of Stoics
225	Eratosthenes of Cyrene (polymath) and Ariston of Ceos (Peripatetic philosopher) active

235–222	Cleomenes III king of Sparta; he reforms Spartan state in 227
223	Antiochus III succeeds to Seleucid kingdom
221	Philip V succeeds to kingdom of Macedon Ptolemy IV succeeds to kingdom of Egypt
219–217	Fourth Syrian War between Ptolemy IV and Antiochus III Egypt is saved from conquest by Egyptian native troops at battle of Raphia

ROME

THE EAST	THE WEST	CULTURAL DEVELOPMENTS

The Conquest of the Mediterranean

'There can surely be no-one so petty or so apathetic in his outlook that he has no desire to discover by what means and under what system of government the Romans succeeded in less than fifty-three years (220–167) in bringing under their rule almost the whole of the inhabited world, an achievement which is without parallel in human history' (Polybius). About 200 Rome began to develop a culture of its own, heavily dependent on Greek models.

THE EAST	THE WEST	CULTURAL DEVELOPMENTS
	218–201 Second Punic War / Hannibal invades Italy	
	217 Hannibal defeats Romans at Lake Trasimene	
	216 Hannibal defeats Romans at Cannae	
215 Philip V of Macedon allies with Carthage	215 Hannibal in south Italy / Roman victories in Spain / Carthage allies with Syracuse	
214–205 First Macedonian War between Rome and Philip	213 Romans besiege Syracuse	
212–205 Antiochus III campaigns in the east in an unsuccessful attempt to reconquer Parthia and Bactria	212 Romans besiege Capua	
211 Roman alliance with Aetolian League	211 Hannibal marches on Rome / Capua and Syracuse fall / Roman defeats in Spain	
209 Attalus I of Pergamum allies with Rome against Philip	211–206 Scipio Africanus defeats Hasdrubal in Spain	
206–185 Revolt and independence of Upper Egypt	204 Spain divided into two provinces / Scipio invades Africa	204–169 Ennius active at Rome as poet and teacher
204 Ptolemy V succeeds in Egypt	203 Hannibal recalled from Italy	204 Plautus' *Miles Gloriosus* performed / Career of Plautus 204–184
203–200 Philip and Antiochus make a secret alliance against Egypt; fifth Syrian War; Antiochus seizes Syria	202 Scipio defeats Hannibal at battle of Zama / Carthage becomes a dependent of Rome	202 Fabius Pictor writes first prose history of Rome in Greek

Date	Event	Date	Event	Date	Event
200–197	Second Macedonian War between Rome and Philip	202–191	Roman conquest of Cisalpine Gaul	200 onwards	Greek art begins to become known to the Romans
196	Rome declares the freedom of the Greeks at the Isthmus of Corinth	197–133	Wars in Spain	200	Aristophanes of Byzantium (scholar) becomes head of Library at Alexandria
196–179	Philip rebuilds the power of Macedon				
194	Romans evacuate Greece				
192–188	Syrian War between Rome and Antiochus				
187	Antiochus III dies			186	Senatorial edict against Bacchic rites
				184	Censorship of the Elder Cato
179	Philip V dies and is succeeded by his son Perseus			179	Basilica Aemilia and Aemilian Bridge built at Rome
175	Antiochus IV Epiphanes succeeds to Seleucid empire				
171–167	Third Macedonian War				
170–168	Sixth Syrian War				
167	Battle of Pydna ends kingdom of Macedon; Rome divides territory into four republics	167	Direct taxation of Roman citizens abolished	167	Polybius the historian arrives in Rome
	Rome orders Antiochus IV out of Egypt				
	Rome declares Delos a free port				
	Desecration of Temple at Jerusalem brings to a head Jewish resistance against Antiochus' policy of hellenizing the Jews; Maccabean Revolt			166–159	Plays of Terence produced
164	Death of Antiochus IV; book of Daniel composed				Great Altar of Zeus and Athena built at Pergamum

ROME (*cont.*)

	THE EAST		THE WEST		CULTURAL DEVELOPMENTS
		155			Carneades (head of the Academy) comes to Rome on an embassy and introduces the Romans to philosophy
		150			Agatharchides of Cnidus (Ptolemaic geographer) flourished
148	Fourth Macedonian War and war against Achaean League Corinth is sacked and Macedonia becomes a Roman province	149–146	Third Carthaginian War; Carthage, destroyed by Romans; Africa becomes a province	149	Publication of Cato's *Origines* or history of Rome

POLITICAL EVENTS

The Late Republic

The history of this period is the history of Rome *domi militiaeque*, at home and abroad. Rome exploited ruthlessly her control of the Mediterranean world; her generals led her citizens to ever richer conquests. But at home the strains of empire began to destroy republican government. Culturally Rome became the centre of patronage, and Latin literature flourished.

	POLITICAL EVENTS		CULTURAL DEVELOPMENTS
		145	Aristarchus (scholar and head of the Library) and other intellectuals flee from Alexandria on accession of Ptolemy VIII
142	Independence of the Jews	144	Panaetius (Stoic philosopher *c.* 185–109) arrives in Rome
141	Parthians attack Babylon		
133	Attalus III of Pergamum bequeaths his kingdom to Rome; it becomes the province of Asia (129)	135	Nicander (medical poet) active
130	Antiochus VII dies fighting the Parthians	118	Polybius dies soon after this
		100	Philo of Larissa becomes head of the Academy
88–85	Mithridates VI of Pontus massacres Roman citizens in Asia and seeks to free the Greeks from Rome	95	Meleager of Gadara (poet and collector of earliest epigrams in the Greek Anthology) active
86	Sulla in the East captures Athens and Greece		

88–68	Antiochus of Ascalon becomes head of the Academy at Athens; Philo of Larissa leaves for Rome
87–51	Posidonius (philosopher, historian, and polymath) active in Rhodes and at Rome
75–35	Philodemus (poet and Epicurean philosopher) active at Rome; Aenesidemus (Sceptic philosopher) active
60–30	Diodorus of Sicily compiles his *Historical Library*
50	Andronicus of Rhodes discovers and begins editing the lost works of Aristotle; foundation of our modern knowledge of Aristotle

83–82	Second Mithridatic War
74–63	Third Mithridatic War
66–63	Pompey defeats Mithridates and reorganizes the East. End of Seleucid monarchy (64) and of independent kingdom of Judaea; provinces of Bithynia, Cilicia, Syria, Crete organized, and client kings established elsewhere
60	'First triumvirate' formed between Pompey, Crassus, and Caesar
51	Parthian invasion of Syria
49	Civil War: Caesar crosses the Rubicon and Pompey leaves for East
47–44	Dictatorship of Caesar
44	(15 March) Caesar is murdered

THE ROMAN EMPIRE

POLITICAL EVENTS	CULTURAL DEVELOPMENTS

The Second Triumvirate and the Age of Augustus

Caesar's heirs struggled for control of the Roman world; the final victory of his nephew Octavian (later Augustus) saw the establishment of monarchy under the guise of a 'restored Republic'. His long reign was marked by consolidation and reform in every sphere of politics and culture. The great age of Latin poetry began with the Triumvirate and continued into the Augustan age.

POLITICAL EVENTS		CULTURAL DEVELOPMENTS	
		44–AD 21	Strabo (geographer and historian) active
42	Republicans defeated at battle of Philippi; Brutus and Cassius commit suicide		
41–32	Antony in the East	40	Didymus (last great Alexandrian literary scholar) active
31	Octavian defeats Antony at battle of Actium		
30	Antony and Cleopatra commit suicide		
	Annexation of Egypt by Rome		
27	'The Republic restored': the first constitutional settlement.		
	Octavian given the name *Augustus*		

The Julio-Claudian Dynasty 14–68 A.D.

Despite the excesses of individual Emperors in Rome, the imperial governmental system was consolidated under a dynasty which claimed hereditary descent from Augustus.

TIBERIUS (14–37)

19	Death of Germanicus
23	Death of Drusus, Emperor's son
26	Tiberius retires to Capri
31	Sejanus, praetorian prefect and effective ruler of Rome, executed

GAIUS (CALIGULA) (37–41)

CLAUDIUS (41–54)
43 Invasion of Britain under Aulus Plautius

NERO (54–68)
54–62 Burrus and Seneca control the young Emperor
58–62 Conquest and loss of Armenia
59 Murder of Agrippina on Nero's orders
61 Revolt of Iceni in Britain under Boudicca
62 Death of Burrus and end of Seneca's influence
64 Fire in Rome for nine days; persecution of Christians
65 Pisonian Conspiracy against Nero
66–73 Jewish Revolt

40 Philo (Jewish writer) active

The Flavian Dynasty 69–96

With the Flavian dynasty power shifted to the bourgeoisie of Italy; luxury became unfashionable at Rome as the Emperor displayed 'old-fashioned standards'. Literature gives way to government as the art of Rome.

70 Destruction of Temple at Jerusalem

The Age of the Antonines 96–192

'If a man were called to fix the period in the history of the world, during which the human race was most happy and prosperous, he would, without hesitation, name that which elapsed from the death of Domitian to the accession of Commodus' (Edward Gibbon). Culturally the Greek world began to revive as city life prospered.

Dio Chrysostom (Greek orator), Epictetus (moralist), and Plutarch (essayist and biographer) active in Greek literature

TRAJAN (98–117)
115–17 Jewish Revolt

HADRIAN (117–38)
131 Hadrian establishes the Panhellenion, based on Athens, as a league of the Greek cities
132–5 Bar Kochba's revolt leads to final dispersal of Jews

Appian (historian), Lucian, (satirist), and Ptolemy (astronomer) active in Greek literature

THE ROMAN EMPIRE (*cont.*)

POLITICAL EVENTS	CULTURAL DEVELOPMENTS
ANTONINUS PIUS (138–61)	
	143 Pausanias writes his description of Greece
	Herodes Atticus (Greek orator) and Fronto (Latin orator) consuls
	144 Speech of Aelius Aristides (Greek orator) in praise of Rome
	148 900th anniversary of founding of Rome
MARCUS AURELIUS (161–80)	
162–6 Parthian Wars of L. Verus	165 Apuleius (Latin writer) and Galen (doctor) active
165–7 Plague spreads through the Roman Empire	Justin (Christian apologist) martyred
	174–80 *Meditations of Marcus Aurelius*
COMMODUS (161–80)	

The Severan Dynasty

'Our history and the affairs of the Romans descend from an age of gold to one of iron and rust' (Cassius Dio, contemporary historian). The causes of the decline and subsequent transformation of the Roman world are complex. Militarization of the Empire and a shift of power from centre to outlying frontiers as barbarian pressure increased, brought strains which began to emerge under the Severans.

POLITICAL EVENTS	CULTURAL DEVELOPMENTS
SEPTIMIUS SEVERUS (193–211)	Philostratus (literary biographer). Herodian (historian), Sextus Empiricus (sceptic philosopher), Alexander of Aphrodisias (commentator on Aristotle), and Clement of Alexandria (Christian writer) active
CARACALLA (212–17)	
212 The *constitutio Antoniniana* grants citizenship to all inhabitants of the Empire	200–54 Origen (Christian philosopher) active
SEVERUS ALEXANDER (222–35)	
226 Ardashir the Sassanian, crowned King of Kings in Iran, inaugurates 400 years of intermittent war with the Roman Empire	229 Cassius Dio (Historian) consul for the second time with the Emperor

The Late Empire

Fifty years of military anarchy (235–84, with nearly twenty Emperors) were ended by Diocletian's reforms and the establishment of the Tetrarchy. But intractable problems of frontier defence, heavy taxation, inflation, and excessive bureaucracy remained, and were not affected by Constantine's conversion to Christianity. The Late Empire was a new world in which from time to time Emperors such as Julian, or literary figures, sought to recapture the values of a lost society. Only a few leading events are mentioned in this brief list.

267	Heruli invade Greece		249–51	Decius' persecution of the Christians
			258	Martyrdom of Cyprian
			270	Death of Plotinus (Neoplatonist philosopher)
284–306	Diocletian re-establishes central power and founds the Tetrarchy		271	Aurelian Walls of Rome built
			303–5	Great Persecution
306–37	Career of Constantine the Great		307–12	Basilica of Maxentius in Rome, completed by Constantine
312	Constantine wins battle of Milvian Bridge under the sign of the Cross: Christianity declared official state religion		313–22	First Christian basilica built in Rome
324	Foundation of Constantinople			
360–3	Julian the Apostate Emperor			
378–95	Theodosius the Great Emperor			
395	Division of the Empire between the sons of Theodosius			
410	Sack of Rome by Alaric the Visigoth			
	Rome formally renounces Britain		430	Death of Saint Augustine
439	Vandals conquer Carthage and Africa			
476	End of Roman Empire in the West			
527–65	Justinian, eastern emperor, seeks to reconquer Italy and Africa		529	The *Digest* of Roman Law is compiled
				Justinian orders the closure of the Academy at Athens
633–55	Arab conquest of Syria, Egypt, and the Sassanid Empire			
1453	Conquest of Constantinople by the Turks and end of the Eastern Roman Empire			

LIST OF ILLUSTRATIONS

COLOUR PLATES

BLACK-AND-WHITE ILLUSTRATIONS

INDEX

References followed by grid letters (e.g. 368 Bd) are to maps. References in italics are to illustrations.